For

Bob

mio fratello

whose wrists have always been ready when
I've leapt out into the void

THIS UNION MAY NEVER BE PERFECT,
BUT GENERATION AFTER GENERATION HAS SHOWN
THAT IT CAN ALWAYS BE PERFECTED.

> —*BARACK OBAMA*
> *"A More Perfect Union"*
> *Delivered at National Constitution Center,*
> *18 March 2008*

OH! DO MY JOHNNY BOWKER,
COME ROCK 'N' ROLL ME OVER
OH, DO ME JOHNNY BOWKER DO!

> —*"JOHNNY BOWKER"*
> *Nineteenth-century halyard sea chantey*

LIFE, ART AND IDENTITY ARE, OF COURSE,
MUCH MORE COMPLICATED. HOW DO I KNOW?
I HEARD IT IN A BRUCE SPRINGSTEEN SONG.

> —*BRUCE SPRINGSTEEN,*
> *Letter to the New York Times Book Review*
> *Published 31 July 2005*

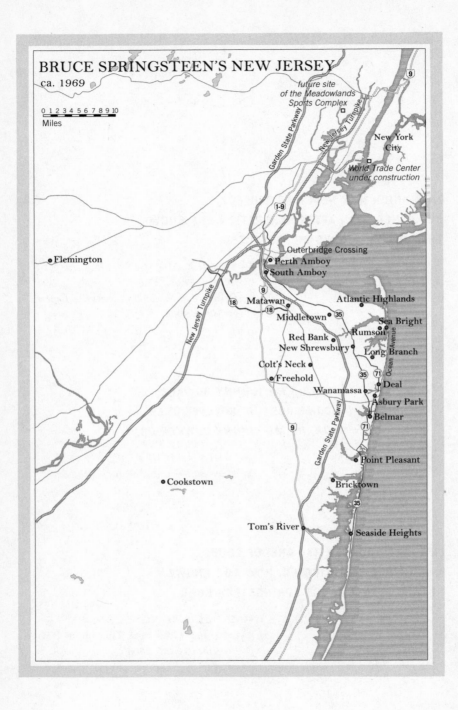

BRUCE SPRINGSTEEN'S NEW JERSEY
ca. 1969

0 1 2 3 4 5 6 7 8 9 10
Miles

future site
of the Meadowlands
Sports Complex

New York
City

World Trade Center
under construction

Garden State Parkway

New Jersey Turnpike

I-9

Flemington

Outerbridge Crossing
Perth Amboy
South Amboy

9

18   Matawan
18   Middletown
35

Atlantic Highlands

Sea Bright
Rumson

Red Bank
New Shrewsbury

Colt's Neck
Freehold

Wanamassa

35 71

Long Branch

Ocean Avenue

Deal

Asbury Park
Belmar

71

9

New Jersey Turnpike

Garden State Parkway

Cookstown

Point Pleasant

Bricktown

35

Tom's River

Seaside Heights

CONTENTS

Walk-In Music: Seven nights to rock   xi

PART ONE I COOKMAN AVENUE

---

1. I'm quick to learn (1964–1968)   3

2. I pushed B-52 and bombed 'em with the blues (1968–1971)   24

3. Dethrone the Dictaphone, hit it in its funnybone (1971–1972)   52

4. Endless juke joints and Valentino drag (1972–1975)   78

5. Tonight's gonna be everything that I said (1975–1976)   122

PART TWO I THE POWER STATION

---

6. I'll be there on time and I'll pay the cost (1976–1979)   137

7. Ain't nobody like to be alone (1979–1982)   167

8. This gun's for hire (1982–1986)   198

PART THREE | THRILL HILL

9. What I need is some proof tonight (1986–1992)   239

10. I'll keep movin' through the dark (1992–1995)   278

11. Look in their eyes, Mom, you'll see me (1995–1997)   309

PART FOUR | THE FAIRGROUNDS

12. Baptized in these waters, and in each other's blood (1997–2005) 339

13. A million different voices speaking in tongues (2005–2008)   386

14. Come tomorrow, none of this will be here (2008–2009)   420

House Lights Up: Meet me in a dream of this hard land   439

Acknowledgments   445

Sources and Notes   448

Permissions Credits   493

Index   495

WALK-IN MUSIC:
SEVEN NIGHTS TO ROCK

A rock 'n' roll audience, February 1957,
New York, NY. © Bettmann/CORBIS.

ROCK 'N' ROLL IS HISTORY: SEVEN DECADES OF MUSIC, AT LEAST four decades of institutionalization, and several distinct cycles of adolescence and maturation. The bare phrase "rock 'n' roll" shows up in popular music as early as the mid-nineteenth-century halyard sea chantey "Johnny Bowker," but the music that we usually call rock 'n' roll grew out of the cross-cultural stew of 1950s post-network radio. When everybody could suddenly hear everybody else's music, particularly late at night, the neat little categories into which *Bill-board* magazine had previously tried to divide it up—"Country &

Western" (formerly "Hillbilly Music"), "Rhythm & Blues" (formerly "Race Records"), and "Best Selling Singles" (implicitly songs favored by upper middle-class urban white people)—suddenly made a lot less sense. Since that first giddy explosion of intercultural hybridity, rock 'n' roll has been declared dead three or four times, usually when one generation's music has grown stale and is just about to give way to its children's.

For some, though, all of that music, from the 1950s to now, is part of a continuum. They can trace a direct line across all those generations from Little Richard to Ke$ha, from Chuck Berry to Muse, from Bo Diddley to Jay-Z, and from Elvis Presley to the Yeah Yeah Yeahs. For those people, rock 'n' roll is unity: a common, ever-evolving discourse that has had its ups and downs in the increasingly fractured culture of our last half century. But if you are one of those people, you can play with the Boston Irish punk band the Dropkick Murphys one night and Stax legend Eddie Floyd another. You can play jazz with Ornette Coleman, country with Joe Ely, folk with Pete Seeger, R&B with Alicia Keys, indie rock with Arcade Fire, and even have your songs sampled by the rap group 2 Live Crew, and there is no contradiction, because all that music flows out of the same vital sources.

Conceived in this way, rock 'n' roll is a kind of faith: a ritual and communion that replaces older forms of religion for generations that have grown skeptical of them. Like all music (and much religion for that matter), the best rock performances are in search of that elusive moment when the familiar once again becomes vital, when the rush of what is happening now is as strong as it was the first time that you heard it. *Spirituality* is present in such moments *as home and as quest*, as a past tradition in which a performer and his audience anchor their actions and as a motivation that propels them through those actions into the future. *How do you find God*, one musically devout performer has suggested, *unless he's in your heart, in your desire, in your feet?* Like most faiths this side of antinomianism, faith in the power of rock is simultaneously individual and communal. Whether the specific style of the music is old-school rockabilly, neo-funk, or Viking death metal, it is by transcending the quotidian together that both artist and audience succeed in moving on up a little higher.

But even if you are one of the faithful, if you are also honest, you must admit that all too frequently such rituals can seem rote, like the thousandth time you've played air guitar on "Jumpin' Jack Flash" or done the spelling dance to "YMCA." In those cases, rock 'n' roll is little more than nostalgia. In those cases, the music provides not vital transcendence but rather a dead longing for a golden age that always seems to exist at that exact point in the past when our independence far exceeded our responsibilities, when *music provided you with a greater sense of unity, a greater sense of shared vision and purpose than it does today,* as one true believer has put it a little more charitably. This is the sort of rote faith that keeps us following the same artists, going to the same clubs, and listening to terrestrial, satellite, and mobile phone–launched radio stations so narrowly conceived that we are virtually guaranteed never to hear a song that we don't already like. This is, of course, the exact antithesis of the sweet chaos that was 1950s radio, the rude, cross-fading juxtapositions that gave birth to rock 'n' roll in the first place.

In this counterview, rock 'n' roll is product, and always has been. It packages acceptable rebellion for each generation until it has success-fully bred the next generation of consuming rebels. It is sold to us the same way that soap is, the same way that politicians are packaged as the friend or neighbor we never knew we had. When you learn the details, it is often shocking how much the planning of a political cam-paign can be like the launch of a rock album, and vice versa. As the generation that embraced rock 'n' roll at its outset has grown first to voting age and now to golden-ager status, the association of musicians and their songs with specific political campaigns has become its own little subindustry. Politicians and their staffs frequently seek rights to songs that their authors protest do not embrace those politicians' val-ues. The ensuing disagreements say a great deal about both popular music and politics, not to mention the visions of society that inevitably underlie both fields.

For our most popular music is not just product, anymore than it is just faith. Despite what those post–World War II parents may have thought the first time they heard "Long Tall Sally" or "Summertime Blues," rock 'n' roll is also thought, thought as deep as its authors' words and feeling can make it. It may begin with a vision of what makes for a great Saturday night at the club, but it extends as its artists and audiences mature to a larger vision of what makes for a good society. Do we come together tonight because of what we have in common, or because of what makes us different from the people outside? Does the band's frontman tell us what to think or do, or are we in the audience the ones who call the tunes? Are we each dancing for ourselves, or do we all dance together? Are the best nights of our lives ahead of us or behind us? We embrace certain musicians, as we embrace certain politicians, because they echo and anticipate our own evolving worldviews. "[A] unique life," as cultural critic Raymond Williams once suggested, "in its place and time, speaks from its own uniqueness and yet speaks a common experience; speaks in a work in language, in a common language, that in its shaping becomes its own but is still common, still connects with others."

Since the 1970s, it is hard to think of an American popular musician whose songs and vision have been embraced as widely as Bruce Springsteen's. Like rock 'n' roll, his career is supposed to have been dead and buried three or four times, but he has reemerged again and again as an artist whose work is a touchstone for many who have very little else in common. He is a widely popular artist in a postmodern, niche-ridden age that is supposed to have outgrown such figures, and he consistently speaks to a continuum of popular music from the 1930s to the present that goes directly against the grain of our self-consciously alternative culture. In "Thunder Road," one of Springsteen's most famous and beloved songs, the music that the characters hear is familiar and conventional. It's Roy Orbison's "Only the Lonely," pure product, mere nostalgia, already fifteen years old back in 1975 when Springsteen wrote his song. But that commercially familiar music nevertheless serves as a call to action for his characters, rather than as an excuse to remain in generationally subdivided complacency.

Trying to coax an old friend away from a beach house haunted by nothing but memory, the narrator of "Thunder Road" declares, *Well I got this guitar / And I learned how to make it talk.* In those two lines, we have the challenge and achievement of Bruce Springsteen's career—making the guitar "talk," as well as the piano, the pump organ, and the ridiculously oversized band; making them say what he wants them to say; speaking to large numbers of people, again and again, so that they actually have a chance of receiving his meaning, so that the highly conventional form of their common language does not overwhelm his deeply felt content.

Rock 'n' roll can be history, unity, faith, nostalgia, product, or thought, and it has been all those things to Bruce Springsteen, at different moments of his life. But rock 'n' roll can also be life, not all of it, but a surprisingly large part. In itself Bruce Springsteen's life is neither representative nor exemplary, but telling the story of his life in rock 'n' roll is a slantwise way of telling the history of our times, how we have come together and divided over the last half century, how we have changed what we think of ourselves as a people. Song by song, album by album, concert by concert, that story has been shaped by subtle but crucial "structures of feeling" (to use Raymond Williams's phrase), unspoken ideas about the world that underlie both the life-or-death controversies of our twenty-four-hour news cycles and the guilty pleasures of our shuffling iPods.

But no matter what some English professors might tell you, that slantwise story does not begin with words, in any language. It begins with three chords and a beat.

PART ONE

COOKMAN AVENUE

—

The Upstage, Cookman Avenue, Asbury Park, NJ.
Photo by Dan Eitner, from *For Music's Sake* by Carrie Potter.

I'M QUICK TO LEARN
(1964–1968)

BRUCE SPRINGSTEEN IS THE FIRST TO ADMIT THAT WHAT HE DOES is a job—but one that he's lucky enough to enjoy most nights. When a concert really clicks, when he feels a real connection with the music, the band, and the audience, he often lengthens the encores, playing other people's songs for ten or fifteen minutes more than he had intended, just to draw out a last bit of fun from that temporary burst of communal energy. If he is having so much fun that, after he has ended the encores, he still wants to go back out onstage and play just one more song, nine out of ten nights it's the same song: "Twist and Shout." *It's the first song I ever learned to play on the guitar,* he has told audiences at least a dozen times. In that statement, in that ending to so many of Springsteen's best performances, lies the beginning of his life in rock 'n' roll.

For some, rock 'n' roll "faltered" in the late 1950s and early 1960s, with "Elvis in the Army, Buddy Holly dead, Little Richard in the ministry, Jerry Lee Lewis in disgrace, and Chuck Berry in jail," but the truth was that it had just gone underground. In the wake of local and federal investigations that showed how heavily influenced some DJs could be by gifts from record companies, many radio stations had switched over during these years to a Top 40 format, which gave disc jockeys less leeway to pick the songs that they played. Increasingly, many stations relied on Bill Gavin's *Record Report* and *Confidential,* two industry newsletters that compiled local requests and airplay in an attempt to spot potential national hits. Gavin put together his charts more quickly and informally than *Billboard* did, and this led to two differences between their surveys of the contemporary pop landscape: Gavin's picks were more pointed toward potential airplay than toward sales; and as a result they reflected the tastes of a younger audience.

The oldest members of the baby boom generation were just ten years old when Elvis Presley hit it big. They didn't have too much spending money to drop on records, but they had plenty of time to listen to the radio once their homework and chores were done. The *Billboard* singles charts for 1957 were hardly rock 'n' roll heaven. Perry Como, Tab Hunter, Johnny Mathis, and Debbie Reynolds occupied the no. 1 slot much more that year than did Elvis, Buddy Holly, Buddy Knox, or the Everly Brothers. By 1963, however, Steve Lawrence, Bobby Vinton, and the Singing Nun could barely hold their own at the no. 1 slot against the raucous likes of Jan and Dean, Little Stevie Wonder, and the Angels. In most cases, the Gavin *Report* predicted these sorts of "younger" hits earlier than the *Billboard* charts did. By 1963, the oldest boomers were turning seventeen. They were driving cars now and starting to buy records of their own. And there were even more teenage consumers coming along in their wake.

In many ways, "Twist and Shout" was the soundtrack for this counterinsurgent takeover of American pop music by the young during the late 1950s and early 1960s. During an era in which rock 'n' roll was (for the first but not the last time) allegedly dead and gone, "Twist and Shout" was quite simply The Little Song That Could. It first hit the *Billboard* Hot 100 in early 1959, but back then it wasn't even "Twist and Shout." It was "La Bamba," the B-side of "Donna," Ritchie Valens's no. 2 hit for Del-Fi Records, a B-side that got as high as no. 22 on its own. (Then as later, ballads always charted higher than party songs, because they usually had more crossover appeal.) Valens didn't write "La Bamba"—it was a traditional Mexican wedding song—but he knew how successfully it could rile up a crowd at a dance. Two years later, in 1961, Phil Medley and Bert Berns came up with a slightly altered version of the song for the Top Notes to record over at Atlantic Records. In terms of notes and lyrics, if not performance style, Medley and Berns's version is the "Twist and Shout" that we know today. But despite the fact that the Top Notes released their single in a year when virtually anything with the word "twist" attached to it seemed like a license to print money, it never charted. In 1962, after the twist craze had peaked, Berns produced a new version of the song for Wand Records, featuring the Isley Brothers, who sang it as a call-and-response number that serendipitously referenced "Shout," their recently reissued two-sided single for RCA. Once again, the song was initially intended as a B-side, but, powered by the Isleys' secularized gospel fervor, this time the song went all the way to no. 17. Cracking the Top 20 in the United States meant that the Isleys' version of the song would inevitably make its way across the Atlantic to Liverpool, where local teenagers thrived on the 45s that visiting American merchant marines left behind in the city's junk shops. When the time came in February 1963 for the Beatles to record their first full album for Parlophone Records, producer George Martin wanted to capture the fervor of one of their live shows, even if he had to do it in the studio. He ended up laying down eleven tracks in a single ten-hour session, about half originals and half covers, just as the group probably would have done down at Liverpool's Cavern Club. Consequently, the Beatles' first album ends the same way that Bruce Springsteen would end so many of his best live shows during the next half century: with a manic, blissfully ragged version of "Twist and Shout."

"Twist and Shout" is as far from a Tin Pan Alley song as you can get. As with the Marketts' "Out of Limits," the Trashmen's "Surfin' Bird," Major Lance's "Um, Um, Um, Um, Um," and especially the Kingsmen's "Louie Louie" (four of the *Billboard* Top 10 singles for the first week of February 1964), the gleeful inarticulateness of this song seems to be part of its point. Are there even lyrics there? There are around forty words in the song, many of them simply repeated. Perhaps because of this, "Twist and Shout" is a song that transcends local cultures and even languages without ever becoming homogeneous. As with "Louie Louie," you can put any words on top of that music— the point is the beat, and the way the musicians use it to pull their audiences together. What other song could liven up the most raucous parties in Chicano Los Angeles, African American Cincinnati, and working-class Irish Liverpool?

Not to mention subsistence-level Freehold, New Jersey. When the

Beatles made their three legendary appearances on CBS's *Ed Sullivan Show* in February of 1964, Bruce Springsteen was fourteen years old, midway through his first year at Freehold Regional High School. He lived at 68 South Street, where he and his family rented half of a house from John Duckett, who owned the Sinclair gas station next door. Like many American families, the Springsteens had moved several times during the 1950s and 1960s as their family had gotten larger, but none of those houses had been particularly palatial. For the first five years of Bruce's life, he and his sister Ginny (who was a little more than a year younger than him) lived with their father and mother in the home of their paternal grandparents, a shotgun house on Randolph Street that was still heated by a wood stove. After that, the family lived in its own tiny mortgaged house on Institute Street for just eight years, moving to Duckett's South Street rental in 1962, when Bruce's younger sister Pam was born. They needed the extra room, but South Street was a main drag in Freehold, and the gas station next door was noisy all night.

If the American economy was expanding and ripe with opportunities during the 1950s and early 1960s, you sure couldn't prove it by Bruce's father, Douglas Springsteen. Doug didn't have a career. He had jobs. In the nearly two decades since he had gotten out of the Army, he had held over half a dozen jobs, ranging from cab driver to jail guard to working on the assembly line at the A&M Karagheusian Rug Mill up on Spring Street, on the other side of the railroad tracks. None of these jobs gave Doug much chance to feel pride in his work, and he lived more for his hours off the job, behind the wheel of the family Buick or sharing a few beers with his friends. But the cars Doug could afford were always used, and sometimes they wouldn't even work in reverse. There was at least one Sunday afternoon when Bruce's mom took him to several dark Freehold bars *searching for my father*. When Bruce was younger, his dad occasionally played catch with him, but by the time he entered high school, for the most part when Doug wasn't working he kept to himself. He also decreed that it would be lights out and heat off throughout the home on South Street after ten every night, to save what money the family had.

It was Bruce's mom who got him interested in pop music. A legal secretary with a local land title company, Adele Zirilli Springsteen was as bright and lively as her husband could be brooding and dark. *She was no stiff with the rock 'n' roll*, Bruce explained on one occasion; *she liked the music.* She sang and danced around the house even as she made everything in it run, while putting her hair up in curlers at night or making the family's breakfast in the morning before she left for work. In 1957, she let Bruce stay up to watch Elvis Presley on the *Sullivan* show, which led to his immediate interest in playing guitar. He quit the instrument after a few lessons, because his hands were too small to make many of the chords, but his interest in pop music abided. A few years later, Adele even took Bruce and his sister Ginny to see a daytime Chubby Checker concert on the Steel Pier, downstate in Atlantic City.

Bruce was a quiet kid, as brooding as his dad, but possessed of a remarkable memory, which he used to get through the tedium of school with a minimal investment of time and energy. Publicly, he often seemed more focused on baseball than on music. (When he was eleven, his team the Indians had the first undefeated season in local Little League history.) At home, though, Bruce listened to WINS and WMCA, two of the New York–area Top 40 stations, almost obsessively, carefully tracking chart positions, and he watched the after-school music shows that local television stations aimed at teenagers. About six months after his family had moved to South Street, Bruce became interested in the guitar again, possibly because of the popularity of such surf music hits as the Chantays' "Pipeline." He took money he had earned by painting houses, bought a secondhand acoustic guitar at a local auto supply store for eighteen bucks, and easily persuaded his cousin Frankie to teach him some chords.

As Springsteen has admitted, the real first song he learned to play on guitar, the one he learned from his cousin Frankie, was "Greensleeves," but it is "Twist and Shout" that he mentions more frequently. That song changed playing guitar from something he might want to do into something that he simply had to do. Given his pop interests, Springsteen probably knew Valens's "La Bamba," and almost certainly knew the Isley Brothers' "Twist and Shout," so why was it the Beatles' version that kicked his interest in music into overdrive?

To put the question in a slightly broader way, why were the early Beatles so important? From the *Sullivan* appearances in February 1964 to the historic moment two months later when *Billboard*'s top 5 U.S. singles were all Beatles songs ("Can't Buy Me Love," "Twist and Shout," "She Loves You," "I Want to Hold Your Hand," and "Please Please Me"), all through 1965 and well into 1966, American Top 40 radio was dominated by Beatles records, imitation Beatles records, and records from the loosely affiliated group of performers that music journalists would collectively dub "the British Invasion." David Crosby— eight years older than Springsteen and a founding member of the Byrds, a group that first cracked the Top 40 in early 1965 with "Mr. Tambourine Man," a Bob Dylan song played as if it were a Beatles song—has told of how he and his bandmates went to see *A Hard Day's Night*, the Beatles' first film, and treated it almost as an instructional feature on how to succeed in popular music.

Musically at least, the Beatles were not doing anything new. If anything, they were feeding a stew of found American sounds from the last ten years back to the land of their origins. By late 1963, even some American groups (most obviously the Beach Boys) were already doing that. Still, in early 1964, the Beatles' music did sound revelatory to pop-trained young American ears like Springsteen's, as did ensuing recordings by the Dave Clark Five, Gerry and the Pacemakers, Herman's Hermits, Manfred Mann, Them, the Animals, the Zombies, the Yardbirds, the Searchers, the Who, and the Rolling Stones. Looking at photographs of these groups now, particularly ones taken early in their careers, one finds it hard to understand how such seemingly clean-cut, frequently uniformed performers could be seen as agents of cultural revolution. This was, after all, before psychedelia, before the Beatles grew beards and adopted false identities, before the Rolling Stones invoked the devil on multiple occasions. Yes, their hair was a little longer than Bobby Vinton's, but was it really long enough to transform a generation?

To answer that question, you cannot just look at the performers as they were back then. You have to listen to them, particularly to Bobby Vinton, who still dominated the Top 40 (if no longer the Top 10) during that last year before the Beatles arrived in America, as well as to Bobby Vee, Steve Lawrence, Andy Williams, Al Martino, the Rooftop Singers, Peter, Paul, and Mary, and Ruby and the Romantics, all of whom had Top 40 hits in 1963. Taken as a group, these performers all sound too casual, too precise, to twenty-first-century ears. Simply put, they do not sound desperate enough. They lack even the suppressed edge of Peggy Lee or Frank Sinatra, not to mention the borderline hysteria of the first true king of American pop music, Al Jolson. While some of these performers were very accomplished technically, they all sang with the same passion that most factory workers who like their jobs feel when they punch in for work. To choose only one example from that oh-so-polished pre-Beatles moment, on paper "I Will Follow Him" might have seemed like a deeply felt tale of romantic obsession, but when Little Peggy March sang it, you were not sure if she cared deeply enough about the boy in question to follow him down to the corner, let alone "forever forever forever."

In contrast to all this excessive polish, the early Beatles, as well as the other British bands that succeeded in their wake, sounded as if they were really enjoying themselves, as if they might get some of the notes wrong but did not care. By 1964, pop songs had been building their lyrics around adolescent concerns for almost a decade, but the new records that these British bands were releasing sounded as if they were being *made* by adolescents, adolescents who were having the time of their lives. When the Beatles sang "Twist and Shout," when the Animals mercilessly tore into "The House of the Rising Sun," when Manfred Mann added a second "Diddy" to "Doo Wah Diddy" and produced that old Bo Diddley song's wholly unrecognizable bastard child, they all sounded as if they were singing along with records and the radio or playing along with them in their crowded homes. If early-1960s American pop had indeed decanted the biracial party music of the previous decade so thoroughly that it was once again safe for white teenagers to imbibe, the bands of the British Invasion took all that safe pop and redistilled it.

And that is why the song on which Springsteen would later center the memory of his conversion experience was the Beatles' version of "Twist and Shout." "Twist and Shout" was the sound of teenage boys' energy busting out of its institutional restraints. It immediately struck a lifer like young Bruce Springsteen as the kind of sound that he wanted to make himself. After that February Beatles broadcast, Bruce spent much of the rest of the year actually practicing on his used secondhand acoustic. It was the most interest he had ever shown in anything, and his mom noticed. That Christmas, she went down to the loan company, as she usually did around that time of year, and took out a loan for $60, the cost of a Kent guitar that Bruce had seen in the window of Calazzo's Music Store downtown. It was cheap and it was Japanese, but it was new, it was electric, and it came with an amp. Christmas morning, it was his. He started practicing even harder than before.

ACROSS CENTER STREET from Calazzo's, about five blocks away from the Springsteens' place, a factory worker by the name of Gordon "Tex" Vinyard lived in yet another Freehold duplex with his wife, Marion. In the spring of 1965, a few months after Bruce received his Kent, Tex couldn't help noticing the racket that a bunch of kids were making next door at the Haynes place. The Hayneses' son Bart was apparently the drummer in a new band called the Sierras that he and a few of his friends had formed. Tex went over and politely asked the boys to dial down the noise a bit—it was bothering Marion. They did, and a few nights later George Theiss, the band's vocalist and rhythm guitarist, came by to make sure everything was okay. Even though Theiss seems to have known almost nothing about Vinyard's own taste in music, he also asked the older man during this second conversation if he would be interested in managing the band. Maybe the walls were thin both ways, but somehow George knew that the older man's union was on strike at the factory and that he currently could use a little extra income.

Tex said yes and dove into his managerial duties with gusto, scheduling regular rehearsals for the band in his own living room and soon firing all its members except Bart and George because they were the only ones who regularly showed up for practice. (Around this time, the band was renamed "the Castiles," after George's favorite brand of soap.) Now the band no longer had a lead guitarist, not to mention the microphone and amp that that guitarist had brought to their practices when he did show up. They didn't have a bassist either, since even before the mass firing their original bass player, Vinnie Roslin, had defected to the Motifs, a more successful local group fronted by singer Walter Cichon. Tex found a bass player by the name of Frank Marziotti who was closer to his own age than the boys', but he was musically solid, and he owned an amp. Frank could also play lead if they needed it, but George kept mentioning this one kid at school who was pestering him about an audition. He was sort of funny-looking, with lots of pimples, and his clothes were pretty worn and never seemed to fit exactly right—but his younger sister Ginny sure was cute.

Bruce showed up at Tex's house for his audition on a rainy night in June, less than six months after his mother had given him the new Kent. When Tex saw the instrument, it looked so worn he assumed that it was "an old [one] that [Bruce]'d borrowed." In Tex's version of the story, though, no matter how hard Bruce had been playing the guitar for the last five or six months, he wasn't necessarily turning out music, just bits and pieces of recent pop songs. If he did complete a song that night, it was almost certainly "Twist and Shout" (which was probably the first song he ever learned to play on *electric* guitar). Impressed more by the boy's enthusiasm than by his technique, Tex suggested that George try to play with him.

When Bruce played solo for Vinyard and the boys, he sounded like a misfit, a wannabe. Before he left, though, he played with George, Frank, and Bart, and Tex heard what had been missing at rehearsals these past two or three months: a band. Promising as the four of them sounded together, though, Tex was still cautious. He told Bruce to "come back when he'd learned say, four or five songs." Bruce came back the next night and played at least seven songs for Vinyard, blowing him away even without using an amp. Not for the last time in his career, Springsteen gave a more impressive audition the second time around, when he could taste how close he was to getting what he'd always dreamed of.

In central Jersey in 1965, there were a lot of teenage boys with exactly the same dream, many of them awakening to it as Springsteen had after watching British bands on American television. About a year before, in Middletown, New Jersey, fifteen miles northeast of the Vinyards' house, Boston-born, fourteen-year-old Steve Van Zandt had seen the Rolling Stones perform Muddy Waters's "I Just Want to Make Love to You" on ABC's *Hollywood Palace* and heard the call: he got a guitar, learned to play, and formed a three-piece band called the Whirlwinds. Over fifty miles northwest of Freehold, in outlet-laden Flemington, New Jersey, another fourteen-year-old, an adopted kid by the name of Danny Federici, had already joined a band called the Legends when he saw the Animals' U.S. premiere on *The Ed Sullivan Show* the following October. Watching Alan Price tear through "Baby Please Don't Go" and "Don't Bring Me Down" got Danny thinking about switching from accordion to electric organ. By the fall of 1964, it seemed as if the teenagers were taking over American television, with shows like ABC's *Shindig* and NBC's *Hullabaloo!* specifically devoted to the sort of music that had been marginalized in prime time just a year before. And in living room after living room across America, the same conversion scene played out again and again. The new groups that teenagers formed in emulation of this new lively music would be called "garage bands," but that assumed that all American families were well off enough to afford a garage. If your family wasn't, you played in the basement or in the cleared-out living room of a laid-off factory worker like Tex Vinyard.

The Castiles rehearsed like crazy throughout July 1965 and had their first paying gig in August, at a swim club on East Freehold Road, where they closed out their set with a rock arrangement of Glenn Miller's "In the Mood." A wedding reception they played that October is the first Bruce Springsteen gig ever for which we have a probable setlist. There the Castiles played just one original song ("Sidewalk"). Otherwise the band performed current Top 40 hits ("You've Lost That Lovin' Feelin'," "I Got You Babe"); surf music covers ("Wipe Out," "Walk Don't Run"), some old soul ("What'd I Say"); one quasi-folk song that had cracked the pop charts ("500 Miles"); and, more than anything, songs from the Kinks ("Tired of Waiting for You"), the Yardbirds ("For Your Love"), the Rolling Stones ("Satisfaction," "Play with Fire," "The Last Time"), even covers of the Beatles covering other artists (Barrett Strong's "Money" and Meredith Willson's "Till There Was You"). As at the swim club gig, there were also some songs for the older crowd ("In the Mood" once again, "Sentimental Journey," "Stranger on the Shore," "Moon River," "What's Your Name," "The Third Man Theme"). It was, in other words, a typical setlist for a late 1965 wedding gig, up-to-date with a little bit of something for everyone.

By that fall, the Castiles had gotten a good enough reputation that they drew the attention of Norman Seldin, the most important music promoter in Monmouth County, who had just gotten the Motifs a chance to record their own single. This wasn't enough for Bart Haynes, though, who was never comfortable in the same place for too long. He quit the Castiles (although he stayed in touch with the band off and on for the next year or so) and was replaced on drums by Vinny "Ski-bots" Manniello. All through Bruce's junior year at Freehold Regional, the band plugged on, making a little more money each time, just enough for Bruce to trade in his already worn Kent for a relatively new Epiphone electric.

At school, Bruce seemed even less interested in his classes, if that were possible. He grew his hair out, the way all his favorite musicians appeared to be doing that year, and he started going for long drives at night with friends. (They were sixteen now, old enough for New Jersey learner's permits.) Some nights they drove up to Manhattan, which took at least two hours. Other nights they slept on the beach or over at the Vinyards' after practice. Sometimes Ginny slept there too, anything to be away from the cold house on South Street.

The tide of Monmouth County rock 'n' roll was rising, however, and the Castiles were rising with it. Around this time, the band stopped wearing uniforms, just as so many of the British bands they emulated were doing, and Frank Marziotti (who had gotten mistaken at least once by a fan for Bruce's father) was replaced on bass by the more age-appropriate Curt Fluhr. Now all the bands' members were juniors at Freehold Regional. In April of 1966, the ever canny Norman Seldin scheduled a countywide Battle of the Bands at a roller dome in

Matawan, with two dozen teen bands playing in competition. In later years, Tex Vinyard would show visitors the piece of paper in his scrapbook that he insisted listed the "results" of the battle that someone had slipped him shortly after it started. Whether those results were fixed or not, the Castiles came in third. Their prize was to open for the Crystals at the same location a week later, but before that could happen the Crystals canceled and Seldin canceled the entire event.

Salvation came in the form of two new venues that opened in Monmouth County that year, both of them specifically targeted at teen audiences. The first was the Surf 'n' See Club, which had its grand opening the first weekend in July down on Ocean Avenue in Sea Bright. The idea was to have a club where kids could surf all day and listen to rock 'n' roll at night. The ever popular Rogues were hired as the house band at the Surf 'n' See, and just hours before their first scheduled performance, they hired the Castiles to be their opening act. This meant that a week later the Castiles got to be introduced by WMCA DJ Gary Stevens and to perform on the same stage as Johnny Tillotson, the Jive Five, the Tymes, and the Shangri-Las. These were the sorts of artists the newer British bands had pushed off the charts, the ones who had made the music that, three or four years before, Bruce had listened to on the radio in his room late at night or in the car with his mom. Soon after that first WMCA show, the Castiles played a second one with Little Anthony and the Imperials, another blast from the pre-Beatles past. These were all artists currently riding out the back ends of their pop careers (which was why they were playing the Surf 'n' See in Sea Bright on a Saturday night in summer), but they were still performers who had at least temporarily achieved the kind of national success that the Castiles dreamed of.

In pursuit of that dream, a few months back, the Castiles had gone to Mr. Music, a storefront recording studio in Bricktown, and laid down two tracks of their own, "That's What You Get" and "Baby I." George Theiss sang lead vocals on both songs, as he still did at most of the band's performances, but George and Bruce shared writing credit on the two songs, just like Lennon and McCartney. In May of 1966, however, Springsteen and Theiss were no Lennon and McCartney. Even if these recordings had attracted the attention of a major label,

"That's What You Get" and "Baby I" contain almost nothing that would have struck a contemporary audience as noteworthy. What words one can make out in the first track are virtually interchangeable with those of almost any guitar pop single from the period, and the second track not only swipes harmonies from the Beatles but also steals the two most frequently repeated lines in its lyric outside of the chorus from "Cathy's Clown," an old Everly Brothers song. If these tracks do not come close to attaining the clichéd originality of the best British Invasion singles, neither do they approach the plodding insanity of the Kingsmen's "Louie Louie," the gold standard for garage band antiverbalism. Words do not even matter as noise for the Castiles, let alone as conveyances of self-expression. Obviously, the point is the harmonies and the guitars, and in that sense we are clearly listening to a knockoff.

A knockoff, though, was just perfect for the kids at the Surf 'n' See, as well as at Le Teendezvous, a "teen country club" that had opened two years before on Route 35 in New Shrewsbury. The Castiles headlined the latter club at least once in the spring and opened for the Rogues at the former at least twice during summer vacation. Just before the Surf 'n' See closed for the season, the band finally got what was probably its first headlining gig there too, which may have led to its first semipermanent headlining gig at the new Hullabaloo Club, about seven miles north of the Teendezvous on Route 35 in Middletown. Because these clubs were explicitly intended for teenagers, they were open Friday and Saturday nights and featured a cheap admission and soft drinks rather than alcohol. As Springsteen later remembered it, the clubs were painted *fluorescent orange* and bands that worked there were predictably expected to perform strictly covers. By the fall of 1966, even older businessmen who might not like the Beatles themselves had realized that the torrent of enthusiasm that teen rock unleashed could be channeled and managed into a steady source of profits.

But how steady, and for how long? Teenage life can't last forever, no matter how much fun it may seem. Even more restless with central New Jersey than Bruce was, drummer Bart Haynes, who had quit the Castiles about a year before, decided in late 1966 that what he wanted to do next was join the Marines. After he enlisted, he came next door to Tex's house to show all the members of the band how he looked in his brand new uniform. As Bruce told an audience almost two decades later, Bart *didn't even know where [Vietnam] was.*

FOR THE REMAINING CASTILES, the most beckoning horizon lay a lot closer than Southeast Asia, about fifty miles north on the island of Manhattan. A month or two after their first date at the Middletown Hullabaloo, Tex Vinyard finally got the band the one thing its members had been bugging him about for months: an audition at a club in Greenwich Village. Tex's comments to Dave Marsh suggest he may have picked the Café Wha? just because it was in a Manhattan neighborhood with a number of other active clubs, Macdougal Street back then being the equivalent of Ludlow Street in our time, but he could hardly have picked a more momentous location for rock 'n' roll history. Six years earlier, on his first day in New York City, Bob Dylan had played a set of Woody Guthrie songs at the Café Wha?, and three months later he was opening on the road for blues legend John Lee Hooker. Just four months before the Castiles' audition, in early July, Jimi Hendrix (then calling himself Jimmy James) had used this "lowest club on the [Village] totem pole" to break out of being an eternal sideman and into fronting his own band.

The Castiles' audition wasn't for a regular gig at the Café Wha? like Hendrix's, and it wasn't even an audition to play any evening shows. It was to become part of a pool of young bands that would play on Saturday or Sunday afternoons, alternating sets for five hours with one or two other bands. In other words, it was to do still more teen-only shows—but they were teen-only shows in Manhattan, with the tantalizing if remote possibility of an opening slot at night much, much farther down the line. When he scheduled the audition with Tex, the club's manager had told him that there would be only thirty chances to play all winter and a hundred bands that wanted to play there. This was probably not an exaggeration, given the explosion of bands that had formed locally over the last two years: both the demand and the supply for teen rock were enormous during the mid-

1960s. Nervous as he was at the audition, Bruce told Curt to turn out some lead bass—not a foundation, but a lead. Curt started the Who's "My Generation," and by the end of the song the Castiles had made the list.

Bruce spent his last semester of high school traveling north and south along the Garden State Parkway. That winter, the Castiles alternated gigs at the Café Wha? (while Frank Zappa was playing just down the street at the Garrick, on his first East Coast swing with the Mothers of Invention) with gigs at the Middletown Hullabaloo (where they alternated most weekends with a wholly forgotten teen band called the Chlan). They were also getting more gigs connected to Freehold Regional: a sweet-sixteen party at the American Hotel in December, the senior farewell dance ten days before graduation in June. If Bruce was forced to make a choice, however, it was Manhattan over Monmouth every time. He ditched the graduation itself for a trip to New York, although when he got home the next morning Doug insisted he go back to the school and pick up his diploma.

At first, leaving high school didn't seem to change Bruce's life, which was still centered on guitar and whatever gigs the Castiles could pick up. That summer, they alternated between the Café Wha? and the Surf 'n' See, making sure they went up Ocean Avenue to Asbury Park after one of their gigs at the latter club to catch the triple bill of Herman's Hermits, the Blues Magoos, and (especially) the Who at the Convention Hall. It was the first time that they had actually seen any of the British bands live, and at seventeen it was clear to Springsteen that the promoters didn't share his own taste in music: the always unpredictable Who were billed second for the Convention Hall show, below the much safer, more acceptable Herman's Hermits.

By the summer of 1967, over three years into the British Invasion and counting, the sound was changing, and the change could be seen in the tagline that the promoters gave to the Blues Magoos, the third act on the Convention Hall bill: "First Psychedelic Rock Group in U.S." Whether it was the increasing use of hallucinogenic or psychedelic drugs or simply yet another attempt to dig out a new kind of sound, British groups like the Beatles and the Kinks were now trying to make their guitars sound like Indian sitars, and the Animals were no longer trying to sound like Delta bluesmen but were singing instead about "San Franciscan Nights." By 1967, the geographical center of American pop had shifted back to California, to the northern part of the state now rather than to its southern part. During the mid-1960s, San Francisco was producing an extraordinary stream of musicians— including Moby Grape, the Grateful Dead, the Jefferson Airplane, and Big Brother and the Holding Company, to cite only a few of the most obvious early examples—as well as a new musically distinct sound that was less snappy than early British Invasion pop had been. From the start, many of these new American groups, along with such British contemporaries as Procol Harum and Pink Floyd, were labeled "psychedelic music," but from a twenty-first-century perspective it may be more useful to think of them as "jam bands." Their perfor- mances were more rangy and discursive than the rock of a few years before had been, less about the bopping pleasures of the beat than about the bending pleasures of an exploratory solo.

In the summer of 1967, new teen clubs offering this kind of music were popping up all over south central Jersey, and older, alcohol-free clubs like the Surf 'n' See were advertising "Freak Out Shows" in an obvious attempt to pull in younger, trippier fans. The Castiles even got to headline the opening weekend of one local teen club—although it was admittedly a place called "the Left Foot," which an Episcopal priest by the name of Fred Coleman operated out of his parish center. "Hear the Sounds," the club's flier announced in the self-consciously Gothic print that seemed to pop up all over the place during the late 1960s. The flier listed not only the Castiles but also the Rogues, the Motifs, and the Chlan, some of the same bands that Springsteen and Theiss's group had been trading gigs with for over two years now.

Thanks to the good Reverend Coleman, who had the perhaps providential foresight to keep a tape player running for the Castiles' two appearances at the Left Foot, we can hear what the band sounded like in late 1967: it had the same five musicians who had cut "That's What You Get" and "Baby I" (Springsteen, Theiss, Manniello, Fluhr, and Popkin) along with a newer, sixth member on organ (Bob Alfano), but their performance style was noticeably different, as different as 1967 felt from 1966. The words still did not matter as much as the sound for the Castiles, but the jangling guitars of a year and a half before had been replaced by more of an amplified sludge. In the Castiles' hands, Sam and Dave's 1966 hit "Hold On I'm Comin'" becomes a stomp, Manniello's drums more insistent with each new measure, Alfano's organ following a path that it seems could amble on forever. The guitar line is less important in the Castiles' interpretation of the song than it was in the Stax original, but Springsteen still remained at the center of the action for this and many of the band's other performances at the Left Foot. By this date, he was sharing lead vocals with Theiss, perhaps because the music that the Castiles now performed was more suited to his voice's undeniable rough edges.

Much of the new music of 1967, especially the acts coming out of San Francisco, was slow to enter the Top 40 in America, in part because the performances were hard to boil down into neat three-minute singles. And that is probably the biggest difference between the songs the Castiles played in September 1967 and those that they had played a little less than two years before: over half the covers they performed at the Left Foot were originally album tracks, not singles. Recently released songs from such San Francisco bands as the Grateful Dead ("Morning Dew") and Moby Grape ("Omaha," performed both nights) were prominently featured, as were the Yardbirds' "Jeff's Boogie," as well as "One by One," a noncharting track by the Blues Magoos. It was also clear that there were two recent LPs to which someone in the Castiles was paying very close attention: the Blues Project's *Projections* and *Are You Experienced?*, the debut album from the Jimi Hendrix Experience. Between the two Left Foot dates, the band covered two songs off the first album ("Steve's Song" and "Wake Me Shake Me") and three off the second ("Fire," "Purple Haze," and "Hey Joe"). Even when the Castiles played a more conservative rock song like "Eleanor Rigby," they extended and developed it instrumentally so that it clocked in at almost seven minutes, well over twice as long as the Beatles' original recording of the song.

Stylistically, the Castiles were spreading their wings, but it wasn't necessarily clear where they were flying. By February 1968 at the latest, the Café Wha? dates definitely ended. The Castiles got an evening slot at the club at least once before they left, but no famous music industry types ever saw them and whisked them away to record in London or tour with famous bluesmen. The acetate of the single they had recorded almost two years before had never been pressed for mass distribution and now probably wouldn't be. They were back to playing teen clubs in New Jersey: the Teendezvous again, as well as the three Hullabaloo clubs that the Jersey Shore now boasted, in Middletown, Asbury Park, and Bruce's hometown of Freehold. (In March, they played the opening of that third, newest one.) The audiences at the teen clubs seemed to have changed over the last year or two, however: they appeared more restless than the teenagers of 1965 had been. *[I]f you ever played a Hullabaloo club,* Springsteen once remembered onstage, *the drummer had to keep the beat . . . so that there wouldn't be any fighting.*

The Castiles were a little older than their audiences now, in the way that a year or two can seem like eons to a teenager. Only organist Bob Alfano was still in high school, and he was going to graduate in a few months. The other guys were thinking about settling down, and Tex made the mistake of suggesting to Bruce that he get a day job, as most of the other Castiles had done. The suggestion was not well received. That fall, Bruce was scheduled to start classes at Ocean County Community College, down in Toms River, about a year after most of his graduating class from Freehold Regional had moved on. He was no more keen on education than he had been in high school, but enrolling at OCCC probably kept Adele and Doug off his back for a while.

It also put him in line for a draft deferment. In the fall of 1967, Bruce turned nineteen, the prime age of most of the young men being inducted and sent over to fight in Vietnam. The war was not an abstraction to him now, as it may have been just a year before. Bart Haynes was killed in action in Vietnam in November of 1967, about a month after the Castiles' gig in the Reverend Coleman's church basement.

IN BIOGRAPHY, AS IN HISTORY, time unspools on multiple levels. Close up, there is the day-to-day accumulation of minor, often repeated events: gigs, arguments, nights out with friends, cold hours in phone booths talking to absent lovers. From a distance, though, there are larger, subtler movements across time. It's the way that a parent or sibling may not notice how much a child has grown, but a relative who visits once a year will spot that growth instantly. While the same old trivia seems to happen every day, the world is spinning through its epic revolutions.

Between 1967 and 1969, on a week-to-week basis, Bruce Springsteen was playing fairly steadily, but in terms of the larger movement of his life, he was essentially in a holding pattern. His music changed only as the records played on the radio did, and the new covers he learned during this period were seldom of songs that he regards nostalgically now. The one overwhelming, often reiterated event of Bruce's life during this period was his never-ending argument with his father. For two men both known for their relative silence, Doug and Bruce Springsteen appear to have fought long, loud, and constantly during the late 1960s. The arguments always seemed to start the same way, with the father asking his son *what did I think I was doing with myself.*

Some of Doug's impatience with Bruce may have been projection, a father's natural desire to make sure that his son didn't repeat his own past mistakes. In the late 1960s, Doug was still having problems finding or keeping a job. Some nights, he just sat in the kitchen of the South Street house, drinking beer, with all the lights off. When his elder, unmarried daughter, Ginny, got pregnant at the age of seventeen, it probably didn't help his mood much either. By the end of the decade, Doug's frequently depressive doubts, not to mention his larger sense that there was nowhere to go in central New Jersey but down, would lead him to clean out the family savings account, pack up the car, and drive Adele and Pam all the way to San Mateo, California, in search of sunnier prospects.

But Doug's angry concern about his son's future wasn't all projection. He had a point. What did Bruce think he was doing with himself? If he was honest, he had to admit that he didn't know where to go next or how to move on. Playing at the Café Wha? had been an eye-opening experience: most successful bands didn't do covers; they wrote their own songs. But in 1967 songs like "That's What You Get" and "Baby I" just weren't going to cut it. Neither were "Mr. Jones" or

"Look into My Window," the two originals the Castiles had performed at the Left Foot.

In late 1967, Bruce started writing songs that weren't for the Castiles, at least a dozen songs with titles like "New York Morning Love," "The Virgin Flower," and "A Winter's Revelation in 9 Illusions." We don't know what the music of these songs sounded like, but we do have some of their lyrics, which are far more self-consciously wrought than those of the five previous songs that Springsteen had had a hand in writing. An audience probably could not have followed their more opaque forays into figurative language even if Bruce had shouted them as loudly as he could over all that sludgy organ and guitar that the Castiles had been offering lately. Consequently, Bruce performed these songs solo at the Off Broad Street Coffee House. The Off Broad Street was next to the post office up in Red Bank, only a fifteen-minute drive from Le Teendezvous, but it must have seemed like an entirely different musical culture. So must have a new teahouse on Cookman Avenue in Asbury Park called the Green Mermaid, where Bruce may also have spent time during the summer before he entered college. In most American cities and college towns, the coffeehouse boom in fact predated the teen club boom, just as *Hootenanny* predated *Shindig* on ABC's prime-time schedule. "By 1962," as biographer Sheila Weller has suggested, "coffeehouses with folksinger entertainers could be found in most major North American cities." Probably through television, Bruce was vaguely aware of this phenomenon, but while he was at Freehold Regional it wasn't an important part of his musical landscape. Even when he was playing in Greenwich Village, surrounded by some of the most respected folk venues in the world, the only music on which he really focused was rock. By 1968, however, both Bruce and Monmouth County were catching up. It made perfect sense that, as Bruce prepared himself to attend college that fall, he simultaneously prepared himself to appreciate, and possibly play, "college music" as well. The Off Broad Street held some rock nights, at which the Castiles played, but they started to hang out there when they weren't playing too, and Bruce performed at the club solo at least once that summer.

He made money, though, by being in the Castiles, now so senior a group around Monmouth County that they were *judging* Battles of the Bands at local YMCAs. They were still playing the same clubs they had been playing for the last two or three years, with at least half a dozen dates at Le Teendezvous through the end of that summer. No matter how much they changed their music to fit shifting fashions, the Castiles were still very much a high school band, and by that point all its members had probably outgrown it. In August, they cut the cord: they played their last professional engagement, at Le Teendezvous, of course. Within a week, Bruce graduated to a new band, whose other two members (John Graham and Michael Burke) had never attended Freehold Regional. They would be starting classes with him a few weeks later at OCCC.

CHAPTER 2

I PUSHED B-52 AND BOMBED 'EM
WITH THE BLUES (1968–1971)

THE NEW BAND WAS CALLED "THE EARTH BAND" AT FIRST AND then simply "Earth." Springsteen, Graham, and Burke had played together several times informally at the Off Broad Street during the summer, and come fall they played some quiet shows on campus and at coffeehouses, covering songs by such acoustic favorites as Tim Buckley and Leonard Cohen. But Bruce was not making a complete break from his precollegiate musical past, not yet. For one thing, there are some surviving publicity materials that baldly announce, "The Castiles will now be touring as The Earth Band," as if the new group merely picked up from where the old one had left off. Moreover, for many of the new band's dates, Bob Alfano was present on organ. On those nights, half of Earth consisted of ex-Castiles.

There are no surviving recordings of Earth, but the reminiscences and setlists that we do have suggest that the group further developed the electric jamming impulse that had overtaken the Castiles at least a year earlier. If anything, Earth was getting even closer to the music that the Castiles had latterly embraced, the music of Jimi Hendrix and the Blues Project. On the nights when Alfano was absent, Earth was a "power trio," as the contemporary term had it, playing not just such Castile-era holdovers as "Get Out of My Life, Woman," "Fire," "Purple Haze," and "Jeff's Boogie" but also a number of Cream songs, most notably "Outside Woman Blues," "Swlabr," "Toad," and "Politician." At the height of the British Invasion, bands could have four, five, or even six members, with a rhythm guitar and keyboards filling out the chords of a song. In a power trio, though, chords were not the point, nor were words. In power trios, instrumental prowess was emphasized above all else, with individual band members taking distinct solos as they did in jazz.

That fall, Earth enjoyed a certain measure of success. In November, the band even sold out the 1,800-seat Diplomat Ballroom in New York, thanks to two fans who were OCCC undergraduates (and who had impulsively made the booking), not to mention the college's administration (which was somehow persuaded to pay for buses to transport students to the concert). In December, Ooze and Oz Productions, Earth's new managers, even got them a gig playing Bill Graham's Fillmore East—for a low-budget movie that happened to be shooting there, though, not for a real concert.

By early 1969, Bruce Springsteen had been playing guitar for pay for three and a half years. Except for the Café Wha? and Diplomat Hotel dates, however, he had never played for an audience more than a half an hour away from his parents' house in Freehold. His world was "the Shore," a nebulous area that to most New Jerseyans means everything east of the Garden State Parkway in Monmouth and Ocean Counties, even those areas that are ten or fifteen miles from the Atlantic Ocean. Routes 18, 35, and 71 are the three main north–south roads that run almost parallel to the parkway in that area, and in the late 1960s and early 1970s most local nightclubs were located on one of those three roads. Drive southeast from Woodbridge through the Amboys on Route 35, and you got to Middletown, where the fluorescent Hullabaloo Club sat three or four miles from the bay. Drive fifteen minutes south from there, and you were in Red Bank, where the Off Broad Street Coffee House was. Drive another ten minutes south of that, and you were in the faux country club atmosphere of Le Teendezvous. Drive another half hour, probably switching over to Route 70 where the two routes crossed in Brielle, and you were at Bruce's new college in Toms River. People were born, lived, and died in this geographical circuit, without seeing all that much else of the world except on television. For such people, New York City was just a rumor, unless one of your maiden aunts treated you to the Rockettes at Christmas-time. But you couldn't support yourself playing music if you lived that restricted a life.

Earth sounded different from the Castiles, but for the most part it was still playing the same types of gigs. Its steadiest engagement throughout late 1968 was at the good old Le Teendezvous, which was apparently happy to absorb every new shock to the musical status quo. The band also played the Freehold Hullabaloo at least once. And its members kept trading bookings with the same other performers their age, even if the bands to which those performers belonged had undergone personnel mitosis over the last three or four years. In the initial wake of the Beatles revolution, each shore town had developed its own distinct music scene, in part because the teen clubs were meant to cater primarily to high school students who could not travel far from home and did not have much money to spend on cover charges. Thus each town ended up having its own reigning popular bands: in Freehold, it was the Motifs and the Castiles; a little farther east in Asbury Park, it was Sonny and the Starfires; up north in Red Bank, it was the Shadows. By late 1968, however, few of these bands remained; they had been done in by time, trends, and the unignorable fact of the draft. Those young musicians who were left all seemed to be moving in the same direction as Earth was, away from quick pop songs and toward a sort of extended jamming. Given all this stylistic convergence, it was only a matter of time before somebody got the idea to build some kind of shorewide "supergroup" across all these microscenes.

In February of 1969, Earth was booked to play a "St. Valentine's Day Massacre" concert in Long Branch. Springsteen probably did not know it at the time, but he was being scouted at this concert by Vini Lopez, formerly of Sonny and the Starfires, lately of the Moment of Truth, who wanted to form a new band. Around the Jersey Shore at that time, everybody had a nickname, and Vini's was "Mad Dog," a sobriquet inspired as much by his flamboyant performance style as by any colorful offstage behavior. In an era known for its emotional drummers, Lopez was still a standout, his long hair whipping in all directions as his drumming increased in furor. He hadn't been impressed by Springsteen the first time he saw him (at the Battle of the Bands in Matawan, almost three years earlier), but lately he had been hearing better things about him, especially since the formation of Earth. Seeing Springsteen live confirmed the rumors. After the concert, Lopez said hello and asked Springsteen if he would be interested in forming a band together. If he was, Lopez said, he should come down to the Upstage.

If the infamous Stone Pony (which didn't even open until 1974) would eventually become the St. Peter's Basilica of Asbury Park rock 'n' roll, then the Upstage was its catacombs: the place where the hard work of building a faith first happened, before a structure and a certainty could be erected on its foundations. Actually, the club was on the third floor, in a windowless storage room above the Green Mermaid teahouse, which was itself above a Thom McAn shoe store on Cookman Avenue, a few doors down from a local salon where Margaret and Tom Potter, the owners of both clubs, sometimes worked as hairdressers. That strictly commercial stretch of Cookman was seven blocks in from the boardwalk and only a block away from the railroad tracks, not where the action usually is in a shore town. But even though the Upstage was open only on Friday, Saturday, and Sunday nights, it was not primarily a place for weekenders. It was for musicians.

Most weekend nights at the Upstage, there was a 9:00 p.m. show for the under-eighteen crowd with Margaret and the Distractions (the house band that Margaret Potter fronted). At midnight they kicked the kids out, cleaned the place up, and then reopened at 1:00 a.m., when the real fun began. The Upstage quickly became famous around the shore as the place that was open when all the other clubs closed. Musicians would come there after their own separate gigs and play together for the rest of the night, once the VFW Hall out back on Bond Street was empty and there wouldn't be any complaints about noise. In time, people were lined up around the block at three in the morning to get in. As one frequent denizen of the club remembered it, "The Upstage was the cheapest motel room in town. Two bucks to get in and you could hang out until dawn when you could go to the beach and sleep there all day—legally."

Being a great crash pad is not enough to make a classic music

scene, though. Every hole-in-the-wall rock club that becomes legendary has to have at least one unique feature that makes it technically
appealing to aspiring musicians. In the case of the Bowery's CBGB
(still just a gleam in Hilly Kristal's eye in the winter of 1969), the dis-
tinguishing feature was the first-rate onstage monitors: for a small,
crowded, dirty little dump, it was amazing how well a band could hear
itself onstage there. For Asbury's admittedly less legendary Upstage, it
was not the quality of the equipment but the quantity. Yes, there was
fluorescent paint all over the walls, just as in the Hullabaloo clubs, not
to mention the black lights and strobe lights that invariably accompa-
nied such paint in contemporary décor. But there was also an entire
wall of speakers, as well as amps and all kinds of sound equipment for
everyone, not to mention house instruments that were as good as any
a local musician could probably afford. The only person who got paid
for this postmidnight session was the one who ran the jam, who
received the princely sum of five bucks. The only currency that got
you into the jam was talent.

These late-night sessions at the Upstage were, after a fashion, merit-
ocratic, if decidedly male. Among the young men at least, there
seemed to be a true openness to each other's talent, even the talent of
relative newcomers. When he started playing in these jams about a
year later, in 1970, David Sancious was a fifteen-year-old keyboardist,
and he found the Upstage incredibly welcoming, even though he was
one of the few African Americans present. "In those days," as a local
guitarist once remembered, "if you were in a band you were already
friends. If you had long hair, you were friends. There were so few
freaks, as we were known, that there was a common philosophy before
you spoke to each other." This philosophy was upheld by the half-
jokey rules that Tom Potter had posted on the wall of the Upstage,
whose first commandment declared, "If you can't love your nabor [sic],
you must respect him or get out." The Upstage was a rock 'n' roll mis-
fits' utopia. Your clothes, your looks, your family, your home—none of
that mattered. If you could play, you were in.

Perhaps as soon as a week after Vini's invitation, Bruce arrived at
the Upstage early, "shortly after midnight," one witness remembers,

before a lot of the regulars even arrived. He "came up very politely," as Margaret Potter would tell the story, "and said 'Excuse me, but would you mind very much if I borrowed your guitar? The gentleman down-stairs said it would probably be okay.'" At the Upstage, the house gui-tar was a Fender Stratocaster, the same instrument that Eric Clapton played, the same instrument that Jimi Hendrix had burned in tribute at the Monterey Pop Festival two years earlier. By late February of 1969, Bruce had traded up guitars again and was now playing a Gib-son Les Paul, but a Stratocaster was an even better instrument, just one step away from the Telecaster that he promised himself he would buy if his career ever really took off. Margaret gave him permission to play the Strat but watched carefully as he plugged it in and learned his way around her husband's eccentric sound system. Then he started playing: "some blues thing" was the colorless way she would later describe it. She ran down one flight to the Green Mermaid, where some of the regulars were playing Monopoly while waiting for the usual 1:00 a.m. jam to start. "Hey guys," she yelled out, "there's some kid up there who can really play."

Rock improvisation, like the blues improvisation on which it is based, is an extraordinarily limited exercise. You were always free to play anything you wanted, but then as later improvisation was usually judged within some shared set of musical conventions. In 1969, at the Upstage and throughout the United States and Europe, those conven-tions derived mostly from what was loosely called "the blues revival." The blues had been in rock from the beginning, from rhythm and blues through rockabilly straight into the British Invasion, but now rock musicians were self-consciously turning back to the work of elder blues players as a model for current performance. This was true not only for such established British artists as Eric Clapton and the Roll-ing Stones (who made their blues roots more explicit as their careers went on), and for such rising California stars as Janis Joplin and the Doors (who had included the "Kosmic Blues" and Willie Dixon's "Back Door Man" on their respective debut albums), but even for such noisier young bands as Iron Butterfly, Steppenwolf, Black Sabbath, and Led Zeppelin (all of whom would eventually be gathered under the newly coined rubric of "heavy metal"). Over the last few years, even the musically discriminating Miles Davis had become more enamored of the electric blues.

Indeed, the blues were so central to American music in 1969 that they inspired several distinct, only mildly overlapping performance styles. These styles could sometimes come into conflict within a single concert. That same year, Iggy Pop, only two years older than Springsteen, opened at the Boston Tea Party for the English blues revival group Ten Years After (whose song "Help Me" was on Earth's list of frequent covers). Both that group and Pop's group, the Stooges, focused much of their performance on "the blues," but the blues Pop came to play apparently weren't the ones that Ten Years After's fans wanted to hear. Their audience was mostly collegiate, and their quiet, almost studious receptivity—"sort of chi-chi-chiffon and guitar worship, with heavy overtones of derivative music worship"—infuriated Pop so much that it inspired him to try stage diving for the first time that night, not to mention verbally taunting the audience and cutting himself and bleeding on them. "[I]f I wasn't going to get a positive reaction," he remembered, "I was DAMNED well going to get one that wouldn't let them sleep at night."

The blues were simple, anyone could play them, but there were many, many kinds of blues. As Newark's LeRoi Jones had observed before the blues revival really took off, the blues "was a music that arose from the needs of a group, although it was assumed that each man had his *own* blues and he would sing them." Because so much of the genre seems the same from song to song, nuance looms large in blues performance. The trick is to bend the very sameness of its music toward one's own individuality—to take the song and the guitar and "make them talk," to rephrase Bruce Springsteen's famous line.

For a young man who seems to have been as uncomfortable with words as Springsteen was in the late 1960s, it must have been a relief to express himself in some way other than brooding silence or barely articulate mumbles. According to Margaret Potter, one of the Monopoly players down in the Green Mermaid that first night was Vini Lopez, who may not have expected Springsteen to come by so soon, or so early. By the time Lopez entered the Upstage, Springsteen was already front and center running a jam.

That first February night at the Upstage, Bruce finally played with Vini Lopez, as well as with bassist Vinnie Roslin (sometimes known as "Little Vini," in order to distinguish him from Lopez) and keyboardist Danny Federici. Springsteen may not have played with Roslin before, but they certainly knew about each other: Roslin had been in the Motifs, the only band in Freehold more highly regarded than the Castiles. In fact, he had been in the Castiles back when it was still the Sierras but had left the band before Bruce had even joined it. Federici, though, who had been in two or three Asbury Park bands with Lopez, had barely heard of Springsteen before his bandmate started talking him up as someone with whom they might be able to play. Once he saw Springsteen play, however, Federici became a true believer. This was definitely another musician with whom he wanted to work.

Adopted in the late 1940s by an Italian father and a Polish mother, Federici was probably destined as a child to study accordion. Over time, though, he had wisely turned his talents to rock 'n' roll, shifting from an old-fashioned 128-button strap-on to the horizontal Farfisa keyboard favored by surf and pop bands like Gary Lewis and the Playboys. What he really wanted was a Vox Continental, like the one that Alan Price of the Animals played, but the Farfisa (like the Kent guitar that Springsteen's parents had initially bought for him) was the best that Mr. and Mrs. Federici could afford. At least when you laid the Farfisa down on an amplifier, it looked like an organ. This was a definite improvement, since, in Federici's words, "[t]he girls were not going for the squeeze box."

At that moment in American pop, the organ was as important as bass and drums in laying the foundation on which vocal and guitar improvisations could be built. Clearly, Lopez and Federici had formed a powerful bond building that foundation together in a succession of groups. The late-night sessions at the Upstage provided a way of trying different combinations of other players until they found a complete group that clicked, and it took only two of those sessions in late February of 1969 for this newest shore band to form. After one performance,

Big Danny Gallagher asked Lopez, "Hey man, are you sure you and [Springsteen] didn't rehearse that stuff you just played?" Lopez laughed and denied it. "I didn't care if I made any money," Federici recalled about his instantaneous decision to join up with Springsteen. "He had a drive and a determination that was so strong that I believed in what he believed in." Within a month, Earth was dissolved and Child was born. It featured Springsteen, Lopez, Roslin, and Federici, and in this band there would be no question who would be both the guitarist and the lead vocalist.

Even more significant for Springsteen's professional development, Child would not be a cover band but would perform original songs, all of them written by Springsteen alone. Indeed, if Danny Federici's testimony can be believed, the sheer volume of songs that Springsteen produced may imply that he was fishing around for a mode in which he felt comfortable composing. The band would sometimes perform as many as sixty original songs in a single weekend. Building on the success of both Child and Sonny and the Starfires, it began to get bookings almost immediately. Back in February, a new all-ages club called Pandemonium had opened in Wanamassa, just west of Asbury Park on Route 35 at the Shore Motel, and within a few weeks of its formation Child played its first of many dates there that year.

In mid-May, a week before the band started its second multiweek stand at the Pandemonium, there was a shooting on South Street in Freehold, just blocks from where the Springsteens lived. It was around this time that Bruce's father, Doug, decided to move his wife and youngest child out of New Jersey altogether. After his family's departure, Springsteen continued to live in the house on South Street, and Danny Federici lived there with him for a while, until they were evicted, maybe for a broken window, maybe because they were long-haired freaks without a responsible adult around. *A weekend outing at that time*, Springsteen recalled several decades later, *was still filled with the drama of possibly getting your ass kicked by a total stranger who disagreed with your fashion sense.* In that emotionally charged climate, the mere sight of Bruce's long hair might have been enough, as one biographer has attested, to lead truckers to "[try] to run him off the road."

Not that things were any better indoors that summer. The crowds could be pretty rough at the Pandemonium. Child *played behind a U-shaped bar [there] that was just three feet and spitting distance from many of the patrons.* All summer long, there was *rarely a night without a fight* at the club, as *[r]ough kids just out of high school, who hadn't been snatched up by the draft just yet, truck drivers heading home, south into the Jersey pines, who weren't gonna make it—not that night at least—and a mixture of college and working girls, women with bouffant hairdos, and a small but steady hippie contingent* mingled gingerly in a thick climate of cultural dissonance. The tension built until 20 July, when Vini flipped out because the crowd decided they would rather watch the moon landing on the bar's TVs than the live performance of his band. With that Mad Dog outburst, Child lost the Pandemonium gig.

The band also played the more comfortable Le Teendezvous several times that summer, as well as one date at the Hullabaloo Club in Asbury Park, which was much closer to the beach than the Upstage but far less hip. Fairly soon, that particular Hullabaloo Club would close and reopen under new, savvier management as the Sunshine In. Another good music club, called the Student Prince, would open up right across Kingsley Avenue from it. Like Margaret and Tom Potter, the owners of these two new clubs were not necessarily averse to making money, but they did seem to have a sense of just how much youth music had changed since the long-ago days of "Love Me Do." Five years after the Beatles had first inspired him to get serious about the guitar, Bruce Springsteen was no longer playing in a band that sounded like a British Invasion knockoff. His new band, as one friend would suggest to an interviewer in the early 1980s, was a heavy metal band, an early one but very much of the same type as Black Sabbath and Iron Butterfly, both bands with whom it would later share a stage. Child's music took off from its blues foundation into extended instrumental riffing, or "shredding," as it would be called in later decades. Rather than playing snappy pop songs, Child often seemed to prefer exploring one continuous dour mood through a succession of brooding songs for an hour at a stretch.

———

IN AN ODD WAY, THE VIETNAM WAR—or at least the protests against it—
provided a real opportunity for up-and-coming bands like Springsteen's. After Lyndon Johnson's departure from the White House in
late January of 1969, there was actually a brief lull in antiwar activity on
most college campuses, so much so that both the *New York Times* and
the State Department, two institutions that increasingly found themselves on opposite sides of most contemporary issues, could agree that
"interest in" and "pressure over" the war had somewhat vanished.
When the *Times* revealed in early May that the newly inaugurated
Richard M. Nixon had ordered secret bombing raids on Vietcong bases
in Cambodia (a step that even the bellicose Johnson had been unwill-
ing to take), the protests returned with a vengeance. On 15 October,
perhaps as many as ten million Americans across the country participated in Vietnam Moratorium Day—including the members of Child,
who gave their second performance at Monmouth College that year as
part of the day's antiwar activities. A month later, they performed briefly
at the college's Student Union Building as part of a daylong buildup to
a midnight bus ride down to DC for an antiwar rally on the National
Mall, exactly the kind of noisy young mob that President Nixon asked
"the great silent majority of my fellow Americans" that November to
help drown out. Whether because of all this antigovernment behavior
or not, that fall Child certainly had a much higher profile, especially
for a band that hadn't even existed six months earlier. By November,
they were opening concerts for such name performers as the James
Cotton Band, Iron Butterfly, and the Chicago Transit Authority. They
had also begun touring regularly outside of New Jersey, in particular to
Richmond, where they had begun to develop quite a following.

But there was a downside to all these college dates, especially for
Springsteen, the band's main songwriter. He wasn't a college boy—he
had lasted only about three semesters at OCCC—and he certainly
wasn't disposed to write songs like one. The earliest surviving recording of Child is from a September 1969 concert in Richmond, and this
recording offers the first chance one really gets to appreciate Springsteen's work as a lone songwriter. The overall impression is that he was
trying too hard at this point in his career to write "important" songs.

The worst of these is "The War Is Over," a faux fairy-tale allegory about the Vietnam War that is as generically representative of late 1969 as "Baby I" is of early 1966. Despite the song's good intentions, the progress of its lyric seems more motivated by the demands of a simple rhyme scheme (including one sequence of lines ending with *outside, side, cried, died,* and *hide*) than by trenchant ideological analysis. The same may be said of the thirty-minute-long "Garden State Parkway Blues," which is undoubtedly one of the "epics" that Danny Federici later recalled from this period. To a knowledgeable ear, this song sounds like a shotgun marriage between the MC5's "Kick Out the Jams" and the Mothers of Invention's "Brown Shoes Don't Make It." Not explicitly about the war, this longer piece is one of many 1960s rock songs (the most famous probably being the Rolling Stones' "Mother's Little Helper") that were written from the viewpoint of a middle-class conformist parent in order to satirize it, skewering vitamin supplements at breakfast and punching time cards at work. Unlike Frank Zappa, however, Springsteen seemed unable to keep up the impersonation for the duration of his fairly long piece, slipping out of character at least once when he laments that he doesn't own his guitars outright.

Indeed, even if he was not doing it consciously at this point, Springsteen's best work here lies in material that was closest to his own experience—beyond the driving and garage talk in "Garden State Parkway Blues," which presages all the car songs for which he would become famous. "Sister Theresa" (on which Lopez plays that classic Nixon-era instrument the recorder) sits near the beginning of a budding tradition of Catholic virgin songs that eventually produced such strong masculinist declarations of the obligation to copulate as Billy Joel's rollicking "Only the Good Die Young" and Night Ranger's insidious "Sister Christian." Better still was the song with which Child followed "Sister Theresa" in concert: "Resurrection," a more thoughtful but still iconoclastic consideration of Catholicism. The subtlety with which Springsteen would later analyze America's involvement in Vietnam may have been absent from the songs he wrote during the war itself, but his complicated relationship to both faith and religion is already there in embryonic form in his lyrics to this latter song.

"Resurrection" is an interesting song for another reason as well: it shows the beginning of Springsteen's fascination with sounding southern. The content of the song's lyrics clearly comes straight from Springsteen's own experience, but on this early recording we can hear him sing those lyrics in the sort of faux Pentecostal accent that would become a regular feature of his performances at the turn of the twenty-first century. The result is manifestly uneven, but this first try at filtering papist experience through evangelical diction is surprisingly effective, particularly on the sing-along choruses.

Although in later years Springsteen referred more frequently to the country and western music to which his mother had exposed him as a child, the most obvious contemporary influence that would have led him to suddenly try to sound southern was the Allman Brothers Band, which had actually formed a month later than Child and whose eponymous first album had just been released in late 1969. This is further proof that Springsteen's tastes were moving away from singles and the Top 40: not only did the Allmans have no charting singles until early 1971, but even their legendary first album didn't hit the *Billboard* charts until four months after this Richmond concert. In some ways, such self-consciously "southern" music was merely an extension of the direction that Bob Dylan and the Band had been taking over the last two or three years, but the tightness of Child as a combo (even during the extended blues jams on most of their songs that would have led many other bands to just be an aggregation of soloists) put them clearly in Allman territory, which fell somewhere between the perfect down-home singles of Creedence Clearwater Revival and the seemingly endless musical runs of the Grateful Dead. Duane Allman, the band's lead guitarist, liked to jam, but he hated the "heavy metal" direction that guitar-based rock was taking in the late 1960s. When he and his original band, Hourglass, had gone out to LA a year earlier to meet with record executives, that was all they kept hearing about. "Fuck this whole thing," his brother Gregg remembered Duane telling the music industry representatives. "Fuck wearing these weird clothes. Fuck playing this 'In-a-Gadda-Da-Vida' shit. Fuck it all." Duane liked wearing his hair long, sure, but he also liked playing bottleneck slide guitar, and he didn't see any contradiction between those two stylistic preferences.

For Duane Allman playing the way he did was a matter of staying true to his southern roots, but for a bunch of Jersey boys like Bruce Springsteen and the members of Child, it was a matter of trying on yet another musical style. That style seemed to fit them better than Zappa-esque art-rock or pseudo-medievalism, especially since Danny Federici had now switched from the surfers' Farfisa to a Hammond B-3 organ, the preferred keyboard of Ray Charles, James Brown, and Spooner Oldham, the celebrated sideman who sat at the core of the Muscle Shoals band that had backed up Aretha Franklin, Percy Sledge, Wilson Pickett, and many other soul singers on some of the greatest American recordings of the previous decade. The Allman Brothers Band was linked more directly than Child to the Muscle Shoals sound—both lead guitarist Duane and drummer Jai Johanny Johanson had actually played on a number of sessions at the legendary FAME Studios—but both bands were driven by much the same impulse: finding a way to play the "white man's blues" without adopting either the distanced gourmet's approach of Cream or the self-involved weightiness of Iron Butterfly. Quite simply, both bands were trying to return the electric blues to its former role as party music.

When Springsteen and company were professionally recorded for the first time, in January of 1970, all three of the tracks that they laid down were in this new, pseudo-southern style. The best song of the three is probably the shortest: "Guilty (Send That Boy to Jail)," a taut, seven-minute-long, soul-based piece, which takes off from a powerfully sung *All rise!* and finds surprising variety in a single riff on which the band plays a series of seemingly spontaneous variations to which its members nevertheless stuck amazingly close throughout all the song's other performances that year. The other two tracks they recorded that day were considerably less impressive. The first, a twangy piece called "The Train Song," was as nakedly generic as its title. The band's country ruse worked a little better on a third, bluesier number, "Goin' Back to Georgia," which was their most obviously Allmanesque song. In the end, though, this track also sounds like mere posing, even if one were unaware that none of its performers had ever been south of Richmond.

These recordings were made in San Francisco, of all places, during a two-month-long trip to the Bay Area that at least some of the band's members considered a semipermanent move. (By the time of this trip, they had renamed themselves Steel Mill, after they found out about a Long Island–based band called Child that had a deal with Roulette Records.) "We'd thought we'd go to California and stay there," Vinnie Roslin told Robert Santelli. "Back in the late '60s, . . . [s]o many bands broke out of [that] city. It was where everything was happening that we wanted to be a part of." In December, they had packed up their manager's equipment truck and an Oldsmobile station wagon and headed west with no more than one guaranteed booking at a New Year's event at the Esalen Institute in Big Sur. Over the next two months, they scored a number of other dates in Northern California, including a few at Kentfield's College of Marin, as well as at such San Francisco clubs as Marty Balin's Matrix and Bill Graham's Fillmore West. The Matrix gig yielded a tremendously positive review from Philip Elwood of the San Francisco *Examiner*, and the Fillmore date led to the recording session, at Graham's Fillmore Recording Studios.

After hearing the three demos that the band had laid down on Washington's Birthday, Bill Graham (or at least someone in his organization) offered Steel Mill a recording contract, but the $1,500 advance that Graham's people promised was only about half of what the band could currently make at a typical college gig. So, five days after the Fillmore recording session, Steel Mill were back in Richmond, breathless and a little crazy from a breakneck drive. Steel Mill did two dates at Free University in Richmond that weekend, once again adding new songs to the set with incredible speed, including two ("California Blues" and "On the Road") that obviously drew on very recent experiences.

The band members were living communally now, in a space that they also owed to their manager. Throughout 1969 and the early 1970s, Tinker West worked as a shaper at Challenger East Surfboards in Wanamassa, and by October 1969, a few desperate months after Springsteen and Federici had been kicked out of the house on South Street, Challenger East had become both the band's rehearsal space and its new home. "[Tinker] had like three or four bathrooms in the back," Federici remembered. "They were fairly large, so we slept in them in sleeping bags." At the surfboard factory, the band had thrown one last concert in December in order to raise money for the trip out west, and to the surfboard factory they returned the following March, after the Bay Area trip and the Richmond gigs.

Upon its return to the East Coast, Steel Mill also acquired a new member: Steve Van Zandt, an Upstage regular who was probably most famous around the Jersey Shore for playing guitar in Red Bank's late lamented Shadows. For his first twenty years, Van Zandt had seemed to be following a steadily southward path. He was born in Boston, raised in Middletown, played guitar in Red Bank, worked his way into the late-night jams in Asbury Park, and actually played his first date with Steel Mill in Richmond. His nickname—"Miami"—pointed even farther south and referred to a loud print shirt he had once been caught wearing when he came back from a trip to Florida. No matter how far south his destiny might lie, however, Van Zandt seems to have met his psychic twin in Springsteen. The two guitarists had a great deal in common, from their Dutch last names and strong Italian mothers to their musical passage from the British Invasion to Stax/Volt soul. That may have been why Van Zandt agreed to join Steel Mill, a band in which he would play a subordinate role. Even though Lopez had originally recruited Springsteen to start Child, by the winter of 1970 it was clear that Springsteen was the one in charge of Steel Mill. He approached Van Zandt and asked him if he wanted to replace Vinnie Roslin—in some ways a bizarre request, since Van Zandt had always been a guitarist, not a bassist. But like Danny Federici, Van Zandt found it very easy to put his trust in Springsteen. This was definitely someone with whom he wanted to perform.

By mid-April, this second incarnation of Steel Mill was playing college gigs in New Jersey, and its setlists seem to have stabilized for the first time in the band's history. "Guilty" and "Resurrection" were usually featured, the former typically somewhere near the top of the show, probably since its *All rise!* opening was a great way to start things off. "Jeannie I Want to Thank You," a slow blues ballad that had worked well as a basis for a jam at the Matrix shows back in January, sometimes appeared near the beginning of the set, while "Goin' Back to Georgia" occasionally came in the middle. At a quickly scheduled concert at Monmouth College in late April—the band was filling in for a canceled performance of *Hair*—"Goin' Back to Georgia" was followed by a new song called "The Wind and the Rain," which was probably Steel Mill's best attempt to create its own original blues number. The shows could still close out with either the grand thesis-statement "Garden State Parkway Blues" or the blues standard "Goin' Down Slow," which the band had been using as a show closer at least since September.

If there is a real story in these shows, however, it lies not in the original songs but rather in the covers. Their return after the fall and winter focus on almost exclusively original sets suggests that the band, and its principal songwriter, now felt secure enough in their identities to try performing others' songs as well. Quite a few of these songs were originated by African American performers, particularly Dyke and the Blazers' "Funky Broadway" (which they may have heard via Wilson Pickett's almost instant cover). On the whole, these new covers were songs that had originated not with blues performers per se but rather with rhythm and blues and soul performers from the pre-Nixon era. In other words, they were instant nostalgia, longing for a time that was only three or four years in the past. The sudden appearance of these songs in Steel Mill's concerts may have something to do with the band's addition of Springsteen's fellow soul lover Steve Van Zandt, but there may have been other causes for their selection as well.

As the spring of 1970 turned into the summer, there was ample reason to long for the seemingly more carefree days of the mid-1960s. Since the autumn of 1969, there had been 250 politically motivated bombings in the United States ("an average of almost one per day," as historian James T. Patterson has noted), including three in Manhattan during February of 1970 at the headquarters of Mobil, IBM, and Gen Tel. American culture was suddenly beset, as Daniel Patrick Moynihan put it in a White House memo written in response to those bombings, by "diffuse, decentralized, irrational, even psychotic groups." Moynihan was speaking in this memo about the tactics of some who opposed the political establishment, but the same irrationality could be easily glimpsed in the actions of some who defended it as well. On 4 May, National Guardsmen posted on the campus of Kent State University in Ohio with orders to prevent political demonstrations of any kind fired sixty-seven shots in thirteen seconds, striking down thirteen unarmed students, four of whom died and one of whom became paralyzed. Not all of those struck down were actually taking part in the protests; they just moved at the wrong time.

It was a paranoid year, a violent year, and the intensity of that violence is singularly hard to explain. In retrospect, conservatives and liberals alike reflexively blame each other for that intensity, but in many conflicts that year, the most extreme actions on one side would be eagerly seized on by those who wished to respond with a corresponding extremism on the other. In later decades, such conflicts would be seen as part of the so-called culture wars, but in 1970 this literally was a war, an armed conflict that could flare up at almost any moment, at any provocation. Four days after the Kent State shootings, at a demonstration in front of Federal Hall on Wall Street in Manhattan, an immature protester's simulated blowing of his nose into an American flag led nearby construction workers to arm themselves with iron clippers and other implements and proceed to lay into the demonstration, stomping, kicking, and punching both its participants and a number of sympathetic bystanders, as members of the NYPD observed the violence without intervening. "These hippies are getting what they deserve," one of the construction workers present said, and one of his colleagues hit a clean-cut young man in the crowd who had the nerve to voice disagreement.

Indeed, no matter how it may have started, by 1970 this was a war about culture, no longer just about politics or Vietnam. This tension had been building for several years, certainly since the period when Bruce was worried about getting run off the road because of the length of his hair, but now it was more easily focused and always closer to flash point. Every day, that underlying tension was as inflamed by style as by substance. Transcending specific politics, programs, and even customary interest groups, the sudden flare-ups of violence in 1970 could be white on white, white on black, even black on black, as happened that July when Tommy Smith, the African American acting police commissioner of Asbury Park, ordered his officers to crack down on teenagers congregating on Springwood Avenue, the main drag of

the city's African American West Side. The West Side had much rational cause for anger in 1970—racism, segregation, inflation, declining
employment—but there was nothing rational about the riots that dev-
astated Asbury Park for almost a week that July, anymore than there
had been anything rational about the rampaging mob of construction
workers on Wall Street the previous May. A returning vet like John
Fogerty looked around at the United States in 1970 and almost found
it more frightening than Vietnam, as he testified in Creedence Clearwater Revival's April 1970 hit "Run through the Jungle."

During the week of the Asbury Park riots, Bruce Springsteen
watched from a water tower near Challenger East as his new hometown was destroyed by its own longtime residents. He was "[n]ot surprised," as one of his interviewers summarized his reaction. "[A]fter
all, this kind of thing had been happening all over the country. Not
surprised, but stunned by the sheer magnitude of the event." Everything had changed—not just in a broader political or cultural way but
also in the very palpable sense of how a twenty-year-old man who had
no home but a surfboard factory could support himself playing rock 'n'
roll. If you connected the dots, this wasn't a war of white versus black,
conservative versus liberal, or middle class versus poor. It was a war of
the old against the young. A few years earlier, loud, long-haired bands
like Earth or Child could play college, high school, even eighth-grade
events with little incident, but by mid-1970 that was no longer the
case. Steel Mill wasn't a big part of the violence of 1970 anymore than
the Rolling Stones had been at Altamont in 1969. No matter how high
they cranked it up, Steel Mill's music was not the music of revolution,
but rather the music of retreat. It was the music of those who locked
themselves away in a windowless room, dancing "[n]ot the tight strut
that went with soul music, or the more controlled steps that people
were doing to Top Forty songs, but a languid, wheeling hop and skip
that paid less attention to the beat than to the texture of the loud, loud
music." No matter how they were intended or enjoyed, however, such
furious, proto-metal sounds could seem awfully violent to nonsympa-
thetic, paranoia-soaked 1970 ears, especially when those sounds were
made by unashamedly long-haired freaks.

Very rapidly in 1970, the rules under which Steel Mill performed seemed to be unraveling. A few weeks after the Kent State shootings, the band encountered resistance at Virginia Commonwealth University in Richmond, where it had played before with no incident, from administrators who now wanted the band to turn down its volume. *[T]here's a weird thing going on between your officials and us*, Springsteen announced from the stage at one point. At 11:00 p.m. sharp, the officials cut Steel Mill's power, but Lopez (the only one whose instrument did not need electricity) kept playing and was arrested for disorderly conduct. In September, while Lopez was in jail and Steel Mill was making do with a substitute drummer, the band headlined a four-act outdoor concert at the Clearwater Swim Club in Atlantic Highlands in order to raise money for his defense. This time, the police suddenly changed the curfew time, so that the show was now required to end at 10:00 rather than 11:00. The concert went on with its full, advertised lineup, and the police cut the power with very little warning shortly after 10:00 in the middle of Steel Mill's headlining set. When a techie tried to plug the sound back in, so that an announcement could be made to calm the crowd, three police officers clubbed him. Danny Federici remembered that he "saw red and just tossed my amplifiers off the stage and onto those cops." The organist got away that time, and on two other occasions (earning him his own Asbury nickname "the Phantom"), but when police officers started regularly showing up at Steel Mill concerts in order to execute the warrant for his arrest, he eventually realized that he had to turn himself in.

According to Federici, the Atlantic Highlands fiasco in September 1970 was the beginning of the end for Steel Mill. For the rest of the year, they would play the usual gigs in New Jersey and make a few trips out of town when its members got the rare chance to open for acts that they admired like Roy Orbison or Ike and Tina Turner. They even opened at the Sunshine In for Black Sabbath on its first U.S. tour. In December, though, Springsteen finally made it official. He was going out to Northern California again to visit his family for Christmas, and he was going alone. The band had a few engagements booked for the beginning of 1971, but that was it. By the end of January, Steel Mill, Bruce Springsteen's fourth band in three years, was history.

AFTER THE BREAKUP of Steel Mill, Bruce was in no hurry to form a new band. Instead, that winter he did what Asbury Park musicians between bands always did in those days: he jammed, mostly at the Upstage, but perhaps even once downstairs at the acoustic Green Mermaid. Then an opportunity popped up that he just couldn't resist: the Allman Brothers Band was scheduled to play the Sunshine In the last week of March, and he really wanted to play on the same bill as the Allmans. He talked the club into booking an opening slot for "Bruce Springsteen & the Friendly Enemies," and then he looked around to see who those Friendly Enemies might be. There is no indication that he thought such a lineup would be permanent, but he didn't want to let the chance to jam with the Allmans slip through his fingers.

Naturally, he used the Upstage regulars as his talent pool. He had played with most of them, and they with each other, so there would be less time wasted figuring out a common musical language. For the core of this pickup band, Bruce borrowed from two of Steve Van Zandt's side projects: Funky Dusty and the Soul Broom and Steve Van Zandt and the Big Bad Bobby Williams Band, two groups that gave Steve ample opportunity to indulge in his love of '60s soul and R&B. (In Asbury, everybody other than Bruce seemed to have more than one band going at that point. Sometimes the same performers would play in different combinations at different clubs on the same night.) In March, about a week before the Allmans hit Asbury, Bruce tried out a new five-man group at a YWHA-YMHA dance at the Deal Park Recreation Center. It featured Steve and himself on guitar, Vini on drums, and two performers with whom he had never before played a paying gig: Garry Tallent on bass and David Sancious on keyboards.

Tallent, the more experienced of the two, had played with Van Zandt in the Jaywalkers (the guitarist's last band before Steel Mill) and in both the Downtown Tangiers Rhythm and Blues Band and the Moment of Truth with Vini Lopez and Danny Federici. Tallent had taken his first steps as a musician on the tuba, an even geekier instrument than Federici's accordion, but he had been smart enough to figure out that, while just about every rock band needed an electric bass, in many cases no one wanted to play it. Among the tallest of the musicians around the Jersey Shore, he undoubtedly stood out onstage next to such height-challenged bandmates as Van Zandt and Lopez. Sometimes jokingly called the "Tennessee Terror"—his family had lived there for two seconds once—Tallent in fact had exactly the right temperament for a bass player: quiet and steady. For close to a year, he had silently stared at Springsteen during the jams at the Upstage. When they finally started talking, it was clear that they had to play together.

Tallent was also the one who brought David Sancious into this new grouping, having worked with him (Tallent appears to have worked with almost everyone down the shore) in the recent band Glory Road. "This is my friend, Dave," he told Springsteen another night at the Upstage. "I met him a couple of weeks ago, and we did something." Born in Long Branch, Sancious was still a teenager when he first played with Springsteen. (He and his friend Johnny Luraschi used to walk to the Upstage from Belmar, where they both lived, and even though those under eighteen were usually kicked out at midnight, Sancious somehow worked his way into the jams.) Danny Federici at first took him for a "terrible piano player," but in truth Sancious was a classically trained pianist who was well versed in both jazz and funk. By the time of his first, underage visit to the Upstage, he had already been jamming for five years at the Orchid Lounge up on Ridgewood, the best soul and R&B club in Asbury. What brought him down to play with the white freaks on Cookman was the music of Jimi Hendrix, which was undeniably black but still not terribly popular on the West Side. If Davey initially sounded amateurish to Danny, it was probably because he was learning how to play an entirely different type of music.

The new, five-man outfit worked well, but for the Sunshine In gig the following week, Bruce wanted to do something a little grander—a little sillier actually. After a particularly crazy, fun night at the Upstage that winter, one apparently devoted to the music of the 1950s, Bruce said, "Hey, why don't we just take everybody we know and party on the stage while we're playing?" For the Allman Brothers gig, he did exactly that, with an outsize outfit he now dubbed Dr. Zoom and the Sonic Boom.

And who were Dr. Zoom and the Sonic Boom? Well, Springsteen

himself was clearly Dr. Zoom. (*Are you ready in the ambulance?* Steve asked the audience at the opening of a later gig. *When Zoom does his thing, they take 'em out by the hundreds.*) Lopez, Van Zandt, Tallent, and Sancious formed the core of the Boom, backing Springsteen at the Sunshine In date as they had done at Deal the week before, but the now enlarged unit for this gig had two guitarists, two keyboardists, and three percussionists, one of them (Tinker West) not even technically a musician. Among the nonmusical personnel were "the Sonic People," women and men (including one baton twirler) who performed comedy bits and joined in on backing vocals. And then there were the other four Upstage regulars, including Big Danny Gallagher and Big Tiny, the Upstage's bouncer, who played Monopoly onstage throughout the performance, except for one song during which Springsteen vocalized while sitting on the game board. "We tried to get a guy to fix an engine onstage," Gallagher remembered. "But he said it was too much of a hassle to do it for just a few songs." Even without the mechanic, that made for almost twenty people onstage.

Had Dr. Zoom and the Sonic Boom first appeared three years earlier, they might have been deemed a happening. From all accounts, to call them a party band would have been a gross understatement. (Indeed, it might be more accurate to call them a party masquerading as a band.) Obviously, they were a quixotic attempt to bring a typical late show at the Upstage out into a relatively normal concert setting. No audio survives from that first weird performance—apparently the only one to feature either Monopoly or baton twirling—but we do have Duane Allman's reported verdict: "That's one cookin' band, man." Backstage between shows, Allman listened to one of Tinker West's tapes of Steel Mill and talked with Van Zandt about playing slide guitar.

To no one's surprise, the Boom lasted only two more performances. Thankfully, its last performance was recorded, so we can hear just how right Duane Allman was. This band does cook: loose where it's good to be, tight where it has to be, ranging all around the last thirty years of American music, mixing covers and originals to the point where it all sounds like one organic seventy-five-minute-long sound. In a way, the setlist for this gig was an archaeology of the blues, but not in the droningly studious manner of some of the English bands that Earth had covered in the fall of 1968. These songs surveyed the communal aspect of blues performance that was intended more to get people dancing than to make them notice the guitarist. After a shrewdly chosen Dylan cover (the barrelhouse blast of "It Takes a Lot to Laugh, It Takes a Train to Cry"), there was the Chicago blues of "Southside Shuffle"; a folkish meditation called "Look toward the Land"; Steel Mill's faux Allman song "Goin' Back to Georgia"; a fast Texas shuffle called "Last Night in Tulsa"; King and Goffin's old Shirelles plea "Will You Still Love Me Tomorrow?"; a proto–New Wave blues called "Jambalaya"; and a heavy metal wail called "Lady of Boston," which might have fit right in at the Matrix gig back in early 1970. And then, of course, there was the "Zoom Theme," a Zappaesque reading of Irving Berlin's sixty-year-old chestnut "Alexander's Ragtime Band" (with new lyrics) that finally allowed Garry Tallent to employ his extensive training on the tuba in an unequivocally rock setting. About the only thing missing from this survey was some '50s guitar rock, the music that had been played on the night when Springsteen allegedly got the idea for this grouping, but a recovered setlist in Springsteen's handwriting suggests that there may have been some Bo Diddley and Chuck Berry songs in the set at the Sunshine In the night before.

A band this large couldn't last, though. If nothing else, by the time you sliced the band's take up into that many pieces, you might just as well pay everyone in Monopoly money. Springsteen and Van Zandt had been playing in jams and smaller combinations at the Asbury clubs since January, and that practice continued straight through the spring. For months, there were short-term gigs and long-form jams, but Springsteen was still taking his time pulling together a band to play on a more permanent basis.

In July 1971, however, his new band finally appeared. In a significant display of confidence, it was simply called "The Bruce Springsteen Band." Describing it to an interviewer a few years later, he spoke of it as "my band." "I gave it my name," he bragged. It was a ten-piece group, half the size of the full-on Sonic Boom, with all of that group's richness and much less of its silliness. Not surprisingly, it included Van Zandt, Sancious, Tallent, and Lopez, the same four players with whom he had been working steadily since March, as well as two horns (Bobby Feigenbaum again on sax, Harvey Cherlin on trumpet) and two backup singers (Delores Holmes and Barbara Dinkins). The horns were probably the most purposeful part of the new arrangement, since he had been telling friends since the breakup of Steel Mill that he wanted horns to supplement the usual guitars. For the Bruce Springsteen Band's first gig, at Brookdale Community College, on 10 July, however, Tinker West was still on congas, so some of the Zoom-era silliness remained.

There were covers at the Brookdale gig, some of which ("C. C. Rider" and "Down the Road Apiece") reached farther back in pop music history than the songs the band had played at its dates in the spring. There were also some holdovers from the Steel Mill's later repertoire ("Last Night in Tulsa," "Goin' Back to Georgia," and the frequent show-closer "Jambalaya"), just as there had been when Springsteen switched from the Castiles to Earth. But there was a raft of new songs, too, a number of which (including "You Mean So Much to Me," "Natural Magic," and "Dance Dance Dance") tilted the band even more toward soul than blues. This was the music that Steel Mill had started uncovering toward the end of its existence, the kind of biracially appreciated mid-'60s songs that were probably aided now in performance by the fact that the musicians who performed them as the Bruce Springsteen Band were a multiracial group, with a Latino drummer and African American keyboardist and vocalists.

Springsteen and the other musicians didn't make a big deal about the band's mixed-race composition. "It wasn't like we had this thing of, like, okay . . . we're the only integrated band," as Sancious clarified for Daniel Wolff. Such an arrangement ("Just five or six guys playing this music and just having a ball") wouldn't have been an issue just a few years before. Throughout the 1960s, Booker T and the MGs, which was the house band at Stax Records, and the Muscle Shoals rhythm section at FAME Studios were biracial groups. Over the last three years, however, both groups had broken up, partly over disputes over fair compensation and partly because of the interracial tension and violence that had lately led to riots all over the United States. In 1968, on the day after the assassination of Dr. Martin Luther King Jr., a simple conversation on the street outside Stax Studios between (white) bassist Duck Dunn and (black) songwriter Isaac Hayes had attracted the attention of police officers who drew shotguns on Hayes because they thought he might be accosting Dunn. "I mean," the bassist told music historian Peter Guralnick, "the cops jumped in because we were white. It makes you feel like shit."

Of regularly charting bands still recording in 1971, Sly and the Family Stone and Eric Burdon's post-Animals group War were biracial, but in each of those cases the composition of the band was a self-conscious statement about the contemporary deterioration of race relations, as their respective early-1970s releases *There's a Riot Goin' On* and *The World Is a Ghetto* would suggest. In 1971, the closest thing to the sort of old, naturally evolving pre-1968 mixed-race band was probably the Allman Brothers Band, which was self-consciously southern rather than self-consciously biracial. Drummer Jaimoe Johanson was an African American veteran of many great FAME sessions, and as Charley Daniels observed, "I think the Allman Brothers having a black guy in the group at that time was a real eye-opener for a lot of people outside the South."

How self-conscious was Bruce Springsteen's decision in 1971 to make the first band with his name on it 30 percent African American? It's hard to say. He had opened his first concert in Asbury Park after the previous summer's riots with "Dancing in the Streets," and at the end of the song he had announced, *It's all happening out there in the street, so what are we doing in here?*, as if he wished to declare himself in solidarity with those in revolt. Yet looking back thirty-five years later, Springsteen admitted to Daniel Wolff that he was oblivious at the time about "what it must have been like for the singers [in his new band] to cross Asbury's racial lines."

The likely truth is that Springsteen cared most about the music, far more than about making a racial statement through the membership of his band. In going as far as he could from the proto-metal of 1970, what Springsteen was apparently trying to do with the Boom and the Bruce Springsteen Band was assemble an R&B-style "show band," much like those that Sam Cooke, James Brown, and even Jimi Hendrix had fronted during the 1960s. Forty years later, when introducing

Sam Moore at a concert in Madison Square Garden, Springsteen would proudly attest to seeing Sam and Dave play the Satellite Lounge in Cookstown, just outside of Fort Dix, around this time and thinking about whether he could model his own performances on theirs. Sixties soul was just another kind of music that Springsteen loved, and one that he hadn't tried to play yet.

The new band had bookings almost from the second it emerged, but aside from a performance at Damrosch Park in Lincoln Center (Springsteen's first Manhattan gig in three years), all of those bookings were in predictable locations. The Bruce Springsteen Band played Richmond, Rutgers, South Amboy, and Long Branch, even a Catholic Youth Organization dance in West Long Branch at St. Jerome School that must have seemed strange for a bunch of young men in their early twenties. Over time, the band got whittled down from ten to nine to seven to five. Soon there were no backup singers or even horn players, just Springsteen, Lopez, Van Zandt, Tallent, and Sancious, but the new style that Springsteen had been cultivating remained intact. They were now a five-piece band that sounded as if it were a ten-piece band. The more they played together, the farther away their sound moved from 1971, and the closer it got to the mid-1960s. By the end of August, they even had a permanent gig: four solid months of weekend bookings at the Student Prince (where they were still advertised as "The Bruce Springsteen Band, formerly Steel Mill"). Their sets were approximately half covers and half Springsteen originals, but among the originals there were no more fairy tales about the Vietnam War or half-hour deconstructions of the New Jersey bourgeoisie. The band's whole attitude could be summed up in the title of one lyrically forgettable Springsteen song that their audiences would groove to many nights that fall: "The Band's Just Bopping the Blues."

IT WAS IN THE MIDST OF THIS NEW ACTIVITY that the unthinkable happened: Margaret and Tom Potter announced that they were closing the Upstage. Margaret would stay in town, but Tom would soon move away, and for some young musicians in Asbury Park it might have felt as if Mom and Dad were getting divorced. But Sonny Kenn, who seems to have been in a band with every local musician except Spring-steen at one point or another, found a better metaphor when trying to describe his time at the Upstage some years later: "Upstage, when you think about it, really was a school. Better yet, for those of us who used to play at Hullabaloo and the teen clubs, it was almost a college of sorts." They were all studying the history of American popular music, working back from the pop that had set their imaginations on fire when they were in high school to the rhythm and blues and even blues that had given rise to it.

By the time of the last night at the Upstage, the Beatles, the Animals, Moby Grape, the Blues Magoos, the Blues Project, Iron Butterfly, and a host of other bands that had influenced Springsteen, Van Zandt, and their whole generation of Asbury Park musicians were all things of the past. (Nearly all those groups would have halfhearted reformations and reunions over the coming years, but none came close to recapturing the thrill of their original incarnations.) Gone, too, were the Castiles, the Rogues, the Motifs, the Shadows, Sonny and the Starfires, the Downtown Tangiers Rhythm and Blues Band, Glory Road, the Source, the Jaywalkers, the Moment of Truth, Earth, Child, Steel Mill, Funky Dusty and the Soul Broom, Dr. Zoom and the Sonic Boom, and the Sundance Blues Band—if not quite yet the simply named Bruce Springsteen Band. And by then, too, Jimi Hendrix, Janis Joplin, and Jim Morrison were all dead. So was Duane Allman (who died in a motorcycle accident near his home in Macon the night before the Upstage closed), not to mention Walter Cichon, Bart Haynes, and far too many of the other teenage boys who had once filled the Monmouth and Ocean County Hullabaloo clubs.

As Steve Van Zandt later said, "The [Rock 'n' Roll] Renaissance would end with either the Who's 'Won't Get Fooled Again' in 1971 or the Stones' *Exile on Main Street* in 1972, take your pick." Consciously or not, when trying to date the definitive death of rock 'n' roll, Van Zandt named two widely known records that marked off a single year's length—from July 1971 to June 1972—that also saw the rise and fall of the less well-known Bruce Springsteen Band. And it's more than reasonable to ask, if rock 'n' roll was essentially over (again) by the fall of 1971, why would anyone want to keep playing it?

CHAPTER 3

DETHRONE THE DICTAPHONE, HIT IT IN ITS FUNNYBONE (1971–1972)

*A*S IT TURNS OUT, NEITHER SPRINGSTEEN NOR VAN ZANDT WAS at the Upstage that last night, nor were Lopez, Tallent, or Sancious. Some of them had probably played in the club's penultimate jam the night before, but on Saturday, 30 October, they were all in Richmond, where the Bruce Springsteen Band was opening for Cactus at Virginia Commonwealth University. Two weeks later, they were back in Asbury Park, playing three nights a week at the Student Prince for the rest of the year, probably for locals. Even in better days, few out-of-towners came to Asbury Park past Labor Day.

When the band opened for Cactus, nearly half its set was made up of covers—not current Top 40 hits but old electric blues numbers, particularly from the Muddy Waters catalog. On the one Student Prince recording we have from that fall, however, only the opening number was a cover (Marvin Gaye's "Ain't That Peculiar"), probably used as a way of warming up the crowd with an old favorite. After that, the rest of the set was made up of originals, all in the style of Chicago blues and soul: harp, organ, and electric guitar. It's hard to say how much of the audience was composed of regulars, but it is worth noting that the club produced "Find the Song Titles of the Bruce Springsteen Band" placemats for this gig, which presumed a certain degree of familiarity with the group's repertoire.

Despite this clever marketing gimmick, the eleven songs listed on the placemat were relatively undistinguished, hardly any of them worth remembering from week to week, let alone decades later. Most of them were just extended jams with interchangeable words tacked on, words about getting away, dancing, halfhearted relationships starting and breaking up—words that reflected the audience's probable concerns back onto them in a generic fashion. The chords of these songs provided a serviceable excuse for improvisation, but the lyrics lacked even the epic badness of a pretentious Steel Mill song like "Resurrection," let alone the sweet play that the words of "Guilty (Send That Boy to Jail)" had fed into its express-train soul.

One of the listed songs, though, does hold some interest. Musically, it's more a highwayman's folk-rock song than a rousing Chicago blues. Lyrically, it actually dares to traffic in metaphor, a technique that Springsteen had pretty much eschewed ever since he started hanging out at the Upstage. Actually, this lyric employs a double layer of metaphor, with underwater images standing in for tropes from the western. Judging by the way he performed this song, Springsteen seems to have been proud of its lyrics. He emphasizes them in the two or three recordings of it that we have. This stands in stark contrast to the way he usually shrugged his way through the lyrics of a piece like "Funk Song" (also known as "The Band's Just Bopping the Blues").

Western metaphors keep popping up in Springsteen's songs during this period, which is not surprising. He was part of the early crest of boomers whose consciousnesses were structured around the stark landscape of the post–World War II cycle of film and TV westerns, a landscape in which gunslingers for hire like Shane and Jimmy Ringo figured much more prominently than in earlier iterations of the genre. As far back as Bo Diddley, rock 'n' roll performers had linked the careers of those rootless figures and their own lives of perpetual touring. In the early 1970s, though, such self-conscious mythologizing almost served as a form of conservative iconoclasm. Like that of the Band, the Byrds, and Peter Fonda and Dennis Hopper (who named their *Easy Rider* characters Wyatt and Billy in order to create deliberate western echoes), Springsteen's repeated adoption of a "cowboy" persona in Richard Nixon's America allowed him to dissent in a traditional manner. In this period, if one was a cowboy, one could still be an American, but not an uptight one.

At its most casual, this cowboy persona led to a Bruce Springsteen

Band song like "Don't You Want to Be an Outlaw (Just like Jesse James)?" a fun, loping piece in which the highlighted guitar solos between verses seemed to serve as a positive answer to the lyric's frequent questions. On a slightly more self-conscious level, it leads to a song like "If I Was the Priest," which uses a western setting to flirt with Catholic subversion without ever engaging in any substantive cultural analysis. If most of the songs that Springsteen had written since the end of Steel Mill were focused on mastering the instrumentals, these western songs by contrast seem concerned mostly with rediscovering the power of figurative language. In the end, though, they don't seem to be "about" anything beyond their playful verbal surfaces.

Only one possibly autobiographical theme seems to unite all these songs, one well suited to the western genre: the desire to get out. Five years before, Springsteen might have desired to get out from under his parents' thumb on South Street, but now he had been living on his own for several years. In the last verse of "If I Was the Priest," when Sheriff Jesus (playing John Wayne perhaps to the young man's Ricky Nelson) asks Bruce to come with him to help clean up Dodge City, the singer tells the savior that he is needed elsewhere. By the end of 1971, it was clear that Springsteen needed to get out of Asbury Park. As had happened repeatedly during his half-dozen years as a professional musician, his career had fallen into a rut: the Castiles had mastered the British Invasion sound, Steel Mill had mastered heavy metal, and the Bruce Springsteen Band was currently the perfect bar band. Now what? As his songwriting efforts then as later seem to suggest, Springsteen was never thoroughly happy working in a single pop genre. As his increased lyrical longing to light out for the territories during this period might also suggest, he was not happy being the uncrowned monarch of a place as small and unnoticed as Kingsley Avenue either.

IT WAS AT this point that Springsteen met one of his most pivotal—and controversial—collaborators. Ten years earlier, Mike Appel would have been a fairly typical figure in the music industry. Born in Queens during World War II, Appel was an old-school pop fan who eventually wrote two or three songs that cracked the *Billboard* Hot 100. Like his contemporaries Carole King and Neil Diamond, Appel signed on with a larger music publishing company as a writer and producer and eventually found a partner, in his case Jim Cretecos, a performer whose credits straddled the worlds of rock and theater. In time, they came to work for Wes Farrell, whose career path offered an attractive model for the two young writers. From the mid-1950s through the mid-1960s, from Leiber and Stoller through Bacharach and David, this was the way the music business worked, particularly in New York: songwriters became producers and then CEOs. It was the old Tin Pan Alley model reconceived for the era of multitrack magnetic recording. In this system, the performers weren't really an essential part of the culture factory—they were more like the eighteen-wheelers or container ships that made sure the product got from the producers to the consumers.

It was a sweet deal for Appel, except for one small detail: he got in on it about ten years too late. In retrospect, the early 1970s have been dubbed the era of the "singer-songwriter," but that bare rubric doesn't quite capture the significant shift in the music industry that this entailed. Bob Dylan and the Beatles initiated the change in the mid-1960s, and it really took off after 1968, when performers who wrote their own material were no longer a liability in the pop marketplace but a highly coveted commodity. Dylan may have been lying fallow in the early 1970s, but three out of the four Beatles were now recording successfully as solo, "singer-songwriter" acts. More significant, such behind-the-scenes songwriters from the previous decade as Neil Diamond and Carole King were now full-fledged pop stars: Diamond had three albums in the Top 20 in a little over a year, and King's album *Tapestry* spent most of the summer at no. 1, slipping after a season into the slot formerly occupied by George Harrison's *All Things Must Pass*. *Tapestry* went on to become the best-selling album of the year, the decade, and for a while of all time.

Appel and Cretecos may have been slow on the uptake, but they eventually caught on. After writing a one-off hit for the Partridge Family, they produced a sequence of acts in the early 1970s that suggest that they were trying to hitch a ride on a succession of trends in popular music: a heavy metal trio from Brooklyn called Sir Lord Baltimore;

a folk-rock group called Montana Flintlock; and a soft-spoken singer-songwriter named Tony Azito. They may have had their doubts about Azito, however. According to Vini Lopez, in the fall of 1971, it was common knowledge among some of his musician friends that there were these two guys from New York who were "looking for singer-songwriters." The East Coast rock world being so much smaller then than it is now, when Lopez mentioned this to Tinker West, it turned out that West knew the two guys in question: he did sound for and managed Montana Flintlock as well as Bruce's band. Springsteen's version of what happened next suggests that he and West visited Appel on a whim, but that characterization sounds disingenuous. Since the moment he first saw Elvis Presley, Springsteen had always been acutely aware of the pop marketplace. He wanted to sign as a solo artist, and, much like Appel and Cretecos, he knew what kinds of solo artists the music industry was currently looking for.

So it was back to the coffeehouse notebooks, but the coffeehouses had never been where Springsteen had thrived. As one might expect, the biggest stars to come out of the singer-songwriter movement had worked for years at being acoustic troubadours, just as Springsteen had worked for years to form and lead the ultimate bar band. In other words, by going to see Appel and Cretecos and selling himself as a "singer-songwriter," he was trying to take his hobby and turn it into his main line of work. It would be as if James Taylor (whose *Sweet Baby James* had made it all the way to no. 3 on the *Billboard* pop albums chart back in March) had suddenly decided to chuck it all and see if he could front a Muddy Waters cover act, perhaps slipping "Steamroller Blues" into the setlist to see if anybody noticed.

On 29 November 1971, when Springsteen and West arrived in the music publishing offices of Pocketful of Tunes, the subdivision of the Farrell organization that Appel and Cretecos ran, Don McLean's *American Pie* was the no. 1 album in America. The two songs Springsteen performed in the office that day would not have seemed stylistically out of place on a McLean album. They weren't playful like "If I Was the Priest" or even soulful like "Cowboys of the Sea," two songs that Appel would not hear for another three months. Even if Bruce did "grab his guitar" before he left New Jersey, when he got to the office in

Manhattan, he sat down at the piano to perform his songs. This was something few Jersey Shore audiences had ever seen him do, but it was very much in keeping with a self-conscious shift from party-hearty rock 'n' roll to would-be introspective singer-songwriter material.

Springsteen played two turgid, draggy, self-absorbed songs with undistinguished lyrics that wore their emotions and highlighted language on their sleeves. We don't know for certain what song Springsteen performed first, only that, according to Appel, it was dreadful. Considering that this man had recently written for the Partridge Family, that was probably saying a great deal. We do know what the second song was, though: a slow number called "Baby Doll," about a sort of distaff equivalent of the Who's Tommy. The music to which these questionable lyrics are set is derivative, but in this case the imitation in no way captures the charm of the original. Incredibly enough (especially if one has heard "Baby Doll" in its entirety), the song caught Appel's attention. It had a line or two in it that he liked, maybe the only good lines in the song, about how the protagonist danced without music with her boyfriend, the narrator of the song. "It was a very weird line," Appel later remembered, "and [it] stuck in my head." So did Springsteen's delivery, which was both committed and vaguely desperate.

Springsteen was desperate, of course. Springsteen had already recorded two singles and gone as far as he could on the local circuit. If he couldn't convince Appel and Cretecos that he was a better Cat Stevens knockoff than Tony Azito, the one they already had signed, his career really was over. And even if he didn't know how to write good lyrics yet (or how to pick the right songs for Manhattan auditions), the last six years had certainly taught him how to connect with his audience. If he had chosen to play guitar rather than piano for the audition, he probably would have made an even more riveting impression.

On the whole, Appel liked the kid, but he didn't know whether there was any real future in him. Unconsciously echoing Tex Vinyard's verdict on Springsteen seven years earlier, Appel told the young man that he needed more songs. Springsteen, of course, had already written dozens of songs, but not of the type that he assumed (mostly correctly) Appel and Cretecos wanted to hear. By his own account, Appel also told Springsteen the blunt truth: "these were the worst two songs I ever heard, utterly devoid of any pop potential." The two men agree that Springsteen received Appel's assessment fairly stoically and tentatively said he'd be back, maybe with "more songs."

When Springsteen left Appel's office, both men probably thought that they would never meet again. Appel was mostly being polite, and Springsteen had already been forming a plan to try to advance his career in a setting more vital than the declining bars of Asbury Park. It was almost Christmas, time to visit his family in San Mateo again, time to get away from the Shore and some girlfriend problems. He told the band he didn't know when he would be back. Just before Christmas, he and Tinker drove cross-country to California, as they had done with Steel Mill two years before.

This time, Bruce came back east in just a little over a month, chastened by the highly competitive coffeehouse circuit in Northern California. Thank God his band had never really broken up. He got its members together again, but probably only for the immediate income. He still had his eye on a solo career. A few weeks after he got back, he called Appel, who may or may not have remembered him from the November visit. Appel told him to come back and he'd listen to him.

The second time Springsteen visited the Pocketful of Tunes offices, it was Valentine's Day 1972. This time, he did not bring Tinker West, but he brought—and played—his acoustic guitar. Although Appel later remembered it differently, the first song Springsteen played may have been "Cowboys of the Sea," which he could have played back in November if he had been a better judge of material. He also performed the similarly experienced "If I Was the Priest" as well as "The Angel," a song that was perhaps newer. Like "Hollywood Kids," another song he performed that afternoon that he may have written while in California, "The Angel" is slow and tentative, the lyrics always freighted with self-importance, and Springsteen approached the performance of such songs differently than he did his usual full-band numbers. After seven years of playing the bars of south Jersey, Springsteen usually assumed that the words of a song were basically disposable. But if he had indeed tried playing solo gigs near his parents' home in San Mateo during early January, however, he probably had a very fresh memory of how much more attention a solo acoustic performer receives from his audience.

There were two gems among the songs he played in Manhattan that February afternoon, both "twisted autobiographies," as Springsteen would later classify so many of the songs he wrote during this period, and both almost certainly written within the last month or two. Of the two, the more clearly autobiographical was "Arabian Night," even though its metaphorical code can at points be difficult to crack. The lyric has a tighter structure than most Springsteen songs of this period, proceeding through three mythologized autobiographical moments. The first is Bruce's argument with his mother over a dark-skinned girlfriend (possibly the Latina, rather than Arabian, Maria Espinoza, who would be immortalized by name twenty-five years later in the oft-bootlegged comical autobiographical song "Freehold"). The second verse of the song leaves family behind and brilliantly captures the pervasive air of violence that hung over the summer 1969 stand at the Pandemonium, as well as the trouble with the police in Atlantic Highlands the following summer. The key to the third verse's imagery is more obscure: it depicts "Duke" (Wayne?) battling the devil in a perpetual knife fight right outside the singer's bedroom window.

In terms of specific autobiographical events, "It's Hard to Be a Saint in the City," the second gem that Bruce premiered that afternoon, is much less revelatory than "Arabian Night." Yet like that song, it communicates a feeling, in this case a general fear of not being tough enough to survive in an artistic environment that was more competitive and brutal than the bars of Monmouth and Ocean Counties. Years before male and female fans would mistakenly fall for the singer's image and believe that he really was a gang member or a hot-rodder, this song makes clear that masculine toughness is little more than an attitude one adopts in order to hold one's own, the way a sensitive actor puts on a costume in order to appear in a biker movie. Springsteen could be singing about coming into the city six years earlier to play all those teen-only shows at the Café Wha?, or he could be singing about coming to the music publishing office that very day and trying to pass himself off as a seasoned professional ready for the big time. Either way, it's clear if you look behind this song's verses that his superficially tough attitude carries with it a strong undercurrent of anxiety.

"It's Hard to Be a Saint in the City" is not written in pure rambling verses, nor is it written in the simple verse/chorus alternation that many folk singers took up during this period in unashamed imitation of so many revered nineteenth-century ballads. Instead, this song adopts what musicologist Charles Hamm has called "the venerable AABA form," the compositional DNA of so much twentieth-century pop music, from Tin Pan Alley straight through to the Beatles. Almost classically, this song presents us with an eight-bar theme (A_1), followed by its reiteration (A_2), then a "bridge" that complicates the original theme both musically and lyrically (B), completed by a final section that reiterates part of the earlier section and may or may not resolve the tensions raised by the bridge (A_3).

Not only is "Saint in the City" written in the AABA form, but it puts the hidden anxiety in the song's scenario, the jackpot surprise waiting to pop out, exactly where a Tin Pan Alley or Broadway songwriter would have put it—in the bridge: this is where the singer peels back his white hustler's disguise to show the fear that lies buried just underneath, a fear of the city that turns into claustrophobia during a subway ride. Even formally, however, the threat is much more disturbing in Springsteen's song than in a more classically composed AABA song like Lerner and Loewe's "If Ever I Would Leave You," precisely because of the long lyrical lines that the young songwriter was beginning to favor. We do feel crowded, maybe even trapped, in this bridge, the way the singer feels trapped in the subway. Musically, the tension of this section is not resolved until almost its last measure, appropriately enough on the word *on*, the moment (one assumes) at which we are safely back aboveground, where a tough-seeming young man can continue to playact without fear of exposure.

"It's Hard to Be a Saint in the City" was, quite simply, the most perfect song that Bruce Springsteen had yet written. In years to come, it proved almost foolproof, instantly adaptable to any number of styles: slick and cool as played by a tight four-piece combo on the studio take released on Springsteen's first album; redone as a harder-edged electric guitar duel between Springsteen and Van Zandt on the singer's tours during the late 1970s; and perhaps most memorably as a blue-eyed soul Phil Spectorish fantasia that David Bowie cut in 1975 but did not release until the mid-1980s.

That first February afternoon, though, what allegedly caught Mike Appel's attention about this song—and in the process launched Bruce Springsteen's subsequent career—was a simple simile of just five bare words. Appel asked him to play the song again, possibly slower. "This time when he finished," Appel later remembered, "I just looked at him and repeated out loud, slowly, *Like a Harley in heat.*" Appel knew enough about songwriting to realize how great a line that was.

WHAT HAD CHANGED in the last three months? Why was Springsteen suddenly turning out memorable lyrics that even a would-be professional songwriter wanted to savor? Well, for one thing, Springsteen had known that he needed to concentrate on his lyrics if he wanted to succeed in the contemporary marketplace, and he had written all the words to these songs first. His new lyrics-first policy explains why these songs were so much more polished than most of the ones he had written in the past, but what was the explanation for his new approach to language? The metaphors in these new songs seemed lighter, less weighed down with heavy meaning. They were more likely to roll at their audiences in a cascade of subtly connected imagery than to drop on their heads like an allegorical anvil.

According to Dave Marsh, Springsteen's earliest biographer, around this time the young singer bought Tony Scaduto's new life of Bob Dylan, despite not being a book reader, and dove into it with gusto. Dylan had actually played Asbury Park in August of 1963 (with Joan Baez), but predictably Springsteen had been a fan of his work only since the summer of 1965. He had come to Dylan not through folk but through pop, having first heard the singer "in the car with my mother listening to WMCA." "[O]n came that snare shot that sounded like somebody had kicked open the door to your mind." He devoured "Like a Rolling Stone" and eventually all of *Highway 61 Revisited*, even covering "It Takes a Lot to Laugh, It Takes a Train to Cry" once or twice with the Bruce Springsteen Band.

But—and this cannot be stressed enough—in the six and a half years since that supposedly life-changing moment listening to AM radio in the family car, Springsteen had never really used Dylan as a role model for his career. You can hear traces of the Allman Brothers Band, the Byrds, the Buffalo Springfield, even Dylan's famous "backup" group the Band in many of Springsteen's performances during the early 1970s, but it's awfully hard to hear Dylan per se in any of those performances except for the rare occasions when the singer was actually covering Dylan. Moreover, to pick Bob Dylan as a professional role model in 1972, of all years, was almost perverse. Even many fans might have said at that point that Dylan's career was over, and that the Scaduto biography just served as a postmortem. Since *Nashville Skyline* three years before, Columbia had been putting out Dylan greatest-hits collections, Dylan cover albums, abandoned Dylan tracks, and alternate Dylan takes, but the living Dylan had essentially squirreled himself away in Woodstock or Greenwich Village, much like the protagonist of Don DeLillo's 1973 novel *Great Jones Street*.

For all their interpretative differences, most Springsteen biographers see the impact of Scaduto's volume on Springsteen in pretty much the same light: Scaduto's book showed the young singer a possible career path and even gave him a name (John Hammond) of someone at a major label who liked to discover new talent. But one cannot underestimate the personal reassurance that the young singer may also have derived from Scaduto's book, over and above any practical career tips he may have gleaned from it. At such a personal dead end, Springsteen could easily have found the portrait that the journalist sketched of the young Robert Zimmerman from Hibbing, Minnesota, oddly comforting: the silent, brooding kid, who was always closer to his mother than to his disapproving father; who always wanted a motorcycle and got one as soon as it was legal; whose life was changed forever by a mass media intrusion of rock 'n' roll (Bill Haley and the Comets in *The Blackboard Jungle* rather than Elvis Presley or the Beatles on *The Ed Sullivan Show*); who, once he got a guitar, was almost literally inseparable from it; who registered for three semesters of college but really attended only one; who honed his craft by picking things up from other musicians at after-hours mob scenes (midnight hootenannies at Gerde's Folk City rather than late-night jams at the Potters' Upstage). Most comforting of all may have been Scaduto's unidealized characterization of the young Dylan as someone who sought out fame, almost to the exclusion of anything or anyone else. "Of all the guys around who were playing," one high school friend of Dylan's recalls early in Scaduto's biography, "Bob was the only one with a specific goal in mind." Ten or fifteen years later, old friends from the Asbury Park scene would be saying very similar things about Springsteen.

Scaduto's new biography of Dylan was the right book for Springsteen to encounter at exactly this time. It may even have become a guidebook for the twenty-two-year-old performer, in much the same way as Woody Guthrie's *Bound for Glory* had served as a guidebook for the nineteen-year-old Robert Zimmerman ("probably the only book he'd read since getting to [college in] Minneapolis," Scaduto suggests). If Scaduto's young Dylan wrote "lyrics first, scratching them out on ruled legal-sized yellow paper, later fitting a melody to the words," Springsteen would sit in the abandoned beauty parlor and "write the verses, then pick up the guitar or sit at the piano and follow the inner rhythm of the words." If Scaduto's young Dylan didn't adopt a "conscious journalistic approach" but wrote about the things he saw in a more "poetical," "intuitive," "emotional" fashion, Springsteen would let his new songs "[find] their seed in people, places, hang-outs, and incidents I'd seen and things I'd lived," developing them "impressionistically and [changing] names to protect the guilty." If the young Dylan tried to channel that intuitive flow as rapidly as possible, even going so far as to write a single like "Mixed-Up Confusion" "on the way to a recording session," Springsteen would write a song like "Does This Bus Stop at 82nd Street?" in almost stream-of-consciousness fashion on his way to a friend's crash pad in Manhattan, responding with immediacy to the rapidly passing bread advertisements and X-rated marquees of the early-1970s Times Square.

For most singer-songwriters of the early 1970s, maybe even for many of the "folk rockers" of the time, Bob Dylan was chiefly a forerunner of their current work, someone to be name-checked but not exactly pored over at that particular moment in musical history.

Whether you were Joni Mitchell or Crosby, Stills, and Nash, you revered Dylan as you might a tribal elder, but you didn't necessarily try to write like him—unless you were a young man at a crossroads by the name of Bruce Springsteen. Even if the young singer did not sit in that abandoned Asbury Park beauty parlor memorizing Scaduto's book chapter and verse, when he says of his early 1972 burst of songwriting that he "worked to find something that was identifiably mine," he means something very close to what Dylan had tried to describe to Scaduto when he had finally given him an interview the previous fall, praising his later, "unconscious" writing over his earlier, self-conscious work. Those "unconscious songs came from inside of me and I didn't have to stop to write them."

For even though many of Springsteen's new songs were indeed covertly autobiographical, they were not primarily based in self-revelation, as the songs of Mitchell or her current opening act Jackson Browne were. What made Springsteen's songs "personal" was not so much their specific autobiographical details or insights as the vision that they communicated of the observed world. When Simon and Garfunkel took their listeners on a bus ride across "America" in 1968 or Crosby, Stills, and Nash offered their audience a chance to ride on the "Marrakesh Express" in 1969, what they communicated to their fans—rather directly, in fact—were the self-conscious thoughts and feelings to which the passing sights gave rise in them. But when we join Bruce Springsteen on a bus trip uptown through Manhattan on a day when he thinks he might just have a chance to finally become a big-time recording star, we are not really privy to the singer's conscious thoughts and feelings. We just see the world through his incredibly excited eyes. It is the difference between writing like George Eliot or Henry James and writing like James Joyce or Virginia Woolf. Both forms of writing are "personal," but the latter privileges the experience of consciousness over its direct analysis or articulation.

Less than a year after the release of *Highway 61 Revisited*, Bob Dylan told Nat Henhoff, "My older songs, to say the least, were about nothing." "[T]he newer ones," he added, "are about the same nothing—only as seen inside a bigger thing, perhaps called nowhere." More than any other American songwriter who came after Dylan, Springsteen took up this particular—albeit obscure—authorial challenge. At least at this early stage of his career, in his lyrics Springsteen neither analyzed society's current ills (as Dylanesque protest singers had done), nor excavated its cultural past for greater understanding of the present (as Dylan's folk-rock spawn were doing), nor even revealed deep truths about his most private relationships (as the singer-songwriters were almost required to do on a nightly basis). Instead, what the reborn Springsteen of 1972 did was sing about a shared nothing in the context of a highly personal nowhere.

He also seems to have picked up one other thing from his engaged reacquaintance with Dylan that spring, something he would desperately need to escape the gravitational pull of the most dominant aspects of the current singer-songwriter mode: *speed*. Being slow, thoughtful, and intimate with a guitar or a piano may have helped lend flight to the talents of James Taylor, Jackson Browne, or Joni Mitchell, but, as we have seen, that sort of performance style tended to weigh down Springsteen's talents with portentousness. By contrast, in a Dylan song like Springsteen's cherished "Like a Rolling Stone," the words, as music critic Greil Marcus has shrewdly observed, sound "cheap, broken, as if the writer was in too much of a hurry to get it right, or didn't care, and the song trips over it, momentarily goes blank as the words are sung. And then the next line is sung." This sort of writing was as much of a breakthrough for Springsteen in 1972 as it was for Dylan in 1965. Keep putting one line after another, without looking back too much, and eventually you achieve escape velocity from your own excessive self-consciousness. As Springsteen would say in concert six years later as a spoken transition between performances of "Growin' Up" and "It's Hard to Be a Saint in the City," *It was bye bye New Jersey. We were aiiiiir-borne . . .*

LESS THAN A month after their second meeting in Manhattan, Springsteen signed with Appel and Cretecos. To be precise, he signed an exclusive recording agreement with Laurel Canyon Productions, a new corporate entity that Appel had formed with Cretecos, almost solely in anticipation of the prospect of recording Springsteen. After the signing, Springsteen went back to gigging with his old band for ready cash, but in between gigs he was by all accounts still writing like a madman, "travel[ing] to New York City on the bus, trying whatever I'd written latest out on Mike and Jimmy." These repeated trips were even affecting the content of his songwriting. For the young man from Monmouth County, Lindsay-era Manhattan became the twilight setting of cooler songs like "Jazz Musician" and "Two Hearts in True Waltz Time." Even though he had previously played in New York on and off for a year, now the city was a place about which he was rapidly acquiring more sensory details, and yet it remained unfamiliar enough to serve as a setting for his stylized fantasies.

While Springsteen wrote, Appel hustled, calling around town to record companies and seeing who might be interested in his exciting new solo act. The person Appel really wanted to see at Columbia was its president, Clive Davis. In Davis's five years heading the label, it had signed Big Brother and the Holding Company, Laura Nyro, Santana, and Blood, Sweat and Tears. Davis wasn't around, though. He then called John Hammond's office and then apparently charmed Liz Gilbert, Hammond's secretary, by calling Springsteen a "longevity act" like Barbra Streisand. Gilbert put a brief meeting with Appel and Springsteen on Hammond's calendar.

And so it was on the morning of Tuesday, 2 May 1972, that John Hammond, like many executives in the entertainment industry, came into his office, looked at his desk calendar, and realized he had absolutely no idea who the person was with whom he had an appointment in a few hours. At eleven o'clock sharp, he found out.

Two men filed in, and Appel did the talking, while his scruffy, initially anonymous client sat in the corner with his guitar. Piecing together Appel's later account with the one Hammond gives in his autobiography, it seems clear that Springsteen's new manager was a little nervous about trying to make a sale to a living legend. In his pitch, Appel understandably stressed Bruce's newfound skill with words. Hammond nodded but seemed to be growing impatient.

Hammond's version of this meeting differs from Appel's on a number of points, but its most interesting detail is the way that the music executive characterizes the young Springsteen: not just as quiet or recessive, but as "grinning easily while Appel and I clashed." The singer may very well have been just as nervous as Appel, but for him the meeting also had a certain sense of unreality about it. Even if it had not been his manager's original intention, here he was auditioning for the man he had just read about a few months before. When you don't come from a world (as Carly Simon, for example, did) in which people read, write, and even appear in books with a certain amount of regularity, you're not as prepared for something like this to happen. No wonder Springsteen was grinning: it was almost like the sort of fairy-tale moment that he had forced himself to stand apart from and analyze in a recent song like "Arabian Night."

Although Hammond never said it, one wonders whether it was Springsteen's less volatile demeanor, his marked contrast to Appel's aggression, that caused the music executive to be intrigued by him. "Now, I haven't got much time," he remembered saying to Appel. "Who's your boy?" Upon finally learning Springsteen's name, Hammond supposedly said, "Why don't you take out your guitar, Bruce, and start playing before I get more irritated?"

The song Bruce probably led off with was, not surprisingly, "It's Hard to Be a Saint in the City"—"an extraordinary piece," as Hammond later called it, "filled with street imagery." Springsteen might not have known the music industry yet, but he certainly knew audiences. If "Saint in the City" was the song that had won over Appel, then it was probably a good choice to lead off with for Hammond. According to Appel, after that first song Hammond turned to him and said, "You were right," then asked Springsteen, "Got any more songs, son?" We don't know all the songs he sang that morning, but among them were probably two pieces he had written in the two months since he signed with Appel and Cretecos: "Mary, Queen of Arkansas" (another plodding number à la "The Angel," which Hammond later claimed not to have liked) and "Growin' Up" (another "twisted autobiography" that had the same three-verse structure as "Arabian Night" but whose lyrics were less specifically personal and a little more broadly comprehensible). Then Hammond asked, in his words, "if [Bruce] had anything really far out," something he wouldn't perform live. Bruce promptly responded with "If I Was the Priest"—which he had performed live at the Student Prince, of course, but no one else in the room knew that. "Bruce," Hammond remembered saying, "that's the damnedest song I've ever heard. Were you brought up by nuns?" "Of course," Bruce replied, charming the music executive in a much lighter way with his performance than Appel ever could have attempted with his earnest sales pitch.

Hammond later remembered this meeting going on for over two hours, but other accounts place it at well under an hour. At the end, the music executive may have made a vague commitment to sign Springsteen, but he still wanted to see Springsteen perform live before the signing was official. Somehow, someone made a phone call, and around six-thirty that evening Springsteen and his guitar were in front of a small audience at the Gaslight au Go Go. This "new" club had opened less than a month earlier in an attempt to merge the resources and audiences of the old folkie Village Gaslight and the more poppy Café au Go Go, on the Bleecker Street site formerly occupied by the latter of those two clubs. He sang for under a half hour to a sparsely populated room—offering "Saint in the City," "Growin' Up," "Arabian Night," and maybe one or two other songs—but Appel thought it was all a waste because he could see neither hide nor hair of Hammond. The next day Hammond told Appel that he had been there, "and we loved him." On Wednesday, Bruce came back to Columbia to cut some demos. All in all, he recorded twelve songs that day in under two hours. Two of the songs, both performed at the piano, required a second take, but all the others he just blazed through with a growing self-confidence you can still hear on the surviving tape.

Despite his commanding air, the declining Hammond did not in fact speak for his entire label, and a definitive contract with Columbia was not immediately forthcoming. While they were waiting, Appel decided it would be a good idea to shop Bruce around to other labels, particularly A&M and Elektra. At the worst, maybe a little competition would get Columbia to up its price when it finally did sign Bruce. To this end, Appel and Cretecos had Springsteen sign a publishing agreement with Sioux City Music (their new music publishing company, the sole artist on its roster Bruce Springsteen) and begin recording his songs. Such recordings served two functions. First, they allowed Appel and

Cretecos to assemble a professional-sounding audition tape to send to labels other than Columbia. Second, the songs themselves could be sent to artists who did have recording contracts as possible material to fill out their own albums. Joni Mitchell and James Taylor had both broken into the recording industry that way, and when you were as broke as Springsteen was at that point, there was certainly no harm in pulling in a few publishing royalties when you were waiting for your ship to come in.

All that became moot, however, a little over a month after the Hammond audition. On 9 June 1972, Columbia Records entered into an agreement with Laurel Canyon Productions to record Bruce Springsteen. Assembling an album of original songs for wide release was no longer a dream or a long-term prospect for the young singer. It was now an urgent necessity. Almost the first thing Bruce did after the signing was finally buy himself a Fender Telecaster—a factory "mistake" actually, with an Esquire body and a Telecaster neck, that he found at a guitar shop in Belmar. Then he started assembling a band.

THE BAND HE CALLED UP was the same one that he had been performing with on and off since the fall: Vini Lopez on drums, David Sancious on keyboards, Garry Tallent on bass, and Steve Van Zandt on rhythm guitar and harmony vocals. Several weeks after the CBS contract was signed, the five musicians rehearsed for three days in a Point Pleasant apartment complex and even gave a warehouse concert at the end of the rehearsals for about a hundred people. It's not clear how advanced the song selection for the album was at this point, but even though Bruce had been playing with these musicians for years, it was almost certainly the first time that they had played most of these songs, maybe even the first time that they had heard them. Throughout the prior six months, Springsteen had carefully kept his band and his new material separate. He may have used the Point Pleasant rehearsals to determine which new songs worked best when played with others.

In fact, this material was so new to the four other musicians that the first time Appel heard them play with Bruce, he thought the singer was crazy to want to record with them. Like Hammond, Appel had only heard Bruce play solo, which was impressive in and of itself.

When he finally heard Springsteen play with his band, Appel's reaction was almost as negative as it had been to his disastrous first audition back in November. Appel thought the other musicians were detrimental to the songs that Springsteen had crafted and that Appel honestly admired. Appel suggested that Springsteen didn't need them, but Springsteen insisted. He wanted the band in the studio with him.

When the recording sessions for the album were finally scheduled, it turned out that Van Zandt couldn't make them: he had a prior commitment playing guitar for the early-'60s Philadelphia group the Dovells during an oldies stand in Las Vegas. Three years later, Bruce would turn the story of his dwindling early-'70s band into an amusing onstage anecdote (from seven members to six to five—*you get down to your boys when you're starving*), but when he walked into 914 Sound Studios in Blauvelt, New York, in July of 1972, it may not have seemed like much of a joke. The last year had been a long slide away from the free-for-all jams at the Upstage. Fourteen months earlier, he had opened for the Allman Brothers Band at the Sunshine In, fronting an assembly of seventeen musicians (and Monopoly players). Now he would be making his first album with just three.

Perhaps logically, it was his livelier songs that ended up receiving the full-band treatment. The sheer giddiness of "Growin' Up" and "Does This Bus Stop at 82nd Street?" worked beautifully with a four-piece band performing at full throttle. In fact, as good as his CBS demo of "It's Hard to Be a Saint in the City" had been two months before, the song may have worked even better with Bruce singing against Davey Sancious's fluid, crashing runs on the piano rather than just against his own guitar work. The professionally loose band lent a similarly orchestrated urban claustrophobia to "Lost in the Flood," a recent song about returning Vietnam veterans. Ultimately, there was only one song recorded during these July full-band sessions that might have warranted a slightly different treatment. For many Springsteen fans, the up-tempo studio recording of "For You" made that July is less preferable than the statelier version of the song that he would later perform on tour by himself at the piano. Oddly enough, Bruce may have finally produced a song that could have worked in the performance style he had so incorrectly adopted for his initial meeting with Appel and Cretecos.

The band sessions were efficient, done in under two weeks with very little waste. Then came a week or two of solo sessions, during which at least eight tracks were laid down, almost all of them songs that Bruce had already recorded for either CBS or Sioux City. For whatever reason, "If I Was the Priest" didn't make the cut, but "Cowboys of the Sea" was deemed worthy of a solo rather than a full-band recording. "Arabian Night" and "Lady and the Doctor," "The Angel" and "Mary, Queen of Arkansas," "Jazz Musician" and "Two Hearts in True Waltz Time" all received solo recordings, as did a song written in June called "Visitation at Fort Horn," which clocked in at almost eight minutes and (like many of Hollywood's recent anti-westerns) tried to use the tropes of American frontier mythology to comment obliquely on the current predicament of the U.S. Army in Southeast Asia.

Other solo tracks may indeed have been laid down at 914, but even if it was just these eight, the contrast between the solo sessions and the ones held with the full band earlier in the month is striking. "Growin' Up," "It's Hard to Be a Saint in the City," "Does This Bus Stop at 82nd Street?," and "Lost in the Flood" all work as a musical and thematic unit. They sound alike and are rooted in an analogous, white boy's would-be R&B style. Even if one is not familiar with the details of their author's life, these four songs (and possibly even the misarranged "For You") can easily be read as sequential chapters of a single story, almost like a mildly happier version of the etchings in Hogarth's *The Rake's Progress*: good-hearted, innocently rebellious kid from the sticks comes to the big city, is tempted, succeeds, sees the fates of the fallen. By contrast, the solo tracks that Bruce laid down in late July could almost have issued from different acts or artists, from an ersatz masculinized Joni Mitchell ("The Angel" and "Mary, Queen of Arkansas") to a proto Steely Dan ("Jazz Musician" and "Two Hearts in True Waltz Time"). Springsteen, Appel, and Hammond had certainly done a good job culling the singer's incredible wealth of recent material. At least half of these solo tracks *were* worth releasing. The question was whether they all belonged on the same album.

By the second week of August, a consensus about the album had been reached—a compromise really, because it tried to have things both ways. Bruce's first album would have five band tracks (the style that Springsteen preferred) and five solo tracks (the style that Appel and Hammond preferred). It's not clear whether the intent at this point was to set this division out starkly in the completed product, with one side of the released album explicitly devoted to each style, as with Dylan's 1965 album *Bringing It All Back Home*. What is striking, though, is the fact that in all probability every one of the band tracks that had been cut was being used, even though CBS and Laurel Canyon had nearly forty minutes' worth of solo material recorded, enough to fill an album by early-1970s standards.

Once this selection had been made, the album began to be prepared for release. It was probably at this point, in mid-August, that assorted tweaks were added to several of the selected tracks—but then CBS president Clive Davis finally weighed in. Before the recording sessions, Davis, like Appel and Hammond, had never heard Bruce with a band. On the other hand, he probably had a better sense of the contemporary market for popular music in 1972 than those other two men put together. And his response to Springsteen's proposed ten-track debut album was simple: he preferred the band material over the solo tracks, tipping the previous debate over the album's content now very heavily in Bruce's favor. More important, he said he didn't hear a hit. Appel and Hammond may have been shocked by Davis's assessment, but Springsteen by all accounts received it in much the same way that he had received Appel's suggestion the previous fall that he write more songs. He got to work.

Could Springsteen write a single quickly, especially if his big-time album release was on the line? Of course, he could. In 1972 coming up with new songs was never a problem for him. His problem that August was coming up with a band: Van Zandt was still in Vegas (although he might be back soon), and Tallent and Sancious had a regular gig down at Alpha Studios in Richmond that they could not steal any more time away from. Lopez was still available, but to make a single that would be fun enough to catch the ears of listeners flipping along the radio dial, he would need more than just drums to back his guitar work. Moreover, if the track was really going to cook, he couldn't just rely on session men, no matter how good. It had to be somebody he knew, probably from the Asbury Park scene.

Springsteen's connection with saxophonist Clarence Clemons has been excessively mythologized, first and foremost by Springsteen himself. In his onstage raps of the late 1970s, the singer would spin elaborate tales of their first meeting, with Clemons rising out of the boardwalk mist, and electrical charges passing between them the first time they touched. Much of this mythologization has been attributed to Clemons's status as the only person of color in Bruce's band, but back in 1972 this actually was not the case: Davey Sancious was African American, and Vini Lopez was a fairly dark-skinned Latino. In truth, Clemons's special status in the band's mythology probably derives from the fact that he was a unique addition at a unique time. Although he had recently played in various Jersey Shore clubs, the Norfolk, Virginia, native had not come up through the local Monmouth County bands the way that Springsteen's other bandmates had. He also wasn't recruited through advertised auditions as Roy Bittan, Max Weinberg, and even Patti Scialfa would be in later years. In other words, Clemons was what you might call a familiar stranger: someone who moved in the same musical circles as Springsteen but whom he had not known and jammed with for the last several years.

One version that Clemons tells of his first meeting with Springsteen is marvelously succinct: "He was playing in a bar down the street from where I was playing. And it was a dark and rainy night—it was cold. I walked out on the street and saw him and asked if I could sit in with him." By comparing local performance dates for the Bruce Springsteen Band and Norman Seldin and the Joyful Noize, the band in which Clemons was then playing, zealous Springsteen aficionados have determined that this meeting probably occurred in early September of 1971, near the beginning of Springsteen's extended residency at the Student Prince. In his 1999 Rock and Roll Hall of Fame acceptance speech, Springsteen tells a similar story, but one that takes place in a more exaggeratedly symbolic climate: "The door literally blew off the club in a storm that night, and I knew I'd found my sax player."

In September of 1971, of course, Springsteen had *not* been looking for a saxophone player. He probably hadn't even been looking for one when he returned the favor and joined Clemons onstage with the

Joyful Noize twice during the summer of 1972, during the band's extended stay at the Shipbottom Lounge in Point Pleasant. In mid-June and early July, when Bruce sat in with them, he was probably just looking for a break from rehearsals for his own upcoming album. Those spontaneous team-ups probably weren't about business; they were about fun, because music could be both for Springsteen, even in different moments of the same day. Underneath all the exaggeration, it seems clear that, from the first, these two men genuinely enjoyed playing with each other. Although it might not have been mystical or electrostatic in nature, there was clearly an instant connection, and that is the kind of thing a serious performer never forgets.

So when Springsteen realized that he needed at least one more band member for his single, Clemons was the person he called. This time Bruce was going into the studio not with seventeen musicians, not with ten, not even with seven or four or three, but with just *two*. The last tracks for his first album would be recorded by a trio—like Earth, but not like Earth. The difference was not just the substitution of a reed instrument for a stringed one. It was also a difference between blues-based jamming and pure party music. Being explicitly asked to make a single freed Bruce up in a way, because for this track, at least, he didn't have to worry about being a "serious" singer-songwriter.

"Spirit in the Night," which Springsteen recorded with Clemons and Lopez that August, is an unabashedly fun song. Even though it is almost certainly goofier than the other five band tracks that had by that point been locked for the album, it did fit stylistically with them. It featured the same sorts of characters that we meet in songs like "Growin' Up" and "Does This Bus Stop at 82nd Street?," and its giddy lyrics are also of a piece with the elongated, colorful lines of those songs. Always a compositional recycler, Bruce even found a way to reuse the only conceit that had impressed Appel on their first meeting, as the *silent band* of the atrocious "Baby Doll" becomes the much sharper but still imagined *soul fairy band* to which the revelers of this song find themselves dancing. This is perhaps the greatest lesson that Springsteen learned upon signing to CBS and recording the album. Back in the fall and winter, he had turned to somber, solo songs as a way of being taken seriously as a songwriter. Intricate lyrics, he assumed, were wasted on the members of a Saturday night bar audience who are only half listening to the house band anyway. The beauty of "Spirit in the Night" is that it tosses that assumption to the winds. Fun singles can still have complicated lyrics. A richness of imaginative detail doesn't have to present a barrier to audience identification.

And that song wasn't even intended as the main single. Springsteen, Lopez, and Clemons cut a second track, this time with session man Harold Wheeler on piano, that was even stranger. As Bruce would do a number of times in the future when pressed to come up with more tracks at the last minute to complete an album's emergent concept, he wrote a song about the state of his art, about where he stood at this odd moment in his career. The lyrics for "Blinded by the Light" are as hermetic in their colorful references as the lyrics of "Spirit in the Night" are open in theirs, and yet it too fits on this album of twisted, motor-mouth autobiographies. In later characterizing how he composed it, Springsteen would speak of *sitting on my bed with a rhyming dictionary in one hand and a notebook in the other* in his spare Asbury Park room, the rhyming dictionary *in flames* by the end of the process, as he raced against the clock to come up with one last song.

More than those of any other song on Springsteen's first album, the words of "Blinded by the Light" make it almost impossible to understand what the singer is talking about most of the time. The opening line alone refers obliquely to both Vini Lopez (by his nickname "Mad Dog") and Bruce's childhood Little League team (the Indians). The second verse deals, in part, with the YMCA dances at which Bruce first kissed Maria Espinoza, the third verse with late-blooming New Jersey campus radicals and their inevitable attempts to avoid FBI surveillance. Yet somehow, through all these incomprehensible lines, a feeling is conveyed. The speed at which the author is now working is the point of the song, as is the glee with which the words pour out of him, an overflowing emotion that is wonderfully doubled by Clemons's unrelenting saxophone part. You don't have to know what the singer is saying to know that you understand him; you don't have to follow all the lyrics in a bar band song to have a good time on Saturday night; and you don't have to comprehend everything that happens in your scattershot career for things to work out for the best. *Don't over-think the whole thing*, Springsteen would later caution fans in the midst of his most extended exegesis of these lyrics. Over a century and a half earlier, John Keats had called this sort of unreasoned self-assurance "negative capability." In the 1970s, they called it "going with the flow," and you didn't have to be an ex-hippie in the age of Nixon to see that sometimes it might actually be a good idea. More than anything, the point of "Blinded by the Light" comes in its last two lines, which Springsteen has called its "best lines," whose import any listener can understand: *Mama always told me not to look into the sights of the sun / Oh but mama that's where the fun is.* And blissfully blind to the whatness of it all, we ride off with the singer on the heady trail of Clarence Clemons's manic riffing.

In the final arrangement of Springsteen's first album, "Blinded by the Light" would lead it off, a clear harbinger of the breathlessness that most of the album's songs would adopt. Along with "Spirit of the Night," "Blinded by the Light" would mercifully bump off the album the new, pretentious "Visitation at Fort Horn" (the only song Spring-steen ever recorded that includes the utterance *What ho!*). Inexplica-bly, "Mary, Queen of Arkansas" and "The Angel" were kept on the album, while "Jazz Musician" and "Two Hearts in True Waltz Time," better songs that fit in more obviously with the other songs' frequently urban settings, were cut. The eventual loss of "Arabian Night," how-ever, made sense. Although that earlier song was an inspired one, it came out of Springsteen's prior understanding of his situation, an understanding that had now been superseded. Now, in a song like "Blinded by the Light," the life of a working musician could be seen as silly rather than gothic, rife with the potential for comedy rather than for violence. Here Bruce could insist at the end of each insane verse that the featured character was *gonna make it all right* and sound as if he meant it.

By early September, nearly all the tracks for the album were com-pleted. (Steve Van Zandt even got back from Vegas at the last minute and helped capture the perfect street noises for the abrupt opening of "Lost in the Flood.") In the end, the album had nine tracks, two solo and seven band tracks. For years, John Hammond would insist that this decision was a mistake. He thought that Springsteen should have just released the solo demo recordings he had laid down back in May.

But the debut album Springsteen finally assembled from all these fevered months of songwriting wasn't just about an individual, about a lone voice speaking to lone listeners through the medium of an LP first heard through bulky early-1970s privacy-inducing headphones. It wasn't a diary passed intimately from one special friend to another. It was a true *album*, a collection of snapshots that shared one individual's vision of a unique world. The title it eventually received was inspired: *Greetings from Asbury Park, N.J.* It is a postcard from a friend you never knew you had, about the strange new world that he has seen.

CHAPTER 4

ENDLESS JUKE JOINTS AND
VALENTINO DRAG (1972–1975)

I N EARLY AUGUST OF 1972, BRUCE SPRINGSTEEN FINALLY WENT
back in front of a live audience. For six nights that summer, he did two
half-hour sets a night at the bottom of a three-artist bill at Max's Kansas City, at that point still one of Manhattan's hottest clubs for live
music. Given his promising but still currently stalled career, the young
singer probably wouldn't have gotten a gig that impressive if the featured act on the bill (folksinger Dave van Ronk) hadn't been an old
friend of his new mentor John Hammond. Springsteen became casually friendly with Hammond that summer, frequently dropping into
his Columbia office without necessarily calling first, much as he had
shown up so often during the spring at Pocketful of Tunes.

Springsteen performed solo for these twelve sets. The first night at
Max's, the MC introduced Springsteen as "a very fine young songwriter with special talents." The singer then took the stage nervously,
adjusted the microphone (*Is this your mike?*), and gave exactly the sort
of ill-at-ease, on-the-money introduction to his first number that was
so typical of singer-songwriters during the latter-day coffeehouse era.
This is a song about being new in town, he says about "Henry Boy," a
lively piece about a young man trying and mostly failing to make it as
a performer in New York City.

"Henry Boy" had been recorded for the Sioux City publishing
demos back in the spring, but it had probably never been seriously
considered for the album. Opening at Max's, however, it must have
seemed like an inevitable choice. Obviously, Bruce is Henry, and the

predicament of the song is almost exactly the one in which he finds himself. He's still looking around, still trying to get the feel of things, even if he does not stand at the corner of Forty-second and Broadway (as the protagonist of the song does) and scream *Up scope!* He sings sitting down, over two dozen blocks downtown from Times Square, upstairs at 213 Park Avenue South, a long way from the now shuttered Green Mermaid Teahouse, and he keeps things very uncomfortably low-key. Somehow, it doesn't seem like the right place for him to bust out the sort of broadly comedic persona that he had used at Lincoln Center a little over a year earlier as Dr. Zoom. At times, his onstage patter between songs can be almost cringe-inducing:

> *This is a song about becoming a man—which everybody's supposed to be doing—particularly you guys—it could be a song about becoming a woman too—I don't know. . . .*

Awkward as the young singer's spoken words are, though, everything changes the second he starts to play. Strumming a guitar, he clearly knows what he's doing. His skills are even more in evidence when he plays his set-closer, the well-honed "Growin' Up," which those awkward words were meant to introduce. Less than a month before, Springsteen had recorded a fuller arrangement of this song with Sancious, Lopez, and Tallent out in Blauvelt, but closing his set at Max's he slips back easily here into performing it by himself. This solo performance of the song is, if anything, even more assured than the one he gave back in May at CBS. He knows the song is good, and he knows he sounds good playing it.

Bruce may have played a few more solo shows at Max's that fall, but by the time he got around to planning a tour to support *Greetings*, the entire idea of the album had, of course, changed. To play most of the songs that ended up on the album in its final form, he would need to have a band, including Lopez and Tallent from his old band and Clemons from the sessions in August. Davey Sancious wasn't available to fill out the keyboards, so Bruce once again turned to Danny Federici. In late October, this five-piece touring band rehearsed in the same Point Pleasant apartment complex that Bruce had used for prerecording rehearsals just a few months earlier. They played several one-off gigs that fall, opening for Cheech and Chong one time and Crazy Horse another, and headlining a Halloween concert in Long Branch for two bands that Tinker West managed: Tumbleweed (the rechristened Montana Flintlock) and a retro act named Odin. In December, Springsteen's newly configured band took up its first regular gig: six nights at Kenny's Castaways, on Manhattan's Upper East Side.

Kenny's wasn't Max's, but it was in the same league. Aerosmith would play one of its first New York club dates there, and the New York Dolls, Patti Smith, and Blondie would all play there by the end of the decade. The newspaper ads for the club self-consciously advertised "FOOD AND BOOZE," but Kenny's was never a dive. Like Max's, it was the closest thing to a dive that many of its more affluent customers would probably be willing to enter. The week after Bruce, John Hartford was scheduled to play the club; the week after that, Rick Roberts (from the now extinct Flying Burrito Brothers) and Liam Clancy. As for Springsteen, Kenny's omitted any mention of his band in the advertising and spelled his last name—as some others would do for the next year or two—as "Springstein."

The sets on this tour were designed to duplicate the experience of the album. For each one, Bruce would come out onstage alone, play a few songs solo, and then bring out the band for the bulk of the performance. In the solo segment, he might perform "Circus Song" or "Song of the Orphans," pieces that had been recorded for *Greetings* but had not made it onto the final version of the album. The other members of the band would join him as needed, Tallent on his first instrument, the tuba, for "Circus Song," Federici on accordion for a goofy new song called "Bishop Danced." This song, as Springsteen explained before one performance that winter, was about

a bishop and his wife and this violin player in West Virginia, how a daughter lost her mother to mathematics out on a business trip in Detroit, pancakes and this guy named Muskrat who lives in Richmond, Virginia . . . who I met when I was playin' down there (he plays saxophone), James Garner when he was very popular years ago [on Maverick], *this little boy who told his father that the Indians are still in the woods, only nobody sees 'em, and the sexual pathos of elderly choirboys in Butte, Montana*

—among other things.

Throughout these early dates, Springsteen began to hone a slightly different stage persona, using loose variations on the same seemingly improvised material every night between songs. That meandering introduction to "Bishop Danced," for example, was from a New York date in late January, but earlier in the month, he had introduced the song almost identically when he appeared with band members on Maxanne Sartori's afternoon show on Boston's WBCN, at that point the most important FM rock station in New England. Reproducing a reduced version of his current stage show for the Boston radio listeners, they performed six songs on the show, only two of which were actually on Springsteen's first album.

In part, this was because the album had come out just four days earlier. CBS had pushed the original November 1972 release date back to 5 January 1973, in the hopes that it wouldn't get lost in an end-of-the-year flood of new releases. Now that the album was out, until it built up some kind of momentum, the band would support itself by touring as an opening act: for Brownsville Station in Ohio; for Travis Shook and the Club Wow at the Main Point in Bryn Mawr; and now for David Bromberg at Paul's Mall in Boston, which the band's WBCN appearance was meant to publicize. (For the Boston stand, the club billed the new artist in ads as "Rick Springsteen.") Independent of CBS's efforts, Mike Appel was planning his own mad promotional schemes to get Springsteen some attention, including a concert at Sing Sing (which actually happened in early December, around the time of the Kenny's stand, and during which Bruce assured the inmates, *When this is over you can all go home!*), not to mention a spot opening the Super Bowl, just before Andy Williams sang the national anthem (which didn't happen, to no one's surprise but Appel's).

Through it all, Springsteen kept writing like a fiend. That was the other reason why the new content in his shows wasn't surprising: Bruce constantly had new songs, dozens of new ones at many rehears-

als, including quite a few for which we have no surviving recordings.
That winter, however, he did return to 914 Studios to lay down solo
versions of at least four tracks—"The Ballad of the Self-Loading Pistol," "The Saga of the Architect Angel," "Janey Needs a Shooter," and
"Winter Song"—all possibly recorded purely for music publishing purposes. The first three of these songs continued his interest in western
themes. Indeed, if those three songs had been combined with "Arabian Night," "Circus Song," "Cowboys of the Sea," "Song of the
Orphans," and "Visitation at Fort Horn" (all of which he had already
recorded), as well as "Bishop Danced" (which he was now performing
almost nightly), he would have had the core of a second, fairly unified
album, much of which could have been adapted both to band and to
solo performance.

That was the sort of album that Springsteen would have recorded
if he had gone back into the studio in the fall. Once he began touring
with a band again, however, he started turning back to more songs
rooted in R&B rather than folk-rock. He was going back to the sort of
music that he had been playing a little over a year earlier at the Student Prince, but the lessons of the intervening summer had not been
lost on him. Even if he wrote a song that sounded like "Quarter to
Three" or "Seven Day Weekend" its lyrics would be more densely
populated than the fairly simple words to those early-1960s chart burn-
ers had been.

Take "Thundercrack," for example, a song that Springsteen probably premiered in late January when he returned to Max's Kansas City,
this time with the band. "Thundercrack" was a party song, about a
stripper, but she didn't work in a place as sketchily defined as the
merely name-checked "Basin Street" in Gary U.S. Bonds's 1960 hit
"New Orleans." This dancer worked a *lightning shack* on *the Inner
Lake,* and among her devotees were *them dancehall hacks from the
west side of the tracks.* As "Thundercrack" plays out, such lyrics prove
to be more than just rhyming slang. They are traces of an intuitively
complete, if imperfectly glimpsed, world that Springsteen's audience
had never encountered before, one that could easily be just down
Route 88 from the characters in "Spirit in the Night." As with *Greasy
Lake* and *go-cart Mozart* in the last two tracks Springsteen had

recorded for *Greetings*, such references were not meant to call up generically familiar images, even of New Jersey, but rather to create an overall impression of a new and wacky world.

In terms of sheer performance, the January stand at Max's was a triumph. The difference between the awkward young man of August and the quirky bandleader onstage now could not have been more striking. Even during the opening solo set, knowing that the band would be coming out later made Springsteen a little more comfortable to goof around than he had been the last time that he was at the venue. The new sets now had a place to go: from the quiet of his solo work to the full force of the band's power. A new set-closer like "Thundercrack" combined the best of what Springsteen had learned with both Steel Mill and the Bruce Springsteen Band: clocking in at over eleven minutes, it was at least half as epic as the former band's "Garden State Parkway Blues," but just as catchy (and twice as ambitious) as the latter band's "Funk Song." Coming at the end of a relatively brief, sixty-minute set opening for the now long-forgotten Biff Rose, it was also an undeniable *band* song, one that gave all the musicians a chance to show off and make the audience want to come back for more. Indeed, it was during this second stand at Max's that David Bowie, a friend of Rose's, first saw Springsteen and was wholly unimpressed by his solo performance. The band, however, had him riveted, and he felt that Springsteen was immeasurably better when he performed with them as well.

February brought more one-offs: headlining at colleges and small clubs in the Northeast and opening for better-known acts in far-afield parts of the country. In friendly, more intimate surroundings, like the week they headlined at Oliver's in Boston, Springsteen would follow his muse. He would try out more stylistically varied songs: the R&B number sometimes called "The Fever" (which sounded as if it had been written two years before, when he was deep into his boardwalk soul phase); the whopper about Santa Ana, Sam Houston, Kid Cole, the devil, and a contessa (yet another western number that had the musical and thematic scope of the new set-closers); or the dreamy song about a skid row character named Diamond Jackie in contemporary New York City (which gave him a chance to play off Clemons's saxophone as some of the other smaller numbers had given him a chance to play off Tallent's tuba or Federici's accordion). Until they were recorded, many of these songs didn't even have titles: they were just things Springsteen was playing around with when he thought the audience might give him the chance to do so.

As an opening act, though, Springsteen and the band were far more likely to stick to a regular setlist or to throw in cover songs to keep the crowd's attention. The supporting nature of many of the former gigs led Bruce to change the shape of his band's usual set. Whether they were opening for Dan Hicks and His Hot Licks in Richmond (billed as "Bruce Springstien") or for Blood, Sweat and Tears in Berkeley and Santa Monica, the audiences had come to hear big bands, even heavy bands, not intimate, quirky, or subtle performances. Consequently, Springsteen led off with a heavier sound as an opening set than he might have used in a more intimate club like Max's, Kenny's, or even the Troubadour in LA. More typically now, he would open the show with a full-band number like "Lost in the Flood" and save the slower, acoustic numbers for changes of pace during the set.

That spring, Springsteen and his band opened for Sha-Na-Na and Lou Reed in Rhode Island, for Stevie Wonder in Pennsylvania, for the Beach Boys in Virginia, for Richie Havens in Connecticut, for Chuck Berry and Jerry Lee Lewis in Maryland, and for the Eagles and Billy Preston in Ohio. Even if the crowds at most of these concerts had no idea who this strange bearded dude from New Jersey was, Don Henley, one of the two frontmen of the Eagles, had already heard about Springsteen from his friend Jackson Browne. After watching just one performance, Henley became yet another convert. "I remember thinking to myself," he has said, "that this was a guy that wasn't gonna be warming up the crowd for us—or for anybody—for very long." That prediction would end up proving true, but not in the way that Henley probably meant it.

FOR THE MOST PART, the critical reaction to *Greetings from Asbury Park, N.J.* was truly underwhelming. In the early 1970s, when a new singer-songwriter was being launched every week, the role of rock journalists and FM DJs as tastemakers for the general buying public could hardly be underestimated. In Springsteen's case, his label's determination to market him aggressively as "the new Dylan" prejudiced many of those tastemakers before they had ever heard a second of Springsteen's music. When Springsteen played a CBS showcase at LA's Ahmanson Theatre that spring, one reporter jokingly asked in the title of his review, "Was Bob Dylan the Previous Bruce Springsteen?" Similarly, *Rolling Stone*'s first profile of Springsteen, also published that spring, was mockingly titled "It's Sign Up a Genius Month." From the Columbia people's point of view, they were just trying to sell Springsteen as they would any other product, but their specific approach wasn't getting his songs on the radio, which was essential if they wanted to move his albums.

And in May came even worse news from Columbia for Springsteen: Clive Davis was out, fired as president of CBS Records. With John Hammond currently hospitalized after his fifth heart attack in the past decade, dangerously close to mandatory retirement age, and admittedly less enamored of Springsteen's full-band and electric material than of the acoustic stuff, the young singer was now almost wholly friendless within his record label. According to Appel—who was admittedly known on occasion to be a trifle paranoid—Charles Koppelman, one of the executives whose star at CBS had risen after Davis's departure, was a big fan of Billy Joel, a more traditional singer-songwriter, whose first solo album, *Cold Spring Harbor*, had been marred on its release by a problem with the speed at which the original recordings had been mastered. (He ended up sounding like a very earnest, self-aware chipmunk.) Koppelman, among others, may have felt that Springsteen had already gotten his shot, and that a performer like Joel now deserved a push. On the other hand, the company still had a five-year, ten-record deal with Springsteen, which amazingly enough was standard practice in the early 1970s. It had already spent over $60,000 on him, he was constantly writing songs, and studio time at 914 Studios in Blauvelt was pretty cheap, particularly in the middle of the night, which was the only time the singer was usually up anyway.

So, in mid-May 1973, Springsteen returned to 914 Studios with his touring band to record his second album. The first number they laid down was probably "The Fever," the male torch song they had pulled out of the trunk at Oliver's, but after that they seem to have concentrated on recent epics like the always fun "Thundercrack." "Circus Song" was recorded again, this time with the full band and now called "Wild Billy's Circus Story," as were "Santa Ana" and two other cowboy numbers: "Evacuation of the West," a piece about the transition of Texas from nationhood to statehood that sounded as if it had been built on the ruins of last summer's "Song of the Orphans"; and "Phantoms," a more modern outlaw number that kept returning to the image of jet fighters streaming *over the hills of St. George*. The title of this last song may be a coded reference to the nickname Danny Federici had first earned by ditching the cops during the Atlantic Highlands riot. Indeed, most of the songs that Springsteen chose to record that spring seem to be enamored of both Federici's Hammond B-3 organ and Clemons's tenor and alto sax. While he had toured all winter waiting for his first album to be released, Springsteen was clearly enjoying having different sounds with which to mess around in performance—and more important, to have different sounds for which to compose.

This was an important shift in Springsteen's compositional strategy. The songs on his first album had been written words first, with incredibly long lyrical lines. At least initially, most of those songs had been meant to be performed solo. By contrast, the songs he had been writing since the fall were meant to be played with his band. They were less likely to cram in as many syllables per line. They used fewer grace notes and kept the words more often within the meter laid out by the music. With a full band behind him, Springsteen didn't have to rely solely on his words to paint a picture. He could know that other instruments would be there to fill in his vision in a more musical, nonverbal fashion. The last five or six months of touring had also taught him the importance of letting instrumental breaks take over a song when its feeling needed to go beyond words. The set-closers he had evolved on this tour had far more distinctive lyrics than any of his Student Prince songs, but they also gave his bandmates more room to stretch out and leave their mark than the wall-to-wall hyperverbosity of the *Greetings* pieces had done. Even in the officially recorded version of an admittedly slight song like "Thundercrack" (which would never be as good in the studio as it was when performed live), the organ, sax, guitar, and drums fill in all the delightfully dirty details about the protagonist's specific movements that the song's words somehow choose to omit.

The band spent a week in Blauvelt that May, almost entirely on the graveyard shift, but there's no indication that anyone thought the album would be finished in that little time. It had taken three or four weeks to finish the less ambitious *Greetings*, and they had at least another four days' worth of recording coming in mid-June. In between, they had to fulfill what was probably their most high-profile touring commitment up to that point: opening for the "jazz-rock" outfit Chicago for a dozen dates along the eastern seaboard.

In a highly superficial way, this pairing of acts might have seemed to make sense, but Springsteen has since called the 1973 mini-tour with Chicago one of the lowest moments of his career. By all accounts, it apparently was the worst two weeks of his performing career, and it includes the only occasion on which an audience verifiably booed him at length. The band had a forty-five-minute opening slot and usually performed around half a dozen songs, which should have been fine for a Chicago crowd. Onstage in practically the biggest halls that Springsteen and his bandmates had ever played in their lives, they played wall-to-wall band-burners on these twelve dates, full sets (in essence) of set-closers—and at nearly every performance, it didn't work. A reviewer of their show in Binghamton, New York, called their opening set "musically cluttered and distorted at times" but (damning them with faint praise) "long on enthusiasm." At the Spectrum in Philadelphia, allegedly the worst night of the tour, the crowd threw toilet paper, even a beach ball during one of the quiet numbers. The booing was so bad that night that Bruce flipped the Pennsylvania audience off throughout the performance and left the stage after only half an hour.

According to one fan, Springsteen and company may have stolen the show from Chicago a few nights later at the Boston Garden, but back in New York City a few days after that, the disrespect was just as bad. Max's fans tended to come crosstown to the new Madison Square Garden for basketball and not music, just as Main Point denizens in eastern Pennsylvania tended to go to the Spectrum for hockey and not rock 'n' roll. The audience reaction the last night with Chicago at the Garden was bad enough that Appel later remembered Springsteen running offstage screaming and crying. He said he didn't want to play big halls and vowed he'd never be an opening act again. He would go back to playing small clubs if he had to. Then, according to one version of the story, he punched his fist into a brick wall and took off into the night.

Two nights later, they were all back in Blauvelt for the next scheduled four dates of studio time, laying down additional instrumental tracks and sweetening the ones they'd already recorded, but not really getting anywhere. No matter how much tinkering they all did, the half-dozen or so songs they had at this point still weren't enough for a real second album. It was like the sets they had been doing all year as an opening act: big finishes, but no real singles and no real progression across the tracks.

After a three-night stand in late June on familiar ground—at Fat City in Seaside Heights, although the club still billed Springsteen at least once as "Springstein"—they then went back into the studio for another week's worth of dates. In a reverse of the winnowing process by which *Greetings* had been recorded the previous summer, for the second album the band seemed to be getting larger as recording went on. When a children's choir didn't show up to add backing vocals for one song, Suki Lahav (the wife of Louis Lahav, the engineer at 914) was enlisted to lay down a number of vocal tracks to get the same multi-voiced effect. Before the summer was over, Richard Blackwell would be enlisted to augment Lopez's percussion, and the band's sound manager Albee "Albany Al" Tellone (who had actually played in Dr. Zoom and the Sonic Boom two years earlier) was eventually asked to play baritone sax. Most important, David Sancious was once again available for recording. In reenlisting Sancious to help record his second album, Springsteen may have been hoping that lightning would strike twice.

It did, and in one of the most unlikely of places. At one of the spring recording sessions, there had been a stab at a full-band version of "New York Song," the subdued, lugubrious piece that Springsteen had done once or twice in performance as an opening duet with Clemons. Usually, Springsteen played acoustic guitar on this number, but at a radio station in Richmond back in the middle of the hellish Chicago tour, one of the first times that this new six-man outfit had played together, he tried doing the song on piano. Now in Blauvelt, Sancious, who may have actually heard the song for the first time that day of the radio broadcast, tried to add his own piano part.

The first minute of the final studio version of "New York City Serenade" (as the song would soon come to be called) is electrifying. Sancious's opening quasi-classical run seems to take in the whole keyboard of a grand piano and immediately changes the scope of a song that up to that point was undeniably small. Shifting fluidly from one musical mode to another, Sancious tries out a series of possible openings—with echoes of Beethoven's Emperor Concerto, '30s boogie-woogie, '50s Erroll Garner, and more—and finally settles on a gentle, almost rippling figure that serves as an undulating backdrop against which the song's narrator can begin to tell his stories. Sancious's part in this recording cannot be adequately characterized as mere accompaniment. His virtuosic opening sets the pace and ground rules for what will follow. His piano part provides the structure within or against which the other instruments and vocals will have to emerge. It may technically be Springsteen's song, but in this recording at least it is Sancious's number.

Perhaps inspired by his bandmate's enlarged ambitions, Springsteen decided to enlarge the song itself. He took the first verse of "New York Song" (including its instantly memorable instruction that *It's midnight in New York City / This is no time to get cute*) and cast its other two verses as well as all of its undistinguished music aside. He then combined the one retained verse of that song with the words and music of another New York song that he had written the year before, called "Vibes Man." That song hadn't even made it past the Sioux City demos, and yet it came from the same compositional place as his other recent New York fantasias. "New York Song" and "New York City Serenade" share some lyrics, but the former song, with just guitar and saxophone, was slight and intimate. With another tune and Sancious's ambitious piano part, suddenly those tiny little words seemed epic. This was the landscape that Springsteen needed to fill in—not the remembered, desiccated Old West of his favorite movies and TV shows, but the gloriously dangerous streets of 1970s New York at night, a decayed but sublime environment glimpsed as only someone from *out of town* (as one version of "Vibes Man" put it) could really appreciate it.

For most Americans during the 1970s, New York City may have suffered by comparison with even the Black Hole of Calcutta. In retrospect, however, that time and place has achieved a certain mythic status. For all its dirt and decline, the badly kept city in default of that era ended up giving us many of the decade's most lasting American cultural artifacts, particularly when it comes to popular music. As had been true for most of the twentieth century, those essential artifacts were crafted not by women and men who had been born in Manhattan but by those who had come to the artistic core of Manhattan from its more peripheral, outlying communities. Even if one restricts oneself to rock 'n' roll circa 1973, David Johansen, the frontman for the New York Dolls (a band that had played many of the same local clubs as Springsteen and whose essential first album came out that July) was from Staten Island; Lou Reed (for whom Springsteen had opened in the spring and who was still touring in support of his greatest, Bowie-produced album *Transformer*) was born in Brooklyn and grew up on Long Island. In 1973, these two figures were the city's reigning kings of glam rock, but many of the central figures in the local flowering of punk a few years later would be similar outlanders in Abe Beame's Manhattan. All four of the original Ramones (who would form their makeshift band in about a year, early in the summer of 1974) attended high school together in Forest Hills, Queens. Chris Stein (the eventual guitarist for Blondie) was from Brooklyn, and Debbie Harry (the group's eventual lead singer, who in 1973 was fronting a postmodern girl group called the Stilettos) was from Hawthorne, New Jersey. Tom Verlaine (né Miller) of the Neon Boys and Television, and eventual Springsteen friend and collaborator Patti Smith (in 1973 still mixing poetry and R&B covers in her occasional, small performances at Manhattan hotels), both hailed from the much-maligned Garden State too.

Technically, all these women and men qualified as what one might call "the bridge and tunnel crowd." Yet it was precisely their proximity to Manhattan during their formative years that allowed these artists to see the glory beyond the dirt—the glory *of* the dirt—that escaped those who glimpsed the city from either too near or too far. As even such late 1970s, shot-on-location films as *The Wiz* and *Saturday Night Fever* would capture, for those for whom the privileged heart of Manhattan had always defined the horizon, that space, even if now dirty, was still the Emerald City. It was still the earthly locus of both heaven and transcendent success.

As Springsteen performed it in the spring of 1973, "New York Song" is just a pair of character sketches: of Diamond Jackie, at least a thief and possibly a prostitute; and of Blacky, her thirty-year-old *dirty big daddy.* These characters may or may not be African American, but either way the narrator of the song paints them in broad strokes without a moment's hesitation as to whether he might be exaggerating their seamier qualities in order to conform to his view of what the city's demimonde should be like. In "New York City Serenade," by contrast, the narrator's perspective becomes more overt as the verses go on. With each verse portrait, the young, out-of-town narrator is less a voyeur in relation to the Manhattan scene that he witnesses and more a participant in its nightly interactions.

Musically, the arrangement of "New York City Serenade" captures this feeling exquisitely: Springsteen's singing and guitar playing do not dominate the world that this track creates, as they did in "New York Song," but clearly respond to it. Given the song's possible racial overtones, it's interesting to note that the two musicians to whom Springsteen is primarily responding here are both African American: David Sancious, whose piano begins and ends the track and provides the grounding for its sonic world; and Clarence Clemons, whose saxophone enters this arrangement at the exact point in the second verse (*Won't you take my hand / Walk with me down Broadway*) when Springsteen's narrator begins to interact with that world's inhabitants. Musically at least, the track seems to tell us that this is Sancious's and Clemons's world, not Springsteen's.

"New York City Serenade" was one of three songs that Bruce and his new five-piece band premiered when they returned to Max's Kansas City in late July, and it provided a clear public indication of how much this new band was influencing Springsteen's songwriting. So did another of those three premieres, the not-quite-finished "4th of July, Asbury Park (Sandy)," the first song Springsteen ever wrote that is clearly and specifically about New Jersey, with no coded allusions to *Greasy Lake* or sketchily referenced racing drags.

On its surface, the song is about the end of a summer romance, but few of Springsteen's fans have noticed how oddly timed this valediction is. Usually the end of summer, not to mention summer romances, comes somewhere around Labor Day, not Independence Day. Early September, not early July, is when vacations end, school begins, and unsupervised adventures in hot weather give way to duty and resumed routine. Who but the most pessimistic and lethargic of young lovers sees the end of the affair coming a full two months in advance?

But "4th of July, Asbury Park" isn't just about summer lovers or boardwalk attractions, of course. It's about how lovely it is to look back on the romantic past, even to see the present *as* past while one is living it, *the aurora rising behind us* as the song's lyric famously puts it. And this is why the song's first public performance at Max's is so interesting, because Springsteen chose to sing and play acoustic guitar with just Danny Federici accompanying him on accordion. This mode of performance lays bare the secret of the song's arrangement, even in the full-band studio version: just as the piano part is the heart of "New York City Serenade," the accordion part is the heart of "4th of July, Asbury Park." In both cases, the narration of Springsteen's acoustic guitar more properly arises in response to his bandmate's highlighted instrument. In the latter case, to sing about the present with Federici's Old World instrument playing in the background is to vertiginously glimpse how this week's youth will in time become a faded tintype— or a Polaroid of bell bottoms and stringy hair that your children will find hilarious. Springsteen has characterized this song as a farewell to his Asbury Park days, but even that suggests how precocious his nostalgia could be: he was only moving to Long Branch, not the other side of the world.

Among aficionados, the July 1973 shows at Max's are legendary, not least because Springsteen's opening act for this headlining gig was the Wailers, fresh from the Springsteen-friendly Paul's Mall in Boston for their first dates in Manhattan. Lou Reed and Patti Smith saw both acts that week, as did Steve Van Zandt. The audience reaction at Max's was certainly better than the one Springsteen and his band received the following week at a convention for CBS sales reps in San Francisco, when he chose to immediately follow a bombastic, special-effects-laden set by Edgar Winter's White Trash with an acoustic rendition of "4th of July, Asbury Park." At this gathering, each act was supposed to play a tight fifteen-minute set for the men who were largely responsible for getting their music to consumers, but Springsteen and company willfully chose to do four songs for a lengthy forty minutes. Even customary Springsteen booster John Hammond thought his performance was a disaster. The music executives could barely understand the ornate lyrics that were whizzing by them, and they soon grew impatient for the next act to come on.

The next three months were a blur of canceled dates, wedged-in recording sessions, and rescheduled performances, at least one of these at a venue that ignominiously reminded the band in its advertisements that they were "Direct from [the] *Chicago* Tour." It had taken four months, six separate rounds of recording, to get to this point, and still in the second week of September Springsteen's second album was only half ready. Even a song like "Rosalita," which the band had been performing live since January, took two nights to mix down just by itself. A song like "Kitty's Back," which had sounded amazing in rehearsal for months, hadn't even made it to the live show yet, let alone been satisfactorily recorded. Tallent and Sancious were nodding off in the studio, waiting to be called for yet another retake of their parts.

Since Sancious rejoined the band back in July, however, there had at least been a clear idea of what the album was about. "New York City Serenade" was the key. This was a New York album, but a full-band album too, one on which such solo New York songs of the previous summer as "Jazz Musician" and "Two Hearts in True Waltz Time" could not fit. It was an album of funk, soul, and jazz, of a biracial band playing black urban music, with reeds and even brass brought into the mix. (Not only did Tallent play tuba on several tracks, but Lopez took up the cornet for another one.) In a throwback to Springsteen's "more is more" aesthetic of two years earlier, the band took full advantage of the fact that it now had two keyboardists, with Federici and Sancious both playing organ on "Kitty's Back" at different points and both playing piano at different points on another tragic late-night New York track called "Incident on 57th Street."

"Incident" seems to have been the last track completed for the album, but late in the process Springsteen also once again wrote a song that obliquely commented on the shape of his career. It was called "The E Street Shuffle," named (as one legend has it) after the street in Belmar on which Sancious's mother lived. Musically, it was spun off of Major Lance's 1963 hit "The Monkey Time" and was an attempt, Springsteen has said, to come up with the perfect song for "a dance with no exact steps." The song could almost be a theme song for this new funkified band, as well as an overture for what the rest of the album would contain. If a late addition to Springsteen's first album like "Blinded by the Light" had hidden the real names and events of early-'70s Jersey Shore life under cryptic, highly personal codes, "The E Street Shuffle," the second album's equivalent, hid the real people and places of Asbury Park behind figures drawn in the fashion of myth. Springsteen could do that now because, as "4th of July, Asbury Park" would testify, *that boardwalk life [was] through*. With the Upstage now two years in the past, everyone who hung out there could safely be turned into larger-than-life legends.

This late-completed homage to the now gone jams of Asbury Park ended up leading to the title of this second album, *The Wild, the Innocent, and the E Street Shuffle*, which on the whole held together better as an album than *Greetings from Asbury Park, N.J.* had done. Much of that stylistic cohesion resulted from Springsteen's more conscious writing for the individual members of his band, but it was also the fruit of his obsessive work on the mixing and mastering of all the album's tracks, the first time he had ever shown any interest in the nuances of production.

A year earlier, when Clive Davis had raised concerns about his first album, Springsteen had written new songs. Now, when Charles Koppelman voiced much stronger objections to the working version of his second album, Springsteen didn't write any new material or even trim any of his gargantuan tracks by more than ten or fifteen seconds each.

Instead, he remixed the tracks that Koppelman had declared unreleasable. He brought up his own vocals and guitar more in the mix, making the whole project sound more like the kind of singer-songwriter album that the label had expected.

The pictures that appeared on the sleeve of *Wild and Innocent* when it was released ended up reflecting this change in perspective. On the back of the album is a photo of the band hanging out on a stoop. In it, Vini is the one who catches your eye. His shirt completely unbuttoned, he stands at the center of the frame, with Davey and Danny, the band's two keyboardists, sitting at his feet. Garry stands to their right, and Bruce is almost lost in Clarence's shadow on their left. That was the image of what Springsteen's musical life was really like in 1973: inseparable from his interactions with the members of his band. The front cover of the album, however, showed Springsteen as his label perceived him: in close-up, with his hand to his bearded chin, as if he was musing over some eternal mystery or another. For CBS, it was all about Springsteen and the stream of his thoughtful words; the band was what led to self-indulgent performances like the one at the Ahmanson.

Springsteen's second album was personal, but its autobiographical revelations lay as much in its soul-and-funk performance style as in its fast-talking lyrics. If *Greetings from Asbury Park, N.J.* had been scrupulously particularized autobiography locked inside wall-to-wall codes, *Wild and Innocent* offers its listeners a slow-dissolving autobiography, in the gradual removal across its seven tracks of the white soul brother's protective mask. Although the album's first track, "The E Street Shuffle," is set in New Jersey rather than New York, it is tied to later, urban tracks on the album by its linguistic embrace of jive. On this song and on the similarly late completion "Kitty's Back" (which also appeared on the album's first side, coming third), Springsteen's use of urban slang matters more than his words' specific meanings. It is as if the narrator of "It's Hard to Be a Saint in the City" thoroughly bought into his own self-contrived image, as if he really thought he was the tough dude he pretended to be.

In a digital age, no one thinks about album sides anymore, but the divide between this album's first four tracks (which made up side 1 of the original LP) and its latter three tracks (side 2) is a brilliant one. The second part of the album looks a little harder at the boasts of an East Coast summer night, as if it had gotten a little later in the night between sides 1 and 2. "Incident on 57th Street" and "Rosalita," the first two songs on side 2, are both fairy tales of love, but tragic and farcical ones that pay fair tribute to the real world that makes such fairy tales so hard and so necessary. In the end, the album builds toward the spot where everyone knew it had been going since July: "New York City Serenade," in which the singer lets the tough jive mask of side 1 unmistakably fall away, and he cops to being the bridge-and-tunnel romantic that any sharp listener has spotted him for long before.

A few years later, when Springsteen finally hit it big, the great rock critic Lester Bangs reported a friend's telling distinction between Springsteen's songs about the city and Lou Reed's: "When I listen to Bruce Springsteen, I hear a romanticization of New York. When I listen to Lou Reed, I hear New York." Bangs's friend missed the point: of course, the songs on an album like *Wild and Innocent* are romantic. They are self-consciously romantic, as the changes Springsteen made to turn "New York Song" and "Vibes Man" into "New York City Serenade" clearly indicate. They do not pretend to capture how New York City "really was" in 1973 (as Bangs's friend might have thought that a recent Lou Reed hit like "Walk on the Wild Side" might have done), but rather how a young man from the sticks might respond to that reality. As Springsteen had said when opening a show with "New York Song" back in April, *Last summer I got stuck in New York too much, and these are some of the things that should've happened, or shouldn't. . . . Wild and Innocent* is a fantasy, a romanticization of New York and New Jersey in an exceptionally dirty and dangerous era, and yet it is also an act of obscured self-revelation. Once again, Bruce Springsteen turned his album into a personal statement—a more unified personal statement, in fact, than his first album had been.

The problem with the album, though, is that it is very easy for careless listeners to take its self-conscious myths for reality: for sensitive souls to act too hyperrealistically tough; for musicians to playact at being criminals; for white boys to pretend that they really are black or

Latino. If by the early 1970s the excessive navel-gazing of the coffee-house children of Bob and Joni could sometimes degenerate into barely musicalized narcissism, this white dabbling in funk personae could sometimes devolve into self-parody too. Pursued relentlessly and less than cautiously, it could end up being little more than latter-day minstrelsy. You could say Bruce was just playing a role, but how could he be sure his audience knew that?

IN MID-OCTOBER, SPRINGSTEEN and his band did a dual headlining concert with Jackson Browne at Villanova University. Like Springsteen, Browne had a second album that was about to drop, and as a more successful performer he could easily have pulled rank. But the two men genuinely enjoyed each other's music, and each act performed at Villanova for an hour and a half. The next night, Browne shared a bill at Avery Fisher Hall in Lincoln Center with Bonnie Raitt, the Radcliffe-educated, blues-living daughter of John Raitt, the biggest star on Broadway two decades earlier. Raitt's second album was about to drop too: all three singers had been recruited by their labels a year or two before in the rush to harvest a new crop of rising singer-songwriters. As had happened at the Bitter End the previous fall, Browne invited an unannounced Springsteen onstage to share part of the set. He clearly saw all three artists as equals and kindred spirits.

In the fall of 1973, however, the record industry did not see things that way, nor apparently did the record-buying public. In the fall of 1973, Jackson Browne was beginning to enjoy the sort of career arc that record companies liked. Helped by a season opening for Joni Mitchell, Browne's self-titled first album had gone to no. 53 on the *Billboard* albums chart the previous year and had actually landed two singles on the Hot 100, one of them ("Doctor My Eyes") even going to no. 8. Raitt, while less successful than Browne, was also clearly on the same path. As Appel had understood when pitching Springsteen to Hammond's secretary, in the 1970s labels like CBS and Warners wanted "legacy" artists, acts that might start up slowly but would eventually yield steady back-catalog sales of albums from all stages of their careers. In Browne's and even Raitt's case this already seemed to be a shrewd gamble, but in Springsteen's case there was less evidence that the strategy would work.

In terms of sales, the release of *Wild and Innocent* in early November made even less of a ripple in the pop market than the release of *Greetings from Asbury Park, N.J.* had done in January. In terms of critical reception, however, the outlook was slightly better. It seemed as if it was only now, late in the year, that Springsteen was finally digging himself out from under the effects of the critical backlash against CBS's "New Dylan" propaganda. When *Greetings* came out, virtually the only influential fans that Springsteen had were the editors of *Crawdaddy*, the first regularly published U.S. magazine devoted to rock 'n' roll: Paul Williams and others at *Crawdaddy* saw potential even in Springsteen's first, almost atypical album, and the magazine consequently published two profiles of the singer in a little under a year. After the release of the more ambitious *Wild and Innocent*, however, support for Springsteen started increasing, particularly among FM DJs, without whose favorable opinion an early-1970s rock 'n' roll performer could not possibly succeed. If Dave Herman, the morning DJ at WNEW, didn't even listen to *Greetings*, Richard Neer, the overnight DJ at the same station, ate up *Wild and Innocent*, and loved playing side 2 in its uninterrupted entirety during his shift.

The importance of such converts to Springsteen's career went beyond mere publicity, however. The boy from Freehold who had never really paid much attention in school was deadly serious about music, and throughout these early, leaner years he would talk about it to any knowledgeable and approachable person who would listen. Much as he had hung out at Pocketful of Tunes and then John Hammond's office at CBS during 1972, during 1973 he frequently dropped in at the *Crawdaddy* offices when he was back in New York. He also had many late-night conversations with Richard Neer over WNEW's listener line. An overnight DJ like Neer was exactly the sort of person Bruce could talk to, and their conversations with each other would often go on for hours while Neer actually ran his program, going off the phone for a minute here, a minute there, to change records, load commercials, and the like. In all these conversations with record executives, music journalists, and disc jockeys, Springsteen was by all accounts seldom focused on promoting his own work. Rather, he was learning, from anyone who could teach him anything about popular music and how it became popular in the first place.

A few well-placed adherents, however, didn't make a mass movement; critical attention on Springsteen was increasing, but his album sales did not yet reflect that. Mike Appel, of course, didn't think Springsteen was the problem. Appel would proselytize about Springsteen to anyone who would listen (and many who wouldn't). He believed that it was live performance, not albums, that turned people into true Bruce believers, and so he and Sam McKeith, Springsteen's representative at the William Morris Agency, planned out a rigorous touring schedule for the fall of 1973: forty-five dates through the end of the year, frequently college dates on the weekend and residencies at familiar clubs like Oliver's, the Main Point, Max's, and My Father's Place in the New York area, and Childe Harold in DC during the week. Given all those unredeemed advances from the label, this relentless touring wasn't just evangelical—it was also economically necessary.

With no disposable income and all that traveling, there was nothing else to do but work on the act. The sets on the new tour were less variable than they had been in the spring, and for eight months (from August 1973 through March 1974), as Springsteen and his band toured incessantly to drum up interest in his second album, there is no record of his introducing any newly written songs. Instead, the new numbers performed tended to be covers. It had all begun with the way the band slipped "Fun Fun Fun" into "Rosalita" at least twice that spring. That may have been intended as preparation for a gig opening for the Beach Boys in April in Clemons's hometown of Norfolk, Virginia, but it also served another useful purpose. A stand-alone cover is just an easy crowd-pleaser, but folding a cover into an original number has a different effect: it connects the new music that the crowd is hearing with older songs that they already know. When Springsteen and the band integrated covers into their sets in this way, they suggested to their audiences, in effect, how they might fit into the already established categories of pop music. In other words, they answered exactly the sorts of branding questions that music executives, critics, and consumers were still struggling with at that point whenever they pondered the taxonomic conundrum that was Bruce Springsteen.

In early 1973, the covers seemed to be one-time-only performances, but by the end of the year specific covers had become a reiterated, structurally integral part of the band's sets. In October, they premiered their versions of Rufus Thomas's "Walking the Dog," the Marvelettes' "Beechwood 4-5789," and Bobby Bland's "Call on Me." For the Christmas season, they introduced a number that would become a Springsteen perennial: a version of "Santa Claus Is Coming to Town" that was unabashedly indebted to Phil Spector's arrangement of the song for the Crystals. Then, in January, another trio of rehearsed covers entered the act: Johnny Cash's "Ring of Fire," Fats Domino's "Let the Four Winds Blow," and Junior Walker's "Shotgun." Some already confirmed Springsteen fans objected to this: Clyde Hadlock, when reviewing a gig at Kent State during which Springsteen opened for Black Oak Arkansas, decried the incorporation of one such number into "Rosalita" (as well as the band's extended introductions), likening such practices to "slapping a bumper sticker on a Dali painting."

A true Bruce believer like Hadlock may have feared that Springsteen was simply cashing in on a craze of the moment. In the bleak times of fall 1973 and winter 1974, rock 'n' roll oldies were suddenly gold. The last year or two of Richard Nixon's presidency saw an extraordinary outpouring of generalized American nostalgia, much of it centered on the post–World War II period. *The Golden Age of Rock 'n' Roll* (Sha Na Na's most popular album), the original stage productions of *Grease* and *The Rocky Horror Show*, and the first season of *Happy Days*, to choose just a few handy examples from 1973 and 1974, all presented their audiences with simulacra of the 1950s. Even such works as George Lucas's film *American Graffiti* and Richard Price's essential Bronx novel *The Wanderers*, both of which are technically set in 1962, seem stylistically to take place in the 1950s as well. These are all doo-wop stories, glances back at the boundary between propriety and sensuality as it supposedly existed during a moment in American culture just before it seemed poised to crumble.

While Springsteen's pop nostalgia may have paralleled this reembrace of 1950s youth music, in truth it had a slightly different chronological and stylistic focus. The seemingly random collection of covers that Springsteen began performing in 1973 and 1974 are not 1950s songs, like the ones that seemed to be popping up everywhere in that era, but instead came from a later, fairly tiny sliver of time, the five years between 1961 and 1966, which almost exactly demarcate Springsteen's time as a teenager. When Paul Williams suggested to Springsteen during a second interview with *Crawdaddy* that early-'60s music was as bad as it was in the current moment, the singer seemed to concur, but then again all the performers that Williams named pejoratively to make his point were white—and very few of the early-'60s artists that Springsteen chose to cover in the fall of 1973 and the winter of 1974 were white. What Springsteen missed most about the 1960s was a time when white and black music seemed to be part of the same movement, the golden age of "monopop," as critic Robert Christgau has called it, during which (as Springsteen would most clearly state thirteen years later) *music provided you with a greater sense of unity, a greater sense of shared vision and purpose than it does today.* In early 1974, the white music on the charts was white (the Carpenters), the black music was black (Isaac Hayes), and never the twain could meet.

The more Bruce thought about it, the more he played these treasured hits of his adolescence, the more he decided that what he needed was a single. *Wild and Innocent* had proved that he could record an album his way. Now he needed to make a record with lyrics as intricate as the ones that he had been writing for the last two years but with the sound of the good old pop singles that he had heard and worshipped on WMCA a decade before. In the same way that he had forced himself two years before to write the words to his songs before the music in order to improve his lyric-writing skills, he now began to think about what the recording of a song would sound like before he ever brought it in front of an audience. In the lead-up to the next album, live performance would give him "an opportunity to feel out the arrangement" for the songs, but from the beginning these new songs would be "the first piece[s] of music [he ever] wrote and conceived as a studio production." With the new Christmas number fresh in his head, he suggested to Appel that the next album might have "a Ronettes-inspired sound," invoking the kind of act in which both the Carpenters and Isaac Hayes might glimpse their primitive musical roots. Springsteen began to plan a simpler song cycle than his last album offered, nine or ten songs that would be loosely autobiographical but that would sound more like hits.

The question was whether he would ever get a chance to record them. While Springsteen and Appel were elaborately planning how to hatch that perfect mixing of mainstream pop and autobiographical art, CBS (among others) was just about ready to cut its losses in the matter of Bruce Springsteen. By early 1974, the label was easily out at least six figures on him; the increased critical attention still wasn't translating into actual sales. Koppelman was starting to suggest that Springsteen ditch the band and record his third album in Nashville with session musicians and songs by other writers. That, at least, would be cheaper. Even one of his managers agreed: around the time of the CBS sales convention in Nashville, Jim Cretecos left Laurel Canyon, cashing in his financial interest in Springsteen's music publishing for just $1,500.

And then there was the band: five young men constantly on the road, underpaid, overbooked, and living on the edge. Even at a gig as retrospectively amazing as the double bill with Browne at Villanova, people didn't fill the seats. After that date, Appel wanted to just pay the band's expenses, but Lopez complained to Springsteen, who talked Appel into giving each band member $35 a week on top of that. In 1974, each of them, like Springsteen and Appel, cleared no more than $8,500 for the whole year, before taxes. Yes, Appel was supposed to be covering their expenses, but cash flow being what it was, sometimes the checks went out a little late. The rent on the band house down the Jersey Shore where three of them lived was in arrears. In January, police officers showed up backstage at a performance somewhere on the perpetual road, maybe in Ohio, and arrested Clemons for failure to pay child support. Lopez called Appel back in New York, and the manager did straighten things out in enough time for Clemons to play that night, but bad blood certainly lingered between Clemons and Lopez.

In early February, just before a show at the University of Kentucky, Lopez (who, by all accounts, frequently lived up to the nickname "Mad Dog") got into a fight backstage with Mike Appel's brother Steve, predictably over money. Money was so tight by that point that

Steve was the band's road manager and Appel himself was doing sound and lights. Lopez had been with Springsteen longer than anyone else, playing with him for years in almost every imaginable kind of early-'70s pop or rock outfit. He was the one, back in 1969, who asked Springsteen to join his band. After this climactic fight, Mike Appel convinced the singer that his old bandmate should be fired. That job Springsteen didn't delegate. Almost five years to the day after the drummer asked the singer to help him form Child, Springsteen told Lopez that he was out of the band.

The next three dates on the tour were canceled, and less than two weeks later the band had a new drummer: Ernest "Boom" Carter, yet another Upstage refugee. In fact, Carter was one of the few Upstage regulars who had actually been born in Asbury Park and not a neighboring shore town. He played drums, but he also played guitar and had been friends with the similarly multi-instrumental Sancious for years, swapping off instruments both in the crowded Upstage jams and in much smaller sessions, making whatever sound felt right for a particular moment. When the Asbury scene fell apart, Carter followed Sancious and Tallent down to Alpha Sounds; when they in time rejoined Springsteen, Carter followed his opportunities to Atlanta, where he became the drummer for Little Royal and the Swing Masters, a southern-based R&B band. Carter wouldn't have been that good a fit with Springsteen in early 1970, but four years later the funky stew he served up for Little Royal was exactly the sort of beat that Springsteen then needed.

Not insignificantly, like Sancious and Clemons, Carter was African American. Now the six men onstage every night were a mathematically biracial band: three black men playing with three whites, a living, breathing testament to Springsteen's vanished monopop dream. They wanted more time to rehearse before their first public gig, but Carlo Rossi, the owner of the Satellite Lounge in Cookstown, where they were booked in late February, was apparently a stickler for contractual obligations. So the band played that date after only one rehearsal with their new drummer, doing even more covers than usual until Carter got his parts on Springsteen's songs down. Then back to the Main Point for two shows, at least one of which Springsteen performed sitting down because he had the flu. Then three shows canceled because of Springsteen's illness, followed by a gig at Georgetown, then two or three weeks in the Southwest, then back east for more college gigs in Pennsylvania and New Jersey, then back up to Boston . . .

IN THE ONGOING BATTLE between Springsteen's rapidly falling fortunes with his record label and his slowly rising popularity with the critics, the spring of 1974 seems to have marked a turning point, even if that critical acclaim still had not translated into album sales. By the spring of 1974, disc jockeys like Richard Neer and Scott Muni at WNEW in New York, Marianne Sartori at WBCN in Boston, Ed Sciaky at WMMR in Philadelphia, and Kid Leo at WMMS in Cleveland were now regularly telling their listeners to check out this Springsteen guy. At the same time, writers like Dave Marsh in *Creem*, Ken Emerson in *Rolling Stone*, and Janet Maslin in *New West* were actively attempting to reverse the hasty dismissals of Springsteen's talent that a number of critics had voiced a year earlier.

In the second week of April (eight weeks and thirty completed sets after Vini Lopez's departure), Springsteen and his band were booked in Cambridge, Massachusetts. They were supposed to play Joe's Place in Inman Square, where they had done three shows back in January, but that firetrap had burned down a week earlier. Instead, they played Charlie's Place in Harvard Square, two shows a night for four days running. (The last night they agreed to play for free as a benefit for the "Joe's Place Disaster Fund.") Between sets on the second night, Springsteen went outside to read a recent local review of *Wild and Innocent* that the club's owners had posted in the window. It was bitterly cold in Massachusetts that Wednesday night, and Springsteen, dressed in just a T-shirt, hopped around on the Bow Street sidewalk just to keep warm.

The *Real Paper* review called Springsteen "the most impressive new singer-songwriter since James Taylor" but suggested that his talent still needed polishing: better production on his albums and more singles (Clive Davis's complaint again). While Springsteen was reading the review, a man in his midtwenties came up and asked him what he thought of it. "It's one of the best I've seen," Springsteen spontaneously offered. "This guy's got his shit together. It's pretty good." Then the stranger introduced himself: he was Jon Landau, the author of the review. Landau had been a music critic for the old *Cambridge Phoenix* and stayed on to write for the *Real Paper* at the same time as he headed up the review section at *Rolling Stone*. He had also written for the eight-year-old *Crawdaddy*. Springsteen may already have heard about Landau, particularly from the *Crawdaddy* crew, but this was the first time that the singer and the critic actually met. Given his habit of picking up interlocutors and teachers in all branches of the music business, it was not surprising that Springsteen wanted to have an extended talk with Landau once he knew who he was.

Inside the club, Landau introduced Springsteen to Dave Marsh, the Detroit-born critic who was also writing for the *Real Paper* at that point and who, like Landau, had come to see Springsteen perform live for the first time that night. Springsteen, in turn, introduced the two writers to his manager, Mike Appel. Appel, acting even more like the Jewish Joe Pesci than usual, proved defensive, reacting to Landau's conversational familiarity with Springsteen the way he had reacted to Hammond's seeming intrusion two years earlier. Landau was shocked at the vehemence with which Appel laid into his review, but he explained some of his problems with *Wild and Innocent*'s production: the instruments, he thought, were excessively separated at points; the recordings also lacked "punch" in both the high and the low ends of the sonic spectrum. Coming from the man who had produced the MC5's second album, *Back in the USA*, four years before, none of this was surprising. According to Landau, at this first meeting Springsteen just listened as he and Appel hashed it out, almost exactly the way that he had sat on the sidelines when Appel first met Hammond. "He just was—" Landau later remembered, "after a while he was just sort of observant."

When Springsteen came back to Cambridge about a month after that for two shows in one night, opening for Bonnie Raitt at the much larger Harvard Square Theatre, he definitely had Landau in mind. Tickets for the later of those shows were waiting at the box office for Landau, his then wife, Janet Maslin, and their friend Ken Emerson, all of whom had burnished the singer's critical reputation over the last six months. The early show that night was recorded, so we know that Springsteen saved three new songs, all from the projected song cycle that he intended for his next album, just for the performance that Landau was slated to see. Since the later show, the one Landau attended, wasn't recorded, we have no way of knowing for sure which new songs were the ones the critic admiringly called "street trash rockers" in his eventual review. It's fairly certain, though, that the song Landau said had "a 'Telstar' guitar introduction and an Eddie Cochran rhythm section" was "Born to Run," the piece that had started Springsteen thinking about composing for studio production in the first place. It was another "getting out of town" song, written in the pop-friendly AABA format and located in a more thoroughly imagined landscape than the similarly themed "She's So Fine" (another proposed song for the next album, which Springsteen had performed in Houston about a month before and may have performed that night as well). The reference in "Born to Run" to *Highway* 9 and *the Palace* clearly set it in the same locale as *Wild and Innocent*'s "4th of July, Asbury Park," a fever dream of the Jersey Shore where every abandoned amusement center was a repository of a desperate narrator's dreams.

A few days after the Harvard Square shows, before Landau had even written his review of the performance, Springsteen obtained the critic's phone number and called him, engaging now in the discussion that Appel and Landau had started at Charlie's the month before. "I noticed in your review," Springsteen said once the two finally connected, "you mentioned production. I don't really know what *production* means. What is it that producers do?" Although Landau may not have known it at the time, when Springsteen made this call, he was almost certainly back in the recording studio, trying to get the songs in his head for his third album captured adequately on tape.

But the summer at Blauvelt had mostly been for naught. The band attempted a number of songs during these early sessions, including repeated tries at capturing "Jungleland," a nine-minute bridge-and-tunnel epic about a guy from Harlem called the Magic Rat who has an ill-fated liaison with a barefoot girl from New Jersey. As with "Born to Run," Springsteen was still intending to wrap "Jungleland" in an ambitious Phil Spector–style production, with a string section and even more elaborate harmonies on the background vocals. While the most winning music on Springsteen's second album was dialogues between different instruments or sections of his band, for this third album he clearly wanted a more "symphonic" sound. All the pieces or parts of the music on each track were meant to add up to a unified whole, frequently with dozens of overdubs laid on top of the original, base recording.

But making "a Phil Spector record" had been much easier at Gold Star Studios in LA in 1964 than at 914 Studios in Blauvelt a decade later. The "unseparated" sound that Jon Landau had suggested Springsteen needed, something very close to Spector's infamous "wall of sound," was hard enough in the age of stereo recording—and it got even harder to achieve with each new overdub that Springsteen and Appel planned. None of the tracks for the new album sounded like jams, like musicians responding to musicians. Instead, they seemed much more like sound collages. Springsteen even persuaded Brooks Arthur, the owner of Blauvelt, to keep one of his pianos "slightly detuned to Bruce's specifications." "We used a bit of Eventide on the piano as well," Arthur recalled, alluding to an early, predigital line of music processors. "We also had this AKG spring echo unit, which Bruce loved—so much so that we began referring to it as the 'Spring-steen.'"

Two years earlier, Springsteen had spent four weeks in the studio and produced *Greetings from Asbury Park, N.J.* A year earlier, he had been in the studio on and off for four months and produced *Wild and Innocent.* But in August of 1974, after six months in the studio, all Springsteen and Appel had to show was one single: "Born to Run," the new song that had wowed Landau back in May. "Born to Run" was only a single, but it was a perfect single, almost exactly what its author had had in mind when he conceived it six months before. Even better, Springsteen and Appel brought it in at under five minutes, so it actually had a shot at the Top 40. If anything, the compression of the song made a more powerful impact on the listener than the more elongated set-closers that he had been writing a year before.

Desperate for product, and aware of how devoted their small but growing fan base at the live dates was becoming, Springsteen and Appel wanted CBS to release the single right away, but the label said no. No matter how nostalgic Bruce may have been that year for the early 1960s, this was the 1970s, and the business model for pop music was entirely different. CBS would not release a single, no matter how good, unless there was an album ready to launch right behind it. In-house at CBS that summer, there was considerable debate about Springsteen's future, with some contending that he should simply be "released" from his contract. Probably because of Springsteen's growing support among DJs in influential markets (rather than his growing base of fans at the live shows, who would be less relevant to any further promotional efforts that CBS might launch), a compromise was reached: Springsteen would receive a little more support, $50,000 to spend on his third album. If that album did not turn a significant profit, however, enough to make up for the lost advances of the last two years, the consensus was that Springsteen should be let go from the label.

As if this ultimatum weren't enough, to top it all off, Sancious and Carter were leaving the band. Back in Richmond, they had played clubs together as Cinnamon and now they wanted to start a slightly larger group called Tone with Gerald Carboy, another Upstage veteran, and one or two other friends. They would play jazz fusion, which was probably closer to their hearts than Bruce's brand of rock 'n' roll. They told Bruce near the end of July, but he seems to have hoped that they'd have second thoughts. In mid-August, shortly after this briefest incarnation of Springsteen's band (Tallent, Sancious, Federici, Clemons, and Carter) finally captured a satisfactory base take of "Born to Run," Sancious and Carter performed with Springsteen and the others for the last time at a show in Red Bank. Then the never-ending tour took a breather. Bruce didn't appear in front of an audience for another month, the longest he'd gone without performing in two years.

EVEN AS SPRINGSTEEN was trying to persuade Sancious and Carter to stay, he or Appel had already placed an ad in the Musicians Wanted section of the *Village Voice*. By the summer of 1974, the Upstage refugees had scattered to the winds, so Springsteen and Appel decided to cast their net a little farther north. Bruce almost certainly had a hand in drafting the ad that finally appeared, because it laid out his musical tastes pretty squarely. He was looking for another drummer, but not a prima donna, someone who could play in a range of styles. They would need a piano player too, someone every bit as eclectic as Sancious, and they might even change the band's instrumental lineup. Given the way Bruce's last album had turned out, and the way his current one was evolving, he was ready to consider the addition of a trumpeter or a violinist. Before the month was out, Springsteen, Tallent, Clemons, and Federici would try to play with over four dozen musicians. In most cases, they started the audition with a James Brown song, then moved into a blues shuffle, and ended up with one of Bruce's own pieces, which (one would assume) any musician in his right mind would have worked up before she or he ever got into the room.

Actually, one of the most promising drummers they saw that August barely knew Springsteen's music at all. Max Weinberg, at twenty-three, was a little younger than the rest of the band, but he had been playing drums for pay since he was seven. Before Bruce was even in the Castiles, Weinberg's band the Epsilons had played a date at the New York World's Fair. In the decade since, he had recorded an album with a band called Blackstone and had had a steady gig in the Broadway production of *Godspell*. Like many professional musicians, though, Weinberg had spent much of his life in cover bands, and it was only because he had worked so much on the other side of the Hudson that he even knew any of Springsteen's songs. A New Jersey native (born in Newark, upstate in Essex County, not downstate in Monmouth), he had been inspired to play rock 'n' roll by seeing D. J. Fontana back Elvis on *The Ed Sullivan Show*.

When the band did the shuffle test on Weinberg at his audition, they used "Let the Four Winds Blow," which the other four musicians had been performing on and off since January. Weinberg didn't know their arrangement, but he knew what a drummer was there for. As he told an interviewer ten years later, "if you're doing your job as a drummer, you're solid but you don't stick out." He found his place among the organ, bass, saxophone, and guitar, kept moving along with them, and paid attention. Suddenly Springsteen stopped the band, then raised his arms. Experienced as he was, Max got the message. He restarted the song after the brief break as smoothly as if he had played with the other four men for years. That quickness, among other things, got him the drummer's slot.

It may have taken Weinberg only one audition to get the job, but a number of other musicians were called back at least twice. With all due respect, the band had already been through two drummers in less than a year. It could probably adjust to a new, third one fairly easily. David Sancious, though, would be much harder to replace. His sound had been essential not just to the band's live performances but to the stylistic crystallization of the first two albums. And yet the wording of the *Voice* ad suggests that, as long as he had to find a new pianist, Springsteen might have been looking for someone slightly different from Sancious. The ad asks for somebody who can play "classical to Jerry Lee Lewis," even though the latter end of the spectrum had not necessarily been Sancious's strong suit. Although the band's recent covers (and even the songs they used for auditions) were resolutely tilted toward soul and R&B, Springsteen may have been thinking of other old rock 'n' roll styles into which he might want to expand, particularly rockabilly. The classical training, however, was still an essential requirement in a potential pianist. With Federici on the other side of the stage playing organ or accordion, the band would need a pianist who could lend structure and even grandeur to Springsteen's music in much the same way that Sancious had.

Unlike Max Weinberg, Roy Bittan did know Springsteen's music: he had played piano for Niki Aukema, an obscure singer-songwriter who had opened for Springsteen three nights at Max's Kansas City. He was two years older than Weinberg, still a musician living from gig to gig, currently staying with his parents in Far Rockaway—"the New York shore," he would later point out, not the Jersey Shore. In truth, Rockaway Beach had scarcely fallen on as hard times by the early 1970s as Asbury Park had, but Bittan nevertheless felt a strong connection to Springsteen's songs. He had two good auditions, but the band was taking its time. Finally, he did the one thing job seekers are never supposed to do when waiting for a decision from potential employers—

he called them. Currently unemployed, he truthfully told Mike Appel that he had just been offered a job playing for the still-touring Crystals, at $275 a week. That was almost twice as much as anyone in Springsteen's band (including Springsteen) was currently making, even in the best of times. The next day, he was offered the pianist spot. Even with the substantial pay cut, he jumped at it. Whether they just hadn't attracted the right kind of horn players or whether the auditions had made up their mind, in the end the band didn't add a full-time trumpeter to their lineup.

They did add a violinist, though, for a high-profile engagement at Avery Fisher Hall in early October. This booking was yet another sign of the prevailing ambivalence regarding Springsteen. The singer might not be able to finish more than a single track for his third album, but his fan base seemed to be growing more and more fanatical with each albumless month. In July, when he and the band had been booked as a late replacement for Boz Scaggs at an inexpensively ticketed Schaefer Music Festival date in Central Park, three-quarters of the 5,000-person audience apparently showed up to see Springsteen—and left after his set, reducing putative headliner Anne Murray (who had just had her third Top 10 hit of the decade) to tears. Three months later, Springsteen's Avery Fisher Hall concert was announced with an ad that quoted CBS's favorite line from Jon Landau's *Real Paper* review of the Harvard Square show back in May, now blown up to screamingly hyperbolic all capital letters: "I SAW ROCK AND ROLL FUTURE AND ITS NAME IS BRUCE SPRINGSTEEN." You never could have told by that ad, and similar ones taken out in *Rolling Stone* and other publications during the summer, that Springsteen was in almost constant danger of being dropped by his label. On the other hand, in the wake of Clive Davis's departure, it sometimes seemed as if different divisions at CBS were working from entirely different game plans, particularly when it came to Springsteen.

The violinist at the Avery Fisher Hall performance was a familiar face: Suki Lahav, wife of Louis Lahav, the main engineer at 914. That night at Avery Fisher Hall, Lahav played violin on "New York City Serenade" and the ever-evolving "Jungleland," among other songs, but the impermanence of her situation can be gleaned from the fact that,

on a surviving recording of this performance, Bruce introduces Weinberg and Bittan as *a couple of new boys* in the band, but does not mention Lahav (or indeed any of the band's other three, established
members). Nevertheless, Lahav brought not only violin and backing
vocals but a very distinct sexual tension to this performance, which
enhanced a number of songs, particularly the more smoldering ones
that Bruce was prepping for his next album. A week after the Lincoln
Center performance, Lahav joined the band on a more permanent
basis and began to serve frequently as Bruce's onstage foil.

The stage show was evolving even further, becoming more polished and professional. On tour, Louis Lahav was now handling the
sound and a quick young man named Marc Brickman, whom the
Appels had essentially picked up on the road in California in July, was
now handling the lights. When Appel had been handling them, his
approach to the lights was pretty much the same as his approach to
recording: keep it cheap and simple, don't get fancy. Brickman, however, had other ideas, even on the band's radically limited budget. He
began, for example, to use an overhead spot, and Springsteen among
others understood the possibilities. He would act out the songs more,
most spectacularly in the case of "Jungleland," at the end of which he
would simulate the character's death.

The addition of Lahav and Brickman to the tour that fall, as well as
the arrival of the receptive Bittan and the Broadway-experienced
Weinberg, changed the nature of Springsteen's stage show. On the
most superficial level, his band was much whiter now, none more so
than the blond, blue-eyed—albeit Israeli-born—Lahav. In a radical
change from just two months earlier, Clemons was now the sole African American onstage, and he began to stand out more in performance, much as Lahav did because she was the only woman. In
reviewing two separate Springsteen performances in Pennsylvania
during November, both Michael Sangiacomo and Lloyd Traven didn't
even bother to mention anyone else onstage other than Springsteen,
Clemons, and Lahav.

Along with being more theatrical, Springsteen's shows were less
improvisational, more deliberate, than they had been a year or two
before. His sets were plotted now: they had a beginning, a middle, and

an end, and they built nicely through them. Once again, Bruce began to add spoken introductions to his songs, preambles that varied only slightly from night to night. As his occasional late-night phone buddy Richard Neer recognized, Springsteen "presented his songs like an FM jock, explaining and embellishing their meanings." Through his narration, Springsteen guided you through the music and showed you how it seemed through his own eyes, juxtaposing songs for rhetorical effect, much as a memorable DJ would have done. This was a far cry from the shows a year earlier, when the play between musicians was much more central to Springsteen's performances. As with his emerging third album, jams and grooves were less important to his shows now than advancing a through line across all the songs, a cohesive vision that united them.

Springsteen's show was so tight now that, even with the band changes, he was continuing to build momentum and generate both critical and popular buzz. Praise was mounting, interest was rising— and he still didn't have an album. The new band went to Blauvelt in late October, made stabs at "Jungleland," "She's the One," a runaway boy-and-girl song called "Lovers in the Cold," "Backstreets" (a late-night betrayal song) and "So Young and in Love" (an up-tempo number). They even tried using full string sections again on "Jungleland" and "Backstreets." None of it worked. According to his contract with CBS, Springsteen should have had at least five finished albums by the fall of 1974. A live album, possibly two or three discs' worth, started to be batted about as a stopgap measure until the third album came into focus.

It was at this point that the ever-hustling Mike Appel hatched what may have been his most brilliant pushy scheme ever. When Irwin Segelstein, the new president of the domestic division of CBS Records, again definitively refused to release "Born to Run" as a single, Appel made forty cassette copies of the recording. Then, in early November, when Bruce was appearing on his new friend Ed Sciaky's show on WMMR in Philadelphia with Tallent, Weinberg, and Bittan, Bruce gave him a copy of the tape. Test pressings of unreleased Springsteen songs had been circulating for over a year now, especially the May 1973 studio recording of "The Fever" (which, like the fresh "Born to

Run" tape, Sciaky played on that afternoon's show). What Springsteen was doing here, however, was something entirely different: he was deliberately going against his record label's wishes and releasing his new single on his own. Thirty years later, he could have just posted it in on MySpace or downloaded it onto a file-sharing network, but in 1974 this was strictly a hands-on transaction.

Over the next month, Appel and Springsteen distributed copies of the song to Scott Muni in New York and Maxanne Sartori in Boston. They got a copy to Kid Leo, and by Thanksgiving the song was the most played record on the radio in Cleveland, even though nobody could buy it. After the first of the year, they sent out another twenty copies of the recording, all to FM DJs in major markets, and later in the winter still more. All across America, rock-buying consumers were frustrated that they couldn't purchase the record, and rival radio stations in all those markets were wondering why CBS wouldn't give them copies, too. From the record company's point of view, what Appel had done was (as usual) totally insane. Springsteen's record might be attracting interest on all those stations, but the only ones who were making money off it were the people who owned the stations, not CBS and not Springsteen or Appel. When Bruce attended a Billy Joel concert at Rutgers in mid-December, Joel dedicated his current no. 34 single, "The Entertainer," to his less successful labelmate, making some of the song's lines even more resonant.

By the time Bruce and his band played a benefit for the Main Point in early February 1975, many of those in the audience had the still unreleased "Born to Run" committed to memory. That was mostly thanks to Ed Sciaky, who introduced the Main Point show and on whose station, WMMR, the concert was broadcast later that night. At this point, the band's shows lasted two and a half hours, but they weren't self-indulgent. This new incarnation of the band was ready to turn on a dime. At the Main Point, the band did much the same stage show that it had been doing for the last month or two, particularly numbers like "Incident on 57th Street," "Jungleland," and its new cover of Bob Dylan's "I Want You" (off *Blonde on Blonde*), all of which allowed Springsteen to notably interact with Lahav onstage.

There were, of course, a couple of extras for the Main Point show, the sorts of goodies Springsteen usually offered when he knew he was with a friendly crowd. "Born to Run" was in the set, as was the first recorded performance of another new car song meant for the third album. In this incarnation, it was called "Wings for Wheels," and it was an extensive reimagining of the fall's "Lovers in the Cold," reset now from Manhattan's Lexington Avenue to a dirty road in a seasonal town. Its first verse (*The screen door slams . . .*) is almost identical to the opening of a better-known Springsteen song, right down to the shambling way that its lyrics finally fall into regular prosody after a dozen, grace-note-ridden opening lines. Much of the rest of the song, though, is different from the piece that would open Springsteen's third album. In this early version, it sounds as if the song might belong on the same album as last year's "She's So Fine," a collection that could almost take its title from a song that Manhattan's Dictators were currently recording for their first album: "I Live for Cars and Girls." The narrator of this early version doesn't sound as if he wants to get out of town, as the narrator of "Born to Run" simply *has* to do. It sounds more as if he simply wants to take *Angelina* (as his female interlocutor is called in this version) for a diverting ride, such as the one the characters in "Spirit in the Night" like to take. And, at least in this version of the lyric, his *4/4* (a car in this case, rather than a time signature) feels much more real to us than the barely individualized *Angelina*.

A month later, *Angelina* became *Chrissie*. Even though such a casual name switch might make it seem that the songwriter felt that all his former girlfriends were interchangeable, the fact is that in this second version of the song, the narrator's interlocutor becomes much more vital. In the original version of the second verse, the narrator devoted only a single line to halfheartedly considering *Angelina's* situation. In Springsteen's revised version, he spends more time trying to imagine what it must feel like to be *Chrissie* than he spends talking about himself (or his car). He even admits some of the reasons she might have to be cautious of him.

If Springsteen had simply made the song about *an* old girlfriend, there would have been no guarantee at this early stage of his career that he would actually capture her individuality in his lyrics. By widening his perspective, however, and trying to capture what any woman might feel in that sort of situation, his lyrics became simultaneously less specific to the scenes of his own life and more concrete and more resonant. Although still a song from a resolutely male perspective that focused on the narrator's rescue of a mid-Atlantic rock 'n' roll damsel in distress, this song in revision became less like "4th of July, Asbury Park" and more like "For You." You could believe in Chrissie's existence as more than the mere object of the narrator's desire.

By this point, the dirty road in the song had acquired a name and the former "Wings for Wheels" its better-known title: "Thunder Road." With "Born to Run" already locked, this now became the song that Springsteen and the band had to get right for the third album. Springsteen wanted the new album to have a sense of unity, and one plan called for it to both open and close with this song. The opening version would feature Springsteen singing the song solo on acoustic guitar, something he had avoided on *Wild and Innocent*. The surviving take of the song that we have using this approach is haunted, an effect that is sharpened by its use of double-tracked vocals, which allow Springsteen to sing harmony with himself. On this simpler version, Springsteen sounds like a post-rock troubadour along the lines of Gordon Lightfoot or a less overproduced Johnny Cash.

At this stage of the process, though, the full-band take of the song meant to close the album proved less successful at capturing its spirit. If on the best *Wild and Innocent* tracks Springsteen and his band had seemed to be in dialogue, on all these early band versions of "Thunder Road," live and recorded, they often appeared to be performing at cross-purposes. In the live version at the Main Point, Lahav's violin part works in counterpoint against Springsteen (much like David Sancious's piano parts on "It's Hard to Be a Saint in the City" and "New York City Serenade"), almost as if it embodies Angelina's unverbalized half of the conversation. Similarly at the Main Point, Clemons's saxophone breaks into a busy cha-cha-cha near the end of the song, almost suggesting that all the two lovers need to get out of their funk is a happening Gary U.S. Bonds–style dance groove. That kind of sax break was perfect for a song like "The E Street Shuffle," which was about pulling the listener into an ongoing celebration, but it undercut the more solitary perspective of a song like "Thunder Road."

And then there is the matter of Springsteen's guitar, which is almost entirely absent from these early band versions of the song. At the Main Point, when Springsteen sings the hopefully triumphant *Well I bought this guitar and I learned how to make it talk*, he is answered musically not by his own guitar but by Federici's organ. On the full-band Chrissie version in the studio, the guitar indeed kicks in at the beginning of the bridge, but it is lost among all the other instruments. Sonically shared in this way, "Thunder Road" seems like a song not about a man desperate to get out of town, or even about a man and a woman in desperate straits, but rather about a celebration that's starting just down the block.

Since he signed with CBS, Springsteen's greatest personal breakthroughs had usually come in moments of artistic fusion, realizing late in the process of recording *Greetings*, for example, that a Mitch Ryder song could have Bob Dylan lyrics, just as he would realize when recording *Wild and Innocent* that his artistic vision wouldn't suffer if he brought a little bit of the Upstage into a professional recording studio. What this third batch of songs required, however, was something entirely different: he needed to be epic and personal at the same time, far more so than he had been even on the socially self-aware "New York City Serenade." Making "Born to Run" work in this way had at least been imaginable: that song was about a fairly simple form of desperation, so it only needed to project a single breakneck feeling through its massive, overloaded arrangement. "Thunder Road," however, took a number of distinct emotional turns during its nearly five minutes. Springsteen needed the band to convey those twists and turns, but to convey parts of a mind with their performances, rather than parts of a world, as on the *Wild and Innocent* tracks.

In a way, it all came down to the piano part. At the Main Point in February, and even back in the preevolved form of "Lovers in the Cold," the piano part was the cornerstone of this song, much as it was for "New York City Serenade." Of the three keyboardists with whom Springsteen had worked most, David Sancious challenged his creativity, Danny Federici drew out the depth of his feelings, but Roy Bittan musically extended Springsteen's vision in the way that he needed to complete his elusive third album. It took a while for him to find the right way to do it, however. At the Main Point, Bittan's piano, even if it was not quite virtuosic, projected an emotional temperature entirely different from that of Springsteen's lyrics. It was playful, taking off with cut-time, jazzy, even honky-tonk riffs of its own that didn't echo the singer so much as challenge him to bop his blues away. With each successive version of the song, Bittan's playing got closer and closer to the narrator's emotions rather than to the mere chords and notes through which they were expressed. On the simplest level, Bittan's piano part increasingly extended the figures of the main vocal line of the track, rather than existing in dialogue or counterpoint with them. It made the melodic fragments and other musical figures of the vocal line more elaborate, more complex, offering a more evolved but not really alternative perspective. Conceived this way, the piano line in "Thunder Road" is less like the narrator's critical interlocutor than like a piece of the narrator's musical clothing, something he dons to lend himself greater presence.

For his first two years with CBS, Springsteen had been billed for most concerts simply by himself. The ad for one date in Beverly, Massachusetts, in December of 1973 went so far as to designate the featured performers as "Bruce Springsteen and his Studio Musicians," probably to make clear that it wasn't an acoustic show. For Springsteen's fans, however, these musicians will always be the "E Street Band," and there is considerable debate about when that legendary entity actually began. The name at least may have gone back to the earliest *Greetings* gigs. E Street was where Davey Sancious lived with his mother in Belmar, and he was inevitably late when the rest of the band came to pick him up. According to Clemons, it was in late October 1972, on the day the band had to drive to East Chester, Pennsylvania, for a set opening for Cheech and Chong, when Bruce declared, "This band has spent so much time parked on this fucking street, we should call it the E Street Band."

If the name was indeed privately coined then, however, it wasn't really used publicly for at least a year and a half. Near the end of the recording of the early show at the Harvard Square Theatre in May of 1974, it does sound as if Springsteen is referring to his musicians collectively as *the E Street Band*, but this is a rare exception. The first time the name appeared in print advertisements was in August of 1974—with the last concert that David Sancious and Boom Carter played with Bruce in fact. In CBS's blaring "ROCK & ROLL FUTURE" ads that fall, the musicians were called "the E Street Shuffle Band," and it was not until mid-1975 that they were simply called "the E Street Band."

In general, the fall of 1974 seems like an appropriate moment to see the band's identity crystallizing. Coming out of a common grounding in the same clubs and hangouts of the Jersey Shore scene, the Lopez-Sancious bands had been Springsteen's partners, and their common feeling had led to more collaborative performances. By contrast, the Bittan-Weinberg band members functioned as accompanists rather than as collaborators. They amplified Springsteen's thought and feeling, and their creativity was in the service of his specific vision. Like his current model Phil Spector, Springsteen saw other musicians at this point in his career as a means to a highly personal aesthetic end. From the fall of 1974 on, Springsteen was definitively a bandleader, if not necessarily the Boss. As Clemons would tell a reporter about a year later, "You hook on to Bruce on that stage and you go wherever he takes you. It's like total surrender to him."

Well, maybe not total surrender. Over the last three years, the band had changed much as Springsteen's songs had. At first, it was a local thing, a continuation of the Upstage with coded references in the lyrics that only true Asbury Park veterans could get. Now its members were bound by less tangible, more archetypal ties: the New York shore as well as the Jersey Shore; north Jersey as well as south Jersey; a shared love of the sort of records you didn't hear enough on the radio anymore. They weren't all old friends now; they were co-workers. In March 1975, as the touring and studio time stretched on, all of it in the service of one man's quest to make the sounds in his ears perfectly match the ones in his head, two members of Springsteen's original touring band were now making their own rumbles about getting out. Twenty-hour days at the Record Plant, hearing Bruce sing out the sax solo he envisioned for "Jungleland" note by pulled-tooth note probably didn't help matters. Even before all the changes in the lineup, Clemons had asked Appel if he could get him a solo deal, and now Federici was interested in one as well. Simultaneously, CBS may have been asking Appel if it was possible, since their recording contract through Laurel Canyon was technically only with Springsteen, to sign the band to its own, separate contract.

In the end, of course, they stayed, and this points to the paradox of the E Street Band, a combination of circumstances that has made it virtually unique in rock history. For more than ten years during the late 1970s and early 1980s (and again in the first decade of the twenty-first century), the E Street Band presented a remarkably stable lineup. Fans could name each band member in turn and enjoy seeing them function as familiar, featured characters in Springsteen's stage shows. On the other hand, the E Street Band was not a band in the sense that the Beatles, the Rolling Stones, the Who, or the quickly imploding Cream were. It was something between those blessed, semi-egalitarian leagues of known, idiosyncratic talents and the autocratic and mostly anonymous soul-style "show bands" that commanding artists like James Brown and even Jimi Hendrix had fronted. After the fall of 1974, each member of the E Street Band was valued for his individual gifts and seen as essentially irreplaceable, even by Springsteen. But make no mistake: their unique gifts were harnessed to serve Springsteen's ends. It was his band, his show, his songs, and his world.

Nowhere was this truer than in the final, released version of "Thunder Road," the turning point that spring in the recording sessions for Springsteen's third album. The instruments once again came in one by one, but in this version not to party. All of them play their parts in the songwriter's overall statement, none more so than Bittan's piano, which extends and complicates the musical figures of Springsteen's main vocal in this take without drawing any attention away from them. Merging the best of the two Chrissie versions of the song, this final, "Mary" version offers up neither a stripped-down solitary statement nor a feel-good rave-up. The narrator's vision once again starts out shambling and small, the separate instruments once again join the song piecemeal, but this time the arrangement takes shape as the narrator's vision similarly clarifies. Framed this way, the narrator grows in stature as his resolve and his world grow larger. It is as if a curtain is being drawn back to reveal more and more of a bigger picture. *The band always makes me think broader for some reason*, Springsteen mused after a solo performance of the song at the *DoubleTake* concerts in 2003. *When I write for them, I always open up into Cinemascope.*

Within these broad instrumental horizons, the key instrument for this ultimate arrangement of "Thunder Road" is the one named in its lyrics but so long deferred in earlier performances: the guitar. It kicks in between the first and second A parts, when the narrator finds his more assured voice. At the beginning of the third A part, it pointedly answers that voice when he speaks about *making it talk*. The full-on fury of "Born to Run" had required wall-to-wall guitars, but waiting for the instrument to enter on this track perfectly conveys the song's gradually dawning hope.

And one last touch had to be added before the song was finished. On all available prerelease takes of the song with the full band, "Thunder Road" had begun with Clemons playing half a dozen bars of the bridge on tenor sax. For the final mix, Bruce played the same snatch of music on harmonica—playing it like Bob Dylan rather than Little Walter, establishing the song as personal rather than communal well before the well-timed appearance of his rhythm guitar. "Thunder Road" finally proved that singer-songwriters like Springsteen didn't have to go it alone. You could still be highly personal with five other musicians backing you.

CHAPTER 5

TONIGHT'S GONNA BE EVERYTHING
THAT I SAID (1975–1976)

T HE SPRING OF 1975 WAS THE TURNING POINT FOR BRUCE SPRING-
steen's third album, mostly because of a surprising surge of support
that the singer suddenly received at that time from his record label.
Three years into his contract, CBS finally figured out who Springsteen's target audience was: not people his own age so much as college
students up to a decade younger, the same students whose bookings
had been keeping him so busy on weekends for the last year or so. In
particular, Irwin Segelstein, the president of the label's domestic division, got an earful from his college-age son after the boy had read
Springsteen's negative comments about CBS in a college newspaper.
He particularly complained about CBS's not releasing "Born to Run"
as a single in advance of the album, knowing full well from Springsteen's interview that his father was the person ultimately responsible
for that decision. Sometime after this conversation, Segelstein agreed
to meet Springsteen and Appel in a Manhattan restaurant. The record
executive had decided that Springsteen now could get more support
from the record label, but he had to record in Manhattan, at a state-of-
the-art facility like the Record Plant. For most of 1974, the singer had
been under the gun to prove himself to CBS. Now that he had the
label's support, the only constraints that he was still under were the
ones imposed by his own perfectionism.

By April, Springsteen and the band were installed at the Record
Plant, trying to make the album come together. By that time, both
Lahavs had returned to Israel, but Springsteen was joined by another

ally in the studio: Jon Landau. In the fall, Landau finally moved to New York, as did fellow Springsteen booster Dave Marsh. Springsteen had enjoyed talking to Landau in May, and in early October they met again and talked even more about music, life, and how they had gotten to where they were. By February of 1975, Springsteen was inviting Landau into the studio to ask his advice on the ever elusive "Jungleland." By the time Springsteen and his band definitively moved from 914 to the Record Plant, Landau had quit *Rolling Stone* and signed on as coproducer of Springsteen's third album, along with Springsteen himself and the ever suspicious Mike Appel.

If Landau made one crucial contribution that spring, it was his reported declaration that they should make a "rock 'n' roll album" and feature electric guitars, something that Springsteen had not done on either of his first two albums despite his musical background. But by the time the former journalist joined Springsteen's production team, at least five of the eight tracks that would end up on his third album had already been selected, and several of them had base or fairly finished recordings. The most feverish work that spring was with the overdubs, and it probably helped a great deal to have yet another set of winnowing ears in the studio, ears that came with Landau's considerable rock credentials. As he had done for the prior three years, Springsteen eagerly solicited opinions from those who might know more about the music business than he did. In the race to complete his third album, however, it was the same with these advisers as with the band: they didn't give Springsteen ideas; they helped him complete the ones he already had.

The tone Springsteen wanted for the album was clear now. These weren't just jokey songs about cars and girls anymore. They were about claustrophobia, desperation, getting out, and the crimes and betrayals that women and men will commit in order to make their escape from a dead-end environment. The people and scenes of "Thunder Road," "Born to Run," "Backstreets," and "Jungleland" all clearly belonged on such an album. In fact, they would nail down the corners of the album's two sides, with the former two leading off sides A and B with the promise of relative hope and the latter two ending those sides with stories of intimate betrayal. The style in which the emerging album painted its world could almost be called industrial gothic, glowing with the sort of garish, probably waste-derived colors that true New Jerseyans will tell you make their sunsets more vibrant than those in any other part of the eastern United States. For the most part, these songs are set in New Jersey rather than in New York, but the Emerald City is off in the distance of most of them, as a lure and a potential target for flight. A song like "The Heist" (whose title was changed at almost the last minute to "Meeting across the River") fits into this world perfectly: its story of two economically struggling young men who place all their hopes on a meeting with mobbed-up guys in Manhattan encapsulates exactly the sort of desperate, probably hopeless hope at which all the characters in these songs seek to grasp.

With "Thunder Road," "Backstreets," "Born to Run," and "Jungleland" serving as its cornerstones, this was not going to be the sort of album onto which you can slip a feel-good single in order to lighten the mood. The happiest song on the album ended up being "Tenth Avenue Freeze-Out," which was, stylistically at least, much more in the spirit of *Wild and Innocent*. It was yet another one of Bruce's late-addition numbers about making music, but its function on *Born to Run* was closer to the one served by "Rosalita" on the second album: it is a comic myth that echoes the tragic variations in most of the other tracks. Its title may remain a mystery to many listeners, but as Daniel Wolff has shrewdly pointed out, there is no Tenth Avenue in Asbury Park, just the lake that serves as the city's western boundary. In other words, this is yet another song about Getting Out.

In June, CBS executives listened to a rough cut of the album and felt positive enough about it to green-light a major promotion campaign. As Mike Appel probably would have liked to remind them, they didn't have to start totally from scratch when promoting Springsteen. Over the last three years, he and the band had built up a considerable network of journalists, club owners, DJs, and fans who were all true believers in the cult of Bruce. To snare a wider audience, though, CBS decided to spend $40,000—more than had been spent to make either of Springsteen's first two albums—to take out ads on FM stations in a number of major markets. The ads were designed to use *Greetings from Asbury Park, N.J., Wild and Innocent,* and the Landau quotation to build up interest in the forthcoming *Born to Run*. That summer, while the new album was still being mixed (and mixed and mixed and mixed, at Bruce's behest), these ads achieved an even more impressive feat: they got people to buy Springsteen's first two albums in significant numbers. Two years after their release, they finally entered the *Billboard* albums chart, barely breaking above no. 60 but doubling their previous sales, staying on the chart for the better part of the next year, and eventually going double platinum.

Now the label and the mass market were behind Springsteen. All he had to do was finish the album. This year at least, the band had been good about not canceling live dates because of studio commitments, but no matter what CBS thought, Bruce continued to record, mix, and refine his tracks, even if it meant twice postponing a scheduled performance in Geneva, New York. Even the songs that had been around for close to a year proved, to his ears, elusive in the studio until almost the last possible moment. On 19 July, Bruce laid down vocals on "She's the One," as a satisfactory mix of the epic "Jungleland" was finally produced in another room at the Record Plant.

Then at three o'clock on Saturday afternoon, a little more than a day before a Sunday night booking at the Palace in Providence that they simply couldn't reschedule, the band finally began to rehearse for its upcoming tour. The musicians hadn't played live in close to three months, and repeatedly laying down overdubs is not a good way to keep in the habit of listening and reacting to your fellow musicians. They practiced straight through for nineteen hours until ten in the morning on Sunday, until Bruce was satisfied. Then they left for the gig, at the Palace Theatre in Providence, which fell on the sixth anniversary of the first lunar landing (not to mention the day that Vini Lopez blew up at the Pandemonium). Springsteen's first spoken words to the Providence audience that night were *This song is something from our new album—it should be out next month—I'm sure.*

But over the next month Springsteen proved similarly obsessive as the engineers back in New York tried to turn all those mixes into masters. They would send the masters to Springsteen on the road in Washington, Richmond, and other towns, and he kept rejecting them, at least a dozen according to Dave Marsh. One master he allegedly threw out the window of his hotel room and into the nearby river. He was driving everybody crazy, and Jon Landau was apparently the only person who could talk sense to him. In early August, after repeated discussions with Landau, Springsteen let go. Close to two years after the release of his second album, he finally had a third.

IN THE SECOND WEEK of August, Springsteen and his band played a five-night stand, two shows a night, at the Bottom Line in Manhattan. Max's Kansas City had fallen on bad times and was in the midst of a change in ownership, but the Bottom Line was still going strong. The band was now back up to seven members, with Steve Van Zandt having been added in the spring as an additional guitarist, vocalist, and all-around musical guru. At the early show on the second night, Springsteen told a long, exaggerated version of the story of the night he met Clemons, as an introduction to a very slow version of "The E Street Shuffle" rather than the show-opening "Tenth Avenue Freeze-Out." The album was still two weeks away from its release, so almost half the set was made of *Wild and Innocent* songs, but the road-tested "Born to Run," "Thunder Road," and "She's the One" made it into the set, as did a couple of songs from *Greetings*. And, of course, there were covers, spaced throughout the set for maximum impact, all from the pre-Castiles 1960s.

The Bottom Line could seat four hundred people for each performance, and over three thousand of the seats for those ten shows sold out in three and a half days, a volume almost unheard of in the days before Ticketmaster, robo-calling, and the internet. The other thousand or so seats were bought up by the record company and distributed free to journalists, DJs, stars, anyone who might be considered a "tastemaker." It was a naked play for Springsteen's record to arrive with a big splash. Some in the business who had grown tired of the "New Dylan" hype accepted the tickets but entered the club as confirmed skeptics.

By any standard you might want to use—artistically, socially, economically—the Bottom Line shows were a shrewd move. Dave Herman, who came on after Richard Neer to do the morning show at

WNEW and who had refused for over two years to play any of the tracks on *Greetings*, actually went on the air the morning after he saw one of the Bottom Line shows and apologized. One of the Bottom Line sets was simulcast on WNEW and then relayed to Philadelphia for WMMR to run as well. From the beginning of the concerts, fans lined up for blocks outside the Bottom Line in hopes of snagging standing room tickets for any of the shows. Even for Springsteen, that week felt like a momentous occasion. Years later, when NYU was preparing to shut down the Bottom Line to make room for more university facilities, the singer declared, "When I think of the most memorable nights of my own career, few match the week of shows we did there in 1975."

CBS's big push worked. The preorders on *Born to Run* were double what the label had been expecting—350,000 units—more than twice as many for this third album as the company had sold to date of the first two albums combined. The moment the singer had been dreading for two years had finally arrived: he had to start playing bigger halls, often to three thousand people a night.

But the tour went on, to the Municipal Auditorium in Austin, the Convention Center Theatre in Dallas, and a dozen other stops between interviews and photo sessions to promote the new album. New songs like "Night" and "Meeting across the River" were worked into live versions, while older songs like "New York City Serenade" and "Blinded by the Light" were eased out of the set. A gig at the Roxy in Los Angeles in October was attended by Hollywood royalty: Ryan and Tatum O'Neal, Wolfman Jack, and Neil Diamond, as well as fellow Monmouth County transplant Jack Nicholson. In the same month, Springsteen finally met both Bob Dylan and Phil Spector, and he and the band actually sat in on a session Spector was producing for Dion (whom Van Zandt had backed onstage at one point during his several wandering years). "Born to Run" began to move from FM over to AM, and a lifelong dream of Bruce's to hear one of his songs on a car radio was finally achieved. Within two weeks of its release, *Born to Run* entered the *Billboard* album chart and almost immediately went to no. 1 in some markets. It would remain on that chart for over two years and ultimately sell six million copies. Mightily helped by its AM airplay, "Born to Run" entered the Hot 100 singles chart, only climbing as high as no. 23 but staying on the chart for the next three months.

The critical response was even more fervent than the popular one. A few days before *Born to Run* was released, *New York Times* music critic John Rockwell hailed it as a masterpiece of "punk poetry" and "one of the great records of recent years." Greil Marcus, writing a few weeks later in *Rolling Stone*, called it "a magnificent album that pays off on every bet ever placed on [Springsteen]—a '57 Chevy running on melted down Crystals records that shuts down every claim that has been made." The next month, Lester Bangs praised Springsteen in similar terms in *Creem*, specifically declaring the old Another Bob Dylan tag to have been in error and suggested instead that the singer was really another Neal Cassady, with the sort of firsthand knowledge of textile mills, "yea-saying" delinquency, and "joyrides" that a self-styled "intellectual" like Bob Dylan could only dream of. Bangs, whose 1970s criticism would swing forever in a real death waltz with his most cherished and hated icon Lou Reed, found in Springsteen an alternative figure, a rock 'n' roll punk who could inspire him to hope without getting sappy, a rebel who wouldn't be boxed in but wasn't self-destructive either.

All of this enthusiasm crested in what was then and may still be an unprecedented media event. In late October, Springsteen simultaneously appeared on the covers of both *Time* and *Newsweek*. The magazines' dueling stories recycled the same material, the same interviews, but they took two slightly different tacks. *Time*'s story, written by critic Jay Cocks, was more of a "local boy hits the big time" type of a piece, while *Newsweek*'s article, a team-reporting effort by Maureen Orth, Janet Huck, and Peter S. Greenberg, was a blunter attempt to use Springsteen as an example of how the music industry manufactured pop stars. A few weeks after John Rockwell's rave in the *New York Times*, Henry Edwards wrote an article for the newspaper entitled "If There Hadn't Been a Bruce Springsteen, Then the Critics Would Have Made Him Up," and the *Newsweek* team built on this journalistic counterresponse, focusing more on CBS's efforts to promote the singer than on those spearheaded by passionate critics.

Such a backlash against CBS's successful promotion of Springsteen was probably inevitable, but it was interesting how many of the articles seemed to think Springsteen was an overnight success who had been plucked out of obscurity and molded to his label's wishes. That fall, Bob Greene and Mike Royko in Chicago questioned the singer's true working-class credentials and reportedly hurt Springsteen's ticket and album sales in that city. Langdon Winner, in the formerly effusive *Real Paper,* called *Born to Run* "the complete monument to rock and roll orthodoxy" and headlined his article "Bruce Springsteen's Nobel Prize Bid." A quarter of a century later, former *Rolling Stone* and *Newsweek* writer James Miller would go so far as to declare the Springsteen hype of 1975 to have been the definitive death knell for the kind of rock 'n' roll he had grown up loving. "With the successful mass-marketing in the United States of Bruce Springsteen, American Superhero (the very image of redemptive innocence), following on the heels of the successful mass-marketing in England of Ziggy Stardust (the very image of redemptive self-destruction), the age of innocence in rock was well and truly over—probably forever."

In a way, it felt like the spring of 1973 all over again—only bigger—but there were two crucial differences this time. First, Bruce's records were finally selling, which probably softened the blow somewhat. Harsh criticism is bad, but most would agree that dwelling in what George Orwell once called "the suburbs of poverty" while hearing it always makes it worse. Second, at least this time, Bruce wasn't being sold as what he wasn't. *Born to Run* reflected his vision. Its songs and its sounds were in no way the result of a calculated record-label strategy, as Charles Koppelman's proposed Nashville solo project would have been. When CBS's marketing division finally took notice of Springsteen, what it did was figure out a strategy to sell his self-expression, not encourage him to express himself in a more salable manner. You could reject the vision that Springsteen projected on *Born to Run,* call it adolescent, overblown, or bathetic if you wanted, but to call it inauthentic or impersonal was just plain ignorant.

Still, the criticism was hard to take, especially for someone who had been pretty anonymous for most of his life. With all the benefits of fame—and Springsteen would be among the first to admit that there are a *lot* of them—there is still something odd about that first season of celebrity, in which you become an entity wholly separate from your self. Now that he had the success that he had been dreaming of for over a decade, he found himself with mixed emotions. The Edwards article particularly stung. In early October in Detroit, on the day Edwards's piece appeared in advance copies of the *New York Times'* Arts and Leisure section, Springsteen almost didn't want to go onstage, but the band got him through his funk.

Continuing the tour that fall, Springsteen tried to take it all in stride. When introducing "Does This Bus Stop at 82nd Street?" in Pennsylvania that December, he joked, *Seasons come, seasons go, you get your picture on the cover of* Time *and* Newsweek, *but the bus never stops,* and then launched into a musical memory of a time when the idea of a big break was still fantastic and undilutedly exciting. He told one reporter that calling him the "future" of rock had been wrong and that he "would like to strangle the guy who thought that up"—presumably meaning not Jon Landau, but whoever it was in the Columbia marketing division who had decided to make that claim the cornerstone of Springsteen's "brand." In early November, the singer told people at his label that, with album and ticket sales going so well, he thought it was time to pull back a little on the hard sell. Shortly after that conversation, he arrived in London for his first European gig, which should have been a triumphant moment, and was enraged to see "Finally the world is ready for Bruce Springsteen" posters all over the lobby of the theater, as well as boxes of "I have seen the future of rock 'n' roll at Hammersmith Odeon" buttons ready to be passed out to all who attended. He ripped down the posters himself and demanded that the buttons be put away. The label passed out *Born to Run* buttons with a picture of a pair of sneakers on them instead, which it had presumably been holding in reserve for just such an eventuality.

While *Newsweek's* charge of whole manufacture was obviously ludicrous, Henry Edwards's barbs at Springsteen dug in a little deeper. Was the singer some kind of rock 'n' roll messiah dreamed up by rock critics and DJs, because they didn't like the music that they had to deal with on a daily basis? The key piece of evidence that Springsteen's most cynical critics would cite to support this claim was the increased importance of Jon Landau to his career over the year and a half leading up to his popular breakthrough. Not only had Landau penned the infamous line that had inspired CBS's successful marketing campaign, but since the night he met Springsteen at Charley's he had become a friend, an adviser, and eventually a record producer to him. In the *Newsweek* article, he was even misidentified in a photo caption as Springsteen's manager. Journalist John Sinclair, writing in the *Ann Arbor Sun* that October, seems to have been the first to claim that, in Fred Goodman's words, "Marsh and Landau were co-conspirators on a massive Springsteen hype," but he was by no means the last. Sensitive to such criticism, *Rolling Stone*, in fact, did not put Springsteen on its cover in 1975, despite his enormous success, specifically because of his notable connection with Landau, one of that magazine's best-known former editors.

Obviously, Jon Landau did not "create" Bruce Springsteen, nor did he (as Mike Appel, for one, might later claim) divert his talent to other directions. It would probably be more accurate to say that Landau "discovered" Springsteen, but it was a personal rather than a professional discovery, coming as it did at a particularly low point in Landau's life. As it happened, the Harvard Square show had been on Landau's twenty-seventh birthday, and it had made him feel nostalgic. (Only a passionate devotee of youth music can feel that nostalgic before he turns thirty.) Landau didn't even mention Springsteen until the thirteenth paragraph of an eighteen-paragraph piece, but instead used the lead of his article to set down his rock 'n' roll autobiography: the records he had worshipped, the bands he had been in, the concerts he had attended, and the publications he had written for. The piece could have come off as narcissistic, but it didn't. It felt like the honest confessions of a critic who was too tired to pretend to be objective anymore. In the sense that H. L. Mencken used the word to describe his own criticism a half century earlier, Landau was displaying his "prejudices" in this review—where he found aesthetic pleasures in popular music and how wistful it made him that he found those pleasures less and less with each passing year.

This kind of nostalgia was different from the kind that Richard Nixon, Ronald Reagan, or even George Lucas might have felt in the mid-1970s: a nostalgia for a time when a pure product of the American

culture industry could honestly move you to strong emotions. Like
Dave Marsh, Richard Neer, Ed Sciaky, and so many others of their
generation, Landau didn't want to give up on pop, let alone rock 'n'
roll, as a meaningful art form. It had given him a voice and a purpose, and he wanted to believe that it could do so again. Like all
those others, Landau recognized in Springsteen a kindred spirit, but
frankly one who could do the one thing in popular music that he
might be able to do a little but would never do well: *perform*. Springsteen could give form and voice to the inchoate feelings that such
old-school pop fans had about their music and their culture. They
had as much to gain from encouraging his talent to reach its full
potential as he had to gain from soliciting their opinions about what
makes for good rock 'n' roll. On both sides of such exchanges, the
least important part of that "gain" had to do with monetary rewards.

In late January of 1976, the same week as "Tenth Avenue Freeze-
Out" entered the Hot 100 for what would end up being a fairly short,
three-week stay, Robert Christgau published a piece in the *Village
Voice* that was probably the most balanced treatment of the controversy surrounding Springsteen's talent and promotion. Entitled "Yes,
There Is a Rock-Critic Establishment (But Is That Bad for Rock?)," it
took a commonsense approach to the swirl of the last six months and
put Springsteen in the context of other artists who had received similarly favorable treatment from U.S. critics. Bette Midler, David Bowie,
Randy Newman, Lou Reed, Patti Smith, and Bob Dylan, Christgau
pointed out, had all been pushed by critics, but they had seldom gone
platinum, as it looked at that point that Springsteen was about to do.
He named names and facetiously referred to Springsteen as "the first
victory of a brand-new grouping of five journalists who for want of a
more felicitous term I have decided to label the rock-critic establishment," namely John Rockwell, Paul Nelson, Dave Marsh, Jon Landau, and—himself.

Christgau's piece was by no means a rave. He took Springsteen to
task on a number of counts and expressed a frank preference for *Wild
and Innocent* over *Born to Run*. Nevertheless, he boldly asserted that
rock criticism for those who practice it primarily is, and almost has to
be, "fannish." "The stock explanation," Christgau wrote, "of why suc-

cessful media professionals like Landau and Marsh and Nelson . . . identify so intensely with an idealized youth rebel like Springsteen is that they want to preserve their own youth, but this is stupid. Say rather that they want to preserve their rebellion." And rebellion in success was very much the paradox that rock 'n' roll fans whose minds had been dazzled when they were children and adolescents by Elvis Presley wanted to embrace. "[M]y colleagues," Christgau noted, "both thrill to a fellow winner and identify with his loser rebel persona, forgetting in the rock and roll moment how much the winner in them shares with what the fighter was fighting against."

This paradox would be at the heart of both Springsteen's art and its promotion for the next decade. Springsteen was singing his own songs, making his own statements, and yet he had arrived at exactly the right moment for a nation slipping rapidly into industrial decline, full of people who wanted to feel as good as they could without denying how bad things really were. "He's able to say what we can't about growing up," said Jon Bordonaro, a telephone dispatcher from the Bronx, when he had been interviewed by the reporters from *Newsweek* the previous fall. "He's talking about hanging around in cars in front of the Exxon sign. He's talking about getting your hands on your very first convertible." "The peace and love movement is gone," Bordonaro's friend Chris Williams added. "We have to make a shot now or settle into the masses." Illusory or not, Springsteen's songs captured a world and a feeling with which many listeners—particularly male listeners—in the declining industrial Northeast could identify. It may have been Springsteen's world, but his growing legion of fans also recognized it as their own.

Back in September, when the album came out, Springsteen had thrown a house party at his place in Long Branch. A lot of his friends from the Upstage days were there, including Southside Johnny Lyon, whose newest band, the Asbury Jukes, now had its own deal with CBS Records. During one break in the party, he had cause to look out the window and saw "all these people waiting to get a glimpse of Brucie, just sitting under the streetlights, not saying anything." With the release of *Born to Run*, Springsteen finally crossed over into stardom, and those fans who creepily waited on the street outside his house party were just the tip of the iceberg—the flip side, if you will, of going double platinum and getting to meet Bob Dylan and Phil Spector. Years later when Springsteen ran into Brooks Arthur, the man who ran the wretched 914 Studios out in Blauvelt, he told him, "You know the Blauvelt Diner? That was the last place I could get breakfast and read the paper!"

PART TWO

THE POWER STATION

Bruce Springsteen, Wembley Stadium, London, England, 4 July 1985.
© Neal Preston/CORBIS.

CHAPTER 6

I'LL BE THERE ON TIME AND I'LL
PAY THE COST (1976–1979)

On 29 APRIL 1976, BRUCE SPRINGSTEEN AND THE E STREET BAND played the Ellis Auditorium in Memphis, Tennessee. It was their fifth show in the state in a little over a week, part of a monthlong southern swing that would subsequently take them through Alabama, Arkansas, Mississippi, and Louisiana—the motherland of American music, even for a bunch of boys from Jersey. The previous night they had played the Grand Ole Opry's new digs in Opryland. The 4,500-seat hall was only two-thirds full, but a reviewer from the *Nashville Banner* gave the performance a solid rave.

The bulk of the show that night in Memphis was pretty typical for this second leg of the *Born to Run* tour, which had begun four weeks earlier, in March, and would run through the end of May. The set began with "Night." The band had rarely performed that song in the fall, but they now found it useful as a full-on stem-winder for unfamiliar audiences in bigger venues. All the other songs from the new album were predictably in the set, except for the quiet, spare "Meeting across the River," which they had tried only two or three times and which never really worked in halls this large. There were three songs each from *Greetings* and *Wild and Innocent*, and a lively cover to end the show: what the band had taken to calling the "Detroit Medley," a ten-minute mash-up of Mitch Ryder and the Detroit Wheels' greatest hits.

Most striking about the sets on this tour, compared with Bruce's performances even as recently as a year ago, were the onstage monologues. Especially after Marc Brinkman's addition as lighting director and the reconfiguration of the band into its current lineup, Bruce had been using onstage anecdotes to set up or bridge between songs. Starting in the fall, though, the anecdotes had changed: they became more personal, more frankly autobiographical. In mid-September, Bruce started telling a long story to introduce the band's dreamy cover of Manfred Mann's 1966 hit "Pretty Flamingo." The story took place in the summer of 1969, between the time Bruce's parents had moved out of the house on South Street and when he had gotten evicted from it. The first recorded version of the story featured Steve and Mad Dog (his bandmates at the time), but by the time he got to Memphis, Bruce had turned it into a tall tale, with Clarence (whom he didn't even meet until 1971) riding by on a bicycle in short pants and playing saxophone with no hands. Still, the core of the story was plausible, and personal. It was about not having the nerve to ask a pretty neighborhood girl her name and finding an echo of one's shyness in a recent pop single. *I never, I never found out what her name was or anything, you know, but that's good,* he told the audience in Memphis that night, *I still think about her sometimes, you know . . . We had this name at the time that we used call her, remember that name, Steve?,* and with that question Bruce slid very smoothly from his seemingly rambling story into the song.

Coincidentally or not, more personal anecdotes had started to enter Springsteen's set just as he was about to hit it big, when he was clearly poised to move from a cult club success to a bona fide rock star. Even if it wasn't a conscious strategy on his part, telling such stories was a good decision: they humanized him and brought him back down to normal size even if the halls he was playing had gotten larger and larger. Even the story he told about hitting the big time, to introduce "Growin' Up" and "It's Hard to Be a Saint in the City," emphasized his formerly plebeian status. As in Nashville the night before, in Memphis Bruce introduced the songs as if he were speaking to aspiring musicians. *You go to New York to get your big break,* he told the crowd, *you gotta have a manager, you gotta have an attorney.* Such stories probably reflected both the way Bruce wanted the audience to see him and how he wanted to see himself at that time, even as his new celebrity status was changing his life forever: as a guy like any other and a New York outsider who had just happened to hit it big.

But another significant story had also entered the set in the fall. It introduced the band's cover of the Animals' "It's My Life," and it was nowhere near as warm and fuzzy as the saga of the lost flamingo of Freehold's South Street. Bruce had added it at the very end of the first leg of the tour, so on this spring swing even most repeat concertgoers were probably hearing it for the first time. This story took the singer's audience inside the former Springsteen home for the very first time. He told what it was like to find his dad waiting up for him, a beer in one hand (not his first of the night), and a lit cigarette in the other providing the only light in the room:

> *If we came in around 10 or 11, it was never too bad. If we came in around 1, 2 in the morning, past midnight, I'd always have to hope I can make it through the kitchen before he'd stop me and make me sit down with him and talk to him about something, whatever was on his mind. First, he'd just start talking to me about what was going on in school, but pretty soon, he'd start asking me where I was getting my money, who I was out with, where I was, what I was trying to do with myself. Pretty soon we'd be screaming at each other and my mother'd be running in from the front room, try and keep us from fighting with each other. I'd be running out the back door, telling him how it was my life and I could do what I wanted to do.*

At that point, Bruce launched into a particularly lugubrious reading of the first verse of the Animals' 1965 hit. His performance of each verse of the song enacted the same emotional journey that he had taken during the monologue that preceded it: starting out low and slow but rising to a height of crashing anger, with Max's drums doubling his passion as the barely contained explosion of feeling spilled out of him. On surviving recordings, the routine is a little unnerving. Both the song and the story that preceded it set loose in Springsteen an extraordinary rage to which his audience hadn't been party before, neither during this particular performance nor in his previous stage personae. A month before the Memphis date, in a concert at Duke University, the students had listened with mouths literally open as

Springsteen went into excruciating detail about what life had really been like on South Street back in 1967. Wailing about *suicide machines* and *last-chance power drives* in all their mythic glory was one thing, but talking about actual knockdowns with your real-life alcoholic father was something entirely different.

Where was all this rage coming from? Repeated every night, it was clearly a performance, but it still didn't seem like an act. Springsteen was usually a collegial performer, one who typically liked to stir up only safely energetic emotions in his audience. At first glance, it seemed out of character for him to ask fans to help him work through his oedipal strife, the way a performer like Lou Reed or the late Jim Morrison had been only all too eager to do. And just last August, when talking to Jay Cocks for the *Time* article, Bruce had seemed at peace with his father.

"It's My Life" usually served on this tour as a transition between "Spirit in the Night" and "Thunder Road," between a song about aimless partying and one about purposeful escape, and that was one hint why this particular song mattered enough to be included in almost every concert that Springsteen gave for a year. Viewed in context, the performance seemed, more than anything, like the singer's reaction to the backlash of the last six months. He'd never comment on his harshest critics directly, at least not onstage, but he was always willing to use a song to express how he felt, particularly if it was a cover. Springsteen could be as kind as can be to his fans, but when critics started asking whether he was talentless, prefabricated, and undeserving of his "sudden" success, it may have felt as if he was back in that dark kitchen on South Street, trying to justify his decision to make music his career. And if Springsteen's stage show was turning into an act of theatricalized self-revelation, in early 1976 his rage at those who called him an overrated phony had to be included in it too.

The rage, though, rated just one song out of eighteen that night in Memphis. Most of the concert was about sheer fun and non-autobiographical dramatics. The main set, as usual, ended with "Rosalita," and when Bruce came out to do the encores, he had a surprise for the audience. Since the success of *Born to Run*, Bruce had been meeting his idols one by one—back in March at the Beacon

Theatre in Manhattan, Carole King had even invited him up onstage to join her in her encore performance of "The Loco-Motion"—but tonight was something different: Eddie Floyd, one of Springsteen's favorite musicians, was agreeing to come up on *his* stage and perform with *him*. Three weeks earlier, Bruce and the band had started using Floyd's "Raise Your Hand" as one of their rotating choices for the encores, but tonight they tried his "Knock on Wood" as well, with a little bit of the less well-known "Yum Yum I Want Some" thrown in for good measure. As Floyd left the stage before the band launched into the show-closing "4th of July, Asbury Park" and "Detroit Medley," Bruce once again paid tribute to the elder musician. *[T]hat's the man that wrote the book*, he exclaimed. *Oh yeah goddamn, that's the man that wrote the book there.*

Springsteen, as one sniping critic had put it, "certainly respect[ed] his elders." He was, as he himself had recently screamed at the end of a concert in Louisville, *just a prisoner . . . of rock and roll!* So since he was in Memphis and never got to sleep until dawn anyway, after the concert he, Steve, and Glen Brunman, the CBS publicist for the tour, happened on what must have seemed like an obvious course of action: take a cab out to Graceland and go jam with Elvis Presley. The fact that they hadn't been invited was a mere technicality. As with Floyd's music, Bruce had been slipping a cover of one of Elvis's songs ("Wear My Ring around Your Neck") into his encores on and off for a year and a half now. And surely the King of Rock 'n' Roll must read either *Time* or *Newsweek.*

On the night the E Street Band played the Ellis, Elvis Presley was onstage at the City Auditorium Arena in Omaha, giving a performance that was nothing at all like the one that had dazzled Bruce in front of his parents' television set nearly two decades before, let alone like the one that Springsteen himself had given that very night in Memphis. "[W]hen he first walked onstage," one backup singer later recalled of this particular Presley tour, "he'd be half asleep. If you watched his show, you'd sometimes see him looking over at us, pleading with those eyes. We'd make more racket, try to get him going, he'd pull through it somehow. I've seen him sometimes when he was glassy-eyed. I thought, he is gonna fall."

None of this mattered to Bruce Springsteen in April of 1976, and the contradiction in that is vaguely touching. Even this early into success, he already didn't like it when he was abstracted and turned into a type, whether negative or positive—but he was still perfectly comfortable reducing his childhood idol to a type without thinking on his own dislike of it.

Bruce, Steve, and Glen didn't make it past the security guards at Graceland that night, let alone to the Jungle Room. Bruce did jump the fence, though, in true Jersey fashion, and stood on the lawn just to say that he had done it.

SPRINGSTEEN'S LOOK HAD changed since moving to bigger venues. He had taken to wearing suits onstage—never with ties, sometimes with jackets, and always perfectly planned. That night at the Ellis, he had worn matching black pants and vest, with the collar of his white dress shirt pulled out over the vest the way so many men would wear it in a disco back then. It was a far cry from the blue jeans and multicolored T-shirt he had worn in Lenox, Massachusetts, the previous summer on the third night of the tour (even if he sometimes still donned his trademark oversized newsboy cap, which worked equally well with both kinds of outfits). It was around this time that Springsteen also began paying close attention to the band's appearance as well as his own. "You wouldn't wear anything that Bruce didn't want you to wear," as one close observer of the backstage rituals on a subsequent tour would observe. "Springsteen and the E Street Band were going to sound and look like a cohesive group of individuals." Not that any particular look would be set in stone, though, either for Springsteen or for the band. He hadn't found the exact look he wanted yet, and he was always tweaking it. After the *Born to Run* tour was finally over, he made an even more radical change: he shaved. One night, visiting Davey and Boom backstage at the Main Point after a Tone gig, he had a beard, and the next night he didn't. The next time he sat in at the Stone Pony, some people in the audience didn't even recognize him.

And even bigger changes were afoot. Early 1976 was the first time that the business of Bruce Springsteen turned a profit, at least in a theoretical sense. In the first quarter of 1976, the singer moved over one million units for the record company and was finally earning more in artist royalties than he was receiving in advances. That was a profit for that quarter, however, not for Springsteen's overall accounting. He and his manager still owed the label for all the monies advanced during the previous three and a half years, particularly during the big publicity push surrounding the launch of *Born to Run*. Even after the expensive marathon recording sessions at the Record Plant to finish the album were already completed, between July 1975 and March 1976 over $445,000 had been advanced to support and promote Bruce Springsteen and the E Street Band, 15 percent more than had been advanced during his first three years at the label combined. CBS's big gamble that summer and fall had paid off, but the true cost of that promotional jump-start was meant to be amortized over the next few years' worth of sales and touring. For right now, even as a star, Springsteen himself still wasn't making much money.

All through the winter and spring, various projects were envisioned as follow-ups to the big success of *Born to Run*: broadcasts, concerts, tours, studio albums, live albums, even a biography (which ultimate true believer Dave Marsh had already begun to write, using the Bottom Line shows of the previous August for his opening). Old Tin Pan Alley hand that he was, Mike Appel was thinking that spring about striking while the iron was hot. Before Bruce's star faded—how long did rock stars last anyway?—he wanted him to cash in and pay off Laurel Canyon's considerable debt. He was thinking he could get half a million dollars for a radio broadcast; a million dollars to headline a New Jersey Bands concert at JFK Stadium in Pennsylvania; sky-high fees for a six-thousand-seat tent tour of colleges during the summer that they could organize themselves. Maybe they could finally do a two- or three-disc live album, which Appel had been trying to sell CBS on for years. Bruce, for his part, wanted to go back into the studio: he had some new songs he wanted to record. Moreover, he emphatically wanted to go into the studio again with Jon Landau, who more than anyone else (including both Steve Van Zandt and Mike Appel) knew when to defer to Springsteen's stubborn instincts.

In retrospect, both Appel and Landau have been portrayed as greedy during this period of Springsteen's career, each trying to steal the singer away from the other solely for the purpose of hoarding the goose that laid the golden eggs. Judging by the totality of their actions, however, especially during the lean years, both men appear to have been sincerely true believers in the First Church of Springsteen. They just differed about where Springsteen should go from there, now that they were no longer wandering in the wilderness. Landau, for his part, thought it was too early in Springsteen's career for a live album: it would lock him into a certain stage show for a year or two, which was madness when he was still so productive. In the end, Landau's view prevailed on this and on a number of other issues, not necessarily because it was Landau's view, but probably because it was closer to Springsteen's.

The last straw for Appel seems to have been the news that Springsteen was planning on going into the studio in August to record his fourth album with Landau as his sole coproducer. In early July, Appel notified CBS Records president Walter Yetnikoff that, per his contract, Bruce could not record for CBS without the participation of Laurel Canyon (that is, himself or a producer approved by him as his representative). Three and a half weeks later, Springsteen's new lawyer Bruce Lundvall filed suit against Mike Appel, Laurel Canyon Management Ltd., Laurel Canyon Ltd., and Laurel Canyon Music Inc. (the renamed Sioux City Music) for "Fraud, Undue Influence, Conversion and Misappropriation of Funds, Breach of Trust, and Breach of Contracts and for an Accounting," as well as compensatory and punitive damages in the amount of one million dollars. Two days later, Appel countersued Springsteen, with the manager pretty much asking for the converse of what the singer now wanted.

The crux of this conflict lay in the contracts that Springsteen and Appel had signed in the spring of 1972, when the idea of having a hit record, let alone being on the covers of both *Time* and *Newsweek*, seemed like a far-away pipe dream. Bruce had never signed directly with his record label, only with Laurel Canyon, and Laurel Canyon had in turn signed agreements with CBS Records. Consequently, Appel seemed to be completely within his rights to say that Springsteen could not record with CBS Records without his explicit approval. More troubling still for Springsteen was the fact that, through Laurel Canyon Music, Appel held at least a half interest in all of Springsteen's music publishing for his songs. Clause 8 of the contract even allowed Laurel Canyon (that is, Appel, since Jim Cretecos had bailed out of that two-man corporation two years earlier) to make "such changes, adaptations, dramatizations, transpositions, editing and arrangements" of Springsteen's work as it deemed fit without any input from the songwriter himself, right down to "the setting of words to the music and the music to the words."

Thirty years later, Springsteen would tell an interviewer that the contracts he signed with Appel were "not evil but naïve." Garry Tallent, even more shrewdly, called them "old school," which was exactly what they were: they reflected the music business as Mike Appel had understood it when he entered it during the 1960s. Back then, before the singer-songwriter boom, this sort of producer/manager/publisher arrangement was fairly standard. As late as 1968, when David Geffen had helped Laura Nyro break an earlier publishing contract, her new arrangement with Geffen awarded him a quarter of her publishing royalties. This was considered good management, even though Geffen never claimed to know a thing about songwriting. In 1975, though, such a contract increasingly seemed atavistic, which was why Springsteen's attorneys had persuaded him to file such an extravagant lawsuit against his manager.

Did anyone in this situation really think that Mike Appel had somehow squirreled away a million dollars over the last few years? Probably not. The man was notoriously frugal, even in his private life. The full accounting that Springsteen's lawyers demanded in the suit ended up showing that Appel hadn't made much more than Springsteen had over the last four years: most of the Laurel Canyon money had been plowed back into the business of spreading the gospel of Bruce. What Springsteen, Landau, Yetnikoff, and Lundvall probably expected was that the high sum of money demanded in the lawsuit would make Appel blink. They were all forgetting, however, how stubborn the manager could be, even in the face of overwhelming evidence that might make his stubbornness seem ill considered. If Mike Appel had been prone to easily acquiescing, Bruce Springsteen's recording career probably would have ended sometime in early 1974. In the summer of 1976, Appel certainly wasn't happy that Lundvall indicated in his correspondence that Laurel Canyon was responsible for Springsteen's legal fees as well, since it seemed to be the lawyers who were most stridently implying that he had cheated the singer. Every week, more lawyers, accountants, and record executives were offering their two bits about what should happen next with Springsteen's career, which must have driven a hands-on, waste-free manager like Appel crazy. Against all conventional wisdom within the music industry, Appel did not blink at the lawsuit. He dug in for a fight.

For decades, Appel would insist that the suit was something that CBS and Landau had talked Springsteen into, in order to break his original contracts and negotiate a new, direct deal with the record label. But there was more to it than that on Springsteen's side. During the depositions, Springsteen's true ambivalence about his new success became clearer. At times, the lawsuit seemed to be a way for him to work through the first steps of what his new, more successful life was going to be like. To begin with, Springsteen was clearly uncomfortable having so many people working for him. When a band has no money, you all just pile in the van and drive from gig to gig. When he was called on it, Springsteen was more than willing to grant that all the people who now traveled with the band should get paid well for what they did—but that was the heart of his problem with Laurel Canyon too. "I have been cheated," he interjected at one point during the legal proceedings, technically off topic. "I wrote 'Born to Run,' every line of that fucking song is me and no line of that fucking song is his. I don't own it. I can't print it in a piece of paper if I want to. I have been cheated." Springsteen's extemporaneous wording on this occasion makes it clear that he was not just talking about monetary royalties. Far more important to him was free and clear ownership of his art, and the autonomy to do with it whatever he wanted.

In the wake of stardom, Springsteen was enraged, even depressed. Success seemed to leave him less in control of his life rather than more, as he made clear in a new, dolorous song he premiered at the Monmouth Arts Center in Red Bank on 3 August 1976. Technically, "The Promise"—or "The Loser," as it may have been called at that first performance—was another car song, about four buddies (Johnny, Billy, Terry, and the unnamed narrator) who had raced cars in the distant past. But from that very first version of the song, one of the friends (Terry) *worked in a rock 'n' roll band*, and ever since most fans have assumed that rock and not cars is what the song is really about. The narrator of the song *won big once and hit the coast*, but now for some reason *spend[s] a lot of time alone*. For the narrator of "The Promise," success is a Pyrrhic victory: when you *win big*, you also *pay the big cost*: the *broken spirits* of those you leave behind, as well as the precious, hand-built creations that don't belong to you anymore, because you traded them away for money. At the beginning of the song, what the narrator has foolishly sold away is a hot rod, the *Challenger*, that he *built . . . by myself*, but by the second verse we realize that he has lost something far more valuable than a mere car: *I lived a secret I should've kept to myself*, he tells us. *But I got drunk one night and I told it.*

Springsteen's live performances that fall (variously called the "Chicken Scratch tour" or the "Lawsuit tour") were a practical necessity. With recording shut off, record sales slowly dropping, and debts to CBS still outstanding, he needed a steady stream of current income. The Red Bank shows that launched the tour occurred one week after Springsteen's lawyers filed suit against Appel and about two weeks before his first deposition in the case. For the first leg of the tour, August through November, Springsteen and the band traveled with a horn section: the "Miami Horns," who normally played for Southside. They brilliantly augmented the core E Street Band sound, especially on "Tenth Avenue Freeze-Out" and "Raise Your Hand." The sets became even tighter than they had been on the *Born to Run* tour, with a core of about eighteen songs that were played most nights. These included at least three regularly performed new songs ("Somewhere in the Night," "Frankie," and "The Promise") that suggested that Springsteen's next album would be more wistful than the last, although still centered on hot rods near the beach.

I've got like a half of the next album written, Springsteen told the audience on the second night of the tour, but four months later he suggested something very different during a further deposition in *Springsteen v. Appel*. "I have started countless numbers of songs," he reported in his testimony, "which I have been unable to develop to their potential for lack of a proper recording opportunity." Up to then, he had never gone into the studio without at least half a dozen good songs from which he could work his way toward a common thematic or stylistic thread, the sort of seed idea around which he could pull together an album. This time, except for "The Promise," none of the new songs he'd premiered live was up to the admittedly high standard that he had set with *Born to Run*, not even "Rendezvous," the fun date song he played second every night on the tour, between "Night" and "Spirit in the Night."

Between legs of the Lawsuit tour, the Asbury Jukes recorded their second album, almost exactly one year after the first, much more like the sort of schedule that CBS would have preferred for all its artists. Bruce could not legally perform during these sessions, but he and Steve did cowrite three songs for the album. Writing songs for the Jukes was as easy as playing in somebody else's band: you didn't have to worry about what you wanted to sound like or say. You just fit into somebody else's groove. In January, Bruce did play during the sessions that Steve supervised for Ronnie Spector, including the recording of "Say Goodbye to Hollywood," a song that his labelmate Billy Joel had written especially for the singer on whom so many white boys of their generation had had crushes in their teens. The single was released as being by "Ronnie Spector and the E Street Band," but Bruce was in there too, as everyone except Appel seems to have known at the time.

In February, Bruce even had his first no. 1 single—as a songwriter. Manfred Mann had returned the favor for Bruce's frequent covers of "Pretty Flamingo" by recording a cover of "Blinded by the Light." Whether it was the track's pulsing synth riff, its significant lyric change (*douche* for *deuce*), or the fact that the song was now slow enough that you could actually follow, if still not understand, many of its words, the single shot straight up the U.S. charts. Back on tour again at that point, Springsteen significantly did not perform the song—he didn't play it at all that year—but he did add two more new songs to the set: an instrumental party song called "Action in the Streets" and a straight-ahead guitar rocker called "Don't Look Back." This last song fruitfully paired the get-out-of-town hopefulness of "Thunder Road" with the explosive rage of the "It's My Life" monologue (including the echoing fury of Max Weinberg's drums).

Finally, in May, ten months after the suit and countersuit had been filed, Mike Appel agreed to a settlement. He was winning the legal case but losing in the court of public opinion, largely as a result of Landau-sympathetic articles that were appearing throughout the music press, particularly in *Rolling Stone*. (As Robert Christgau might have agreed, this was in fact a much truer proof of there being a "rock critical establishment" than the initial success of *Born to Run* had been.) Under the terms of the settlement, Bruce was released from all his Laurel Canyon agreements. In return, Appel would get $800,000, a five-year production deal for the now Springsteen-less Laurel Canyon at CBS, and shares of the profits from Bruce's first three albums. In practice, the first of these terms was the only one that mattered: CBS wasn't really interested in any of the manager's other acts, and Appel ended up selling his share of the publishing rights (now reduced to 25 percent) back to Bruce several years later when his management business went south. Appel had started the job by taking Springsteen seriously as an entertainer, but it was now Jon Landau's turn to finish it by taking him seriously as an artist.

The day after the settlement, Bruce and Steve drove to Philadelphia to see Elvis Presley play the Spectrum, where they had played with the E Street Band almost exactly six months earlier. The concert was disappointing, but they still thought it might be fun to write a song for Elvis, so Bruce created a low, smoldering song that would be perfect for Elvis's sneer. The plan was to record a demo during the sessions for the next album and send it out to Presley later that summer. Maybe they'd get to see the Jungle Room yet.

WHEN LANDAU, SPRINGSTEEN, and the E Street Band finally entered the studio in early June, they hit the ground running. In later years, legend would hold that the band laid down twenty tracks the first night in the studio, but that is almost certainly an exaggeration. Springsteen did come into the studio, however, with at least seven songs already written: the five that he and the band had worked into the live set over the last year or so ("Rendezvous," "The Promise," "Frankie," "Something in the Night," and "Don't Look Back"); the

Presley number ("Fire"); and a slow, longing song called "Drive All Night," which had grown out of a half-sung monologue that Bruce had recently been slipping in near the end of performances of "Backstreets." There were also an almost crooning ballad ("One Way Street") and two fun rockers ("I Wanna Be with You" and "Outside Lookin' In") that seem to have been fully formed fairly early on.

These songs were finished, but very quickly Springsteen turned his attention in the studio to songs that were not, songs for which (unlike those on his first three albums) he had written music first. One extensively worked-out early track was simply called "The Fast Song." Other early instrumentals were attached to one or another of the titles that Bruce kept in lists in his songwriting notebooks. Even when he later superimposed a separate vocal track onto such a recording, some of the lyrics were still clearly placeholders. In a reverse of what happened on his first album, this time the music came first, the words second.

In similarly sharp contrast to the recording process for his last two albums, the sound for the next album came into focus very quickly that summer. Two and a half years of touring with Springsteen had made the E Street Band a very precise and responsive unit for the interpretation of his songs. He depended on the specific gifts of each band member, particularly Roy's supple piano playing and Max's clockwork drumming. Indeed, the drums were rapidly becoming a more important part of the arrangements for this album than they had been on his first three. Springsteen also benefited from the regular presence of Steve in the studio, as well as Jon, both of whom probably led to this emerging album sounding more like what the average 1970s American fan would have called a "rock" album, with highlighted guitar solos, crashing drums, and the like. On many tracks, the obligatory E Street Band sax solo almost sounded like an afterthought. This time, anything even vaguely Spectorish was simply out of the question.

Even with almost a year's leadtime, Springsteen still wasn't sure what he wanted to specifically say on his fourth album. However, he did know the general sort of material he wanted to touch on. In later years, Springsteen has said that he went into the studio that summer explicitly intending to sing in some way about class on his next album.

As his output with Steel Mill would suggest, though, social or political songwriting had never been his strong suit, no matter how "Dylanesque" people might have found him to be. Like learning a more artful use of figurative language five years earlier, learning how to write about class in a less than heavy-handed fashion would take time for Springsteen, and a lot of trial and error.

After several frustrating months at Atlantic Studios, the band began recording at the Record Plant, and fairly rapidly a number of tracks for the new album began to fall into place: first "Don't Look Back" in July, then "Something in the Night," "Badlands," "Streets of Fire," and "Prove It All Night" in the early fall. All these tracks shared an emotional temperature: the tempered rage that had powered Bruce's performances of "It's My Life" for the last year and a half. Even the originally wistful "Something in the Night" acquired in the course of multiple revisions an enraged howl at the end of its choruses. In terms of its general instrumentation, the music on this emerging rock record certainly sounded "whiter" than the tracks on *Wild and Innocent*, but the soul shouting that Bruce affected in his vocals on many of the tracks was clearly rooted in 1960s African American singing styles. You could hear James Brown in the concluding shouts of "Badlands," as well as the "cornbread singing" of such favorite vocalists as Solomon Burke and Sam Moore throughout a track like "Streets of Fire." Bruce was now undoubtedly singing about the circumstances of his own life; and he was far less likely than on his first two albums to adopt the vocabulary or verbal tics of a subculture in which he had not actually lived. In these specific senses, the content of the new album was undeniably "white," but the sound of the vocals that communicated that content was still surprisingly "black."

Like "Daddy Raised a Cain" (or "Adam Raised a Cain," as it would come to be called by the end of the fall), all these new shouting rockers were not just about class, but more specifically about class resentment. They were about the situations of restricted possibility into which you were *born*. If "Born to Run," "Thunder Road," "Rosalita," and all the other get-out-of-town songs of the last five years had emphasized the urgent present, these songs emphasized the scarring past, as well as the people left behind who were not going to get out. These were songs not just about *cages* and *death traps* but about "Rat Traps," as Dun Laoghaire's Boomtown Rats would put it in a single of that title that they were laying down on the other side of the Atlantic that summer, "and you got—caught." As a result of this thematic focus, fathers became crucial to Springsteen's new project in a dual sense: as objects of oedipal rage (as in the Steinbeck/Kazan-inspired "Adam Raised a Cain") and as objects of filial pity (as in the more plaintive "Independence Day," which Bruce and the band laid down in September). The impossibly looming fathers in these songs have both maintained the larger trap into which their sons have been born and fallen victim to as well.

Aside from *Daddy's house*, the other setting that looms over these songs is "the Circuit," the loop formed by Kingsley and Ocean Avenues, just west of the boardwalk in Asbury Park. After the closing of the Upstage, nearly all the clubs left that mattered were on those two streets—the Sunshine In and the Student Prince were across Kingsley from each other; after they closed, the Stone Pony opened just around the corner on Ocean—but the music wasn't necessarily why the Circuit mattered. During the week, Asbury Park was pretty much a ghost town, but weekend nights it was along those streets that hot-rodders raced. The Circuit was the named setting of "Something in the Night" and was the implicit setting for one of the more successful slow songs that Springsteen was developing for his fourth album.

In terms of Springsteen's emerging album, "Racing in the Street" provided a necessary contrast to a brasher, more confident breakout song like "Badlands." Its lyric offers yet another glimpse of characters much like those from "Thunder Road," now seen two or three years on. In the wake of Springsteen's extraordinary intervening success, the song posits a haunting "what if" situation. What if you can't get out of town? What if you have to stay there and get a boring job and have a life? Maybe weekends are the only escape you have, but this song does not present us with a mere bacchanal of respite as "Spirit in the Night" does. As in "The Promise," here we see the rebuilding of cars as a creative endeavor, with the specific details of the car's reconstruction proudly noted out of a craftsman's pride. In the former song, the construction of the emblematic *Challenger* was purposefully set out as an aesthetic parallel to the construction of a band's *million-dollar sound*. In the latter song, the components the narrator uses in each version convey the attention he gives to the smallest aspects of his necessary leisure: knowing the difference between a *'32 Ford [with] a 318* in one case and *a '69 Chevy with a 396* in the other is as important for the song's narrator as choosing between a Stratocaster and a Telecaster was for his creator.

As so often happened with Springsteen, the way the arrangement of this song evolved in the studio implicitly sharpened the meaning of its lyrics. In one early take of "Racing in the Street," the band's sound rises and rises with each ensuing verse of the song, creating a sense of increasing triumph, as the final studio arrangement of "Thunder Road" had more appropriately done. In this case, however, such a one-dimensional reading of the song would reflect only the situation of the narrator. In the arrangement that finally made it onto the album (and has been in effect for virtually every live performance of the song since then), the first and second verses rise triumphantly, but the sound steps down, becoming quieter and more minimalist, when it reaches the song's final verse. In what are probably the most remarkable lines of the lyric, the narrator tells of his girlfriend: *She stares off alone into the night / With the eyes of one who hates for just being born.*

One of the reasons why "Racing in the Street" was so essential to the thematic structure of this project was that it implicitly admitted in this last verse that such individualistic efforts may not be enough: the narrator may have racing on the Circuit to keep him sane and whole, but his girlfriend doesn't have anything like that. At a number of points, "Racing in the Street" echoes the themes and even the words of Brian Wilson's 1964 Beach Boys hit "Don't Worry Baby," but the nonracing young woman in Springsteen's song has so much more solidity than the one in Wilson's. As in "For You" and "Thunder Road," the few details we pick up about her in the lyric make us want to hear more. Even with the little we do learn about her in this lyric, it seems more than possible that a *ride to the sea* won't be enough to solve her problems, especially if it's only a block away from the narrator's beloved Circuit.

By early October, Bruce and the band had two-thirds of a good album done. As usually happened when Bruce spent this much time in the studio, he began to let off steam by spitballing songs he would probably never use in this particular project. He kept the more personal discards, but he gave away several of the better pastiches. In what had become an annual ritual now, Southside would get "Hearts of Stone" and "Talk to Me" for the third Jukes album, while neo-rockabilly star Robert Gordon would get "Fire." Elvis Presley had died in mid-August. Whether Springsteen's demo of "Fire" ever got to him before his death is, at this date, still a matter of urban legend.

At the end of October, the album needed at most one or two more tracks to be finished. One came in the form of "The Promised Land," another song like "Racing in the Street" that would be overtly anchored on record and in performance by Roy's vaguely countryish piano. From its title forward, the song feels like an answer to "The Promise" (which was still in consideration for the album at this point), or like a further evolution of its thoughts. By early November, they had a satisfactory take of "The Promised Land," and it seemed as if they might have an album. It would be called *Badlands*, and mock-ups were even made of a possible album sleeve with a brooding Bruce on the front cover and a far-from-cuddly Clarence on the back, both dressed in almost solid black. It would be a short album, only eight tracks, as *Born to Run* was, but with briefer songs on the whole, and with three of the quieter completed tracks left off: "Something in the Night," "Drive All Night," and—most significantly—"The Promise." As happened with the western-themed album that he might have released five years earlier, Bruce had simply outgrown his own thoughts of only a year before.

Still, into November he puttered, recording at least one song with the band ("Give the Girl a Kiss") that felt like a throwback to *Born to Run*. The undistinguished ballad "Let's Go Tonight" was stripped of its lyrics and changed into Bruce's most sympathetic father song yet, a short number simply titled "Factory," which drew on Doug Springsteen's time working at Freehold's A&M Karagheusian Rug Mill. Another slow song already slated for the album shifted gears, as pieces of "Candy's Boy" and "The Fast Song" were strapped together to create the unrelenting and not at all loping "Candy's Room." Then, as they were mixing down *Badlands*, Bruce suddenly presented everyone with a new song, "something like a tone poem," as he would later call it.

"Darkness on the Edge of Town" was probably one of those titles that Bruce had had kicking around in his notebook for ages, but the song that ultimately bore that title seemed to come together very quickly that November. Of all the songs on the album, of all the songs he had ever written to this point, this one took place more than any other in a highly personal Nowhere that could be called nothing but Springsteenland. The song's references are specific without being particular. To show how much sharper Springsteen's lyrics had become since *Greetings from Asbury Park, N.J.*, there is no problem following what he is saying here, even if we are left to ponder some of the lyric's more elliptical implications. There are *Trestles* in this town, as well as the invented and biblically named *Abram's Bridge*. The narrator in this song may be the same one as in "Racing in the Street" (just as the narrator in "The Promise" may have been the same one as in "Thunder Road"), and so the [ex-]*wife* in this song may be the so-called *little girl* in that lyric. But the place where she now lives, the rotely named *Fairview,* could be located in so many communities in the United States that its name serves as both a cliché and a universal symbol.

This landscape is sketched in the song's first verse, and in the second the narrator tells us how he got there. Like the narrator of the now discarded "Promise," the narrator of "Darkness on the Edge of Town" has a *secret*. This second verse implies that he ended up under the bridge because he let that secret *drag him down*. Much time can be wasted on speculating exactly what the narrator's secret is in this song, but in such an emblematic landscape, the most important thing he tells us is that in this he is not unique. *Everybody's got a secret Sonny,* he informs us at the beginning of the verse, *Something that they just can't face.* It's a weight, a millstone or sandbag, that some people— perhaps even the narrator's ex-wife—*cut loose* in order to rise above it.

But if the narrator's ex-wife has truly risen, and the narrator has correspondingly fallen, then why in the third verse of the song does he sound so triumphant? As the warier "Arabian Nights" had given way during the completion of *Greetings* to the giddy "Blinded by the Light," so now the depressive success of "The Promise" gave way as Springsteen finished his fourth album to the victorious failure of "Darkness on the Edge of Town." The narrator of this later song doesn't sit by a window bemoaning his fate, even though it would seem to be much worse than the one that so shattered the narrator of "The Promise." He stands *on that hill with everything I got,* neither running out of town (as the narrator of "Thunder Road" did), nor resigning himself to a flickeringly meaningful existence (as the narrator of "Racing in the Street" might do). He stands his ground, with eyes wide open about exactly who and where he is. *That kind of character,* Springsteen said years later, *comes forward and he asserts his will,* which is *the only thing he has . . . the only thing he can give out.* With that last verse of this song, Springsteen has said, "I'd found my adult voice."

IN THE LATE 1970s, Bruce Springsteen wasn't the only one trying to figure out what extraordinary success might have to do with rock 'n' roll. A month after Springsteen finally found his Yes in thunder in the completed base take of "Darkness on the Edge of Town," newly crowned rock god Johnny Rotten (né John Lydon) actually did what the narrator of "The Promise" only dreamed of doing: he *took it all and threw it all away.* On 17 January 1978, Rotten's band, the Sex Pistols, played Bill Graham's Winterland in San Francisco, a 5,000-seat hall at which Springsteen and the E Street Band would also play two dates later in the year. This was the Sex Pistols' last show of a brief, perversely scheduled U.S. tour, during which both their manager, Malcolm McLaren, and the mainstream U.S. press had treated them as more of a traveling freak show than a rock band. By the last night, Rotten was clearly fed up.

"You'll get one encore and one encore only," he told the audience when he came out at the end, "because I'm a lazy bastard." The Pistols programmatically played the same encore they did every night on this tour: a cover of the Stooges' "No Fun." "This is bloody awful," Rotten declared at one point during the song, and he was right: his mate Sid Vicious was a drug-addicted cartoon on bass and Paul Cook and Steve Jones were, as always, there to pick up a paycheck. Finally, Rotten simply said to the audience, "Ever get the feeling you've been cheated?" and walked offstage, thus ending the Pistols (for the next few decades at least) and creating a true rock legend. Within a year, Neil Young would link Johnny Rotten with the recently deceased Elvis Presley in the lyrics of "Hey Hey My My," the song that framed his classic 1979 album *Rust Never Sleeps* in acoustic and electric versions, the song that Nirvana's Kurt Cobain would quote in his 1994 suicide note.

When you read most histories of rock music, Bruce Springsteen and Johnny Rotten are something of an either/or proposition. If you emphasize one, you deemphasize the other, because, of course, Springsteen was "classic rock" and the Sex Pistols were "punk." In the most common twenty-first-century view, those two forms of music are supposed to have nothing to do with each other. Back in the late 1970s, though, when rock 'n' roll was trying to resurrect itself after yet another alleged generic death, matters weren't quite so clear. For one thing, it's important to remember that whatever "punk" may have meant to later generations, in 1975 it didn't mean to most people what it means now. Many of the reviews of *Born to Run* that fall (most notably Lester Bangs's review in *Creem*) had used the word "punk" to describe Bruce Springsteen's persona. "Punk" was a leftover term from 1950s greaser culture, Bowzer or the Fonz without the edges rounded off. Moreover, throughout the late 1970s, Springsteen remained very much embedded in the milieu of what later came to be seen as "New York punk."

Most important, though, Springsteen and the more successful punks like Lydon faced the same late 1970s career choices. The process of institutionalization that had so affected rock by the time of the Hullabaloo clubs during the late 1960s reached its zenith during the late 1970s, as rock 'n' roll became one of the biggest businesses around. Depending on how you looked at it, punk was either the greatest challenge to that commodification or its greatest exemplar. Once you started playing 5,000-seat halls on an extended tour, you'd have to be a fool not to notice that you were a product, packaged if not necessarily made by a multinational corporation, and very much pre-identified by your audience before they ever heard a note of your music. If (like both Springsteen and Lydon) you weren't just in it for the money or the laughs, but rather because you thought you had something to say, this was troubling. Was it possible to be an artist, or even just a soul with an individual message, when your audiences entered your concerts with such a predetermined idea of what you were going to do?

This dilemma by no means originated in the late 1970s, even if it did seem to peak then. Indeed, it had been outlined in considerable detail months before the Sex Pistols ever played their first gig by rock critic Greil Marcus in *Mystery Train: Images of America in Rock 'n' Roll Music*, a book that Dave Marsh for one later insisted had been the primary influence on "The Promise." In his book, Marcus stressed the covenant or "promise" between the rock star and his audience. "The best popular artists," Marcus suggested, "create immediate links between people who might have nothing in common but a response to their work." This, he theorized, presented the popular artist with a "choice": ignore the audience that has gathered around him (which gives his work "all the vitality and strength it had when he knew it mattered to other people"); or accept their "image" of him and "lose himself in the audience." In terms of the artists that Bruce Springsteen had grown up idolizing, these choices were respectively embraced by Bob Dylan and by Elvis Presley: run away from fame and hole up in upstate New York so that there will never again be even a fleeting possibility that anyone will ever mistake you for the voice of a generation; or become a bloated parody of yourself when you were young and cool, in Las Vegas and other assorted unchallenging venues. John Lydon, for one, knew he did not want to end up like Elvis Presley, so he left the Sex Pistols, pulled a Dylan, and formed Public Image Ltd., an entirely different sort of band, with his friend Jah Wobble.

When Springsteen wrote "The Promise" in 1976, he might have been willing to do the same thing, just as he had been willing to go back to basics years earlier after the frustrations of the Chicago tour. But something in him changed during the *Darkness* sessions. They burned away the anger and depression he had felt in that first burst of stardom and allowed him to conceive a third alternative, a more mature grounding for his future relations with his audience. After all, "The Promise" betrays a certain romantic naïveté about being a rock star: it insists that art is a *secret* that is lost if shared, a credo that seems better suited to a career in avant-garde poetry than to one in popular music. The real challenge, the one that both Dylan and Presley had stared down and blinked first at, was to see if you could continue to create true art while being a booming business as well.

To do this, you couldn't go out onstage and repeatedly deliver the kind of rote set that had eventually driven John Lydon to chuck his previous work altogether. You had to work within your audience's expectations and yet advance them to another level, continually enlarging both their understanding and your own. To put it another way, you had to remain familiar to your audience but still never be fully or flatly "known."

As Springsteen has made clear on a number of occasions, "Darkness on the Edge of Town" is not a song about homelessness or substance abuse, even though it is certainly possible to read many of its lines in that way. For him, this is another of his songs about art, the kind of song he frequently wrote when he was getting ready to finish up an album. "Blinded by the Light," "The E Street Shuffle," and "Tenth Avenue Freeze-Out" had all captured stages of Springsteen's distancing himself from Asbury Park, turning the place where he had learned how to be a musician and performer from coded present to mythologized past. "Darkness on the Edge of Town," by contrast, is in no way a song about memories of the Upstage. *That last verse*, Springsteen observed during a 2003 concert, *always reminds me of the artist's promise to his audience, and the challenge that he throws out to his audience too: that if I'm going there, you're coming with me. I'll be on that hill with everything I got*, he says, throwing down the gauntlet to fans who may just want him to write good-time party songs. If you want my truth, my *secret*, you can have it. That's my job. *I'll be there on time and I'll pay the cost.*

But, as he would tell a reporter from *Crawdaddy* when *Darkness on the Edge of Town* was finally released, as far as he was concerned, there was a transaction cost on the audience's end too. "You wanna ride, you gotta pay," he told the interviewer. "And maybe you'll make it through, but you ain't gonna make it through 'til you been beat, you been hurt, until you been messed up. There's hope, but it's just the hope of, like, survival." As both Springsteen and his narrator in this song truly believe, in the *darkness* is the one place where things of consequence can happen, there *on the line where dreams are found and lost*. Only when there is enough true risk can true gain be possible, not just for the widely popular artist but also for his ever-growing audience.

THE TEST OF THIS wager came in the tour Springsteen made to support *Darkness* during the second half of 1978, one of the most legendary tours in the history of rock 'n' roll. The band hit the road in late
May with an embarrassment of riches. Ten tracks from the Record
Plant sessions were released on *Darkness,* but there were two or three
times as many other tracks that were just as strong but had been
rejected as not being quite right for the album. Not only was Bruce
regularly including many of these unreleased songs in his sets, but
thanks to about a dozen FM simulcasts of his concerts that year (not
to mention the bootleg albums that those broadcasts inevitably
spawned), it was almost as if fans were getting a full second album's
worth of Springsteen music. By the end of the tour, he seemed to
expect that the audiences would know not only his officially released
songs but the unreleased ones that he was performing regularly as
well. He treated "The Fever," "Fire," and "Because the Night" as if
they were old favorites, even though none of these songs had ever
appeared on an official Springsteen album.

On 1978's *Darkness* tour, Bruce Springsteen and the E Street Band
gave 112 concerts, performing 74 different songs. By comparison, four
years earlier, when the band first appeared in this configuration, they
performed only 24 different songs during the entire fall tour. During
the late 1970s, the peak of "arena rock," such variation was the exception rather than the rule. For example, during the same seven months
that Springsteen toured, Black Sabbath mounted a tenth-anniversary
tour in support of its recently released album *Never Say Die!* At 93
American and European dates, Black Sabbath, with only two or three
exceptions, performed the same 17 songs at every performance.
Granted, it performed a shorter set, with bands like Van Halen and the
Ramones opening for them at different points on the tour, but still the
disparity is striking. Even with sets averaging around 23 or 24 songs,
the E Street Band kept at least three times as much material ready as
it actually needed on any given night.

The broader structure of the sets on the *Darkness* tour was pretty
much the same from the first date to the last. The concert was broken down into three parts: two main sets separated by an intermis-

sion, each set containing about ten songs and always lasting over an hour, the latter set followed by an encore of about half a dozen songs that usually lasted at least half an hour. Bruce gave each of these segments tent poles, clearly planted songs that rarely varied from night to night, much like the "four corners" he had by now learned to lock in place when finalizing the contents of a two-sided LP. Indeed, the sets on this tour almost always started the same way *Darkness* did as an album, with "Badlands." It was a great way to get the crowd's energy up, to get their butts out of their seats and their minds out of the parking lot. Through the end of August, the second set opened with a similarly lively new song, "Paradise by the C," an instrumental iteration of the same basic musical idea as the lately recorded "So Young and So in Love." For his set closers, Bruce eventually chose more familiar songs off *Born to Run*, although by no means that earlier album's more triumphant songs or singles. Just as the new "Badlands" inevitably came at the beginning of the first set, "Backstreets" nearly always came at the end of the second, sending the audience into the brief darkness just before the encores with one last burst of tortured emotion.

Early in the tour, before the new album was out, Bruce followed the opening explosion of "Badlands" with a considerable helping of older songs early on, as a way of getting audiences acclimated. For the most part, though, the older Springsteen songs functioned on this tour much as the covers had on the last one. Once the album was out and familiar to Bruce's audiences, he could juxtapose older and newer songs as a way of demonstrating the links between the ideas he had put forth in 1975 and those that he was putting forth in 1978. Following "Badlands" with "Night" and "Spirit in the Night" placed Springsteen's new credo that *it ain't no sin to be glad you're alive* in the context of two earlier, less socioeconomic articulations of the same impulse. Similarly, for the first month or so of the tour, Bruce purposefully juxtaposed "Born to Run" and "The Promise" during the encores, introducing "The Promise" on 26 May at the Spectrum in Philadelphia, for example, as *the first song I wrote after* Born to Run.

What made this reiterated journey feel like more than mere numbing repetition was the way Springsteen's presentation of his mediated thoughts and feelings would vary from concert to concert in response to the reactions of the fans who attended. As he found his own voice and mature personality as a performer, Springsteen discovered that he was neither Bob Dylan nor Elvis Presley, but he wasn't Johnny Rotten either. He was ultimately more collaborative with his audiences than any of those three performers, which is why an album like *Darkness on the Edge of Town*, great as the songs on it were, was ultimately incomplete when it was merely recorded and not yet performed.

Indeed, the care that Springsteen gave to adjusting and fine-tuning the setlists on this tour from night to night suggests that, even though he had finally gotten out of the studio in May of 1978, he was still tinkering with this material straight through to the end of the year. John Sayles, with whom Springsteen would collaborate during the mid-1980s, has spoken of his own multiple jobs as a filmmaker as separate stages of the compositional process, likening the screenwriting, directing, and editing of any of his films to the customary three drafts he writes for any of his novels. In terms of music, the same seemed to hold true for Springsteen from this point on. First there would be the songwriting, then the recording, and finally the tour—three distinct but linked sequential phases through which he articulated and sharpened his artistic vision.

Near the end of the tour, on 15 and 16 December, Bruce and the band played two shows at Winterland. Back in July, they had played the Berkeley Community Center, another, smaller Bay Area venue owned by Bill Graham, for many of the same audience members. In fact, Springsteen's comments from the stage on 16 December suggest that there were even people who came to both of his Winterland concerts, the beginning of a common pattern of behavior among die-hard fans. Springsteen knew this, and he made sure that the two Winterland shows were notably different, two distinct performances with certain common elements, which bore a fraternal rather than an identical resemblance to each other.

The first concert, on Friday, the fifteenth, was the starker one. Four songs in, Springsteen dedicated "Darkness on the Edge of Town" to author/activist Ron Kovic, who lived in San Francisco and whose arresting Vietnam memoir *Born on the Fourth of July* he had read the previous year. Most nights on this tour, the song after "Darkness" was a tribute to Springsteen's father, and on this first, more somber night at Winterland, when he knew his dad was across the bay in San Mateo listening to the simulcast on KSAN, he offered a rare live performance of "Factory," invoking in his speech before it the haunted house on South Street once again. Two songs later, he grimly introduced "Prove It All Night" by rapping *I remember when I was a kid . . . I used to think . . . that if I was ok, everybody else would be too . . . and that 'long as when I went to bed and I said my prayers that everything'd be all right . . . but you find out . . . you gotta prove it all night, every night.* Throughout the concert, songs like "Streets of Fire," "The Ties That Bind," and "Mona" lent the proceedings a general air of gloom that even the band's seasonal cover of "Santa Claus Is Comin' to Town" (performed both nights) could not completely shake off.

On Saturday, the sixteenth, however, the mood was entirely different, from the second Bruce stepped out on the stage. *How many of you guys were here last night?* he asked at the top of the show, receiving a surprisingly loud volley of cheers. *Who* wasn't *here last night?* he quipped, and there was another volley. *Well, this is tonight,* he announced. He then proceeded to open the concert not with "Badlands" (which came second this night) but with a cover of "Good Rockin' Tonight," one of Elvis Presley's first singles on Sun Records and a cover itself of Wynonie Harris's 1949 original. The fun only continued from there. Two songs later, "Rendezvous" replaced "Streets of Fire," making "Badlands" and not "Spirit in the Night" the tonal odd song out early in the set. Three songs after that, "Independence Day" replaced "Factory" as the song for his father, with a quicker, less lugubrious dedication, simply noting that this was another song that had been left off *Darkness.* On Saturday, when introducing "Prove It All Night," he didn't cast any dark shadows on either the song or his memories of his childhood but instead called out engagingly, *Is San Francisco ready to prove it all night?* This second concert felt much more like the kind of house party that most of the shows on the fall 1975 tour had been.

Most of these selections were variants that Springsteen had already worked out in earlier concerts, choices he and the band could make depending on how they read the mood of a particular audience. The most striking of these options was the different ways they presented "Racing in the Street," a song that they appear to have performed at every stop on the tour as the third song before the end of the concert's first set. Some nights he'd let the song slip by with a vague dedication to drivers, people who never had a car when they were young, even his sister Pam, who had just gotten her learner's permit. Other nights he'd speak at greater length about the Circuit back in Asbury Park, lending his desolated former neighborhood a sort of epic grandeur.

Some nights, though, Springsteen did not give his audience a thematic context for "Racing in the Street" until after he had sung it. On Saturday night at Winterland, during the instrumental stretch that Roy used to modulate between that song and the next, Bruce told a variation on a story he had been using since the Roxy shows down in LA the previous July:

> *Back in 1974, 1975, I was walking by this movie theater, and it had this poster of this Robert Mitchum movie. It was this great picture and I took the title of the movie and I wrote a song, but I never thought there was any place that was like this—you know, like this song. . . . And me and Steve, we drove from Utah down to Reno, Nevada [last year], and along the side of the highway, we came upon this house that this Indian had built out of stuff he'd scavenged off the desert, and it had a big picture of Geronimo out front. Underneath it, it said "Landlord," and it had this big white sign painted in blood-red. It said "This is the land of peace . . . love . . . justice . . . and no mercy," and it pointed down this dirt road . . . that said "Thunder Road."*

Suddenly, with the harmonica glissando that followed those words, both "Racing in the Street" and "Thunder Road" were now about a lot more than cars. The juxtaposition between them, and the anecdote that connected them, brought the wider themes of Springsteen's new album to light, almost serving as a thesis statement just before the end of the first set of this second Winterland show. If the early blast of

"Badlands" just after "Good Rockin' Tonight" had made defiant survival in an unforgiving environment seem like fun, then "Racing in the Street" and "Thunder Road" showed the characters further on, maybe worn down, maybe suddenly renewed, but in no way as cockily defiant as that earlier narrator had seemed. After this, the first set ended, as usual, with "Jungleland," in which the desperate scramble for some kind of meaning is raised from a personal to a societal level, in which a whole state's worth of characters *take [their] stand* against a world that seems stacked against them.

The Winterland shows of December 1978 are fondly remembered by Springsteen fans, and the Friday night show in particular would probably make most fans' lists of the top four or five concert bootlegs of his career. It's important to note, though, that neither of these was a "historic" concert, as the Sex Pistols' stand in the same venue eleven months earlier had most assuredly been. In terms of Bruce Springsteen's career, however, the *Darkness* tour marks an unmistakable turning point. Now that he had begun to grow accustomed to playing larger venues, Springsteen found a way to make his concerts part ritual without being rote. By the latter part of the tour, he was regularly taking his audiences on a journey backward through time: from his most recent songs in the first set, through earlier and more obscure material in the second, to his feel-good hits and greatest influences in the encores. Such concerts were an act of reconstruction, rather than deconstruction, in which the performer rededicated himself on a nightly basis to his youthful dreams, realistically placing them within the more troubled context of his late 1970s adulthood. On this tour, direct autobiographical revelations like the "It's My Life" story didn't matter as much as they had two or three years earlier. The form itself of the concerts now allowed the singer to pick apart his musical, and sometimes even personal, past in a far less explicitly revelatory fashion.

Even at the first, more somber Winterland show, the encores celebrated the sort of raw, live energy that had led Springsteen to dedicate himself to rock 'n' roll in the first place. During the climactic rendition of Eddie Floyd's "Raise Your Hand," he refused to accept that members of his audience could feel tired or listless—even if they weren't actually in the hall.

*I wanna tell everybody who's listening at home. . . . I want you
to get up, I want you to turn up the radio as loud as it'll go. . . .
I want you to open up all the windows in Sacramento and
Eugene and Seattle and Portland and San Francisco, if you're
driving your car, roll down the window, when you get to the
light, jump, jump out, dance around in the street, get back in,
hit your head on the steering wheel, and drive on . . . and if the
cops come knocking at your door, send all your complaints to
Bill Graham care of Winterland, San Francisco.*

This was a goof, of course, near the end of a show that lasted nearly
three hours, but underneath the joke was an implicit contract that
Springsteen now took very seriously. If pop stardom as Greil Marcus
had theorized it three years before was going to work to its best rather
than its worst effect, then Springsteen's audience had to be as fully
committed to the act of live creation as he was. He could make no
hermetic Dylan withdrawals, but they should expect no dead Elvis
rituals either. What was the point of rock 'n' roll if you weren't all alive
in the now?

CHAPTER 7

AIN'T NOBODY LIKE TO BE ALONE
(1979–1982)

*B*Y THE TIME THE *DARKNESS* TOUR ENDED IN CLEVELAND ON New Year's night 1979, Bruce Springsteen was one of the most widely respected American rockers of his generation. He might not be to your taste, but anyone who heard or saw him knew that his performances were sincere, passionate, and committed.

But you couldn't call him satisfied. Something was missing, something he still wanted. On the most superficial level, beyond his current critical success, there was a wider popular success that still eluded him. He was an FM hit but not an AM hit; a rock star but not yet a pop star. For an old WMCA fan like Springsteen, some of it may have been a matter of numbers, for there was still one long-held professional goal that he had never attained: he had never had a Top 10 single. In fact, he hadn't even had a Top 20 single. For all the publicity, "Born to Run" had peaked at no. 23, and none of his other five singles had even come close to being that popular. Instead, his songs seemed to yield big hits for other people. According to photographer Lynn Goldsmith, Springsteen's girlfriend from late 1977 through early 1979, he was particularly upset about the notable success of the Pointer Sisters' "Fire," which had rapidly followed Robert Gordon's version, sold a million copies, and spent two weeks in the late winter of 1979 perched at no. 2 on the pop singles chart.

Early 1979 was a strange time for an almost thirty-year-old rocker with Springsteen's tastes. Disco and other kinds of heavily produced dance music overwhelmingly dominated the American singles and albums charts. An old favorite from a decade before like "Knock on Wood" was becoming better known in Amii Stewart's tricked-out, technified remake than in the original Stax version by Bruce's idol Eddie Floyd. Both the Rolling Stones and Rod Stewart were self-consciously embracing the new style, the former for a few tracks on the prior year's *Some Girls*, the latter for an entire album on the currently popular *Blondes Have More Fun*. A surf-loving CBGB band like Blondie was having a spectacular success with "Heart of Glass," a number that had begun as a parody bluntly called "The Disco Song." Frank Zappa, perhaps the ultimate cult rocker, was having the biggest hit of his career (so far) with an even more overt disco parody called "Dancing Fool." The previous year at the Universal Amphitheatre, *Saturday Night Live*'s Dan Aykroyd, in the aggressively retroed persona of Elwood Blues, had decried the recent rise of "pre-programmed electronic disco"; and come summer, old-school rock fans would hold a "Disco Demolition Night" in Chicago's Comiskey Park, lighting a pyre of 12-inch dance singles before a White Sox–Tigers game.

For his part, Springsteen didn't mind disco. He embraced it, as he tended to embrace nearly every movement in popular music as it came along—he would even write a song for Donna Summer a few years later—but he also knew enough to understand that he and the E Street Band were not going to make a disco record the way the Stones had. And the one thing of which Springsteen was most certain as he sat down to imagine his fifth album in the winter of 1979 was that it needed to be a "band" album, not a solitary artistic statement with band backup as all his albums up to this point had been. Springsteen had come off the 1978 tour with a renewed appreciation of the musicians with whom he regularly played, and in this next round of recording, he wanted to show them off at their best. His last two albums featured songs about confinement and desperation. Maybe now it was time to make an album about fun.

He already had a good place to start: all the tracks he had rejected for *Darkness*, the good songs he had discarded in his dogged quest to provide that album with a unified thematic feel. Before even stepping back into the studio, Springsteen had at least a dozen solid unreleased songs that existed either in polished studio takes or in well-worked-out live arrangements. In the first half of 1979, he made private solo record-ings of two dozen other, new songs, laid down for the most part on a cheap cassette player in his house in Holmdel, New Jersey. Few of these early-1979 home recordings are aesthetically interesting in and of them-selves, but taken together they give a suggestive glimpse of what Spring-steen may have thought a "good" pop single needed to sound like.

More than anything, what Bruce seemed to be hearing most as the sound of potential hits was the music of the Byrds. That band had been officially split up for six years now, but their peak had really only been from 1965 to 1967, a lifetime ago in popular music. Their influ-ence, however, had run fairly deep: they had been one of the first post-British Invasion American bands that had proven to be more than just one-hit wonders. Tom Petty, a Floridian four years younger than Springsteen, had had three hits in the last year that were clearly inspired by the sound of the Byrds and especially by the unmistakable rhythm guitar work of Roger McGuinn, the group's founder and leader. For Springsteen's purposes, the Byrds' combination of jangly guitars and subtly complex vocal harmonies was a good model for him to use in his own work now that Steve would be performing alongside him on a regular basis. Harmony vocals in particular had been a con-sistent part of Springsteen's music from the Castiles through the Bruce Springsteen Band, but it had been almost wholly absent from his first four albums, as he pursued a solitary, singer-songwriter path. Using the Byrds' sound as a model (rather than Phil Spector's or Van Morri-son's), the E Street Band could now begin to contemplate making music with Bruce Springsteen rather than just for him.

In the lead-up to recording *Darkness*, rehearsals at Springsteen's house in Holmdel had been a necessity, since he couldn't legally record until his lawsuit with Mike Appel was resolved. Two years later, in late March of 1979, Springsteen began the process for his fifth album with rehearsals at his home as well, using these sessions to determine which new songs might work best with the group. At least eight songs never made it out of those rehearsals. Others fell into place very quickly, particularly "The Ties That Bind," a harmony- and multiguitar-laden track that could easily have been written in 1967 and that the band had already performed a few times on the *Darkness* tour. There was also a song about a girl who watches too many movies and expects her real-life relationships to conform to what she sees on the screen that Springsteen kept reworking under various names that spring: first as "White Lies" in April, then as "Mary Lou" in May, and finally as "Be True" in July. These two songs, along with such other tracks recorded during this period as "Hungry Heart," "I Wanna Be with You," and "Bring on the Night," are as bright and sparkling as the *Darkness* tracks are dour and enraged. When a song clicked during these sessions, it frequently clicked in a single base take, in part because Springsteen wasn't trying to create a new sound with such songs but rather to revisit an old, familiar one.

Still, even if many of these early-1979 tracks worked as bar band numbers or garage band tributes, as examples of Springsteen's song-writing they represented something of a step backward. For the most part, they possessed neither the densely populated texture of the *Greetings* songs nor the sparer symbolic resonance that Bruce had begun to court on *Darkness*. Few of these songs are about anything in particular, as the best Byrds, Creedence, and even garage band singles of the previous decade usually were. They lack the specificity of place, feeling, or relation that made even the cheesiest Sun, Motown, and British Invasion hits lodge firmly in American cultural memory. In the first few months of recording at least, Springsteen's fifth album didn't have a theme to hold it together—it had a sound.

In June, Springsteen and the band went out to LA for Marc Brinkman's wedding, and at the reception they jammed with such other Brinkman clients as Ricky Lee Jones and Boz Scaggs. Springsteen was never one for religion, but something about the rabbi's remarks at the service moved him. As he would relate onstage repeatedly during his next tour, *the rabbi got up and he said that till you go out and make that connection with somebody, until you meet a girl or you go out and meet just a friend or a person, all the things that you dream about when you're a kid and all the fantasies that you have of making your life as complete as it can be, they just stay dreams and fantasies. If you don't go out and make that connection,* Springsteen emphasized, voicing a theme that would dominate his work for the next three decades, *you end up just being like a ghost, like nobody can hear you, nobody can see you . . .*

Inspired by what the rabbi had said, that night in his hotel room Springsteen wrote a haunting song called "Stolen Car," about a man in a troubled marriage who drives around estranged not just from his wife but from everyone he sees. Although it was not necessarily a fan favorite, Springsteen has repeatedly cited this song as an essential transitional work for him. From a technical standpoint, it represents one of his first successful attempts to imagine the inner as well as the outer lives of one of his characters, particularly of a human being whose experience differs from his own.

It's also worth noting, though, that "Stolen Car" is the third in a series of songs (almost certainly the most interesting ones that Springsteen had written so far that year) in which he tried to imagine what it might be like to be married, maybe even to be a parent. In the home demos he had recorded back in the winter, there were four takes of a song called "Oh Angelyne" that were based on the current situation of his brother-in-law, who had married Ginny twelve years earlier after she had gotten pregnant with his child but who had recently been laid off from his construction job. That song was mournful, eerie, but Springsteen still hadn't completed it to his satisfaction, so it never made it to the band rehearsals, let alone the Record Plant sessions. But the very first track he and the band had completed at the Record Plant in April was "Roulette," which reimagined the recent failure of the nuclear reactors at Three Mile Island through the eyes of a father who fears the incident will lead to the death of his children. It says something about Springsteen's state of mind in early 1979 that the married and parental reality in such songs seemed much more real than the countless variations on dating and single life in many of his other, more colorless songs from this period.

Until the trip to LA in June, marital and parental connection had not been a theme on which Springsteen had chosen to focus in his songwriting. It just kept popping up. Once he and the band returned to New York after the Brinkman wedding, however, such themes became more prominent. New songs like "The Price You Pay" and "Loose Ends," of which there are no recorded traces before late July, still contained the sweet late-'60s harmonies that had prevailed during the spring recording sessions, but the lyrics sung to those harmonies now focused on older, more shattered, less optimistic characters than those in the earlier songs. "Stolen Car" was attempted at least three times in late July, and it was also around this time that the sole available take of "The River" (the completed version of "Oh Angelyne") was recorded. In a clear sign that Bruce seemed to be reaching the end of some process, there now emerged spin-offs, songs that differed markedly in style from the bulk of what had been recorded so far. In this case, Bruce's spin-offs seemed to be more overtly "country" songs: a new "roadhouse" number called "Ramrod" about motorcycles; a rockabilly take on "You Can Look But You Better Not Touch" from the winter and spring demos.

By mid-September, there was general agreement that the album was almost finished, and a Christmas release was even planned. Of the over two dozen songs that the band had been playing since April, ten were picked for the album's two sides. The first side would feature mostly "up" songs (including "Hungry Heart" and "Be True"), while the latter would feature more contemplative ones (including "The Price You Pay" and "Loose Ends"). Nearly all of the selected songs fell in that same Byrds-like stylistic vibe with which Springsteen had begun the project. The only exceptions were the country-tinged "Stolen Car" and "The River," which stuck out here as much as "Mary, Queen of Arkansas" and "The Angel" stuck out on *Greetings*. But Springsteen liked and was proud of these songs, even if they didn't fit in with all the rest. When he and the band headlined two charity concerts at Madison Square Garden on 21 and 22 September for Musicians for Safe Energy (MUSE), "The River" was the only new song that they played.

As had happened repeatedly in the past, Springsteen's creative impulses were a moving target. Shortly after the MUSE concert, the singer declared that *The Ties That Bind* (as the initial version of his fifth album was supposed to be called) needed to be rethought. "The exuberance of the audience at MUSE," as Dave Marsh has paraphrased one version of Springsteen's thinking, "had just made the [planned] album inadequate." This was a vague complaint, however, and Springsteen's subsequent attempts at resolving this nebulous "inadequacy" proved similarly vague.

Two years earlier, the eleventh-hour reformulation of *Badlands* into *Darkness on the Edge of Town* had been a matter of focus and clarity. This time, however, the pullback and rethinking didn't focus Springsteen's forthcoming album. Instead, it made it sprawl. Rather than using a few songs as a core and homing in on a mood or a style, Springsteen began duplicating the moods and styles of multiple previously recorded tracks, as if he were trying to finish three or four albums at once. There were at least a dozen new songs, probably written that fall, that never made it past the home demos, and another dozen that never made it out of a second round of rehearsals in Holmdel. A number of *Darkness* rejects suddenly returned during this second round of recording, including "Sherry Darling" (which had appeared in both MUSE sets), "Drive All Night," and "Independence Day." "Stolen Car" was reworked and cut again. Bruce and the band kept recording on and off for another seven months, eventually spending over a year in the studio. Then Bruce went out to Los Angeles and stayed there for another five months mixing the tracks, making for a year and a half of production, another two and a half years between albums.

Springsteen simply seemed incapable of turning out an album a year, the way that virtually everyone else in the music business (Tom Petty or the Rolling Stones, for example) tended to take for granted. In this case, it wasn't even clear why Springsteen was delaying his next album: it was supposed to be a fun batch of songs that could be played by a bar band, not an epic thematic statement as his last three albums had been. Indeed, in the final form in which it was released in October of 1980, *The River* (as it was called) was a two-record set, one disc per year for the time since *Darkness*, but neither disc had the conceptual or stylistic unity that fans expected from Springsteen. Both the songs and the sequences in which they were arranged seemed almost haphazard. Viewed in its totality, *The River* was at best an album with (as the title of one of its songs puts it) "Two Hearts." As Robert Hilburn would point out, one set of songs on the album evinced a form of optimism or "idealism," while another set presented a countervailing sort of fatalism or "realism." When Hilburn suggested this to Springsteen during an interview, the singer admitted that this collection of songs presented a "certain happiness that is, in its way, the most beautiful thing in life" side by side with a "hardness and coldness and being alone" that he felt was also at the heart of rock 'n' roll, every bit as much as the joyous rave-ups of a good Saturday night.

Schizophrenic grab bag that it was, however, when *The River* was released that fall it did exactly what Springsteen had intended. Despite its double-disc size, within two weeks the album had hit no. 1, the best-selling and fastest-selling album of Springsteen's career so far. More important, a week later, "Hungry Heart," the first single from the album, reached no. 5 on the *Billboard* Hot 100. Bruce finally had his Top 10 hit and was in regular rotation on AM radio.

IN THE SAME WEEK that *The River* hit no. 1, in a seemingly unrelated event, Governor Ronald Reagan of California was elected the fortieth president of the United States, garnering a whopping 489 Electoral College votes, while incumbent president Jimmy Carter received a mere 49. During the last days of the campaign, Bruce Springsteen and the E Street Band were on tour, of course, still promoting the month-old *River*, but they had election night off. The next night, on 5 November, they played a concert at Arizona State University in Tempe that was virtually identical to the one they had played in Los Angeles the previous Thursday—except that it was longer. *All you guys in the aisle find your seats, ok?* Bruce announced three songs in. *There's gonna be a real long show.*

That night Springsteen rambled, more than usual. Before the postindustrial triptych of "Independence Day," "Factory," and "Jackson Cage" midway through the first set, he began a long monologue, although not about his father, whom he frequently talked about before "Factory." Instead, Springsteen used this opportunity to talk about his love of pop music, about what it had meant to him growing up. Spontaneously, falteringly, he offered the most coherent argument he would ever make for the essential unity of the two distinct compositional strains that had flowed into *The River*, its idealistic and pessimistic "hearts":

> I *never did good in school, never did good, and they always figured that if you're not smart in school, it's because you're dumb.*

*But I always felt that I never really learned anything, or learned
anything that was important to me, till I started listening to the
radio back in the early 60s. And it seemed that the stuff that I
was hearing off the radio in all those great songs was stuff that
if they knew how, they'd be trying to teach you in school . . . but
they just didn't know how to. They always talked to your head,
they could never figure out how to talk to your heart, you know.
And it seems that, like all those singers and all those groups,
there's one thing that they just knew: what it was about. And
when I started listening, I found out that the first time . . . that,
instead of the fantasies that you have when you're a little kid, I
had dreams now and that they were different, it was different,
and that if that was possible, that I didn't have to live my life the
way that I was, that things could be better. If you just go out,
take a chance, find out what's going on. . . .*

It was only toward the end of the first set in Tempe that Springsteen
finally addressed the election. *I don't know what you guys think about
what happened last night,* he said as a transition between "The River"
and "Badlands," *but I think it's pretty frightening. You guys are young,
there's gonna be a lot of people depending on you coming up, so this is
for you.* When you listen to recordings of this concert, during this
speech you hear scattered cheers from the crowd, but nowhere near as
strong as when Springsteen actually started the next song.

Springsteen's comments before "Badlands" in Tempe that night
were virtually the first recorded statement he ever made about politics.
At the MUSE concerts a year earlier, he was practically the most apolitical performer on the stage. He had played a small acoustic benefit
for George McGovern's campaign at the Red Bank Drive-In in 1972,
but there is no other record of his ever endorsing a political candidate
up to this point, or even expressing displeasure with one as he did in the
wake of Reagan's election. In subsequent interviews, he would admit
that he had maybe voted once, but no more than that. Like the draft or
Kent State, politics was something that happened outside of his life, to
his life, while he was trying to make his dreams come true. And he was
obviously not the only American who viewed politics that way, espe-

cially not in the fall of 1980. Ronald Reagan's victory, much closer in the popular vote than in the Electoral College, reflected the will of about a quarter of the electorate; only a little more than half of those eligible to vote had done so that year. Like Bruce Springsteen, many other Americans at that point in our history were essentially apolitical.

But there's a subtle difference between politics and ideology, between elected officials and the policies they enact on the one hand and the underlying principles that cause people to trust or distrust politicians on the other. You can live your life without ever having an opinion on any elected official or legislative body, but you cannot live your life as an adult without having some notion of what a better world would look like. In the late 1970s, as the two dominant political parties in the United States reacted to contemporary economic crises by dissolving into ever greater procedural disarray, such utopian visions of what might work better suddenly became far more important. In 1979, however, only the college professors called this "ideology." The word that both First Lady Rosalynn Carter and the Reverend Jerry Falwell of the Thomas Road Baptist Church started using that year was "values."

In 1979 and 1980, as Bruce Springsteen crafted *The River* and began touring to support it, his politics were virtually nonexistent, but his ideology—his "values," if you must—was all over his songs. Springsteen believed in "freedom," in as vague a sense as any American would define it, in the freedom to head out where you wanted when you wanted with whomever you wanted with no bossman or exaggerated patriarch telling you what to do. On Springsteen's first four albums, his ideal world was the road, the way to the next great place but not necessarily the place itself, because all fixed places had the potential to trap you. In Springsteen's songs, success was seldom material success (no matter how much the singer might want it in real life). In most cases, the success his characters dreamed of or attained was mere survival, making their stand in an environment that was constantly trying to grind them down.

Half of *The River* reinforced this view, not only such *Darkness* survivors as "Sherry Darling" and "Independence Day" but such newer songs as "Ramrod," "Jackson Cage," "Out in the Street," and "Cadillac Ranch" as well. There were also all the new songs about connection ("I Wanna Marry You," "Fade Away," "Stolen Car," "The Price You Pay," "Drive All Night," and "Wreck on the Highway"), but they were about personal commitments rather than communal ones. Both these aspects of *The River* were undeniably ideological, but they were not political; they sought no help for their characters through governmental or collective action. Even in the album's title track, the characters' situation seems more mythic than political. In that song, Springsteen sings, *Lately there ain't been much work on account of the economy*, but there is no sense here that these characters' problems could be fixed by a government stimulus package or a cut in the mortgage rates. Their problems are synchronic rather than historical and must simply be endured.

But during this same period, as the nation around him felt adrift in an uncertain and uncommitted age, Springsteen was crafting his first specifically topical songs in almost a decade, since the trendy, epic antiwar songs he had written during the Nixon era. The most obvious of these was "Roulette," written in a white heat during the first week after the event at Three Mile Island but by all accounts never seriously considered for the album. Almost a year later, toward the end of the *River* sessions, Springsteen had also written the little gem "Held Up without a Gun," which managed to turn the most pressing political issue of the late 1970s—the exorbitantly rising price of gasoline—into a rocking good joke.

Indeed, with the gas crisis of the Carter years, history practically forced Springsteen to consider the political implications of his apolitical, personal ideology. In his pre-1979 songs, as in rock songs since at least Chuck Berry, cars and motorcycles were the vehicles of the individualized freedom that he craved. In the late 1970s, however, ration-starved cars and motorcycles became much more specific cultural symbols, emblems of how Americans saw their personal freedom limited by current events. Gas prices had been rising since the beginning of the decade, and in one day, 28 June 1979, OPEC raised the price of a barrel of crude oil by 24 percent. That summer, as Springsteen labored at the Record Plant, blocks-long lines at gas stations became a common, even violent occurrence.

Suddenly, Springsteen's favorite form of mindless fun had taken on economic, political, and even international significance. The two roadhouse numbers he and the band cut that fall, "Ramrod" and "Cadillac Ranch," spoke about the sheer fun of driving, in purely sensual terms that were a world away from the desperate tales of escape he had trafficked in on his last two albums. Simultaneously, though, in songs like "Stolen Car" and "The River," it was also becoming clear that cars could take you nowhere as well, that they could signify escape in the sense of avoidance rather than freedom. In many ways, the great lost album that Springsteen could have released but didn't in 1980 was a single disc of songs about cars, taking in the freedoms and restrictions that they made possible for his fellow citizens. It would have been a perfect project to release during a year in which driving was an implicitly ideological act.

The one song that would have tied all this together may have never made it out of the second round of rehearsals in Holmdel. "Chevrolet Deluxe"—a song whose individual title would also have made a great overall title for a car-themed album—was apparently one of the many songs that Springsteen wrote after the MUSE concerts. There were five aborted tries and one completed version of it on the second round of home demos, in which its eeriness makes it sound like a perfect companion piece to the similarly haunted "The River." As happened with many other songs, though, the band changed the way the song sounded: the two full-band rehearsal takes of it that we have from 15 November 1979 give "Chevrolet Deluxe" an even more appropriate, dreamy, Byrds-like feeling. In fact, the arrangement on which Springsteen and the band finally settled in the second of these takes is very reminiscent of the Byrds' 1967 version of Bob Dylan's "My Back Pages."

At its simplest level, "Chevrolet Deluxe" is a love song to a car, one more convincingly drawn than the narrators' girlfriends in such frivolous *River* tracks as "Crush on You" and "I'm a Rocker." At the age of seventeen, the narrator falls for the car immediately when he sees it on the lot, and he buys it and uses it to drive his friend Billy (yes, the same name as in "The Promise") to basic training at Fort Bragg. He drives it to businesses and factories, and later to streets full of closed stores, and he complains in the choruses about how he can no longer afford to keep it.

Obviously, this is not just a song about a car. It uses the car, an American car, to take the audience on an implicit journey through the last fifteen years of American culture and society, tracing a number of stages of the contemporary feeling of disempowerment shared by many white male members of the American working class: the Vietnam War that killed Bart Haynes, the deindustrialization that drove Doug Springsteen to leave New Jersey; the inflation and gas rationing that made the promised freedom of a beautiful automobile seem like a lie and a prison. Implicitly, what the narrator *buys* in this song is not just a product of the declining American auto industry but also a bankrupt American dream. In 1980, "Chevrolet Deluxe" was, without question, the most successful political song that Bruce Springsteen had yet written in his career, more pointed even than "Roulette" and more successful in capturing the dilemmas of its moment than any of his overtly antiwar efforts with Steel Mill.

And he decided to leave it off *The River.* He left off "Roulette," too, and "Held Up without a Gun," all three of the recently written songs that dealt most directly with the American working-class male's increasing sense of cultural impotence. Without these three specifically topical songs, what prevailed on the album were Springsteen's two ahistorical hearts: the optimistic, gleeful Saturday night rocker, who had heard the cry of freedom on WMCA radio and had hit the road for the last fifteen years to make his dreams come true; and the brooding, wistful, Sunday morning country fan, who increasingly feared that independence might end up being no more than disconnection.

Like many other Americans of his era, Springsteen was caught up in the "crisis of the American spirit" about which President Carter had spoken during that same brutal summer of 1979. This was another part of Springsteen's dissatisfaction during the late 1970s, a more abiding need than could be solved by a simple Top 10 single. He knew that something was missing in his life, that just driving off into the night wouldn't fill the absence he increasingly felt in his soul, but he was still nowhere near embracing Carter's solution to this crisis: increased civic involvement. "In a nation that was proud of hard work, strong families, close-knit communities, and our faith in God," Carter had declared, "too many of us now tend to worship self-indulgence and consumption." Springsteen obviously believed in hard work, but the only community he had ever been a part of was the Upstage. Ever the proud individualist, he was innately suspicious of virtually all systems, structures, clubs, and experts, even if they claimed they were trying to help him.

In other words, Springsteen's criticism of Ronald Reagan from the stage in Tempe was in no way a too-late endorsement of Jimmy Carter. It was simply a voiced suspicion of Reagan, who had been clearly labeled a public enemy of rock 'n' roll since Jeffrey Shurtleff's mockery of him at Woodstock at the absolute latest. Given his later admissions of political apathy during the 1970s, it is doubtful that Springsteen was acquainted with too many of the specifics of Reagan's political plat-form. He just seemed like the kind of person who wouldn't be too comfortable with "freaks."

Nevertheless, there was more truth than Springsteen realized to his knee-jerk statement that he didn't know what his fans thought about what had happened the previous night. What Springsteen probably didn't know at that time, but would become clear once the 1980 elec-tion results were more closely analyzed, was that the youth vote broke slightly for Reagan, with many of the youngest baby boomers casting their first presidential votes that year for the former California gover-nor. Moreover, Reagan received 49 percent of the Catholic vote, 40 percent of the union vote, and 24 percent of the votes cast by registered Democrats, all groups to which Springsteen had strong personal ties.

We will never know for sure, but statistically there is an excellent chance that many of the young women and men in Springsteen's audi-ence in Tempe who had voted the previous day had voted for Ronald Reagan. This may have seemed inconceivable to Springsteen, but if you weren't listening carefully, it was surprisingly easy to be a fan of both men that fall. Like Springsteen (not to mention the pop singers of the 1960s whom he so admired), Reagan *spoke to the heart, not the head*; he "made sense of the world narratively"; and he thought that structures and institutions tended to get in the way of individual effort—all attitudes surprisingly consonant with the ethos of a song like "Out in the Street," for example. The night before the election, Governor Reagan had even declared that he would be honored to lead what he called "the freest society the world has ever known." Until Bruce Springsteen started telling audiences what he thought about the Soviet Union or the size of the federal budget—until he told them specifically what he found *frightening* about the president-elect, which he did not do that night in Tempe—it was perfectly understandable for his more casual fans to think that he might be a "Reagan Democrat" too.

EVEN IN A PRE-INTERNET AGE, word of Springsteen's brief comment at Tempe spread, and the rock critical establishment was pleased. "[I]t is an almost certain bet," Greil Marcus wrote in *New West* seven weeks after the concert, "that the songs Springsteen will now be writing will have something to do with the events of November 4. Those songs likely will not comment on those events; they will, I think, reflect those events back to us, fixing moods and telling stories that are, at present, out of reach."

When Greil Marcus was shocked by the election of Ronald Reagan, he could collect his thoughts by writing an essay in which his usual twin concerns of democracy and rock 'n' roll could be intertwined with a consideration of Springsteen's forthcoming world tour. But even if Springsteen's ideas on these topics had been clear in the fall of 1980—and they weren't—he was not going to sit down and write an essay about them. He wasn't used to articulating his politics, or even his political ideology. He processed the election more performatively: not by writing new songs of his own, as Marcus and others wished. (It was too early for that.) Instead, he covered other people's songs.

These were a number of one-off covers that fall, sometimes performed to provide a local reference in the setlist, always added to change things up on a tour that seemed surprisingly stable. But by the time Springsteen returned to Madison Square Garden on 18 December, he had a new cover, one that would prove to be as much of a staple on this tour as "It's My Life" had been on the *Born to Run* tour: Creedence Clearwater Revival's "Who'll Stop the Rain." From the first, he placed the song in the body of the set rather than in the encores, indicating that it was not an afterthought but very much in keeping with the overall worldview of his own compositions. Ten days later at the Nassau Coliseum in Uniondale, Long Island, he dug farther back in the American song bag than he had ever done before, putting his own spin on Woody Guthrie's "This Land Is Your Land" and turning the tail end of the band's first set—which also featured, among other songs, "The River" and "Thunder Road"—into something of a harmonica showcase.

Unlike the one-off covers that Springsteen and the band had played during the first two and a half months of the tour, these two songs were keepers: they would perform them at most of their concerts in North America and Europe over the next nine months. Usually, either or both songs appeared in close proximity to "The Promised Land," Springsteen's self-consciously American credo of three years earlier. But while that song might be mistakenly tagged by a casual listener as vaguely Reaganesque, these Creedence and Guthrie songs were less individualistic and more collectivist in spirit. Both songs emerged from protest movements, in the late 1960s and late 1930s, and both implicitly took their listeners to task for not being involved in their nation or community. In introducing the Guthrie song, Springsteen repeatedly made it clear that he didn't see it as a safe third-grade sing-along number. He didn't necessarily sing the song's fourth verse (which questioned the presumptive sanctity of private property), but he did invoke the interpretation of the song that Joe Klein had advanced in his recent biography of Guthrie: that "This Your Land Is Your Land" was written as an "answer song" to Irving Berlin's "God Bless America." On New Year's Eve, Springsteen told an audience at the Nassau Coliseum that *this is a fighting song for you in the New Year.*

There were other, subtler changes in the tour as well. From its inception, the "Detroit Medley" had begun to occasionally include an "I hear a train" thread that ran through a roll call of all the tour's stops. Sometimes this would even provide an occasion for a song or a verse with a local reference. When the tour resumed after a break in January, the band also changed the style of the All Area Access passes that the musicians handed out for their shows. Instead of just having a single, common image for all stops on the tour, they began using local variations: the arch for St. Louis, Missouri; a corn cob for Ames, Iowa; a badger for Madison, Wisconsin; and so on. Few members of Springsteen's audience would see such passes, of course. Like the list of tour stops during the encores, this was a perhaps perfunctory acknowledgment of the individuality of each new audience, but it was a necessity for performers like the E Street Band who were seeing so many audiences in so many arenas, so many of which must have seemed virtually the same. Ultimately, such superficial gestures were probably there more for Springsteen than for the people who came to listen to him.

During a second break, in early April, just before the band started the first leg of its European tour, Springsteen did take a stab at writing some new songs, and they were not specifically about the election or its aftermath. Musically, these songs showed Springsteen continuing in a country vein, as he had begun to do for two or three songs on *Darkness* and for at least a full album side during the *River* sessions. Lyrically, for the first time in nearly a decade, he returned to the outlaw myths of the Old West with a brief snippet about "Robert Ford and Jesse James." Another, more developed song, "Fist Full of Dollars," took its title from a Sergio Leone western that had been released when he was in high school. The song itself, however, was set recently, measuring the impact of New Jersey's decision five years earlier to legalize gambling in Atlantic City. The song's first line, *Well they blew up the Chicken Man in Philly last night*, was taken almost literally from an *Asbury Park Press* headline about the Mafia-sanctioned bombing on 15 March 1981 of former Angelo Bruno lieutenant Philip Testa in South Philadelphia. This was the sort of writing that had yielded "Roulette" two years before: an immediate response to a current event.

Almost none of the other germs for songs that Springsteen worked on during this 1981 break ran for over a couple of minutes, but "Fist Full of Dollars" received two extended tries, first with a reliable Bo Diddley beat and then with a more rambling Bob Dylan–style accompaniment, à la the songs on *Bringing It All Back Home*. In a reverse of what had happened with the earliest songs on *The River*, this time Springsteen had a glimmer of the subject for his next album (violent crime), but he was still fiddling around for a sound.

The European tour through April and May continued Bruce's slow evolution away from the would-be party monster of just six months before. These were his first European concerts in almost six years, featuring more dates at larger venues than he and the band would have been able to book back then. Another Creedence song ("Run through the Jungle," John Fogerty's time capsule of the violence of 1970) was added to the set, opening most concerts for several weeks, and a John Fogerty solo single ("Rockin' All Over the World") tended to close the encores. After three years of trying, Springsteen finally found a reggae song he could make his own—Jimmy Cliff's "Trapped"—and on 11 May in Manchester, England, he dedicated "This Land Is Your Land" to Bob Marley, who had died in Miami that day, a little under two months after the Testa bombing and nearly eight years after he had shared a stage with Springsteen. Along with Reagan's political ascendancy, the deaths within a few months of both Bob Marley and John Lennon seemed to signal the end of a certain generous spirit in global rock and pop. Aside from the No Nukes movement and intermittent punk action against racism, popular music seemed as wholly separated from politics for most other popular musicians as it was for Springsteen.

Significantly, though, the dead artist about whom Springsteen spoke at greatest length that night in Manchester was neither Marley nor Lennon, but Elvis Presley. On this leg of the tour, Springsteen had begun to show a renewed interest in Presley, covering both "I Can't Help Falling in Love" and "Follow That Dream" at separate dates in Paris during late April. In Manchester, on the day of Marley's death, he premiered a song that suggested his own highly delayed reaction to Presley's death, introducing it by saying, *I think everybody remembers where they were when they heard that Elvis died. It's a hard thing to understand.*

Technically, "Johnny Bye Bye" had started as yet another cover, a revision of an old Chuck Berry song that had served as a quasi-prequel to the guitarist's "Johnny B. Goode." In Springsteen's hands, though, the song became a meditation not on Berry's "little country [read 'colored'] boy" but on Presley. In this reinvented form, it was no longer a consideration of how a mother might have felt about her son's huge success but rather a consideration of how fans might have felt when such success unraveled. Like "The Promise," "Johnny Bye Bye" is about stardom, but this time viewed from the fan's side of the equation. Willfully placing himself in a role he hadn't occupied in over half a decade, in writing this song Springsteen may very well have been trying to ensure that he didn't make the same mistakes that Elvis had. It wasn't the drug addiction that Springsteen was worried about. (He was notoriously drug-free.) It was the isolation and estrangement of which such addiction was usually a symptom.

"Johnny Bye Bye" was the only unrecorded song that Springsteen premiered on the entire *River* tour (as opposed to the wealth of unrecorded tracks that he had performed on the tour to support *Darkness*), and his most articulate statement about what the song meant to him came very near the end of the tour:

> *I remember when I was nine years old and I was sitting in front of the TV set and my mother had Ed Sullivan on, and on came Elvis. I remember right from that time, I said—I looked—I said "I wanna be just like that."*
>
> *But I grew up and I didn't wanna be just like that anymore. . . . I remember I was sitting at home when a friend of mine called and told me that he'd died, and it wasn't that big a surprise at the time, 'cause I'd seen him a few months earlier in Philadelphia. I thought a lot about it, how somebody who'd had so much could in the end lose so bad, and how dreams don't mean nothing unless you're strong enough to fight for 'em and make 'em come true.*

Springsteen made these remarks at a very special concert, a benefit that he and the band did at the LA Sports Arena on 20 August 1981 for the Vietnam Veterans of America Foundation. It had been nearly two years since the band's last benefit performance, at the MUSE concerts, and the transformation in Springsteen's stage persona could not have been starker. Although he had not said a word about politics at his concerts since the previous November, on this occasion Springsteen spoke about the Vietnam War, about how it felt this year to be an American abroad, even about what "Who'll Stop the Rain" meant to him. Since the band had started playing the song the preceding fall,

Springsteen had never given it a spoken introduction or explained why it fit with his own works. At the VVA benefit, he explicitly linked the song (written by John Fogerty, probably the greatest rock 'n' roller who was also a Vietnam veteran) to the war, and to his own guilt over not caring about the war as long as he knew that he himself would not have to fight in it. He confessed that his meeting with VVA members the day before the concert had felt awkward:

> I'm used to coming out in front of a lot of people and I realized that I was nervous, and I was a little embarrassed about not knowing what to say to 'em. It's like when you feel like you're walking down a dark street at night, and out of the corner of your eye you see somebody getting hurt or somebody getting hit in the dark alley but you keep walking on, because you think it don't have nothing to do with you and you just want to get home. Well, Vietnam turned this whole country into that dark street. Unless we're able to walk down those dark alleys and look into the eyes of the men and the women that are down there and the things that happened, we're never gonna be able to get home. . . .

Unlike the speech in Tempe, that night's speech about rock 'n' roll was attached to a song about a rock 'n' roller, and the speech about the struggle to end conflict that night was attached to a song about ending conflict. Shot through both public statements were profound, honest emotions on Springsteen's part: fear that stardom inevitably turned you into some kind of a zombie, and guilt over his lack of civic engagement. In the conclusion of his "Who'll Stop the Rain" rap, Springsteen even explained what specifically *frightened* him about Reagan's election and why he thought the younger generation would need a *fight song* to live through the coming years, ideas that he had left unspoken in briefer statements from the stage at previous concerts, as he trailed off into ellipsis before beginning to play a song: *You guys out there, you're 18 or 19 years old*, he said, singling out his youngest fans as he had done the night after the election: *it happened once, and it can happen again.*

In the nine months since he was visibly shaken by Ronald Reagan's election, no matter what his most ardent fans among rock critics might have wished, Springsteen hadn't seemed to do much that was very political. He read a few books, wrote a few songs, took to playing an additional few songs written by other people. He toured. But what he was unconsciously doing during all that time was returning to touchstones: the songs of Elvis Presley, who had always defined the thrills and perils of what it meant to be a rock star; the songs of Creedence Clearwater Revival, which had gotten him through the violent summer at the Pandemonium; the archetypes of the Old West, which would forever define masculinity for both his generation and Reagan's; Chuck Berry licks; country songs; even reggae. He took the measure of all these familiar, cherished things to see what they meant in an altered world, a world that he viscerally believed was about to be plunged back into the civil war of the early 1970s.

With the even grander success of *The River* and the tour to support it, Springsteen was now unequivocally a pop star as well as a rock star. If that wasn't all that he wanted, if he didn't want to end up like the elder Elvis Presley, it was time to hold on to himself and fight for the rest of his dreams.

OVER THE LAST SIX YEARS, those who worked closely with Springsteen had gotten used to planning their life-altering events around his recording and touring commitments. Max got married back in July, between the European dates and the last American leg of the *River* tour. In September, ten days after the tour ended, there was another wedding—Clarence's this time, his second. As for Springsteen, although he wasn't getting married, he had his own major commitment to make that fall. He went house hunting. Ever since he moved out of the "band house" in 1975, he had been renting or leasing.

Springsteen's quest for home ownership would not be completed for another two years. "I've probably seen every house in the state of New Jersey—twice," he joked. It was during this same period, in the fall of 1981, that he found himself repeatedly drawn back to Freehold, to the house on Institute Street where he had lived between the ages of five and thirteen, the only house in New Jersey that his father had ever owned. *There was some missing part of me that was there that I still couldn't find,* he'd later confess, *and I'd . . . walk up the street and re-trace the cracks that I used to walk on when I was a kid . . . and I'd look at all the houses and they'd be all lit up and I'd imagine like at night when the houses are lit, they would always look so safe inside . . . and they look happy.* Even he knew that this was abnormal behavior. He realized that he didn't know how to live off the road, "that all my rock 'n' roll answers had fizzled out," and he did what would have been unthinkable for anyone in his old neighborhood growing up: he began to see a therapist.

Whether it was another round of depression or simply an attempt at rock 'n' roll detox, for the whole final quarter of 1981, Springsteen mostly kept to himself. He moved into yet another rental, this time in Colts Neck, a Monmouth County township, didn't do any drop-ins at the Fast Lane or the Pony, and spent some time writing new songs, experimenting with a range of material, from soul to rock to country to straight-up folk. He might begin a song like "Open All Night" with the germ of a discarded *River* song like "Living on the Edge of the World," or reset an old Elvis song like "Follow That Dream" with a new set of lyrics and call it "Baby, I'm So Cold," an even more radical alteration of the original than "Johnny Bye Bye" had been.

As had been true in the spring, lyrically Bruce now seemed particularly drawn to songs about crime and violence. "They Killed Him in the Street" and "Ruled by the Gun," songs whose lyrical content can be safely inferred from their titles, both received extensive workouts that fall, as did "James Lincoln Dear," a song about an Indiana man whose underemployment drives him first to crime and then to prison. Bruce also slightly altered "Fist Full of Dollars" to become the less derivatively titled "Atlantic City." The original song's prospective gambling changed to an ambiguous *favor,* perhaps along the lines of the *favor* (more clearly a heist) in 1975's "Meeting across the River." The self-consciously balladic "Nebraska" was about Charles Starkweather's 1957–58 murder spree, and in order to write it Springsteen had called up Ninette Beaver, a Midwestern journalist who was an expert on the case, to make sure that he got all the details right. "Johnny 99," "Downbound Train," and "The Losin' Kind" were all songs that similarly focused on rootless individuals who drifted from the suburbs of poverty into the seemingly handy solution of criminal activity. These thematically linked songs represented the sort of rapid homing in on a theme that had characterized the development of Springsteen's best albums in the past, but had been notably absent during the preparation of *The River*.

Given the temper of the times, writing songs that engaged these themes was a serendipitously political act, much like writing about cars during the gas crisis. Crime in America was almost at an all-time high: there were 22,000 murders in the United States during the year, and a full third of the nation's households had been affected by violent crime. Since the crime rate had begun to rise during the mid-1960s, many conservatives saw a clear link between it and the greater leniency in sentencing, drug use, and sexual promiscuity evident in American society during that period. In February of 1981, as the E Street Band was barnstorming through the Southeast, Chief Justice Warren Burger went so far as to label current conditions a "reign of terror in American cities." As the new president took office, only 10 percent of violent crimes in America resulted in incarceration. "Why," Justice Burger asked, "do we show such indignation over alien terrorists and such tolerance for the domestic variety?" Given these epidemic conditions, crime was not just a conservative issue. People who could remember what the United States, especially its cities, had been like just two decades earlier were legitimately terrified.

Although Springsteen had begun using sympathetic imagination during the *River* sessions to conjure up the texture and experiential details of lives that he himself had not led, these new crime-focused songs may have taken that process a step too far. Why imagine yourself in the place of a thief, a statutory rapist, or a mass murderer? As one self-professed Springsteen fan, a Rhode Island police officer, later said, these songs "sure brought me to a complete halt!" Not only were they perhaps the least commercial songs that Springsteen could have been writing; they may also have been the least Reaganesque songs that he could have written at that moment. Reagan had made "law and order" (along with lower taxes and a tougher stance toward the Soviet Union) one of his touchstone issues, declaring as far back as late 1976 that Americans should "start treating 17 yr. old muggers, robbers, rapists & murderers like muggers, robbers, rapists & murderers." Reagan was vehemently opposed to the "sociological fairy tale . . . that poverty causes crime," pointing out that during the 1930s "we had possibly the lowest crime rate in our history at a time when poverty was most widespread." By contrast, Reagan liked to point out, in the third quarter of the twentieth century, "poverty dropped by 55% [and] crime increased by 160%."

Although many of the songs Springsteen wrote in 1981 do run directly counter to such comments, all available evidence suggests that Springsteen did not write them for a specifically political purpose. When he described them to Jon Landau a few months later, he stressed that these were new subjects for him, not political ones. He was attracted to these characters not merely because they were criminals, but rather because he believed that criminals are so radically estranged from society. That was exactly how he felt off the road between tours. He wasn't exploring his murderous or violent side in these songs so much as exploring the sociopathic or schizophrenic aspects of his personality.

By mid-December, he had at least two dozen new songs, enough to bring into the studio when he and the band were scheduled to record again in January. This time, though, he wanted to record a little more efficiently. Even he would admit he took too long in the studio. On his early albums, this was a question of obsessive overdubbing, but it also happened on his last two albums, which were supposed to have been stripped down and simple. Rehearsing with the band in advance of recording the last two albums didn't help with this problem either, as he proceeded to run through dozens of songs in the studio, searching for the right combination that would make up an album. He needed to get all that work done faster, and well in advance of an overly extended stay in one Manhattan recording studio or another.

So, just before Christmas, Mike Batlan, Springsteen's guitar technician, helped the singer set up a home recording studio in the spare bedroom of his new place in Colts Neck, making a few minor acoustic modifications to the room itself and installing a Series 144 Teac Tascom 4-track recorder, as well as two microphones and stands. With four tracks, Springsteen could fill out his demos a bit more, recording himself in stereo first, but singing or playing along with that base track on the two that remained. Under these conditions, he was his own recording engineer, mixing the sound through an old Gibson Echo-plex and pulling a Panasonic boom box into service as a mix-down deck. The result was something that sounded very much like the discarded acoustic version of "Thunder Road" with its haunting double-tracked vocal. Indeed, this rudimentary setup was, in many ways, the culmination of the process that Springsteen had begun with the composition of the earliest *Born to Run* songs. If those were the first songs he had ever written with an eye to multitrack recording, now he was creating multitrack recordings on his own, ostensibly as a guide for later, more professional versions.

In *Songs*, Springsteen would later claim that he wanted to record this way because he "found the atmosphere in the studio to be sterile and isolating," but that seems a trifle disingenuous. How much more sterile and isolating could a Manhattan recording studio be than a spare room in a house you rent because you can't commit to a permanent home, sitting alone for hours on end in the middle of the night with nothing but a collection of sound equipment to keep you company? For whatever combination of logical and unconscious reasons, Springsteen was recording songs about estrangement and isolation under what may have been the most solitary conditions he had ever known. Under these conditions, he achieved total artistic control, but it was at the cost of the only community that had ever really meant anything to him: the collaborative community of his fellow musicians.

After at least one trial run with the new equipment (during which he sang harmony with himself on the white gospel standard "Precious Memories"), on the night of 3 January 1982, Springsteen recorded a sampler of fifteen of his new songs for Jon Landau, purposefully omitting half a dozen songs that he knew he wanted to work out in more detail with the band. Given the way that Springsteen's songwriting had been progressing during the last year, it's interesting to note that only about half the songs he recorded that night were about criminals. Making the cut for the Landau tape were not just songs about crime per se but songs about both victims and victimizers who felt cut off from the society in which they lived. More significant, in what seemed a predictable culmination of the way Springsteen's music had been moving for the last five years, over half the tracks he recorded that night were based in country music, and many of the rest in rockabilly.

In retrospect, Springsteen has referred to the songs he recorded that night as being his most autobiographical. That seems odd, given not only their intermittently violent content but also their rural flavor. But truth be told, while "Bye Bye Johnny" and "Nebraska" are both clearly set well west of New Jersey, nearly all the other songs he recorded that night are either set in the Garden State or draw their geographical referents from it. Two of the songs he recorded that night ("Used Cars" and "Mansion on the Hill") are the most literally autobiographical songs he had written up to this point, and all the songs are generally autobiographical, in the sense that they capture his estrangement during this period, the disconnection and rootlessness that began to feel more and more like a prison to him than like freedom.

Moreover, in Springsteen's mind, the mood of dread and imminent disaster in these songs had a specific chronological focus within his own life. For him, these songs resonated neither with the adolescence of his South Street years nor with the grade school imprisonment he had experienced in the house on Institute Street that he had been visiting obsessively during the fall. They echoed instead the haunted time of his early childhood, which he had spent on Randolph Street in Freehold, where Doug, Adele, Bruce, and Ginny had lived with Doug's parents during the early 1950s. For Springsteen, the house on Randolph Street, virtually his entire world for the first five years of his life, was almost like a home out of time. In generalized historical memory, the 1950s are supposed to present an overflowing cornucopia of shiny home appliances, but the elder Springsteens' house was heated by kerosene and coal. Recent decades seemed irrelevant there, as if they were all still living in the Great Depression. The only picture anywhere in the house was an old photograph of Doug's sister, who had died as a child decades earlier, and the house's most abiding presence was Bruce's grandmother, whom he described in one of his early-1970s coffeehouse songs as cold and flinty.

No one would ever confuse Freehold, New Jersey, with Butcher Holler, Kentucky, or Sevierville, Tennessee, but for the allegedly industrialized Northeast, Springsteen's grandparents lived during the early 1950s in surprisingly primitive and impoverished conditions. When Springsteen had tried to write directly about these experiences during his singer-songwriter period ten years before, the resulting song ("Randolph Street," sometimes known as "Master of Science") had overreached and its metaphors had been overripe. In these new songs, though, he finally processed those childhood years artistically, without ever mentioning any specific details from them but rather conveying his general feeling of that time, during which optimism had seemed an unimaginable luxury. In all the songs he recorded on 3 January 1982, he was going back, way back, past the rock 'n' roll dreams that his adolescent self had once thought would be his salvation. Locking himself away in the fall and winter, Springsteen had dug down through all his brash, imagined criminals to the little boy who had cut himself off from the rest of the world in the first place. At what should have been a moment of triumph, he was remembering a very frightened, dark part of his life that he had spent most of it trying to forget. Whether superficially happy or sad, all the songs he recorded that night are based in the black cloud that overshadowed his childhood, the overwhelming sense (as one of their lyrics puts it) of *a meanness in this world.*

Musically, Springsteen was traveling back in those tracks to a style that many considered more adult than rock, more capable of expressing an individual's problems past adolescence. Old-school country felt right for describing this world, because of its sparseness and tenuousness, as well as the mixture of traditional connection and current alienation that had characterized the best country songs over the years: from the Carter Family's "Will the Circle Be Unbroken" straight down to Porter Wagoner's "The Cold Hard Facts of Life." When previously explaining how he had come to write "The River," one of his first successful stabs at country music, Springsteen emphasized not only his overt debt to Hank Williams but also the direct influence of a songwriter like Johnny Cash. In the songs Springsteen recorded for Jon Landau that January night, his five-year interest in country music reached its fullest creative expression.

Even here, though, there was a more personal, autobiographical resonance for Springsteen than mere generic considerations might suggest. Not incidentally, Randolph Street was the first place where Springsteen had heard country music. There was a "displaced Alabaman next door" to Bruce's grandparents, from whom, as Christopher Sandford has suggested, Springsteen got to hear his earliest country, folk, and gospel tunes. He hadn't really indulged that taste until well into his twenties, however, when he was secure enough in his present that he could really start to think about the past from which he was trying so hard to rock away.

WHEN SPRINGSTEEN FINISHED mixing down a single cassette of these fifteen songs from his four-track experiment, he gave copies of it to Jon, Steve, and Chuck Plotkin. Plotkin had mixed *Darkness on the Edge of Town*, played an even more central role in getting *The River* ready for release, and was now helping Steve produce his long-deferred solo project. All three men were startled by what they heard on that crude recording. Steve thought it so perfect as it was that he explicitly wondered whether Bruce really wanted to rerecord this material with the band.

Nevertheless, in February the band reassembled. Roy was using synthesizers now, and even if Max had not jumped on the recent drum machine bandwagon, he was playing more tightly than he had on tour. All that session work was a good thing for the band, because the musicians were now much more familiar with how to get specific effects in a studio than they would have been if they had lain totally fallow between Springsteen's albums and tours. Tape rolled all the time in the studio, and a quickly improvised song like "I'm on Fire," with its Tennessee Two feel, just emerged from the sparks that flew between all these musicians as they reunited after half a year off.

The songs that Bruce had intended to record with the band, however, came much more sporadically. "Downbound Train," which he had described to Landau as an "up-tempo rocker," now swung and hung back a little more than it had done solo. The Flannery O'Connoresque "Child Bride" became the more fun "Working on the Highway," in which Roy's synth riff once again seemed to propel the song forward in a way that a solo acoustic guitar and tambourine never could. "Glory Days," a song about looking back on the past from your midthirties that was also recorded during these early-1982 sessions, was almost certainly one of the songs that Bruce had held back to work out with the band. In practice, it became a happier, less mournful song than it was on the monaural solo demo that he had made during the fall, with a verse about Doug Springsteen's lifelong underemployment that was deleted from the final product.

But probably the greatest triumph of these early-1982 full-band sessions was a song that actually got heavier rather than lighter when it moved away from its original solo acoustic version. "Born in the U.S.A." was one of the songs that Bruce had worked on hardest in the fall. Originally titled "Vietnam," it was a darkly picaresque story of a returning Vietnam vet that Bruce had started writing shortly after the VVA benefit back in August, but by the following February the song had been reconceived in a more offhand 1950s style. Not only did the song's unfortunate narrator end the lyric by declaring himself to be *a cool-rocking daddy*, but the song's third verse unmistakably echoes the lyrics of "Summertime Blues," one of Bruce's favorite rockabilly covers. The resulting song in the solo version was both serious and fun, a mixture of emotions that may not have captured exactly what Bruce had wanted to say about the plight of the Vietnam veteran. Although he didn't tell Bruce this at the time, Landau actually considered "Born in the U.S.A." a stillborn song, whose separate elements never quite added up in an artistic sense.

All that changed when the band got into the studio. As Dave Marsh has observed, these early-1982 sessions centered on Bruce, Roy, Max, and Garry, with Danny, Clarence, and Steve supplying mostly "coloration" for the band's four-piece core. And from the first take of "Born in the U.S.A.," Roy and Max's assault on this song was brutal. For once, Roy's synth riff is relentless rather than rallying, and in the track's final minute Max's drums get closer to Ginger Baker (or Keith Moon, for that matter) than ever before. Surrounded by this heavy instrumentation, the wail with which Springsteen concludes his vocal for the song sheds the faux James Brown coolness of the solo recording and gets much closer to the cry that ended "Jungleland"—a long scream taking over when even the simplest, most finely observed lyrics could simply communicate no more. This was a song that needed the band to complete it. It needed, as Landau later put it, "that turbulence and that scale." Like many of the tracks that did work that spring, this one was finished very quickly. When it was done, Springsteen invited Bobby Muller, the president of VVA, into the studio to listen to it, and his grinning approval was all the singer needed. Springsteen had accurately captured an experience in song that he had notably avoided in his actual life.

"Born in the U.S.A." was pretty much the exception, though. By that point, about two weeks into the sessions, it was clear that many of the songs that Springsteen had recorded in January didn't work with the band, no matter how many ways they tried to do them. Not surprisingly, "Nebraska," "Johnny 99," and "Atlantic City," the three songs that had received the most extensive workout on the January solo tape, seemed the most resistant to full-band arrangements. As it turned out, Bruce *was* recording faster in the studio this time than in the past. He just wasn't recording, for the most part, the songs that he had labored over so hard in the fall.

By the last weekend in April, Springsteen had come to a decision about his next album. Earlier in the month, he had given Toby Scott, his recording engineer, a copy of the January four-track cassette, idly wondering whether was any way they could just release that. A few weeks later, Scott got back to him to say yes, maybe they could. Steve was right: these songs *were* an album. The three songs that seemed to work with the band could be peeled off from the project and saved for a later venture. On 26 April, Springsteen recorded "My Father's House" and "The Big Payback" in the same style and under virtually the same recording conditions as those of almost four months earlier. With those last two tracks, the solo album was done, and it was the most painless recording experience that Springsteen ever had.

They went back and forth on what to call this solo album—"Open All Night" was considered, as was the stark "January 3, 1982." Ultimately, the decision was made to call it *Nebraska*, signaling the elevation of that particular single and the location radically different from that of *Greetings from Asbury Park, N.J.* Upon its release that fall, *Nebraska* was greeted with ecstatic reviews. Steve Pond in *Rolling*

Stone gave the album 4½ out of a possible 5 stars and called it "the bravest of Springsteen's six records." John Rockwell, writing in the *New York Times*, singled it out as the singer's "most personal record, and most disturbing," which he clearly meant as a compliment. "It's been a long time," the critic noted, "since a mainstream rock star made an album that asks such tough questions and refuses to settle for easy answers—let alone an album suggesting that perhaps there are no answers."

Nebraska was received, by critics at least, as the political album they had been expecting since Springsteen's remarks at Tempe two years before, as a deliberate response to Ronald Reagan's ascendance to the presidency. A reviewer like Pond was closer to the mark, however, when he called it Springsteen's "narrowest and most single-minded work." *Nebraska* was more a personal album than a political album, as auteurist a work as any rock star had made up to that point. As such, it inevitably reflected the way that Springsteen looked at the world: the terrors, fears, and suspicions he had, which did have political implications in the current environment, but were first and foremost the deep structure of his emotional architecture.

For all his focus on the marginalized citizens of the United States on *Nebraska*, in the fall of 1982 Bruce Springsteen still didn't have a coherent set of political views. If pressed, he couldn't explain in detail what he thought should be done about poverty or unemployment, let alone what might constitute a system of more progressive taxation. Nor was he any closer to committing to a permanent home, let alone someone with whom he might want to share his life. Springsteen may have understood in theory that his old rock 'n' roll answers had played out, but in practice they were still pretty much all he had.

CHAPTER 8

THIS GUN'S FOR HIRE (1982–1986)

*N*EBRASKA WAS SPRINGSTEEN'S SIXTH ALBUM, BUT IT WAS HIS first to be released without an accompanying tour to promote it. If you wanted to see him play live in 1982, you had to be down at the Jersey Shore. Clarence had a new club in Red Bank called Big Man's West, and a lot of Saturday nights Bruce sat in with whoever was playing there: Beaver Brown, Sonny Kenn, Billy Chinnock, and C. himself. By the end of the summer, he was sitting in almost regularly on Sunday nights at the Pony with Cats on a Smooth Surface, Bobby Bandiera's new band. That's where he was on 19 September, the night before *Nebraska* was released, and that's where he was two weeks later, on 3 October, at the beginning of the week during which (according to *Billboard*) it was against all odds the third-best-selling album in the entire United States.

For those familiar with the ups and downs of the music industry, *Nebraska* looked like a typical succès d'estime by a well-established artist: it shot straight to the top of the chart very quickly, but it didn't have a hit single to give its sales legs. Overall, the album sold decently (one million copies), but its sales were nowhere near Springsteen's recent ones. Whereas Bruce's last three successful albums each spent about two years on *Billboard*'s top pop albums chart, *Nebraska* slipped off after a little more than six months. There's no record of Springsteen's reaction to the sales dip, but he was so proud of the album that he may not have minded.

During the half year that *Nebraska* made its desultory journey down the albums chart, both Clarence Clemons and Steve Van Zandt were touring behind their first solo efforts, and their album and ticket sales almost certainly benefited from the two or three E Street–less years that had passed since the release of *The River.* The *River* tour had made Springsteen such an icon that even people who didn't care about rock 'n' roll knew who he was. In 1982, replacement Springsteen music was everywhere. New songs by him appeared on albums from Donna Summer and Gary U.S. Bonds, and pastiches of the E Street sound were surprisingly common: from "Bruce Springstone and the Bedrock Band"'s raspy-voiced cover of the *Flintstones* theme (complete with a "Factory"-style opening monologue) to the soundtrack that Beaver Brown (soon to be rechristened "John Cafferty and the Beaver Brown Band") was currently recording for the MGM movie *Eddie and the Cruisers.* At Universal Studios, Walter Hill was about to start shooting a postapocalyptic "rock 'n' roll fable," as he called it, "what I would have thought was a perfect movie when I was in my teens," with such late-'50s and early-'60s derived elements as "custom-cars, kissing in the rain, neon, trains in the night, high speed pursuit, rumbles, rock stars, motorcycles, jokes in tough situations, leather jackets, and questions of honor." In a sign of how pervasive Springsteen's influence was at that cultural moment, the title of Hill's picture was *Streets of Fire,* even though Bruce's *Darkness* song of that name would not actually appear on the film's soundtrack.

Not many people knew it, but there had actually been some talk back in the summer of 1982 about putting out two discs again, one of Springsteen solo and one with the E Street Band, but Springsteen ultimately nixed it. He felt that releasing band songs simultaneously would give people an excuse to ignore the acoustic songs. Still, during the five months of sessions at the Power Station the previous winter and spring, he and the band had recorded over a dozen polished tracks, all of them at least as good as most of the songs on *The River.*

But Springsteen wouldn't even discuss a band album during the months just after *Nebraska's* release. He spent most of that time, from November 1982 to March 1983, in Los Angeles, in his new house in the Hollywood Hills. (Apparently, buying a house in California was an easier step for him to take than buying one in New Jersey.) Now out of high school, his younger sister Pam had decided to give movie acting a try, and sometimes she would stay in the house too. Bruce drove around town, took in some concerts, and was apparently making a few lifestyle changes, as a highly physical performer in his midthirties usually needs to do. One reporter who saw him at a Prince concert in LA during this period noted that Springsteen's "muscles have swelled to Popeye size since he embarked on a weight-training program . . . and one source says that he's even passing up junk food." The only time Springsteen headed back east during those five months was for weddings: both Southside and Steve got married in 1982.

That fall and winter, Springsteen continued his self-imposed isolation, much like the one of the year before, only this time he was on the West Coast. In December of 1982, almost exactly one year after Mike Batlan had set up the home studio in Colts Neck, Bruce asked him to install a more elaborate setup in his LA place. He wanted to make more home recordings, and he once again declared that they were in preparation for possible band sessions in the new year. This time, he didn't record the songs in one digested burst, as he had the *Nebraska* songs, but instead laid them down over a period of about six weeks and added drum machines to the tracks to give them a less folky feel. Tellingly, the most affecting songs in this round were those that dealt with alienation ("Fugitive's Dream" and "Unsatisfied Heart") and with a generalized longing to settle down, without a specific person with whom to do it ("Little Girl Like You"). These were the same themes Springsteen had been wrestling with since the three breakthrough songs leading up to *The River*, but there still didn't seem to be a way to make an album out of such material, especially not with the E Street Band.

Briefly, Springsteen considered releasing the best of these LA home recordings as a second solo project. Given the expectation built up about the next E Street Band album, however, such a plan would have been professionally perverse. Next, he talked with Jon Landau and others about issuing the best of the band's unused recordings from the spring of 1982, adding just one recent solo recording (of the long-nurtured "Johnny Bye Bye") and using five of the best of the new home recordings as B-sides. In what had become a familiar pattern, however, he ultimately decided that something was missing. In April 1983, he headed back east to record with the band, just as *Nebraska* was finally slipping off the *Billboard* albums chart.

Like those of the preceding year, these new sessions apparently began with reworkings of recent solo material: "Cynthia" and "Your Hometown" (now called "My Hometown") were slowed down; "Pink Cadillac" was now speeded up, in an arrangement so close to Henry Mancini's "Peter Gunn Theme" that it almost felt like an homage. In the space of about two weeks in late May and early June, the band turned out at least three songs that fell into a countryish or honky-tonk groove: "Car Wash," "TV Movie," and "Stand on It." The last featured Roy doing his best Johnny Johnson on a song that owed more than a little in structure and execution to Chuck Berry's "Brown Eyed Handsome Man." As on the best 1982 band recordings, Roy, Max, and Garry were the core of this track, with the piano becoming even more central in its final mixes. Indeed, what seemed to hold the best tracks together at this point wasn't their words or ideas (as it had been with *Nebraska*) but rather their sound—the tight four-piece arrangement that had produced the band's best studio work since *The River*. But was a sound enough to transform ten or twelve songs into a single work?

In June, the E Street Band stopped recording, mixing began . . . and once again Springsteen still didn't think he had an album. Even with at least two dozen solid tracks in the can now, he would keep recording on and off with the band for another eight months. Truth be told, we have no idea exactly how many tracks the E Street Band recorded during this period, because this is the point at which the veritable bounty of Springsteen studio bootlegs dries up. Demand for the new Springsteen album was so great that someone smuggled out a tape of the version that Springsteen had mixed down and considered releasing in spring 1983 (variously called *Murder Incorporated* or *This Hard Land*). By summer, vinyl copies of this rejected album were in record stores throughout the Northeast, and this led to increased security when band sessions resumed at the Hit Factory that fall.

From the tracks that Springsteen has released from this period, though, we can glimpse a slight progression of themes. "Brothers under the Bridges," "No Surrender," and "Bobby Jean," all from the fall of 1983, look back at adolescence and fond memories of finding kindred spirits to run with, whether it be riding in cars or listening to records. In "Thunder Road," written when he was twenty-five, Springsteen had tried to imagine middle age, but these new songs were the sort that only an artist in his midthirties could really produce. When you're thirty-four years old, your mind and body tell you every day that you're no longer fourteen, and while there are a great many good things about that, you also wonder if you've moved too far from where you started. These songs are more wistful and earnest than the jolly songs about the Upstage he had written on his first few albums. Unlike "Blinded by the Light," to choose only one example, these new songs emerged from the awareness that maybe everything isn't going to be alright, but that it's good to go down fighting.

By contrast, the two discarded songs that Springsteen has released from early 1984 deal more with his continuing hesitation to charge forward into the big time. For the most part, "Rockaway the Days," for example, is a Jimmy Buffett–flavored rewrite of "Hungry Heart," but its last verse ruefully observes:

Well rich man want the power and the seat on the top
Poor man want the money that the rich man got
Honey tonight I'm feeling so tired and unsure
Come on in Mary, shut the light, close the door . . .

Whether the echo here of "Badlands" (*poor man wanna be rich*) is intentional, the shift in tone from seven years before is striking. This narrator isn't defiant, he's just resigned. "Man at the Top," which Springsteen recorded a few weeks before "Rockaway," leaves the listener with a similar impression. The lyrics speak loudly of ambition, but as always with Springsteen you need to hear the music and its arrangement as well as the words. In this case, the music seems wistful rather than triumphant and suggests a continuing ambivalence with regard to success. It holds back and stands as detached from the prospect of a happy near future as "4th of July, Asbury Park" stood detached from its retrospect of the romantic recent past. For the last eight years, Springsteen had been alternately attracted and repulsed by the idea of becoming an even bigger star. These were the same themes he had been writing about for the last two or three albums, and with each further iteration they sounded more tired, more exhausted, almost as if even Springsteen didn't care about them anymore but still couldn't let them go.

As usual, Jon Landau was the practical, if still artistically sensitive, voice in Bruce's ear. In late January or early February, echoing Clive Davis's words from the summer of 1972, Jon told Bruce that he might have an album but he didn't have a single. What did a hit single sound like in early February of 1984? Despite the presence of such self-consciously retro singles as John Mellencamp's "Pink Houses," Elton John's "I Guess That's Why They Call It the Blues," and (most of all) Billy Joel's "An Innocent Man," most Top 20 hits then were starting to embrace early digital technology. On the most obvious level, the singles chart was now awash with synthesizers, from the Euro peace pop of Nena's "99 Luftballons" and the Nuevo art rock of Yes's "Owner of a Lonely Heart" to the reimagined Brill Building dreams of Cyndi Lauper's "Girls Just Want to Have Fun" and the updated garage band sound of the Romantics' "Talking in Your Sleep." Even Van Halen's biggest hit, "Jump," was built around a synthesizer riff, and not even the most paranoid suburban parent could possibly label the song heavy metal. Generally speaking, the lyrics of the Top 20 contained denser narrative details than they had five years before, with even dance songs like Shannon's "Let the Music Play" laying out a sequence of events rather than a merely static lyrical state. The second British Invasion of punk and new wave was beginning to see the end of its reign on the American pop charts, with the Pretenders' "Middle of the Road" (a song about rocking despite aging that Bruce might have wished he had written) and the Police's "Wrapped around Your Finger," showing how small combos could still produce compelling sounds.

According to Max Weinberg, it was a few days after he had seen what would be one of the last Police concerts for a quarter of a century that he and the band were called into the studio to record one last song, the potential "single" that Bruce had written at Jon's behest. Measured against the likes of "Born to Run" or "Thunder Road," "Dancing in the Dark" might seem, at first, a relatively minor song. It's hard to say if it's really about anything, except the situation that Bruce found himself in during the winter of 1984: stuck. Viewed more closely, however, it is actually one of the most autobiographical songs that Springsteen had ever written, especially in terms of the quotidian details of life, right down to *getting up in the evening* and *coming home in the morning,* a more likely work schedule for a rock star than a novelist.

In other words, in writing the last song for his seventh album, Springsteen was doing what he had done for at least five of the albums preceding it: giving his personal state of the union address as an artist. "Blinded by the Light" captured his feeling at being poised on the edge of the big time; "The E Street Shuffle" and "Tenth Avenue Freeze-Out" mythologized the vanished Asbury Park music community that had helped form his sound and worldview; "Darkness on the Edge of Town" threw down a poststardom challenge to his listeners; and "My Father's House" marked the ways in which he was trying to let go of his personal, haunted past. If the first three of these songs were cries of giddiness, the fourth a measure of defiance, and the fifth an accommodation with adulthood, this new song was much more like a formal surrender. *Man I ain't getting nowhere / I'm just living in a dump like this,* Springsteen sings, which takes on special resonance if you realize that, around the time he recorded this track, the singer finally purchased his first home in New Jersey: a huge spread in the rich Monmouth County suburb of Rumson. The *dump* to which he refers here is almost certainly the moping slough of authorial despond in which he spent the time between albums for most of the last five years, the isolation that yielded *Nebraska* but little else. The narrator is tired of staying indoors and being serious. He wants to head out with his partner and have some Fun.

But this raises the most interesting question about the song: to whom is "Dancing in the Dark" addressed? Yet another of Springsteen's sketchily drawn "little girls"? Not if it's a song about songwriting. This is, in some ways, the answer song to "Darkness on the Edge of Town." If in that earlier song Springsteen asked his audience to join him in the challenge of making modern rock more than an easy good time, in this song he's asking them if they want to just go out and find *some action.* Given the whole drama surrounding *Nebraska,* Springsteen clearly understands how contradictory this turnaround looks.

There's a joke here somewhere, he admits, *and it's on me. I'll shake this world off my shoulders,* he promises, *come on baby this laugh's on me.*

In retrospect, Springsteen has called *Born in the U.S.A.,* the album for which "Dancing in the Dark" ended up serving as the lead-off single, a "grab-bag," even though it holds together better stylistically than *The River.* He has stated that it "contains a group of songs about which I've always had some ambivalence," a statement he would never make about the contents of a thematically focused album like *Darkness* or *Nebraska.* But clearly the last two, three, five, seven, even nine years had worn the singer-songwriter down. Springsteen didn't just want to be serious and respected; he also wanted to be a star, an even bigger star than *The River* had made him. Since the success of *Born to Run,* he had swung back and forth between these twin goals, so it was only logical that the succès d'estime of *Nebraska* would cause him to make his most naked bid for superstardom. It had taken him a long time to come around: two-thirds of *Born in the U.S.A.* (including its entire first side) had been in the can for two full years, a lifetime in pop music. Now, however, he was all in, ready to do whatever it took to kick him up to the next level. *This gun's for hire,* he unapologetically sang, *even if we're just dancing in the dark.*

A FEW WEEKS AFTER cutting "Dancing in the Dark" at the Hit Factory, Springsteen spent the weekend at his new place in Rumson with a houseguest: Chicago-born guitarist Nils Lofgren. Two years younger than Springsteen, Lofgren had known Bruce for almost fifteen years. In 1970, Lofgren's band Grin, formed with his brother Tom, was present at the same Fillmore East audition as Steel Mill. Lofgren spent the 1970s working with Neil Young among others, on *After the Gold Rush,* *Crazy Horse,* and *Tonight's the Night.* He also recorded with Steve Stills and Tim Curry. Still, his real passion was Grin, which recorded four albums in the early 1970s before their label gave them the kiss-off "best of" treatment at the end of the decade. Shortly before that weekend in Rumson, Lofgren was dropped by MCA, leaving him without a recording contract.

It might have seemed like a busman's holiday, but even when taking a break between recording and touring, Springsteen loved nothing more than playing and talking about music. That weekend, he and Lofgren went to bars, played together informally, talked about their careers, and watched TV together—MTV, which was still something of a novelty in early 1984. The video music channel had launched in the summer of 1981, during the *River* tour, and its viewership was so small at first that it hardly seemed worth noticing. By the time *Nebraska* came out, MTV had grown enough that CBS had wanted to release a video on it in order to promote the album. At that time, Bruce decided he didn't want to appear in any videos, so director Arnold Levine cut together some raw location footage to accompany "Atlantic City." Just a year and a half after that, however, MTV was the highest-rated basic cable network in the country, with 22 million teenage and young adult viewers. It was also a crucial part of every record label's strategy for promoting new pop releases.

As Springsteen and Lofgren watched, they heard the announcement that Steve Van Zandt would be leaving the E Street Band. Van Zandt had actually left the band almost two years earlier, after it became obvious that the Power Station sessions weren't going to translate into a new album anytime soon, but the formal separation had become public knowledge only recently. MTV News stated that Van Zandt's replacement would be from New Jersey, but Springsteen told Lofgren that that wasn't true. Sensing an opening, Lofgren volunteered that, if the band needed another guitarist, he'd like a shot. Given Lofgren's musical résumé, Springsteen could hardly believe the offer, and he filed it away for future reference.

As usual, the next few months were spent mixing down the album and preparing for both its release and the tour that would promote it. The tour would begin in late June, the album would drop three and a half weeks earlier, but the single needed to be out about a month before that, in order to build interest first. In addition to preparing a traditional 7-inch single of "Dancing in the Dark," the label also prepped a 12-inch single that featured "Blaster," "Radio," and "Dub" remixes of the song. These "dance mixes" (dance-targeted remixes of seemingly nondance songs) were produced by Arthur Baker, in many ways the most influential record producer of the early 1980s. Three years earlier, he had helped Afrika Bambaataa hone "Planet Rock" into the perfect 12-inch single that it was. More recently, he had remixed Cyndi Lauper's "Girls Just Want to Have Fun," reenvisioning Lauper's original recording in a way that Springsteen had liked. When given the assignment of remixing "Dancing in the Dark," Baker said he wanted to produce something that was more like "Bruce's old stuff," but almost the first thing he did was essentially remove the E Street Band, replacing Garry's and Max's work in the studio with new bass, drums, and rhythm. He also added chimes and reverb to the track, as well as enough backing vocals to make it sound even more like the rejected, "Beach Boys" version of "Born to Run."

Between the proliferation of "dance mixes," the rise of MTV, and the tightened playlists now in force at most FM stations, popular music in 1984 seemed much more focused on singles than even as recently as four years earlier. What all these changes added up to was the return of Top 40. There was one crucial difference, though, between the music world in which Bruce had started out and the current one. Financially, as a result of the standard contracts that had come into use during the 1970s, record labels still had a long-term rather than a short-term interest in artists. One-hit wonders, whose albums couldn't be counted on to yield steady catalog sales over time, couldn't justify such contracts. Moreover, singles were for the most part still released on vinyl, but it was the new compact disc (CD) format that was proving to be a financial gold mine for the recording industry. So even if dance clubs, cable television, and radio were now promoting singles, the record companies needed to sell albums, albums so full of arresting singles that they seemed to be worth $16.95 (the current list price for CDs).

Consequently, the major labels were now intent on turning as many albums as possible into mega-albums, with Michael Jackson's 1982 *Thriller* the presumed model. *"Thriller,"* as one music publicist active in the early 1980s remembers it, "was like Moses carrying all the Jews across the Red Sea." It established what music industry historian Steve Knopper has called a "video-driven blueprint" for keeping an album near the top of the sales charts for at least an entire year. The videos drove the radio airplay, the remixes made sure that that airplay transcended narrowly defined FM formats, and it all drove the CD sales, which would always perk up again when the next video/single was released. To achieve this level of success during the album-oriented 1970s, a release like Carole King's *Tapestry* had needed to be considered a generational touchstone. *Thriller*'s success, on the other hand, could be more easily copied (if not fully duplicated), given the right promotional campaign.

Even though Springsteen and Landau saw only one or two singles on *Born in the U.S.A.*, the label saw at least half a dozen possible singles, which could be promoted by turning them into dance mixes and music videos. The album could keep going for a year and a half, and Springsteen could keep touring for all that time too, especially if he moved from indoor arenas to outdoor stadiums for the tour's later stages. The singles and videos would promote the tour, and the tour would promote the singles and videos. "Cover Me" (the song Landau had stopped Springsteen from giving away to Donna Summer two years earlier) would be the second single. It sounded enough like the other music on the radio and on MTV to fit into the mix nicely. More contemplative and stereotypically E Street songs like "My Hometown" and "Glory Days" could come later, and there were plenty of *River*-style outtakes to go on the B-sides of the 7-inch singles to keep more confirmed Springsteen fans happy. The early singles' main purpose was to grab the attention of people who had never really listened to Springsteen before.

"But you don't have to worry about this," Al Teller, the senior vice president and general manager of Columbia Records told Springsteen in the spring of 1984. "Go out and do what you do great." Springsteen's willingness to go along with this strategy—to let the label worry about dance mixes, music videos, and what would make people who didn't like him yet like him—shows how much he wanted success on the level that only a musician like Michael Jackson had really enjoyed. Ceding control of some aspects of his career like this was almost the exact opposite of locking himself in a spare room, being his own recording engineer, and not touring to promote an album. Both impulses, though, were authentic ones, both parts of Springsteen's character. During the last few years, he had out-Dylaned Dylan. Now it was time to out-Elvis Elvis.

But if Springsteen was going to tour, especially for that long, there was still the matter of the band. Aside from the occasional wedding, they hadn't played together live in two and a half years, and it was obvious that they would have to practice before they hit the road. Moreover, he needed to finally decide whether he would bring in another second guitarist to replace Steve Van Zandt, who had played on two-thirds of the tracks on *Born in the U.S.A.* and provided crucial guitar and harmony vocal support on the last tour. In early May, with the album release and tour less than two months away, Bruce called Garry, Danny, Clarence, Roy, and Max back for rehearsals, to be held on the premises of Clarence's now closed club in Red Bank. He also called Nils Lofgren and asked him to join them.

Was Lofgren brought in to "replace" Van Zandt? At the risk of cliché, no one could replace Steve Van Zandt for Bruce's purposes, just as no one could replace Jon Landau, if it ever came to that. Steve was a friend and a sounding board, someone who, even when he differed with Bruce, arrived at his opinions by reasoning from the same musical and cultural principles. And if the second guitarist in the band was going to be there solely for musical rather than personal reasons, one could ask in fairness whether the band even needed him. True, sometimes Bruce needed someone else to play the guitar parts so he could throw himself fully into the vocals, but the other six members of the band had played pretty well as a unit for a year or so in the mid-1970s, just before the release of *Born to Run.*

Most important, even in the narrow instrumental sense, Nils didn't "replace" Steve in the sense of duplicating his style or sound. Instrumentally, one might even say he surpassed him. He was undeniably more accomplished on steel and six-string electric than Van Zandt or Springsteen were. He was, as Bruce would call him some years later, "the most over-qualified second guitarist in show business." Moreover, his voice, while beautiful, was much higher and purer than Van Zandt's, lending his harmony vocals a more ethereal quality than the blue-eyed soul earthiness that Van Zandt had provided. So, this was no matter of mere replacement, but rather a more meaningful shift. Adding Lofgren to the band after Van Zandt's departure was like changing from David Sancious on piano to Roy Bittan: both men were fine musicians, but their interactions with Springsteen produced very different sounds.

There was also a second addition to the band that spring, but this one Springsteen held off announcing until almost the last possible moment. Born in Deal, New Jersey, Patti Scialfa was four years younger than Springsteen, and it seemed as if they had been running into each other for decades. Scialfa attended high school in Asbury Park, and according to Springsteen they first met back then, during his Steel Mill days, just before Scialfa left Monmouth County to attend the jazz conservatory at the University of Miami. Within a few years, she transferred to NYU, and between classes she waited tables and played music on street corners with her friends Soozie Tyrell and Lisa Lowell in a group informally called Trickster. In 1974, during her last year at NYU, she was one of those whom Springsteen auditioned to replace Suki Lahav, when he was briefly considering adding a female background vocalist to the regular E Street lineup. In the late 1970s and early 1980s, Scialfa picked up session work in New York but remained closely tied to the Jersey Shore music scene. She sang with Tone, the group Davey Sancious and Boom Carter had left Springsteen to form, and with Tyrell and Lowell she recorded and toured with the Asbury Jukes for two years. In the spring of 1984, she could often be found Sunday nights singing at the Pony with Cats on a Smooth Surface, a group with whom Springsteen had sat in dozens of times over the last two years.

So by the spring of 1984, Springsteen and Scialfa had certainly performed together informally a number of times, but it's unclear exactly when he formally asked her to work with him on his own music. According to Scialfa, at some point in the late winter or early spring Springsteen asked her to sing background vocals on a recording of "Dancing in the Dark," but unless she is one of the voices in the Arthur Baker remix (and it doesn't sound as if she is) that version of the single is still locked in the Sony vaults. On 24 June, Scialfa took part in the E Street Band's penultimate rehearsal in Red Bank before the tour, supposedly as a fill-in for Lofgren, because his then current bout of mononucleosis allowed him to play guitar but not sing harmony vocals. Scialfa, however, has suggested that Springsteen had made her an offer by this point, almost certainly by the end of this rehearsal, four days before the tour was set to start. "I wanted to tell him that I had to wash my hair," she later joked to Dave Marsh, "that I didn't have time to get ready."

Certainly, Springsteen sprang the decision to add a female vocalist on the other members of the band very suddenly. Retelling fifteen years later a version of what must have happened at that late June rehearsal, Springsteen remembered saying, "Okay, fellas, there's gonna be a woman in the band. We need someone to sing the high parts. How complicated can it get?" As with the enlistment of Lofgren, it is entirely possible that Springsteen had been mulling over the addition of Scialfa for weeks before he mentioned it to anyone else. As in 1974, the last time Springsteen was forced to change the E Street lineup, he saw the occasion as an opportunity to consider different sounds that he might want to add to the mix. Lofgren's muscular guitarwork was one of those sounds, and the hard attack of Scialfa's mezzo harmonies was another.

The new eight-member E Street Band—two guitars, two key-boards, bass, saxophone, and more vocalists than you could shake a stick at—rehearsed one more time in Red Bank and then flew out to St. Paul, Minnesota, where they began work on the "Dancing in the Dark" video in the city's civic center one day before they started the tour there. Originally, Springsteen had been set to shoot a conceptual video for the song with Jeff Stein, the director of the Cars' video for "You Might Think" (which had won MTV's first-ever Video of the Year award the previous fall), but that was the one time during the whole spring publicity blitz that Springsteen apparently put his foot down. After a little bit of shooting with Stein, Springsteen said it didn't feel right not having the band around him, so he, Landau, and friend Brian De Palma cooked up another idea for a video, one that would take place at a Springsteen concert. This first day in St. Paul, De Palma would shoot close-ups with a few hundred extras. This footage could be edited together with film shot during the real concert at the civic center the following night.

In one sense, the video that the band shot in St. Paul that June wasn't necessary. "Dancing in the Dark" had been released almost two months earlier and was already peaking that week at no. 2 on *Bill-board*'s Hot 100 chart. Arthur Baker's three remixes of the song would end up being the highest-selling 12-inch single of the entire year. Ultimately, though, the video for "Dancing in the Dark" proved popular in its own right. It launched the career of actress Courteney Cox, who played the spotlighted girl in the first row of the video's faux crowd, and created an in-concert ritual that Springsteen had never before practiced: selecting an audience member with whom he would dance.

Moreover, although this was almost certainly not its intention, the video probably sold concert tickets as well as CDs. It made a Springsteen concert seem like a much more wholesome place than previously circulating performance clips might have led many people to believe. In addition to "Atlantic City," MTV sometimes played a few pro-shot Springsteen clips from a 1978 concert in Phoenix, but in the Phoenix footage even a fun song like "Rosalita" looked grungy and dark. Except for Clarence's suit, everything from that concert seems black and gray and shrouded in shadow. By contrast, the film De Palma shot in St. Paul, in keeping with the dominant cinematographic palette of the mid-1980s, was brightly lit and filled with pastels and vivid primary colors: the powder blue of Nils' striped shirt; the pink shirt and white vest that Garry is clearly wearing even though he is only briefly visible; the sprightly red-white-and-blue of the tour shirt that Cox is wearing (and which we saw her character purchase during a nonmusical prologue that has seldom been available since the video's original release). The stage lighting for both videos is the same warm pink wash, but the high-key lighting that De Palma added for the video shoot makes the 1984 concert seem hyperreal rather than verisimilar.

Most important for MTV's purposes, the video for "Dancing in the Dark" showed off the New Bruce. Audiences hadn't really seen the singer in three or four years, since the end of the *River* tour. He had been highly attentive to his public image for almost a decade now, and in these last four years, even as he had courted solitude and seclusion, he had also gotten a new haircut, had his teeth fixed, and started pumping some serious iron. His biceps were truly impressive in the video, and, thanks to De Palma, the short-sleeve white thrift-store shirt from which they emerge practically glows as he sings. No longer the scruffy guy who slept in a surfboard factory, the brooding Elvis wannabe, or the goofy dude with unkempt hair in the "Rosalita" clip, in mid-1984 Bruce Springsteen looked like a clean-cut firefighter or auto mechanic. No, wait a minute. In De Palma's clip, he looked like *Hollywood's* idea of a firefighter or an auto mechanic, or like Kevin Bacon on the poster of *Footloose*, one of the biggest movies so far that year. That was it: the man who ten years earlier had been king of the street punks now looked like a movie star.

SINCE SPRINGSTEEN HADN'T toured for *Nebraska*, he found himself in a similar position to the one at the start of the *River* tour four years before. He had two discs of material out (both *Nebraska* and *Born in the U.S.A.*) that his fans hadn't seen him perform live. Add to that the half-dozen released and planned B-sides, not to mention the almost three dozen officially unreleased tracks that he had written and recorded during the last three years, and you realize that Springsteen hit the road in 1984 with almost sixty new, untoured songs. He could easily have done a distinct all-new set each night during his multinight stands, but canny showman that he was, he knew enough to slip in some old songs with the new. Most nights, just under half the songs performed were ones that had not been featured on previous tours. That was still an extraordinary percentage for an established artist who did two full sets and a half set of encores every night without an opening act.

From the first real concert in St. Paul, the *Born in the U.S.A.* shows had a clear structure, with the usual fixed tent poles that allowed for a certain amount of variation in between. "Born in the U.S.A." and "Thunder Road" usually sat at the two ends of the first set, although they sometimes swapped places. In second and third position were "Prove It All Night" and "Out in the Street," two tested stem-winders that may also have been intended to mirror the audience's own feelings about coming to the concert. Four songs in, after Bruce had broken the ice with the audience, he would usually perform two or three songs off *Nebraska*, most often "Atlantic City" and "Open All Night," since they were both "c'mon baby" songs that fit well into the mood established by the evening's earlier numbers.

Although few fans knew enough to appreciate it, it was interesting to listen in those first sets to the album that Springsteen might have released two years earlier. They reached the public on record nearly two years apart, but songs like "Atlantic City" and "Born in the U.S.A." sprang from the same impulse, the same moment in late 1981 and early 1982 that had marked such a notably creative burst in Springsteen's songwriting. Most nights, the songs from that earlier period ended up in the concert's first set, regardless of which of his two recent albums they had been released on. The songs he had written during the two years after that, in his continuing attempt to fill out the elusive band album (songs such as "Dancing in the Dark," "No Surrender," and "Bobby Jean"), tended to end up in the concert's second set. If *The River* had shown Springsteen to be of two minds within a single historical moment, the *Born in the U.S.A.* tour (if not necessarily the album that it was intended to promote) showcased his distinct moods during two barely separated historical moments: just after the *River* tour, during the depths of the Reagan recession; and in the time since then, as the economy recovered and as he geared up for the full-market assault that CBS planned for him.

On 12 July, two weeks after the video shoot in St. Paul, Bruce and the band were eight shows into their U.S. tour, playing the first night of a two-night stand at the Alpine Valley Music Theatre in East Troy, Wisconsin. By that point, *Born in the U.S.A.* had just begun its nearly three-year residency on the *Billboard* albums chart. Nevertheless, at Alpine Valley, the Wisconsin audience greeted the opening bars of a *Nebraska* song like "Used Cars" with enthusiastic applause rather than polite indifference. Some of that was due to the die-hard fans in the audience, but some of it was also due to the thoroughness with which Springsteen constructed, every night, a little island of acoustic restraint in his sea of loud electric theatrics.

During the second set on 12 July, the crowd at the Alpine got to hear an even rarer revision of a recent song. Many of Springsteen's songs had been improved on this tour by the addition of Lofgren and Scialfa's backing vocals, but none perhaps more than the previously discarded "Man at the Top." In the recording made six months before, the country-lite accompaniment on the track was almost willfully simplistic, as was Springsteen's ersatz ingenuous vocal. One could almost envision the singer performing the song on *Sesame Street*, perhaps as a prelude to joining Elmo in a duet on the Red One's eventual cover "Barn in the U.S.A." In Wisconsin, however, in one of only two known live airings of the song, "Man at the Top" started out with Bruce on unaccompanied acoustic guitar but then added answering harmony vocals on the later choruses, with the *all rights* and *oh yeahs* providing a gentle comfort for which the song's narrator may not even be looking. Reconceived in this way, the song is no longer nursery school pabulum, but an overachieving capitalist's stripped-down version of Paul McCartney's "Let It Be." If this interpretation reflects Springsteen's view of his career at this early stage of the tour, he seems more at peace now than he did during the last-minute recording of "Dancing in the Dark." Then he was fuguing in hopped-up frustration; now he seems more willing to sit back and let his career just roll on.

Like "Dancing in the Dark," "Man at the Top" gives obvious clues that it is a quasi-autobiographical song. Live, though, Springsteen tried to deflect some of the song's attention away from himself and toward other contemporary American status seekers. He introduced it that night by saying *this is a song for an election year* and changed one line of the lyric to say, *From the movie star to the as-tro-naut*, clearly referring to that year's presidential race. Ronald Reagan (*the movie star*) was running for reelection, and John Glenn (Springsteen's *as-tro-naut*) was one of the many contenders for the Democratic nomination that year, whom the press had collectively dubbed "the Seven Dwarfs." Much as "Man at the Top" on record may have been about Springsteen's own doubts about impending megastardom, in performance he presented it as a joke about the presidential campaign, and the ways in which it seemed to be more about celebrity than politics.

Springsteen's introduction and revised lyric at Alpine Valley were mere throwaways, by no means a serious attempt at political critique, but they did in fact strike very close to the truth. In 1980, Ronald Reagan ran for president mostly on what he considered the most important issues: lowering taxes, shrinking the federal government, rebuilding U.S. defense in the face of what he deemed a détente-emboldened Soviet Union. That year, his campaign aired cheap-looking TV spots in which the candidate spoke directly to the camera about soaring energy costs in front of a fake-looking shelf of books, as if he were a personal-injury lawyer looking for new clients. Four years later, however, after closely reading the poll data, in-house pragmatists like James Baker counseled the president that his long-standing supporters would vote for him no matter what. For the reelection campaign, Reagan's team focused on images rather than issues, particularly in its advertising, which featured suburban homes, rural churches, forests, and gardens, all of them signifying a bucolic America that the ad copy suggested the president had restored. In 1980, the campaign had sold Reagan. Four years later, it was selling a putatively reborn America, in order to pull in voters who didn't agree with the president already on specific political policies.

So, just as Bruce Springsteen and his advisers were plotting in the spring of 1984 to snag the broadest possible segment of the record-buying public, Ronald Reagan and his advisers were planning that same season in strategically similar ways to pull in the largest possible portion of the electorate. Reagan might be proceeding from the House Un-American Activities Committee–based right and Springsteen from the Monterey Pop–based left, but in 1984 each man was seeking to go beyond the loyal base that he had painstakingly built during the 1970s in order to capture the hearts and minds of the much wider American center. Viewed side by side, their relaunches look strikingly similar at points, particularly in terms of the visuals they presented. Like Springsteen's "Dancing in the Dark" video, "Morning in America," Reagan's most famous 1984 reelection ad, was filled with pastels and variations on the American tricolor: pretty red roses, a true-blue sky over the District of Columbia, and dazzlingly bright white picket fences and wedding gowns. A casual observer might think that Springsteen was trying to cynically cash in on the contemporary rise in patriotism, but the reverse was actually true: Reagan and his team were, like Springsteen, trying to put on a good show. Walter Mondale might have sought to be the rock 'n' roll candidate of 1984 by using a Crosby, Stills, and Nash song in one of his advertisements, but the sad truth of that year's presidential campaign is that Reagan knew how to throw a better arena-style concert than Mondale did. Skydivers, hot-air balloons, and forty thousand people chanting "U.S.A.!" may not have been how Franklin Delano Roosevelt would have kicked off a reelection campaign, but it did sound like one hell of a finale for a Van Halen concert.

Politically, Springsteen's sympathies may have been more with the Democratic camp, but when Democratic politicians spoke about America, none of them seemed to describe the country found in Springsteen songs. At the Democratic National Convention in San Francisco in mid-July—a month after Bruce's stand at Alpine Valley—Governor Mario Cuomo challenged Reagan's invocation of John Winthrop's "shining city on a hill" by speaking about "the other part of the city [where] there are more poor than ever, more families in trouble, more and more people who need help but can't find it." Two nights later the Reverend Jesse Jackson famously spoke to the convention of "our Nation [as] a rainbow." What both Reagan and Springsteen understood in 1984, however, was that, after the last fifteen or twenty years of battering national history, most Americans didn't want their nation to be two or many. They wanted it to be one. As one Reagan aide remarked in a memo written on 8 March (while Arthur Baker was adding aerobic-friendly rhythms to the already synth-heavy "Dancing in the Dark"), "If we allow any Democrat to claim optimism or idealism as his issue, we will lose the election."

Ronald Reagan's most deeply held ideological tenet, far more important than any specific policy that might have grown out of it, was his belief that the United States was a nation of individuals. In his acceptance speech at the Republican National Convention on 23 August, Reagan contended that the core change that his administration had made during the last few years was to shift the government from a philosophy of "statism" that only viewed "people in groups" to one that advanced "the ultimate in individual freedom consistent with an orderly society." For the casual listener, how different was that from Springsteen's current variation on the Elvis Presley freedom speech from four years before, now used to introduce "Born to Run" (in this case, in Largo, Maryland, two nights after Reagan accepted the Republican nomination)?

> *When I was a kid growing up, and I first heard the music of Elvis Presley, the main thing it did for me was it set my mind free a little bit. I could dream a little bit bigger than I had been. His music and the best of rock 'n' roll always said to me "Just let freedom ring," and that's what we're here for tonight. But remember you gotta fight for it every day.*

For the most part, this was as political as Springsteen got in the summer of 1984. Despite the presence of two or three *Nebraska* songs every night, Springsteen's most notable response to contemporary politics on this tour so far was his decision to cover the Rolling Stones' "Street Fightin' Man" during his encores many nights, as significant an addition on this tour as "Who'll Stop the Rain" had been four years earlier.

That night at the Capital Centre in Largo, "Street Fightin' Man" directly followed "Born to Run" during the encores, its first appearance after a two-week absence. In the audience that night was syndicated columnist George Will, who had been invited to the show by Max Weinberg's wife, Rebecca, who was a fan of his tag-team punditry with Sam Donaldson on Sunday morning TV. For his first and only Springsteen concert, Will wore a bow tie, double-breasted blazer, and dress slacks rather than the increasingly de rigueur denim. At Rebecca's suggestion, the columnist also stuffed cotton in his ears. In general, Will found Springsteen androgynous, noisy, and surrounded by pot smokers, yet in the end he concluded that the singer was "a wholesome cultural portent." As a political commentator, Will may not have cared about rock 'n' roll's future, but he did see Springsteen's abundant success as an emblem of a robust American present.

Although his columns that year never made this clear, George Will was in fact an off-the-books adviser to the president's reelection campaign. He seems to have come up with the idea of linking Springsteen with Reagan, but his genuine reaction to Springsteen's concert was very much in keeping with the Reagan camp's wider reelection strategy—don't divide, co-opt. In attempting to seize many formerly liberal strains (even ones associated with the 1960s) and claim them for their own, Reagan's advisers were piggybacking on a larger, hegemonic shift that had been building in U.S. society for the last year or two. In retrospect, historian Gil Troy has dubbed this shift "the Great Reconciliation," which evidenced itself, in his words, "in the rise of the corporate activist, the consumer with a conscience, a society filled with people yearning to earn like Rockefellers, but occasionally live and sometimes even vote like Beatniks."

Very much in this spirit, Will essentially announced in his column that rock was not rebellion. It was hard work. "Backstage," he noted, "there hovers the odor of Ben-Gay: Springsteen is an athlete draining himself for every audience." Moreover, he classified Springsteen's brand of rock as a well-made American product, one that produced large profits and need not be shipped overseas (except on well-managed tours). "If all Americans," Will continued, "—in labor and management, who make steel or cars or shoes or textiles—made their products with as much energy and confidence as Springsteen and his merry band make music, there would be no need for Congress to be thinking about protectionism."

Whether it was just a lucky accident due to Will's vacation schedule or a more purposeful delay to help out the president's cause, Will's column on Springsteen finally appeared in print on 13 September: over a month after the concert he had attended; a week or so into the official presidential campaign; as "Dancing in the Dark" sank down to no. 50 on the Hot 100, "Cover Me" rose to no. 15, and John Cafferty and the Beaver Brown Band's ersatz E Street track "On the Dark Side" sat between the two genuine articles at no. 37. On 19 September, less than a week later, Ronald Reagan made a scheduled stump appearance in Hammonton, New Jersey, a fairly rural community about an hour's drive southwest of Freehold and half an hour northwest of Atlantic City. At this appearance, Reagan's standard stump speech was altered as usual to include a local reference or two. In this case, the president noted, "America's future rests in a thousand dreams inside your hearts. It rests in the message of hope in [the] songs of a man so many young Americans admire—New Jersey's own, Bruce Springsteen. And helping you make those dreams come true is what this job of mine is all about."

Over the weekend, between shows, Springsteen tried to make light of Reagan's comments, but the impression persisted that Reaganism and Springsteenism were one and the same. When you heard Springsteen extol unrestricted individualism as he did in the *Let freedom ring* rap before "Born to Run," or speak about the Revolutionary War monument in Freehold as he frequently did before "My Hometown," you could easily understand why. Generationally specific as Springsteen's remarks before "My Hometown" might be, they were still stylistically in tune with the similarly honorific remarks that the president had made in France in early June on the fortieth anniversary of D-Day, not to mention the tribute to the Statue of Liberty with which he had concluded his speech in Dallas.

By the night of Springsteen's next performance, at the Civic Arena in Pittsburgh on 21 September, it was clear that the singer's Reagan problem was not going away. That night, almost the first thing Springsteen mentioned to the audience was Reagan's appropriation of his music. *Well, the President was mentioning my name in his speech the other day, and I kind of got to wondering what his favorite album of mine must've been, you know? I don't think it was the* Nebraska *album,* Bruce concluded, *I don't think he's been listening to this one,* and he led the band into their customary rave-up on "Johnny 99."

Throughout the concert that night, Springsteen made his displeasure at the current administration known, as he had done briefly after Reagan's election and during the VVA benefit. It's important to note, though, that in the ensuing three or four years the specific *fight* that Springsteen had hinted at back then had never really come. In 1980 and 1981, Springsteen implicitly feared another culture war, like the one the nation had experienced during the early Nixon years. But in its rhetoric, the Reagan administration stressed unity rather than division, especially during this election year. Rock 'n' roll was not a designated enemy for Ronald Reagan (as it might have been for a previous Republican like Spiro Agnew); pessimism was. Springsteen seems to have prepared himself for a *fight* that wasn't even an open disagreement.

That night in Pittsburgh, in trying to definitively distinguish him-self from Reagan, Springsteen went somewhere he had rarely gone before: into the politics of class—not the division of the world into conformists and free spirits, but rather its division into haves and have-nots. Pushed to articulate his political convictions, Springsteen finally moved beyond his 1960s rock 'n' roll individualism, back to the New Deal communalism he had instinctively absorbed from his parents. Now, as he once again reformulated the monuments story before "My Hometown," he made his most directly anti-Reagan comment yet:

> *It's a long walk from the government that's supposed to repre-sent all the people to where we [are now. It] seems like some-thing's happening out there where there's a lot of stuff being taken away from a lot of people that shouldn't have it taken away from them. Sometimes it's hard to remember that this place belongs to us, that this is our hometown.*

This was a start. If actively articulating his political concern for those less fortunate, those who might benefit from a larger federal government, was all it took for Springsteen to distinguish himself from the president, then a statement like this should have solved his prob-lems of misperception.

But despite Springsteen's increasingly explicit political statements as the tour rolled on, the ideological similarities between the two men remained. Springsteen could tell you better than anyone else that music speaks louder than words, and arrangements and setlists often speak louder than both. Every night, Springsteen took his audience on the same phased journey from the bad times of late 1981 to the good times of 1983–84, precisely the same historical journey on which Pres-ident Reagan took his audiences during his stump speeches; from the *Nebraska*-esque days of "drift" and "torpor" to the promise of "you young people." "[M]y generation," Reagan declared near the end of his standard stump speech that fall (almost setting his audience up for a rendition of "Born to Run," his allegedly favorite Springsteen song), "and a few generations between mine and yours . . . grew up in an America where we took it for granted that you could fly as high and as far as your own strength and ability would take you." In the end, when you compared Springsteen's fall 1984 tour with Reagan's, no matter how different their political visions were supposed to be, their rhetoric seemed a lot alike.

Bruce put in more appearances that fall than the president, whose campaign had restricted his stumping to two or three well-chosen photo ops a week. Springsteen was still introducing "Born to Run" by saying *Let freedom ring* but now added *but it's no good if it's just for one. It's gotta be for everyone.* More effectively, he started making room at his concerts for representatives of local food banks and political organizations, giving a shout-out from the stage of the Tacoma Dome to Washington Fair Share, a local coalition dealing with the results of toxic-waste dumping in the Northwest. By that point in the tour, the rock critical establishment (in the person of Jersey Shore–born soon-to-be MTV employee Kurt Loder) had stepped in to try and reburnish Bruce's liberal reputation. As the tour made its way down the coast to Los Angeles, Loder conducted Springsteen's first extended interview with *Rolling Stone*, giving him a widely distributed, rock-friendly forum in which to make his differences from the president clear.

None of it, though, made any difference, at least not in terms of the presidential race. On Sunday, 4 November, two days before the election, Bruce and the band finished up a seven-night stand in Los Angeles, pulling out a rarely performed "Shut Out the Light" as a dedication for audience member Ron Kovic. Four days later, they were right back where they had been almost exactly four years earlier: onstage at Arizona State University in Tempe, looking ahead to four years of Ronald Reagan in the White House, this time elected by a wider margin than any nominee since Franklin Delano Roosevelt nearly half a century before. This time, Bruce didn't say anything from the stage about the election. In the introduction to "My Hometown," he didn't even mention Freehold by name, let alone the town's Revolutionary War monument.

Instead, he dwelled on the People's Clinic in nearby Clifton, Arizona, which had been set up to help those who were currently striking against the Phelps Dodge Corporation. *They can use your help,* he declared, sounding neither nostalgic nor Reaganesque. *You know, there's people out there fighting for their lives and their homes and their families and the communities that they live in. I hope that if you believe that the business of America is Americans, you can find some way to give 'em a little support out there tonight. I know they can use it and they'd appreciate it and I'd appreciate it.* At the beginning of the encores, just before "Born to Run," he reminded the audience about the People's Clinic again, saying not a word about Elvis Presley or what pop music had meant to him as a child. *This is your town,* he simply added, *so fight for it,* finally beginning to make clear what he had meant for all the last four years when he gave his audience that charge.

The week of the Tempe show, with "Cover Me" slipping down the *Billboard* Hot 100, it was time for the album's third single to arrive. In the week of Reagan's triumphant reelection, "Born in the U.S.A." entered the singles chart at no. 52. The next week "Tender Years," another of John Cafferty and the Beaver Brown Band's ersatz Springsteen songs from the *Eddie and the Cruisers* soundtrack, slipped onto the chart at no. 72, and soap star Rick Springfield's "(They Call Me) Bruce," a song about getting confused with Springsteen because of the similarity between their last names, slipped on at no. 81. By the end of the year, 1. 3 million people had seen Springsteen perform live on this tour. Meanwhile, as the Christmas season approached, "Born in the U.S.A." climbed all the way up to no. 9 on the charts, as Arthur Baker's 12-inch "Born in the U.S.A. (Freedom Mix)" was unleashed on the public, glockenspiel, full-court brass band tracks, and all.

ON 27 JANUARY 1985, less than a week after Chief Justice Burger swore Ronald Reagan in for his second term as president of the United States, Springsteen and the E Street Band ended the initial, arena leg of the *Born in the U.S.A.* tour in Syracuse, New York. After the concert, they had two months off before they set out for Australia and their first tour of Japan. A few hours after the break started, Bruce flew back to New Jersey and slept. When he woke up the next afternoon, he flew out to California. That night in LA, "Dancing in the Dark" won Best Single at the American Music Awards, but Bruce wasn't in town to attend the ceremony. Shortly after his plane landed, he drove over to A&M Studios and the recording session for the charity single "We Are the World," joining probably the most fully biracial performing group of his career.

According to Ken Kragen (the manager of Harry Belafonte, the late Harry Chapin, and many others who had organized the session), Springsteen was the key "get" for this session. Once he said yes, a lot of other people came aboard. Moreover, in Tom Bahler's vocal arrangement for the song, Springsteen occupied an anchor position, kicking off its second chorus and eventually being dubbed into a spliced duet with Stevie Wonder at the recording's climax. Springsteen's singing on the track was even more gospel-inflected than usual, and not just because he was surrounded by so many African Americans. Exhausted and hoarse from the arena tour, Bruce couldn't have crooned on the recording the way Kenny Rogers or Billy Joel did even if he had wanted to. As usual, though, guesting on somebody else's recording was still much less stressful than authoring his own. Rather than playing the perfectionist and taking three years to lay down a track, Bruce waited his turn, did his take, and left the studio the way he came, without an escort.

Springsteen stayed in California for the whole tour break, and soon his fans found out about another reason why he was spending so much time in LA. When he attended the Grammys at the Shrine Auditorium in late February, his date was Julianne Phillips, a high-end model who had just begun getting acting parts in TV movies. Anyone who saw the two together at the ceremony knew that this was no one-night black-tie relationship. Bruce had been introduced to Juli by Barry Bell, one of his agents since the Gaslight days, after an October show in LA, and they had gone out for dinner. Bruce told one of his friends that the second he saw Phillips "I knew." They started dating almost immediately, moved in together by the end of November, and were already talking marriage during a trip to Rumson over the holidays. Shortly before the Grammys, they even went to Oregon so that Bruce could meet Juli's parents. He wore a suit and tie for the occasion, and one family friend who was present during the visit said that the singer was notably respectful and unflamboyant.

On the face of it, Springsteen and Phillips seemed to have only two things in common: they were both gorgeous, and they had both been raised Catholic. If Springsteen had grown up in "the suburbs of poverty," Phillips had just grown up in the suburbs—and fairly ritzy ones at that. Ten years younger than her beau, Phillips was given to peppering her conversation with self-help nostrums (for instance, "I'm taking a dip in the lake of me"), while Springsteen was more likely to quote lines from cowboy movies. Just before Bruce met Juli, he had told Kurt Loder, "*Someday*, I'd like to have the whole nine yards—the wife, the kids," and the emphasis on *someday* was wholly his own. "I'm just not really lookin' to get married at this point," he quickly cautioned. "I've made a commitment to doin' my job right now, and that's basically what I do." Given how fast things were moving with Phillips, one wondered how long "this point" would be. He also told Loder in the same interview that he purposefully "stayed in New Jersey" in order to keep himself from getting lost in the isolation of stardom—and here he was essentially living in the Hollywood Hills whenever he was off the road. It was almost as if he was saying one thing these days so that he could then go off and do the opposite.

In the spring, during the month-and-a-half break between the Japanese stadium tour and the European stadium tour, the band finally got to see Bruce do something that he had been watching them do for close to a decade: get married. On 3 May, back in the States, Bruce formally proposed marriage to Juli. They told friends and family the news on 6 May, and everyone decided that the best place to get married would be at Our Lady of the Lake, the local church in Oswego, Oregon, where Juli's mom was the regular organist. So many paparazzi flew into Portland, site of the nearest airport, that the ceremony had to be moved up by a day and half, to just past midnight on Monday, the thirteenth, almost the first minute that the couple's marriage license would be legal. The next day there was a reception at the local country club, of which Bill Phillips was a member. After the wedding, Juli and Bruce flew off to Lake Como, to stay in a villa lent to them for their honeymoon by Gianni Versace. For the world's biggest pop star and his new model wife, a week in Cape May or Atlantic City was out of the question.

By 27 May, though, the new couple was back in New Jersey—for a video shoot with John Sayles at Maxwell's, a bar on Washington Street in Hoboken that was locally famous for its intimate live music. The sound system may not have been as good as the one across the Hudson at CBGB but the actual acoustics of the back room at Maxwell's were much, much better. Nevertheless, despite having gone on record as disliking the lip-synched simulacrum of live performance he had given in the "Dancing in the Dark" video, eleven months later Bruce decided to go with the lip-synched version of "Glory Days" too. It was his fourth video in a year, for his album's fifth single, and within a week the song entered the *Billboard* Hot 100 at no. 48, while "I'm on Fire" slipped down to no. 72. The wheels of the machine just kept on moving.

A week and a half later, the E Street Band was playing for the first time in Ireland, at Slane Castle in county Meath, to an audience of almost 100,000 people, double the size of the audience in Brisbane, Australia, a little over two months earlier, and easily Bruce's largest audience ever. This was followed by a month of dates across Europe, all of them in stadiums, culminating in a three-day stand at Wembley Stadium in London. The last two Wembley dates were made even more enjoyable by guest appearances by Steve Van Zandt on "Two Hearts," one of his standard duets with Springsteen on the *River* tour.

As it turned out, during the break between his second and third albums, Steve was planning a massive team-up single of his own, although at first he didn't want to presume and ask Bruce if he would sing on it. Steve's first album, *Men without Women*, was all about relationships as its title suggested, but on his second album, *Voice of America*, his writing started to turn more toward global politics, with song titles like "Solidarity," "Los Desaparecidos," and "Checkpoint Charlie." In "I Am a Patriot," which would end up being his most frequently covered song, Van Zandt simply declared, "I know but one country, and it is freedom." When Springsteen spoke of "freedom," his meaning could frequently seem vague. When Van Zandt used it, though, on an album filled with songs inspired by specific political situations around the globe, the word had a more historically specific charge. Such specifically political songs were the greatest justification for Van Zandt's breaking off from Springsteen and going solo. These weren't just songs he needed to write; they were the kinds of songs that one would never hear on an E Street Band album, let alone an Asbury Jukes effort.

The all-star song Van Zandt wanted to record wasn't a charity single like "Do They Know It's Christmas?" or "We Are the World," although it would raise money for a worthy cause. It was a politically explicit protest song the likes of which pop music had seldom heard, fueled by anger, not guilt. "Sun City," the song he wrote and whose recording he subsequently produced with the still-ubiquitous Arthur Baker, took the rising, vibrant anti-apartheid movement and implicitly used it as a club to beat some of his hypocritical fellow musicians over the head. Sun City was a showplace resort in the middle of Bophuthatswana, a "phony homeland," as the song's lyric put it, to which the South African government had relocated blacks, subsequently claiming that it was not actually in South Africa. Naïvely and conveniently taking this dubious statement at its face value, such otherwise reputable performers as Linda Ronstadt, Rod Stewart, Queen, Ray Charles, and the O'Jays had performed at the resort and received enormous paychecks as a result.

Van Zandt's goal in recording "Sun City" was awareness first, fundraising second. He wanted to make sure that no other musician could claim ignorance in playing Sun City. Van Zandt wrote the song as a solo piece and then, at the suggestion of journalist Bill Schechter, decided to bring others into the project, taking months, not days, to make his invitations. By the end of July, he had gotten acceptances from dozens of artists, many of them New York–based. Because he was going for maximum impact rather than maximum sales, there was nothing bland about the recording that these sessions produced. Throughout the month of August, over three hundred separate tracks were laid down, not only by such mainstream rock and pop stars as Hall and Oates, Bob Dylan, Pat Benatar, Peter Gabriel, and Jackson Browne (as well as members of U2, the Beatles, the Rolling Stones, the Who, and Midnight Oil), but by an impressive lineup of old-school pop and soul stars (David Ruffin, Eddie Kendricks, Darlene Love, and Bobby Womack), jazz legends (Herbie Hancock, Miles Davis, and Nona Hendryx), reggae pioneers (Jimmy Cliff and Big Youth), cross-

over Latin artists (Ruben Blades and Ray Barretto), at least one funk
master (George Clinton), a world-class blues performer (Bonnie Raitt),
two downtown rock legends (Lou Reed and Joey Ramone), and some
of the most essential artists in the fast-growing field of hip-hop (Kool
DJ Herc, Grandmaster Melle Mel, Afrika Bambaataa, Kurtis Blow,
Run DMC, and Gil Scott-Heron). Van Zandt created a powerful stylistic as well as lyrical statement about the ways in which heterogeneity
enhances life and culture. If this is what it sounds like when all these
varied people get together, who would ever want to go to a place where
they aren't allowed to?

Springsteen was one of the last artists to record his part for "Sun
City," only a few lines of which are distinct in the finished single. He
came into Manhattan to do it in late August, when one of his shows at
Giants Stadium in the Meadowlands had to be canceled because of
rain. Now he was playing stadiums in the United States too, unthinkable even as recently as four years earlier. But as a man who wanted to
be an artist as well as a star, Springsteen had to wonder: after fourteen
months on the road, how many of those in his newly enlarged audience actually understood a word that he was saying? Steve's politics
were increasingly clear in his work, as were Peter Gabriel's and Jackson
Browne's, but they played to smaller audiences these days than he did.
Every night in a venue like Giants Stadium, there were the chants of
U.S.A.! U.S.A.!, as if the lyrics weren't obvious enough on their face.
And there was also the odd way that tens of thousands of well-fed
young people in the richest and most powerful nation on earth were
pumping their fists in the air so many nights on the title word of Jimmy
Cliff's "Trapped." The stadium shows were great fun at points, but
they had become as much of a predictable ritual as the pre–Vatican II
Mass that Bruce had parodied in "Resurrection" fifteen years before.

The *Born in the U.S.A.* tour ended with four dates at the Coliseum
in Bruce's new hometown of Los Angeles. The one new song he added
for those dates was a cover, of course, but it had apparently been Jon
Landau's idea. A year earlier, around the time of the Reagan incident,
Jon had suggested that he and the band do Edwin Starr's "War." It was
as clear and lively a protest song as "Sun City" (which would be out in
a month or two) and as overt a piece of pop dissent as "Street Fightin'

Man" had been an evasion of it. Coming into the home stretch of the tour in late 1985, Springsteen finally found a way for his band to do the song. The first night at the Coliseum, Bruce taped the song's words to his arm and slipped it in right after "The River."

That first night, the two songs seemed unconnected, but the next night Bruce revised the "River" monologue yet again, talking about his experiences with the draft back in the 1960s, using a little bit of the material about Bart Haynes that had appeared in the "My Hometown" monologue over a year before. The third night in L.A., Bruce switched around the setlist, omitting all but one *Nebraska* song but creating a sequence of five songs written across fifteen years ("Johnny 99," "Seeds," "Darkness on the Edge of Town," "The River," and "War") that made it clear as a group that the failure and loss that many Americans had suffered since his childhood days were more structural and less individualistic than the current administration might claim. He continued not to mention the president by name onstage, but his charge to the young people in the audience at the end of that sequence was no Reaganesque "Born to Run"/just-follow-your-dreams spiel: Instead, he brusquely declared, *Blind faith in your leaders can get you killed*, and then tore into "War," achieving a bluntness and clarity that he seemed incapable of as a writer.

Of course, he picked a girl out of the audience to dance with that night—it was expected, everyone had seen the video—but for this last night of the tour, the girl was Juli. After the last encore, they went to the Marquis on Sunset for the end-of-tour party. "I'm happy," Bruce said as he left the Marquis, "the bubble is in the middle of me." The phrase sounded more like Phillips than like Springsteen.

SOON AFTER THAT, Bruce and Juli headed back to Rumson, although Juli had started talking about their getting an apartment in Manhattan. Obviously, they could afford it, and it would allow her to be closer to work. Her acting career had already been on the upswing when they first met, and with all the recent publicity it was really taking off. Both personally and professionally, she was now "Julianne Springsteen."

As for Bruce, although he was off the road, he still wasn't finished with *Born in the U.S.A.*, a project that, in one way or another, had taken up the last four years of his life. CBS thought he could pull one more single off the album, ensuring that over half its tracks had been spun off as separate 45s. Their candidate was "My Hometown," probably the best-known of the six tracks that hadn't already been turned into singles. There would be no dance remix for this song, and a video could be culled from footage shot at one of those last few shows at the Coliseum. The problem was that they needed a B-side, and many of the most usable castoffs from the 1982–84 sessions had already served as flip sides for the six earlier singles.

Thinking, as always, of the last thing he had done that he had really liked, Bruce suggested they use a live cover of "War" from one of the Coliseum concerts, which would have made for an interesting, purposeful juxtaposition with the shrugging resignation at political conflict of "My Hometown." So Jon took down the tapes from those concerts and listened to them. The song did sound good, especially on the third night—too good, in his opinion, to waste as a B-side. Since the people at the label had already said that they wanted "My Hometown" as a Christmas release, Jon suggested that they use a 1975 live recording of "Santa Claus Is Coming to Town." It had been circulating for years on bootlegs and on promotional releases handed out to radio stations, but up until then there had been no legal way for fans to buy it. At the same time that he proposed this, Jon sent Bruce a tape of four songs from that sterling third night at the Coliseum ("Born in the U.S.A.," "Seeds," "The River," and "War") and suggested that the singer listen to them.

Sending that four-song tape was a very shrewd move on Landau's part, proof if anyone still needed it that he knew his client almost better than Springsteen knew himself. Bruce had been recording his concerts for years, since even before Jon became his manager, and for at least a dozen years, his label had been after him to release a live album. For all that time, he said no. He barely listened to any of those recordings, but he nevertheless kept on taping. Very shortly after the LA shows, Jon brought the topic up once again, and Bruce said no once again, even though he was proud of those shows and knew that they had been professionally taped.

When live albums had been discussed in the past, the idea was to preserve from start to finish specific performances, many of them already available on widely circulated bootlegs. What Jon sent him was something different: four songs from the same concert, but not four songs that Bruce had sung in a row. Rather, they were four songs out of the first eight that he had sung that night, a neat compression of the usual opening quarter of one of Springsteen's concerts into a little under half an hour of concentrated music. Basically, what Landau sent him was an album side.

Presented in that way, a possible live set didn't seem like something that Bruce had done already, not even in performance. This was about making something *new*. In a way, it was also about putting together the ultimate setlist, which Bruce had been trying to do for well over a decade. Even better, this was an album that Bruce could put together in his living room rather than locked away in a studio. (That was one of the major reasons why he had bought the big place in Rumson. It had a lot of land, and Bruce wanted to build a real home studio on it, so that he wouldn't have to waste his summers driving back and forth to Manhattan.)

The "My Hometown"/"Santa Claus Is Coming to Town" single was released on 18 November. Well before the end of the year, the single's B-side predictably zoomed to no. 1 on *Billboard*'s annual holiday chart. By then, though, Bruce's mind was on other matters, and the last *Born in the U.S.A.* single was no more than an afterthought in the singer's rearview mirror. By Christmas, he and Jon had laid out what they thought should be the live album's first side: the solo piano version of "Thunder Road" from one of the 1975 Roxy shows; "Adam Raised a Cain" and "Spirit in the Night" from a show at the same venue almost three years later; and "4th of July, Asbury Park" from the legendary New Year's Eve show at the Nassau Coliseum in 1980 (one of about half a dozen individual shows that had often been mentioned as a good candidate for a live album).

As this second, joint selection of tracks indicates, a month or two into the project several key decisions had already been made. First and foremost, the album wouldn't be drawn from a single show or even a single stand. More interestingly, it wouldn't be drawn from a single year or even a single tour. Just on the two sides that they had already programmed, Landau and Springsteen had committed to using tracks drawn from across a decade, the decade that had seen the band's slow and steady rise from mere stars to undeniable superstars.

One last decision that had probably also been made about the live album by this point was its size. Clearly, this wasn't going to be merely a single LP, because the two sides that Landau and Springsteen had already programmed could not reasonably coexist on the same slab of vinyl. The difference was just too stark. If the goal was to create the quintessential Springsteen concert, then they would need at least three LPs for that, with maybe a fourth for encores. In October 1985, Bob Dylan, still very much Bruce's idol, would release *Biograph*, his own career retrospective, but Springsteen and Landau probably knew well in advance that CBS had cleared that project to be released on a full five LPs. If *Biograph* was to be Bruce's model, then he had eight sides left to program.

By the new year, Toby Scott had determined they had usable recordings of fifty or sixty shows, two hundred hours of music that had to be whittled down to a little over three and a half. For the moment, Bruce stayed in New Jersey, waiting for Chuck Plotkin in LA to listen through all the tapes. Even though he wasn't really working on the live album yet, Bruce wasn't spending too much time with Juli during this period either. (Currently, she was working even more than he was.) Instead, he was devoting much of his off-tour energy to drumming up sympathetic publicity for the workers at the 3M plant in Freehold, which was due to be closed the following year. There were workers at the 3M plant who had come there from the Karagheusian Rug Mill, the plant whose closing "My Hometown" was about. Bruce's father and grandfather had worked in that plant, the one Springsteen also memorialized in "Factory." Perhaps most symbolically resonant of all, the 3M plant made audio and video tape, products that Springsteen bought and sold in sizable quantities. This was the kind of cause to which it was almost impossible for him to say no.

In late January, shortly after a twelve-hour concert at the Pony to raise funds for Oil Chemical and Atomic Workers Local 8–760 (which represented most of the employees at the 3M plant), Springsteen flew out to LA to meet in person with Plotkin, who had spent at least a month listening closely to all the live shows they had been able to find. Through most of February, Springsteen treated the live set as his day job, even if he never left the house. For two or three weeks, he and Plotkin sat in his living room five days a week, six hours a day, listening to the assembled recordings. "One of the things that happens when you work for Bruce," Plotkin told *Rolling Stone* just before the live set was finally released, "you go down—as if in a submarine—for a period of time, and when you resurface, you realize that you've let the rest of your life go to seed."

Springsteen and Plotkin were hoping to document Bruce and the band's history, but more than anything at this stage they were just listening for the best takes. By the time Landau joined them in their discussions, they had whittled that mountain of recordings down to around fifty songs, only about 25 percent more than they probably needed. After Bruce made a quick trip back to New Jersey for another Pony show and to lay down a guitar solo for a recording by Garry Tallent's charity supergroup Jersey Artists for Mankind, the three men sat down once again and started figuring out the best order in which to put the tracks they'd picked.

As finally programmed, the live set is divided into three distinct movements, each documenting one of Springsteen's last three tours. After the acoustic "Thunder Road"—the only recording on the set that is drawn from the first three or four years of the E Street Band's existence—there follow ten tracks (sides 1 through 3 of the LP release) that are exclusively drawn from the 1978 *Darkness* tour. In the set's second eleven-song grouping (sides 4 and 5 and one song on side 6), all the performances are drawn from the 1980–81 *River* tour, although over half of the songs being performed date back to the recording sessions for *Darkness*. The set's third grouping (the rest of side 6 and all of sides 7 through 10) disproportionately emphasizes Springsteen's recent work by presenting a full seventeen songs from the 1984–85 *Born in the U.S.A.* tour, most of them from its final stadium-enlarged performances. Dave Marsh, perhaps echoing Springsteen's own views, has characterized these groupings as reflecting a club phase, an arena phase, and a stadium phase of Springsteen's career. In terms of mood, the three phases are also distinctly different, as indicated by the encores with which each section closes out: the first, most fun phase ends with a rousing version of Eddie Floyd's "Raise Your Hand"; the second, darker grouping with the earnest Nassau Coliseum version of "This Land Is Your Land"; and the third, bittersweet arc with a wistful rendition of Tom Waits's "Jersey Girl."

When measured against the actual setlists from these three tours, just three covers in a prototypical Springsteen concert seems fairly sparing. The number of monologues that Springsteen preserved on the set seems similarly culled, with at least two instances (the 7 July 1978 version of "Backstreets" and the 5 November 1980 version of "Badlands") in which memorable monologues have been edited out. While there is one purely fun monologue early on in the set (the extended injunction to radio listeners during "Raise Your Hand"), at least three of the remaining four extended monologues have one thing in common: Bruce. Taken together, these three monologues, one per movement, cast the singer's story in a three-act structure: Act One, "Growin' Up" (despite the doubts of parents and other authority figures, Bruce hits the big time); Act Two, "This Land Is Your Land" (once he does hit the big time, he feels the need to educate himself); Act Three, "The River" (Bruce realizes that his personal problems are indicative of larger societal problems).

The coda to this three-act movement comes with "War," the track that directly follows "The River" in sequence, even if it ultimately couldn't be jammed onto the same album side. Here Bruce offers a political lesson for his young audience from his own personal experiences, drawing an inescapable conclusion from the personal-political syllogism laid out in his three earlier speeches: you don't have an obligation to your government, but you do have an obligation to your community. This may be another reason why Springsteen didn't want to use any recordings from before 1975: the story he wanted to tell didn't end with stardom; it began with it. The live set, in other words, was his public autobiography, far more than *Biograph* was Bob Dylan's. Like many autobiographies, it was reductive, emphasizing a very limited view of Springsteen's life. It omitted the long road to success, his frustrations with girlfriends, and especially his inability to find a place he wanted to call home. It focused instead on what happened when he first became a media sensation, and started to wonder what he could do to live up to that changed state.

The imminent release of the live set was announced in September, and the marketing frenzy that had abated somewhat during the last six months was now back in full swing, as was a rising Springsteen backlash. Even his fellow musicians were now getting in on the act. Van Morrison was intimating that Bruce had stolen his shtick, Keith Richards was mocking the overindulgent length of his shows, Bob Geldof was questioning his claims of political wisdom, and even occasional friend Pete Townshend was publicly wondering whether Bruce was turning into a parody of himself, "a combination of Apollo and Bugs Bunny," as novelist William Gibson so memorably put it some years later. "After the car-stereo bombast of *Born in the U.S.A.* (album and tour)," critic James Wolcott would note in the upcoming December issue of *Vanity Fair*, "Bruce Springsteen certainly needs to undo his bandanna and let his mighty brow cool."

Walcott and all the others had no way of knowing, but that was precisely what Bruce Springsteen was currently planning to do. On 13 October, Nils and Danny joined Bruce at the 17,000-seat Shoreline Amphitheatre in Mountain View, California, to perform an acoustic set at a concert to benefit the Bridge, Neil and Pegi Young's charity for autistic children. The mixing on the live set had been completed a little over a week earlier, and it may have been around this time that Bruce assembled the band at his home in Los Angeles—in the bedroom of his home, as the most salient account of the incident puts it—and presented each of them with copies of the new album's first pressing. He reportedly told them that "when they were all old and gray, they could play it for their grandchildren as a way to illustrate what those days were like." Rolling in wealth as he was at that point, Springsteen then gave each of them a $2 million bonus and told them that they were now free to pursue other projects. He might call on them now and again, but for all intents and purposes, the E Street Band was no more.

That was funny in a way, because the live set, simply titled *Bruce Springsteen & the E Street Band Live/1975–85*, was the first of Bruce's albums that was formally credited to both him and the band, implicitly suggesting that what emerged from the studio was ultimately authored by Springsteen while what happened onstage was more fully collaborative. A handwritten note reproduced in the set's souvenir booklet thanked "the E Street Band for 1,001 nights of comradeship and good rockin'." Springsteen's note went on to call the band "the best bunch of people you can have at your side when you're goin' on a long drive," but in retrospect it seems significant that the cover photo for the set shows Bruce alone onstage looking off into the space where the album's title is printed. At least one biographer would call this set a coffin, but what the cover looks most like is a gravestone, with the birth and death dates clearly marked and displayed in the place where Bruce's finally co-billed collaborators should be.

The set marked another kind of ending as well, because it may have been the last album that Springsteen conceived of as an LP release. Despite his careful work arranging ten album sides, many of those who bought the album did so in a three-CD rather than a five-LP set. Much of the construction of the set was lost on them. The three discs didn't even divide along the lines signaled by the set's three movements. Disc 2, for example, ran from "Cadillac Ranch" to "Seeds," slicing the four-song set from the LA Coliseum that started off the whole project into two distinct halves.

In the fall of 1986, Bruce Springsteen was richer than he ever could have imagined back on Randolph Street, but there were plenty of other things in his life that didn't seem to be running quite as well as his career—maybe his marriage, definitely his attempts at social change. Despite over a year of opposition, 3M was still cutting three-fourths of the workforce at the Freehold plant: with the rise of the CD, cassette sales were declining as well as vinyl, and there simply wasn't the demand for audio tape that there had been during the 1970s. So much for the perks, power, and influence of being a rock star.

PART THREE

THRILL HILL

—

Bruce Springsteen, Thrill Hill West, Los Angeles, CA,
c. 1994. © Neal Preston/CORBIS.

CHAPTER 9

WHAT I NEED IS SOME PROOF
TONIGHT (1986–1992)

O N 5 NOVEMBER 1986, BRUCE SPRINGSTEEN WAS ONSTAGE AT LE Zenith in Paris performing with two of the many other participants in "We Are the World": Huey Lewis and Bob Geldof. Just a month before, Geldof had been making fun of the Cult of Bruce, and backstage at this show both he and Lewis teased Springsteen about the marketing-stoked anticipation for his forthcoming live set. Still, there was no one else on the planet who could throw together an instant pop cover the way Bruce could. The song they decided to perform was Robert Parker's twenty-year-old hit "Barefootin'," a song without a hint of social significance, which Pete Townshend was also known to enjoy covering now and again. The performance was ultimately broadcast on VH1, the U.S. cable channel that Viacom had launched almost two years earlier to serve those music fans who had grown too old for MTV.

Lewis was in Paris because his band was on tour there; Geldof lived a channel away and frequently visited the city; but Springsteen's reason for being in France was more sober and personal. His wife, Juli, was shooting the Alain Delon film *Sweet Lies* in the city, and he was there to be with her, perhaps to try to salvage what was left of a relationship that had begun two years before in a fever and was by this point almost ice cold. For as long as Springsteen and Phillips had been together, onlookers had been searching for signs that they might break apart, but as counterintuitive as the match between them might have seemed, they clearly enjoyed each other's company, at first. If nothing else, they seemed to really like taking vacations together. Comments from family and friends suggest that their relationship foundered in time on the shoals of a more mundane kind of existence: the two-career marriage. When Juli wanted to relax, Bruce was off scribbling down songs or planning a box set. When Bruce wanted to relax, Juli was off shooting a movie. There were days when she huffily headed out the door with a suitcase, and nights when he broodingly hopped in a car and drove off into the dark.

Moreover, according to some observers, there was an even larger issue looming between the two of them: starting a family. Before Springsteen and Phillips had ever met, nearly everyone who knew him could have told you that his longing for fatherhood was clearer and more insistent with each passing year. Just as surely, many of her friends could have told you that, for her, children were something that she wanted well in the future, if ever. She might have played the mother of Bruce's children in John Sayles's video for "Glory Days," but that was the closest she intended to get to motherhood for quite some time. That neither Springsteen nor Phillips thought this fundamental disagreement would be a strain on their relationship suggests that each of them had entered their marriage in a spirit of willful blindness at best. Perhaps each believed that the other could be won over in time to a more sensible point of view.

Three days after the Le Zenith concert, Springsteen flew back to New York on the Concorde with Matty DiLea, a friend who ran a motorcycle shop in New Jersey and who had driven west with him in the fall of 1982 just after *Nebraska* was released. Phillips remained in Paris. According to at least one Springsteen biographer, from that point on Phillips and Springsteen's marriage was "a sham," the two seldom living under the same roof or even making common plans.

By no purposeful design, Springsteen and DiLea arrived back in the United States on the day of the live set's release. The singer wasn't needed for any of its prerelease publicity (especially back in those days, when he never appeared on television), so he spent this momentous day of his career just hanging out in Manhattan with his friend. Dave Marsh in particular has noted the incongruity of Springsteen wandering around the city relatively unrecognized, eating cheeseburgers and seeing movies, while an even greater publicity push than had greeted

Born in the U.S.A. was just reaching its frenzied peak. You could see Springsteen's face all over record stores and billboards that fall, but apparently it wasn't quite as recognizable when glimpsed in real life. The star was more widely recognized than the man.

Throughout the United States, most retail outlets sold out their initial shipments of *Live/1975–85* on that first day. In Europe, a truck bearing a shipment of the album was hijacked. Radio stations were announcing "All Bruce Radio," and despite its size and higher cost, the album debuted on the *Billboard* chart at no. 1, making it only the fourth album in the history of the chart ever to do so. Perhaps more gratifying to both Springsteen and Landau, "War" (on the A-side, with the 1980 Nassau Coliseum performance of "Merry Christmas Baby" on the flip) entered the *Billboard* Hot 100 two weeks later, eventually rising to no. 8. After over a dozen years on the label, Bruce Springsteen finally turned into the surest of sure things for CBS. If Bruce was willing to keep feeding E Street mania, this golden goose could keep on laying eggs at least through the end of the decade.

But Springsteen wasn't willing to do that. He was serious about trying to restart his career, or at least redirect it. In January, on the night before "Fire," the second single off the live set, entered the Hot 100, he helped induct Roy Orbison into the Rock and Roll Hall of Fame. A few weeks later, he publicly guested on one of Steve Van Zandt's solo tracks (the reggae-flavored "Native American," which would eventually appear on Van Zandt's album *Freedom No Compromise*). And then he was back in Rumson, cutting a batch of new songs, recording them as he had recorded *Nebraska*: solo and in his own home, where if a car drove by a little too noisily he had to start another take. His mood since returning from Paris that winter was dark and removed, and the songs he now recorded grew out of that mood. They further worked the vein he had first explored seven years earlier in "Stolen Car" and "The River": they treated the rise and fall of relationships, how what at first seems like intimacy can over time turn into intimate disconnection.

The difference now, of course, was that he had actually been in such a relationship, a relationship that he had taken to the point of marriage. The question was: how honestly could he write about such material, about emotions that were closer, rawer, and more anxiety producing for him than any he had ever tried to capture before? After all, the dangers of intimacy were why both Springsteen and his protagonists so often hopped into those night-bound cars alone in the first place. It would have been much easier for him to keep writing songs about young working-class men waiting for their big break—but after the megastardom of the last few years, it would also have been more laughable. "Rosalita" worked best as a time capsule now. Any vital writing he might produce from this point on needed to emerge from his current situation.

Springsteen later reported that the songs that eventually appeared on his eighth studio album were written and recorded in the space of three weeks, but one may imagine that, like the songs that he had turned into *Nebraska* five years earlier, many of these new songs had a long foreground. If one includes the discarded material from this period that was later released on *Tracks*, however, one can see a certain progression of themes across a relatively short stretch of time: from the generic relationship pop of "When You Need Me" to the specifically autobiographical "The Honeymooners" and "The Wish" to the darker and more troubled "Lucky Man." If these four tracks are indeed indicative of a larger progression, then, starting with an explicit theme, Springsteen moved within a very short span of time from pastiche to personal portraits of those he loved to actually digging down into his own insecurities.

If this next album was intended to reintroduce Springsteen to his fans as a songwriter, it ended up highlighting two slightly different aspects of his creativity: the songs based in 1960s pop that were most apparent on *The River*; and the more personal compositions that were featured on *Nebraska*, the pieces in which the singer explored the dark places of his life even when he wasn't being directly autobiographical. Perhaps inspired by Dave Marsh's simultaneous work *The Heart of Rock and Soul: The 1001 Greatest Singles Ever Made*, Bruce produced on the pop side an Elvis pastiche with a Bo Diddley beat ("Ain't Got You"), songs whose titles echoed early-'60s hits by Lou Christie ("Two Faces") and Frankie Valli and the Four Seasons ("Walk like a Man"), and one song ("All That Heaven Will Allow") that would have been perfect for

Gene Pitney. As far as the autobiographical songs were concerned, there was the first song he had ever written about his mother ("The Wish") as well as what would turn out to be the last publicly released song that he would ever write about his father ("Walk like a Man").

"Walk like a Man" is an obvious instance of how pop and personal history overlapped for Springsteen in this project, but these two strains fused much more meaningfully in "Brilliant Disguise," his most universally praised song from this period and the one that he would eventually designate as the "center" of the album. Formally, "Brilliant Disguise" is wholly in keeping with the principles of early-'60s pop. Rhythmically, it is based around the Brazilian *baion* beat: a dotted quarter with an eighth note going into a quarter. Twenty-eight years before Springsteen decided to use this rhythm, Jerry Leiber and Mike Stoller had labored to put it at the heart of the Drifters' "There Goes My Baby," creating, as Kenneth Emerson has so memorably put it, "the Italian bastardization of a Brazilian samba to an ersatz Russian string orchestration on a rhythm-and-blues record by an African-American quartet." In so doing, they had influenced dozens if not hundreds of records that issued forth from Manhattan's studios over the next five years. If in "There Goes My Baby" Lieber and Stoller had stolen the beat from Latin American culture and applied it to Tin Pan Alley pop, in "Brilliant Disguise" Springsteen took that transformed beat and combined it with elements of the guitar-based post-Dylan pop that had essentially replaced the kinds of songs with which Lieber and Stoller had for a while dominated the airwaves.

"Brilliant Disguise" draws not only its rhythm but its sense of presumed values as well from the Top 40 songs that Springsteen absorbed in his youth. This is one of the things that make it such a marvel of composition. As always, Springsteen is seeing the world through ears and eyes trained by Drifters, Lou Christie, and Bruce Channel singles, and yet he is nonetheless seeing it clearly. The song's original bridge was almost a placeholder lyric, interchangeable with dozens if not hundreds of other "what are you doing to me baby?" pop songs, which feature slightly softened noir femmes fatales who rob their protagonists of all will (and conveniently relieve them of all responsibility in the process). At best, this original bridge is a vague memory of the opening lines of Elvis Presley's 1969 hit "Suspicious Minds," but without the musical insistence that underpinned those bare words.

In revising the bridge, however, Springsteen went "Suspicious Minds" one better by changing the singer's position:

> *Now look at me, baby*
> *Struggling to do everything right*
> *And then it all falls apart*
> *When out go the lights*

In revision, the bridge becomes the pivot on which the song turns, as all good B parts should be in classical pop songwriting. Now it's not a song about a two-dimensional woman who has deceived the foolish singer, but rather a song about how two flawed, three-dimensional people deceive each other. *I wanna know if it's you I don't trust*, the narrator of the song tells his suspect beloved, *'Cause I damn sure don't trust myself.*

Without ever mentioning either of their names or any details of their lives, Springsteen captured in the final lyric of this song the reality of a troubled marriage like his own, an uncommunicative ongoing exchange between two professional performers. More than a mere pastiche, "Brilliant Disguise" was a song that could stand with Carole King and Gerry Goffin's "Will You Still Love Me Tomorrow?" as proof that traditional pop could be more than least-common-denominator drivel. Moreover, casting aside another criticism frequently hurled at pop songs, "Brilliant Disguise" was most assuredly not a song that was primarily aimed at teenagers. For persons under the age of adulthood, such lines as *God have mercy on the man / Who doubts what he's sure of* were probably not as resonant as they were for their elders.

One thing that makes Springsteen's declaration that all these songs emerged in a quick burst more likely is the fact that only seventeen songs survive from this period, with an eighteenth that later showed up in live shows and was probably recorded during those three weeks as well. These seventeen or eighteen songs chart male-female relationships from their most youthful and optimistic to their most decayed and dark, but one significant theme is almost wholly absent from the group, quite notably so, given Springsteen's earlier work in this vein, as well as the conflicts that had reportedly marred his marriage: children. In earlier songs like "The River," "My Hometown," and "Roulette," Springsteen directly connected children with the fact of being married, as if one inevitably entailed the other. Here, however, at his most self-exploratory, he had the presence of mind to separate out love from procreation, to understand that whether his wife did or didn't want to have children had nothing to do with the larger problems in their relationship. The only children in these new songs were Bruce himself in the two songs about his parents, the pointedly abandoned son in the blues-tinged "Spare Parts," and the child the singer implicitly longs to have in "Valentine's Day."

Even in this last song, though, the problem in the characters' relationship isn't the presence, absence, or possibility of children. It's the narrator's own compulsive solitude. [H]e travels fastest who travels alone, he believes in spite of his best hopes, and oddly he asks his presumed love to be his lonely valentine, with the oxymoronic adjective lending depth and special poignancy to the too often candy-colored noun. Again and again in these songs, the characters' problems stem not from current conditions but from preexisting fears, deception, and failed communication, You me and all that stuff we're so scared of, as Springsteen so pithily put it in "Tunnel of Love."

When Bruce left Paris in November, he had essentially given up on his marriage. In the songs he had written since then, he learned to take responsibility for his own interpersonal failures. Inevitably, Tunnel of Love, the album on which twelve of these songs were released, would in time be compared to Blood on the Tracks, the 1974 Bob Dylan album that may or may not have been inspired by the slow disintegration of that singer's marriage to Sara Lownds. In many ways, though, Tunnel of Love was a more mature album than Blood on the Tracks, if not necessarily a more accomplished one. With the exception of the relatively weak "When You're Alone," Springsteen indulges in no petty revenge or jealousy on any of his songs. Instead, he seizes a moment of personal failure as an opportunity for greater self-knowledge. Locked in a room with just a tape machine and a guitar again, he simply had nowhere left to run.

———

TUNNEL OF LOVE came together quickly, as *Nebraska* had, but there don't seem to have ever been any plans to release Springsteen's home recordings of these new songs as is. In the late spring, he was joined at A&M Studios in Los Angeles by a trio of country musicians: harmonica player Jimmie Wood, fiddler Richard Greene, and pedal steel guitar player Jay Dee Maness of the Desert Rose Band. Some of Bruce's new songs (most obviously "Spare Parts") would have lent themselves quite easily to a country arrangement, while others (such as "Brilliant Disguise") might have been changed drastically. Whether it was because this new stylistic approach didn't work, or because Greene went public with the fact that the sessions were taking place, the only fragment that was even used from these LA sessions was Wood's harmonica overdub on "Spare Parts." By July, Bruce was back east and dropping in at Key Largo, the Green Parrot, the Deck House, the Columns, the Tradewinds, and the Pony. And as *Tunnel of Love* was being prepared for release, first Patti, then Max, then Danny, then Roy, then Garry, Nils, and Clarence were brought in to the Hit Factory to add overdubs on the solo recordings that Bruce had cut at home six months earlier.

Despite his dramatic gesture the previous autumn, Bruce had never really let go of the E Street Band. How could he? Back in April, some of the band had played with him, Jon Bon Jovi, and members of Cats on a Smooth Surface, Patti's old group, at the Stone Pony. In August, even more of them were back for two more dates at the club. While Bruce was working on the new album, sales of the live set fell off precipitously. Did the potential audience for Springsteen that *Born in the U.S.A.* had artificially inflated to megastar proportions finally settle back down to normal? Or did Springsteen fans simply want something new? Would a new Bruce Springsteen album à la *Nebraska* be enough? Or did they really want a new E Street Band album?

They would all find out soon enough. In August, Bruce delivered his eighth studio album to the label. Still thinking in terms of LPs or cassettes rather than the increasingly dominant medium of CDs, Bruce laid out a two-sided journey for the new album, as he had on *Wild and Innocent*, from the youthful cockiness of "Ain't Got You" and "Tougher than the Rest" (a thematic rewrite of "None but the Brave," one of the many sweet discards from the 1983 band sessions) to the interpersonal desolation of "Brilliant Disguise" and "One Step Up." In September, Bruce shot the first of three planned videos for the album on a soundstage in Sandy Hook, a comfortable drive from his place in Rumson. It was for "Brilliant Disguise," and for practically the first time since he had agreed to start doing videos, he would be singing live when the cameras rolled rather than lip-synching to a recorded track. A second video, for "Tunnel of Love," was shot in November at the abandoned and appropriately haunted Palace Amusements on the boardwalk in Asbury Park. A third video was shot three months later at the Wonder Bar, just four blocks away on Ocean. For this album at least, the promotional images were true New Jersey.

One of the nice things about videos was that they let Springsteen put off the question of whether he was going to tour, and with whom. Thanks in no small part to Bruce's continued presence on MTV and VH1, "Brilliant Disguise" went to no. 5, "Tunnel of Love" to no. 9, "One Step Up" to no. 13. More user-friendly than *Nebraska* at least, *Tunnel of Love* was Bruce's third album in a row to go to no. 1, and his fourth overall if you skipped *Nebraska* and went back to *The River*. As the promotion machine played itself out, Springsteen spent the fall and early winter playing his favorite types of gigs: quick guest shots (with U2 in Philly and both Bobby Bandiera and Cats at the Pony); benefits (for homeless children at Madison Square Garden); weddings (Danny's second); funerals (John Hammond's); and tribute concerts (for the living Roy Orbison and the deceased Harry Chapin). On Halloween, he and the whole band except Nils and Clarence played a surprise midnight gig at McLoone's Rum Runner in Sea Bright, even premiering three songs off the new album. But, as with *Nebraska*, no formal tour was announced.

Come the New Year, though, as the album's sales began to decline, the decision was made to put a brief tour together—an "Express" tour to "small venues." In mid-January, Springsteen's people announced that he would "perform either solo or with a few musicians" on the tour, but within a few weeks he had apparently bowed to the inevitable. Yes, he would tour with the E Street Band—but only to arenas, no stadiums this time, and for no more than two dates per city. There would also be a bit more of a stage set (a ticket seller's booth, a bench, etc.), so maybe this tour wouldn't end up being quite so small after all.

Going out on tour with the band again, he needed to find something new to keep the shows from being too predictable. For the first time in over a decade, he and the band would bring along the Miami Horns, the horn section that frequently toured with Southside and the Jukes, which would make some of the more familiar songs sound different. Since he had put out only one disc of new material since the last tour, plus two or three new songs on the live set, Springsteen also decided to dig back into the past and add some B-sides to his sets, as well as some unreleased songs that had slipped through the cracks. All that, plus the new album's emphasis on relationships, would allow for a show different enough from the one he and the band had done to death in 1984 and 1985. He would also be changing around the way the band was arranged onstage, most obviously bringing Scialfa up front to permit more direct male-female interchanges on songs like "Cover Me" and "Brilliant Disguise." Like the addition of a horn section, this stage arrangement was reaching back almost a decade and a half to the pre–*Born to Run* tours that had so prominently featured Suki Lahav.

In late January, the band reassembled at the Expo Theater in Fort Monmouth for the first of several tour rehearsals. Given what had allegedly transpired in Bruce's LA bedroom fifteen months earlier, at least some of the band members must have been surprised to find themselves back together again. They rehearsed a number of songs off the new album, taking two stabs in particular at "Valentine's Day" but never quite nailing it. They hauled both "From Small Things" and the Donna Summer giveaway "Protection" out of the closet and tried out two fairly interesting covers: a brief attempt at the Four Tops' "Something about You" and a radical rewrite of Gino Washington's 1963 single "Gino Is a Coward."

When Bruce and the band started the *Tunnel of Love* Express tour four weeks later, however, most of the experiments they had tried out in rehearsal weren't there. The Washington song was, now called "I'm a Coward When It Comes to Love," but at least a quarter of the songs they had practiced never made it in front of a paying audience. The set was enlivened by fresh E Street renditions of "Be True," "Roulette," and "Light of Day," not to mention a new reggae-style evolutionary number called "Part Man, Part Monkey." On opening night, Bruce and the band performed eight of the twelve songs on *Tunnel of Love* but definitely favored the album's sunnier first half over its more troubled second half. In general, the setlist was noticeably lighter than the brooding album that this tour was supposed to be promoting, and the omission of some of the band's Fort Monmouth experiments (particularly "Valentine's Day" and "Protection") certainly reinforced this impression.

Yet from that first night, 25 February, longtime fans could see that something about Bruce had changed over the last few years. At the beginning of the tour at least, his marriage seemed to be back on—Juli attended several early performances; Bruce made ersatz casual comments onstage now about being married—but that wasn't what was different. The monologues seemed more personal than they had been in a decade. Before "Spare Parts," for example, Bruce detailed the spousal abuse that a childhood neighbor named Audrey had suffered. It was a story that reached back to the beginning of the decade, to the compulsive visits to Institute Street in Freehold that had led him to begin psychotherapy. The way Springsteen told it to the opening-night audience in Worcester, however, such visits had been healing, not neurotic. *One night*, he remembered, *when I walked back down that street, I felt different. . . . I got in my car, and I drove home to my house and to my family because I knew that street wasn't mine anymore.*

At the time the anecdote probably took place, in the fall of 1981, Springsteen had almost been too paralyzed to decide where he wanted to live. Over six years later, although Bruce may have jocularly pretended otherwise, he knew that there was no one waiting in his house for him, and no family other than his parents and sisters, all of whom were across the continent from him. His big house in Jersey was a place to store his clothes, guitars, cars, and motorcycles. It wasn't really a home.

The way in which that absence, that loneliness, ate away at Spring-

steen was also apparent in the even more personally revelatory introduction to that night's encores:

> *I know one of the hardest things for me over the past ten years
> has been trying to understand what growing up and being a
> man is about; trying to find out how to make some sort of home
> for myself and then trying to hold on to it, which is a hard thing
> for anybody to do. I know that my dad did his best to show me
> what that is about, and things get pretty confusing.*

At this point, restless fans were probably wondering what song he
was going to play after this moody introduction. He had come out alone,
without the band, with just an acoustic guitar and a harmonica rack.

> *Now, when I was twenty-four years old, I wrote this song and it
> was about a guy and a girl who wanted to run and keep on run-
> ning, and as I got older, I realized that that is my song and
> maybe that was your song too. But I also realized, as I got older,
> that I didn't want it to be, that I wanted to learn how to make a
> home for myself, learn how to fit in, 'cause there's really nothing,
> there's nothing in being homeless.*

There was a pause, awkward for both Springsteen and his audience.

> *So, anyway, I wish you luck on your trip, and I do this for you.*

And with that Springsteen started to play "Born to Run"—but it
was a version unlike any other he had ever done before. Even at its
most suicidal, "Born to Run" (which had been written on piano, not
acoustic guitar) had always been a song about exuberance and escape.
This version was slow and brooding, far more trapped than even the
acoustic "Thunder Road." In this version, only a fool would think that
either the singer or his Mary would ever get out alive. Played this way,
the song was almost a prior echo of "Fast Car," Tracy Chapman's song
about two doomed homeless lovers who would run if they only had
the wheels.

This brooding acoustic version of "Born to Run" is fairly unique, a passive-aggressive performative act at which even Bob Dylan or Johnny Rotten would probably have to marvel. *I do this for you,* Springsteen told his audience, almost explicitly saying that he was tired of singing one of his most famous songs. Then he proceeded to perform that song in such a way that he broke down his audience's familiarity with it, thus denying them the most basic form of gratification that old pop songs customarily give us. Moreover, his introduction to the song specifically repudiated its lyric, saying that it carried a message to which he no longer subscribed. A few nights later, he softened his introduction, calling "Born to Run" *my favorite song . . . I don't know if it's my best song*—but once again, he sang the brooding version. Many fans left these concerts puzzled. Even some of his most open-minded fans, while they may have appreciated the experiment that Springsteen was offering up, hoped that he would play the song the "real" way the next time he swung through town.

But the sets on the *Tunnel of Love* Express tour mostly sounded the same from night to night. Fans who bought tickets for multiple dates in the hopes of hearing notably different concerts were sorely disappointed. On this tour, if you wanted to hear Springsteen try something a little different, you had to come to the sound checks. On previous tours, sound checks had been the places to briefly thrash out arrangements that would make it into the actual performances a few days later, maybe even that night. This time, though, they were more like the alternate songs that Springsteen had tried back in the late January rehearsals: interesting deviations from the tour's rigid structure, but ones that he seemed to try only when playing to an audience of dozens, not thousands. When no one but the band and crew was listening, Springsteen was playing a much wider variety of covers than he could usually get away when he sat in at the Pony. Before the second date in Chapel Hill, he essayed the Byrds, Dylan, Van Morrison, and the Everly Brothers; the second night in Cleveland, it was Johnny Cash and Hank Williams; the last night in Atlanta, more Morrison, Cash, Dylan, and the Everlys, with some Animals and Sam Cooke thrown in for good measure.

Throughout March and April, two songs kept showing up consistently during the sound checks. The first was "Tunnel of Love," which Springsteen and the band obviously did perform for their audiences: it opened the show every night. That song may have been practiced repeatedly because the opening was keyed to a stage set, the first that Springsteen had ever used for his concerts. Its most prominent feature was a ticket window, staffed by Jersey Shore veteran Terry Magovern. The band walked onstage singly and mimed buying tickets from Magovern, thus literalizing the song's central metaphor. Every band member had his own unique bit of business, and Scialfa even walked in with a bouquet of balloons. As a rule, the more stage business you have, the more can go wrong, so that may have been why they needed to practice this song at almost every hall they visited.

The other song that kept showing up in sound checks, however, was one that they weren't performing for audiences yet: the six-year-old "Across the Borderline." Ry Cooder had written it for the soundtrack of *The Border*, a Tony Richardson film that starred Jack Nicholson as a guard on the Mexican border who goes from taking payoffs to caring about those who try to cross over into the United States illegally. While the film's story would clearly exercise a greater influence on Springsteen's work a few years later, on this tour it was Cooder's song that fascinated him. When Steve Pond of *Rolling Stone* sat in for the sound check at the Omni in Atlanta, a crew member confirmed that Springsteen was obsessed with Cooder's song, not only playing it in the sound checks but repeatedly playing it on the tour bus between gigs too. In hindsight, it's clear why the song fascinated him. "Across the Borderline" was an older, wiser answer to songs like "Badlands" or "The Promised Land," the songs of defiant faith that he had written a little over a decade before, songs that were wholly absent from his repertoire on this tour for the first time since then. Much like "Sun City," "Across the Borderline" was a relatively recent song that so perfectly described Springsteen's own views that it must have seemed incredible to him that he hadn't written it himself.

On 27 April, the fourth of five nights at the LA Sports Arena, the band finally premiered "Across the Borderline," which Springsteen had been running them through during sound checks for at least six weeks. Interestingly enough, even though it was a cover, it didn't go in the encores. It appeared in the second set, in the spot where "Walk like a Man" sometimes went, and it changed the emotional temperature of the set as it slid rapidly toward the one-two punch of "Dancing in the Dark" and "Light of Day" just before the encores. "Walk like a Man" acknowledged Springsteen's own fears about not being able to make a relationship work, while Cooder's song pointed out that an idealized object may prove disappointing when it is actually attained. Either mood led naturally into the jumpy last-ditch anticipation of "Dancing in the Dark," an invitation to engagement from a man who is long used to being solitary.

"[T]he type of connection you can make in your show," Springsteen had told Steve Pond for the *Rolling Stone* story, "which is *enormous*, you can't live there," but Springsteen's behavior on this tour made it seem even more as if he did. In the elaborate staging for "Tunnel of Love" that opened all these spring concerts, Bruce came out last, duded up and carrying a bouquet of roses that he threw into the audience, saying something like *Wanna date?* or *Are you ready to ride?* By opening his first sets in this way, and by making "Dancing in the Dark" (during which he plucked a dancing partner from the same section into which he had thrown the roses) almost the last song in the second set, he structured the entire concert as much around his relationship with the audience as around the more general idea of intimate relations between women and men. It made it seem as if he were dating the audience, trying each night to make their relationship work.

Slowly but surely, the setlist was changing—not the body of the concert so much as the encores. They were getting longer, some nights as many as ten extra songs when there were only twelve songs in each of the two main sets. It was as if the encores were becoming an entirely separate set of their own, a fun one without the baggage of the tour's stated themes. There were very few one-off experiments, though, the kind one might have seen on previous tours. Once a song got in, it usually stuck: "Have Love Will Travel" and "Across the Borderline" were now reasonably permanent parts of the show, as was a cover of John Lee Hooker's "Boom Boom" that owed more than a little to the 1965 version by the Animals. As on the *River* tour, all the new songs added were covers. As far as the unperformed songs from the new album were concerned, Springsteen and the band tried "Cautious Man" once, but "Valentine's Day" and "When You're Alone" never.

After five nights at Madison Square Garden in May, there was a two-week break before the tour headed off to Europe. In the States, the "two dates per city" rule had been dropped. In Europe, the "no stadiums" rule also fell by the wayside, perhaps because European cities didn't have the same sort of medium-size indoor arenas that their American counterparts favored for basketball or hockey. The European leg of the allegedly express tour opened at the Stadio Comunale in Turin on 11 June with a setlist and performance, right down to the flowers, that was pretty much the same one that the first audience in Worcester had heard more than three months earlier.

And then on 15 June, the storm broke. In Rome, where Springsteen and the band did two virtually identical concerts at the Stadio Flaminio, Bruce and Patti were photographed nuzzling in their underwear on a hotel balcony. The whispers that had been flying back and forth for months quickly turned into gossipy shouts: Bruce's marriage with Juli was a lie; Patti and Bruce looked suspiciously close onstage; Patti had set her sights on Bruce from the moment she joined the band; Bruce had been involved with Patti for years . . .

By mid-June of 1988, Springsteen and Scialfa were definitely involved in a sexual relationship. When that relationship began, however, and how intimate it was, even during that summer, is known to only them. They may have become more than co-workers as early as the winter of 1987 (when, as Christopher Sandford shrewdly notes, Springsteen shifted his nickname for Scialfa from "doll" to "darlin'"), or they may have remained fascinated with each other but technically apart until as late as the spring of 1988 (when Julianne Phillips left the tour huffily after a few dates and Springsteen was ending his phone calls to her, according to conflicting accounts, either in tears or slamming down the phone and saying, "Whatever"). For all the personal breakthroughs Bruce had theoretically made during that cold and lonely winter in Rumson, it was still too easy for him to slip back into old habits and old assumptions. For the first few months of the tour, he seems to have talked himself back into trying to reestablish his marriage with Phillips, just as he had somehow talked himself back into touring with the E Street Band. By late April, though, it seemed clear that whatever new arrangement he had tried with Juli had effected even less change in the state of his marriage than his rearrangement of onstage personnel had made in his public performances. One cannot know for sure, but it seems probable that by 10 May, when Springsteen first replaced the youthfully sweet "Be True" in the no. 2 slot of the first set at one of his concerts with his rawly sexual cover of "Boom Boom," he had decided to exchange a ten-year-old idea of fidelity for a recent rediscovery of the joys of lust.

Throughout that time, though, Springsteen had never really deceived anyone—well, certainly not his audience. Every time he had a chance on this tour, he spoke about how difficult marriage was, and his new songs couldn't have been any blunter about how ill suited he might have been for the institution. He and Phillips were separated in every sense but the legal one for the better part of a year, and it is almost certain that Springsteen's more personal relationship with Scialfa, whatever its nature, didn't begin until after that separation occurred. True, the few times Phillips attended shows on this tour, she left angry at Springsteen and Scialfa's onstage interaction, but given all that passed between the actress and her husband, that may simply have been a matter of being publicly embarrassed.

After the circus of the last four years, not to mention the rumors that had been flying since the tour began, it seems incredible that Springsteen didn't know that paparazzi were following his every move on this tour. Then again, maybe he did. Three and a half months into this grueling "express," maybe he was tired of playing an offstage role as well as an onstage one. On 16 June, the day after the photos from the hotel balcony were published, Springsteen permanently dropped "Be True" from the second slot in the setlist, where it had been swapping places with "Boom Boom" for over a month. For the rest of the tour, he regularly followed up "Tunnel of Love" with Hooker's explosive conveyance of sexual desire. Phillips filed for divorce in August. Scialfa was at Springsteen's side both onstage and off for the rest of the summer, and paparazzi were always following them.

Escape from this traveling sideshow came, for Springsteen at least, in a reembrace of politics. A few days after the incident in Rome,

Bruce and Clarence participated in the SOS Racisme! concert at the Château de Vincennes in Paris, and they performed four songs ("The Promised Land," "My Hometown," "Blowin' in the Wind," and "Bad Moon Rising") that Bruce had not yet performed at any other concert that year. Then on 3 July, Springsteen announced from the stage in Stockholm that he and the band would be participating in Human Rights Now!, a concert tour for Amnesty International that fall to celebrate the fortieth anniversary of the UN Declaration of Human Rights. Like that of Steve Van Zandt's "Sun City" single, the goal of the tour was publicity first, fund-raising second. Two years earlier, Springsteen had declined the organization's request to join its first rock venture, the Conspiracy of Hope tour, but in the summer of 1988 the time suddenly seemed right. After the year he'd had, Springsteen could certainly do worse than dive back into politics, where less of his self needed to be laid bare onstage.

In August, Bruce and the band returned to the States for a break between the end of their own tour and the beginning of Human Rights Now! Late in the month, Bruce did one of his drop-ins at Madison Square Garden, performing with Sting, another participant in the Amnesty tour, who joined him in an earnestly country rendition of "The River." Sting and Springsteen apparently hit it off immediately, not least because they shared a similarly jokey attitude toward being pop stars. At the informational press conferences at each stop on the tour, they mocked each other's public personae almost relentlessly. "I play my songs," Bruce told one group of reporters, "and between sets Sting lectures me on what's wrong with all of them." Tossing the self-conscious joke right back at him, Sting responded, "I'm going to be a better person for having known you, Bruce." The two men might sound different in their press releases, but the fact was that the ex-English teacher from Wallsend and the ex-house painter from Freehold had more in common than most casual observers might suspect. Born within two years of each other, they were also both currently dating women whom some fans incorrectly blamed for the ends of their first marriages. Most important, although neither of them was probably aware of it yet, both men were currently in the midst of a three-year patch of writer's block, brought on in Sting's case by his reaction to his father's recent death. Certainly, he and Springsteen had a great deal to talk about between gigs.

With five acts on the Human Rights Now! bill, Bruce and the band had time for only fifteen songs most nights on the tour, but it was clear from his reaction that he preferred this kind of touring. Yes, they were playing stadiums, but at least they did not play more than two dates per venue. They were barnstorming around the world: Europe in less than two weeks, North America in just ten days; and places like Costa Rica and New Delhi where the E Street Band had never performed before. Most moving of all for the entire band was playing the National Sports Stadium in Harare, Zimbabwe. For all Bruce's passionate commitment to a biracial society, the audiences at most of his own concerts were still overwhelmingly white. In Zimbabwe, they found that they could move primarily black audiences with their music too.

Amnesty International was a cause seemingly made for Springsteen, far more than any political party or candidate. Its most legendary tactic—individuals writing letters on behalf of individuals—was ideally suited to a man who was innately suspicious of any kind of formal organization. As he told reporters at the tour's press conference in Barcelona, "If you believe that an individual can make a difference and that a single human spirit is a powerful thing, Amnesty International, in a very tough, pragmatic and realistic way, gives you an opportunity to put your ideals in service in a world in which they are so badly needed." At dates in English-speaking countries, he blended these ideas, in almost identical language, with the "let freedom ring" speech that he had used to introduce "Born to Run" early in the *Born in the U.S.A.* tour four years before. This new hybrid speech introduced "My Hometown," offering up a course of action in the face of injustice that the song's well-meaning but impotent narrator could have used.

The longer the Amnesty tour went on, the closer many of the performers got. Davey Sancious was part of Peter Gabriel's touring band, and some nights he provided a third keyboard on E Street songs like "Glory Days" or "Cadillac Ranch," on which he had never played before. By trial and error, Bruce found the Police's "Ev'ry Breath You Take" better suited to him than "Message in a Bottle," and Sting continued guesting on "The River," with Gabriel's violin player joining them at least one night. In New Delhi, Springsteen played harmonica with sitarist Ravi Shankar on one of Shankar's songs. Springsteen became, in a way, the head cheerleader of the tour, persuading his tourmates to join him at the end of the show in a condensed version of Bob Dylan's "Chimes of Freedom" many nights, as well as a cover of Bob Marley's "Get Up Stand Up." The last night, in Buenos Aires, Bruce's set was almost half encores, with Branford Marsalis from Sting's band adding a second sax on "Raise Your Hand" and all the headliners joining in on "Twist and Shout," several of them in Springsteenesque blue jeans and bandannas.

It was fun, but in mid-October, after six weeks and five continents, it was over. And now, finally off the road after eight whirlwind months, all the insights Springsteen had had twenty months before were still there waiting for him. Back in the winter of 1987, he had grasped some deep truths about himself, but he hadn't really acted on any of his insights. He had ended a failed marriage, yet even that was a decision that he had deferred for a year and a half and essentially backed his way into. Once he was back in the States, this passivity continued for the better part of a year. For at least eleven months after the end of Human Rights Now!, he couldn't finish a song. Every piece he started sounded like a darker, inferior outtake from *Tunnel of Love*. During that time, he performed quite a number of drop-ins, by now a familiar indication that his creativity was spinning its wheels. He played with John Prine; Southside Johnny Lyon, Nils Lofgren, and Neil Young; at the Pony; at the Waldorf Astoria for the Hall of Fame bash; at the Rubber Club, Mickey Rourke's joint in LA, and at Roy Bittan's wedding at the Carlyle Hotel in Manhattan.

He was living with Patti all this time, in Manhattan, Hollywood, and Rumson. She worked on her long-deferred solo album, while Bruce acted just as he had with Julianne Phillips when the two had begun living together. When the times came for quotidian intimacy, the hard work of any relationship, Bruce started checking the exits, which may explain all his spontaneous gigging that year. "Oh, I'm going out of the house for a little while, and I'm going down . . . ," he later said, parodying his own standard line. But if Bruce responded to their first year of living together by being typically Bruce, Patti's response to his behavior was nothing like Juli's. She didn't have to head out the door for her work. She dug in, calling Bruce on his evasions, challenging him to put some effort into the relationship he allegedly wanted to have.

It all culminated in what appears to have been a most unpleasant summer, the first summer of the first Bush presidency, which Bruce spent (as usual) near the Jersey Shore. The drop-ins that summer became almost compulsive. At Cheers in Long Branch that August, the man who had played to 100,000 people four years earlier dropped in for a rendition of "Willie and the Hand Jive" with Bobby Bandiera in front of about 30 patrons. Bruce also had a flu he couldn't shake that summer and experienced serious respiratory problems. He was grumpy, moody, and picking fights with friends and co-workers. On 23 September 1989, a little less than a year after the end of the Human Rights Now! tour, Bruce threw himself a fortieth birthday party at the Rum Runner in Sea Bright, a venue convenient to his place in Rumson. The band was there, even Little Steven, and they sang Chuck Berry, Ben E. King, Ray Charles, Sam Cooke, and Beatles songs. They even did one Bruce Springsteen number ("Glory Days").

The next day, Bruce hopped on a brand-new blue-and-silver Harley and headed west, toward Route 70 and inevitably, almost mythically, toward Route 66. "You know," he told a friend from Missouri, "you can always get off the wheel . . . it really *is* your land." Traveling with Bruce was Matty DiLea, the same friend who had flown back from Paris on the Concorde with him nearly three years before, as well as Matty's brothers Tony and Eddie. Not every stop or activity on their itinerary is known—there appears to have been at least one very pleased female fan in Texas, for example—but they did make good time. Less than a week after starting out from Jersey, they walked into Matt's Saloon in Prescott, Arizona, asking where the "greaser chicks" were, and Bruce made the acquaintance of Brenda "Bubbles" Pechanec, a barmaid who had been married eight times. As he took the stage to join the members of the Mile High Band for the inevitable drop-in performance, Bruce declared, *I'm here in Prescott to take Bubbles away and be her ninth!* Among the songs he performed that night with the astonished band for a handful of attendant Hells Angels was "Sweet Little Sixteen," which he had done with the E Streeters at his birthday party.

On 18 October 1989, after his bike trip with the DiLeas was over, Springsteen called each of the members of the E Street Band individually and told them that the band was over, really over this time. Some were shocked, but after the last three years they shouldn't have been. As one of them later remarked, "All of us needed to get off the jet." Around the same time, Bruce and Patti decided to have a baby. Now Bruce was almost exactly where he had wanted to be three years earlier: free of the burden of E Street assumptions and ready to start a family. There were two crucial differences, however: the woman in his life was not Julianne Phillips; and in working through the end of his relationship with Phillips, he had in theory gained a certain amount of self-knowledge. Now it was time to see whether he could apply it in practice.

ONE OF THE FIRST THINGS Springsteen took to that year was therapy. He had seen therapists off and on for at least seven years, but now he decided to get serious about it. As he had understood for close to three years, a great many of his problems with other people were not necessarily their fault. Once you get to the other side of forty, what goes on in your head can't plausibly be laid down solely on your parents, no matter how many great songs they've provided you with material for. By then it's time to admit that a fair share of what you don't like about your life probably stems from you, and by that age you should finally get serious about dealing with it.

For an artist, however, psychotherapy can be tricky. In any medium, the difference between competence and inspiration, between craft and art, is most often instinctual. The more self-conscious an artist becomes, the harder it can be to make art that isn't studied or mannered. That's not a problem if you're an avant-garde novelist, but if you're an artist who has and wants to continue to have a wide following, it can pose a conundrum. "I questioned all my motivations," Bruce later said of his intensive dive into therapy. "Why am I writing what I'm writing? Why am I saying what I'm saying? Do I mean it? Am

I bullshitting? Am I just trying to be the most popular guy in town? Do I need to be liked that much?" Trying to write popular songs with all those questions buzzing around your head is not unlike trying to walk while thinking about all the individual movements within your body that enable walking. It can't help slowing you down. The best thing might have been for Springsteen to take time off from writing while he worked all this out, but he had already lost almost three years and wanted to get going again.

Fortunately, he stumbled upon a way of tricking himself into being relaxed about writing again. He and Patti were living in California now rather than New Jersey (which both of them thought would relieve a certain amount of pressure), and Roy and his wife were living out there too. One day when Bruce was visiting the Bittans, Roy played him a few instrumentals he had written. Bruce had an idea: he could write words to Roy's music. He wrote genre pieces at first, old soul and R&B songs like the ones he so much enjoyed covering. That way, there was no pressure to make "a statement" while his mind was still rearranging itself around the insights emerging from concentrated psychotherapy and the serious, truly intimate relationship with Scialfa. Perhaps inspired by his recent cover of Elvis Presley's "Viva Las Vegas" for a charity album—the first recording made under his name with a band that contained no past or present E Street Band members—Springsteen came up with a nifty assemblage of love-as-gambling metaphors that he titled "Roll of the Dice." Another of Bittan's tunes inspired a by-the-numbers seesaw sort of song called "Trouble in Paradise," about a doomed marriage that didn't bear too much resemblance to Springsteen's one with Phillips.

More telling, however, was a third collaboration from that November called "Real World." From a technical standpoint, the lyrics Springsteen wrote to this Bittan tune are almost the reverse of the ones for "Roll of the Dice": a tangle of competing metaphors rather than a single metaphor worked to death across four minutes. If the *Darkness* songs had their *fields* and the *Tunnel* songs their *roads* and *rides*, this song had *roads, rivers, carnivals,* and *tumbling dice* to spare. Still, there is a sweet taste of middle-aged acceptance in a couplet as seemingly contradictory as *If love is hopeless, hopeless at best / Come on, put on your party dress.* Such lines represent a mature evolution from the singer's wish fifteen years earlier to *die with you Wendy on the streets tonight / In an everlasting kiss.* They are also much closer to an apocalyptic party song like Warren Zevon's "Monkey Wash Donkey Rinse" than a more casual listener might suspect.

If the lyrics' metaphors and even ideas seem confused, that is only because they reflect Springsteen's state of mind when he wrote the song in the fall of 1989. "Real World" isn't a thesis statement song like "The Promised Land" or "Reason to Believe," written toward the end of the periods during which he composed the material for *Darkness* and *Nebraska,* respectively. Rather, this collaboration with Bittan voices an explicit wish to *find* a thesis statement for his ninth album:

> *I'm searchin' for one clear moment*
> *Of love and truth*
> *I still got a little faith*
> *But what I need is some proof tonight*
> *I'm lookin' for it in your eyes*

In terms of songwriting (if not life writing), in December Bruce kicked off the training wheels. At first, he wrote a lyric called "Soul Driver" to one of Roy's stray tunes, but he later decided that he could come up with a much better tune for it himself. Then there was a song called "Man's Job," which he wrote without any input from Roy. It was yet another ersatz pop standard, which worked a single idea for its duration without the sort of coded or anthropological specificity that had previously distinguished Springsteen's lyrics.

But the tricks were working. After woodshedding these songs for a while, Bruce and Roy would go into Bruce's home studio (much more elaborate than the one he had had six years before) and lay down a four-track recording with Bruce doing vocals and guitar and Roy doing keyboards and bass to a basic drum track. Before the year was out, they were ready to head over to Soundworks West and record with two other musicians: on drums, Jeff Porcaro of Toto (who had also played on the "Viva Las Vegas" cover and with whom Bruce had felt a connection); and on bass, Randy Jackson (a senior vice president of A&R

for Columbia Records who had also played bass for Journey for a year around the time that Bruce was putting together the live set). Sometimes the four men played live, sometimes Porcaro and Jackson added parts to the recordings that Springsteen and Bittan had already laid down in his home studio. Come the New Year, Davey Sancious was called in to temporarily replace Roy on keyboards for the rewritten "Soul Driver" and the *Tunnel* tour staple "Part Man, Part Monkey."

Then the real guest stars were brought in. This whole project had found its voice in Bruce's embrace of soul and R&B records, old genres that were just on the verge of turning peculiarly hot again. Although the earliest tracks laid down for the project featured Bruce singing backup for himself, once he laid down solid drums, bass, and keyboard tracks, the next sound he knew he wanted to layer on top of them were harmony vocals. What he wanted, though, was not the sort of female backup vocals that Patti had provided on the last album and tour. He wanted male backing vocals, tenor baritones that could support his best attempt at blue-eyed soul, and serve as alternative yet reinforcing versions of pop masculinity. For this, he turned to two men (Sam Moore of Sam and Dave and Bobby Hatfield of the Righteous Brothers) who had made this sort of male duetting a staple of 1960s soul and pop, as well as a third (Bobby King) who had formed a latter-day soul duo with Terry Evans in the late 1980s that was simply called "Bobby King and Terry Evans." King sang on "Roll of the Dice," Moore on "Real World" and "Soul Driver," and both men created an impressive three-way call-and-response with Springsteen on "Man's Job," probably the most accomplished recording, but not song, from this early phase of the project.

Most of the songs continued in this neo-soul vein, with "Leavin' Train," "Gloria's Eyes," "All or Nothin' at All," "30 Days Out," "Trouble River," and "Seven Angels" all piling up as Patti passed from the second trimester of her pregnancy into the third. As usual with Springsteen, though, he was writing songs in another generic vein at the same time, a quieter vein that reached its purest pop form in a country-styled, wistful jealousy number called "I Wish I Were Blind" (the track on which Hatfield guested). An even more interesting example of this quieter style was "With Ev'ry Wish," one of the few songs for which we can be certain that the core recording, stripped of drums, bass, and trumpet, stemmed from those initial duet sessions with Bittan at Bruce's home studio. In a way, "With Ev'ry Wish" was Springsteen's attempt to write his own version, finally, of "Across the Borderline." Here, though, as in "Real World," the weary singer draws the courage to believe yet again from *someone waitin' with a look in her eyes. Tonight I'll drink from her waters*, he sings, *to quench my thirst*, once again admitting to a personal insufficiency at which an older song like "Because the Night" merely hinted.

If, at this point in Springsteen's songwriting, Scialfa was still only an object of enabling desire, that would have indicated that he hadn't made much interpersonal progress at all. Among the songs Springsteen completed in early 1990, however, are two that suggest that he really was working at his relationship with the mother of his soon-to-be-born child, working in a way that he had probably never worked at any other relationship before. More than any other lyric from this period, "Human Touch" seems at first glance most marred by Springsteen's dive into therapy. The bridge in particular could almost be lifted right out of a self-help book: its insights are admirable, but that doesn't mean they're good songwriting. In fact, such lyrics may be less artistic precisely because they are so "on the nose."

Nevertheless, "Human Touch" represented a quantum leap forward for Springsteen as a human being, and perhaps as a songwriter as well. In "The Long Goodbye" (another probably autobiographical song from this period) Springsteen explicitly looked back on his prior mistakes and reassessed them, but in "Human Touch" the singer is taking his interlocutor to task for his self-pity, fears, and lack of intimate human connection. Despite the gender of the pronouns in the latter song, it makes sense only within the context of Springsteen's life in the early 1990s as a song addressed to Springsteen himself, respinning the connection rap that Springsteen had laid on Steve Pond during his *Rolling Stone* interview a year and a half before, with a dose of tough love tossed in for good measure.

One way to view "Human Touch"—especially since it is the only track from this period for which Springsteen felt the need for female backing vocals, including Scialfa's—is that in writing this song he was adopting Patti's voice, perhaps echoing, not his psychotherapist's insights, but the ones Scialfa had offered when she challenged him on his fear of engagement the previous summer. Nor is this the only song from this period that would seem to adopt Scialfa's perspective regarding Springsteen. "Sad Eyes," which was recorded in late January of 1990 but wasn't officially released for nearly nine years, similarly makes no sense when seen as a song from Springsteen's perspective on an emerging relationship. Even back in the 1970s, Springsteen was never one to let a relationship develop slowly, as the narrator of this song does. He was much more like the quick-pickup narrator of "One Step Up," one of the songs on *Tunnel of Love* that felt embarrassingly close to life. The idea of a slow-burning desire that blossoms into full physicality when it's *good and ready* was virtually unknown among Springsteen's relationships—except for his relationship with Scialfa.

In the best songs on *Tunnel of Love*, Springsteen faced some hard truths about his own fear of honest, intimate engagement with another human being. But just being honest about what's going on in your own head is only half of love. If that's all you do, you're just being a clearheaded solipsist. As the authors of both "Sad Eyes" and *The Autobiography of Alice B. Toklas* could tell you, the other part, the best part, of love is trying to see the world as much as possible through another human being's eyes—to grasp that other person's difference and embrace her self as something that enriches your life precisely because it is wholly foreign to the way you looked at the world before you met her. Children see everyone they know as embodiments of their own mental ideals or fears, but adults are supposed to know better. Certainly a forty-year-old man without a care in the world but his own neuroses should tumble to it. Writing at least two songs from Patti's perspective was quite possibly the most important step that Bruce took in early 1990, finally getting himself out of his own admittedly brilliant but deeply solipsistic head.

In April, as the arrival of their child drew nearer, Bruce and Patti moved from Hollywood to Beverly Hills, to a half-acre home on Tower Drive with a separate home studio but no pool. Bruce had been recording with Bittan, Porcaro, and Jackson for months now, but in so desultory a fashion that they had laid down tracks in at least three different

LA studios. Bruce still liked to record through the middle of the night, but the days of block-booking weeks of studio time appeared to be over. When he had something from his home studio that sounded promising, he'd call up the musicians and see what space was available. If Randy Jackson wasn't on hand when the time came to record "Leavin' Train," Bob Glaub from the "Viva Las Vegas" combo could fill in on bass. If Jeff Porcaro wasn't on hand when the time came to record "Seven Angels," Shawn Pelton could fill in on drums. Some of those participating in the sessions weren't even sure whether they were contributing to Bruce's ninth studio album or Patti's first. Still, by June, Springsteen had at least nineteen tracks recorded for his project, more than enough for two sides of an album and a handful of B-sides. He would also have his usual leftovers (maybe quieter songs like "With Ev'ry Wish," "Sad Eyes," and "I Wish I Were Blind") that might point the way toward a second, more countryish album that he could quickly pull together as a follow-up to the big soul-with-guitars release.

As usual, though, Springsteen appeared to have no intention of assembling an album on anybody's schedule but his own. Besides, come June, he had more important things than music on his mind: it was time for Scialfa and him to prepare for the arrival of their son. When the contractions started, Springsteen *figured the situation would get tense*, he recalled later that year, *so I [thought] it was kinda my responsibility to lighten things up*. In late July, a few days after Patti's birthday, he stopped in a drugstore to look for some silly novelty item that might break the tension during the delivery. He settled on a jokebook called *How to Be an Italian*, thinking, "*Gee, when it gets really tight, I'll crack out some Italian jokes*."

When the time came, though, he didn't, and Scialfa was probably grateful for that. Around 5 a.m. on Wednesday, 25 July 1990, Evan James Springsteen was born. In anticipation of the event, Sting, ever the former English teacher, had given his recent friend a copy of Dylan Thomas's *Under Milk Wood* as a gift, and after the boy's birth, he incorrectly assumed that Bruce and Patti had taken their son's name from a character in that work (an undertaker, actually, called Evans the Death). The truth, however, was that the name was yet another of the many fruits of Springsteen's year of intensive psychotherapy.

One therapist had encouraged him to get rid of the "ego validators and nuts" of old, and the initials of that jargony slogan apparently yielded his son's first name.

New age self-help slogans aside, Evan's birth was a watershed event for Springsteen. If a true connection with Patti had come slowly and with effort, what he felt when he first met Evan was something sudden and extraordinary. In describing the event, he always recalls it as "night," their firstborn arriving in the hour just before a midsummer dawn. In talking about what he felt at that moment with an interviewer a few years later, he instinctively compared it to the thrill of live performance, the feeling that he had previously thought was the greatest he could ever know. "I've played onstage for hundreds of thousands of people," he said, "and I've felt my own spirit really rise some nights. But when [Evan] came out, I had this feeling of a kind of love that I hadn't experienced before." And that feeling also scared him, he knew. It made him "afraid to be that in love." *I stood down there looking at him*, he told an audience a few months after Evan's birth, *and it was amazing because I seen the first time he cried, and I caught his first tear on the tip of my finger.*

From Evan's birth on, live performance would never again be the addictive escape for Springsteen that it had been up to that point. Western society raises girls to be mothers far more than it raises boys to be fathers, but for some men becoming a father turns out to be the greatest adventure of their lives. In spite of, maybe because of, all the dark things he had written about the relationships between fathers and sons, Bruce Springsteen greeted the arrival of his own moment of fatherhood with a zeal he hadn't exhibited since he first saw the Beatles on *The Ed Sullivan Show.* The greatest advantage that his considerable wealth could bring him that year was the fact that he didn't have to work, at anything. He could spend the time with his spouse and newborn child that so many other, less well-off parents wished they could.

From June to December the only recordings Bruce made were two children's songs, and in all of 1990 there were just two drop-in performances, both before Evan was born. After Evan's birth, maybe the only two performers who could have gotten Springsteen out of the house and up on a stage, particularly by himself, were Jackson Browne and Bonnie Raitt, both of whom had been not just colleagues but friends for almost twenty years. The benefit at which they wanted him to perform was for the Christic Institute, a DC-based public-interest law firm that had taken the lead in publicizing the Reagan administration's continued covert assistance to the Contras in Nicaragua, among other alternative issues. When it was announced that Springsteen would be topping the bill for a mid-November benefit for the institute, giving his first scheduled performances in over two years, the six thousand seats in the Shrine Auditorium sold out in forty minutes, as did the inevitable second show when it was announced.

In terms of Springsteen's career, the Christic Institute benefits weren't just his first scheduled concerts since the end of the Human Rights Now! tour. They were also the first concerts he had performed solo in at least eighteen years. Between the time he had spent away from performing and the ways in which he was trying to wean himself off so many unhealthy attitudes associated with his stage persona, Springsteen took the stage for the first concert on 16 November nervous, even exposed. *It sounds a little funny,* he told the audience before he started off the set with an acoustic rendition of "Brilliant Disguise," *but it's been awhile since I did this so if you're moved to clap along, please don't. It's gonna mix me up.* Before he started "Darkness on the Edge of Town," the next number, he reiterated, *I'd appreciate if during the songs I'd get just a little bit of quiet so I can concentrate.* That night, much of his between-songs patter consisted of similar apologies: for bad notes in a slow version of "Tenth Avenue Freeze-Out" and for forgotten lyrics in, of all songs, "Thunder Road." After "Mansion on the Hill," one enthusiastic fan shouted, "We love you Bruce," and the newly self-conscious performer immediately replied, *But you don't know me.* On the page, such statements might sound petulant, but when you listen to recordings of the event there is a vulnerability in Springsteen's voice that simply wasn't present in earlier performances, not even when he was telling the Freehold story before "Spare Parts" at the beginning of the *Tunnel of Love* tour.

Of the songs Springsteen performed at the first Christic concert, a third were from *Nebraska,* which made sense given the solo nature of the performance. There was nothing from *The River,* his ultimate band album, two songs from *Born to Run,* and one each from *Wild and Innocent, Darkness, Born in the U.S.A.,* and *Tunnel of Love.* Most interesting of all was the fact that he premiered four new songs that night, three of which he hadn't even recorded yet. These three songs ("57 Channels and Nothin' On," "Red Headed Woman," and "When the Lights Go Out"), which he had apparently written since Evan's birth, had one theme in common: sex. The latter two were also among his most sexually explicit songs, making what are almost the first uncoded references in Springsteen's work to female genitalia. It doesn't seem like too much of a stretch to conclude that, since the birth of his child, Springsteen was enjoying not only the newness of fatherhood but also the resumption of conjugal relations with Scialfa. The next night he played a slightly different set, including the premieres of the more metaphorically inclined "Soul Driver" as well as "The Wish," the song he had written about his mother nearly four years before. He may have been nervous, even a little off, but on the whole the two Christic shows were extraordinary, his finest and most spontaneous performances in years, and a powerful argument that he should have stuck to his guns and just toured for *Tunnel of Love* solo.

In December, he resumed recording, laying down studio versions of "57 Channels" and "When the Lights Go Out" (but probably not "Red Headed Woman"), as well as two newer, less impressive songs called "My Lover Man" and "Over the Rise." By early 1991, he had laid down about two dozen tracks in a little over a year, certainly more than enough for an album. He could have released an all-neo-soul album, for example, or an album (to keep thinking in predigital terms) that gave the listener one soul side and one paranoid rockabilly side. Still, he continued to sit on the project. The album wasn't finished yet.

For the first time since childhood, maybe the first time ever, music took second place in Bruce Springsteen's life. For the first half of 1991, he seems to have been most heavily invested in the good, the bad, and the ugly of daddy duty. Many days, he and Scialfa would drive down Highway 10 into the desert with their son and simply enjoy being together in nature. In early June, they invited a little under a hundred people to their place on Tower Drive for a small, Unitarian wedding.

During the ceremony, which the formerly postreligious Springsteen self-consciously understood as a "ritual," the groom smiled broadly and wept happily. As Scialfa walked down the aisle to meet him, she was about three months pregnant with their second child. Little Evan was going to have a baby sister.

FOR MOST OF 1991, Bruce Springsteen interacted with contemporary popular music largely as a consumer rather than as a producer. At first glance, the Hot 100 around Labor Day that year didn't look that much different than it had three years before when he had checked out of the music business temporarily just after the hellish *Tunnel of Love* express tour. Bonnie Raitt was at no. 24 on the chart, enjoying the greatest success of her career with *Nick of Time*, her wonderful comeback album produced by Don Was. Paris singing partner Huey Lewis was at no. 23, Bob Seger at no. 44, and Tom Petty at no. 47. A remarkably retro vibe was running through the American pop charts that year, with both Rod Stewart and Philadelphia harmony group Boyz II Men placing in the Top 20 with songs that referenced the heyday of Motown in their titles ("The Motown Song" and "Motown-philly"). New Orleans stalwart Aaron Neville was back in the Top 40 more than two decades after his first hit, and even a relatively young performer like Lenny Kravitz was playing guitar as if the last twenty years hadn't happened. At Springsteen's own label, the hottest artist of the moment was Tommy Mottola protégée Mariah Carey, whose second album showcased her retro-soul diva skills even more expansively than her debut album of the previous year did. Also at Columbia, the similarly popular Michael Bolton sang (and was received by some) as if he were the second, long-haired, white coming of Percy Sledge.

But there was more going on in the charts than that. In retrospect, the early 1990s clearly mark a moment of profound cultural change—from the political leadership of the "Greatest Generation" to the dominance of the baby boomers, from the end of the Cold War to the beginning of the War on Terror—a feeling summed up almost programmatically in Jesus Jones's popular single that fall,

"Right Here, Right Now," in which the end of the Cold War is likened to "watching the world wake up from history." On a much more superficial level, the years of the presidency of George Herbert Walker Bush also mark the beginning of one of the usual periodic shifts in American popular music. Some might say that these years marked the end of Robert Christgau's ideal of "monopop," the relatively unified pop culture that had dominated American life for most of the last half century. Certainly, it would be fair to say that they marked the end of the Top 40 revival in the American music industry that post–free-form FM and the arrival of MTV had helped to usher in a decade before.

Looking at the Hot 100 in the fall of 1991 another way, you saw the slow, inevitable rise of rap artists (Salt-N-Pepa and Naughty by Nature, for example, not to mention 3rd Bass engaging in a high-profile feud with LL Cool J) and "college bands" (like REM and Siouxsie and the Banshees), artists who were emerging from what had been the musical underground of the High MTV era. Over time, MTV had added shows like *Yo! MTV Raps* and *120 Minutes* to cater to the niche audiences for groups like these. Increasingly, though, this music wasn't at the margins of American pop. It was inexorably redefining the mainstream.

On some level, Springsteen understood this. Like most professional musicians, he generally embraced a wider variety of music than his fans would often accept. When asked what recent music he liked, he spoke in detail about Sir Mix-a-Lot, Queen Latifah, Social Distortion, and Faith No More. It's not that he wanted to make music like these younger artists, necessarily, but he unquestionably appreciated their achievement.

But where did that achievement leave Springsteen and his comrades? For these key transitional years also marked the inevitable popular decline of a number of artists of Springsteen's own generation whose careers had boomed during the 1970s and 1980s. This was only natural, the elder generation passing out of the way to make room for the rising generation. In the words of a song that Elton John cowrote a few years later for a Disney film (that in itself an unthinkable possibility back in the days of Paul's Mall and Max's Kansas City), it was "the

circle of life." Two years earlier, Dave Marsh had almost perfectly captured this end-of-an-era moment with *The Heart of Rock & Soul,* a
book whose chronological center of gravity was 1965, the year when
the triple blast of the Beatles, Dylan, and Motown shot Springsteen,
Van Zandt, and so many other young men of their generation toward
the dream of a career in music. Now, though, over a quarter of a century later, while the Bonnie Raitt and Tom Petty songs that charted
that fall ("Something to Talk About" and "Learning to Fly") could
fairly be ranked among those artists' best works, the current hits by
Rod Stewart, Bob Seger, and Huey Lewis ("The Motown Song" "The
Real Love," and "It Hit Me like a Hammer") were all deeply minor
tracks, singles that rose up the charts because of residual good will or
consumer inertia.

The career of Michael Bolton, most of all, pointed to a sickness at
the heart of contemporary American pop. For a while after the introduction of compact disc technology, the record companies could
count on fans' buying fresh digital copies of all their favorite vinyl
albums. After a certain point, though, the companies needed to sell
new product, which you couldn't do if all people wanted to listen to
was music they already had. So you had to sell them new music that
sounded like the old stuff. But if all one wanted to hear was a performer trying to sound like Otis Redding, why not just listen to the
copies you already owned of the real thing? Such a strategy could
work, but only for so long, and it was no surprise that newer sounds
were replacing the old ones on the charts. It had happened in the mid-
1960s, as the late decadent phase of swing definitively gave way to the
most creative phase of what was now called "classic rock," and it
appeared to be happening all over again in the early 1990s.

But you couldn't prove that by Southside Johnny Lyon, who after a
decade or so in the wilderness decided in the summer of 1991 to cash
in on the current retro feeling and put together a comeback album.
Steve Van Zandt, who had spent that same decade exploring the more
political side of his songwriting, was happy to mend his rift with Lyon
and appear on, produce, and arrange the album, as well as write two-
thirds of its songs. Other than Southside, the membership of the Jukes
had always been fluid. For this album, Steve called in the currently

unemployed Max Weinberg and Garry Tallent to provide an E Street rhythm section to back up Lyon, and relative Jersey whippersnapper Jon Bon Jovi agreed to do a duet on one song and provide backing vocals on another. At some point, either Johnny or Steve asked Bruce whether he might want to contribute.

Like the Human Rights Now! opportunity three years earlier, the timing of this professional request in terms of Springsteen's personal life was just perfect. About a month after their wedding, Bruce and Patti had come back to Rumson with Evan. The bad memory of two summers before had been effectively wiped out by the hard work of the last two years, and somehow it felt safe now to spend a summer near the shore. Once he was in Jersey, Bruce did do a few drop-ins, but for the most part his life continued to be firmly centered on Patti and Evan.

He did contribute to Southside's comeback album, though, quite enthusiastically. He offered Lyon a song called "All the Way Home," which may or may not have been a reject from his still-gestating ninth album. He sang backing vocals on that song and formed a fore-grounded trio with Southside and Steve on the album's most anthemic number, "It's Been a Long, Long Time." This song was almost a sequel to "I Don't Want to Go Home," the biggest hit that Steve had written for Southside. Both that older song and Bruce's 1976 liner notes for the album that bore its name paid tribute to the lost, mythic days of the Upstage, which Van Zandt's lyric for this newer song now made sound like some kind of virtual *La Bohème* for the Blues Magoos generation. Southside's album would end up being called *Better Days*, after a phrase that runs both as a line within "It's Been a Long, Long Time" and as the title of Steve's most politically minded song for the album.

By the fall of 1991, Bruce Springsteen had been sitting on the pieces of his ninth studio album for almost a year and a half. "I still felt I needed another song," he later recalled of this period, a thesis statement to sum up the album. Some reports suggest that the release of Bob Dylan's *Bootleg Series, Volumes 1–3* in late March of 1991, particularly the set's final track, "Series of Dreams," had pushed Springsteen even further to come up with a grand summing-up for this album. According to Springsteen, the song that eventually gave him the summation he sought was "Living Proof," which captured, in his words, "the common strength it takes to constitute a family." After that song, at least nine other songs came pouring out of him, nine songs that he claims were written and recorded in just three weeks, during the fall of 1991.

The question was: why then? If the catalyst for Springsteen's compositional breakthrough had been solely Evan's birth, then he could have written all these songs before the Christic shows. If the catalyst had been solely the inspiring example of Dylan, he could have written them even before his wedding.

Although "Living Proof" was undoubtedly the breakthrough thesis song that Springsteen was looking for, there is nevertheless a tempting possibility that the song that jump-started his songwriting that fall, after at least eight dry months, was "Better Days." Most obviously, Springsteen's title for this song is a clear echo of Steve's title song for Southside's new album. More centrally, though, Springsteen's "Better Days" is almost an answer song to Southside's entire project. It is his renewed look at "Glory Days" almost a decade after he wrote it, a few months after he heard "All Night Long," Southside's own accomplished if deeply dark take on that earlier song's conceit. If in "Glory Days," Springsteen wrote laughingly about washed-up baseball players and high school beauties, ten years later Lyon sang soulfully about old good-time club denizens who turned in middle age into prostitutes, alcoholics, and unnervingly born-again Christians.

That may have been Southside's experience of the early 1990s, but it certainly wasn't Bruce's. Nor, as he specified in "My Beautiful Reward," did he wish to use music as a *drug* to ease his pain, as Lyon's latterday narrator clearly does. *These are better days*, Springsteen insisted in his song of that title, rejecting the idea that he was "freer" back in the days of the Upstage and refusing to sentimentalize the time of his mixed-up youth.

Traditionally, as pop musicians settle down, they are supposed to get quieter, but what is striking about the tracks Springsteen recorded that fall in this burst of testifying bliss is how loud they are, how prominent and joyous his electric guitar playing is, not just on full-band tracks like "Better Days" and "Living Proof" that he recorded at A&M

Studios but even on a home-recorded track like "Lucky Town." Maybe on this album more than any other, in the ten tracks Springsteen cut that autumn, he made his guitar *talk*, and it spoke of his exhilaration not only at marriage and family but at being over all his own accumulated bullshit. "Local Hero," possibly based on a dime-store visit the previous summer, is the funniest bit of self-effacement that Springsteen has ever perpetrated, parodying not only the MegaBruce of the mid-1980s (*First they made me the king, then they made me the pope / Then they brought the rope*) but also, in the lyric's most brilliant lines, even the allegedly New and Improved Bruce of the current moment (*These days I'm feeling all right / 'Cept I can't tell my courage from my desperation*).

In general, these songs find Springsteen more at home with human frailty than he had ever been before, warning against hypocrisy in judging others' sins ("The Big Muddy") but acknowledging that his past actions made it reasonable to regard his own promises skeptically ("If I Should Fall Behind"). On a personal level, all these ideas had been clear in Bruce's head for some time, but for an artist personal breakthroughs can often precede or even follow compositional ones. If the fall of 1989 had found him flipping through his old 45s in search of artistic inspiration, the ten tracks he recorded two years later felt more as if the listener were flipping through his private photo album. They captured the shock of stardom ("Local Hero"), the birth of his children ("Living Proof" and "My Beautiful Reward"), and the day of his wedding to Scialfa ("Book of Dreams").

Unlike the pastiches with which he started the project, the best of these late songs clearly seem to be happening in a specific place, not a mythologized Monmouth or Ocean County, let alone a South or a West that he had only driven through on a tour bus or a motorcycle. These songs take place in the hills and desertscapes through which he now traveled every day. The one explicitly political track on the album, "Souls of the Departed," another remarkably loud track from the home studio sessions, connects the details of the singer's current life with the specificity of an American soldier's last moments in an Iraq firefight and the school-yard death of an East Compton boy who dies before his time. Springsteen could still write about the poor and disenfranchised, but to do so honestly he had to cop to the altered truth of his own situation. To keep his songs honest, he had to admit on some level that he was a millionaire, and stop *pretending*, as the lyric of "Better Days" puts it, to be *a rich man in a poor man's shirt.*

On the whole, it is remarkable how self-contained the recording of these songs was, much more so than *Tunnel of Love*, if less than the admitted fluke of *Nebraska*. Randy Jackson was brought in to play bass on one track, Roy to provide keyboards on three others, but otherwise the keyboards, guitar, and bass on most tracks are all Springsteen. This was rock auteurism, the closest to a purely personal statement that this singer-songwriter had ever made. For half of the tracks, he headed down to A&M Studios to record backing vocals—female backing vocals this time, on which the very pregnant Patti was joined by her old New York friends Lisa Lowell and Soozie Tyrell. No longer interested in staying in studios late into the night, Springsteen recorded and mixed the new album from two to six in the afternoon, almost as if he had a part-time job. No matter what he was working on, he always made it home for dinner by seven.

In the liner notes for *Nebraska* and *Tunnel of Love*, the credits simply read "Recorded in New Jersey." On this new album, for the first time, the credits said "Recorded at Thrill Hill Recording." It's not clear when Bruce first gave his home studio this name, but it's not surprising that his Los Angeles setup received it before the one in Rumson did. Fittingly for Springsteen, the name was a reference to the old-time rock 'n' roll of Fats Domino, but it also had an echo of his own invocation almost a decade earlier of the old country trope of the "Mansion on the Hill," which he could no longer deny that he had come to live in. Most important, the name signaled his own emotional state now. *Nebraska* and *Tunnel of Love*, his two other mostly solo works, were lonely howls of pain and isolation, both recorded a short drive away from his beloved Jersey Shore in the dead of winter. This new solo work, which he would rightly call *Lucky Town*, was something entirely different: a loud cry of joy over his incredible good fortune.

In mid-January 1992, a few weeks after the New Year's Eve birth of Scialfa and Springsteen's daughter Jessica Rae, Bruce and Roy went into the A&M Studios to record "Happy," one of the most blandly direct songs Springsteen had ever written. But "Happy" was not only a minor and reiterative act of songwriting (even musically it sounded like a redraft of the superior "My Beautiful Reward"). At this point, such a direct affirmation on Springsteen's part was unnecessary, in a way that it wouldn't have been when he had purposefully moved to Los Angeles a little over two years before. Both personally and artistically, he now lived on Thrill Hill.

CHAPTER 10

I'LL KEEP MOVIN' THROUGH THE DARK (1992–1995)

M AYBE IT WAS THE SLEEP DEPRIVATION THAT COMES FROM LIVING in a household with both a newborn and a toddler, but shortly after cutting "Happy," Bruce Springsteen made one of the most unfortunate artistic decisions of his entire career, a decision even worse than keeping "The Angel" and "Mary Queen of Arkansas" on *Greetings from Asbury Park, N.J.* or reforming the E Street Band to tour behind *Tunnel of Love.* It wasn't the release of his most recent recordings as a separate album that was ill advised. As in the winters of 1982 and 1987, in the fall of 1991 Springsteen experienced an impressive, solitary burst of creativity. It made sense for those recordings to be packaged as a single artistic unit. No, the ill-advised decision was to release *two* records in the spring of 1992: one called *Lucky Town*, which collected that most recent batch of recordings; and one called *Human Touch*, which selected at most half of the recordings that he had made during the previous two years. Unlike the *Lucky Town* sessions, this earlier group of recordings did not spring from a single artistic impulse but rather from a series of them. Like *Tunnel of Love* and *Lucky Town*, the albums that preceded and immediately followed it, *Human Touch* is often grouped as one of Springsteen's "relationship" albums, but all that really indicates is that most of these songs aren't primarily concerned with work or politics.

On the face of it, Springsteen had a sound professional reason for not wanting to release just one album: whenever possible, he liked touring with at least two albums' worth of new material, enough to make sure that a new tour wasn't just a retread of one of the old ones. But even if it was wise for him to issue two albums that spring, one can still question his specific selection of songs for *Human Touch*. Of all the tracks on the album, Bruce clearly needed to release both "Human Touch" and "Pony Boy" for personal reasons. Among the early soul pastiches, "Roll of the Dice" and "Man's Job" were probably the most fun. But was there any reason to include such stiff, relatively uninspired songs as "Real Man" or "All or Nothing at All" and leave off a true barn burner like "Trouble River"? As *Lucky Town*'s companion piece, this second album needed to complement that more rapidly completed work either musically or autobiographically, but many of the songs ultimately included on *Human Touch* did neither. As sheer pop songwriting, "Sad Eyes" (a discard from early 1990) was a much better piece of work than such *Human Touch* tracks as "Cross My Heart" and "Gloria's Eyes." As far as autobiographical songwriting was concerned, "Goin' Cali" (a discard from early 1991) was a much more specific and arresting piece of self-revelation than a relatively slight *Human Touch* song like "The Long Goodbye," which merely echoed finer autobiographical tracks on both albums.

While Springsteen's specific selection of material may have been questionable, the speed with which Springsteen, Landau, and others prepared the two albums for release was still impressive. By late January the announcement was made, and Bruce and Patti made a brief visit to New Orleans to shoot a video for "Human Touch." In early March, a second video was shot on a Hollywood soundstage for "Better Days" (which would be released as the "second A-side" of "Human Touch," presumably to promote both albums with the same single). Both videos were rapidly made available to MTV, VH1, and all other appropriate services. The full albums, it was decided, would be out at Easter. A world tour, without the E Street Band, would follow in the summer. Originally, Springsteen may have wanted to travel with his session men—Roy was a given, and it was rumored that he had offered Jeff Porcaro a million dollars to join the tour—but he eventually decided to assemble a band of young but "seasoned 'road guys.'"

For his tour band, Springsteen seemed to want a basic five-man rock combo: a second guitarist, bassist, and drummer to add to Roy and himself. For the second guitarist, Bruce pretty much knew whom he wanted: Shane Fontayne. An Englishman born with the name of Mick Barakan, the rechristened Fontayne was ten years younger than Springsteen but had been making records for almost exactly as long. For the first fifteen years of his career, he played with Mick Ronson, Ian Hunter, Garland Jeffreys, Billy Burnette, and others, but he had risen to prominence over the last five years after becoming the guitarist for Lone Justice, the LA rock band fronted by Maria McKee. An opening slot with U2 for part of the *Joshua Tree* tour gave Lone Justice a great deal of exposure, as did the band's 1986 appearance on *Saturday Night Live*, which was when Fontayne caught Springsteen's attention. As frequently happens in the music industry, the two guitarists eventually connected through a producer, mutual friend Jimmy Iovine. Fontayne had a flashier, harder attack on guitar than Lofgren did, but then again Nils Lofgren hadn't sounded like Steve Van Zandt.

Finding a bassist and drummer to tour with was harder. Chuck Plotkin scouted possibilities, and Roy's home studio became a place to audition people. Tommy Sims, the bassist Springsteen eventually settled on, didn't have any road experience, which was the one paramount credential announced prior to tryouts. He hadn't heard Springsteen's music until fairly recently, and the first Springsteen album he owned was *Tunnel of Love*. His strongest credits were in the emerging field of Christian pop, most notably on tracks by its biggest crossover star, Amy Grant (although he also recorded with the far less angelic Divinyls, among other bands). Zach Alford, who finally got the drummer slot, was the one New York–based performer in this, Springsteen's first LA-based band, and he flew out to California at least four times in March and April for tryouts. Around the same age as Fontayne and Sims, Alford was more a product of New York's downtown avant-garde scene than the metal-oriented clubs on LA's Sunset Strip. "I never had any of [Bruce's] records," he told an Italian journalist later that year, "but of course you know a lot of his songs: he's had so many hits, you just know them." When viewed alongside Springsteen and Bittan, Fontayne, Sims, and Alford practically boxed the compass of early-1990s rock and pop. Like most pop musicians of their time, they had common roots in the rock 'n' roll of Springsteen's childhood and adolescence, but it would be pushing it to say that they were part of a common musical movement or even that they shared a style.

The five men first met face to face in mid-April of 1992, just as Columbia was preparing to release *Human Touch* and *Lucky Town*. Almost everyone who heard about this lineup commented on how notably younger than Springsteen the three new members of the band were, but almost no one mentioned another difference that was even more manifest: Sims and Alford were African American. If 60 percent of Springsteen's new band was under the age of thirty-five, it was also true that 40 percent of it was black.

In the eighteen years since Davey Sancious and Boom Carter left the E Street Band, rock—whose two most fundamental guitarists, Chuck Berry and Jimi Hendrix, were both black—had been getting steadily more and more white. Awash in the wake of the late 1970s racist antidisco movement, during the early 1980s MTV and many FM rock stations were initially reluctant to play the music of Prince, for example, whom most rock performers would have named as one of the greatest electric guitarists of his generation. In 1985, guitarist Vernon Reid, with whom Tommy Sims had toured Europe, joined with others to found the Black Rock Coalition, but in terms of pop impact their campaign for equal recognition was very much an uphill battle. In the spring of 1992, the very idea that African American artists could call rock their own was directly addressed in the lyrics of "Free Your Mind," a track on En Vogue's Top 10 album *Funky Divas* (which would be a Top 10 single in its own right the following fall). In another two years, John Mellencamp would crack the Top 10 even more self-consciously by recording a duet version of Van Morrison's "Wild Night" with bassist and BRC member Me'shell Ndegeocello. For the most part, though, in the days of George H. W. Bush, black America and white America were divided. They were in effect "two nations," as the title of Andrew Hacker's book of the time put it, and division by musical instrumentation was hardly the worst of it.

In Los Angeles, you couldn't miss it, particularly on Thursday, 30 April, the second day that Springsteen's new band rehearsed together. At 3:15 on Wednesday, 29 April, a predominantly white Southern California jury had concluded a week of deliberations by declaring four members of the Los Angeles Police Department not guilty of assault in the videotaped, sustained beating of African American motorist Rodney King. The incident occurred over a year earlier, around the time that Springsteen was finishing up the *Human Touch* sessions, and because of the intensive local media coverage the trial was moved from Los Angeles to Simi Valley, with a jury pool drawn from the surrounding San Fernando Valley. Within a half hour of when the acquittal was announced, protests against it formed—in front of the Los Angeles County Courthouse, which was closer to where the protesters lived than Simi Valley. In early-1990s Southern California, you couldn't even get justice, or be denied it, without driving north on the 101 for a couple of hours. The region's freeways, where King had been beaten within an inch of his life, were the very symbol of the last four decades of white flight, creating what Douglas Massey and Nancy Denton would soon dub (with a nod to George, rather than Bill, Clinton) "chocolate cities with vanilla suburbs."

In the hours after the surprising verdict, spontaneous crowds started to form at two more Los Angeles locations: the Parker Center, the headquarters of the LAPD, and the intersection of Florence and Normandie Avenues, in the predominantly African American district of South Central Los Angeles. Over the past few years, South Central had become the most famous and infamous section of the city for those who didn't live there, a late twentieth-century mythologized equivalent of Wyatt Earp's Tombstone or Eliot Ness's Chicago. Those who did live in South Central saw things a little differently. While they deplored well-known street gangs like the Crips and the Bloods, they also felt such gangs were too often an easy explanation that outsiders used for anything that went wrong in their part of town. In the minds of many residents, the LAPD was part of the problem in South Central much more than part of the solution. As the rap group NWA had put the same local sentiment three years earlier in "Fuck tha Police," the most widely circulated track on their debut album *Straight outta Compton*, "They have the authority / To kill a minority."

As a matter of tactics, the LAPD chose to hold its officers back that night of Wednesday, 29 April. At the courthouse, the Parker Center, and down in South Central, citizens continued to gather with absolutely no direction, either by experienced activists and community organizers or by law enforcement personnel. Three and a half hours after the verdict, a white driver by the name of Reginald Denny, who was hauling twenty-seven tons of sand, stopped for a traffic light at Florence and Normandie—where he drove almost every day, sometimes stopping to buy cookies or little cakes from the Muslim vendors on the corner—and was dragged from his truck by at least four people. His skull was hit with cinder blocks and pieces of concrete. Someone drew a gun. Bob and Marika Tur, two reporters for the LA News Service, flew overhead with a video camera and transmitted images of the beating live, as a city, a nation, and a world watched. One viewer, Bobby Green Jr., an African American man who lived nearby, saw the scene on TV and ran out to do something about the atrocity he was witnessing. Green, Larry Tarvo, Lee Euell, and one other South Central resident pulled Denny away from his attackers and drove him to the hospital in the sand-hauling truck from which he had been dragged.

When the sun came up Thursday morning, many people (at least those who didn't live in the affected areas) assumed that the worst of the fighting was over. That was the thing about LA, as opposed to East Coast cities like New York or Boston: the freeways cut areas up so much that you didn't have to pass through other people's neighborhoods. Still, even the images on TV that morning were frightening enough. As recent LA transplant Bruce Springsteen recalled, "people were scared. People were really scared." "It really felt," he told a reporter a little later that spring, "like the wall was coming down," referring not to the wall between black and white but rather the wall between tentatively maintained civilization and outright civil war. Springsteen had seen this kind of civil disorder before, during the Asbury Park riots in the summer of 1970, but now he watched it happening in a larger city on a much larger scale. When he addressed an LA audience about four weeks after the riots, he got even more specific about what he thought they had done: *the veil got pulled away,* he said, *and you got a chance to see how profoundly estranged from each other we really are.*

That Thursday, Springsteen had an album climbing up the charts, his newly formed band had two high-profile gigs scheduled in New York in a little over a week, but there was a riot going on half a dozen blocks from the Hollywood Center Studios where he and the band were rehearsing. It was "Street Fightin' Man" on the widest possible level. Springsteen and the other four musicians practiced songs about personal redemption, as parts of the city in which the singer had finally found that redemption were being burned to the ground around him.

On Thursday, the fighting rippled out from South Central to touch much more of Los Angeles. The dippier news outlets latched onto the fact that Frederick's of Hollywood was being looted, as if one quirky story about stolen celebrity lingerie would somehow make everybody feel better about injustice and pervasive disorder. In the White House Briefing Room, President Bush tried to speak to both sides of the issue, simultaneously voicing "a demand for law and order" and declaring that "in the American conscience, there is no room for bigotry and racism." The National Guard and the Highway Patrol were brought into Los Angeles. Mayor Tom Bradley declared a dusk-to-dawn curfew. On Friday, a visibly dazed Rodney King went on television to call for peace, famously using variations on the phrase "can we get along" four times in well under a minute. On Saturday, four thousand U.S. Army and Marine troops arrived to supplement the four thousand National Guard members already on the ground. Mayor Bradley's curfew held until Monday, but local, state, and federal officers stayed in certain sections of Los Angeles for days, even weeks, after that.

When the smoke cleared and what passed for order was restored, 53 people had died, 2,000 people had been injured, 3,600 fires had been set, 1,100 buildings had been destroyed, and $1 billion in property had been damaged. For all the global fear that the transmitted images of the riots had engendered, most of the damage to persons and property was predictably centered in South Central Los Angeles, an area that had already been hit disproportionately hard by the current recession. To an area native like NWA's Ice Cube, "[t]he looting that was done in South Central was nothing like the looting done by the savings and loans." As the rapper told Robert Hilburn, the premier music critic for the Los Angeles Times, that week, "You take everything that happened in fact and it was just a smidgen of what has happened to [local] blacks all these years."

By Wednesday, 6 May, a week after the Simi Valley verdict, Bruce Springsteen and his new band were in New York, playing a showcase for a few hundred Sony executives at the Bottom Line. On Saturday, the ninth, the day most federal troops were removed from Los Angeles, Bruce and his new four-man combo performed on *Saturday Night Live*. It was Springsteen's first scheduled television performance, even if his new second guitarist already knew his way around Rockefeller Center's Studio 8H. Like most *SNL* musical guests, Springsteen appeared twice during the show, but on neither occasion did he perform either side of his current single. (It had peaked at no. 16 a month earlier, before he had even finalized the membership of his touring band.) During the first segment, Bruce tore through "Lucky Town," a song that, oddly enough, provided a great showcase for Shane Fontayne. The younger man's guitar work was rawer and consequently more interesting than any heard at a Springsteen show in well over a decade. The song sounded fuller this way than on the officially released album, with Zack Alford's drumming similarly looser than Gary Mallaber's on the Thrill Hill track.

The real surprise, though, came in the second musical segment. After guest host Tom Hanks's introduction ("Ladies and gentlemen, once again, Bruce Springsteen"), the next voice the audience heard belonged not to Bruce but to President Bush. "I want a kinder, gentler nation," the president intoned, in a sound bite taken from "The Mission," his acceptance speech at the 1988 Republican National Convention. This was followed by at least half a dozen more sound bites, most of them relating to the events of the last week and a half: the president's declaration nine days earlier that there was "no room for bigotry" in the United States; U.S. Attorney George L. Phillips's November 1991 admonishment of the LAPD in the wake of the King beating to "just do what is right"; a generalized, buried newscaster's announcement that "anger burns in Los Angeles"; and a jokier message from a newscast on 30 April in which the anchor smirkingly announced that "Frederick's of Hollywood is being looted." Somewhere in the middle of all that, there was a snippet from the Home Shopping Network or QVC announcing satin comforters on sale. After this sound collage came Tommy Sims's bass, and Bruce launched into the song that had long been designated as his next single, "57 Channels (and Nothin' On)."

But this was a new version of "57 Channels," not the one that had been released on *Human Touch* a few weeks before. Its opening use of sound samples from the last week and a half made it sound more like a new track from Public Enemy than the next single from a 1970s rocker. It ended in an implosion of guitar feedback, and the second musical segment of the night didn't quite end there. Over the applause that followed the harsh end of "57 Channels," Zach Alford struck out a steady beat and Bruce began to sing the one song that had brought his ambiguous two-year project to an end: "Living Proof." Like the other two performances that night, this one was smoking, although for once it wasn't Shane Fontayne that drew your attention. It was Bruce and the conviction with which he sang his new credo. Taken together, the three songs were an impressive reintroduction of Springsteen to an American audience after he had spent four years out of the public eye. If nothing else, they suggested that the singer's forties weren't turning him soft.

NO ART EXISTS in a vacuum. Culture frequently changes even "finished" artworks in ways that their creators can seldom expect. It's interesting to wonder, for example, how "Born in the U.S.A." would have been received if it had been released in 1982 (when Springsteen first wrote and recorded it) rather than in 1984 (when the album *Born in the U.S.A.* was released). In the fall of 1982, in the depths of the Reagan recession, audiences might have heard more clearly the song's lament for the plight of the Vietnam veteran. In the summer of 1984, in the midst of not only the Reagan reelection campaign but the nationalist hoopla that surrounded the Olympic Games in Los Angeles, "Born in the U.S.A." ended up sounding more patriotic than it actually was.

Although not as well known a Springsteen song, "57 Channels" underwent a similar semantic transformation between Springsteen's first public performance of it in November 1990 (at one of the Christic Institute shows) and its next public performances in May 1992 (at the Bottom Line showcase and on *Saturday Night Live*). Despite the way that Springsteen presented the song in those later cases, he had not initially intended it to be a political work. At the Christic Institute show, one of the most politically charged shows that Springsteen had ever played, he framed "57 Channels" as a comic, personal number. He introduced it with an anecdote about Bob Dylan's being told by a film director, "*Just be yourself,*" to which Dylan had responded, "*I was wondering 'Which one?'*" *I knew just what he meant,* Springsteen continued, and then he insisted that *this next song [*"57 Channels"*] is the real me . . . just in case you were wondering.* What he meant, of course, was that "57 Channels" was a stage exaggeration of his real life, nowhere near as real as the more directly revelatory "The Wish" or even "Red Headed Woman," both of which he also performed that night.

As presented at the Christic shows, "57 Channels" was a goofy rockabilly piece, which invoked *the blessed name of Elvis* in its climactic shooting of a troublemaking television set. Most of its attention was focused on the narrator's lost chance to *get all hot and horny . . . upstairs* with his disengaged *baby.* The song's arresting opening lines (*I bought a bourgeois house in the Hollywood hills / With a trunkload of hundred thousand dollar bills*) are the clearest autobiographical reference in the song, poking fun at Springsteen's new "mansion on the hill" as such *Lucky Town* tracks as "Local Hero" and "Better Days" would poke fun at other aspects of his prosperity and image making. In the Thrill Hill recording of "57 Channels" that Springsteen made in December 1990, the song became less loping and goofy, more cool and ironic, than it had been live. But even in the recorded version, the song is still a shaggy-dog story, another one of Springsteen's dozens of Elvis pastiches. Nothing about it screams social commentary.

But in the first week of May 1992, with the National Guard still manning checkpoints in South Central, how could Springsteen possibly sing a song with those opening lines and not be aware of its political implications? If he was going to be honest about being *a rich man in a poor man's shirt,* then the riots would force him to admit how distanced he now was from what happened to the American working class, even in his new hometown. "We've abandoned a gigantic part of the population," he told an interviewer around this time, "—we've just left them for dead. . . . I mean, I live great, and plenty of people do, but it affects you internally in some fashion, and it just eats away at whatever sort of spirituality you pursue."

As "57 Channels" moved from live solo performance to recording and then to live band performance, it became more a song about these kinds of interpersonal disconnection and less a song about a sexually frustrated rich guy. It grew more dissonant and disconnected with each incarnation, as first the separated channels of recording production and later the purposeful distortion of feedback made the song seem more alienated than it had initially been. In its final form, the song is not a joke, but rather an indictment of the culture of spectacle.

For it wasn't just Springsteen or Los Angeles that had changed in the eighteen months since he had written "57 Channels." So had television, which was, after all, the nominal subject of the song. If 1981 was the making of MTV, 1991 was the making of CNN, Ted Turner's previously dubious experiment in twenty-four-hour news coverage. Peter Arnett's and Bernard Shaw's reports from the Al-Rashid Hotel in Baghdad during the first bombing raids of the U.S.-Iraq war changed the way most Americans consumed news, years before many of them even knew what the internet was. Suddenly, the steady stream of information that an around-the-clock cable news network could provide seemed so much more relevant than the mere daily dispatches posted by newspapers and network news divisions.

Even more significant, CNN had been the making of the Gulf War as well, or at least the selling of that war for propaganda purposes to the United States and the rest of the world. This promotional symbiosis hinged on what sociologist Steven Livingston would soon call "the CNN effect," the way in which powerful television images could be used to stir up strong, near-collective emotions on a daily basis. Provide the right, steady stream of powerful images to a television audience, and you could control the narrative of present history that the audience experienced as it unfolded. When Operation Desert Storm commenced in January 1991, mere weeks after Springsteen had cut the studio version of "57 Channels," there were almost a million troops from thirty-four countries in the Persian Gulf—and, along with them, thousands of journalists. Journalistic access to the front lines was severely controlled during combat operations, and so most of those journalists transmitted the images and details to their audiences that the armed forces wanted them to transmit. Indeed, the First Gulf War was designed to provide images ready for television. Coincidentally or not, the bombing raids with which Desert Storm began occurred at the exact time that the three U.S. network news anchors were recording their nightly broadcasts. This was, however, one of the few notable concessions to pre-CNN television journalism during the entire war. From that point onward, the unfolding of history during Desert Storm was managed on an hourly basis as if it were the newest cable miniseries.

A year later, freed from the restraints and censorship placed on it by U.S. armed forces during the Gulf War, this same twenty-four-hour, narrative-starved news cycle quickly turned the LA riots from urban tragedy into mediated spectacle. The beating of Rodney King was videotaped and repeatedly replayed, the trial of those who committed the beating was televised, and the urban disintegration that followed the trial's verdict became a narrativized guilty pleasure for far too many cable viewers for the better part of a week. Never before in American history had the nation's citizens been able to watch chaos break out on such an epic scale. As with Springsteen's joke about his fancy house in the opening lines of "57 Channels," in the wake of such events the song's treatment of television could not be as easily shrugged off as it had been when originally performed. In November 1990, the idea that there was nothing good on TV but we all keep watching it anyway was a cute little piece of observational humor. In May 1992, that thought was as sinister as the song's now foregrounded bass line.

The speed with which Springsteen reinvented his song to fit a changed political landscape is striking. It was much like the sort of instant topical songs that he had written in the late 1970s and early 1980s with "Roulette" and "Atlantic City," except that in this case the commentary came in the arrangement. The lyric of "57 Channels" changed very little in those eighteen months, but the sonic frame within which that lyric was now presented became drastically different after the upheavals of late April and early May. The sound samples at the beginning of the song's live performance are only part of this transformation. The arrangement of the song that Springsteen worked out with his four new bandmates was much angrier than the one that he had recorded, almost certainly because it had been thrashed out in the midst of the riots. Because of the tightness of Springsteen's new band, not to mention Shane Fontayne's particular approach to his guitar part, the live NBC version of "57 Channels" comes off as something close to an electric blues number, a Howlin' Wolf song with more elaborate lyrics, or a young postmodern sibling to the harder-edged *Nebraska* tracks.

Played in this way at this moment in American history, even the song's sampled revolver blast to the television set now felt like more than just a funny little Elvis homage (as it had been at the climax of "Phil the Shill," an episode of *Miami Vice* that NBC aired back in 1985). A little over a week before Springsteen's *SNL* appearance, when the looting in LA was at its worst, electronics stores were among the favorite targets. Television news consumers around the world watched Los Angeles residents steal televisions, on which they could presumably later watch the moving images of their own acts of theft. Given the infinite regress of mediation in this situation, the sound of a bullet shattering a cathode-ray tube could almost be considered the ultimate form of absurdist political protest. The fact that Springsteen made this veiled accusation of American spectatorship during his first scheduled television appearance, at a quarter to one in the morning on a Saturday night, just before the onset of what many insomniacs would consider prime channel surfing time, only made it all the sweeter.

But it is important to remember that this was only half of Springsteen's statement during the second set of his *Saturday Night Live* performance. He followed "57 Channels" up immediately with "Living Proof," which was a very interesting choice for him to make: angry misanthropy followed by his purest hope. It was almost as if Springsteen had disassembled the pieces of "Souls of the Departed," a *Lucky Town* song whose first verse took place in Iraq during Desert Storm; its second in South Central after a playground shooting; and its third in Springsteen's new, walled-in home. "Souls of the Departed" might have seemed more immediately relevant to recent events than the combination of "57 Channels" and "Living Proof," but it would also have been too easy. On that specific night, performing "Souls of the Departed" might have seemed like cultural blasphemy, as if Springsteen were capitalizing on too recent events to elevate his cachet as a "serious" songwriter. In this humbling and disturbing moment, how could he respectfully speak about the disorder of South Central and the harmony of his own life in the same breath?

So instead he gave each truth its own song within which it could be noted. Juxtaposed, the live performances of "57 Channels" and "Living Proof" gave the audience two different Bruces side by side: the insulated rich man in the Hollywood Hills and the loving family man who had finally learned how to actively engage other people; disconnected and connected; guilty and innocent. Ultimately, Springsteen's two-song set near the end of *SNL* was as baffled and contradictory a response to the LA riots as George H. W. Bush's and Rodney King's immediate responses had been the week before. But like those responses, it was as honest and sincere as the man could make it. I doubt that the Bruce of the E Street years could have seen his own minor place in recent events quite so clearly.

See you in the summer! Springsteen declared at the end of "Living Proof," just before the TV show slipped away to more commercials. Now that he had finally gotten his personal life in order, he was ready to try and reengage with the world.

THE FIRST DATE of the *Human Touch/Lucky Town* tour was scheduled for Stockholm a little over a month later. For the Sony showcase, the new band had worked up live versions of about half the tracks on *Human Touch* and nearly all the tracks on *Lucky Town*, which was enough for about half of a concert. After the two gigs in New York, they took a week and a half off and then reconvened at the Hollywood Center Studios Soundstage in a slightly less tense Los Angeles than the one they had left. On 20 June, they began working up enough of Bruce's earlier songs to fill out a setlist.

On Saturday, 23 June, Springsteen added Crystal Taliefero to the band. Taliefero was the sort of "seasoned road guy" he had originally said he was looking for on this tour, even though she obviously wasn't a guy. She was a native Hoosier who had been in John Mellencamp's band almost from the beginning of his career and had subsequently toured with Billy Joel, Bob Seger, and Joe Cocker. Because she was African American and sometimes played saxophone, the more boorish of Springsteen's fans might have thought that she was a replacement for Clarence Clemons. But she played guitar too, and, with formal training in both opera and jazz, she supplied much more outrageous vocals than Clemons ever had. If she was a replacement for anybody in the E Street Band, it wasn't Clemons but Danny Federici. With the other four members of the combo laying down a fairly solid rock foundation, Taliefero's vocals and work on various instruments would play the same role in Springsteen's performances on this tour that Federici's organ and accordion work had played throughout the last two decades. Like Federici, Taliefero was the main improvisatory element in the band's sound, against which Springsteen would vary his own foregrounded performance every night.

Even with the addition of Taliefero, Springsteen still wasn't done enlarging the band. For a few of the *Lucky Town* studio sessions, he had used female harmony vocals, and now he decided he wanted to tour with female backup singers for the first time in twenty-one years. The four singers he ended up hiring—Gia Ciambotti, Carolyn Dennis, Cleopatra Kennedy, and Angel Rogers—were, respectively, a native Hollywoodian who had sung with Charlotte Caffey, Belinda Carlisle, and Patty Smyth; Bob Dylan's soon-to-be-divorced second wife (and mother of his youngest child), who had recently sung Lynn Whitfield's vocal parts for *The Josephine Baker Story*; a former civil rights activist from Birmingham, Alabama, whom Springsteen had met thirteen years earlier when she backed up Graham Nash at the No Nukes concerts; and a lyric soprano from Janis Joplin's hometown of Port Arthur, Texas, who had sung with everyone from Dizzy Gillespie to Paula Abdul and Yanni.

And Springsteen still wasn't finished. On 1 June, two weeks before the tour was scheduled to start and four days before a rehearsal concert that was scheduled to be broadcast on a nationwide radio hookup in order to drum up more interest in the tour, he brought in Bobby King, who had already participated in the studio sessions for "Roll of the Dice" and "Man's Job" and guested on "Human Touch" at the Sony showcase. That brought the total number of performers to eleven. Throw in a Monopoly board, and you almost had Dr. Zoom and the Sonic Boom up there, although this band was blacker and more southern in its origins than any other band with which Springsteen had ever toured. It was also enlarged by voices, not instruments, giving some clue of the direction Springsteen might want to take on this tour.

The broadcast public rehearsal on the fifth went fine. For the most part, it was an expansion of the same setlist that the five-man combo had done at the Bottom Line almost exactly a month earlier, with older Springsteen songs inserted between the main building blocks of tracks from the two new albums. Generally speaking, the *Lucky Town* songs tended to go earlier in the concert, the *Human Touch* songs later. Even more interesting, the bulk of the pre-1992 releases that Springsteen performed with his new band came from *Born in the U.S.A.*, his most recent E Street studio effort, with more songs from that album in this kickoff for the tour than there were from *Human Touch*. With this enlarged outfit, much of the attention in all his old songs shifted, not surprisingly, to the vocals. The full harmonies of all those southern-born singers unearthed the gospel roots in familiar Springsteen songs like "Darkness on the Edge of Town" and "My Hometown," and they highlighted the unglimpsed musicological facets of a seemingly disposable song like "Working on the Highway."

As far as his stage persona was concerned, Springsteen was less desperately autobiographical with this audience, being both more serious and perhaps wittier than he had been at the peak of his fame seven years before. He addressed the riots twice (before "If I Should Fall Behind" and "My Hometown," making the political personal as was his wont) and spoke about Evan and Jess twice too. He joked about how after *two years in Beverly Hills, you can't tune your guitar any more, that's what happens. [O]h, it's a shame, the man, what happened to him?* he cried, deliberately mocking *Entertainment Weekly*'s recent "Whatever Happened to Bruce Springsteen?" cover. He also kidded that he and Patti were *hiring the National Enquirer as our publicists from here on out. [A]nd I'm getting a Calvin Klein underwear endorse-ment also,* he added, specifically making reference to the famous 1988 balcony photos from Rome.

But Springsteen's most widely noted self-mockery that day came in his concluding rap, near the end of a climactic rendition of "Glory Days." Very specifically, he name-checked all his current competition on the pop music charts:

> *I can see those albums, man, I see them going back up the charts. I see 'em rising now past that ol' Def Leppard, past that Kriss Kross . . . I can see 'em all the way past Weird Al Yankovic even. . . . Oh-oh, we're going down, down, out of sight, into the darkness.*

This was a joke, of course, but it was a highly specific one. Like most releases from established artists with a loyal but aging following, *Human Touch* and *Lucky Town* had premiered big on the *Billboard* albums chart but then started sinking back down that chart surpris-ingly quickly. In a robust season that also included U2's *Achtung Baby,* the Red Hot Chili Peppers' *Blood Sex Sugar Magik,* Michael Jackson's *Dangerous,* and TLC's *Crazysexycool,* Springsteen's two new releases also had to contend for record buyers' attention with strong-showing albums by relative newcomers Billy Ray Cyrus and the aforementioned Kriss Kross. By midsummer, even the usually loyal *Rolling Stone* would be calling Springsteen's two new albums "much-publicized failure[s]" in a strictly economic sense.

Some of this relative failure could be attributed to the aging of Springsteen's core audience, as well as his decision to release a mid-dling album alongside a relatively well-assembled one. It is also true, however, that Springsteen may have come afoul of a recent change in the way that the popularity of recorded music was measured in the United States. In the opening decades of the twentieth century, trade journals judged recordings popular by rather ingenuously relying on sales figures provided by the record labels themselves. From the 1930s forward, *Billboard's* charts of popular singles (and later albums) were based on a combination of airplay and sales, but the measurements that led to those charts were once again unverified and self-reported, in this case by radio stations and record stores. In 1991, however, *Billboard* began to take advantage of the early phases of the digital revolution by employing the information accumulated by Broadcast Data Systems (a computerized service that automatically monitored actual radio airplay) and Nielsen Soundscan (which used bar-code technology to obtain point-of-purchase data on actual sales). The *Billboard* albums chart was switched over first in late May of 1991, and the Hot 100 was switched over in late November.

In both cases, the popularity of specific records shifted slightly but noticeably when the new methods of measurement were adopted. Record buyers and possibly DJs were more adventurous than prior industry self-reporting had given them credit for. More specifically, 1990s hip-hop was far more popular now than warmed-over 1970s soul. The biggest surprise, though, came in rock. On the second Hot 100 chart under the new system, compiled 7 December 1991, Nirvana (a band from Washington State that Geffen Records had signed away from the local independent label SubPop) had a single that debuted at no. 40, more than qualifying it as that week's "Hot Shot Debut." It was called "Smells like Teen Spirit," and by the time Nirvana performed the song on *Saturday Night Live* a little over a month later—when Bruce and Patti were enjoying Jessica's first days as a part of their family; a week before Springsteen and Bittan cut "Happy"—it had already shot up to no. 5. For the last fifteen years, rap had been engaged in a slow climb up to Top 40 respectability, but with the swift ascent of Nirvana, the rock underground of the Reagan era seemed to have accomplished that same feat in just a few months. Very quickly after the adjusted charts became available, A& R executives at all the major labels suddenly became enamored of grunge and gangsta, and tried to locate every promising artist in both of those genres who hadn't already signed with a major label.

But even if recording executives were rapidly changing their outlook on popular music in early 1992, not all American music consumers were as thoroughly transformed. Ad-minded local FM stations seemed to grasp this more readily than the record labels did. As the baby boomers entered middle age, Adult Contemporary stations

around the country slid from late swing into soft rock. One reconfig-
ured station in Boston proudly announced in the early 1990s that it
featured "No Rap, No Metal," thereby purposefully rejecting the most
vibrant music of the current moment for the twilight age of post–
British Invasion biracial pop. There were still artists around Springsteen's age who were succeeding under the new *Billboard* measurement
system, including his good friend Bonnie Raitt, whose "Not the Only
One" at no. 37 was her third Top 40 single in the last year. Eric Clapton, to cite an even more salient example, enjoyed the second-highest
charting single of his entire career in the summer of 1992 with "Tears
in Heaven," a song he had written after the death of his son that had
been featured in the film *Rush*.

Raitt and Clapton undeniably released good music in the early
1990s, but they gained wide popularity for the most part by turning
the volume down. Clapton in particular rebooted his career by playing
on an episode of MTV's series *Unplugged*, which had morphed in just
two or three years on the air from a venue for so-called alternative
music to a showcase for long-established artists. Clapton's episode of
Unplugged, taped 16 January 1992 (as Nirvana was celebrating its first
pop success and Bruce was celebrating the newest addition to his family) was notable for several reasons. First, more than almost any other
veteran guest on the show up to this point, Clapton was mostly associated with playing loud and electric. This concert lowered the sound
level. Surprisingly or not, Clapton didn't do too many of his own songs
during the taping, but his reinvention of "Layla" in particular on this
occasion was exceedingly different—"that bossa nova bongo version of
Layla" as the ever charitable Pete Townshend would later describe it.
Second, Clapton used the *Unplugged* concert as a springboard for
future success, not only releasing a recording of it as a CD that would
be the no. 1 seller for three weeks in a row but winning the Grammy
for 1992 Album of the Year.

Technically, Clapton was the second artist to release an album of
his performance on *MTV Unplugged*—a year earlier, Paul McCartney
had released a limited pressing of a recording of his own appearance—
but he was undeniably the first to see such a recording as anything
more than a curiosity. Suddenly, after Clapton's success on the show,

doing *MTV Unplugged* seemed like a very smart move for an established artist whose sales were in a lull. So, when sales of *Human Touch* and *Lucky Town* kept heading south, Springsteen's management booked him to tape an episode of the show in late September 1992, just before a three-night stand at the LA Sports Arena. This was at the height of unplugged mania, a few weeks after Clapton's *Unplugged* album entered the *Billboard* albums chart, a few weeks before that acoustic "Layla" entered the Hot 100.

According to most reports, Springsteen at least initially intended to do an *Unplugged* show. Since the Meadowlands shows a month and a half earlier, he had taken to starting many of his concerts on the 1992 tour with a solo acoustic number before bringing the whole band out. By the time he hit LA, he had a repertoire of at least half a dozen songs he could do quietly and acoustically, with at least a dozen more if you added the Christic material. For whatever reason, though, by the time MTV's cameras rolled at the Warner Hollywood Studios on 22 September (the day before Bruce's forty-third birthday), what he decided to perform for the taping was pretty much a high-energy, slightly concentrated version of his standard concert that year. Clearly, he felt loose on this tour and enjoyed playing with his new band, but unlike Eric Clapton and Mariah Carey (whose quickly issued *Unplugged* EP had already gone triple platinum), he didn't want to make an album during this performance. He wanted to promote one—two, in fact. Moreover, unlike Clapton, who had pored over the alternate takes of "Layla" two years before his *Unplugged* concert while preparing the release of a Derek and the Dominoes twentieth-anniversary box set, Springsteen wasn't ready to quiet down his new songs just yet. He was still in the midst of his new burst of joy.

MTV apparently took the news in stride. "When you have the chance to work with Bruce Springsteen," one of the show's producer said at the time, "he can do what he wants." Viewed twenty years later, the performance Springsteen taped for MTV is a wonderful document of his born-again band, which is livelier and more fun than most die-hard E Street fans would give it credit for. What the new band members lacked in familiar synergy with Springsteen, they made up for in the youthful energy with which they attacked his songs.

At the time, though, this performance, like the two new albums it was meant to support, barely registered on the pop music landscape. Louder than the now distinguished Clapton but softer and more intelligible than Nirvana, Springsteen may very well have had no proper place in the pop music universe of 1992. Maybe it was Boss fatigue, maybe nostalgia for the E Street Band, maybe even some paradoxical but not unlikely combination of those two feelings, but this time around folks weren't buying. By the time Springsteen taped his MTV special, *Lucky Town* had already slipped off the *Billboard* albums chart. When the special (titled *Bruce Springsteen XXPlugged*, with the Xes covering a still legible *Un* in the cable channel's usual logo for the series) aired in November, *Human Touch* had been off the same chart for several weeks. Lucky now in love and family, Springsteen was apparently no longer lucky in pop.

But the tour continued. At various stops, old friends and bandmates joined him for encores—Danny Federici in LA in September; Steve Van Zandt on Long Island in November; Garry Tallent in Lexington, Kentucky, in mid-December; Max Weinberg in Red Bank the following March—but "it wasn't a whole lot of fun," Garry reported. When Max sat in, he was astonished to find that Bruce expected him to play to a click track. The sets were similar from night to night, but there was usually just enough variation in them to allow for a little play—four or five songs would differ between concerts, sometimes more if they were playing multiple nights in the same venue. Bruce seemed to be having fun, although not the same kind of manic need-driven fun that he had derived from the tours of the 1970s and 1980s. Patti, Evan, and Jess traveled with him on the tour, and they were still the center of his world.

After a break over the holidays, the tour geared up for a second, more elaborate swing through Europe, where there seemed to be more support for Springsteen's newer work than in the United States. "This Hard Land" now regularly joined the sets in Europe, as did a shimmering gospel take on Jimmy Cliff's "Many Rivers to Cross" that almost single-handedly justified the current touring lineup. Flying into Dublin a few days before his concert on 20 May, Springsteen caught a performance by country artist Joe Ely at the stadium. After that night, the two men became fast friends, so much so that Ely was the only artist whom Springsteen asked to perform with him at both of the benefits back in the States with which he and his new band were unofficially closing their 1992–93 tour. The first was at Madison Square Garden on 24 June, a benefit for hunger relief, the other was in the Meadowlands two nights later, for an organization funding sarcoma research that was named after Kristen Ann Carr, a friend and former employee of Springsteen's who had died six months earlier.

It had been a good tour, earning more than $30 million in ticket sales alone, with a core band that Bruce wanted to work with again— but not just yet. Patti's solo album, entitled *Rumble Doll*, finally came out that summer, with underplayed assistance from Bruce on two of the last tracks finished. Come July, the two headed back to LA, and Bruce didn't step in front of a paying audience for the rest of the year. Sometime that summer, with Patti pregnant with their third child (another boy, as it would turn out), the two went camping with the kids in the desert, giving rise to another personal song from Springsteen, a quiet coda to the *Lucky Town* songs called "Long Time Comin'." Humbly, it voiced a more knowing prayer than Springsteen might have made even as little as three or four years earlier:

> *Well there's just a spark of campfire burning*
> *Two kids in a sleeping bag beside*
> *I reach 'neath your shirt, lay my hands across your belly*
> *And feel another one kickin' inside*
> *I ain't gonna fuck it up this time . . .*

He had been writing all along. Back in late February, during the break in the tour, he recorded demos of over a dozen songs. These weren't full-on four-track Thrill Hill productions, just stabs at ideas that he caught with a cassette recorder before the inspiration left him. In late August, he made his first serious home recording since the *Lucky Town* sessions a year and a half before, this one a commission from film director Jonathan Demme. Stung by criticism of the more homophobic aspects of his successful thriller *The Silence of the Lambs*, Demme had made a courtroom drama about AIDS and antigay discrimination. The film wasn't meant for art houses, Demme told Springsteen. He "want[ed] it to play the malls," so he asked first Neil Young and then Bruce to write possible themes for the film. He wanted songs that sounded like mainstream rock, something fist-poundingly anthemic in order to enlist the sympathies of those who might otherwise not be inclined to sympathize with a rich young male lawyer who lives with a boyfriend, even if he did have a terminal disease and was played by Tom Hanks. Springsteen said he'd give it a shot, even though he'd never written a song for a film before.

The song Springsteen wrote, however, seems only tangentially related to Demme's film, and particularly tangential to its protagonist. The narrator of Springsteen's song is not prosperous but poor, as were a great many of those with HIV and AIDS in 1993, too poor in fact to afford the recent highly active retroviral therapies (HAART, for short) that had successfully arrested the development of the virus in many wealthier patients. Moreover, although Springsteen's narrator in this song is probably gay, he is also notably homeless. The song is pointedly called "*Streets* of Philadelphia" rather than merely "Philadelphia," as Demme's film was entitled, because, unlike Demme's protagonist, Springsteen's narrator has no apartment.

As it turns out, the greatest influence on Springsteen's lyric wasn't a homosexual man but a heterosexual woman: Kristen Ann Carr, whose death still haunted Bruce seven months later. Daughter of his comanager Barbara Carr and stepdaughter of his biographer Dave Marsh, Kristen had worked with her fiancé to organize the off-duty itinerary for Bruce's band during the initial European leg of the *Human Touch/Lucky Town* tour. The following January, during the break in the tour, she died at the age of twenty-one, and Bruce and Patti ended up singing "If I Should Fall Behind" at her funeral rather than her wedding. Carr died of liposarcoma (which affects the fatty tissues) rather than Kaposi's sarcoma (which most manifestly attacks the skin, and which was one of the most common visible symptoms among HIV-positive men during the early stages of the epidemic). But once you've seen someone *wasting away*, you don't forget it, and the details that Bruce started pouring into his notes for a possible lyric seem drawn from the final stages of Carr's illness.

Writing to order, Springsteen had come up with the words first. Then he tried to set them to the sort of anthemic music that Demme had requested, maybe something as angry and defiant as "Born in the U.S.A.," but for ACT-UP veterans this time rather than for veterans of the Vietnam War. It didn't work, however. After a day of rock-oriented frustration, Springsteen's unfortunate interest in click tracks came in handy. He programmed "a hip-hop-influenced beat" on his drum machine, played some minor chords on a synthesizer, and found the music for his words. Bruce mailed the tape to Demme, and when the director listened to it he cried. It wasn't the song he had wanted, but he found it "exquisite" nevertheless and decided he would put Springsteen's song over the opening titles of his film and Young's even more mournful one over the end titles.

Springsteen's solo demo for the song was completed in late August, and it was obvious that this was not a track that should be recorded with his most recent touring band. Still in the mind-set he had embraced during his last tour, though, Bruce seemed to be focused on vocals rather than instrumentation. He called in Tommy Sims to contribute background vocals as well as a bass part. Even more interesting, renowned jazz vocalist Little Jimmy Scott provided a more elaborate set of background vocals for the record, and jazz legend Ornette Coleman agreed to perform on it as well. Springsteen was the only non–African American in the combo, and the recording fulfilled the jazz potential that critics had glimpsed in such earlier Springsteen songs as "Incident on 57th Street" and "Meeting across the River." The track was cut, Scott was included in the on-location video shoot, and the song was mixed and included on *Philadelphia*'s soundtrack.

And then, almost at the last moment, Bruce made one of his sudden, strategic withdrawals. In mid-December, mere weeks before the movie, video, and soundtrack album were set to be released, the Thrill Hill solo track replaced the Springsteen-Coleman-Scott-Sims collaboration. It was placed over the opening titles of Demme's film (although the four-man version of the song can still be heard at one point during the film), and the video was recut or reshot to eliminate Jimmy Scott's presence. It was odd, to say the least, although one could argue the merits of the Thrill Hill version on aesthetic grounds. Still, it seems notable that, after two or three years of ignoring almost everyone else's ideas about what he should do with his career, Springsteen now issued his most auteurist recording to date. He plays everything on the released version of "Streets of Philadelphia," including drums (via a drum machine) for the first time ever. Even if he intended it as a song that, like Demme's movie, addressed the need to "[tie] disparate communities together," it was nevertheless suggestive how isolated Springsteen's creative process had become.

On 5 January 1994, Patti gave birth to their second son, Sam Ryan, and "Streets of Philadelphia"—the only single that Springsteen had released in the last two and a half years, since "57 Channels"—was suddenly a hit. The week of its release it was the Hot Shot Debut on the Hot 100, and the next week it was the Greatest Gainer/Airplay, and the week after that the Greatest Gainer/Sales. It was nominated for an Oscar, and for that ceremony in late March Springsteen performed it solo (rather than with Roy, Tommy, and Bobby, as he had at a benefit a few months before). He won the Oscar that night, and he used his acceptance speech to make a point about "popular art," insisting that it was the logical medium for helping large, diverse groups of people to overcome their more superficial differences. At the end of April 1994, a month after the Oscars, the single peaked at no. 9 on the Hot 100, making it Springsteen's first Top 10 single in seven years. This was what he had wanted to happen with his last three singles, but for whatever reason they hadn't caught fire. This song had, even if he was donating most of the profits from it to charity. Over the next year, Springsteen would perform "Streets of Philadelphia" at the MTV Music Awards and at the Grammy Awards, being consistently praised and rewarded for the first time in his career for a song that was not intertwined with the E Street Band.

Springsteen appears to have been a little confused by all this. For anyone who knew him, one of the signs of his confusion during 1994 was the frequency with which he returned to drop-in gigs that year: two nights at the House of Blues on the Sunset Strip when it opened and another night in late June; the Stone Pony tent in Asbury with Patti, Southside, Max, and Bon Jovi; the House of Blues again with Fogerty when he briefly returned to LA in September; encores with Dylan and

Young a month later at Roseland in October; and a power pop dream quintet the next night in Sayreville when he sang "Suspicious Minds," "Route 66," and "Gloria" with John Eddie, Greg Kihn, Marshall Crenshaw, and Elliott Murphy. There didn't seem to be problems at home this time, as there had been during the truly compulsive gigging five years earlier, but there may very well have been problems in the studio. By the time of the Oscars, he had written at least three or four songs for yet another "relationships" album, this one possibly influenced by hip-hop (at least rhythmically). He recorded those songs with Bittan, Simms, and Alford, but none has ever seen the light of day. Throughout 1994, Springsteen's only fruitful recording sessions seemed to have been five tracks he did at Thrill Hill for Joe Grushecky, a Pittsburgh rocker whom he had first met thirteen years before when Steve Van Zandt produced one of his albums.

For this period of writer's block—or, more precisely, recorder's block—Springsteen has offered no explanation of what his difficulties might have been. There is a suggestion, though, in the one track he did complete in 1994: "Missing." This song, recorded at Thrill Hill West that fall, is yet another solo production, with Springsteen again combining a hip-hop-influenced drum program with minor chords on a synthesizer. In other words, it is another song in the same mode as "Streets of Philadelphia," which he had written a little over a year earlier and for which he had been so widely praised since then. "Streets" had been commissioned by a film director, but in the case of "Missing," Springsteen seems to have approached a director himself. He went to Sean Penn, who had dated his sister Pam in the early 1980s (when both had appeared in the film *Fast Times at Ridgemont High*) and who had based *The Indian Runner*, the first film he wrote and directed, on Springsteen's song "Highway Patrolman." In late 1994, Penn was in the middle of writing and directing his second film, *The Crossing Guard*, and Springsteen asked him whether he thought he could use this new song for the soundtrack. On the face of it, it certainly looked as if Springsteen was trying to re-create his most recent, unexpected success.

Nearing the quarter-century mark of his recording career, Springsteen didn't want to repeat himself too much, though, nor did he want to coast, but what was there left to do in pop music that he hadn't already done? He was experimenting with jazz and hip-hop, two forms in which he had not yet worked extensively, but he apparently wasn't happy with the results. He could work out singles that sounded fresh for him, but there didn't seem to be enough material for an album. This may have been why recording and performing with Joe Grushecky provided such a release that year: Springsteen knew how to craft a great bar band sound, but he also knew that he didn't want his own next album to sound like that. He'd already done that. Helping a struggling friend come out with his own version of Born in the U.S.A., however, could definitely provide its own satisfactions.

Even more significantly, though, Springsteen seemed to be most pleased artistically in 1993 and 1994 when he made records by himself. Working with others seemed to be unsatisfying—at least if the result was supposed to be a "Bruce Springsteen record." We don't know much about the tracks that he recorded that year, but it's interesting how many of the songs that seem to have been written during this period are about isolation and impenetrability: not only "Streets of Philadelphia" and "Missing" but "Back in Your Arms" (which grew out of one of those fragments on the February 1993 tape) and "Nothing Man" (a song about a secretly suicidal hometown hero). Because these four songs ended up being released on four separate albums, they have never really been perceived as a group, but together they suggest a powerful loneliness in Springsteen's life, a topic that certainly absorbed him thematically that fall. Although "Secret Garden" (another song written during this period) might suggest that this loneliness grew out of abiding concerns about his relationship with Scialfa, "Nothing Man" alternately suggests that it may have been the isolation of celebrity, the theme jokingly hinted at in "57 Channels," that was really bothering him.

Springsteen was grumpy that fall, although nowhere near as off-putting as he had been in the summer of 1989. He watched a lot of TV, jokingly or not offered to serve as a go-between between the parties in the current baseball players' strike, and was vocally concerned about the victims of the Northridge earthquake and the future of O. J. Simpson's children. More purposefully, he visited homeless shelters and soup kitchens and took Patti Smith's son Jackson out for a bike ride shortly after the death of his father, Fred "Sonic" Smith. Reinforcing his own ties to others in this way was both a positive step for Springsteen personally and the sort of noble distraction that could let his art stew.

Still, he hadn't released an album in two and a half years, and people were buying the soundtrack to Jonathan Demme's film to get a copy of "Streets of Philadelphia." It had been eight years since the live set, and if Bruce was currently blocked, Landau suggested it might be time to put out a greatest-hits package. The album would need added value, though, so that fans who already had all his previous albums would want to pick it up anyway. Obviously, "Streets of Philadelphia" could be included, as could one or two of the oft-bootlegged discards from his older albums, particularly "This Hard Land," which had become a staple on the last leg of the *Human Touch/Lucky Town* tour. But Landau also suggested that they might want to record a few tracks with the band—the E Street Band. In some ways, it might feel like a step backward for Springsteen, but it was obvious that he currently wasn't able to finish an album either solo or with his most recent touring band.

Over the last five or six years, Springsteen had played with each of the former members of the E Street Band at least once, and had even invited many of them up onstage for encores during his 1992–93 tour. He had claimed in his last *Rolling Stone* interview that he had better relationships with all of them now than when they were his full-time employees. The fact was, though, that of all the former E Streeters, probably only Roy and Steve had Bruce's home number in LA, where he now stayed most of the time. Some of them were doing well these days—Steve and Garry were producing, Roy had three or four acts other than Bruce who regularly counted on him for studio work, and Max was now the bandleader for *Late Night with Conan O'Brien*—but others were not doing as well. Clarence's solo career and side work had slowed down to a trickle, and the best steady gig that Danny could get was playing keyboards in the house band at the House of Blues. Several of the band members had openly campaigned for a reunion, and they had played together on special occasions without Springsteen twice, in late 1992 and early 1993, just before he formed his new, younger touring band.

As usual, Jon was one of the few people who could get Bruce to overcome his stubborn pride, although it apparently took him at least three months to do so. On 5 January 1995 (oddly enough, during Sam's first birthday party), Bruce called up Steve, Garry, Danny, Clarence, Max, Roy, and Nils individually and asked each of them whether he would be willing to do some recording. For all the bad blood that may have passed between the band members and Springsteen, it is a tribute to what these eight men could do when they played together that four days later they were all at the Hit Factory in New York, diving into Springsteen tunes again. They would need at least four new tracks to get fans to buy the greatest-hits package, but Springsteen and Landau decided that there was one *Born in the U.S.A.* discard ("Murder Incorporated") that was in good enough shape that it could be used without rerecording. In fact, it would make a great first single. Of the other older songs, "This Hard Land," by whose 1982 recording many bootleg owners swore, would also get several new tries, with harmonica, mandolin, and guitar parts adjusted and readjusted as they went along.

Around the studio, Bruce was all goofing and smiles, but he clearly approached this occasion with some "ambivalence." These mixed feelings are unmistakable in "Blood Brothers," the song about the reunion that he wrote just before they met in the studio. Considered in toto, the song is best understood as a tacit apology. Its idealized first verse ends with the promise *We said until we died we'd always be blood brothers*, but the complicating second verse concedes, *We lose ourselves in work to do and bills to pay*, practically admitting that something was lost when the E Street Band changed from a bunch of guys in a van to a minor corporation. Most strikingly, near the end of the song, Springsteen flatly declares, *I don't even know why, I don't know why I made this call*, almost certainly referring to his telephone request to each of these men earlier in the week, *Or if any of this matters anymore after all.*

Although the band members may not have thought so, Springsteen may have been wondering if a completely new album might emerge from these sessions. During them, he trotted out at least five tracks ("Without You," "Blind Spot," "Back in Your Arms," "Secret Garden," and "Waiting on the End of the World") that he had worked over in the studio the previous year with other musicians. Along with salvaging that abandoned "relationships album," he also may have been mulling over a larger societal album, one in keeping with both of the recycled *Born in the U.S.A.* tracks and very much in the same vein as the still-unreleased tracks that he had recorded with Joe Grushecky during the past year. There was a cover of Tim McConnell's "High Hopes," which addressed the excessive commercialization and commodification of society, attempted at these sessions, as well as a new song called "The Ghost of Tom Joad," which spoke to the social discontents of George Bush's New World Order that had persisted into the Clinton years.

Over the next three months, Bruce Springsteen and the E Street Band performed together in public three times, all of them in Manhattan: at Tramps nightclub (for a video shoot for "Murder Incorporated"); on *The Late Show with David Letterman* (playing both "Murder Incorporated" and "Secret Garden," the two designated singles from *Greatest Hits*); and at a label showcase at Sony Studios (during which they premiered the full-band version of "Streets of Philadelphia," as well as a new, jokey Springsteen song called "I'm Turning into Elvis (and There's Nothing I Can Do)"). It was all to promote *Greatest Hits*, of course, but who was going to be picky? These were their first live performances together in over six years and their first club shows in almost two decades. At the Tramps video shoot, in between the six takes they did of "Murder Incorporated" to provide enough coverage, they performed other, older songs, from *The River*, *Darkness*, even *Greetings*, and they closed with a red-hot smoking cover of "Little Latin Lupe Lu," playing off each other so beautifully that it seemed as if they hadn't spent a day, let alone the better part of a decade, apart.

On its release, *Greatest Hits* entered the *Billboard* albums chart at no. 1 and stayed on that chart straight through to the end of the year. Thirteen of its eighteen tracks featured the E Street Band, but that still wasn't enough for many of Springsteen's die-hard fans, who questioned the absence of any songs from his first two albums. They seemed to have missed the point of the album's name: Springsteen had no "hits" before "Born to Run." Fans were happy for "Murder Incorporated," but some contended that the new recording of "This Hard Land" wasn't as good as the 1982 studio version that they'd had on bootlegs for a dozen years now. Much like *Human Touch*, but more predictably so, *Greatest Hits* was a grab bag, with no stylistic unity, and felt like a sampler of Springsteen's work rather than a summing-up. Since the announcement of the February 1995 recording session, some fans had gotten their hopes up for an E Street Band reunion tour, maybe an album. Critics, however, tended to be more skeptical. To Parke Puterbaugh, who reviewed *Greatest Hits* for *Rolling Stone*, the four new tracks on that collection "sound[ed] more like a final coda than a new beginning."

CHAPTER 11

LOOK IN THEIR EYES, MOM,
YOU'LL SEE ME (1995–1997)

*I*NDEED, MOST OF THE NEW SONGS THAT WERE POURING OUT OF SPRING-steen in the winter of 1995 did seem to call for a quieter, more delicate approach than the E Street Band could offer. There was not only the aforementioned "Ghost of Tom Joad," which worked better if kept close around a tightly shared campfire, but also the slowly gestated "Dry Lightning," sections of which he had been working over for about two years. In addition, there was an elegantly crafted song called "Highway 29," which may very well be one of the most consistently underrated of Springsteen's works, even by its author.

As he had a number of times in the past, Springsteen slowly, dimly seemed to be moving toward a common theme, the sort of general idea around which he could build a coherent album's worth of songs. "Highway 29," "Dry Lightning," and "Straight Time" (another song completed around this time) all seem to describe the same kind of protagonist, as do "Brothers under the Bridge" (Springsteen's second song with almost that exact title, this one about homeless Vietnam veterans) and "It's the Little Things That Count" (a song Springsteen would premiere that fall near the beginning of his next world tour and which may very well have been written around this time as well). The shared protagonist of all these songs is not the solitary, alienated man of so many earlier Springsteen works, most noticeably "Stolen Car" and many of the songs on *Nebraska*. Instead, it is a man who tries to live in society, but knows that his presence in it is tenuous. *One minute you're right there*, as the narrator of "Brothers under the Bridge" puts it, *then something slips. You get so sick of the fightin'*, as the narrator of "Dry Lightning" declares, *You lose your fear of the end.*

For the most part, these five or six songs seem to be pointedly about people other than their author. After the relentless self-revelation of his last three albums, it was probably a relief for Springsteen to write about the details and experiences of other people's lives, to channel his art through criminals, veterans, and others living an existence very removed from his own, now sheltered life. Yet, however dissimilar their outer lives, at their core most of these characters possessed certain inner traits that they also shared with their creator. Most obviously, these characters seemed like less fortunate cousins of the humble narrator of a more directly autobiographical recent work like "If I Should Fall Behind": hoping for the best but aware how easily the worst could return.

Even more interesting, Springsteen's later introductions of these songs in concert suggest that more than a few of them sprang from covertly autobiographical germs. "Dry Lightning," he would tell an audience in New Brunswick late that fall, *is a song about one of those relationships where you can't seem to get it right. I had one for about thirty-five years—with different women, but it was the same one. It was really with myself, so, in hindsight . . .* He was even coyer about the origins of "It's the Little Things That Count," invariably introducing it over the next year with one of two entirely different anecdotes about picking up a woman in a bar, even directly asking a Dublin audience, *Do you want the long story or the short story? This is the part of the night where I like to regale the crowd with tales from my life and my loves,* he would often say before he launched into either version, *Of course I make all this shit up . . . and if I didn't make it up, it happened a real long time ago.* In other words, these songs were autobiographical in the way that "57 Channels" was autobiographical: which of Bruce Springsteen's selves did you want to hear about?

Still, the temptation to read these songs autobiographically—to conjure up some literal personal crisis out of whole gossip that might have caused such themes to loom suddenly larger in Springsteen's mind—is almost overpowering. If we would think the worst of millionaire rock stars and their impulses, then the ex-con's life in

"Straight Time" can be viewed as a metaphor for Springsteen's own life in Beverly Hills, right down to *[getting] out of prison in '86* yet still looking back on that time fondly. *[Y]ou get used to anything*, this narrator admits of his time "inside" during the late 1970s and early 1980s, *Sooner or later it just becomes your life*. Despite his frequent affirmations of current sanity and domestic bliss, did Springsteen secretly wish to have his old crazy life on the road back? Is *Mary smiling but . . . watching me out of the corner of her* eye as he *[tosses] his babies high* in the *kitchen* a simple stand-in for Patti, who might have known even better than Bruce what direction he was tending in the winter of 1995?

We can never know for sure, but other factors suggest that things were probably not quite that simple. If the most important thing for Springsteen that winter had been to play rock god again to hundreds of thousands of people, he could very easily have just gone out and done it. With *Greatest Hits* staying longer on the charts than any Springsteen album since *Tunnel of Love*, fans and record executives (not to mention former bandmates) would have loved nothing more than a massive E Street Band tour that could have put him in stadiums again before Evan James's fourth birthday. If domesticity had really felt like a prison for the singer-songwriter, it was one from which he would always have had a handy escape route.

What's more likely is that one of Springsteen's abiding themes was coming to a head now. Previously, Springsteen's awareness of his own alienation had begun faintly with "Stolen Car" and not reached its full development until "Living Proof" a dozen years later. By the same token, his understanding of how close he constantly was to slipping away from his own best self-conception—*When I look at myself I don't see / The man I wanted to be*, as he had written in "One Step Up"—underwent a similarly slow-dawning process. One might say this awareness was the major undeveloped theme on the three relationship albums, most notably in a released song like "The Big Muddy" and its initially unreleased older sibling "When the Lights Go Out," but also in the key switch in perspective during the bridge of "Brilliant Disguise." That shift in awareness (from the lover's sins to the narrator's) is echoed more starkly at a structurally similar moment in "Highway

29": *I told myself it was all something in her / But as we drove I knew it was something in me.*

When introducing "Highway 29" in Dublin a year later, Springsteen specifically called it *a song about self-knowledge,* suggesting as he elaborated that it was this driving epiphany of the narrator's that may have been the most clearly autobiographical moment in the song for him, rather than any specific description of either sexual or criminal temptation. Self-knowledge, he told the audience, *is kind of a funny thing because the less of it you have, the more you think you have. You see, that's its twisted blessing. When I was 22 or 23, I had a shitload of self-knowledge, but I lost it along the way somewhere.* Like so many of these personal introductions on tour, Springsteen's brief revelation to his audience ended there, trailing off into a chuckle, maybe before he gave too much away. Judging by the way he introduced "Straight Time" during the same concert, Springsteen may have been struggling when he wrote these songs in the winter of 1995 to stick to his interpersonal resolutions of three years before, now that the first burst of that blinding "Living Proof" moment had faded into the normality of daily family life. *I think it's hard to lose your old habits,* he told the Dublin audience, *even the ones that've led you wrong or come close to killing you.*

This secularized, lapsed Catholic's idea of original sin—that every seemingly civilized human being may be forever on the verge of dissolving into his solitary worst impulses—had been present in Springsteen's work for almost two decades. But throughout the 1970s and 1980s, this concept lay most frequently on the fringes of his work, brought up (often in bridges) but then left undeveloped in most songs as Springsteen moved on to other, more pressing themes. Because Springsteen was a performer as well as an author, however, someone who not only revisited his older compositions but constantly juxtaposed them with his newer works, one could almost glimpse a gradual teasing out of this theme over the years, as his self-examination and self-consciousness grew.

Most significantly, this teasing out is evidenced in Springsteen's shifting presentations of "Darkness on the Edge of Town," one of his most frequently performed songs. Even in the song's earliest incarnations, this notion of innate human weakness was obviously not only present but was suggested as a source of potential aesthetic power. Around the time of *Lucky Town*, though, almost fifteen years after "Darkness," Springsteen made a significant alteration to its lyrics, one that he has consistently sung in virtually every live performance of the song since then. In its last verse, instead of singing, *I lost my money and I lost my wife*, he began in the early 1990s to sing, *I lost my faith and I lost my wife*, or still more intriguingly, *I lost my faith when I lost my wife*, making the narrator's crisis even less socioeconomic and more existential. If this alteration was autobiographically motivated, then the *faith* to which Springsteen refers here can't possibly be literal religion, since he was parodying Catholicism in his songs at least two decades before he ever got married, let alone divorced. Given the timing of the lyric change, this *faith* is probably the same one referred to in the contemporaneous "Living Proof," *the faith I'd lost in myself*, suggesting that the end of Springsteen's first marriage irrevocably transformed his sense of self, and that he did not regain it until he successfully built a family with Scialfa.

This seems to have been the last phase of Springsteen's personal reinvention: cultivating a purposeful, useful awareness of his own limitations and weaknesses—not a bad trait for a millionaire rock star to possess, when you come to think of it. The five or six songs he wrote around this idea in the winter of 1995 could easily have formed the core of a new album, a more wistful sequel to *Nebraska*, in which the characters *wound up wounded not even dead*, trying to maintain equilibrium amid the dangers and disasters of an ordinary life. Springsteen even found a way to address this theme in another commissioned film song that he wrote that winter, for Tim Robbins's forthcoming anti–capital punishment film, *Dead Man Walking*. In crafting a song in the presumed voice of Matthew Poncelet, a condemned prisoner played in the film by his friend Sean Penn, Springsteen still managed to declare, *Between our dreams and our actions lies this world*, articulating an idea that was more in keeping with his own recent work than with Robbins's or Penn's.

On the whole, films and books seem to have been Springsteen's most fecund source of inspiration during this period, and in far more specific ways than they had previously served him. Such 1970s songs as "Backstreets" and "Be True" may have referred generally to *movies*, and "Thunder Road" may have stolen a title from the poster of an old Robert Mitchum film, but "Highway 29" seemed to take place *inside* a midcentury noir film, and "My Best Was Never Good Enough" was specifically written in the persona of the cliché-spouting psychopath at the heart of Jim Thompson's recently reissued novel *The Killer inside Me*. Robbins's upcoming film led to one of these new songs, the TV adaptation of Lanford Wilson's Vietnam veteran–centered *Redwood Curtain* seemingly yielded aspects of another ("Brothers under the Bridges"), and Springsteen's old favorite *The Border* apparently inspired not one but two songs: "Across the Border," yet another of his attempts to come up with his own version of Ry Cooder's theme for that movie; and the more character-centered "The Line," whose narrator seemed cousin to both Charlie Smith, Jack Nicholson's border guard in that 1982 Tony Richardson film, and Joe Roberts, the narrator of Springsteen's own contemporaneous "Highway Patrolman."

In yet again reworking *The Border*, however, Springsteen made a significant change: the narrator of his song staffed not the Rio Grande crossing in Texas but the INS office in San Diego. That was another thing that all these songs had in common: California. They were clearly set neither in the Northeast nor in an imagined South or West but in the state in which Springsteen had happily lived for most of the last decade. The *Jersey state line* into New York City had been replaced by the Sierra Madre in these lyrics, *the fireroads to the interstate* by the San Gabriel Mountains, and Asbury's Kingsley and Ocean Avenues by Alvarado Street in the heart of Westlake, one of Los Angeles' most densely populated Latino neighborhoods. Indeed, many of these new songs were tinged with Chicano and Latino touches. "Across the Border" took the generalized landscape of a *Human Touch* song like "With Ev'ry Wish" and substituted *corazon* for "heart," additionally drawing a metaphor like *eat the fruit from the vine* from the lives of Mexican-born migrant farm workers.

Given this clear geographical placement, it seemed only logical that, as Springsteen cast about for still more marginal protagonists on whom he could center his songs, he would end up writing about Chicanos. Living in Southern California in the early 1990s, it was almost impossible not to think about immigration from Latin America, and especially from Mexico. The number of legal immigrants to the United States had more than doubled in just twenty years, from 4.5 million in the 1970s to 9.1 million in the 1990s. The overwhelming majority of these new immigrants settled in just half a dozen states (especially California), and over half of them came from south of the Rio Grande. From Mexico alone, 4 million legal immigrants arrived in the last two decades of the twentieth century, with around 300,000 additional illegal immigrants arriving every year. When these numbers grew unignorable, initiative-happy California voters responded in 1994 with Proposition 187, which if it had been implemented would have denied government benefits to illegal immigrants. Nationwide, noises were beginning to be made about denying government benefits even to legal immigrants, as well as turning back the tide of bilingual education and affirmative action by national origin.

In the late winter of 1995, as Springsteen was crafting his character sketches, the *Los Angeles Times*, which he had read every morning for the last six years, featured articles about legal and illegal Mexican Americans almost every day on its front page. For a native New Jerseyan, the Mexican American gay hustlers of San Diego's public parks were both generationally and culturally a world away from a West Side Puerto Rican flyboy like 1973's "Spanish Johnny," but Springsteen made sure he did his research. Fifteen years earlier he may have been happy to tear off "Roulette" or "Atlantic City" (but not "Nebraska") after reading one newspaper article, but now he had his assistant Terry Magovern call Mark Arax, a *Times* reporter who had written a story about the employment of Mexican immigrants in rural methamphetamine production, in order to get more material—"evocative images" and "Spanish-language terms."

On the surface, "Balboa Park" and "Sinaloa Cowboys," the two detailed songs that Springsteen wrote that spring about the Californian lives of recent Mexican immigrants, might have seemed of a piece with the other songs he had been writing in early 1995, but two things about these songs made them very different. First, they were written in the third person, as if Springsteen were cautious about implicitly claiming to fully understand these characters' interior lives. He had no problem identifying with murderers, bank robbers, veterans, and even border patrolmen, but he could apparently be comfortable writing about illegal immigrants only from the outside. More important, these characters were not existentially marginal but sociologically marginal. These protagonists were people whose lives were undone not by their own irresistible worst impulses but rather by an unfair social order. Consequently, the songs in which they appeared ended up being about not universal human failings but rather specific injustices.

In terms of Springsteen's private development as a songwriter, these two songs represented a significant shift, but in terms of the public perception of his career such songs were exactly what many observers had been expecting. For many, Springsteen's public work of the last few years—particularly the "57 Channels" remixes, "Streets of Philadelphia," and his announced contribution to Tim Robbins's film—suggested an increasing tilt toward more politically motivated topics. Even though the song was thirteen years old, the presence on "This Hard Land" on *Greatest Hits* also suggested as much to Parke Puterbaugh, who guessed in the conclusion of his review of the collection that Springsteen's next work would feature him "walk[ing] alone with a guitar and harmonica for companions." In a way, this made little sense—Springsteen may have been working more on his own lately, but his pure solo works of 1993 and 1994 were built on synthesizers and drum machines, not guitars and harmonicas—but one could still see why people got that impression.

When Springsteen came back from his trip to New York promoting *Greatest Hits*, he turned to making a new album and called in several musicians to help him fill out the sound of a few of the tracks. These new sessions turned out to be the closest thing to an E Street Band reunion that Springsteen fans were going to get for at least a few years, employing as they did Danny and Garry, the two longest-standing members of the band. Gary Mallaber (who had played on most of the *Lucky Town* tracks) came in to play drums. Even more notable, however, were the two other musicians whom Springsteen chose for these sessions: Soozie Tyrell (one of Patti's friends who had sung backup vocals on *Lucky Town*) was asked to play violin; and Marty Rifkin, an experienced session performer, was asked to play Dobro and pedal steel guitar.

Given those last two instruments, it seems clear that Springsteen was interested in trying a country approach to his new songs. He had been fascinated with country music for at least two decades. Not only were *Nebraska* and miscellaneous songs on *Darkness* and *The River* most clearly based in country music, but back in 1987 when he first split off from the E Street Band, the first new genre to which he originally turned was country music, with the abortive initial band sessions for *Tunnel of Love* in the spring of 1987. Now eight years later, having dived fully into gospel on his last world tour, he seemed poised to take a similar dive into country music, scratching an itch that had only been vaguely satisfied by his occasional team-ups with Joe Ely. Whether as a warm-up exercise or not, the musicians assembled in Thrill Hill West that spring ran through a number of original rockabilly and country swing songs. At least one of them ("Tiger Rose") was memorable enough for Garry to propose it as good material for Sun Records legend Sonny Burgess when he was producing Burgess's comeback album in Nashville that fall.

But of all the new material, the character sketches did seem to work best, whether performed by Bruce solo or with this country combo. Once they were included among possible tracks for the new album, though, "Sinaloa Cowboys" and "Balboa Park" changed the formative idea of what sort of character sketches might be appropriate for it. Now Springsteen added a song called "Galveston Bay" (significantly written in the third person, like those two songs), which treated Vietnamese immigrants in Texas rather than Mexican immigrants in California and drew at least some of its inspiration from the ten-year-old film *Alamo Bay*. A late-night rediscovery of Dale Maharidge's sociological work *Journey to Nowhere: The Saga of the New Underclass* led Springsteen to write "Youngstown," about the industrial decline of that Ohio city, which led in turn to "The New Timer," about displaced industrial workers riding the rails.

In all probability, Springsteen's early 1995 burst of cloistered new writing had begun with a personal rather than a political impulse. Nevertheless, as his work shifted more and more to sociological issues, an older song like "Dry Lightning," with its lovelorn protagonist, for example, now started to feel out of place in the project. In the end, "Dry Lightning" was retained, but because of the album's increasingly social focus "It's the Little Things That Count" was eventually omitted from its contents, as was the more author-centered "I'm Turning into Elvis." Fairly late in the process, "Brothers under the Bridge" was left off, too, perhaps in order to allow "My Best Was Never Good Enough" to provide a faint touch of humor, even if grim.

When Springsteen had started this project back in February, his new album could almost have been called *Straight Time* or *Highway 29*, but as its focus grew broader, one song seemed to have the potential to pull so many of these disparate character sketches together: "The Ghost of Tom Joad," the song that he had not been able to record satisfactorily at the Hit Factory back in January. In a way, it was the oddest of the new works: it didn't belong with any of these new songs, not even the Chicano ones. It was about a broader vision of society rather than an individual one, and thus should have been a logical candidate for a full-on E Street arrangement, the dark 1995 sequel to the persistent optimism of 1982's "This Hard Land." But the fact remained that it sounded best neither solo nor E-Street style, but when played by a four-man combo. Moreover, it provided Springsteen's project with a much-needed thesis statement, the sort of song that, in the absence of which, *Born in the U.S.A.* and *Human Touch* had both languished unreleased for years.

The quoted words of Tom Joad so dominate the end of Springsteen's song that we may almost forget about the narrator who begins it, a narrator about whom we probably know even less than the narrator of the much terser "Streets of Philadelphia." Indeed, he is remarkably passive for the narrator of a Springsteen song, particularly a song proffered as a summing-up for one of his albums. Desperate as the narrators of "Darkness on the Edge of Town" or "Dancing in the Dark" might have been, they were ready to plunge into the madness around them and give it their all. The narrator of "The Ghost of Tom Joad," though, isn't quite ready to move yet. He is *waiting for a savior to rise up*—exactly what the narrator of "Thunder Road" advised his beloved Mary *not* to do. Significantly, when that savior does arise in the song's last verse, his conclusive words here are not Springsteen's own, but Steinbeck's (as plucked by screenwriter Nunnally Johnson to be spoken by Henry Fonda near the end of John Ford's film adaptation of the novel). If in 1977 and 1984 Springsteen had looked to his audience to help him complete his vision, now he invoked the work of prior artists whom he admired.

Truth be told, "The Ghost of Tom Joad" was more than just a thesis statement for a possible album. It was the germ of a twilight anthem, the kind of song that Jonathan Demme had wanted Springsteen to write for "Philadelphia," a rallying cry for advocacy and conflicts with those in power. Unlike the decidedly unanthemic "Streets of Philadelphia," however, "The Ghost of Tom Joad" had significantly not been commissioned by a film director or political party. Springsteen had written it wholly unbidden, whether other people in American culture wanted to hear it or not.

THE RELATIONSHIP BETWEEN creation and history is a funny thing. Any work of art, if it is any good, arises in some way from the time and place in which it is composed. In some cases, though, the relevant cultural setting for a work is more immediately clear than it is in others. Some works (such as *Uncle Tom's Cabin* and *The Grapes of Wrath*) resonate immediately with their audiences, because they seem to capture the times in which those people see themselves as living. Other works (such as *Moby-Dick* and *Their Eyes Were Watching God*) develop their audiences more slowly, as the less evident patterns of history become clearer. For the first part of Bruce Springsteen's career, most of his works clearly fell into the first of these categories. They chronicled the cultural effects of the essential deindustrialization of the United States, with the split material between *Nebraska* and *Born in the U.S.A.* capturing both the Reagan recession and the beginning of the 1980s postindustrial boom. During the presidencies of George H. W. Bush and Bill Clinton, however, Springsteen seemed more culturally removed from the times in which most other Americans thought they were living. In 1992, in the depths of the first Bush recession, he obliviously sang about "Better Days." Three years later, just as the nation's economy was beginning to pick up, he chose to sing about its impoverished and downtrodden citizens.

Critics have frequently claimed that Springsteen's work is nostalgic, but in these songs it seemed even more nostalgic than ever—or maybe it was just old-fashioned. Most of these songs were set in twentieth-century California, as the last half of Steinbeck's *The Grapes of Wrath* was, but it was hard to say during which decade of the state's history their action took place, caught as this project was from its opening minutes between *the railroad tracks* and the *Highway patrol choppers comin' up over the ridge*. Much like "Christmas in Washington," the song Steve Earle would write almost two years later in the bittersweet wake of Clinton's reelection, "The Ghost of Tom Joad" almost wished that time could be turned back, that the mediated recessions of the 1990s could be swapped for the four-square honesty of the Great Depression of the 1930s. If not an all-out denial of history, these songs certainly express a longing for a simpler time, in which an angry man knew, as the narrator of "The New Timer" puts it (in a line also taken from Steinbeck's epic novel), *the name of who I ought to kill.*

Indeed, nearly all of these new songs seemed firmly rooted in the past, not just the black-and-white midcentury of "The Ghost of Tom Joad," "Highway 29," and "My Best Was Never Good Enough," but also the recent past of the 1980s, during which the problems chronicled in "Straight Time," "Youngstown," "The New Timer," and "Galveston Bay" all occur or begin. Even "The Line" could have been written in the previous decade, although illegal Mexican immigration to California received far more attention during the Bush and Clinton eras. During the months that Springsteen was writing and recording this album, the president and Congress were at odds over the Republicans' Contract for America (which sought to undo the social safety net of the sixty-year-old policies of the New Deal), and the United States suffered its first wide-scale act of domestic terrorism when Timothy McVeigh and Terry Nichols leveled the Federal Building in Oklahoma City with a truck bomb. If Springsteen wanted to address social problems, there were certainly enough current materials on which he could focus, most obviously the currently raging "culture wars." Instead, the most current social issue he seemed to be addressing in these new songs was the rising use of methamphetamine, and even that came up only as a side issue.

Springsteen's seeming anachronism on *The Ghost of Tom Joad*, even while trying to remain topical, is even more apparent when you listen to it side by side with a contemporaneous release like *Mellon Collie and the Infinite Sadness*, the Smashing Pumpkins' no. 1 album released around the same time that fall. For Billy Corgan, the young lead singer of the Pumpkins, "1979" was a moment so far in the past that giving a song that title made it almost appear that its action took place in never-never land. Contrasted with such a work, Springsteen's album seemed oddly archaic, with references that clearly marked it as an artifact of Reagan-era protest movements. Such references made Springsteen seem even worse than an oldies act: it made him look as if he were still living, even in his new songs, in 1985.

The United States had changed a great deal in those ten intervening years, at least on the face of it. In terms of American economic history, 1995 is a signal year. In retrospect, it sits at the center of a ten-year period (from 1991 to 2001) that marks the longest continuous economic expansion in America's history. The U.S. share of the world's industrial output climbed to nearly a quarter by the turn of the twenty-first century, and the Dow Jones Industrial Average more than tripled during that time, climbing from 2,588 in January 1991 to 11,722 just nine years later. More cheeringly, most available evidence suggests that these advances were not merely systemic or wholly removed from daily American life. During this period, unemployment and poverty in the United States both dropped significantly, while home ownership, per capita income, disposable income, charitable giving, and life expectancy all climbed just as significantly for nearly all Americans. Not that all of this was clear in 1995—by some measures, the country was just coming out of a two-year recession, and the greater part of all these gains occurred during the second half of the decade—but it still seems like bad timing on Springsteen's part to bemoan homelessness and poverty among other social ills, just when both were about to be visibly diminished. By 1996 at the latest, most Americans would probably have concurred with the judgment of Springsteen's fellow baby boomer President Clinton, who declared, "The best days of America are yet to come."

That was one story of American culture in the 1990s, a tale of triumph and optimism that began around 1989 (when the Berlin Wall fell, the Smashing Pumpkins formed, and Bruce Springsteen stepped off the road to get his head right) and rolled straight on into 2001, moving for the last hundred yards or so perhaps across President Clinton's famous "Bridge to the Twenty-first Century." But there was another story about what was happening in the United States during the 1990s, particularly to its economy, and that story began earlier and ended later than this more narrowly drawn one. This second, more broadly gleaned story stretched from the economic decline of the mid-1970s straight through to the second President Bush's recession, the one during the late 2000s that was bad enough to be called an economic contraction and quite possibly a second Great Depression. That thirty-five-year story saw the deindustrialization of the United States during the 1970s, with which Springsteen seemed so archaically preoccupied, as a problem that never really went away. The nearly quarter-century soundtrack for this second story could almost be culled from a number of genealogically related sources: Studs Terkel's 1972 interview with union organizer Grace Clements (who worked monotonous shifts on a luggage tank in an ARMCO factory); James Taylor's 1978 song "Millworker" (written for the musical version of Terkel's oral history *Working*, its lyrics based directly on Clements's words); Billy Joel's 1982 song "Allentown" (a Top 20 single about the postwar decline of the American steel industry); Joe Grushecky's 1994 song "Homestead" (whose music Bruce Springsteen cowrote); and Springsteen's own 1995 song "Youngstown" (whose lyrics echo not only Grushecky's and Joel's but Taylor's as well, thus reaching back to Terkel's interview with Clements in the year Springsteen himself signed with Columbia Records).

In the final analysis, the good times of the 1980s and 1990s in the United States were built not so much on production or employment (although both did admittedly increase during that era) as on consumption and investment, both of which were fueled by mountains of personal and corporate debt. Blue-collar work, factory work, millwork, steelwork, was what Americans used to do. We didn't need to make processor chips in the United States; we just needed to know how to use them—and how to invest in them. The Dow Jones rose so markedly during this period because, for better or worse, so many more middle-class Americans were taking an active role in investment. Thanks to increased access to computers, a surprising number of ordinary Americans took up day-trading during the 1990s, hoping to cash in on a brief big chance, like the moment in August 1995 when the price of a share of Netscape, a company that was marketing a promising web browser, more than quadrupled in a single hour.

Many more computer-related stocks than Netscape rose and fell at alarmingly rapid rates during the 1990s. The pronounced market volatility that stemmed from this "dot-com boom" famously led Federal Reserve Board Chairman Alan Greenspan to declare in late 1996 that much of this investment was based on "irrational exuberance"—initially justified optimism that forgot in time how fragile its generative preconditions were. As would become clearer in the first decade of the next century, much of the money made during the Clinton boom existed only on paper. If you didn't cash in your investments at just the right moment, it was as if you had never had all that money, and you might have lost much of the money that you started with too. *One minute you're right there*, in other words, *then something slips . . .*

Seventeen years on, we can now see that much of the increasingly good times of 1995 was as close to collapse as were the hard-won lives of the protagonists of so many of the songs that Bruce Springsteen wrote that winter. Poets, Percy Shelley once famously remarked, see the shadow cast on the present by the future, the same idea that cultural critic Raymond Williams invoked over a century later when he spoke of the as yet unarticulated structures of feeling that lie nascent in the time and place of an artistic creation. In one sense, Springsteen was as removed from American culture in 1995 as he had ever been or ever would be. In another sense, though, in capturing his own mood that winter, he captured a larger, as yet unarticulated truth about his time, about the ways in which the victories won by his generation during the last two decades were built in many ways on hope, sand, and irredeemable debt. Holed up in Thrill Hill, he intuitively grasped a hard truth that had eluded so many of his contemporaries: the unresolved mistakes of the 1970s and 1980s still underlay the temporary comforts of the booming 1990s.

BY JUNE 1995, the band sessions for *The Ghost of Tom Joad* were done. Springsteen tinkered with the album and its contents a little more over the summer, but by September it was all down to mixing. A release date was set for late November, with a solo acoustic tour of the States and Europe scheduled to follow. In preparation for the tour, Springsteen relistened to every song he had ever recorded, much of it in the company of Scialfa, to whom he gave a running commentary of how specific works had been composed.

Still, at times that year, Bruce seemed more focused on the careers of the two Joes—Ely and Grushecky—than on his own. In April, in the midst of the flurry of promotion that greeted the release of *Greatest Hits*, Springsteen made time between New York and LA to visit Ely's home studio in Austin to perform on two tracks for his next album, and he sat in the following fall when the Texan played the Viper Room on Sunset Boulevard. With Grushecky, he finalized the mixes for the long-delayed *American Babylon* (which had finally found a label that wanted to release it) and cowrote four songs for the Pennsylvanian's next album. As far as Grushecky's live performances were concerned, Bruce not only sat in for a combined fifteen-song set in July with the Houserockers at the Tradewinds in Sea Bright, but he did six dates with them that October on their Northeast tour.

And then there were the two really big performances that fall. First, on Labor Day weekend, came a concert in Cleveland Stadium for the long-awaited opening of the Rock and Roll Hall of Fame and Museum right next door on the banks of Lake Erie. Two months earlier, Bruce may have been backed at the Café Eckstein by Wolfgang Niedecken and his friends, but could there have been any doubt that on this momentous occasion he would be playing with the E Street Band? They not only performed "Darkness on the Edge of Town" (from Springsteen's own catalog) and the eternally dirty "Shake Rattle and Roll" (as a tribute to deceased Hall of Fame member Big Joe Turner), but they served as backing band for Bob Dylan, Jerry Lee Lewis, and Chuck Berry—this last over twenty-two years after half the band had previously backed him at a music festival in Ohio.

And in mid-November, three days after *The Ghost of Tom Joad* was released, came a much more surprising guest performance, at a gala concert to celebrate Frank Sinatra's eightieth birthday. In a brief speech to the audience in the Shrine Auditorium before he started singing, Bruce shrugged off the differences between the two performers as well as he could, but the fact remained that Sinatra's music was not really Springsteen's music. When he and Patti visited the Sinatra house for dinner shortly before the concert, Springsteen enjoyed the meal and the conversation but felt awkward when a sing-along began. Instead, it was Patti who sang standards from the prerock Great American Songbook around the piano to Frank and Barbara's delight. "I don't know those songs," Springsteen later told an interviewer; "I can't sing like that."

What Bruce did to honor Sinatra at the Shrine was something very different. Using just his voice and an acoustic guitar, after his speech he performed a reimagined version of one of Sinatra's signature songs, focusing not on his fellow New Jerseyan's sound (as his friend Bono would do that night in his ersatz crooner's ballad "One Shot of Happy, Two Shots of Sad") but on his spirit. *It was the deep blueness of Frank's voice that affected me the most,* he explained to the audience, *and while his music became synonymous with black tie, good life, the best booze, women, sophistication, his blues voice was always a sound of hard luck, and men late at night with the last ten dollars in their pockets trying to figure a way out.* What Springsteen did, in other words, was find that part of Sinatra's work that was closest to where his own art lay that fall, the place where the urban insomnia of a song like Sinatra's "In the Wee Small Hours of the Morning" bled into the early desert rising of a song like Springsteen's "Dry Lightning."

Whether intentional or not, the song Springsteen chose to perform that night was emblematic of many of the commonalities and contradictions between the two men's careers. It was "Angel Eyes," which originally appeared on Sinatra's classic 1958 album *Only the Lonely* but more significantly was the song with which the elder singer commenced his self-imposed—and ultimately temporary—retirement in 1971, turning an unforgettable twist on that song's sweet last line ("Excuse me, while I disappear . . ."). Sinatra retired for two years in the early 1970s because changing tastes in music had all but driven him out of the recording business, at just the same moment as young rock-based performers like Springsteen and his friends were being signed in large numbers to established labels that had grown tired of swing-descended balladeers. Now, less than a decade younger in 1995 than Sinatra had been in 1971, Springsteen's career had grown into his own period of generational irrelevance. For most record buyers in November of 1995, "Glory Days" was as faint a memory that fall as "Nice 'n' Easy" had been in the summer of the Kent State shootings.

TWO DAYS AFTER the Sinatra tribute, with nothing but his acoustic guitar and biker's mustache seemingly the same, Springsteen took the stage on the other side of the continent at the State Theater in New Brunswick, to begin the *Tom Joad* tour. Aside from two songs that he had performed at Neil Young's annual Bridge School benefit in late October, this was the first time that nearly all his new songs received a hearing. *I got a couple of requests before I go on,* he told the audience after opening with "The Ghost of Tom Joad."

> *One is, a lot of songs tonight were composed with a lot of silence, so for me to give you my best, I need a lot of quiet during the course of the evening. In the course of the tunes, if you happen to know the words to some of these songs? I appreciate it. Singing along? Not. Feeling like clapping along? A train wreck, okay? All I'm saying is, I could use your help, to give you the best that I can give you. So, that said, that'll keep me from having to come out in the crowd and slap a few people around and ruin my nice guy image.*

It goes for whistling too, pal, Springsteen responded when someone whistled at the conclusion of this speech. *What do I look like? A juke-box?* he responded three songs later, in vintage Jersey style, when some people started shouting out requests.

It was the beginning of a different type of Springsteen tour: solo, quiet, and amazingly dour. For the first dates of the tour, he leaned heavily on his most recent work: ten out of the twelve tracks on *Ghost* of *Tom Joad* and his movie songs "Streets of Philadelphia" and "Dead Man Walking." In general, the less sociopolitical new songs ("Straight Time," "Highway 29," and "Dry Lightning") came earlier in the concert, interspersed with old *Darkness* and *Nebraska* tracks. For the conclusion of the main set, the four Mexican-American border songs were arranged in a row, as they were not on the new album, with the purposefully hopeful "Across the Border" placed last for maximum impact. The encores usually began with a goofier song from *Greetings*, as a nod to the past, and continued into the renewed faith of "This Hard Land" and "Galveston Bay" (which Springsteen had revised during the summer to make it more hopeful).

Through all its variations, Springsteen's setlist on this tour was the modal opposite of the most common one that he had used on the *Born in the U.S.A.* tour a decade earlier. Here the politics lay in the songs, while the good times and humor lay in the patter in between them. Now as then, the general tenor of his music registered more powerfully with most audiences than his mere interspersed words could probably do. These nearly two dozen songs made for a pretty bleak couple of hours, especially for fans who had first come to Springsteen after seeing him pluck Courteney Cox out of the audience to do a rudimentary twist. Throughout the concerts, audiences seemed so starved for some kind of release that they would laugh at almost anything if it provided a break in the tension. Less than a week into the tour, Bruce added the discarded "It's the Little Things That Count," a song that ended up providing relief only because its character's self-deception was pathetic rather than truly harmful to anyone. Early on in the tour, the heartiest laughs usually came with the last song of the encores, "My Best Was Never Good Enough"—a cute little one-joke number, if you didn't know that it was written in the persona of a psychopath.

In LA in late November, Springsteen performed on *The Tonight Show with Jay Leno*, in New York a few weeks later on *The Late Show with David Letterman*, but in neither case were the songs he performed ("The Ghost of Tom Joad" and "Youngstown") ever considered for release as singles. The new album peaked at no. 11, Springsteen's lowest-chart position since *Wild and Innocent*, and was off the *Billboard* albums chart by the time the tour hit Europe in the spring. At least this time, though, Springsteen obviously wasn't trying for pop success. From the get-go, *The Ghost of Tom Joad* had clearly been intended as a succès d'estime, and storming Europe was obviously part of the plan: five cities in Germany, three nights in the UK's northern industrial cities, a few nights in Ireland, a quick trip back to LA for the Academy Awards ("Dead Man Walking" was nominated for an Oscar but didn't win), then three cities in Italy.

This transatlantic marketing plan clearly paid off. By the end of the spring, *The Ghost of Tom Joad* had moved only half a million units in the United States, but over a million throughout all of Europe. In late April, Bruce played London's Royal Albert Hall the way he would have played the Meadowlands fifteen years earlier, with six shows in one and a half weeks. As usually happened when Bruce played multiple nights in the same venue, the setlist suddenly loosened up considerably in London. The two most notable surprises were Springsteen's first-ever live performance of "The Angel" and the premiere of one of his most legendary unreleased songs: "Pilgrim in the House of Love."

As any fifth century BC Athenian could have told you, the bleaker the tragedy, the sharper the ludic farce you need to follow it. Five months into the *Tom Joad* tour, "Pilgrim in the House of Love" provided the wildly ludic element that Springsteen's 1996 setlists so desperately needed, giving his audience sufficient release through contrast after the increasing downer of the show's first seven songs. Simply put, "Pilgrim in the House of Love" is a song about Christmas Eve in a strip club, with a Santa Claus who may or may not be the real thing but who is definitely receiving oral sex from one of the club's dancers out in the parking lot. Here, it wasn't just Bruce's introduction that was poking fun at himself. The song purposefully deconstructed Springsteen's current public persona as noble, earnest family man and caricatured one of the clearest challenges to Springsteen's flatly honorable persona: his widely known fondness for occasionally visiting strip clubs. After he concluded the song one night in London, he joked, *My wife always tells me "Hey, talk about that in your next interview, Mr. Social Consciousness!"* When he started a week later to regularly follow this new song with a lusty, even dirtier rendition of "Red Headed Woman" than the one on his last tour (a number he now semiregularly introduced as *a great song about a great subject: cunnilingus*), the theatrical effect was even more magnificent. In the midst of the increasingly promulgated image of Bruce Springsteen, Noble Ballad-eer, "Pilgrim in the House of Love" was the perfect way to break the tension, as well as pop the balloon of pretension that his new profes-sional persona appeared to be inflating.

Despite such efforts, however, that flatly noble image seemed to be ever in ascendance as 1996 went on. Like "Streets of Philadelphia," *The Ghost of Tom Joad* brought Springsteen awards, particularly Gram-mys, which he had rarely received during the ten years that people were buying his albums in droves. In the 1970s, Springsteen was the prototypical Neo-Greaser, something between the retro pap of Bowzer and the scary art of Lou Reed. In the 1980s, he had been the Macho American, hardworking in a way that laissez-faire conservativism had coopted and balkanized from former unionist adherents. Now, in the 1990s, as the reductive infotainment-centered iconography of his career continued, Springsteen was going from pop to folk, from Elvis Presley to Woody Guthrie, as if there had never been a performer like Bob Dylan, for example, who had ever tried to contain it all.

In the fall of 1997—in the midst of a second leg of the *Tom Joad* tour that seemed to defy all music industry logic (there could be no more sales in the United States—the album had slipped off the *Bill-board* chart six months before)—Springsteen almost made this neat stylistic transition seem even cleaner by participating in a concert in Cleveland, a little over a year after the Hall of Fame celebration, that featured the work of Woody Guthrie. The nonprofit album that docu-mented the concert was released on Ani DiFranco's independent label Righteous Babe, which ensured its enduring indie cred. At the con-cert, Springsteen sang "Blowing Down the Road" with Joe Ely (as he had done at the hunger benefit at the Meadowlands a little over three years earlier), Jack Guthrie's "Oklahoma Hills" with Ely and Arlo Guthrie, and "Hobo's Lullaby" with Pete Seeger, the éminence grise of late twentieth-century American folk.

For the most part, Bruce's solo performances at this benefit were less interesting than those collaborations. Dipping into Guthrie's song-book, Springsteen essayed "Tom Joad" and "Plane Wreck at Los Gatos

(Deportee)," both of which he had been including in the sets on his own tour for the last several dates. These covers sounded more like "Sinaloa Cowboys" than the version of "This Land Is Your Land" that Bruce had done with the E Street Band so many times on the *River* tour fifteen years earlier. The accompaniment was minimal and non-distracting, the words emphasized above all else. Unlike the hard electric cover of Guthrie's "Vigilante Man" that Springsteen and the E Street Band had contributed to the *Folkways* collection in 1991, neither of these two 1996 performances could be confused with rock—or with any other form of truly popular music, for that matter.

It sometimes seemed as if one of the worst things that had happened to folk music since Woody Guthrie's time was rock—not that rock was bad music per se, but since the mid-1950s at least, folk artists had felt the need to define their work against rock, to define it in a way as "anti-popular." In trying to avoid any seeming taint of Top 40 influence, a folkie like Bob Dylan felt it necessary during the formative stage of his career to hide his early obsession with Little Richard, Joni Mitchell her love of Frankie Lymon and the Teenagers, and Simon and Garfunkel their Brill Building wishes under their early guise of Tom and Jerry. Of course, it's absurd to say that something can be "of the people" and yet anti-popular, but just as post-1950 jazz may have worked a little too hard at not being dance music, post-1960 folk may have worked a little too hard at not being sing-along music. From the 1960s through the 1980s, both these genres became sit-down club music, connoisseurs' music rather than the people's music, songs you understood rather than felt. Just as the chords often mattered more than the melody in post-FDR jazz, the words often mattered more than the music in post-JFK folk. At its worst, such a deformation of the genre shoved plenitudinous detail into endless strings of grace notes, highlighting the songwriter's well-intentioned reportage at the expense of the underlying melody and rhythm that was allegedly supposed to convey it. This wasn't the sing-along folk and brilliant, easily graspable social commentary of Guthrie's "Do Re Mi," let alone the polyrhythmically rejuvenated folk of Ani DiFranco's stunning work. This was the kind of folk music that sent most nonfolkies running for the exits.

Even as Springsteen was indulging in this mode of music (to the point where some former fans were using the words "monotonous" and "droning" to describe his most recent album and his current, seemingly never-ending tour), on some level he still held his long-cherished belief that the most influential music was the music that could be embraced by the widest number. Nearly every night on the tour, the one place where he spoke about *The Grapes of Wrath* was not after the explicitly intertextual "The Ghost of Tom Joad" (which usually opened his shows) but rather just before "Across the Border" (the last song in the main set). He also cited the time in the mid-1970s when Jon Landau had first showed him John Ford's film version of the novel as a signal event in his life. Although he would usually mention subsequently reading Steinbeck's book, it was the movie that had made the stronger impression, particularly the film's last reel—not just the concluding speech from which the last verse of his own song had been culled, but the dance at the sanitary camp that preceded it. As he told an audience at the EJ Thomas Hall in Akron, just four days before the Guthrie tribute,

> There's a scene—Tom Joad's killed a security guard and he's gonna have to leave his family, but he knows he's gonna have to tell his mother that, after she's come thousands of miles and lost her home and lost family members, that she's gonna lose her son now too. Before that, there's this dance scene, and it's great, the music is great. The way that he shot people's faces and the way people are holding one another out on the dancefloor, you know, I always thought that was Ford holding out the possibility of beauty. Where there's beauty, there's hope and where there's hope, there's faith and, and divine love or whatever you like to call it.

Leave it to Bruce Springsteen to find the dance party in a social realist work.

What made this introduction so significant, though—especially since he used almost exactly these words at every performance on the *Tom Joad* tour—was that this speech was ultimately a further evolution of the *let freedom ring* speech that he had given before "Born to Run" and "My Hometown" ten years earlier. During a concert in which he played music that was, for the most part, as far away from "Born to Run" and "Rosalita" as he had ever done, Springsteen instinctively linked that music with his own rising interest as a child in rock 'n' roll. *When I was a kid*, this speech had begun that night in Akron, just before he starting talking about the impression Ford's movie would make on him as an adult,

> *I grew up in a house where there wasn't a lot of talk about books or art. Everybody was kind of struggling to keep their heads above the water, you know. I guess the thing that really first had an effect on me was, my mother always had the radio on when I came down into the kitchen in the morning. I guess when I was in my teens, she was probably . . . I don't know, ten years younger than me. She was but a girl, you know, and she liked that rock 'n' roll music. Every morning we'd be down there, she'd have the local Top 40 station on. . . . Throughout most of my young life, it was the music that gave me a sense of just living and having fun, and that life could be more than what I saw around me, you know, and should be more . . . if you could make it so.*

As he tried to explain on the *Tom Joad* tour with this speech, what seemed contradictory about his work and interests to other people was all of a piece to him. He saw himself in the fictional Tom Joad making a promise in a California sanitary camp to his mother to be noble, and he also remembered himself as the actual little boy in the kitchen of the house on South Street who liked to dance around with his mom to Elvis Presley songs. The thing about art was that it lifted you up, whether it was a square dance at a New Deal sanitary camp or a screaming rendition of "Twist and Shout" on *The Ed Sullivan Show*. On the 1984–85 tour that saw the first performances of songs from both the poverty-stricken *Nebraska* and the nakedly hit-seeking *Born in the U.S.A.*, Springsteen had tried to combine these two kinds of art. For the most part, though, people had taken his work on that tour for what they wanted it to be—pop, not in the transformative sense that

Springsteen had grown to love, but in the pabulumic sense that an old folkie like Pete Seeger despised.

The *Tom Joad* tour wasn't all doom and gloom, of course. There was a sweet benefit concert at St. Rose of Lima School in Freehold in November 1996 that was attended by Marion Vinyard and Sister Charles Marie, and three concerts at the Paramount in Asbury followed a few weeks later that included guest appearances by Patti, Sooz, Steve, Danny, and even Vini Lopez. These concerts succeeded magnificently in large part because they felt like the kind of communal celebration that Springsteen admired so much at the conclusion of Ford's film. These events were people making sad music, happy music, deep music, silly music, but they were doing it interactively, renewing and reforging ties between each other as they performed. That kind of transcendent association through music, whether happy or sad, was for the most part missing on the rest of the *Tom Joad* tour. On this tour, audience members arrived, remained quiet, didn't clap or sing along, and listened to Bruce Springsteen speak truth. No matter how much he might sing about community in such concerts, whatever art they contained was not the result of collaboration between artist and audience. It was about an artist simply telling an audience what he thought.

In May of 1997, just before the final, predictably European leg of the *Tom Joad* tour, Bruce flew to Stockholm to receive the Polar Music Prize. It was a particular honor for him, since one of the few artists who had already received the award in its relatively brief history was his idol Bob Dylan. Some had taken to calling the Polar the "Nobel Prize of music," which seemed fitting, since (like the Nobel Prize in Literature) it was handed out in Sweden and seemed to pay more attention to the content of an artist's work than its form or style. The introductory speaker at the awards ceremony in Stockholm's concert hall stressed Springsteen's "words" and "message" over his music, while Tomas Ledin, in introducing Springsteen to the king of Sweden, who was to present the award, labeled Springsteen a "bard," specifically exalting that status over the popularity of his records. In a congratulatory telegram that was read at the subsequent awards banquet by U.S. Ambassador Thomas L. Siebert, President Clinton echoed these judgments, singling out Springsteen's "poetic spirit and

. . . deep respect for the roots of [his] musical heritage," as if Bruce had been playing folk music in small clubs continuously for the last two or three decades from the Gaslight au Go Go forward.

Bruce, for his part, tried to leaven this one-dimensional treatment of his work with touches of the self-deprecating humor he had been using throughout his last eighteen months of touring. He was humble before his royal hosts, and joked about the urban legend that his 1985 concert at the Gothenburg stadium (particularly the concert-closing "Twist and Shout") had weakened the stadium's foundations. Self-conscious about receiving a lifetime achievement award before he was yet fifty, Bruce *promise[d] to continue to provide you with some fun, entertainment, laughs, something to dance to, to vacuum your floor by, to make love to your baby to, and provide you with a little company on your own trip down Thunder Road.*

But the song he performed at the awards banquet that night wasn't "Thunder Road," which he hadn't performed in front of an audience for at least four years. It was the earnest "The Ghost of Tom Joad," a clear, quiet song about waiting on social justice. *When I started out*, he told the awards banquet audience, almost wholly rewriting his personal history in light of his current enthusiasms, *I wasn't so concerned with instantaneous success or the biggest hits as I was with making music that would find its way into people's daily lives that would become a part of them. I wanted to find my audience*, he continued a little more truthfully, *my spiritual community, my blood brothers and sisters, somebody I could talk to who shared my concerns and my obsessions. That's why I'm here tonight*, he declared, *to thank that audience, for it's the audience that gives my work its deepest meaning.*

The truth was, in the spring of 1997, that Bruce Springsteen had spent the last eleven or twelve years running away from his audience, winnowing it down and training it so that he could be confident that those who remained understood exactly what he was saying, on his terms. The truth was, singing about John Steinbeck to a club full of folkies was easy. Denouncing Ronald Reagan to fifty thousand typical American fans in the Meadowlands was hard. In turning auteurist and turning away from the Top 40, Springsteen had confirmed every intellectual's most dismissive thoughts about American pop: pop music has cycles of up, peak, and down; the smaller the audience, the more meaningful the songs; and so on. As far as the music industry was concerned, Springsteen was simply turning eccentric during his years of decline. He was only delaying the inevitable: cashing in big one last time on the oldies circuit. For most observers, a lifetime achievement award seemed just about right, even if Springsteen still had a couple of years to go before turning fifty. Obviously, his career was over now, at least as a widely popular musician.

PART FOUR

THE FAIRGROUNDS

—

Bruce Springsteen and the Sessions Band, New Orleans Fairgrounds,
30 April 2006. Ozier Muhammad/*The New York Times* (Redux Pictures).

CHAPTER 12

BAPTIZED IN THESE WATERS, AND IN EACH OTHER'S BLOOD (1997–2005)

ON 23 SEPTEMBER 1997, BRUCE SPRINGSTEEN THREW HIMSELF A forty-eighth-birthday party on the field outside the big new farmhouse that he had bought in Colts Neck. The height of Brucemania was now a good dozen years or so in the past, and it seemed safe to come back and live in New Jersey again. Moreover, if Bruce was going to swap coasts on a more or less permanent basis, as a father he needed to do it soon. Evan had turned seven in July (two months after the *Tom Joad* tour had ended), Jess would be turning six just after Christmas, and Sam four a few weeks after that. Millionaire kids or no, it would be good for the three of them to stay in the same school with the same friends from now straight on through their teenage years. The family would live at the Rumson place, but this property just down the road in Colts Neck could house Springsteen's new home studio, as well as a working farm, with horses and other livestock.

Firmly planted back on the East Coast, Springsteen nevertheless chose a fiesta theme for his birthday party. Casting around for a fairly local band that could play thematically appropriate music for his guests, he took Soozie Tyrell's suggestion and phoned a Manhattan-based group called the Gotham Playboys, with whom she sometimes per- formed. Formed by the polymath comic-book artist Arthur Suydam, the Playboys seemed to owe their name to Bruce Wayne and their style to the variegated gumbo that was New Orleans. Their music was mostly acoustic, but not in a dull or solemn way. It was party music for people who didn't feel the need to plug in—perfect, in other words, for a birthday party in a field. Frank Bruno played guitar and Larry Eagle percussion, but the rest of the instrumentation was slightly different from the sort of prototypical rock lineup that Springsteen was used to: Jeremy Chatzy played an upright bass rather than an electric one, Mark Clifford played banjo rather than second guitar, and Charlie Giordano played accordion far more than the B3 organ at which he was also adept.

Springsteen enjoyed the Playboys' music so much that a month and a half later he called them back to the farmhouse to record with him. He had been asked to contribute a track to a tribute album honoring Pete Seeger, and he thought they might be the right band to back him up. When Springsteen received the request, he didn't actually know all that much about Seeger's music, even though he had performed with the elder musician at the Guthrie tribute a little over a year earlier. As usual, though, when he found a wholly fresh project, he dove into it with gusto. As he would later tell it, he "headed to the record store and came back with an armful of Pete Seeger records," listening to them intensively over the next few days. "[T]he wealth of songs, their richness and power," he recalled almost a decade later, "changed what I thought I knew about 'folk music.'"

The significance of this statement has gone largely unnoticed. In 1995 and 1996, all through the *Tom Joad* tour and culminating in the Guthrie tribute, Springsteen's place as a member of the community of American folk singers had become increasingly assured. Despite these seemingly sterling folk credentials, however, when the time came for Springsteen to make a recording honoring the widely accepted dean of late twentieth-century American folk music, he decided he didn't know all that he should about the genre—which was actually a very shrewd assessment. Seeger's music, of course, was *pre*-Dylan folk, wholly unlike many of the songs that Springsteen had probably heard in the coffeehouses of his youth. There wasn't a trace of self-revelation or the confessional in it, for this was "music of the people" in the sense that the artist almost never sang about himself. It was the kind of writing toward which Springsteen had been trying to move when he composed the Mexican American and factory songs late in the *Tom Joad* process two and a half years earlier, but Seeger's songs in that mode seemed much lighter than Springsteen's.

Then again, technically, a lot of them weren't Seeger's songs. That was another one of the points of pre-Dylan folk—you didn't write songs so much as you collected them. You took a song that was already out there, and you put your own spin on it. It was almost like playing in a cover band, except far less lucrative and a lot more respectable. As Greil Marcus showed in his book *Invisible Republic* (released a little earlier in 1997), that was essentially what Dylan did after his 1966 motorcycle accident, after superstardom and the revolutionary triple blast of *Bringing It All Back Home*, *Highway 61 Revisited*, and *Blonde on Blonde* had essentially tapped him out. Seeking to refill his well of inspiration, he dove with Levon Helm and the Hawks into the basement of a rambling house in Woodstock, New York, and played the "old, weird" rural blues and country songs from the 1920s, tossing in sound-alike originals and a few rock 'n' roll tunes for good measure. Although Dylan might later half deny it, Marcus in his book convincingly linked these "Basement Tapes" from 1967 to Harry Smith's classic 1952 *Anthology of American Folk Music*, which collected dozens of those same old songs onto six double-sided LPs organized by genre. Not coincidentally, Smith's *Anthology* was finally issued on CD in 1997 as well, with not only Marcus but Springsteen's sometime stagemates Dave van Ronk and Elvis Costello supplying appreciations of the set in the supplemental liner notes.

We can't know for certain if Springsteen was as fascinated with Smith's *Anthology* in 1997 as his idol Bob Dylan probably had been thirty years earlier, but as an artist who had been associated with Smithsonian/Folkways Records for a decade, he probably had a copy of the reissue either before or shortly after it came out. It was extensively promoted, widely discussed, and generally considered one of the most indispensable releases of the year for anyone interested in the broader history of American music. The crudely recorded songs that Smith had memorialized in his anthology weren't as verbally intricate as Springsteen's own recent attempts at balladeering, but like many of the songs that Seeger performed (and, one hastens to point out, like Springsteen's own prefolk compositions), they were easier for an audience to catch. In many cases, they were easier to sing along to.

The songs that Seeger and Smith collected were also not just pre-

Dylan but even pre-Guthrie folk. While these songs frequently reflected the social conditions from which they emerged, they were far less didactic than folk songs circulated after the Great Depression had been, far less likely to wear their politics on their sleeves. Truth be told, these songs were closer to the sort of sanitary-camp communal spirit that Springsteen had been lauding every night on the *Tom Joad* tour than either Dylan's songs or Guthrie's. Certainly, they were much closer to that kind of music than nearly any of Springsteen's own more recent songs were.

Since he was holding the recording session for the Seeger tribute at home, Springsteen didn't have to book studio time. He just told the musicians to all come to the farmhouse—"Thrill Hill, Boxwood Studios"—on the first Sunday in November. In Springsteen's account, the first song they tried was "Jesse James," a song whose simplicity masks a fairly intriguing musicological history. The take of the song they recorded on 2 November 1997 sounds very close to the version recorded by the Pogues for their 1985 album *Rum, Sodomy, and the Lash.* This may have been because, as Springsteen would later admit, he was making up the arrangements for these songs on the fly, actually calling them out as they were recorded, something he had *never* done in over two decades of making records.

One of the things that made these sessions even more improvisatory was that he wasn't just playing with the Gotham Playboys. He had also called in Ed Manion, Mark Pender, and Richie "La Bamba" Rosenberg, the core players of the Miami Horns (with whom he had been playing off and on for the last twenty years). In essence, at this recording session, Springsteen was combining two distinct bands in order to see what would happen when they played together. With Patti and Sooz also singing and playing, he had a roster of twelve very versatile musicians whose default styles were about half New Orleans and half Asbury Park. It was a lark, and it was incredibly liberating for the lifelong perfectionist. It gave him a taste of the kind of fun he usually had when he sat in with the Houserockers, but this time at a recording session. As he would later tell it, it helped him recapture "the informality, the freeness, and the eclecticism of my earliest music."

Springsteen convened this loose hybrid band only for that one day, but his presumed duties as folk troubadour continued throughout that winter, with a performance of "The Times They Are A-Changin'" in tribute to Bob Dylan at the Kennedy Center Honors in December and a taping of "The Ghost of Tom Joad" and "Across the Border" for a TV special to celebrate the thirtieth anniversary of *Rolling Stone* in January. Certainly, if Springsteen had wanted to stay in resolute folk mode for a while, he could have. In terms of his image, it would have been as easy for him to do in 1998 as the E Street reunion tour would have been three years earlier, even if it wouldn't have made his record label very happy. Throughout the second leg of the *Tom Joad* tour, he had been writing more character sketches, and he still had songs left over from that album and from earlier songwriting bouts. Not only did he probably record a few of these songs ("Reno," "The Hitter," and "All I'm Thinkin' About") solo that winter, but he also evidently recorded at least two of them ("Long Time Coming" and "All the Way Home") with a group very close to the one he had used for the spring 1995 band sessions, including Danny, Patti, Sooz, and Marty Rifkin.

In the end, Springsteen may have recorded as many as a dozen songs during the winter of 1998, but somehow they didn't add up to an album. There was no unifying theme. After *The Ghost of Tom Joad*, it was unclear if there was anything either personal or political that was so pressing that Springsteen felt the need to write about it. He even started writing songs with Joe Grushecky again, usually a sign that his own work was blocked. Finally, in February, he apparently threw in the towel. "Let's do the boxed set," he told Toby Scott, who was at that point engineering the Thrill Hill solo sessions. As he had done when the singer committed to doing the live set a dozen years before, Scott then went to Sony's sound archives in Buffalo to see what they had.

Springsteen had already listened through a great deal of his unreleased material just before going out on the *Tom Joad* tour, to see if there was anything he might have wanted to dust off for his solo performances, but he was looking for songs then, not recordings. When Scott came back, he brought with him 300 different recorded songs, enough to fill a Springsteen "bootleg series" that was at least five times as large as the one that Columbia was periodically releasing for Bob Dylan. Because of an ongoing court case over the 1972 Sioux City recordings, most of Springsteen's early solo work would have to be omitted, but even without those recordings the intended scope of this set was somewhat daunting. The 1986 set had sought to encompass about seven years of live performances, but this set sought to encompass two and a half decades of work in the studio, from the Hammond audition through *The Ghost of Tom Joad*. A 1980 live recording of "Rendezvous" might be used because none of the studio takes of that song had ever quite gelled, horns might be added to the 1982 recording of "Lion's Den," and Vini Lopez might be called in to supply just the right backing vocals for 1973's "Thundercrack," but for the most part the base recordings of these songs would be left untouched. They were remixed but not rerecorded. By summer, Springsteen and Scott had whittled those 300 songs down to 128 tracks (eight CDs' worth), then 100 songs (six CDs' worth), and finally, once label executives had made themselves heard, 66 songs (four CDs' worth).

Simultaneous with his work with Scott on the box set, Springsteen also began collaborating with music journalist Robert Santelli on a book of collected lyrics, with extensive reminiscences in between of how he had composed the contents of each of his twelve studio albums. The book of lyrics and reminiscences would be called *Songs*, the box set of B-sides and outtakes *Tracks*, and while both projects were retrospective it was interesting how little they overlapped. In the end, *Tracks* was a remarkable document, but *Songs* was a much more impressive achievement, almost certainly Springsteen's greatest work as a creative artist in 1998. With Santelli's help, he fashioned a volume that was as much autobiography as collected works, with numerous reproductions from his songwriting notebooks that took his audience far inside the creative process. It was the equivalent of the talk-through that he had given Patti almost three years before when he was preparing for the *Tom Joad* tour, with an openness about the joys and frustrations of songwriting that he hadn't communicated to his audience in any detail since his earliest published interviews.

Simply and without comment, Springsteen dedicated *Songs* to the memory of his father, who had died in late April. On the dedication page, he reproduced a picture of Doug in his army uniform, a cigarette in his hand and looking every bit as much like John Garfield as his son liked to tell people that he did. In fact, Doug looked younger on the dedication page of *Songs* than Bruce did on its cover. When Springsteen and Scott had started preparing the box set, Doug was still alive.

It was probably the roadblock that the new recording sessions had run into that caused Springsteen to suggest finally starting work on *Tracks*, but it may also have been the signal occasion that everyone must have known was coming up. Even though *Greetings from Asbury Park* had been recorded in 1972, it had not been released until early 1973, which made 1998 the official twenty-fifth anniversary of Bruce's first widely released recording. Not only was twenty-five years the sort of round number that made people start thinking about commemorations in general, but it was also the cutoff for eligibility for induction into the Rock and Roll Hall of Fame. For years, Springsteen had been a regular attendee at the hall's induction ceremonies, and Santelli, his current collaborator, was at the moment the chief curator for the hall. (He flew back and forth to Cleveland all through the spring and summer while working on *Songs*.) When the ballot for the next round of inductees was circulated in the fall, was there any doubt that Springsteen's name would be on it, or that he would make the cut and be inducted in his first year of eligibility? Although Springsteen and Scott may not have prepared the four-CD retrospective in this spirit, it now felt like a commemoration in a way that neither the live set nor *Greatest Hits* had ended up being received. It felt like a victory lap, at the end of an increasingly diminished career.

Tracks was released in the fall of 1998, predictably in time for the Christmas season, but when Springsteen began a whirlwind month of interviews in the United States and Europe to promote it, he almost acted as if he were promoting *Songs*. In these interviews, the one number he inevitably performed was the bluesy version of "Born in the U.S.A.," for which he may have attempted a video shoot in Asbury a few weeks before the box set came out. If he added a second song during these interviews, it was "This Hard Land," the other overlap between the two projects and another song featured at most dates on *The Ghost of Tom Joad* tour. If the 1986 live set had represented a monumentalizing of the E Street era of the late 1970s and early 1980s, both *Songs* and Springsteen's early interviews for *Tracks* seemed far more interested in recasting the more widely popular first half of his career in light of its more purposefully populist second half. Springsteen was a solitary Artist, such interviews suggested, and his work was all of a piece.

If you promote a blockbuster as a genteel work of art, however, its sales will be correspondingly genteel. Back in 1986, the marketing of the live set may have been crass, but it certainly got a lot of copies under Christmas trees. Twelve years later, the sales of *Tracks* were far from impressive. In January, Bruce and the label decided to release a less expensive, less massive, one-disc version called *18 Tracks*, which included only three songs that had not been recorded or performed by the E Street Band. As a further incentive, two of the most requested songs that hadn't been included on *Tracks* were put on the new disc: "The Fever" (in its long-circulating 1973 Blauvelt recording) and "The Promise" (which Bruce rerecorded on Lincoln's birthday at Thrill Hill East).

18 Tracks would be released in mid-April, but now another decision had to be made: what about a tour? More immediately, what about the Hall of Fame induction? Springsteen had indeed been elected to the hall on the first ballot, but because it hadn't received a full cover credit from Columbia Records until the live set, the E Street Band was not eligible for induction. Would the band members assemble at the ceremony for a one-shot appearance, as they had done at the Hit Factory and to promote *Greatest Hits* three years before? Or would Bruce have no choice but to perform solo, as he had been regularly doing for the last nine years?

By mid-February, the decision was made. There would be a Springsteen tour, starting in early April and continuing on into the new millennium. More important, for the first time in eleven years, Springsteen would be joined on tour by the E Street Band.

AT THE ROCK AND ROLL Hall of Fame galas, the speeches given by the inductees are usually a lot less fun than the ones given by the inductors. Bruce's acceptance speech at his own induction on 15 March

1999 was no exception to this rule: it was mostly a list of thank-yous. They proceeded chronologically, from Adele and Doug, through the Vinyards, to twenty-five years of recording engineers, tour crews, lawyers, managers, and even top Columbia executives (all of whom came in for a mention, even Walter Yetnikoff). The list climaxed, however, with a tribute to, *last, but not least, the mighty men and women of the E Street Band.*

As he had done for the 1986 live set, Springsteen seemed to assume that the real E Street Band had begun in 1975. Vini, Boom, and Davey got name-checked, but each of the eight performers who had regularly played with him on the tours supporting his albums from *Born to Run* through *Born in the U.S.A.* received a special, extended mention. Even more interesting, Bruce listed these musicians, neither in the order that they had entered the band (he began with Nils, then moved on to Danny and Garry, both of whom had played with him since Steel Mill) nor in what one might have presumed was his order of increasing closeness to them (he ended not with Patti but with Clarence). Instead, he did a roll call as he might do near the end of a second set, in the order that a more casual fan might recognize the members of the band, from Nils, Danny, Garry, and Roy (the foundation of the band's sound but less likely to take part in any onstage funny business) through Max and Steve (both far better known now than during the 1970s and 1980s, because of their current work in television) to Patti and Clarence (easy interlocutors at the front of the stage, unmistakable embodiments of sexual and racial difference). *Rock 'n' roll*, he said, explicitly quoting Steve in his peroration, *it's a band thing.* He ended his speech by calling up *my wife, my great friends, my great collaborators, my great band*—calling them up not to speak, but to perform.

Even though they came out simultaneously, *Songs* represented something of an ending for Springsteen and *Tracks* a second beginning. The book sealed his eleven-year-long reintroduction to his fans and to the public as a serious songwriter, a process that had probably seen its true climax with the acceptance of the Polar Music Prize almost two years earlier. The box set, though, and especially this induction speech, kicked off a slight but still significant reinvention of the E Street Band, a *rebirth*, as Bruce told audiences both at an open rehearsal in Asbury Park three days after the Hall of Fame ceremony and again in Barcelona a few weeks later, on the first night of what would prove to be so much more than just a "reunion" tour. During the Hall of Fame speech, he insisted in mock-preacher tones that he had *reeducated and rededicated, re-animated, resuscitated and reinvigorated [the band] with the power, the magic, the mystery, the ministry of rock 'n' roll.* As Springsteen would make clearer as the tour went on, though, the truth for him was slightly more complicated than that. It was the band, and perhaps the audience, to which he now looked to reinvigorate himself, as he tried to fuse the articulated commitment and connection of his last ten, quieter years to the gargantuan concerts that had previously made him famous.

Arena rock, Springsteen realized, perhaps better than anyone else, needed to be mythic. You just can't fill a space as large as Madison Square Garden if you act the same way you would when performing at the Main Point or Paul's Mall. But the myths of growing up and longing for success that had fueled Springsteen's shows during the late 1970s and early 1980s were by 1999 long past their shelf life. At his current level of wealth and success, songs like "Thunder Road" or "Badlands" couldn't sound as convincingly desperate as they had twenty years before—and with three children of his own in grade school, he was getting a little long in the tooth to keep poring over thirty-year-old fights with his now deceased dad. So on this tour, the focus of Bruce's onstage mythologizing would no longer be himself, and the tall tales he spun onstage would for the most part not be about his life. This time (maybe for the first time since the Bottom Line shows almost a quarter of a century earlier), the anecdotes and underlying narrative of the show would be about the band.

In retrospect, the mock-preacher tone that Springsteen had taken during the induction ceremony was a fairly clear indication of his plans for the tour. The conceit of the 1999–2000 concerts was that they were a touring revival show. *Brothers and sisters, all rise,* Clarence intoned with unmistakable bass gravitas as the lights went out to begin one concert that fall in Los Angeles. *There's going to be a meeeeeting in the town toniiight,* Bruce began half singing and half chanting as the band members took their places for the opening number. At all the shows, the revival motif returned explicitly at least twice, for ten-minute-plus versions of "Tenth Avenue Freeze-Out" (at the center of the show) and "Light of Day" (at the end of the main set). The extended monologues that Springsteen indulged in near the climaxes of both these songs were delivered in full-on preacher mode, although each was concerned with a different object of "revival." The "Light of Day" monologue (which was in place from the first night of the tour in Barcelona) spoke about how the audience might be lost and how it might be able to find *not life everlasting but life . . . right now, through the power, the magic, the mystery, the ministry of rock 'n' roll!* The "Tenth Avenue Freeze-Out" monologue (which first appeared when the tour returned to the States for a fifteen-night stand at the Meadowlands in July) was ersatz Pastor Bruce's own witnessing of how he had been *saved* by rock 'n' roll. As this monologue evolved across the tour, it became a Dantesque narrative—by way of Nick Tosches, perhaps—about how the singer couldn't pass through a dark wood over to the river of salvation until a gypsy woman in an expensive foreign automobile informed him that he couldn't move *because you're alone. What you need is . . . some help, Mr. Independence! You need a band!*

It was a joke, it was a goof, it was one of the most elaborate, outlandish monologues that Springsteen had performed in almost a quarter of a century, and it grew more and more outlandish with each additional date of the tour. It was also, at its core, a surprisingly serious and personal statement. Maybe because he was playing a role, Springsteen got more personal onstage than he had in a long time. As that last quotation might suggest, this monologue took as its theme the same notion of the need for connection that had dominated Springsteen's own personal "revival" of the early 1990s. Speaking of that *river of life . . . and companionship,* Springsteen emphasized to an audience at the Staples Center in LA that fall that *you can't get there by yourself.* "Uh-uh, I'm not going!" he fictionally remembered himself saying. "Man, I'm gonna run 'cause that's what I know how to do. That's what I'm good at, I understand that. I'm not going!" He did this, he explained, *because I knew there were responsibilities that waited with that life on the other side, and I couldn't find the courage to face those responsibilities.*

Underneath the exaggerated diction of this speech was a tacit admission of a specific responsibility to the members of this band. As Springsteen had acknowledged with reference to the now available album discards on *Tracks*, he knew that on occasion his single-mindedness caused him to cast things aside that might end up being aesthetically valuable—things and people. That this tour might, in some measure, be a bit of an apology to the musicians he had dismissed with a phone call ten years earlier became even clearer with a third number that was performed at every stop on the tour, from Barcelona forward.

Although Springsteen always liked to go out on tour with plenty of new songs to perform, he actually didn't end up doing that many *Tracks* songs on this tour, usually no more than one or two per night. Instead, he seemed more interested in trying out E Street versions of the songs that he had written since separating from the band. Most notable among these was "If I Should Fall Behind," which appeared nearly every night in the penultimate spot of the encores, in a rendition that Springsteen's voice framed but did not dominate. He played acoustic guitar throughout this song, but after his initial verse, first Steve, then Nils, then Patti, then Clarence stepped up to sing verses and eventually to harmonize on it. It was a simple but devastatingly effective treatment of the piece, turning a song about romantic renewal into a song about renewing friendship and artistic collaboration.

But it wasn't just his relationship with the E Street Band that Springsteen thought needed revival. It was also his relationship with his audience. *I wanna go there tonight,* he would say to the audience, *and I want you to go with me, because I need to go with you. That's why we're here.* Even more than the tale of being lost in a dark wood, his fired-up pitch about *the ministry of rock 'n' roll* was both a joke and a serious admission on Springsteen's part. Maybe it was the cumulative effect of playing for five or six years to quiet, respectful audiences, but it almost seemed on this tour as if Springsteen was starting to reconsider the possible social value of merely making a joyful noise. A dozen years before, he hadn't been able to control it—the audience had reshaped him, rather than the other way around. Could there be a way, as he cautiously suggested in his preacherly tones, that he and his audience could reshape and even help each other, to "break down," as University of Wisconsin professor Craig Werner had put it the previous year, "the difference between personal salvation and communal liberation"?

When Werner wrote those words, in his book *A Change Is Gonna Come: Music, Race & the Soul of America,* he was describing what he called the "gospel impulse" in American music, which he traced from the clearly labeled gospel music of Mahalia Jackson, Sam Cooke, and Aretha Franklin through to less literally religious music by Roberta Flack, Parliament, and Digable Planets. "No one makes it alone," Werner wrote when characterizing this music. "[I]f we're going to survive to bear witness and move on up, we're going to have to connect. The music shows us how." The echoes of such ideas in Springsteen's onstage speeches were by no means accidental. Werner was a Springsteen fan, who wrote in his book admiringly about Springsteen's live shows of the late 1970s and how they had "created a sense of community that said no in thunder to what was happening in the outside world." He even included "The Promised Land" as the only work by a white artist in his list of forty songs that typified the gospel impulse. When he attended one of the revival shows at the Palace in Auburn Hills, Michigan, in September of 1999, a friend leaned over near the end of the show and said, "Man, this sounds like he's read your book." When Werner was given the chance to meet Springsteen backstage after the show, the first words out of the singer's mouth were "Your idea of the gospel impulse is what I've been looking for since 'The Promised Land.'"

It was a sweet meeting of two mutually admiring white disciples of the essential role played by black culture in American society, but both Werner and Springsteen would probably also admit that their shared dream of salvation through popular music was most assuredly a long shot. For a white professor of African American studies like Werner, the gospel impulse was a powerful argument with which to shape his undergraduate seminars, but for a rocker who had been in the business as long as Springsteen, it was an almost ludicrously naïve (if always sincere) premise on which to operate. This was probably why he felt the need to adopt such an exaggerated onstage persona when advancing it publicly.

Moreover, for Springsteen to call his audience *lost in these waning years of the twentieth century,* as he did nearly every night at the climax of his main set, seemed almost contrary. He called them *downsized,* but that bit of economic compassion was at least five years too late. It probably would have resonated best during his 1992 tour, when Springsteen was asynchronously singing about his own newfound happiness. As the century, and the Clinton administration, drew to a close, the nation (and particularly the aging members of Springsteen's core audience) was enjoying a period of relative prosperity. If you asked many of those who went to see Springsteen in 1999 what they felt they might have *lost,* they probably would have told you their youth, which is why they were more than ready to hear the old songs of fifteen or twenty years before.

Springsteen also sometimes commiserated with his audience for being *Lewinskyized,* referring to the infamous sexual liaison between President Bill Clinton and a White House intern, the slow uncovering of which dominated American journalism and even politics that year. This particular charge of Springsteen's often flew by a little quickly for many of them to catch, but it was a much surer guide to the singer's cultural (if not quite political) concerns on this tour. Springsteen was no more vocal a fan of Bill Clinton than of any other American president, but the spectacle of Clinton's impeachment that year almost certainly disturbed him deeply. Kenneth Starr's grand jury was hearing evidence on the case all throughout early 1999, as Springsteen reassembled the E Street Band and toured with them through Europe. The grand jury was still in session when the tour returned to the States in August and throughout the band's dates up and down the eastern seaboard. By the time Springsteen hit Auburn Hills, Starr had delivered his report, which was now much more about sexual misconduct than about the financial misconduct that he had originally been asked to investigate. That September, the case against Clinton was the one thing about which almost everyone in the United States was talking. For the third time in American history, the second time in Springsteen's lifetime, the House of Representatives began an impeachment inquiry regarding a sitting president.

Like so many public events regarding members of Springsteen's generation, eventually Bill Clinton's presidency was boiled down in cultural discourse to an argument about the legacy of the 1960s: about whether that decade had set loose freedom or license in America, a greater sense of national purpose or a greater wave of personal self-indulgence. At the time, the usual shorthand for this nationwide disagreement was "the culture wars," but it could just as easily have been termed "the history wars," because the argument was seldom about the present and all too often about the past. Liberals who reflexively defended Clinton, especially in the early stages, on occasion analogized between a current "vast right-wing conspiracy" and President Richard Nixon's enemies list, as if the Republicans of the late 1990s were identical with their counterparts of a quarter of a century earlier. As for those who wanted to see Clinton prosecuted to the full extent of the law, few of them framed their argument in terms of sexual harassment (a term that was coined in the mid-1970s and didn't even exist when Richard Nixon took office). Instead, they spoke of twenty-five-year-old Monica Lewinsky as being someone's "daughter" who had been preyed upon by a depraved individual, consciously invoking recent conservative concerns about the sanctity of the family but also unconsciously echoing all the preyed-upon daughters who had preoccupied American culture during the hippie years. For both sides, contemporary wrongdoing mattered most as an echo of the past, of skirmishes and battles from the Nixon era that had ended without being satisfactorily concluded for either side.

When crafting his own response to this increasingly nasty debate, Springsteen reached back not to the late 1960s and early 1970s but rather to the supposedly bucolic world of mid-twentieth-century America, a world that Senator Bob Dole had explicitly promised to bring back to the country during his failed attempt to unseat Clinton in the 1996 presidential race. Back in March, while Kenneth Starr called dozens of witnesses before a grand jury in order to definitively find a crime that Bill Clinton had committed, Springsteen rehearsed at least three new songs with the band, and by far the most frequently performed of these on the subsequent tour was "Land of Hope and Dreams," which ended the encores at nearly all his 1999–2000 concerts. "Land of Hope and Dreams" was yet another "train" song, but it reached back not to the "I Hear a Train" medley, nor to James Brown's revision of Jimmy Forrest's "Night Train," nor even to Elvis Presley's hallowed "Mystery Train" call. It was a deliberate rewrite of the old gospel song "This Train," most indelibly sung in the 1940s by Sister Rosetta Tharpe.

Springsteen's new song was in direct contradiction to the spirit of that old one, however, a purist rebuke that might have found fans in the fieriest precincts of the pro-impeachment camp. "This train," Tharpe sang very sharply in her version, "is a cleeean train," and as the song went on she carefully delineated those who would *not* be able to travel on this morally quarantined vehicle to its promised, heavenly destination. As Werner has noted, Springsteen's train is much closer to the one in Curtis Mayfield's "People Get Ready," but somehow even more inclusive, numbering among its passengers not only *saints and sinners* but *whores and gamblers*, not to mention *fools, kings*, and *lost souls*.

For all his reinvention of his older songs, Springsteen wanted at least one new signature song for this tour, the same way he usually wanted one last song that served as a thesis statement for his albums. Twenty years before in a song like "Badlands," Springsteen may have let out a generalized cry of socioeconomic frustration. "Land of Hope and Dreams," however, more directly confronted the nation's fin de siècle spiritual crisis, embracing neither condemnation nor license but rather forgiveness toward human frailty, the same stance the singer had taken on a personal level eight years earlier with "If I Should Fall Behind," the song preceding "Land" almost every night on the tour. Whether Springsteen's audience understood all this was very much an open question, but one thing became clear fairly early in the tour: "Land of Hope and Dreams" worked well as a sing-along with the audience. In this regard, the song was more of a folk-singing success than most of the *Tom Joad* songs had been.

The best part of the revival tour by far was the band, whose members were playing better than they had on the *Tunnel of Love* tour. The years apart had made them appreciate what they could accomplish together, and the time that so many of them had spent leading their own bands had paradoxically led them to be much better collaborators than they might have been before. There was a new song or two played every night, with "Lion's Den," "Mary, Queen of Arkansas," and

"Dead Man Walking" receiving interesting E Street arrangements. Moreover, many of the more familiar songs received country rather than rock arrangements (most notably "Dancing in the Dark"), showing the influence of Springsteen's increasing experiments in that genre throughout the 1990s. In the late spring of 2000, toward the end of the tour, there were more new songs too, including two songs—"Further on Up the Road" and "Waiting on a Sunny Day"—that the band had rehearsed in Asbury over a year before and to which they were only now returning.

And then, on 4 June 2000 at the Philips Arena in Atlanta, the band premiered another new song, one that Bruce had taken his time writing. It was called "American Skin," and it was another of Springsteen's "occasional" songs, those prompted by commissions or current events, the source of many of his best songs during the last decade. It used as its starting point the shooting on 4 February 1999 of Guinean immigrant Amadou Diallo by four members of the New York Police Department.

If Bill Clinton's sexual misconduct and perjury was the most reported story of 1999, then (in New York City at least) the Diallo shooting may very well have been the second most reported. The plainclothes detectives who shot Diallo were members of the NYPD's Street Crimes Unit, which had originally been formed with funds from the 1969 federal Omnibus Crimes and Safe Streets Act and was expanded mightily in the late 1990s as concerns about violent crime irrationally outpaced the falling crime rate. The SCU's mandate was to send plainclothes officers into high-crime neighborhoods as visible targets to flush out criminals, thus yielding an exponentially higher arrest rate than rank-and-file police officers. When stopped by SCU detectives on 4 February 1999 because he matched the general description of a serial rapist, Amadou Diallo reached into his pocket. The moment he did that, one of the officers shouted "Gun!" and the detectives instinctively fell back on their academy training. They carried semiautomatic handguns loaded with full metal jacket ammunition because some of the criminals they were supposed to catch were armed in that manner, and they set up a kill zone so "effective" that in a matter of seconds (less time than it had taken members of the

LAPD to subdue Rodney King), they fired forty-one shots, hitting their target nineteen times. Diallo's reach into his pocket was advanced as one justification for this behavior, as was the fact that, shortly after the gunfire began, one of the detectives was knocked down the stairs.

After the gunfire ended, however, several things became clear: the detective who fell down a flight of stairs during the shooting had probably been knocked over by a recoil, not a bullet; the only person hit by any bullets during the altercation was Diallo, who was now dead; and the object for which Diallo had reached into his pocket was his wallet. As an immigrant who had lived in at least seven countries before moving to the United States three years earlier, Diallo was as conditioned to provide his identity papers to the authorities when stopped as the officers were conditioned to protect their own in circumstances of perceived danger.

Less than two months after the shooting, in late March, the SCU detectives involved were indicted by a Bronx grand jury. Nine months later, an appellate court moved the proceedings upstate to Albany, New York, to ensure a fairer trial, it was said—the same logic that had led to the change of venue to Simi Valley for the trial concerning the beating of Rodney King in Los Angeles eight years before. In late February of 2000, a little over a year after the shooting, the Albany jury acquitted the New York detectives on all charges. That spring, tens of thousands of New Yorkers protested outside One Police Plaza in Manhattan, and nearly two thousand protesters were arrested. There was talk of Janet Reno's Justice Department filing civil rights charges against the four detectives. By Springsteen's account, the germ of "American Skin" had been in his workbook for most of 1999, but it seems that the early-2000 verdict, as well as the E Street Band's impending eleven-night, tour-ending stand at New York's Madison Square Garden, pushed him to complete it.

Before and after "American Skin," Springsteen was accused of being an isolated millionaire rock star who was out of touch with his less affluent fans. While that may be true in some regards (few of us, for example, can afford to spend hundreds of thousands of dollars on a horse for our teenage daughter), in the specific case of "American

Skin," the charge seems less apt. Springsteen's song begins and ends where any ordinary human being's reaction to the Diallo shooting would, simply repeating *41 shots* over and over again, stunned at the sheer number of bullets that had hailed down on the victim in a matter of seconds. Such quiet repetition does not come at us in the same spirit of assured resistance that an earlier protest song might have done, as it did when Joan Baez unquestioningly sang "then we'll raze the prisons to the ground" in her 1972, Attica-era song "Billy Rose." Springsteen's lyric, instead, is the cry of a numbed brain trying to absorb what should be an extraordinary fact. All the specific details of the Diallo shooting could be explained and accounted for, but for anyone who cherishes human life, the confused reaction must still be the same: *41 shots / 41 shots / 41 shots / 41 shots* . . . You could explain the incident, but that didn't excuse the culture. How did we get here? How did we get to the point where a man who sells socks on the street during the day and takes computer courses at night is by default considered an enemy in the jungle? And how did we get to the point where so many seemingly reasonable people mouth words about "tragic" losses but still count such a death as an acceptable loss in light of other social goals?

Springsteen's gift in "American Skin" was an extension of the way that he had treated such social problems in the past. He made the larger question in this case more immediate by putting himself inside the head of a participant. He had been doing this for over twenty years, since "Roulette" at least, through "Born in the U.S.A." and "Seeds," straight through to the four less successful border songs on his last studio album. The genius of this song, however, was that it was simultaneously individual and collective, in a way that none of those earlier songs were. It was "Souls of the Departed" conceived nationally rather than autobiographically. One verse views the situation from the perspective of one of the shooters, who instantly knows, despite his training, that he has made a tragic mistake. A second verse adopts the perspective of an African American mother instructing her young son how to act in front of the police.

All his life, Springsteen had believed in and preached a biracial America. This song, however, made that biracial reality palpable, as a white police officer and a black mother are gathered up into the same collective, frightened *we*. More radically and successfully than "Land of Hope and Dreams," "American Skin" made it clear how uncomfortable Springsteen was with the increasingly divided America that prevailed during the 1990s. If the quickly assembled "57 Channels" mixes had been his initial response to this phenomenon, "American Skin" was his considered opinion. Not even offering Rodney King's simple dream of all just getting along, eight years after the King beating Springsteen simply uttered a basic fact: we are all in this together, *baptized in these waters and in each other's blood.*

Tied to the bootlegging movement as Springsteen's music has been, it's worth pointing out that "American Skin" was essentially the first of his songs to be leaked to the internet. Enterprising fans recorded it at the Atlanta concert and before they went to sleep that night had it up on file-sharing services like Kazaa and Limewire. Back in the 1970s, if you wanted to hear one of Bruce's new songs, you had to see him live, catch an FM-simulcast concert, or wait for an illegal album to be pressed, but now the song was immediately available. It was like an eighteenth-century crime ballad gone viral in a wired world.

Police officials and reporters for the old print media reacted to the news of the song's existence in many cases before having actually heard it, as if repeating the phrase *41 shots* so many times made the song by definition an antipolice rant. If Springsteen repeated the number of shots fired, he was clearly no better than Ice Cube performing "Cop Killa" with his speed metal band Body Count. To John Tierney of the *New York Times*, Springsteen was a "limousine liberal," too rich and politically naïve to know what life was like for average Americans. Conversely, to Paul Mulshine of the *Newark Star Ledger*, Springsteen's song grew out of the singer's own secret racist fears "of potentially violent felons, loaded guns, and dark vestibules." (Most sane people are afraid of those three things, of course, but only two of them were actually present in the Diallou shooting, and the only loaded guns in that incident were in the possession of the police.) To Bob Lucente, president of the New York chapter of the Fraternal Order of Police, who had not only not listened to "American Skin" but apparently never paid close attention to "Born in the U.S.A." either, Springsteen was a

fallen patriot, once properly respectful but now "some kind of dirtbag
. . . a floating fag."

Not only were most of these reactions based on reports of the existence of "American Skin" rather than on a direct knowledge of the
song, but they were also mutually incoherent. How could the same
song be both not frightened enough and too frightened? Once again,
ideology triumphed over politics, the stories we tell ourselves about
our world taking precedence over our reasoned, documented knowledge of what actually occurs in it. What mattered about Springsteen's
song in 1999 was not any specific statement it might have made about
interracial violence, but rather the fact that it painted Amadou Diallo's
death as tragic. Even more radically, it saw both Diallo and the SCU
members as victims of the same tragic circumstances, a position that
was virtually unique within contemporary culture. Most New Yorkers
who had publicly discussed the Diallo shooting could truly be divided
into merely pro- and antipolice camps. For such commentators, there
could be no *we* in matters like these. There could be only *us* and *them*,
as there were in the public deliberation over Bill Clinton's misdeeds.
For Tierney, Mulshine, Lucente, and thousands of Springsteen fans
who had bought their tickets for the Garden shows back in the early
spring, before the song had even been finished, Springsteen now
seemed to be clearly one of *them*.

By the time the tour hit New York, The Song was the focus of
nearly all public attention on the concerts. The fact that this was
the climax of a reunion tour for which fans had been clamoring for
over a decade, and that two nights of the Garden shows would be
filmed for a possible HBO special, made no difference. "I received
letters," Springsteen later recalled, "from officials asking me not to
play the song," probably the first time in his career that he had ever
received negative requests. Had there ever been this much anticipation and public anxiety over an arena concert by a group of fifty-
year-olds? There was a reasonable expectation (later confirmed by
experience) that some of the audience might very well boo them.
For Springsteen, that probably made the gamble worth it. No one
could say he was playing it safe, pandering to his audience, being a
cartoon of himself rather than an artist. "This is what we were built

for," he told the band one night just before the lights went down, "let's go."

"American Skin" is simple in a way that most of the *Tom Joad* songs are not, and one can easily imagine how it grew out of scraps and pieces into a fully composed work. But it is also a classic example of a Springsteen song that wasn't finished when written. For one thing, it needed to be performed. It needed the E Street Band to give it the same scale that they had given to an earlier song like "Thunder Road," turning private crises into more mythic stories through the instrumental enlargement that turns musical sketches into cycloramic pseudosymphonies.

More important, though, "American Skin" needed an audience, a big audience. If you want to say that there's something deeply wrong about our society, that we are all in this together, you don't say it to a small club full of like-minded individuals. You don't just preach to the leftist choir. As stunning a protest song as Crosby, Stills, Nash, and Young's "Ohio" was, for example, Neil Young had never tried to sing it to an audience dotted with National Guardsmen. When Springsteen took the stage at Madison Square Garden at the end of the revival tour, though, he knew he was speaking unpleasant truths to a significant number of those in his audience. This was indeed what the E Street Band had been made for. Even more essentially, it was what this tour had been made for: to pull together a fragmented culture as only pop at its best can, to remind that culture of its abiding flaws as well as its still beckoning possibilities.

With all the prior anticipation, for The Song to have its desired effect, it also had to come at the audience in the right way: it needed to be properly framed in the setlist. Faced with audience members who liked his "old stuff" but who may have thought that he had gotten too big for his britches, Springsteen needed to connect his prior material with this new piece, just as he had sought to connect up the seemingly distinct fears in the separate verses of "American Skin." Most nights at the Garden, the new song appeared about a quarter of the way into the concert, where the *Nebraska* songs had been placed during the *Born in the U.S.A.* tour: warm the audience up first, then plunge them into the underbelly of that joy. Most nights "American Skin" was followed by a three-song set of "The Promised Land,"

"Youngstown," and "Murder Incorporated," once again tying current problems to the industrial decline and increased paranoia of the late 1970s and early 1980s, as Springsteen had done on the *Tom Joad* tour.

The real question, though, was what song should precede "American Skin." What song would make the audience most receptive to it? For two nights at the Garden, it was crudely preceded by "Point Blank," which made a metonymic rather than ideological connection between an old song and a new one. Many other nights, it was preceded by one of the songs about sons who can't quite break out of their father's problems ("The River," "Independence Day," "Factory," and "Mansion on the Hill"), as if to suggest that our current problem as a nation was an unthinking result of how we had been raised.

Most effectively, though, the song was preceded three nights at the Garden by "My Hometown," a track that more than any other on *Born in the U.S.A.* had seemed to be an endorsement of Ronald Reagan's America. Those like Bob Lucente who had heard that album's opening, title song back in 1984 as a boisterous cry of patriotic pride were clearly only listening to the choruses, but "My Hometown," which closed that album, did resonate strongly with Reagan's emphasis on family values, local community, and individual rather than collective responsibility. The song also contains one of Springsteen's most politically cowardly verses, albeit one phrased almost exactly as a small-town New Jerseyan of the time would have put it. Referring to the social unrest that plagued Freehold, like so many other American cities, during the mid-1960s, he sang, *There was a lot of fights between the black and white / There was nothing you could do.* This was the same kind of Reaganesque shrug that led members of Springsteen's audience a quarter of a century later to regard the shooting of Amadou Diallo as the "tragic" price of "keeping our streets safe."

In the summer of 1984, "My Hometown" had fed a cultural nostalgia that encouraged many Americans to turn away from any social problems that could not be conceived of as issues of punishment rather than renewal. In the summer of 2000, as Springsteen fans heard this song again at Madison Square Garden, their nostalgia was now squared: they longed not only for the simple small-town existence held out in the song, but also for the era in which they had first heard it.

Master showman that he was, Springsteen used this complex emotion. He elongated the song's ending, holding out his microphone to the audience and encouraging them to sing

> Your hometown
> Your home-town
> Your hometown
> Your home-town

over and over again for several minutes, as if the rafters of Madison Square Garden were the night sky above a youth group campground in Cheesequake State Park.

Then he gave the signal, Garry's bassline changed, and before the audience could readjust themselves emotionally, the members of the band were singing one by one,

> 41 shots
> 41 shots
> 41 shots
> 41 shots

The effect on the audience was visceral. Many of them actually recoiled. A stocky gray-haired man in the upper tier one night, a man who could very easily have been an off-duty cop, folded his arms across his chest and told a friend, "I don't need some millionaire telling me how to do my job."

To make this transition—to invite his audience to participate, and then to remind them that a collective responsibility, even a collective sin, goes hand in hand with citizenship—was the most effective political act that Bruce Springsteen had ever committed during a concert. It was as brave as the second verse of "My Hometown" was cowardly, and far braver than the acoustic rewrite of "Born to Run" that he had performed on his last E Street Band tour twelve years earlier. That expectation-thwarting performance had been about removing himself from his audience, about taking back one of his songs that he hadn't wanted to become collective property. In this case, he was doing the opposite. Yes, he was implicitly saying to his fans, we share this music and we share this country, but you can't just pick out the parts you like. My work is all of a piece, and so is our nation. We are not one, we are not two, we are many.

This was a new variation on his old late-1970s gospel of *You want to play, you got to pay,* the idea of an engaged rather than a passive audience to which he had turned in the immediate wake of his newfound celebrity. Now, though, he was raising that belief to a level that exceeded mere performance and connected it to politics and social justice as well. This was the piece of Pastor Springsteen's service that had been missing when the revival tour began, a true sight of communal sin that needed to be acknowledged before rock 'n' roll redemption could occur. Just before the tour's closing, it all fell into place, as the night moved from "Two Hearts" to "Your Hometown" and "American Skin" through "Out in the Street" and "Tenth Avenue Freeze-Out" to "Light of Day" and finally to the two prayers for conscious reconciliation that were the current tour's performances of "If I Should Fall Behind," and "Land of Hope and Dreams."

The obvious question is, "Did it work?" The 1999–2000 tour did see the rebirth of the E Street Band, quite possibly better and more exciting than ever, but what about Springsteen's audience on this tour? Was it revived or merely reunited? Did the audience actually see how the vision embodied in these old and new songs spoke of a different, more tolerant, less partisan America than the current climate encouraged?

Most nights, if you watched the aisles in those big arenas, the answer seemed to be no. Some in the audience may have been moved to greater political awareness, but too many still attended Springsteen's concerts obliviously, hearing the memories they bought their tickets to hear but not listening to what was new in these performances. For all of Springsteen's experimentation with the setlist, a lot of nights you could see many audience members reflexively leap to their feet for old songs like "Badlands" or "Ramrod," then go for a walk to the concession stand when the band gave "Youngstown" or "The Ghost of Tom Joad" the full-on E Street treatment. For too many in Springsteen's audience, the individualistic defiance of the Carter era was a pair of faded jeans into which, they seemed to think, they could always slip.

But the social empathy that Springsteen had cultivated in the years since Reagan had left office? Well, that just seemed like too tight a fit.

AFTER THE REUNION TOUR, many people assumed that Springsteen would finally record more songs with the E Street Band. It had been five years since the brief *Greatest Hits* sessions, after all, and sixteen years since the final *Born in the U.S.A.* recordings. From a business standpoint, it would have made sense for Bruce to strike while the iron was hot and put out a new album as quickly as possible in order to capitalize on the attendant publicity. Moreover, having not released a new studio album in five years, Springsteen certainly had enough material that he was sitting on, even after the vault clearing of *Tracks*.

But the year after those last shows at the Garden found Springsteen mostly in Thrill Hill mode, recording solo tracks, perhaps with the intention of adding on other voices and instruments later. For most of that year Springsteen kept to himself, as he usually did after he'd been on the road for a while. He stayed in Rumson—the Gotham Playboys performed at his birthday party once again that year—and focused more on his family and his community. Indeed, after a year and a half of touring the United States and Europe, his focus now seemed firmly trained on purely local matters. He played only charity gigs that fall, one with Joe Grushecky at the Pony and another with Patti, Max, Jon Bon Jovi, and Bobby Bandiera and his band at the Hedgerow Farm in Middletown, a bedroom community seven or eight miles northeast of Rumson, on the still-essential Route 35.

Just before Christmas, he headlined two concerts at the Convention Hall in Asbury Park that were designed to benefit a host of charities, all based in central and south Jersey. That the current state of the local scene, and of Asbury in particular, was on Springsteen's mind became even more obvious when he introduced a new song at these concerts, "My City of Ruins," which was a naked depiction of the current state of Asbury Park. To Springsteen's credit, he didn't write in this song about the decline of the Circuit or the boardwalk, which would have fit more neatly with his own earlier work. Nor does "My

City of Ruins" focus on the vanished Asbury of young white musicians, as a decade-old Van Zandt song like "It's Been a Long, Long Time" did. Instead, Springsteen focused his song on the city's interior, where longtime residents lived and for the most part worked.

Yet the song is still, in a way, about a lost utopia. Writing about a primarily African American community that suffered in the wake of white flight, Springsteen self-consciously chose to write the song in "the soul gospel of my favorite '60s records." Consequently, this song can be seen as yet another of Springsteen's longings for the lost biracial culture of his youth, for the more communal aspects of the Upstage and the late-'60s boardwalk rather than their musicianship. "My City of Ruins" thus continues the impulse first articulated in "American Skin," focusing now on neglect rather than violence, and calling for action rather than mere understanding. *Come on, rise up*, its lyric declares over and over again. The local charities that benefited from the Christmas concerts at which the song was first performed were an initial indication of what Springsteen thought his audience might want to *rise up* to do, but the lyric's imperative instruction still remained rather vague. As in "American Skin," in "My City of Ruins" Springsteen articulated his sense of loss far more keenly than he did any ideas he might have had about how that loss might be reversed.

Once in the fall of 2000 and once more again in the first weekend of the following March, Springsteen called the E Street Band together at the Hit Factory, where they cut somewhere between half a dozen and a dozen songs, but still no combination of them added up to an album. Springsteen was now stalled with the band as he had been stalled solo four years before. While everyone waited for something new from him, the promised HBO special aired, and a live album and a DVD of the concert were released in April. In the late summer, Bruce met with Brendan O'Brien, a young producer of such recent so-called alternative bands as Pearl Jam and Rage against the Machine, and they sifted through the Thrill Hill recordings that Bruce thought sounded promising. There was no rush, though. They promised to meet again later in the year but purposefully kept the actual date of their future meeting indefinite, maybe in a month or so, maybe down in Atlanta, where O'Brien was based.

As he tried to figure out what he wanted to do next, Bruce returned, as one might have expected, to occasional gigging. In mid-August, he performed three times at the Clearwater Music Festival in Asbury, first an acoustic set of his own, then sitting in with Nils, and later with John Eddie at the Pony. He was back onstage at the Pony two weeks later to help Clarence record a live album with his current band, the Temple of Soul. They were supposed to play two nights, so that the best performances of individual songs from the two dates could be spliced together (as they had been for Bruce's *Live in New York City* set), but there was a bomb scare on the second, so the Sunday night show was canceled.

Nine days after that, ten terrorists flew a pair of 767s into two of the tallest buildings in the world, and it suddenly seemed as if nothing in the U.S.A. would ever be the same. For most Americans, 11 September 2001 was a heavily mediated event, the same video clip played over and over to the point where it became the Zapruder film of the new millennium. Down at the Jersey Shore, though, you could see the damage even without a television. Two dozen miles south across the bays of New York and New Jersey from the spot that would soon be dubbed Ground Zero, the attack had immediately and unmistakably altered the horizon. That morning, Springsteen later remembered, "I went to the beach, and from there I used to have a clear view of the World Trade Center. They were gone. There was a long line of smoke drifting south."

Per capita, the greatest number of victims from the 9/11 attacks came from the northeastern tip of Monmouth County. This was Bruce Springsteen's backyard, the place where he had lived, loved, and played music for most of his life. The area's victims that day were his neighbors, in the moral and in some cases literal sense. As Bruce knew perhaps better than anyone else, Monmouth County contained a wide variety of homes, from working-class households just getting by (much like the one in which he had grown up) to gated estates owned by millionaires (whose children attended classes with his children now at the Rumson Country Day School). Wall Street's financial wizards came to Monmouth County to live because they could get a big spread of land to come home to at night, when they got a chance. The five boroughs' Finest and Bravest came to Monmouth County to live because the commute into the city via the Parkway and the Outerbridge Crossing could be surprisingly quick, especially if you were heading in for an early roll call. Dozens of Monmouth County residents—financial advisers and firefighters, office assistants and police officers—headed in early that morning to be at their desks or do their duty.

According to Springsteen, as he was pulling out of the parking lot at the beach that day, "some kid rolled his window down and said, 'Hey, man, we need ya.'" In the short term, Bruce tried to fill that need by committing to benefits and telethons, both local and national, but the stranger's remark was probably meant to point toward something different: toward the composition of new music that somehow made sense of what had happened. When, at a street fair that Rumson high school students were throwing to raise money for the families of local victims, he was later asked more directly whether he intended to write new songs about the tragedy, Springsteen demurred. "We've lost so many people," he said. "Whatever music we can do, we'll do."

It did seem like the perfect time for at least one of his occasional songs. His friend Neil Young quickly wrote and recorded one of his own called "Let's Roll," about the passenger revolt on United flight 93 that probably saved the White House. Springsteen, for his part, began work on a song about a different kind of heroism, not the bravery of someone who mounts an attack on armed terrorists, but rather of someone who runs into danger to save lives. "Of the many tragic images of that day," he later remembered, "the picture I couldn't let go of was of the emergency workers going up the stairs as others rushed down to safety." With this song (eventually called "Into the Fire"), Springsteen may have been trying to write something deliberately anthemic, something with which an audience could easily sing along.

But the fragments in his notebook didn't quickly add up to anything that worked. For his appearance as the opening act on *America: A Tribute to Heroes*, a two-hour fund-raising telethon set to air on all four major broadcast networks ten days after the attacks, Springsteen instead decided to perform the last great song that he had completed, the year-old "My City of Ruins," with only an acoustic guitar and harmonica as instrumental accompaniment but with vocals backed by the tight harmonies of Steve, Patti, Clarence, and others, including Delores Holmes from the thirty-year-gone Bruce Springsteen Band. The song went by so quickly and its performance was so arresting that probably few in the audience guessed that it hadn't been written for the occasion.

In truth, the attacks of 11 September were such a shock to most Americans that they seemed, for a time, to add new meanings to many preexisting artifacts, particularly seemingly disposable aspects of popular culture. Shortly after the attacks, program directors at a number of radio stations owned by Clear Channel Entertainment started exchanging emails about songs they might not want to play on their stations given recent events. One of the participants in this exchange even created a list of 150 songs that might offend some listeners, particularly songs that referenced flames, fire, crashes, blood, bombs, falling, planes, traveling, Tuesday, the devil, America, or New York in their titles. As far as Springsteen songs went, it was suggested that programmers might want to skip "I'm on Fire" and "I'm Goin' Down" for the near future. In this quickly prepared list, there was also a general frowning on metal bands (particularly such crossover successes as AC/DC, Alice in Chains, Black Sabbath, Megadeth, Metallica, and Rage against the Machine), as well as a suggestion that notorious Muslim convert Cat Stevens's songs "Peace Train" and "Morning Has Broken" be avoided.

But the list wasn't all hardship-denying positivism either. Indeed, the otherwise anonymous Clear Channel employee who prepared it also apparently thought it might be too soon for such inspirational songs as "What a Wonderful World," "Imagine," and "Bridge over Troubled Water." Probably the most sensible comment about all of this was made by Mark O'Brien, the general manager at WWZZ, an FM station that broadcast in the Adult Rock format to the DC area. O'Brien wasn't pulling any songs from his playlist for their titles alone. It was more for their "happy-go-lucky, life is great" attitude. "Anything up-tempo is still off the air today," he told a *Washington Post* reporter a week after the attacks. This was probably the same reasoning that had led that Clear Channel programmer to conclude that "Dancing in the Streets," whether recorded by Martha and the Vandellas or Van Halen, should be given a rest for a while.

Musicians, however, don't think like program directors, and it's probably true that most music fans don't either. Both on *America: A Tribute to Heroes* and *The Concert for New York City,* a free event for rescue workers at Madison Square Garden a month later, it was striking how many of the songs performed were the ones that the more overly cautious members of the broadcasting community might have wanted to keep off the air. During the telethon, Neil Young made John Lennon's proscribed "Imagine" into his own cracked original, and Paul Simon gave one of his most moving renditions of "Bridge over Troubled Water" in decades. At the Madison Square Garden concert, James Taylor took "Fire and Rain," one of the quietest songs that had been deemed questionable by some, and turned it into an arena-sized meditation on personal loss.

As critic Geoffrey O'Brien among others can attest, "Fire and Rain" is not a song about a plane crash, even though its lyrics do speak of "flying machines in pieces on the ground." In the days after 9/11, though, those who cared about music weren't looking to familiar songs for their already established, literal meanings. They were instead turning to them as vessels into which they could pour their own as yet inarticulable meanings. Greil Marcus later reported that he listened to the New Pornographers' "Letter from an Occupant" over and over during that period; I found myself listening to the original cast album of Jason Robert Brown's *Parade.* None of these works are "about" 9/11. Yet they served as touchstones for those trying to sort out their feelings about those events.

In the fall of 2001, a number of Bruce Springsteen's unreleased songs, particularly the recent ones out of which he had been unable to make an album just a few months earlier, were transformed by this same sort of symbolic osmosis. The cry for reunion and revival in the name of a common purpose to which Springsteen had given voice in "My City of Ruins" and throughout the last two years while touring with the revitalized E Street Band was now a cry that had as much relevance for the nation as for Springsteen himself. As the numb initial reaction to the attacks faded that fall, the willed cheeriness of

"Waitin' on a Sunny Day," "Let's Be Friends," and "Countin' on a Miracle" also seemed as if they might be relevant. Even a seven-year-old song like "Nothing Man," which had been born of the same feeling of isolation that had yielded "Streets of Philadelphia" and "Missing," could with a little retooling be turned into a song about a first responder with post-traumatic stress disorder.

Shortly after the telethon, Springsteen started writing new songs. He finished both "Into the Fire" and the haunting "You're Missing" before he headed down to Atlanta for his deferred follow-up meeting with Brendan O'Brien. If "Into the Fire" was a self-conscious attempt at an anthem, "You're Missing" was just as clearly written in the internal mode that characterized the *Ghost of Tom Joad* songs. Almost lazily rhymed, "You're Missing" might seem at first glance to be a direct transcription of unconnected fragments from the songwriter's notebook, but that very numb fragmentation captures the mood in so many Monmouth County homes that late September, as well as in New York City, where the homemade posters that New Yorkers had put up in search of missing loved ones were growing unignorably tattered. Although not as obvious an occasional song as "American Skin," "You're Missing" contains specific details that unmistakably convey that time and place, right down to the *too many phone calls* and *dust on my shoes*. The latter reference may seem obscure, but many who were downtown that day and lived couldn't bring themselves to clean the clothing they'd worn, because they knew what the "dirt" or "dust" on it might be.

As early October's funerals and memorial services gave way to late October's preparations for a U.S. military assault on al-Qaeda bases in Afghanistan, the world of "You're Missing," turned into the world of "The Fuse" and perhaps the world of "Lonesome Day" as well. In this climate of supercharged meaning, an old but still unreleased song like "Further on Up the Road"—at its heart a cowboy song with a narrator who speaks lines that could easily have been put into the halting mouth of John Wayne—now seemed much less antiquated than it might have appeared at the Garden shows a year and a half before.

With the new songs and at least half a dozen of these holdovers that now seemed to carry fresh meanings, Springsteen already had more than half an album. To write the rest of it, he sought out possible character sketches, as he had been doing in his writing for most of the last decade. The most obvious of these is "Paradise," which tried to link three longing consciousnesses on two continents the way that "Souls of the Departed" had done almost exactly ten years before. Indeed, most of the songs Springsteen wrote in the fall of 2001 sounded like the sort of solo writing that he had been doing since 1987, even if the internal sympathies of a song like "Paradise" did find their more social echo in a new band song like "Worlds Apart."

The two best songs he wrote for the project, however, were band songs, even if the first of them may predate 11 September. With a lyric that drew on an old Sam Cooke number and chords that once again openly echoed Major Lance's "The Monkey Time," "Mary's Place" was a house-rockin' party song that could easily have been performed on the revival tour. It is Springsteen's most naked profession of faith in *the power, the majesty, and the mystery of rock 'n' roll,* and all the good that he believes the monopop music of his adolescence could do to heal the wounds of an overburdened soul. Indeed, after *I got this guitar and I learned how to make it talk,* there may be no other line that so perfectly sums up Springsteen's attitude toward pop music as this song's seemingly blasphemous but ultimately devout *I drop the needle and pray.* This, too, is a song about loss and absence, the only real subject for a writer who sought to capture the reality of New York and New Jersey in the fall of 2001, but this narrator is trying to dance that absence away, even if only for a few hours. As NYPD detective John McAuliffe said of *The Concert for New York City* around this time, "Psychologically everyone needed to let loose for a night. After working such long hours for such a long time, the concert was the perfect break. I don't think I sat down all night." The narrator of "Mary's Place" is similarly exhausted by nonstop searching and not knowing, by the unignorable presence of *the black hole on the horizon* that he mentions twice in the song's first verse. He flatly wonders *how do you live broken-hearted.* Like so many of those who were still putting up fliers or checking websites in late October, he knows that it is extremely unlikely that the person he misses is ever coming back. But Bruce Springsteen's faith, much like Saint Paul's, is apparently based on the evidence of things not seen.

As for the best song on the album, the one that would clearly give it its name, that song unified all the communal good that Springsteen sought to do with his work in the last three years, both on the revival tour and in his attempts to write about the recent crisis. From its first verse, "The Rising" is obviously another song about a firefighter. It was "written late in the record," Springsteen relates in the second edition of *Songs*, "as a bookend to 'Into the Fire.'" From the chorus at least, it could also obviously be seen as a song about a preacher, particularly with its emphasis on the laying on of *hands*. The religion in this lyric is Springsteen's usual odd mixture, with equal parts conditioned Catholic imagery and acquired Pentecostal revival.

Less obviously and more crucially, however, "The Rising" is also a song about a performer, someone very much like Springsteen himself. With this song, for the first time since "Dancing in the Dark" almost twenty years before, Springsteen concluded the recording of an album by writing a song about his relationship with his audience. Far more than "Land of Hope and Dreams," "The Rising" is a song about reciprocal redemption. If the narrator of "Dancing in the Dark" has been banging his head against the wall of pop music for so long that he's simply desperate to please, the narrator of "The Rising" has been doing this for so long that he's *Lost track of how far I've gone / How far I've gone, how high I've climbed*. For the fifty-two-year-old rock star, as for the depicted firefighter, the tools of his trade are a source of weakness as well as strength. *On my back's a sixty-pound stone*, he sings, literally denoting the firefighter's gear but figuratively indicating the considerable weight of experience. An ideal stem-winder for concert audiences in a way that the well-intentioned "Into the Fire" never could be, "The Rising" is in many ways Springsteen's finest work song. It's about getting up in the morning and doing your job, whatever it is, and how you draw the strength to do it well from the community that you hope to help with your labor.

With the completion of one last song after "The Rising"—"Empty Sky," in which Bruce circles back to many of his own feelings on the day he sometimes just called "the eleventh"—the album was finished, fifteen tracks laid down quickly and efficiently. The album would launch in late July, as would another world tour, just about two years after the last E Street Band tour ended. The publicity machine swung into action, widely but subtly hyping the forthcoming album as Springsteen's response to 9/11, even though at least half its songs predated the event. Then again, almost a year after the attacks, it was amazing how many people had found ways to incorporate their pre-2001 concerns into the contemporary climate.

THE REVIVAL TOUR had been news in and of itself, and the Hall of Fame induction a perfect launching pad for it. For *The Rising*, however, Springsteen and CBS adopted a wider approach to publicity. On 30 July, the day after the album's release, you could begin and end your television day with Bruce Springsteen and *The Rising*: bright and early in the morning, Bruce did a live broadcast with the E Street Band from the Convention Hall in Asbury Park for NBC's *Today*, and late that night ABC aired the first part of an extended interview that Springsteen gave to Ted Koppel for his short-lived program *Up Close*. Two days later, CBS got its share of Springsteen promotion as well, as Bruce and the band taped two songs at the Ed Sullivan Theater in Manhattan for *The Late Show with David Letterman*. After a month's touring through the same U.S. arenas that they had visited two years before, they ended up back in New York, playing what was probably their most spectacular TV appearance ever: introduced by James Gandolfini (Steve's castmate from *The Sopranos*) as the cold open for the MTV Video Music Awards, playing "The Rising" in front of the recently opened Rose Center and Planetarium at the American Museum of Natural History, as a driving rain poured down on the band and all its equipment. If the telethon appearance a little over a year earlier had brought the definitive performance of "My City of Ruins," this was the definitive performance of "The Rising," with the timing, the occasion, the location, and even the skies themselves whipping the band into an intensity that unlocked the anxious fury that lay at the heart of the song.

The instant success with which both the album and the tour were met seemed to go against the conventional wisdom that Andrew Card voiced in the *New York Times* the following week: "From a marketing point of view, you don't introduce new products in August." Card headed a trade association that represented the most successful Detroit car manufacturers, but in this case he wasn't speaking about the launch of a new SUV or even a rock album. He was talking about the campaign by George W. Bush and his administration to "sell" America and the world on a war with Saddam Hussein's Iraq. Card had been chief of staff for the current President Bush's father in the 1990s, and both he and those who had worked for President Reagan admired the skill with which the current administration put its ideas and goals into public circulation. One of the reasons why the VMA performance of "The Rising" connected with the contemporary audience was its backdrop: here was a song about renewal and rebuilding sung in front of the most striking structure to go up in Manhattan since the Twin Towers had gone down. Less than two weeks later, on the first anniversary of those attacks, President Bush spoke to the nation in prime time, for much the same reasons, from Ellis Island against an even more resonant backdrop: the Statue of Liberty.

As the nation eventually learned, the Bush administration's plans to wage war on Iraq were no more about 9/11 than *The Rising* was. Both projects were rooted in more personal lost causes of the 1990s. While in the past Springsteen's tours had frequently coincided with presidential election campaigns, the tour for *The Rising* would instead parallel the buildup and aftermath of the Second Gulf War. In the fall of 2001, while Springsteen was writing the new half of the album, American troops were seizing Kabul in Afghanistan. In the winter of 2002, as Springsteen and his band were recording their seventeen tracks in Atlanta, Karl Rove, Dick Cheney, and others in the Bush administration were determining that the best way of prolonging the current sense of national unity was to "Focus on war." In the summer of 2002, six days before *The Rising* was released, British prime minister Tony Blair was being informed by Sir Richard Dearlove, the head of MI6, that the Bush administration was bent on war with Hussein, whether he was connected with the 11 September attacks or not, and that in Washington "the intelligence and facts [regarding Hussein] were being fixed around the policy." In October, less than a week after Springsteen made his second appearance ever on *Saturday Night Live* (his first with the E Street Band), the Bush administration's month-long, perfectly run campaign to stir up popular support behind a second U.S. war with Iraq reached its desired conclusion: the House of Representatives and then the Senate voted to give the president an unprecedented blank check in dealing with Iraq.

It may seem flip or trivial to equate a nation's march toward war to the promotion of a rock album, but, as Andrew Card's remark suggests, that is how those who work in government sometimes see such things and have seen them for decades. The three barges' worth of giant Musco lights that Bush's team hauled out to Liberty Island on 11 September 2002, in order to illuminate the full height of Lady Liberty from the base of that statue, were merely more carefully refined variations on the tools wielded by John F. Kennedy's team during the election of 1960. You could admire Kennedy's campaign geniuses for their marketing virtuosity (as Theodore White famously did in *The Making of the President, 1960*) or decry the reduction of democratic discourse to the cynically manipulated "Image" (as Daniel Boorstin just as influentially did in *The Image: A Guide to Pseudo Events in America*), but in the end most Americans objected to such practices only when they were used in the service of a candidate or cause with which they disagreed. At their best, as in Ronald Reagan's 1987 Gorbachev-baiting speech at the Berlin Wall, such moments are indeed sincere, but that doesn't make them any less about marketing.

For most members of George W. Bush's inner circle, 9/11 did not change their opinions about American foreign policy a bit. Those events just gave them a chance to advance ideas that they already held about what would be best for the United States of America. The same may be said of Bruce Springsteen, whose 2002–03 tour for *The Rising* was for the most part a reinvention of the 1999–2000 revival tour. Opening the new concerts with the title track from the new album merely made the last tour's revival theme more obviously manifest. "Empty Sky" and "You're Missing," the two songs on the new album most haunted by loss, now went into the quarter-in slot, where *Nebraska* songs, *Tom Joad* songs, and "American Skin" had gone in the past. "Mary's Place" became the fired-up song to bring everyone together, taking on the role that "Tenth Avenue Freeze-Out" had played on the last tour. "Land of Hope and Dreams" still closed most shows, but now it was usually preceded by "Born in the U.S.A." rather than the multiply sung "If I Should Fall Behind." When other performers guested on this tour (Eddie Vedder in Chicago, Emmylou Harris in Birmingham), they often duetted with Bruce on an acoustic version of "My Hometown" during the body of the set. At least early on, there were more *Born in the U.S.A.* songs and fewer *River* songs on this tour than on the last one—these concerts were more about reviving the nation than reviving the band.

The most visible shift in Springsteen's setlists came the following March. A year and a half before, Springsteen had put a message up on his website that cautiously but unequivocally supported the U.S. retaliatory attacks on Afghanistan. His support for U.S. military action against Iraq was less clear. In fact, on 9 March 2003, at his first concert after the United States, Britain, Spain, and Bulgaria announced a ten-day deadline for Saddam Hussein to divest himself of weapons that were never actually in his possession, Springsteen made his feelings about the matter indirectly clear in his favorite way to do so: he performed a cover, opening the concert with Edwin Starr's "War" instead of "The Rising." As in 1985, performing Starr's song was the bluntest way Springsteen knew to communicate to his audience that, although he loved his country, he never loved it blindly, and especially not its leaders. The second U.S.–Iraq war formally began twelve days after the concert, while Springsteen was en route to Australia. The next night, he cautioned an audience in Melbourne after a performance of "Empty Sky" not to read the song as a statement of his own personal beliefs but rather as a *cry out from the character's anger and grief and sadness.* When he sang *I want an eye for eye,* he insisted, *it was never a call for blind revenge or bloodlust.* At this statement, the Melbourne audience cheered, and it's impossible to tell from a recording of the concert, whether that cheer arose in sympathy with or opposition to *bloodlust.*

In Australia and New Zealand, and back in the States in California, Bruce took to opening the concerts alone with an acoustic version of "Born in the U.S.A.," still his most succinct original statement about misguided American military action. For the next month or so, as U.S. ground operations continued in Iraq, this song was one of a number of openings with which Springsteen experimented. Sometimes the willed hope of "The Promised Land" substituted for the Vietnam vet's anguish, but at other times it was "No Surrender," his song about not giving up on youthful rock 'n' roll dreams. However personally important this song may have been for the singer, it was a bizarre choice that was easily open to misinterpretation in the current climate. On 1 May, during a break in Springsteen's tour before the European leg started, President Bush achieved the mother of all photo ops when he landed an S-3B Viking on the deck of the USS *Abraham Lincoln* (in San Diego harbor) and subsequently gave a speech on the carrier's deck under a banner that read "Mission Accomplished," declaring that "major combat operations in Iraq have ended."

But the fighting in Iraq was not over, of course, and neither was Springsteen's tour. As the *Rising* tour moved through Europe and then back home to the States, Bruce confined his direct political statements to the encores now: a request for donations to local charities before "My City of Ruins" and paradoxically *demanding accountability* from the current administration before singing of forgiveness for *whores, gamblers, fools,* and *kings* in "Land of Hope and Dreams." In George W. Bush's America, Springsteen was clear about his politics, in a way he had never been during Ronald Reagan's presidency. Many in his audience, however, still weren't listening. They took what they wanted from his music and barely even noticed a song like "Paradise" that made the deaths of Iraqis equivalent with those of Americans. Some of the fault for this, though, was Springsteen's. While he sang of *an eye for an eye* in "Empty Sky" nearly every night of this tour, no matter how self-protestingly, he performed the admittedly weaker "Paradise" only once.

The *Rising* tour continued through the fall of 2003, culminating in a series of baseball park gigs, at Dodger Stadium in LA, Fenway Park in Boston, and finally Shea Stadium in Queens. For the last concert at Shea, Springsteen was joined onstage by Gary U.S. Bonds, Joe Grushecky, and Bob Dylan. In fact, he dedicated to Dylan his last performance that year of "Land of Hope and Dreams," a song in which he had tried for four years now to encapsulate what his unified America would look like. Dylan, he told his audience, [*a*]*t a particular time in*

*our country's history . . . was one of those fellas who came along and has
been willing to stand in the fire. His music,* he testified, *really empowered
me and got me thinking about the world, outside of my own little town.*

After these remarks, Bruce repeated a variation on the speech he
had been giving for months now before "Land of Hope and Dreams,"
about how the Bush administration must be held accountable for its
deceptions—but it didn't really make any difference. Name-checking
the protest-song Dylan of the early 1960s, before singing his own most
self-conscious attempt to re-create a civil rights–era sing-along, just
felt too much like old history. Those who agreed with such sentiments
were probably already with him. Those who didn't weren't looking for
this kind of oldies song during the encores at a Springsteen concert.

AFTER THE TOUR was over, Bruce returned to the Jersey Shore, spending time with his family and playing benefits at the Pony and the Convention Center. For the first three-quarters of 2004, nearly all of
Springsteen's live performances were supporting Scialfa, as she toured
behind her second solo album. Meanwhile, he toiled in private with
Brendan O'Brien to fashion a new album of his own out of a dozen or
so of the discarded tracks from the last fifteen years. Unlike *The Rising,* this new solo album was mostly recorded at the two Thrill Hill
facilities, and much of it seemed to merely supplement Springsteen's
homemade tracks with overdubs. Springsteen and O'Brien presumably added session work in hopes of opening up Springsteen's original
base recordings, but the result still sounded too much like a collection
of *Tom Joad* outtakes, almost a fifth *Tracks* disc that intensified that
earlier album's monochromaticism. Like the contents of *Human
Touch,* many of these songs had simply been around too long to hold
interest as anything but curiosities.

The exception was the one undoubtedly new song on the album,
the one that would give this solo collection its title. "Devils and Dust"
is about the second U.S.–Iraq war, probably written during that war's
first year, after President Bush's flightdeck pep rally, when too many
National Guardsmen were hunkering down in Camp Victory for stop-
loss-extended stays. The base recording was made by Springsteen,

O'Brien, and drummer Steve Jordan, superficially the sort of Cream-influenced three-man rock trio in which Bruce had briefly played with Earth thirty-five years earlier, but the sound of the song is anything but rock 'n' roll–ish. Instead, it sounds vaguely countryish. This seems the appropriate genre, since country music (and to a lesser extent hip-hop) proved to be a much more readily suitable genre for songs about this military conflict. Whereas the Vietnam War had yielded such unforgettable soldier's-eye-view rock songs as Creedence Clearwater Revival's "Fortunate Son" and Bob Seger's "2 + 2 = ?," this time rock seemed to catch fire only when criticizing the war at a geographical remove, as in System of a Down's brilliant "BYOB."

Unlike Springsteen's ersatz country song, however, the vast majority of Second Gulf War country songs were wholeheartedly supportive of the conflict. Songs like Daryl Worley's "Have You Forgotten?," Montgomery Gentry's "Didn't I?," and Toby Keith's "Courtesy of the Red, White, and Blue" had a last-stand determination that Springsteen's more hesitant song lacks. Keith's song in particular is more "rock 'n' roll" than Springsteen's, in the sense that it is a much cockier song. It's the sort of number—like "Born in the U.S.A.," one might point out—that seems instantly suited to beer-soaked Saturday night sing-alongs, the sort of number from whose words and music one may draw some measure of courage. However, Keith's Bush-era song surpasses Springsteen's Reagan-era song by far in confidence, since its words as well as its music enshrine the same brand of 4/4 boot-wearing certainty. If Springsteen's earlier narrator is left at the end of his lyric with *Nowhere to run, nowhere to go*, an admission of defeat that trails into an anguished howl, Keith's narrator knows exactly where to go and what to do to shake off his wounds. Just so Keith's audience wouldn't miss the point, he even titled the album on which this song appeared *Shock'n Y'all*, which punned on "Shock and Awe," the well-known operational name for the U.S. armed forces' March 2003 bombardment of Baghdad.

In the aftermath of 9/11, American popular culture, and country music in particular, seemed to find the sort of national unity for which Springsteen had been calling over the last five years, a singularity of purpose missing in our national culture for most of the singer's lifetime.

This should have been precisely what Springsteen wanted. But the common purpose that prevailed during George W. Bush's first term as president was not the broadly inclusive national unity of "Land of Hope and Dreams" (if such a thing were even possible this side of heaven). Instead, it was a relentless binarism disguised as unity, an extension of the divisive culture wars of the 1990s that Springsteen so hated. Underlying this seeming unity was a determination that one was either "with us" or "against us." The rock song that captured this compelled division most piercingly was "American Idiot," Green Day's self-consciously alternative anthem of that historical moment. Billie Joe Armstrong's lyric for it assumes that if one has not been brainwashed by the media into following one's government blindly, then one is by default part of "the faggot America," a term that the narrator uses to describe himself, proudly rather than derisively. Bob Lucente, of course, had consigned Bruce Springsteen to that America a full four years before.

Yet unabashedly based in traditional rock motifs as it is, "American Idiot" is no more a song that Bruce Springsteen could have written than "Courtesy of the Red, White, and Blue" is. As the controversy surrounding "American Skin" had already shown, even when the times called for it, Springsteen seemed constitutionally incapable of a binary citizenship. That is, however, the only kind of citizenship that the United States seemed to offer its citizens in 2004: Red State or Blue State; Toby Keith fan or Green Day fan. American culture was now more divided than ever. Bruce had to have known this during that last leg of the *Rising* tour, as a visibly uninterested audience milled around the ground level of Giants Stadium during what Bruce self-consciously called *our public service announcement for tonight*, hitting the T-shirt concessions before the inevitable rendition of "Rosalita" kicked in.

This points to one of the reasons why "Devils and Dust" is unique among songs of the second U.S.–Iraq conflict, not to mention why it may hold a certain eerie power. At first glance, there is no enemy combatant in this song, neither the caricatured and interchangeable Muslim villains of the right nor the Bush-and-Cheney-led "idiots" of the left. There are only two characters in the song, the unnamed narrator and his comrade Bobbie, and there is an unspeakable tension between them. This is the real conflict in "Devils and Dust": not the war in

Iraq but the war at home with its two Americans looking at each other in close quarters and finding each other increasingly unrecognizable.

Springsteen and O'Brien worked on the album *Devils and Dust* sporadically during the spring and summer of 2004, as President Bush's reelection campaign geared up. By August, it was probably all over except for the final mix downs. Around this time, Kelly Curtis, Pearl Jam's manager, convened a meeting in Washington, DC, of several dozen music industry people, in order to organize an artists' effort to prevent Bush from gaining a second term. The idea they finally hit on was a barnstorming week of concerts, thirty-four shows in twenty-eight cities, centered on a handful of "swing" states, where polling data indicated that the electoral vote could go for either of the two major candidates. One of the first managers Curtis asked to join this effort was Jon Landau. The whole enterprise had Springsteen written all over it, not least because most of the states that the tour would visit were in the Rust Belt, where Springsteen had found some of his earliest and most enduring fans.

Since the McGovern benefit at the Red Bank Drive-In thirty-two years earlier, Springsteen had never publicly endorsed a political candidate. He had endorsed causes (No Nukes, Vietnam Veterans for America) and spoken out on public issues (most notably Proposition 209 in California), but he had never even voiced his casual preference for a specific candidate. Senator John Kerry, however, enthusiastically endorsed Bruce Springsteen almost every chance he got, famously naming "No Surrender" as his favorite song during a September 2003 debate among the pre-Iowa candidates for the Democratic presidential nomination. While Senator Kerry should undoubtedly get some credit for naming an album track rather than a single, a true Springsteen fan might have found his choice a little tone-deaf. "No Surrender" was a song that used old war movies as a metaphor for a career in rock 'n' roll. But Kerry, whose campaign stridently emphasized his military service during the Vietnam War, seemed to take that metaphor for the whole song. "Bruce Springsteen had it right," he told the press at the Democratic National Convention in late July, "'no retreat, no surrender.' We are taking this fight to the country and we're going to win back our democracy and our future." When the senator arrived at the convention (shamelessly riding on a water taxi meant to serve as an unconscious reminder of the swift boat on which he had served during the war), the song that was playing was "No Surrender." When he walked up to the podium the next night at the convention to give his acceptance speech, "No Surrender" was playing again. He also played the song at many of his rallies.

Even with all this flattering attention, Springsteen endorsed Kerry relatively late in the game, just after the Democratic convention, at the time the Vote for Change concerts were announced. Moreover, Springsteen's initial endorsement of the senator was somewhat muted. "I don't think John Kerry and John Edwards have all the answers," he wrote in a *New York Times* editorial. "I do believe they are sincerely interested in asking the right questions and working their way toward honest solutions." For Springsteen, Kerry's war service was probably only half the reason for his endorsement. It was also the way that Kerry had come home from the war and then spoken out against it, as Ron Kovic and Bobby Muller had done. Springsteen had in fact met Kerry through Muller, and while there was no evidence that they had spent much time together, the Vietnam Veterans of America connection was probably the single most important factor in Springsteen's endorsement. Beyond that, the fact that the senator could play a surprisingly good rendition of "Tenth Avenue Freeze-Out" on guitar was probably much less important than the fact that he simply wasn't George W. Bush.

A far more compatible left-leaning Vietnam-era veteran ended up joining Springsteen and the E Street Band for their sets at the Vote for Change concerts: John Fogerty, whose "Fortunate Son" had become an anti-Bush rallying cry for even so seemingly removed a rock group as Portland's riot grrrrrrrl outfit Sleater-Kinney. Fogerty met with the E Street Band in the Asbury Park Convention Hall in late September, rehearsing many of the same Creedence songs with which Bruce, Danny, and Garry had rocked Wanamassa's Pandamonium thirty-five years before. Fogerty also rehearsed a haunting new song about the current war but one that explicitly tied it to the war in Vietnam. Fogerty's new song, "Déjà Vu All Over Again" worked nicely in tandem with "Fortunate Son": the latter was a young man's angry song about war; the former, a middle-aged man's rueful supplement to it.

At those same rehearsals, Bruce tried out a version of "Devils and Dust," but he couldn't make it work live, at least not for these shows. Instead, he decided to open his abridged sets at the Vote for Change concerts with an acoustic instrumental version of "The Star-Spangled Banner." To knowledgeable ears, it sounded a great deal like the troubled acoustic rendition of "Born in the U.S.A." that he had taken to performing on his last two arena tours. Indeed, at each stop on the VFC tour, Bruce's gnarled national anthem was followed by the E Street Band's first regularly performed version of "Born in the U.S.A." in almost two decades. One of the advantages of now being widely labeled a shameless liberal was that Bruce didn't have to worry quite so much about whether his meaning in that overly familiar song was clear.

Springsteen's setlists on this briefest of tours were among the most thematically unrelenting of his career. They were drawn mostly from three albums—*Darkness on the Edge of Town, Born in the U.S.A.*, and *The Rising*—and drew mightily on those works' concerns with economic stagnation, the long journey home for America's veterans, and the cultural crossroads that followed 9/11. In this climate, Fogerty's Creedence songs felt less out of place than "No Surrender" did.

The VFC concerts zoomed by in one crazy week, an even faster blur than the Human Rights Now! shows back in 1988. Two weeks later, Springsteen was once again in many of the same cities performing solo at election rallies for Kerry, nearly always playing "The Promised Land" and the increasingly meaningless "No Surrender." (In a way, John Kerry had now stolen that song away from Springsteen far more purposefully than Ronald Reagan had stolen "Born in the U.S.A.") *We've already had a sax player,* Springsteen joked during at least one stop; *we need a guitar player in the White House.*

IN NASHVILLE A FEW months later, country singer Sara Evans unreservedly declared, "America does not care what Bruce Springsteen has to say about the election." Indeed, all through 2003 and 2004, such conservative commentators as Laura Ingraham and Rush Limbaugh had been quick to tell (liberal) musicians like Springsteen and the Dixie Chicks to "shut up and sing." Probably the pithiest response to such dismissals had been Kris Kristofferson's: "I *am* singing, dammit—shut up and listen!" Bush did win reelection in 2004, of course, but many people forget by how small a margin: less than 3 million votes, around 1 percentage point. In terms of the states where the Vote for Change concerts had been held, Michigan, Wisconsin, Pennsylvania, and New Jersey all went for Kerry, while Ohio and Florida went for Bush.

Bruce, almost more than any other performer involved with Vote for Change, had done what he could. It's important to remember, though, that what Springsteen "could" do for a cause usually meant donating his talent and treasure, not his face time as an activist. Simply put, he wasn't Bono. When reporters interviewed him at press conferences, he was reasonably knowledgeable, but he was not the sort of person who was going to spend half his time reading up in detail on microbanks and the drug trials of recent HIV therapies so that he could lobby Congress or the White House for Third World funding. He would rather perform for a good cause, as he did four days after the election at a Parkinson's benefit at the Pony, a few weeks later at a flood benefit in Pittsburgh with Joe Grushecky, and in late December at Harry's Roadhouse in Asbury for the now-traditional local Christmas benefit. Not that he was trying to oblige Ingraham, Limbaugh, or any of his other critics, but after the unrelenting social consciousness of the VFC concerts and the Kerry rallies, it must have felt nice for Springsteen to unapologetically rock out for a while.

Between the benefits, Springsteen and Landau started poring through Bruce's old recordings again, maybe in preparation for a second edition of *Tracks*. Landau zeroed in on the half-dozen recordings from the farmhouse session back in the fall of 1997. As he had done twenty years before with the four LA recordings that formed the germ of the live set, Landau now asked if there might be the beginnings of an album there. Of course, Springsteen already had an album coming out (*Devils and Dust*), but somehow listening to those six tracks again moved him to do something he had not done in quite a while: schedule a recording session with other people when there was no pressing need for it.

Five days after he inducted U2 into the Rock and Roll Hall of Fame, on Saturday 19 March 2005, Springsteen convened the ten musicians who had been present at that first crazy session, along with Mark Pender on trumpet and Lisa Lowell on vocals. As he had done eight years earlier, Springsteen was still mining the Seeger archive for songs, and while some of his conservative detractors might have thought that that would have led him to pull out an old leftie standard like "Deliver the Goods" or "Talkin' Union," in fact only one of the songs Springsteen chose for this second session, the Irish antiwar ballad "Mrs. McGrath," seemed like anything even remotely approaching political commentary. Instead, he and his makeshift band powered through work songs ("Erie Canal," "Shenandoah," "John Henry," and "Pay Me My Money Down"), gospel-fueled songs of joy ("Oh Mary Don't You Weep No More" and "Michael Row the Boat Ashore") and downright silly songs ("Old Dan Tucker" and "Froggie Went a Courtin'"). They ended up recording nine tracks in a single day, something Springsteen probably hadn't done in at least thirty years. It was fun, it was exhilarating, and it was what music was supposed to be. There was definitely an album there, one that in March 2005 seemed anything but political, despite its origins in the work of one of the most notoriously political musicians in twentieth-century America.

But before that album could be finished, there was *Devils and Dust* to get out, as well as the noisy publicity that would be necessary to promote its quiet tangles. There was a taping of *Storytellers* for VH1 in Red Bank, then a benefit for his kids' school at the Pony, and somewhere around there Bruce would have to decide what he was going to do about the tour.

CHAPTER 13

A MILLION DIFFERENT VOICES
SPEAKING IN TONGUES (2005–2008)

ORIGINALLY, THE *DEVILS AND DUST* TOUR WASN'T SUPPOSED TO be a solo effort. Bruce started rehearsals at the Paramount Theatre in Asbury in early March with a few other musicians, including Nils. These medium-sized arrangements of his music had somehow not sounded right, however, and for the songs from the new album an eight- or nine-piece band would have been too much. "[W]hat tends to be dramatic," he told an interviewer from *Rolling Stone*, "is either the full band or you onstage by yourself. Playing alone creates a sort of drama and intimacy for the audience: They know it's just them and just you." Just as the songs from *Nebraska* and *The Ghost of Tom Joad* had acquired a much stronger social resonance when Springsteen eventually performed them on tour with the full E Street Band, so too would the songs from his better-known rock albums become more "intimate," as he put it to *Rolling Stone*, when he performed them alone.

Throughout these rehearsals, die-hard Springsteenites camped outside the Paramount to hear which songs Bruce was working up. Fans had gathered outside rehearsal spaces before previous tours, especially the last two, but thanks to the internet these fans were now sharing the information that they gleaned from these vigils with Springsteen fanatics around the world, via such well-run fan sites as http://www.back streets.com/, http://www.brucebase.org.uk/, and http://www.brucespring steen.it/. (After the advent of smartphones and Twitter, they would be sharing this information with the world almost instantaneously.) When

Bruce resumed rehearsals at the Paramount in mid-April, after the *Storytellers* taping and the school benefit, fans reported hearing some *Darkness, Nebraska, Born in the U.S.A.,* and *Rising* tunes mixed in with the *Devils and Dust* material. They also heard a few songs that would have been out of place on the *Tom Joad* tour, particularly the *Tunnel*-era discard "Part Man Part Monkey." Perhaps the clearest indication of what was going to be different about this tour came when Springsteen did a photo shoot on the Asbury Park boardwalk on 13 April. As part of the shoot, he went to the Wonder Bar for lunch, and after he'd eaten and posed for some pictures, he played a few songs on the house piano.

Eight days later, Springsteen held an open rehearsal, which was pretty much a win-win situation: if people were going to wait outside eavesdropping on what he was doing, he might as well bring them in, use them to test out arrangements and stage chatter, and send the money they paid for their tickets to World Hunger Year, Harry Chapin's old charity. Now that they could clearly hear it, many fans were surprised by Springsteen's proposed set for this tour. Despite the singer's semijoking injunction up front *that the* Tom Joad*—rules apply—I can use all the quiet I can get during the songs,* he performed only two *Tom Joad* songs, one of them the wickedly funny "My Best Was Never Good Enough." The general grimness of the *Joad* concerts seemed absent. Moreover, this performance did not just feature Bruce on acoustic guitar: he played piano for a fifth of the set, including two songs from *Greetings* ("For You" and "Lost in the Flood"). The next afternoon he held another open rehearsal, with proceeds from this one benefiting many of the same local charities featured at the Christmas shows, and the piano trend continued when "Real World" and "Racing in the Street" joined the set. He also led off with a version of "Reason to Believe" sung through his harp mic, electronically extending the usual blues practice of voice masking and making the song sound like a lost Howlin' Wolf track.

When the *Devils and Dust* tour opened in Detroit three days later, word quickly got out that a chandelier and a Tiffany-style lamp were part of the stage set. Clearly, this was going to be a Springsteen tour like no other. He was talking about his kids, talking about how he had written the songs, being explicit about which songs he felt were connected with which others, but the whole proceedings were much less structured than the *Storytellers* taping for VH1 had been. In Dallas, on the second night of the tour, when he substituted "Two Faces" in the slot where "Tougher than the Rest" and "Real World" had gone for the first few performances, he told the audience, *I haven't tried this one before, we'll see how we do,* a cautionary word that he would essentially repeat before dozens of other songs on the rest of the tour. Springsteen started doing a new song or two every night, adding new instruments and new sounds, playing "Johnny 99" on Dobro, "My Beautiful Reward" on pump organ, "Paradise" on electric piano, and "I'm on Fire" on banjo, making his rock songs sound country, his country songs sound homespun, and his political songs sound slightly techno. He played "Book of Dreams," "Cautious Man," "A Good Man Is Hard to Find," "Iceman," "Wreck on the Highway"—songs you never heard at an E Street Band concert. The one cover he performed (which he premiered in Chicago on 11 May and with which he closed every concert for the rest of the tour) was "Dream, Baby, Dream," a rewrite of a song by Suicide, an obscure band from the thirty-year-gone glory days of CBGB. He played that song on pump organ too, so that the shows now began and ended with that instrument.

It may have been the recent exhilarating day of farmhouse recording that made Springsteen so fearless, but then he had always liked playing around with songs and reinventing them. The acoustic "Born to Run" on the 1988 tour was a darker example of this, but there was also the country version of "Countin' on a Miracle" that he spitballed in the hallway at Southern Sounds during the *Rising* sessions. Thom Zimny's film of that little improvisation ended up being shown on the Jumbotron at the end of the shows on the 2002–03 tour, and the audio of it was included on the third disc of Columbia's 2003 *Essential Bruce Springsteen* set. As for spontaneously adding new songs to a performance, Springsteen would occasionally change the setlist with the E Street Band, calling out "audibles" (as musicians often term them), but it's even easier to add new numbers when it's just you and your tech crew. As long as all your instruments are tuned and you have a cheat screen in case you blank out on old lyrics, you can read the temperature of your audience and move things around to fit. Springsteen's favorite recording sessions had always been the simple ones: the CBS demos, the *Nebraska* session, these recent farmhouse recordings. The 2005 solo concerts weren't quite as loosey-goosey as those, but they were a lot more relaxed than the mammoth E Street Band tours of the last twenty years had been.

The *Devils and Dust* tour was as radical a reinvention of himself as any pop star of Springsteen's magnitude had ever attempted. It was courageous and risky on a nightly basis. On this tour, audiences got to enjoy not the familiar, epic Springsteen but Springsteen the short story writer, who was developed purposefully after the personal break-through of "Stolen Car." Most nights, the songs came overwhelmingly from the years after *Born in the U.S.A.*, during which Springsteen had tried to back away from the caricatures of Brucemania. In this setting, the three relationship albums became essential, not just because their songs were focused on the trials of intimacy, but also because *Tunnel of Love*, *Human Touch*, and *Lucky Town* were mostly solo albums that Bruce had initially promoted with full-band tours. Now, especially on a piece like "Real World," you could hear what these songs were sup-posed to sound like, a fact that Springsteen freely acknowledged. *[This is a song that] kind of got away from me on the record*, he told one audi-ence that spring just before performing "Real World." *We didn't get a good version of it but it was a good song*. Even a relatively successful early-'90s band number like "Lucky Town" took on fresh life during this tour when vigorously played on acoustic guitar.

By the time the tour hit Europe, it had settled into a groove. At the Point in Dublin on 24 May, half of Springsteen's set was drawn from *Devils and Dust* and *The Rising*. The other half contained one or two songs each from most of his other post-1975 albums. At the outset of the tour, the relationship songs had been added intentionally, in part because Springsteen thought that what unified many of the songs on *Devils and Dust* was their focus on *sons and mothers*. Now that he was comfortable with this format, he began adding more *Nebraska* songs— "State Trooper" in Brussels, "My Father's House" in Bologna.

And the fan sites were noticing. "Bruce keeps digging into *Nebraska*," Backstreets. com said in the lead of its 4 June report on the

Bologna concert. "From Frankfurt to Dusseldorf, from Wednesday to Thursday," the site reported on 16 June, *"half of the set changes."* Twenty-five years before, Charles Cross had started *Backstreets* as a magazine, one to which most members of the E Street band and many members of the old Asbury scene gave thorough, thoughtful interviews. Shortly after taking over from Cross as managing editor in 1994, Christopher Phillips established a companion Backstreets website. The internet almost seemed made for fan culture, for the compilation and sharing of tiny scraps of information that add up to a larger, emergent whole. In time, the site would boast forums for swapping tickets and recordings (as long as no money changed hands), but in the summer of 2005 it was mostly a clearinghouse for information on this strangest of Springsteen tours. All through the European swing, one or two new songs at a minimum popped up at each venue—in a number of cases (Copenhagen and Stockholm), it was three or four. By the time Springsteen started the tour's second U.S. leg, Backstreets.com had taken to putting the night's tour premieres in boldface.

By this point in the tour, Springsteen was actually taking requests, something he had rarely done since his Student Prince days, including a hilariously sketchy request for "Empty Sky," for which a fan had simply written "Play 'Everything Is Everything.'" (They probably weren't asking Bruce to cover Lauryn Hill.) *When I get a request like that,* Springsteen joked before complying, *I wonder, like, how much could you like the song if you don't know the title? But, you know, sometimes you only have to hear something once and, like I remember going to the record store . . . It's the same bit of business.* Far from the folkie grinch of the *Tom Joad* shows, Springsteen was trying his best on this tour to be obliging, with only one explicitly voiced exception. *No, I can't go putting it on, man,* he told a fan who shouted out a request for "Happy Birthday" later in the summer. *That's where I draw the line. This ain't a Jimmy Buffett show.*

But all this obliging behavior still wasn't necessarily filling the seats. In Buffalo, tour personnel upgraded many concertgoers' tickets so that most of the audience could be on the floor of the HSBC Arena. *I've been in Buffalo two days,* Springsteen told the crowd in his usual hello spot just before "Long Time Comin'." *You're the first folks I've seen. Where the hell is everybody?* Even with the increasingly polarized views of Bruce's politics, most of the dates on the revival and *Rising* tours had sold out on the day they were announced. But a lot of Springsteen fans, whatever their politics, did not want to see him onstage by himself: they wanted the E Street Band. To whip up interest among fans, Springsteen's organization took a leaf from Backstreets.com's book and started posting his setlists online. They also posted the contents of the three CDs of walk-in music that Bruce had prepared for those who arrived at the concert venues early, a detail that received a paragraph or two of analysis in the *New York Times* Sunday Arts and Leisure section. If with "American Skin" five years earlier, the internet may have taken Springsteen by surprise, by 2005 his management seems to have understood that even an artist who had recorded his first album in the early 1970s was now living in a fully wired world.

Springsteen probably wasn't monitoring all these sites himself, but someone was clearly telling him about them. In his speeches between songs, he seemed to acknowledge the online fan speculation. On 23 July in Atlanta, when he performed "Sad Eyes" and "Valentine's Day," he introduced them as *a back-to-back, never-played-before double header.* Eight days later in Columbus, he spoke before starting "Cynthia" of *a night of debuts, a night of debuts.* In between those two dates, in Greensboro on 26 July, he dedicated "Dream Baby Dream" to the local fans who ran http://www.greasylake.org/, another website that had been following the tour quite closely.

More important, the fans who attended these concerts seemed to be following all these sites too. After the Atlanta premiere of "Valentine's Day," seventeen years after Bruce had rehearsed it for the *Tunnel of Love* tour without ever putting it into the set at any of his concerts, the audience gave him a standing ovation, one long enough to justify turning the house lights up. Over the next two weeks, he worked his way through the remaining tracks on *Tunnel of Love,* almost giving that personally transformative album the solo tour it so richly deserved —and the fan sites were noting it, every step of the way. The houses were slightly fuller now than they had been in the spring, but the real difference was in the quality, not the quantity, of the audiences. The internet coverage had gotten many of those who attended these concerts primed for the tour in a way that they hadn't been for the previous decade's *Tom Joad* tour. They were respectful during the songs but enthusiastic in between, a perfect balance that seemed to push Springsteen to be even bolder. *The audiences've just gotten better and better [on this tour],* he told the crowd in Seattle in mid-August, during a swing through the Northwest on which his son Evan joined him. *It's great to be able to come out here and play like this. It's something I really enjoy, and it takes a dedicated crowd. . . .*

After those concerts, Springsteen took his usual birthday break through September and resumed the tour on 4 October with another rehearsal show at the Paramount in Asbury, a benefit this time for the Red Cross. A little over a month earlier, on 29 August, a category 5 hurricane called Katrina had hit the Gulf of Mexico region, killing over 1,800 people, wreaking over $81 billion in property damage, and flooding 80 percent of New Orleans, a city cherished by anyone who cares about the history of American music. In light of this situation, Springsteen made sure to name half a dozen other New Jersey fundraisers for flood relief, and he pointedly opened the show by using the harp mic to sing "Idiot's Delight," a recently released collaboration with Joe Grushecky that lamented how political malfeasance can ruin public life.

The main job of the night, though, was still musical, not political. *Got a few different things tonight,* he told the audience before trying a rockabilly version of "The Ties That Bind," *so you're the guinea pigs.* He opened the encores now by playing ukulele (*You can laugh,* he told the audience) and changed "Jesus Was an Only Son," which he had played at every concert on this tour, on a whim. *I just played that song in a key I've never played it in before in my life,* he informed the audience, *and in the middle my hands leapt to the right key! It's good to take time off, 'cause when you come back, you have no idea what you're doing, and everything is new. Whoa!*

Bruce was clearly having the time of his life. *I don't think I've played this on the tour yet, I'm not sure,* he said to cheers while a broken string was being changed before "Independence Day" in Rochester two nights later, *I mean I've played about 120 songs. That would mean there's gonna be about a hundred of 'em you're gonna miss tonight. Oh, it's, it's, it's, it's a system, it's a system,* he said, and then dissolved into laughter before getting serious again for the song. And even if he wasn't entirely comfortable with computers himself, he apparently understood that this was now the most effective way to communicate with his fans. *You guys can do me a favor,* he told the crowd in Hartford the following night at the beginning of the encores, *you can get on the internet tonight—'cause I know that's how you get in touch—and ask people not to come to the stage until the end of the set, alright? You only need to run your fingers across those little buttons,* he joked, miming activity at a computer keyboard as only a man who writes out all his lyrics longhand in spiral notebooks can.

During this last leg, the tour became a lovefest between Springsteen and his fans, with many of them getting name-checked from the stage, most notably *Richie from Germany.* Bruce displayed photographs of Richie unveiling Springsteen banners on the summits of Mounts Kilimanjaro and Aconcagua. *I try to stay as far away from these kinds of fans as possible,* Bruce kidded at the top of the encores in Madison, Wisconsin, before good-naturedly playing "Growin' Up." Fans started bringing signs, and Bruce started changing his setlist to suit. *They brought the damn sign, so you know . . . ,* he kidded during the same, goofy bunch of encores. *By the time you make the sign, it's sung.* In Philly in early November, one of his fans (Patty Poppos from Toronto) actually supplied him with a map of his old neighborhood that he could use as a visual aid during the Catholicism rap before "Jesus Was an Only Son."

As usual, Springsteen loosened up even more as the tour went on, digging back and doing such early songs as "The Fever," "Thundercrack," and "Santa Ana." Sony released a thirtieth-anniversary three-disc box set of *Born to Run* in mid-November, and Bruce got into the spirit and started performing more songs from that album, something he had clearly been reluctant to do when the tour started. The November shows in the Meadowlands were awash with dedications, including one to *Scott Greenstein and all the guys at Sirius Radio,* which had recently launched E Street Radio, a satellite radio channel devoted solely to Springsteen. *Yes, I have my own radio channel,* Bruce told the audience. *It's every artist's dream. You turn on the radio and there's nothing but you on it. . . . It's a little unsettling because, as I've listened, I've said "Gee, there are so many things that I have no idea that I ever did." There's a lot of people over there that now know more about me than I know about myself. From now on if I have any questions about myself, I know who to call.*

The satellite radio channel, the internet chatter over the tour, and the release of half a dozen new books on Springsteen seemed to make the singer aware of just how much detailed information about him was now available to the world—so much that a foreign fan could draw a fairly accurate map of the locations of all his relatives' old houses, some of which were no longer standing. A younger Springsteen might have been more resentful of all this disseminated knowledge, but over a quarter of a century after he had pulled Lynn Goldsmith out of the audience at the No Nukes concerts for just taking a picture, he was much more comfortable with the fact that he could not fully control what people saw or knew about him. This, too, was part of the game that he relished on the tour. During one of the last concerts in New Jersey, he gleefully introduced the thirty-five-year-absent "Song for Orphans" as *an outtake from* Greetings . . . *never released . . . so you're not gonna know this bastard! Though some of you may*, he admitted.

When the tour was over, www.brucespringsteen.net proudly announced that Springsteen had played 243 different songs at seventy-two shows, a wider variety of material than he probably would have comfortably done had he been touring with the E Street Band. He did all of *Nebraska, Devils and Dust,* and *Tunnel of Love,* nearly all of *The Ghost of Tom Joad* and *Greetings from Asbury Park,* most of *The River,* not to mention a larger sampling of *Tracks* than he had done on the revival tour that was ostensibly meant to promote it. In doing so, he finally showed off the true range of his songwriting in a way that his self-conscious recordings and tours of the 1990s never could have. "He's finally become a Bruce Springsteen fan," as Dave Marsh quotes one fan concluding.

Between this solo tour and the recordings of folk songs that he'd been making with the thrown-together band at his farmhouse, he had finally found a way to get out from under the weight of being Bruce

Springsteen, to have fun with music again without just slipping onstage at a Grushecky gig. He was also, not incidentally, now as productive as CBS had wanted him to be back in the early 1970s. In the last five years, in addition to the *Born to Run* set, he had come out with four albums (two of them live recordings), another greatest-hits collection (the *Essential Bruce Springsteen*, which included a disc of rarities to make sure that fans bought it), and three live DVDs (of the 2000 concerts at the Garden, a Barcelona concert on the *Rising* tour, and the *Storytellers* taping). All were selling respectably and suggested that, as long as Springsteen wanted to put out product, a significant number of fans would be willing to buy it.

ONE SIGN OF Springsteen's newfound busyness—five tours in five years, something he hadn't done in three decades—was the fact that he didn't participate in any of the Christmas benefits around the Jersey Shore in late 2005. He implicitly passed that baton on to Bobby Bandiera, although he would show up at several of Bandiera's future holiday concerts. On 14 January 2006, he was in the somewhat awkward position of attending a performance of other artists playing through one of his own albums, start to finish. Over the years, *Nebraska* had become something of a cult object, and a group of musicians at the 2006 New York Guitar Festival decided to cover the entire album live. At the end of the performance, Bruce thanked each of them individually but opted to play Jack Guthrie's "Oklahoma Hills" rather than any of his own songs for the requisite encore. When the host for the evening, John Platt, a DJ from the independent but sometimes excessively earnest local FM station WFUV, tried to get Bruce to make some portentous comment about the performances or the album that gave rise to them, the singer just goofed around. Even on *Nebraska*, he jokingly insisted, most of the songs had been written *to get women to pull their pants down*. Like many professional performers, Springsteen was clearly uncomfortable with an occasion that called for him to be someone else's idealized version of his actual self.

What Platt had probably been hoping for was some kind of political statement from the singer. No matter what its origins in Springsteen's own personal crises, twenty-four years later *Nebraska* was now seen by many as a political response to Ronald Reagan's vision of America. As Springsteen had gotten more explicitly political over the last ten to fifteen years, that hastily recorded album was increasingly regarded as a Rosetta stone to the further evolution of his work. More important, the political landscape of the United States was very different in the winter of 2006 from what it had been in the fall of 2004 when Springsteen stumped for John Kerry—and the federal government's fumbling response to Hurricane Katrina in the fall of 2005 had a great deal to do with that. Even without the "liberal media" of the television networks, raw video footage of the neglect and destruction along the Gulf Coast spread faster online than the government was able to come up with rationalizations for it. By late 2005, the United States was simply too vast, too populated, and too wired for the U.S. government to prevent unflattering information about its efforts from getting out, as it had done just a few years earlier in Iraq.

Even in terms of protest music, the internet was changing the rules of the game. When hip-hop artist Kanye West declared on a 2 September 2005 live telethon for flood victims, "You know it's been five days [without aid], because most of the people are black. . . . George Bush doesn't care about black people," an enterprising Houston rapper named Legendary K. O. took that as a cue. He stripped the lead vocal off West's recent hit "Golddigger" and four days later had a song called "George Bush Don't Like Black People." It was the best instant American protest song in decades, and Legendary K. O. distributed it as a free download. His funked-up rage spread around the world within hours.

In early 2006, Bruce was at least a decade past any misguided thoughts about experimenting with hip-hop, but he was clearly thinking about responding to the accumulated messes of the Bush administration. In L.A. on 8 February, he was awarded the Grammy for Best Rock Vocal for "Devils and Dust" before the TV cameras rolled, but he did get a slot on the subsequent Grammy broadcast performing it solo. At the end of that song, about a war that was supposed to have been over before he even wrote it, he simply shouted, "Bring 'em home!" At the end of the broadcast, he led a group performance of "In the Midnight Hour," meant to honor both Wilson Pickett (who had died on 19 January) and the now scattered community of working musicians from New Orleans.

The war in Iraq was obviously egregious, but the neglect of New Orleans may have rankled Springsteen even more. At the open rehearsal in Asbury in October, when alerting the audience to local fund-raisers, he had spoken about what that southern city meant to him. *I don't know if any of you ever been to New Orleans much,* he told the New Jersey audience, *but it's an incredible town . . . It was one of those few places in the country where there was still a place there, and you could literally walk along the street and still hear terrific street musicians, and I just heard a lot of beautiful music down there.* Standing a few blocks from where the Sunshine In had stood, Bruce certainly knew about the importance of a local "scene." As far as musical communities are concerned, the "community" part always comes first. A common history, a common polity, is always the first step toward a common, vibrant musical language.

Moreover, in terms of Springsteen's own relationship with music, the devastation of Katrina could not have come at a more personally resonant time. Thanks to the presence of the Gotham Playboys, the farmhouse recordings that he hoped would make up his next album were as rooted in the enormous musical legacy of New Orleans as in the blue-eyed gospel of Asbury Park. Although the project may have begun with an attempt to come up with a track for the tribute album to Pete Seeger, only one of the songs Springsteen recorded for it was actually written by Seeger. The rest were old-time songs Seeger had "collected," recorded, and made his own, exactly what Springsteen was trying to do with his new, makeshift band. Despite what some commentators would erroneously assume, "the Seeger sessions," as the farmhouse recordings would soon be called, did not begin life as a political project. In fact, the most fruitful sessions, just after the presidential election in 2004, probably stemmed from a desire to get away from politics for a while and just have fun making music. Between the second and third sessions, however, Hurricane Katrina made the performance of old-time American music, particularly played in a horn-swung style associated with New Orleans, a political act in itself.

This was clear in the songs that Bruce chose for the band to cover at their third and final session on 21 January, two days after Wilson Pickett's death. Two rounds of rave-ups weren't quite enough for an album, so Springsteen scheduled a third day of recordings to finish things off. The early-'60s folkie standards "Eyes on the Prize," "Jacob's Ladder," and "If I Had a Hammer" were tried that day, as was Seeger's Vietnam-era "Bring Them Home" (which Bruce would obliquely reference in his Grammy performance), not to mention Seeger's McCarthy-era rewrite of the old Baptist hymn "How Can I Keep from Singing?" and "Worried Man Blues," a Woody Guthrie song about an escaped convict. The one song recorded that day that would have fit in during the last, unpreoccupied session the previous March was the joyous "Buffalo Gals." Even "American Land," Springsteen's livelier rewrite of Seeger's setting of a Slovak-American poem about immigration, was still trying too hard: its many grace notes, awkwardly packing as many syllables into each line as possible, were reminiscent of the late *Tom Joad* border songs.

As it turned out, only two of the eight tracks recorded at this third and last session ended up on *We Shall Overcome: The Seeger Sessions* when it was released in late April, but the issues that had driven Springsteen to choose them were obviously still on his mind. Bruce held five rehearsals with his enormous new band at the Paramount in mid-March and another six in mid-April, and as the setlists leaked out it became clear that he was connecting the material on the new album to both current politics and a number of his old songs from *Nebraska*. The first open rehearsal show on 20 April confirmed this, as Springsteen dedicated "Mrs. McGrath" to Cindy Sheehan, the Gold Star mom who had been arrested for, among other acts of protest, wearing a "2,245 Dead. How many more?" T-shirt to President Bush's State of the Union address in January. During the set, he placed this song after "Devils and Dust" and before a highly effective folk rewrite of Blind Alfred Reed's early Great Depression song "How Can a Poor Man Stand Such Times and Live?" Springsteen's version directly parodied Bush's quick 2 September 2005 visit to New Orleans, during which the president had thought a sly allusion to it as "the town where I used to come from Houston, Texas, to enjoy myself—sometimes too much" would be cute. Even with other people's songs, Springsteen knew how to arrange a cathartic setlist.

But the set wasn't all politics. Springsteen's culling of tracks for the album made it clear that he wanted it to be what he had first heard from the Gotham Playboys eight and a half years before at his birthday celebration: party music. "John Henry," "Jesse James," and "Buffalo Gals" were just plain fun, and most of the Springsteen originals with which he filled out the set were also barnburners. Even the socially conscious "Johnny 99" seemed less so in this new arrangement. Of his own songs, the stunner by far was "Open All Night," which he chose to throw even farther into the past, so that it sounded as if it had been recorded in 1943, with Patti, Sooz, and Lisa serving as New Jersey's answer to the Andrews Sisters. Backstreets reported one fan being reminded of "Walt Whitman's Niece," off *Mermaid Avenue*, Billy Bragg and Wilco's completion of a number of unfinished Woody Guthrie songs (recorded a few months after the first, long-unreleased Seeger session), but they might just as easily have thought of Tom Waits's relentlessly eclectic musical archivalism. Even though Springsteen had played with the horn section of his new band on and off for decades, they swung more on this record, playing with the bop of swing and even Dixieland far more than the funky discipline of the Stax horn sections. Between the folk and the swing, the album was deliberately prerock, even pre-R&B. It was like a Burgess Shale of American popular music, an alternate direction that pop could have taken around the time of Springsteen's birth but didn't.

We Shall Overcome: The Seeger Sessions dropped on 24 April, the day of the second open rehearsal show at the Asbury Park Convention Hall, and the next day the new band did a remote broadcast on *Good Morning America* that was much like the one that Bruce and the E Streeters had done on *Today* for *The Rising* three years before. Except for Scialfa, however, the band was entirely different: the thirteen musicians and vocalists who had worked on the farmhouse recordings were now joined by four others: Greg Liszt (who had pioneered a four-finger-picking technique for banjo and had, until recently, been studying molecular biology at MIT); Marty Rifkin (who had played steel guitar on *The Ghost of Tom Joad* and been part of the early, country sessions for *Tunnel of Love*); Cindy Mizelle (who, like Rifkin, was an in-demand session player who had recorded background vocals with R&B greats from Luther Vandross and Chaka Khan to Mary J. Blige and Alicia Keys); and Marc Anthony Thompson (an Italian-born African American vocalist and guitarist who had once described his own eclectic band, Chocolate Genius, Inc., as "a brothel with free candy"). With these four artists added to the fugitive members of the Gotham Playboys and the Asbury Jukes, Springsteen had assembled a transgeneric supergroup of musicians whom most Americans had never heard of.

The band wasn't just spontaneous at these early appearances; it was rough. *Let's check the key on this one*, Springsteen told the band at the fourth and last open rehearsal, before launching into a version of "Cadillac Ranch" that folded "Mystery Train" into it. *Oh yeah we found it*, he said before starting the next song, the much more straightforward "My Oklahoma Home." *We had to travel through a couple of keys, a few minor heart attacks. You're singing and you're going: "I'm singing it, it's playing," but it's like having your right shoe on your left foot and your left shoe on your right foot. . . . This is what we need*, he added, *We need to fuck up. I'm glad we're fucking up, better now than later.*

Three days later, Bruce and the Seeger Sessions Band were headlining at the New Orleans Jazz and Heritage Festival, a brilliant move from a promotional standpoint but not the most obvious candidate for what Bruce frankly informed the Jazz Fest audience was *our first gig*. This was the first Jazz Fest after Hurricane Katrina, and the festival organizers were as nervous as Springsteen, worried that people wouldn't come to a city still in disrepair. In their performance, Springsteen and his band mostly stuck to the contents of the new album, playing ten out of its thirteen tracks, filling out the set with four of Springsteen's own songs (the now honed arrangements of "Johnny 99," "Open All Night," "My City of Ruins," and "You Can Look But You Better Not Touch"), as well as at least two of the songs that Springsteen had considered adding to the album during the last few months ("How Can a Poor Man Stand Such Times and Live?" and "Buffalo Gals").

Bruce's patter between songs was not as loose as at the rehearsal shows—most frequently, it offered a series of historical notes about the songs and where they came from—but from first to last his comments were directly political. About half an hour into the set, he described "My Oklahoma Home" (which he had first recorded in 1997, when George W. Bush was still governor of Texas) as *a song that was written during the other great American natural disaster in our country's recent history that separated families, that drove Americans from their homes and left them spread out all across the country, the Oklahoma dustbowl.* In introducing "Poor Man" (the one piece he had specifically rewritten in honor of New Orleans), he spoke of walking around the city the preceding day, Friday, 29 April, *from Lake View to the 9th Ward, and I think I saw sights I never thought I'd see in an American city. The criminal ineptitude,* he continued, communicating an articulate political anger that he had never before voiced onstage without masking it in some form of humor or satire, *makes you feel furious. This is what happens when political cronyism cuts the very agencies that are supposed to serve American citizens in times of trial and hardship.* He then finally leavened his vented spleen with a touch of sarcasm, dedicating the actual performance of the song to *President Bystander.*

As could be expected, the New Orleans crowd ate all this up. The twenty-ninth was the eight-month anniversary of the day Katrina hit, and the wounds in the city were still pretty raw. Less than a week after the album's release, the audience was sliding quite naturally into the invited call-and-response of *Blown away* on "My Oklahoma Home." Even the inevitable YouTube video shot from the back of the crowd with someone's cellphone (in this case, of "My City of Ruins") shows an audience that connected more with that song by ways of shouts and swaying hands than any of the crowds at the Meadowlands had done on the *Rising* tour. When Bruce decided to end the concert with a sweet, tentative version of "When the Saints Go Marching In"—*we know,* he admitted to the crowd, *there's about a hundred people around town gonna do it better than us*—the audience accepted the song as the honest gesture of propitiatory benediction that it was.

But the audience's warm reaction was beyond any mere response to Bruce's special pleading to a local crowd. Over the years, Jazz Fest audiences had become accustomed to a broad range of music being subsumed under the more general rubric of "jazz," and they immediately embraced the Sessions Band as the sincere musicians that they were. Although Bruce kidded at one point during the New Orleans concert that he still had some gesture[s] left over from the rock shows, the truth was that Bruce's interaction with this new band was also different from his onstage relationship with the E Streeters. He was less of a frontman with these musicians and more of a bandleader, gladly sharing vocals on a number of songs with Thompson, whose own band Springsteen plugged every chance he got. The result was probably a truer "revival" than Springsteen had ever achieved with his better-known band. "It was hard to imagine," Randy Lewis declared in his review of the concert for the Los Angeles Times, "a more dramatic and exhilarating confluence of music with moment."

The triumph in New Orleans launched Springsteen's second great brief tour in as many years. He and the Sessions Band, as he would simply call it by the end of the tour, played fewer than a dozen dates in Europe and a few more than that in the United States over the next two months, and they just went rolling along, mixing rollicking fun and righteous politics more smoothly than the perhaps excessively mythic E Street Band had ever been able to do. Typical of this was the song that usually closed out their brief set, just before the encores. "Pay Me My Money Down," whose lyrics Lydia Parrish had recorded in 1942 from the stevedores in the Georgia Sea Islands and whose music Alan Lomax had been able to trace back even farther than that, was so firmly rooted in capitalist individualism that it might honestly have passed muster with Ronald Reagan back in his proud "I'm paying for this microphone" days of 1980. At the same time, though, the song was unashamedly pro-worker in a way that the current president's dream of an "Ownership Society" could never be. Most of all, though, the song was unabashedly fun to sing and play along to, for this was usually the number on which Springsteen asked guests onstage to join him on this tour, whether they were professional musicians or not.

The tour also continued Springsteen's use of the internet and digital media. Now he could truly finish an album on tour, which he had not been able to do in the days of Darkness. Back in January, he had been dissatisfied with the new band's arrangement of "Bring 'Em Home" and had recorded another version during the closed rehearsals at the Paramount in April. He then premiered the song live before an audience in Paris in early May, took another stab at his vocals for the recording in Oslo a little over a week later, and had it out as an internet single by the middle of June. "American Land," which he had also tried to cut during that last farmhouse session, premiered at Madison Square Garden in late June and was recorded that night for eventual download as well. Now alternate tracks didn't need to sit in the Sony Archives for decades waiting to be released: they could be made available through iTunes and even repackaged as part of the expanded version of the album, which Springsteen intended to release in early October, just around the time they started the second leg of the tour.

The Seeger Sessions album and tour felt organic, like a project that had been naturally growing for almost a decade but had picked up speed within the last year or two. It felt like *a roll of the dice, an adventure*, as Bruce told the crowd at the Garden State Arts Center in Holmdel in June at the end of the tour's first leg. Part of the fun was in doing something new, but part of it was also in not knowing if it was going to work, which hadn't been an issue with the E Street Band for over thirty years.

For the Jersey audience in Holmdel, Springsteen offered two endings for the concert. The first was "When the Saints Go Marching In," which had closed most of the band's performances over those dizzying two months since the New Orleans Jazz Fest. He told the audience that that song *explain[ed] what we're trying to do*. Its well-known first verse (*We are all trav'lling in the footsteps / Of those that have gone before*) reminded his audience, as this whole tour had done, of the devotion with which he regarded the history of American popular music. The middle verse that Bruce had unearthed in an old songbook (*And some say that this world of trouble / Is the only world we'll ever see / But I'm waiting on that morning / When the new world is revealed*) almost sounded like a prefiguring of "The Promised Land," especially when Springsteen sang it. As with his own song, there could be no doubt that when Springsteen sang this cover, he was sharing a sacred vision of this world rather than the next.

But it was the song with which Springsteen ended the concert that night in Holmdel that told the real story of how he had been reborn on this tour. This final song, which the band had performed at several of the rehearsal shows but not yet on the tour proper, *explained* (Bruce told the audience) *not what we're trying to do but what we're doing.* The song was "The Daring Young Man on the Flying Trapeze," which Pete Seeger had indeed once recorded, and which is probably the only song that has been or ever would be performed by both Bruce Springsteen and Eddie Cantor. The message of this song came at the audience more sideways than most of the others on this tour, but it was still clear: in addition to politics, this tour was about making danger look graceful, about doing something difficult as if it was just being tossed off. *Nothing to it!* Springsteen exclaimed as he finished the song, promising the audience that he and this outlandish band would be back.

PROBABLY THE MOST awkward performance Bruce gave that year was on Friday, 25 August, at the Antique Center, a small shop in Red Bank. The day before, the *New York Post* had gleefully run an unsigned 350-word story in its Page Six gossip column declaring that Springsteen and Scialfa had separated and that their marriage was over, allegedly because of Bruce's involvement with a 9/11 widow. The newspaper's evidence for this was, in part, the fact that Bruce had taken his children to the beach without Patti and that he had been spending a great deal of time not at their home in Rumson but at their property in Colts Neck. The fact that the story ran just around the time of the first anniversary of Hurricane Katrina, when populist liberals of Springsteen's ilk were reminding Americans how mismanaged the Bush administration's response to that disaster had been, may not have been a total coincidence.

Springsteen posted an unequivocal denial of the *Post*'s story on his website, but he and Patti apparently went to the trouble of being publicly seen together that next day at the Antique Center, where they were known to shop both separately and together. It was an oddly homey place for them to provide a handy photo op of marital bliss—there were no cameras around and only a few customers there—but then maybe that was the point. Going to a Manhattan gala together would have been exactly what Page Six readers would expect. Bruce and Patti tuned up some of the instruments in the shop and played a few songs, and Patti hugged the store's owner and commiserated with him. "Isn't this the pits?" she said. "My friends are more upset than I am."

Whoever wrote the Page Six item probably wasn't a Springsteen fan, and not just because of his politics. If you were a true Springsteen fanatic (as opposed to someone who considered him vaguely inter-changeable with Jon Bon Jovi and/or Mick Jagger), the real news in the story wasn't his taking the kids to the beach by himself. Frankly, after eighteen years together as a couple, it would probably have been more suspicious if Patti *hadn't* let Bruce take the kids to the beach by himself, as if she couldn't trust him for too long out of her sight. As fans knew, even professionally, Bruce and Patti were spending a little more time apart these days. Patti had quit the Sessions tour to take care of their children back in mid-May, leaving Sooz to cover most of her vocals for the last few shows of the European swing and nearly all of the American dates. Even though Bruce invariably gave a better performance when Patti was present, her onstage absences would become much more common over the next few years, as first Ev, then Jess, and finally Sam became teenagers. *Patti sends her love,* Spring-steen would tell a Dallas audience on another Scialfa-less night on his next tour, *we have the three teenagers so it gives a whole new meaning to "homeland security," my friends. As I was leaving, the black helicop-ters were dropping kegs of beer to my backyard, the pot cookies were coming out of the oven, and all my favorite clothes were up on eBay. Patti'll take care of that, she'll get it all back!* For Springsteen fans, Patti staying in Rumson while Bruce toured with the rest of his new band was frankly old news.

Far more intriguing for fans was the report that Bruce was spend-ing more time in Colts Neck, where his workroom and studio were. (Rumson was where the family actually lived.) That almost suggested that Bruce was working fairly hard on a new album—which seemed impossible, since he had already released as many albums in the last four years as in the previous decade.

But sure enough, on 11 November, at the top of the encores at London's Wembley Arena, Springsteen sheepishly introduced a new song as *a kind of work-in-progress.* It was a political song, Bruce made clear—over the last five years, he told the Wembley audience, *there was so much destruction done, just to basic principles of democracy, that not only is [America] broken, it needs to be fixed now*—but this new song also resonated with many of Bruce's earlier works that purposefully avoided politics, particularly "My Hometown" and "Independence Day." The new song, called "Long Walk Home," chronicled its narrator's nighttime walk through the town in which he had been born, which had changed utterly. In this early version, the song seemed like the next, exasperated step after 2004's "Devils and Dust," one that metaphorically added the devastation of Hurricane Katrina to the list of recent horrors. In this verse (which Springsteen ultimately discarded), the song seems like another address to his audience—his mass audience, not the ones who had bought tickets to these last two, smaller tours, but rather the wider one to whom he knew he probably owed another E Street Band album. As in "Devils and Dust," the problem in "Long Walk Home" is estrangement.

A few weeks after the Sessions tour was over, Bruce invited Brendan O'Brien up to Jersey to listen to a batch of new songs, all of which fit in one way or another with "Long Walk Home." Bruce's challenge to his audience was removed from that song (which already had enough going on in it) and put front and center in the much noisier "Radio Nowhere." While that song's choruses were built around Bruce's old concert cry *Is there anybody alive out there?,* its main riff was borrowed from Tommy Tutone's 1982 hit "Jenny Jenny," and its whole conceit (that musicians and fans had no real connection anymore) may very well have reflected the singer's personal ambivalence regarding the establishment of E Street Radio. "Radio Nowhere" would end up opening Bruce's next album, its desperate howl for human contact, *I just want to hear your rhythm,* thematically echoed at the album's other end by the reiterated *the beat of your heart* in "Devil's Arcade," the track with which Springsteen had originally intended to close it. As in "Long Walk Home"—and much of Springsteen's earlier work, of course—disconnection and estrangement run through most of these songs.

"Devil's Arcade" was one of three songs Springsteen had written for this project about U.S. soldiers killed in the current Iraq war. Another, "Gypsy Biker," absorbed the misguided hometown jubilation that Bruce had cut from "Long Walk Home," while the third, "Last to Die," took off from then lieutenant John Kerry's 22 April 1971 testimony to the U.S. Senate about the conduct of the Vietnam War. In truth, that last piece would have made a much fierier campaign song for Kerry in 2004 than "No Surrender" had—if only the senator had been as willing to emphasize his antiwar credentials as Springsteen was. Indeed, much of Springsteen's new political material sounded like songs that he probably wished he could have written three or four years earlier, with one song ("Livin' in the Future") touching on the personal shock of the 2004 election and another ("Your Own Worst Enemy") indirectly suggesting the pervasive paranoia and surveillance of the last five years. One of the most devastating songs in this new, political group was the one that would give the eventual album its title: "Magic." Its lyrics hauntingly and evocatively captured the manipulation of reality in which the Bush administration had engaged since the 2000 election, and its music was even reminiscent of John Fogerty's own Bush-era song "Déjà Vu All Over Again."

Indeed, this is how Springsteen and his publicists would spin his fifteenth studio album in press releases and interviews over the next year, emphasizing its political elements, as they had with *The Rising* five years before. But the dozen or so songs on *Magic* aren't quite that simple. Other themes run through them, more personal and less broadly historical ones, and they contain some of Springsteen's most opaque lyrics since *Tunnel of Love* and quite possibly since *Greetings from Asbury Park, N.J.* When Bruce had dipped into his own songbook on both the *Sessions* and *Devils and Dust* tours, *Greetings* was one of the albums that he seemed most eager to rediscover. Many nights on both tours, the songs from that album, along with those from the more obvious solo albums *Nebraska* and *Devils and Dust*, dominated the setlist. The tricky simplicity of a song like "Long Walk Home," for example, seemed indebted to Bruce's songwriting on all three albums, with the bluntness of his more recent songs now suddenly rejoined by the lyrical hermeticism of his early work.

In more ways than one, "Long Walk Home," the song that seems to have given rise to Springsteen's sudden burst of creativity during late 2006, is the signal song for this project: as it becomes more political, it becomes clearer, but as its narrator walks abroad in the world, the listener is still left with the nagging suspicion that there is also something troubling going on at his *home*. If the song's foreground is the politically disconnected world of "Devils and Dust," its background feels a great deal like the intimately disconnected world of "Brilliant Disguise."

Indeed, there is more sex on *Magic* than on any other album Springsteen had released since the administration of the first President Bush. In nearly every case, the sex in these songs is not the pleasure-free kind described in a *Devils and Dust* song like "Reno," and it would be remiss of even the most aesthetically inclined biographer not to ask where all this carnality suddenly came from, especially since the *New York Post* story of August 2006 was not the last one in which someone would allege that Springsteen was sexually unfaithful to Scialfa. In April of 2010, the singer would be named as the "other man" in the divorce proceedings of Arthur and Ann Kelly, a couple from West Long Branch. Ann Kelly attended the same gym as Springsteen, and they had worked out together. According to allegations originally made by Arthur, and subsequently dropped from his complaint, his wife received unsigned Valentine's Day cards in both 2007 and 2008 that he was convinced were from Springsteen.

Whether Springsteen had a sexual relationship with Kelly matters less for our purposes than whether she was the inspiration for a wholly unpolitical *Magic* song like "I'll Work for Your Love." But "I'll Work for Your Love" doesn't sound as if it had sprung from an actual relationship, as a willfully sexual song like "Red Headed Woman" (or even "Candy's Room") had. It sounds like a fantasy, an imagined encounter with an attractive woman running through the head of an otherwise faithful married man. These are the sorts of songs that Springsteen had written both before and after he was married, usually about strippers, songs like "Thundercrack," "Kitty's Back," and "Pilgrim in the House of Love." He had mentioned during the *Storytellers* taping that he didn't go to strip clubs the way he used to, in large part out of respect for Scialfa, but that didn't mean that his mind still didn't wander on occasion. From his first album on, Springsteen's best songs about sex had been drenched in the lust of the body, but these songs were more about the lust of the eye, imagining sex but not necessarily having it. No song on *Magic* demonstrates this more keenly than the languorous "Girls in Their Summer Clothes," who, as Springsteen points out at the end of every chorus, *Pass me by.*

When he was twenty-six, Springsteen had famously declared that *we ain't that young anymore,* but in truth it was only now, when he was fifty-seven, that Springsteen finally copped in his work (rather than in interviews) to the passage of time. He wasn't a teenager anymore, he was a father of teenagers, and the measure of passed time is all over the songs he wrote in late 2006, from the distance he felt from the America in which he had been raised to the wistful realization that he might no longer be an object of teenage lust. Most men reach this latter realization far earlier than Springsteen did, but he was, after all, a rock star.

Less flippantly, Springsteen had another reason to be deeply concerned in late 2006 with the passage of time. About a year earlier, Danny Federici had been diagnosed with melanoma. On 4 October 2006, when the Sessions Band played in Udine, Italy, Springsteen dedicated their tentatively hopeful performance of "When the Saints Go Marching In" to Danny, even though his longtime collaborator doesn't seem to have been in the house that night, or even on the same continent. By the time Bruce gathered the E Street Band to record the songs for *Magic* in March of 2007, the news was more definitive and it wasn't good: Danny's cancer was probably terminal.

No doubt, Danny could be a pill sometimes. He was the only member of the band whose equipment Bruce had actually assaulted. But he was Danny. For twenty-eight out of the last thirty-seven years, he had been behind Bruce, literally, making his music even quirkier than it had been to begin with. As Springsteen later admitted, "If we didn't play together, the E Street Band at this point would probably not know one another. . . . But we do play together. And every night at 8 p.m., we walk out on stage together and that, my friends, is a place where miracles occur . . . old and new miracles. And those you are with, in the presence of miracles, you never forget." "Those you are with who create miracles *for* you," Springsteen added, "like Danny did for me every night, you are honored to be amongst." Firing Danny he could easily imagine (he had already done it at least once), but watching him die, when both he and the band were in a better place than ever, was an entirely different story.

Bruce started working on the new album in Atlanta with Brendan O'Brien in February 2007, almost exactly five years after they had first collaborated on *The Rising*. In early March, Bruce, Garry, Max, and Roy spent an intense five days laying down the base tracks for the album, and the next two months of sessions settled into a desultory routine, with Springsteen and O'Brien usually working during the week, to be joined by band members for specific overdubs on the weekends. This was actually an approach that worked perfectly for Danny, who had never been one for structure. His sly organ part on "Your Own Worst Enemy," which you probably wouldn't notice if you weren't specifically listening for it, was particularly inspired. It made that song much more interesting in a way that his foregrounded organ line for "My City of Ruins" hadn't really done in the studio.

Springsteen and O'Brien purposefully selected songs for this album that they thought would be good "E Street Band songs," but at least half of *Magic* doesn't sound like any previous E Street album, not even the O'Brien-produced *Rising*. Not only had the last few years gotten Springsteen to reconsider his early, denser style of lyric writing, but thirty-one years after *Born to Run*, he seemed ready to reconsider heavily layered production again. All in all, Springsteen seemed less inclined to fetishize "clarity" in his recordings now than at any other point in the last three decades. That was one of the things that would make *Magic* a much more satisfying album artistically than *The Rising* was: in this case, Bruce was enthusiastically bringing production ideas to the table. Several tracks sounded as if they had been produced by a calmer Brian Wilson (with whom Bruce would sing at a benefit in Red Bank in mid-May, while he was still traveling back and forth to Atlanta). Others sounded like something Terry Melcher would have produced for the Byrds back in the days when the Castiles were playing the Left Foot. Not only were this album's lyrics built on the parallax perspective provided by aging, but so was its sound. O'Brien helped Springsteen craft a dozen tracks that sounded like what Phil Spector might have produced if he had been given an iMac for his high school graduation. It would have been easier to set these layered lyrics off with less layered production, but the fact that you know you are listening to a middle-aged re-creation of another era's teenage music reinforces the songs' themes on a preverbal, visceral level.

Magic was done by the middle of June, and its release was set for the early fall. Except for the sweet fluke of the Seeger Sessions, it was Springsteen's most artistically satisfying album since *Lucky Town*, quite possibly since *Tunnel of Love*. At the last minute, a twelfth song was added to the album: a tribute to Terry Magovern, Springsteen's assistant and gatekeeper ("a kind of Cerberus," as one biographer has called him). Bruce wrote the simply titled "Terry's Song" for Magovern's funeral in August, when he couldn't find anything he'd already written that would work. Superficially, adding this song to *Magic* marred the theoretical symmetry of the longings for intimacy that were originally supposed to open and close the album, but it did fit well thematically with a group of songs that were all drenched in mortality. As a coda to the new album, "Terry's Song" stands out, providing a final touch of stark, acoustic directness after the previous eleven songs' extensively produced mystification.

COME SEPTEMBER, Bruce rehearsed the E Street Band hard for the upcoming tour, especially hard considering that they'd spent only three years apart. The now traditional open-rehearsal benefits in late September revealed a fairly conventional show, with seven of the songs from the new album mixed in with predictable standards from *Born to Run*, *Born in the U.S.A.*, and *The Rising*. By this point in Springsteen's career, you could usually tell what kind of a tour it was going to be by whether he favored *River* songs or *Darkness* songs in filling out the setlist. If it was the former, the tour was about fun; if the latter, the tour was about politics. As the rehearsal shows made clear, for this tour it would definitely be *Darkness* songs, essentially picking up the political thread in Springsteen's work from where the E Street Band had left off at the end of the Vote for Change tour.

Politics also dictated the content of Bruce's onstage raps for the

Magic tour, starting with the outdoor concert that he and the band gave in Rockefeller Center for *The Today Show* on 28 September, the album's official release date. The tone the singer took in introducing a frankly unclear song like "Livin' in the Future" was something halfway between the preacher pose that he had adopted during the revival tour and the more specific political voice that he had used with the Sessions Band. In reeling off a list of *the things that we love about America,* he moved in the space of a minute from generalized references (*cheeseburgers, French fries*) to goofy NBC in-jokes (*Tim Russert's haircut, the way that the womenfolk love on Matt Lauer*) to a string of references meant to fire up a fall 2007 New York–area crowd (*the Yankees battling Boston, trans-fats, the Jersey Shore*), with *the Bill of Rights* and *Beachwood Motorcycles* thrown in for good measure. Springsteen then followed this crowd-pleasing list of good things with an alternative list of grievances against King George that wouldn't have been out of place during his performance in New Orleans a year and a half before. *Over the past six years,* he declared, *we've had to add to the American picture: rendition, illegal wiretapping, voter-suppression, no habeas corpus, the neglect of our great city New Orleans and her people, and an attack on the Constitution and the loss of our best young men and women in a tragic war.* This may have been the most direct assault on the administration of a sitting president that had ever been uttered by a musical guest on a network morning show. Probably only Springsteen in full E Street mode could have gotten away with it without being censored in one way or another.

Even though Bruce would joke to the audience at the LA Sports Arena in October about *Magic* being *our smash, smash hit album—for a week or two,* the truth was it was selling respectably that fall. It hit no. 1 on the *Billboard* albums chart in its first week, stayed in the Top 10 for the next few weeks, and would sell steadily about five thousand copies a week well into 2008. That wasn't bad for a fifty-eight-year-old recording artist, especially in the age of file sharing. Springsteen shot several videos for *Magic,* but almost no effort was made to release any of its tracks as singles. Springsteen definitely liked seeing younger people enjoy his music—he and the E Street Band played "Keep the Car Running" with Arcade Fire in Ottawa; he let a young fan propose marriage to his girlfriend onstage the first night in Boston; and he appeared visibly energized when teenagers in the pit got into the show in both Chicago and St. Paul—but he was under no delusions about his importance to twenty-first-century pop. The singles charts now belonged to Justin Timberlake and T-Pain, and the Top 10 "comebacks" of late 2007 were being made by '90s pop bands like Matchbox Twenty. Like most aging rockers of the twenty-first century, Springsteen made a decent amount of money off his albums, and a lot more off his tours.

The sets on the *Magic* tour were short and tight, with no intermission and as many as half a dozen usually unvaried encores. The highlight of the sets, especially for longtime fans, was a swamp boogie version of "Reason to Believe" that was part ZZ Top, part the harp-mic version of the song from the *Devils and Dust* tour, and all country shuffle. It slid out of the eerie "Magic" like a rocket on rails and propelled the audience into a few harder oldies before the full-stop instructional moment of the speech before "Livin' in the Future." After his last two, quieter tours, Bruce was apparently ready to be a rock star again, because the best moments in these sets were loud, almost cacophonous. They were also thematically unrelenting, a further evolution of what the band had done on the Vote for Change tour, and it was only partially leavened at concert's end by five or six feel-good encores. For the most part, it was the political songs from *Magic* that made it onto this tour's setlists, not the songs about love and sex.

Tonally, this approach was very effective, but the sets didn't change much from night to night. They were all tent poles and no tent. When Bruce played the Meadowlands on 9 and 10 October, eighteen out of twenty-three songs were the same between the two nights, not the usual variation that favored repeat customers. Most nights, the real wild card was which song would spotlight Patti, whether it was her own "A Town Called Heartbreak" (off her most recent solo album, *Play It As It Lays*) or one of her duets with Bruce. By late October, she had returned home, to keep an eye on the kids.

As the first U.S. leg wound down that fall, there was a little more variation, much of it centered on Danny. Despite the tight lid that Springsteen's people usually tried to keep on things, there were already rumors about Federici's health, and one couldn't help wondering if the completely apolitical "I'll Work for Your Love" had finally entered the set because it offered the organist a chance to shine. In Albany on 15 November, that song was immediately followed by the seasonally inappropriate "4th of July, Asbury Park," during which there was a spotlight on Danny for the length of the number. In Boston four days later, at the band's last performance before they left for Europe, the show seemed to be all about Danny, with three songs featured from *Wild and Innocent*, the one album on which Springsteen's compositions had been most affected by playing with Federici. On "Kitty's Back" during the encores in particular, Danny played an extended solo that brought the house down. Maybe the organist's illness was supposed to be a secret, but like many secrets it was an open one. At the final bows, Springsteen brought Federici down for a special bow of his own, and the crowd started chanting "Danny!" Less than a week after that second show in Boston, Springsteen was on tour in Europe, with the E Street Band but without Danny. Charlie Giordano from the Sessions Band was subbing for Federici, no one said for how long.

With Sooz subbing for Patti again, this older outfit was starting to look like the Sessions Band, although not necessarily with any of its looseness. If anything, the sets they played in Europe over the next four weeks were even less varied than the ones they had played in the United States. The biggest changes came in the relatively brief stage raps, which could be used to chart Springsteen's week-to-week political concerns. The next presidential election was almost a year away, but it was already on Springsteen's mind. On 8 December, he told the crowd in Copenhagen that he and the band had decided that *all Europeans should vote in the [next] American election. That's right,* he declared, only half joking, *it's everybody's ass!* That was pretty much his message in the "Livin' in the Future" rap through the end of the year, but when the tour resumed with another North American leg later that winter, he told a Montreal crowd in early March during the same spot in the concert, *I do feel a new wind blowing back home.*

What had changed in the last three months? A long shot in the presidential election suddenly became a front runner. In December

2007, in Chicago as well as Copenhagen, two friends talking about the upcoming presidential race could agree that, while they might even like Barack Hussein Obama, the junior senator from Illinois ultimately wasn't "electable." The last two months of Democratic primaries, particularly the ones in February, gave the lie to that hasty conclusion, however. After decisively winning the Iowa caucuses on 3 January, Obama went on to win South Carolina on 26 January, and thirteen out of twenty-two states on 5 February, the "Super Tuesday" of the primary season. For almost a month after that, he was on a hot streak, winning primaries in Louisiana, Nebraska, Washington, Maine, the District of Columbia, Maryland, Virginia, Wisconsin, Hawaii, and the Virgin Islands—ultimately eleven states in a row.

Nothing attracts support like winning, but there was more to Obama's appeal than that. Unlike such previous Democratic presidential nominees as Walter Mondale, Michael Dukakis, and John Kerry, Obama was someone you could see yourself casting a vote *for*, rather than merely against the other guy. From the beginning, Obama's campaign had been a magnet for both young voters and those in the entertainment industry. will.i.am of the Black Eyed Peas had even remade the words of Obama's concession speech after a rare loss in the New Hampshire primary into a free downloadable single called "Yes We Can." As even his critics would admit that winter, the senator possessed a quality that is both overadduced and underappreciated in politics: charisma. On 25 February, five days before Springsteen made his comment about *a new wind blowing*, the *Dayton Daily News* called Obama a "rock star."

It may seem glib to list "star power" as one of the qualities necessary for someone who hopes to lead the most powerful nation in the world, but William Shakespeare for one might be called to support such a claim. (In performance, it can often seem that Henry V succeeds where Richard II failed because the artist formerly known as Prince Hal had learned from his old pal Falstaff how to work a crowd.) In truth, anyone who underestimates how much a modern American president needs to use the media in order to accomplish his goals doesn't understand how political change has actually been effected in this country since at least the advent of broadcasting. The two most far-reaching modern transformations of American government, the New Deal on the left and the Reagan revolution on the right, both succeeded in large part because the presidents spearheading them knew how to work the media of their respective eras. By the late winter of 2008 (or the late summer of 2002, for that matter), being a president like George W. Bush had more in common with being a rock star like Bruce Springsteen than either of those two men would probably want to admit. Both might know a new place where they wanted the crowd to go, but they had to lead them there by familiar paths.

From his first moment on the national stage, Barack Obama had understood this. His keynote speech at the 2004 Democratic National Convention, the one that had nominated John Kerry for the presidency, had flat-out denied that the United States could be divided into Red America and Blue America. "The pundits," he told the crowd in Boston and those who were watching the speech on television and the internet,

> like to slice-and-dice our country into Red States and Blue States; Red States for Republicans, Blue States for Democrats. But I've got news for them. . . . We worship an awesome God in the Blue States, and we don't like federal agents poking around our libraries in the Red States. We coach Little League in the Blue States and have gay friends in the Red States. There are patriots who opposed the war in Iraq and patriots who supported it. We are one people, all of us pledging allegiance to the stars and stripes, all of us defending the United States of America.

Such a statement sounded laughably naïve in the year of Green Day's "American Idiot" and Toby Keith's "Courtesy of the Red, White, and Blue," but Obama kept offering variations on it during the next four years as he moved ever closer to running for president. His earnestness, his seemingly compulsive willingness to embrace all of America rather than just one part of it, actually became an object of derision for at least one of his rivals for the Democratic nomination: Senator Hillary Rodham Clinton, the presumed front-runner. "Making change," Senator Clinton declared in a debate on 5 January 2008, "is not about what you believe. It's not about a speech you make. It is about working hard." "Words," she cautioned, "are not action. As beautifully presented and as passionately felt as they are, they are not action." "No," Senator Obama countered. "The truth is, actually, words do inspire. Words do help people get involved."

Was there ever a presidential candidate who fit better with Bruce Springsteen's worldview? Ronald Reagan may have usurped the aesthetics of a rock show for his presidential campaign, and John Kerry may have enjoyed Springsteen's songs (as Jimmy Carter had enjoyed the songs of Bob Dylan, the Band, and the Allman Brothers Band), but Barack Obama actually thought like a rock star, and the rock star he most frequently sounded like was Bruce Springsteen. The speech at the 2004 convention was his "Land of Hope and Dreams"; his repeated insistence on grassroots involvement was his own version of "You wanna play you gotta pay"; and his greatest speech—"A More Perfect Union," a thoughtful consideration of the role of race in American politics delivered at the National Constitution Center on Monday, 18 March 2008, less than half a day after Springsteen had told a Milwaukee audience, *We need a new wind blowing*—was Obama's own, even more insightful version of "American Skin."

The senator revealed later in the campaign that he actually was a Springsteen fan, although he named the sultry "I'm on Fire" as a favorite, rather than any song that could more clearly be identified as political. Backstage at a fund-raiser that fall, he joked to his wife, Michelle, "The reason I'm running for President is because I can't be Bruce Springsteen." As a young man with visibly dark skin who was raised in a mostly white environment, Obama's teenage years had been as filled with rock as with soul, spent listening as much to Bob Dylan and the Rolling Stones as to Marvin Gaye and Stevie Wonder. As one of the first presidential candidates in American history to be questioned semiregularly on the contents of his iPod, Obama confirmed that his musical tastes were of a piece with his political ones: broader than any FM or satellite radio station could contain and drawn from many seemingly disparate areas of the last half century of American music.

More important, as his autobiography *Dreams from My Father* made clear, Obama had not been born into the "gospel impulse" as Gaye, Wonder, or Aretha Franklin had been. Much like Springsteen, he discovered it during adulthood (at the Trinity United Church of Christ on West Ninety-fifth Street in Chicago rather than at a Sam and Dave show at the Satellite Lounge out on Route 68 near Fort Dix), and he saw that it was the surest path to the world in which he wanted to live. In a passage from the book that he also incorporated into his speech at the National Constitution Center, Obama caught the invigorating mixture of individuals and community that can arise only when those who meet in faith passionately recommit to the weight of the familiar in the rush of the now—Craig Werner's "gospel impulse," in other words, back in its original preconcert setting. "[T]his black church," Obama declared, "on this bright day, seemed once more a vessel carrying the story of a people into future generations and into a larger world." The vessel to which Obama alluded in this passage is probably a ship, but it could just as easily be a train, more like Springsteen's train than Sister Rosetta Tharpe's, boarding as many disparate souls as it can, steaming its way straight to the promised land.

A few weeks after "A More Perfect Union," Bruce Springsteen endorsed Barack Obama for president. The senator stands, Springsteen opined on his website "head and shoulders above the rest" and "speaks to the America I've envisioned in my music for the past 35 years, a generous nation with a citizenry willing to tackle nuanced and complex problems, a country that's interested in its collective destiny and in the potential of its gathered spirit"—a "place," Springsteen added, explicitly linking Obama's campaign to the political sentiments he had recently voiced in "Long Walk Home," "where '. . . nobody crowds you, and nobody goes it alone.'" Not just in his recent speeches but throughout his political career, Obama had repeatedly stated that the primary job of American leaders was "perfecting our imperfect union," and Springsteen clearly concurred. *I've spent most of my creative life,* the singer would declare at one of the senator's political rallies later that year, *measuring the distance between [the] American promise and American reality. I believe Senator Obama has taken the measure of that distance in his own life and in his work.* Springsteen wasn't the first celebrity to endorse Obama, and he wouldn't be the last, but the fact that he came out for him so early in the year suggests a level of engagement with Obama's campaign that may not have existed with regard to John Kerry's candidacy four years earlier.

After his announcement on 16 April, however, Springsteen made no further comment on Obama that week: no joint appearances with the senator, no rallies or performances to capitalize on or generate publicity during that crazy final weekend before the all-important Pennsylvania primary. Instead, he had something far more pressing than politics on his mind.

CHAPTER 14

COME TOMORROW, NONE OF THIS
WILL BE HERE (2008–2009)

*A*FTER ALL THESE YEARS, THERE WAS STILL SOMETHING SPECIAL about the people whom Bruce had first met at the Upstage. He had been playing regularly with Sooz for just four or five years, with Nils and Patti for a little over fifteen years before that, and with Max and Roy for exactly ten years before that. Clarence had become part of his life in the Student Prince and in the recording studio back in 1972. Garry, Steve, and Danny, however, had been there from the beginning, from Steel Mill and the Upstage.

It had been one thing for Bruce to lose his dad eight years earlier—you expect your parents to die before you. Now, though, members of Springsteen's own generation were starting to fall, particularly friends and colleagues from the old Asbury days. Big Danny Gallagher (who had been the Mayor of the Upstage just as surely as Bruce had been its Boss, not to mention an invaluable member of the E Street road crew) died in January of 2008. Two months later, Danny Chinnock (who had been in one band or another during the Nixon years with almost everyone around the Jersey Shore except Bruce) committed suicide rather than face a prolonged death from leukemia.

And then there was Danny Federici. The tour hadn't been the same since Danny left, and that had nothing to do with the substitution of Charlie Giordano, who was a highly talented addition to the E Street Band. Bruce, quite frankly, had been more off than usual. A March show in St. Paul struck some fans as by-the-numbers, and a show in Cincinnati less than a week later was so rushed that Springsteen actually came back out onstage after "American Land," the customary end of the encores, to do one more song. He had also seemed to be thinking a great deal about the past on this leg of the tour. *[T]his is a good building,* he commented at the Blue Cross Arena in Rochester after a particularly hearty sing-along on "Waitin' on a Sunny Day." *Is this a new building or an old building?* The crowd all shouted "Old!" *See,* he answered, assessing the situation from the perspective of a veteran performer, *the old buildings are still the best buildings. [D]on't let them knock this building down,* he said again about an hour later, at the conclusion of the encores. *Keep it up here.*

By anyone's measure, the best of the early-2008 shows was the one in Indianapolis on 20 March. Bruce had been promising Danny Federici's return to audiences all month, but Indianapolis was the place where it actually happened, with no prior publicity, in a barely half-filled arena. Federici was visibly tired, clearly not his old leprechaunish self. He played for only a third of the show, most of it on songs from Springsteen's first three albums, but you could see the spirits of all the other musicians rise as he did so. Before the show, Bruce asked Danny what he wanted to play, and, of course, he said "Sandy." Thirty-five years earlier, Federici had helped Springsteen craft the sound of this precociously nostalgic farewell to the *carnival life* of Asbury Park. On the last day of winter 2008, the valediction sounded twice as bittersweet as it had originally.

That night in Indianapolis was the last time Danny would play that song, and the last time that he and Bruce would play together. Four weeks later, on 17 April, the day after Bruce Springsteen endorsed Barack Obama for the Democratic presidential nomination, Danny Federici finally lost his battle with cancer. That weekend, the band canceled two shows, in Fort Lauderdale and Orlando.

On Tuesday, 22 April, the day after Danny's funeral and the night of the Pennsylvania presidential primary, the E Street Band—all of them, including Scialfa—went back onstage at the St. Pete Times Forum in Tampa, Florida, trying to make music for the first time in a world that would now be forever without their founding organist. The show opened with a video tribute to Danny, cut to the officially released version of "Blood Brothers," the ambivalent tribute to the band that Springsteen had written thirteen years before. Six songs in, they performed "4th of July, Asbury Park," which they hadn't played since Indy, with the ever-precise Professor taking over for the Phantom. *Roy, you better get this one right, man,* Springsteen joked as Bittan stepped out from behind his piano and strapped on an accordion. *Somebody's watching.* The *fairytale* of "Growin' Up" traveled that night to *the highest hill in Flemington, New Jersey,* during Bruce's rap between its second and third verses, and he spontaneously changed the lyrics of the last verse of "Darkness on the Edge of Town" so that he now sang, *I lost my faith when I lost you.* In the encores, Bruce led the E Streeters in a rendition of the old Baptist hymn "I'll Fly Away" that owed a great deal to the Sessions Band's version of "When the Saints Go Marching In," which he had hopefully dedicated to Danny eighteen months before. *Thank you so much for coming out tonight and helping us through,* Springsteen sincerely told the audience before they started the number.

Still a little numb, Bruce and the band played the next two weeks of scheduled concerts in Florida, Virginia, and the Carolinas. Each of them featured a song and monologue in tribute to Danny in the quarter-in slot, where Bruce had been putting any darkness he wanted to purge for over a quarter of a century. In Charlotte, before "Wild Billy's Circus Story," he told an anecdote that he had included in his eulogy, about Danny's car getting towed with a marijuana plant sitting in the shotgun seat. In Greensboro, before "It's Hard to Be a Saint in the City," he brought out the old chestnut about Danny unscrewing elevator buttons in a hotel on tour so he could install them on his organ. In Charlottesville, before "Growin' Up," he cataloged the succession of beat-up vehicles that the band had used to get to gigs back in the early days. At the rescheduled show in Fort Lauderdale, the story was about the brief time the band had spent living in the house on South Street after Doug and Adele had moved out to California. In the first five days after Danny's death, there was an intimate wake and funeral for friends and family, but these concerts in the weeks immediately following felt like a much bigger sort of gathering, at which Bruce and the band could swap memories with the members of what even Springsteen had now taken to calling E Street Nation.

From the earliest shows in 2008, Bruce had seemed to want to shake up this tour, to help the *Magic* sets break out of the tight thematic straitjacket into which he had put them the previous fall, but even a generous helping of *Tracks* songs and audibles couldn't seem to change the vibe. In the wake of Danny's death, there seemed now even more reason to liven things up, and for once Springsteen's fans appeared to know better than he how to fix an off tour. In a holdover from the much looser *Devils and Dust* concerts, fans had started bringing more signs to the *Magic* shows, requesting specific songs, many of them up-tempo or inspirational ones to balance out the noisy dread of the songs that Springsteen was known to play most nights on this tour. No matter what Bruce might have decided the previous fall, his fans seemed convinced that what the tour needed was more *River* songs, particularly "Ramrod" (for which signs had shown up in both Auburn Hills, Michigan, and Hempstead, New York).

It wasn't that audience members were hostile to any of Springsteen's newer songs, as they had been on the revival tour almost a decade before. They did, however, seem to want to hear more of his early work, especially given Danny's absence. In Madrid, twenty thousand audience members saw one fan's sign and shouted in unison for "Thunder Road." "Jungleland" was popular too, as were the "Detroit Medley" and "Incident on 57th Street." *The quality of this sign is very low*, Bruce commented after one particularly slapdash request for "For You" was submitted in Portland, *but we don't let that affect our decision-making processes*. Indeed the same night there was a request for "Jungleland" done up as an elaborately oversized Oregon license plate, as if Bruce were some kind of turnpike-descended Monty Hall choosing contestants for a twenty-first-century rock version of *Let's Make a Deal*. In San Jose, one bald fan even wrote "Glory Days" in marker on his shiny forehead and was brought up onstage beside Bruce, so that everyone could admire his mirror-aided block printing on the Jumbotron. Thanks to the internet, by the time the tour swung back to Europe in late spring, the collection of signs had become an expected part of the concert. On 30 May at the new Emirates Stadium in London, Bruce asked, *Who's got the signs?*, much as he had declared, *Bootleggers, roll your tapes*, thirty years before, now acknowledging this new precondition of his working existence.

In many cases, the songs fans requested were ones the band had done recently or often did, so it was no trouble. This made the sign collection on this tour something like the legendary "Wheel of Elvis" with which Elvis Costello had toured back in 1986. In those concerts, an audience member would spin the wheel to decide the next number, thus seeming to add a wholly random element to the performance—but the Wheel of Elvis held only forty songs, which was a manageable amount of material for a band to learn and keep on tap. Costello's wheel loosened things up on a tour with a slightly new band, but it didn't make things too chaotic. This was pretty much how Springsteen's sign collections worked in early 2008. Once in a while, though, the E Street Band would get requests for which they just weren't ready. Back in Sacramento in early April, Steve (who was always ready to do anything from the *River* sessions and had requested— and gotten—"Loose Ends" on the setlist in Milwaukee) pointed excitedly to a man who was holding a sign for "Held Up without a Gun," but Bruce did not feel ready to play it.

But something changed on 14 June, in Amsterdam of all places, which had never before been the site of a particularly noteworthy Springsteen concert. For some reason that night (it may have had something to do with the Dutch audience's delight over their national team's chances in the World Cup), everyone felt fairly giddy, including the band. So Bruce did his usual sign collection during "Spirit in the Night," laying the cards on the stage, making a new setlist in his mind, picking some songs to do right away, some to slot in later in the show around the ones that were already on the setlist. That night in Amsterdam, one of the signs was for "Summertime Blues," which the E Street Band had done fairly regularly for a while—over a quarter of a century before. That meant Charlie, Soozie, and Nils hadn't done it, and none of the others had rehearsed it since Barack Obama was in college. Nevertheless, in the encores, Bruce called for it, and the band flew—like the Wright Brothers at Kitty Hawk, with dips and lifts, but it flew. The rawness of the performance was so intoxicating for the musicians that at the end of the number Steve started to play the opening chords of Them's

"Gloria," as if he was ready for that one too. The irony was delicious: even though Bruce introduced them many nights as *the best little bar band in the world*, the E Street Band had been a highly organized corporate entity for decades now. Were they really going to go back to being a cover band, the very thing Bruce had fled from thirty-six years before?

The answer appeared to be yes. Two nights later in Hamburg, they didn't do "Gloria," but they did do something even more interesting: "Held Up without a Gun." In Amsterdam, Bruce recovered with the E Street Band what he had regained without them on his 2005 and 2006 tours: the fearlessness of youth. Two nights later in Antwerp, before a banner-requested "Thundercrack," Bruce proclaimed the E Street Band to be *always ready . . . almost always!* Two nights after that in Milan, he was playing "None but the Brave" by sign request, for only the second time ever in front of an audience. If you needed any further indication that Bruce was having the time of his life playing with this level of uncertainty, you got it at the end of the encores in Milan when he called for his old favorite "Twist and Shout."

"Twist and Shout," which the E Street Band had not played in five years, closed out more than half of their remaining concerts in Europe that summer. Not that there weren't missed cues—in Paris, Bruce called out for "Fire," and Max started "I'm on Fire"—but they were all clearly having the time of their lives. When Bruce and the band came back to the States for two months of stadium dates that would close out the tour, they brought their anything-goes attitude with them. With every new stop, the tour became more interactive, and the sign-collection segment became the heart of every concert. *Oh my God*, Bruce said onstage in Hershey, Pennsylvania, two weeks before the end of the tour. *We've created a monster.* Whether it was a representative measure of his audience's preferences or simply Bruce's own inevitable preference for a challenge—*We're going for obscurity*, he instructed Steve in Hershey when he sent him to pick a few of the hundreds of signs—most nights there was at least one unique cover, often one the band hadn't done since the 1970s. The requests for Springsteen songs were now getting fairly unique too. In Jacksonville someone requested and got "Back in Your Arms Again," and three nights later, in Richmond, Bruce got a request that stopped him cold. At the start of the encores, he held up someone's sign for "Crush on You" (a *River* track that the band hadn't performed in twenty-eight years) and proudly announced, *We firmly believe this is the worst song we ever put on a record*, and then led the band through a performance of it.

If the sign collections had just been about Springsteen obscurity or geeky completism, it wouldn't have mattered all that much, but that spontaneity spilled out to affect other parts of the shows that summer. Even as Bruce had sung *Is there anybody alive out there?* in "Radio Nowhere" to open most of the shows on the first half of the *Magic* tour, it had been fair to ask whether there was anybody alive *up here* as well. *Magic* was an exquisitely composed album, but in 2007 and early 2008 the sets on the tour to support it had seemed predetermined weeks before audience members ever got into their seats. In the summer of 2008, not knowing what they were going to do, often changing as much as a third of the setlist onstage after the house lights went down, the E Street Band now made it clear that they were *alive* as well. As the *Devils and Dust* tour had showcased the length and breadth of Springsteen's songwriting, the back half of the *Magic* tour was now showcasing the full history of the E Street Band, from "Then She Kissed Me" and "Little Queenie" down to "Gypsy Biker" and "I'll Work for Your Love." By the last date in the tour, at a festival celebrating the 105th anniversary of the founding of Harley Davidson, Steve could joke at a photo shoot just before the show that they should play "Born to Be Wild" themselves rather than just play a tape of it as they walked off-stage after their performance—and Bruce could take the idea seriously. It didn't matter that they hadn't had time to rehearse the song and that around a hundred thousand people were waiting to see them perform. They were the E Street Band: they could do anything.

And as the band loosened up, so did Springsteen. "On stage," he would say about a year later, "your exhilaration is in direct proportion to the void you're dancing over," and all these sudden, risky changes left Bruce feeling exhilarated onstage that year. As he rediscovered the spontaneity with the E Street Band that they had had back in the beginning, before they were a business, and that he had recently rediscovered as a solo performer, he also eased up on his exaggerated stage personae.

In particular, for one remarkable moment during the concert on 31

July, the last of three nights at Giants Stadium, there almost seemed to be no persona at all, just Bruce. This particular batch of Meadowlands concerts already felt like onstage parties, with family and friends added to the lineup as casually as earlier on the Sessions tour. That last night, though, the proximity of both Patti's fifty-sixth birthday (the night before) and C's fourth wedding (six days later) prompted Bruce to muse on the nature of love and attachment, including the fourteen years he had known Scialfa before falling in love with her. *Let's see,* he said, not even looking at the audience, just at Patti, with his smile growing broader with each passing second, *I first met Pats when I was 20 and she was 17. And then again when I was 24 and she was 21. And again when I was 35 and she was 32. In the meantime, something happened to me,* he drawled, alluding to his brief first marriage without actually mentioning it. *So I guess you can't say,* he concluded, not really looking at anyone for a moment, *that I believe in love at first sight.* Then he looked back at Scialfa and neither spoke, but now both were smiling very broadly, Patti with that "what am I going to do with you?" look she sometimes put on when Bruce tried to drag her into the spotlight when she didn't want to be there.

Springsteen had never made such comments in public before and would never make them afterward. As he said them, they seemed as natural and authentic as his nightly park bench conversations with Clarence on the *Tunnel of Love* tour had seemed forced. Here he sounded as if he was speaking from his heart to his wife and one of his friends—in front of fifty thousand people. And then he called for "Pretty Flamingo," which the band had played only two times in the last three decades. As they played, he shouted out instructions, as he had during the Seeger Sessions, to guide his fellow musicians through the trickier parts of a song that they might not remember.

WHEN THE *MAGIC* TOUR ended a month later, after the boldly improvised cover of "Born to Be Wild" that closed out the Harley Davidson concert, Bruce declared, *Thank you, we'll be seeing you. We're only just getting started!*—and he wasn't kidding. During the few breaks during the last months of the tour, he had already started recording another album with the E Street Band. But another studio album, his fifth in six years, almost wasn't the point. "You are in a manic state," Patti told Bruce in late 2008, knowing him better and in more ways than anyone else on the planet, "running like crazy from, let me think, death itself?"

Clearly, Danny's death, and all the deaths of the last few years (not to mention the ways in which the band and the fans had reacted to them) had triggered something in Springsteen in the summer of 2008, but this wasn't just about death or aging. Bruce's burst of activity and creativity went back farther than the spring of 2008, at least three years back to the spring of 2005 and the awakening of the *Devils and Dust* tour. Before that, Springsteen had been blocked for ten or twelve years, not really knowing where to go after the *Tom Joad* songs. By all accounts, he was still writing, but he found only a fraction of the material he wrote during the late 1990s and early 2000s worth recording or performing. He was happy for the most part during these years, joyously engaged in a loving, committed relationship and delighted to be a father, but as a songwriter and performer his work during that period was too frequently hit or miss.

One clue to what might have caused this difficulty comes in a song that Springsteen wrote and recorded solo in the summer of 2008, as a favor to an old friend. Bruce had been close to the actor Mickey Rourke during the late 1980s, when he had been spending a lot of time in Los Angeles. The intervening years had been much kinder to Springsteen than to Rourke, but the two men had evidently kept in touch. The film director Darren Aronofsky was less a friend than a fan of Rourke's, but he had commissioned the script for *The Wrestler,* a story about a violent, self-destructive, substance-abusing, washed-out star of the 1980s, with Rourke in mind. In May of 2008, when the movie was in postproduction, Rourke contacted Springsteen on tour in Dublin and told him about the part and what playing it meant to him. The way Rourke told it, "[a] while later I got a call in the middle of the night; Bruce said he'd written a little song, for nothing." Both Rourke and Aronofsky attended the "Pretty Flamingo" concert on 31 July, and backstage after the show Springsteen played the song for them.

Nearly all the responses to *The Wrestler* noted its story's strong autobiographical echoes for Mickey Rourke, but almost no one noted how

Springsteen's song for the film (a true Thrill Hill creation, with no other vocalists and instrumentalists and no listed producers other than himself) may also have been a piece of alternative autobiography for the songwriter. As such songs as 1984's "Dancing in the Dark" and 1992's "Local Hero" (to name only two) showed, Springsteen was seldom averse to puncturing his own balloon of self-importance. It may have been easy for him to look at Rourke's character in the film and see an aspect of himself, a road not taken. Like Randy the Ram, both Rourke and Springsteen were associated, rightly or wrongly, with the macho posturing of the Reagan era. In fact, Springsteen had taken the radical step of breaking up the E Street Band—just around the time that he befriended Rourke—precisely because he was afraid of being a *one-trick pony.* And the lesson of the 1990s for the singer was that there was indeed *anything more* than the sheer rush and sometimes impersonal payback of highly calculated live performance for humongous crowds. This suggestion seems even more likely when we note Springsteen's self-reported response to Rourke's initial description of his character in Aronofsky's film: "Well," he said drily, "I know a couple of those guys." As a matter of fact, he had almost been one of them.

As Springsteen told interviewer after interviewer in 1992, the way he kept himself from becoming the rock star equivalent of Randy the Ram was through "connection," but when he said that he meant connection with his friends and family. For over a dozen years, though, he didn't know how to connect with his audience, something that he thought he had instinctively known how to do since he was fifteen. In his forties and fifties, Bruce didn't want to go back to his unthinking, younger ways, but he also felt increasingly estranged from his audience, as songs like "Devils and Dust," "Long Walk Home," and "Radio Nowhere" clearly attested. How could he be *alive* to fifty thousand strangers, and they to him, without its being some kind of glitzy rock star sham? All of this was harder for Springsteen than it would have been for an artist who preferred to court a select, elite audience. He wanted to be truthful and insightful with the largest audience possible, to somehow make art and meaning together with his audience, and to move society forward by doing so.

This was another way in which Springsteen's work ethic more

closely paralleled Barack Obama's than many commentators probably understood. Obama was not just a former "community organizer" (as was Jesus, as one pro-Obama button reminded Republicans during the election). He saw community organizing as an essential model for government, a model that was strikingly at odds with both the technocratic utopia that many of his fellow liberals might endorse and the publicly held corporation that many conservatives implicitly envisioned. One of the many songs that the Obama campaign played at their rallies throughout 2008 was "The Rising." In particular, they played it at the conclusion of the candidate's speech on 7 June, after Senator Clinton finally conceded the race for the Democratic nomination to him. The song fit Obama's candidacy far better than most casual listeners realized. As with "Born in the U.S.A.," if you hear only the choruses of "The Rising," it may seem like yet another song to make people feel good about feeling bad. At its heart, though, the song is about how the leader and the congregation always help each other.

Never has this seemed clearer than on 18 January 2009, two days before Obama's presidential inauguration (and a week after "The Wrestler" won a Golden Globe for Best Original Song Written for a Motion Picture), when Springsteen performed "The Rising" as the first professional musician to take the stage at a celebratory concert at the Lincoln Memorial. On that bitterly cold Sunday on the mall in Washington, facing a world and an economy that had grown worse nearly every day of the two months since his election, the president-elect, like the preacher-firefighter in Springsteen's song, may have known that he had the experience and the skills to tackle the job at hand. Still, no one would have blamed him if he had honestly doubted for a moment, as the singer does in that song, whether he was equal to so massive a challenge. The performance of "The Rising" that day, in which Springsteen on solo acoustic guitar is backed up by the Joyce Garrett Singers, a well-traveled gospel choir, doesn't come close to earlier versions of the song (particularly the August 2002 one in front of the Rose Space Center), but three years after that concert it seems like the one performance on the mall that day that actually caught in advance the dominant tone of President Obama's first two years in office.

Neither Obama nor Springsteen could give up on those fellow

Americans from whom they seemed separated. They needed them in order to succeed. Late in the *Magic* sessions, Springsteen had written a song called "What Love Can Do," which seems like yet another stage in the evolution of his thinking about his wider audience and their differences in perspective. Rapid as they were, the *Magic* sessions can almost be seen as a journey from the estranged departure of "Long Walk Home" to the begrudging challenge of this aggressively optimistic song. Lines like *When the hope you've gathered's drifted to the wind / And it's you and I my friend* recall the *When the party's over* verse that he had ended up dropping from that earlier song. This time, though, rather than walking away from the dispute as the narrator in "Long Walk Home" did, the narrator of "What Love Can Do" stands his ground and demands of his listener, *Let me show you what love can do,* denying the premise of so much public discourse of the last two decades, which insisted that initially opposed points of view were fixed and irredeemably separate. Even though it was only the seed of Springsteen's sixteenth studio album, "What Love Can Do" suggests that the songwriter's new optimism about his relationship with his audience may have predated his 2007–08 tour. Still, it wasn't until the end of that tour, almost a year later, that his actual interactions with his audience seemed to justify such hope.

As Springsteen's sixteenth studio album grew through late 2008, however, it became less a theme-driven project like *Magic* and more of a catchall album like *Devils and Dust.* Carrying over from the giddiness of the last stretch of the *Magic* tour, maybe it was just too exciting to release another album again this quickly to fuss over it too much with deliberation and overplanning. The new album, entitled *Working on a Dream* (after what was probably its weakest song and almost certainly the weakest title song of any Springsteen album) was announced in December 2008 and released in January 2009, with a huge publicity push, including free downloads, Guitar Hero plugins, a Walmart greatest hits collection, and a performance during the halftime at the Super Bowl. "At my age," Springsteen frankly admitted to one music critic, "it is tough to get word of your music out. . . . If we weren't doing these big things, there's no middle things."

In April of 2009, the E Street Band members were back on tour, a little less than half a year after they had wrapped up their last one. Moreover, they were now enlarged by two new backup singers, Curtis King and Cindy Mizelle—new to the E Street Band, but not necessarily to Springsteen concerts. The addition of King and Mizelle meant that half the people onstage during the *Working on a Dream* tour, six out of twelve, had also toured with the Sessions Band. At times, it seemed as if Springsteen was trying to combine those two bands to make this his ultimate tour. Not only was "American Land" still at the end of the encores most nights, but Stephen Foster's "Hard Times" was often at the beginning.

The Foster song was intended less as a Sessions-style reworking of a prerock standard than as an explicit acknowledgment of the current recession. For the second time in his career, Springsteen had released one of his happiest albums at a time when the nation, including his fans, were being plunged into economic misery. Springsteen responded by trying to build the quarter-in spot on this tour around the concerns of the recession, running "Seeds," "Johnny 99," and "The Ghost of Tom Joad" together. Indeed, the crowd seemed to respond much more to the last of these songs on this tour than it had on the revival tour at the end of the go-go '90s.

The sign collections from the *Magic* tour persisted on this one, and once again the crowd seemed to want a less somber mood, even if the economy was in the tank. The requested covers in particular kept getting crazier and crazier, including "I'm Bad I'm Nationwide," "Expressway to Your Heart," "Seventh Son," "I Wanna Be Sedated," "Hava Nagila," and "96 Tears." *They think they're gonna stump the band*, Bruce kidded the crowd in Atlanta on 26 April, *but this is the greatest bar band in the land, and if they don't think we know 96 fuckin' Tears*. The redemption Bruce's fans wanted in the face of 2009 was not the singer's own personal redemption as expressed in the gorgeous "Kingdom of Days" (even though he did perform that song most nights near the end of the main set), nor was it the social and even political redemption of "Badlands" or "The Promised Land" (the latter being one of the songs Springsteen had performed on acoustic guitar at every one of his campaign appearances for now president Obama the previous fall). No, what the crowds wanted was rock 'n' roll redemption, the catharsis that only a mythically enlarged bar band can give.

The Blue Cross Arena in Rochester wasn't the only old box that Springsteen admired on this tour. During the recession, it seemed as if the only large construction projects that could get off the ground in most cities were new sports arenas, tearing down the "old" ones in those cities that were often just about as old as Springsteen's career. The older arenas were usually physically hotter than the new ones, but their acoustics were much better for rock shows, especially the sorts of participatory shows that Springsteen liked to run. On 16 April, Bruce referred to the LA Arena as *the dump that jumps*. A few weeks later at the Spectrum in Philadelphia, on 28 April, the singer praised both that ostensibly obsolete building and the Arena in LA. *They don't make arenas like this anymore*, he declared, noting that the Spectrum was the first arena that the E Street Band had ever played. The next night at the Spectrum, he led off the first version of "Thundercrack" on this tour by declaring, *We're gonna take this one back to the Main Point!*

So when it was announced that they would be tearing down Giants Stadium in the Meadowlands, the scene of at least a dozen legendary Springsteen concerts, fans began to speculate whether Bruce would get to play that joint one last time. No stadium dates were scheduled for the tour at that point, not even in Jersey, just three shows at the smaller, enclosed Izod Center at the Meadowlands. (When Bruce had inaugurated that venue with a series of concerts back in 1981, it was simply called the Brendan Byrne Arena, after a former governor rather than a vendor of alligator shirts.) Sure enough, at the top of the encores at the first Izod show, on 21 May, Springsteen announced that there would be three E Street Band shows in Giants Stadium in the fall, the last concerts ever given in the venue before it was torn down. *Before they bring the wrecking ball*, he declared, *the wrecking crew is coming back.*

The full significance of that sentence wasn't clear until the first of what ended up being five E Street concerts that closed out Giants Stadium. On 30 September, when Bruce stepped up to the microphone to begin the first show, after a preliminary greeting, he added something no one was expecting: *Here's a little something I wrote for tonight.* The song was called "Wrecking Ball," and it was another one of his inspired occasional pieces, this time taking off from the stadium's imminent demolition. As he began the song, Bruce strummed his acoustic guitar lustily, with a big grin on his face, ready for the Jersey audience to respond on the song's obvious applause lines, references to *the swamps of Jersey, the mud and the beer,* the *Giants,* and the legendary size of Meadowlands *mosquitoes.*

But as the song's lyrics went on—and this was one Springsteen premiere whose lyrics the audience could instantly follow, because they were scrolling on a big screen behind the band—it became clear that they weren't just about football or stadiums. One sweet clue to the song's true subject was in its first line: *I was raised out of steel here in the swamps of Jersey, some misty years ago.* If it hadn't been for the scroll, it would have been easy to mishear that line. It wouldn't have taken much imagination for a fan to hear *sixty* there instead of *misty,* especially since Bruce had just passed that milestone birthday about a week before. Also out of sync with a mere local reading of the song was another line in its second verse: *Tonight all the dead are here,* which makes almost no sense in terms of football, but does make perfect sense in terms of the recent history of the E Street Band.

As the revival tour had in retrospect seemed to be inevitably tending toward the as-yet-unwritten "American Skin," so too did the relatively brief *Working on a Dream* tour (and possibly even the latter half of the *Magic* tour before it) seem in retrospect to tend toward "Wrecking Ball," a fabulous, even joyful song about mortality that turned this last Giants Stadium stand into a grand old Irish wake. Curt Ramm— yet another touring member of the Sessions Band, which meant that a majority of people onstage for what inevitably came to be called the "Wrecking Ball" shows had been part of that group's 2006 tour— played trumpet on the song's wordless choruses like a New Orleans– steeped Gabriel who just can't wait for Judgment Day. When Bruce first sang, *Bring on your wrecking ball,* it sounded like something of a barroom boast in the face of Death, but when he was later joined by the full harmony vocals of almost everyone onstage, the effect of the phrase was almost anagogic. *Yeah we know that come tomorrow,* Springsteen's lyric admitted in the bridge, right where it should, *none of this will be here,* but that doesn't mean that you should lie down and stop trying to regularly do the impossible anyway. As the song entered its third verse, the metaphor was drawn even more closely:

When all this steel and these stories, they drift away to rust
And all our youth and beauty, it's been given to the dust
And your game has been decided, and you're burning down the clock
And all our little victories and glories have turned into parking lots
When your best hopes and desires, are scattered to the wind

And hard times come, and hard times go, Bruce went on, and as he sang that line over and over, the sound of Max Weinberg's bass drum became more insistent, doubling up the beat after the first two iterations, as if Death or the demolition crew was already tapping at the door before the concert had even started. *Just to come again,* Bruce admitted, leaving aside his articulated politics for one night to readopt the sort of cyclical view of history he had embraced in his late twenties. *Bring on your wrecking ball,* he exclaimed proudly to fifty thousand fans as the mighty E Street Band backed him up. *Bring on your wrecking ball / Come on and take your best shot, let me see what you've got / Bring on your wrecking ball!*

Much like the band's Super Bowl appearance the previous January, when younger viewers who didn't know Springsteen from Adam were astonished to see him knee-slide across the stage right into the cameraman, a boast like this meant more at sixty than it would have at thirty. One visitor who got to ride with the band out to the Harley Davidson gig the prior summer later commented on how much older they all seemed offstage. "You can't tell from listening to the shows," he observed, "but these men are hurting in the way that men this age hurt." Nils, despite the astonishing acrobatics he had displayed all throughout the *Magic* tour during his extended solo on "Because the Night," had had both hips replaced the past fall. Clarence had had both knees replaced between these last two tours and could barely stand. Max wore a back brace. Even Bruce, who was in excellent condition for a man of his age, sometimes needed to sip a cup of specially prepared tea during the sax solo on "Jungleland" so that he could produce a wholly satisfying wail at the song's end. Within a year, Max would have major invasive open-heart surgery. Within two years, Clarence would be dead.

But here they were, in the fall of 2009, facing death and aging by enjoying their life onstage as much as they could, *dancing together on the high wire*, as Springsteen had written in "The Last Carnival," a song in memory of Danny that was *Working on a Dream*'s penultimate track, using a metaphor that went back to "Born to Run" and even earlier, *breathin' the smoke and the fire / On the Midway*. And the projected lyrics of "Wrecking Ball" meant that the fans could dance with them at these concerts as well, singing along communally, not to a song that they had memorized decades earlier, but to one that had been written to commemorate the here and now. The song began each of the final five Giants Stadium concerts not with ritual but with the true catharsis of collective improvisation. Bruce not only chatted with the crowd in the pit during these shows; he stage-dived and surfed it during "Hungry Heart." And if that isn't an act of faith in his fans on the part of a sixty-year-old rock star, I don't know what it is.

For these Meadowlands shows, Springsteen decided to repeat the satisfying trick the band had performed at a Count Basie Theatre benefit just after Danny's death: they performed some of their best-known albums front to back—*Born to Run* at two concerts, *Born in the U.S.A.* at another two, and *Darkness on the Edge of Town* once. Each time, Springsteen made sure to give bows after the album set was completed to the six musicians present who had originally recorded them, *the guys who made the music. And Phantom Dan Federici*, he always added. The versions of the individual songs on those albums sounded more like the recorded versions than some of his wilder experiments over the years, but they were also inevitably longer than the recorded versions. Virtually every instrumentalist on the stage got an extended solo in one of these performances, even the ones who may not have been around back in the day when Bruce was a lot more of a control freak about his music.

When the tour was extended to include four official final nights at the Spectrum a few weeks later, Bruce brought along the front-to-back album concept with him, as well as a slightly rewritten version of

"Wrecking Ball" that referred to *cheesesteaks* [not mosquitoes] . . . *as big as airplanes* and commemorated a spot where *Dr. J* [not Giants] *played the game*. After continuously touring for almost two years, he and the band still had a few surprises up their sleeves, whether they got signs to request them or not. Those four nights in Philly, they threw in tour premieres of everything from "When You Walk into the Room" (which they hadn't performed since the Chicken Scratch tour) to "What Love Can Do" (which they had never performed, not even at a rehearsal show). When two more dates were added at Madison Square Garden in early November, Bruce decided to do the instrumentally complex *Wild and Innocent* and the double-disc set *The River* front to back as well at those two concerts, even though nobody had been talking about tearing that building down lately. With "Human Touch" and "Living Proof" added for good measure, it was hard to think of a phase of Springsteen's career that wasn't being thrown into the mix.

But, of course, there was one of his classic 1970s albums left that Springsteen hadn't done yet, and it was soon announced that on the last night of the tour, on 22 November in Buffalo, the E Street Band would play—for one time only—*Greetings from Asbury Park, N.J.* front to back, ending this epic tour where Springsteen's recording career had begun. Some fans expected a requiem—how much longer could these guys keep touring?—but Springsteen was having none of it, insisting during his usual rap during "Working on a Dream" that they were *here one last time . . . for a* little *while. It's been just about the best time in our band's work life,* he exclaimed. *We want to thank you for supporting our old music, our new music, our tour.* The play-through of *Greetings* was impressive, as all these album sets had been, even "The Angel," which Springsteen appeared to have finally figured out how to perform thirty-eight years after he had recorded it. That afternoon, he called his first manager, Mike Appel, with whom he had been reconciled for at least a decade, and asked him if he'd like to come up for the concert. Springsteen ended up dedicating the performance that night to Appel, *the man who got me in the door.*

The real story that night of 22 November 2009, though, was Steve Van Zandt's fifty-ninth birthday. *Stevie,* Bruce declared, *is my age, and for years he's been asking to play this one song.* That night, Bruce and the band played "Restless Nights" (a *River* discard that had been included on *Tracks*) for the first time ever, and it sounded every bit like a great lost single. *Dammit,* Bruce proclaimed just after the performance, *he might have been right all these years!* A roadie brought out an enormous birthday cake, with decorations that noted *The Sopranos,* the Disciples of Soul, the Underground Garage, Wicked Cool Records, and several other things that Steve usually did when he wasn't actively enrolled in the E Street Band. Then Bruce led the audience in "Happy Birthday," the very song that he had claimed in this same arena a little over four years earlier he would never add to one of his setlists.

After that, the song Bruce called for was "Surprise Surprise," which many fans held in even lower esteem than "The Angel." On *Working on a Dream,* the song had seemed disposable, juvenile, and almost meaningless, despite its borrowed "All You Need Is Love" riff. The dreaded "Crush on You" was at least catchier than "Surprise Surprise," and the band had performed it only a handful of times before on this tour, just twice in the United States. Tonight, however, the song's lyrics (*Today is your birthday we traveled so far we two . . .*) were drenched in meaning. As they played, Bruce fed Steve cake, and the band members were laughing and smiling at each other. Once again, it felt as if the audience was in on what might easily have been a private celebration. They were all sharing this, and this moment would never happen again.

HOUSE LIGHTS UP:
MEET ME IN A DREAM OF
THIS HARD LAND

A rock 'n' roll audience, June 2011, New York, NY.
CAMERA PRESS/Tina Paul/Redux

*P*REDICTABLY, CELL PHONE VIDEOS OF THE BUFFALO PERFORMANCE showed up on YouTube the following morning. Rock music was a world away from where it had been forty-five and a half years earlier when Springsteen had watched the Beatles demolish "Twist and Shout" on *The Ed Sullivan Show*. Now you didn't need a TV to watch bands, a record player to listen to albums, or a studio like Mr. Music to cut a single. In a few years, Evan James would post two of his own songs on a Myspace page, something that would have sounded like science fiction to his father back in the days when he was writing "Resurrection" and "Garden State Parkway Blues." And he didn't get to do it because his dad was a rock star. Any kid could do it if he had access to a decent laptop. The internet had taken the promise that AM radio had held for kids like Bruce in the 1950s and made it global. Every kind of music is out there now, much of it available for free, and all the freaks can find all the other freaks in the globe if they only know how to surf the medium. With the help of sites like BandCamp and Kickstarter, they can even bypass the record labels.

The digital age has changed the way Bruce Springsteen sells his music, but it hasn't really changed the way he performs it. If anything, as the technology of popular music has grown more elaborate, Springsteen's performance techniques have grown more archaic, as he includes more obsolete and varied musical styles under his unusually inclusive definition of pop. He rarely has a bad word to say about anybody's music, and even now he embraces younger rock bands much more frequently and publicly than he does politicians. Some of these bands (such as the Dropkick Murphys, the National, and the Kings of Leon) go on to greater success, but others (particularly Marah, whose "Float Away" contains one of the sweetest Springsteen guest shots ever) just remain personal favorites, much like their elders Joe Ely and Joe Grushecky. In all these encounters, Springsteen doesn't necessarily seem to cherish bands that sound like his, but rather ones that proceed from a common basis in the music of the 1960s and 1970s and build on that musical foundation in new, hitherto undreamt-of ways.

On 21 January 2009, Arcade Fire, one of the younger rock bands that Springsteen enjoys that would later go on to greater stardom, returned the favor of the E Street Band's cover of "Keep the Car Running" by playing a very loose mandolin-and-accordion-inflected version of "Born in the U.S.A.," under a banner that read "Fulfilling America's Promise." No tickets had been sold for this particular performance at the District of Columbia Armory, which had also featured a set by Jay-Z. It was the Obama staff party, a final thank-you two days after the inauguration for four thousand campaign workers who had helped the junior senator from Illinois become the forty-fourth President of the United States.

Arcade Fire's performance of this cover was obviously a tip of the hat to Springsteen's impassioned support for Obama, but it was also yet another reinvention of a song that had been repeatedly transformed over the last three decades—the song, after all, that had sucked Springsteen into the swamp of American electoral politics in the first place. Since its origin as a vaguely boppy acoustic blues (just after the VVA benefit in 1981), "Born in the U.S.A." had been a synthesizer-driven wail of pain (in the studio in 1982); an opening thesis statement that notably mixed swagger and desperation (on the 1984–85 world tour); and then, after a decade's absence from Springsteen's setlists, a gloomy acoustic blues (on the 1995–97 solo tour) that made the song much less joyous and defiant than it was in its original solo incarnation. Even when Springsteen reunited with the E Street Band at the turn of the twenty-first century, he continued to insist on performing "Born in the U.S.A." acoustically, but now with a far more ornate strumming pattern than he had used on the solo tour. This fifth incarnation of the song reflected, as much of that revival tour did, Springsteen's troubled concern for a country that was now led by members of his own generation, whose service in or protest of the Vietnam War frequently shaped their responses to contemporary problems.

Arcade Fire's 2009 performance of "Born in the U.S.A." took the song and remade it once again, in an unplugged style much like the country stabs at other Springsteen songs that the E Street Band had taken during the revival tour. The song sounded old in this version, not quite old enough for Pete Seeger to "collect," but still clearly a part of the twentieth-century past. For "Born in the U.S.A." was old for this band, as well as for its audience. A YouTube video of the performance shows a crowd of young campaign workers in front of the stage, and as you watch them attend to the song, you can't help thinking that none of them were alive during the Vietnam War, the essential context for the song's narrator and his problems. In fact, it looks as if many of them weren't even alive in 1984 when Springsteen released the original version of the song. For these Gulf War–era youths, the song might just as well be about the Civil War, as so many Band and Dylan songs had been in the late 1960s. The meaning of "Born in the U.S.A." has been debated and reformulated for over a quarter of a century, not least by its own author, but in a performance like this, one wonders if it's just about blind patriotism again, for liberals this time rather than for conservatives (and even if it is sung on this occasion by Canadians).

But no matter what Sha Na Na might have told you back in the 1970s, the golden age of rock 'n' roll is always now. Arcade Fire's performance of "Born in the U.S.A." was a great one, whether it served Springsteen's original intentions for the song or not. It remade the song to fit a new moment, the same way so many of Springsteen's own covers had done over the years. Burning down the second decade of the twenty-first century, on a good Saturday night in a town full of music, rock 'n' roll can take dozens of forms, many of which have no more in common with each other than a faint origin in that mid-twentieth-century explosion of crosscultural, broadcast-assisted musical borrowing. And rock 'n' roll doesn't have to be for or about teenagers, even though they are usually the first ones to discover what new forms of it are coming down the pike. At its best and most transformative, though, rock 'n' roll always lives—with crackling energy—in the present.

"That's what you get paid for," Springsteen has said of his work, "TO BE HERE NOW!" But to be consistently and vitally present, to speak as truthfully as you can to decades of Now on this planet, is a considerable challenge. The defaulting Manhattan of the early 1970s, the deindustrialized New Jersey of the late 1970s; the shame and hope of Ronald Reagan's U.S.A.; the divided communities of early 1990s Los Angeles; the shaky good fortune of Bill Clinton's America; the absence-haunted suburbs of the days after 9/11; the culturally estranged home front of the Second Gulf War—Bruce Springsteen has captured all of these places and times in his best work, and he has done so while trying to appeal to the largest possible audience. Since the end of the *Working on a Dream* tour and especially the "Wrecking Ball" shows, there have been Springsteen reissues, box sets, and interviews, all of them reexamining the glory days of the past, but forty years after he first signed with Columbia Records it is amazing how many people in the world still eagerly anticipate what Bruce Springsteen will do next.

When rock works, whether live or recorded, a performer connects with an audience and they meet in that vital present, that Now. Sometimes, against all odds, the performer can even connect meaningfully with a fairly broad audience. A remarkable performer can shape the audience's perception, a remarkable audience can shape the performer's perception, and together they can be shaped by and even shape the moment itself. All of that is what Bruce Springsteen meant when he boasted at age twenty-six that he *had got this guitar / And learned how to make it talk*. When something like that happens, feeling, thought, and history are all made palpable, for however brief a time. That's what all art does, even rock 'n' roll.

ACKNOWLEDGMENTS

The roots of this book go deep. Bob Lamb, to whom it is dedicated, has joked more than once to me that I've been working on it for most of my life. (That's not writing, I usually reply, that's collecting bootlegs.) My father saw to it that it that I grew up in a house and a world full of music, both live and recorded, and my mother was the first cultural critic I ever knew, although she never would have copped to the job description. My brother, Martin, and sisters, Maryellen and Peggy, introduced me to an even more varied world of art and took me on many of my first, formative trips on the PATH trains over to the Emerald City, back in the down and dirty 1970s. Later, Linda Adams, Tony Davis, and Mary P. Keating all shared their own knowledge of Bruce Springsteen's work; Owen Burley talked from the heart one night about the practical side of being in a rock band; and Andrew Violette taught me over a much longer period what it means to collaborate in performance. So many teachers and friends have left their traces on me, too many to acknowledge in full, but I do want to single out just two more for specific mention: David Herbert Donald taught me about biography and the highly contingent nature of history; and Michael O'Regan first helped me articulate my ideas about popular art. As I wish my parents had lived to read this book, I also wish that Professor Donald and Mike had lived to read it, too.

In more recent years, I have had the good fortune to be surrounded professionally by a remarkable group of people, who have motivated me to push my ideas further than I might otherwise have done. Bob Crozier, Chris Suggs, Marny Tabb, and Alison Pease at John Jay College have been wonderfully understanding and supportive department chairs, never questioning for a second why a professor of English was devoting so much of his time to rock 'n' roll. At the CUNY Graduate Center, my distinguished colleagues in the American studies program, especially Morris Dickstein and Gary Giddins, have done me the extraordinary favor of treating me from the first as an equal and motivating me to be worthy of that designation. The students of both the American studies program and the Ph.D. program in English have graciously served as unwitting but brilliant guinea pigs for many of the ideas in this book, and I am particularly indebted to the students in Gail Levin's seminar on the 1960s, as well as the students in my own seminars on the 1970s and Thomas Pynchon. As Executive Officer of the English program, Provost and President of the Graduate Center, and even occasional fellow concertgoer, Bill Kelly has supported this project since well before either of us even knew it existed. And John Matteson has been a friend and an inspiration, not to mention the right man in the right place at the right time. Among other signal kindnesses, he introduced me to Amy Cherry and Laura Romain, my editors at W. W. Norton, who have moved through this book with brisk assurance. Without them, my words would have fallen so much shorter of their goals.

In the last stages of this project, I incurred a very special debt to Eileen Chapman and Liz Rimassa (of Monmouth University), as well as to Bob Crane (of the Friends of the Springsteen Special Collection). They allowed me the extraordinary privilege of researching at the Jersey Shore Center of Music Archives, months before it actually opened or its existence was even announced to the public. Eileen's generosity with both her time and her intimate knowledge of the shore scene was particularly touching. I find it singularly appropriate that, the night before Eileen and I officially met, we were both in the Stone Pony at the same time without realizing it, watching Vini Lopez join that year's house band (Outside the Box) in a lively version of "Thunder-crack." If all university archivists had that sort of real-world experience of their subjects, scholarly research would be an even more righteous pursuit. In gathering the images for this volume, I have also incurred debts to Jason Federici, Carrie Potter Devening, Pete Russell, Robert

Santelli, and Howard Kramer of the Rock and Roll Hall of Fame and Museum. And while this is far from an authorized biography and was written without any input from either Mr. Springsteen or his management, Mona Okada and Brittany Pollard of Grubman Indursky & Shire patiently guided me through the process of obtaining the necessary permissions after the book was completed.

My wife, Stephanie LaTour, has been hearing Springsteen music around the house literally since the moment we started dating, and she has been remarkably patient with the long, idiosyncratic path that this project has taken to its completion. She has one of the sharpest minds I have ever known, and more than anyone else she has made my ideas tougher and far more politically aware by asking the best sorts of questions. Our sons, Robert and Stephen, take after their mother in this, as in many other regards: all parents know that explaining why you think and do what you think and do when your children ask you about it is almost a second education. This project has grown along with Stephen and Robert, as they have passed from curling on the floor at Music for Aardvarks to taking guitar lessons of their own. Their daily questions about that band from the 1960s or this artist from last week have regularly made me express my ideas about popular music with a minimum of overly academic verbiage. They also remind me every day where the fun is.

And then there's Bob. I've known him longer than anyone else I've listed here except for my siblings, and we've taken a lot of long walks together down unfamiliar streets. Bob is a brilliant teacher, writer, and critic, but I am most grateful to him for the faith and trust that he has shown me as a friend for over three decades now. As Little Steven says, "rock 'n' roll—it's a band thing." Because I know Bob is backing me up, I play much better than I ever would solo.

SOURCES AND NOTES

My work has benefited from the insights of dozens of journalists and scholars who have written about Springsteen before me. Chief among these is Dave Marsh, the dean of Springsteen biographers, whose work is an essential starting point for anyone who wants to learn about the singer. As my notes will attest, I have also drawn on several books by Marc Eliot, Fred Goodman, and Christopher Sandford that sought to correct what their authors saw as Marsh's overly favorable depiction of his subject. As with Marsh's work, I found the relative proximity to the events themselves provided by these three books invaluable, particularly in the case of one of Sandford's multiply cited anonymous sources, whom I suspect is now no longer alive. I have also benefited from the firsthand testimony more recently gathered by Robert Santelli for *Greetings from E Street: The Story of Bruce Springsteen and the E Street Band* (San Francisco: Chronicle Press, 2006), the half-legendary version of E Street events offered in Clarence Clemons and Don Reo's unfairly ignored *Big Man: Real Life and Tall Tales* (New York: Grand Central Publishing, 2009), Jimmy Guterman's fan's-eye view *Runaway American Dream: Listening to Bruce Springsteen* (Cambridge, MA: Da Capo, 2005), Eric Alterman's politically focused *It Ain't No Sin to Be Glad You're Alive: The Promise of Bruce Springsteen* (Boston: Little, Brown, 1999; 2nd ed., 2001), and Rob Kirkpatrick's critically focused *Magic in the Night: The Words and Music of Bruce Springsteen* (2007; 2nd ed. New York: St. Martin's, 2009). A life story can be told many ways, and all of these books, as well as Marsh's volumes, offer alternative versions of Bruce Springsteen's story, emphasizing events and details that I have chosen not to emphasize in my own version of his life.

My work owes a similarly proximate debt to a number of late twentieth-century rock journalists, particularly those whom Robert Christgau half jokingly called "the rock critical establishment." Several of them are characters in my narrative, but that makes them no less valuable for having worked at formulating an aesthetics for an art form that was emerging before their eyes. Writers like Lester Bangs, Ken Emerson, Peter Guralnick, Robert Hilburn, Greil Marcus, John Rockwell, Nick Tosches, and Ellen Willis were to the "classic rock" of the 1960s and 1970s what Giorgio Vasari was to the Italian Renaissance. I have also found Joel Whitburn's compilations of *Billboard* chart data for Record Research Books repeatedly valuable, not just his straightforward reproductions of week-by-week Hot 100 charts grouped by decade from the 1960s through the 2000s, but also *Top Pop Singles, 1955–1999* (Menomonee Falls, WI: Record Research, 2000) and *Top Pop Albums, 1955–2001* (Menomonee Falls, WI: Record Research, 2001). Much of this material is now serially available and searchable online, but particularly in the case of the Hot 100 charts, it is always useful to see data for which one is not deliberately searching.

As far as video is concerned, *The Complete Video Anthology, 1978–2000* (Columbia DVD, 2001) supplements Springsteen's original one-disc 1989 collection of 1970s performance videos and 1980s conceptual videos with a second disc that showcases his 1990s solo work. The eight-disc set *This Is Your Life: Bruce Springsteen* is a useful video archive covering over three decades of Springsteen's work, from 1972 to 2003. (The copy I own lists no video production company of record, but the set does circulate among fans.) Similarly, I have listened to far more Springsteen recordings than he and CBS have officially released, and I will cite the most relevant ones in the notes for each chapter, but two compilations that offer interesting sidelights on Springsteen's early career are *All Those Years* (Templar Records, 5 discs) and *Deep Down in the Vaults* (DDT Recordings, 3 discs), which provide useful supplements to *Live/1975–85* (CBS, 1986, 3 discs) and *Tracks* (CBS, 1998, 4 disks), respectively.

It would be prohibitively expensive for me to quote as much in this book from Springsteen's lyrics as I would like, but the text of the lyrics on his first fourteen albums can be found in *Bruce Springsteen Songs*, which I discuss in chapter 12 and have treated throughout my narrative as a version of his artistic autobiography. For the lyrics of all of Springsteen's officially released songs, including the post-*Rising* ones and those included on *Tracks*, the best place to go is the Songs page of Springsteen's own website (http://www.brucespringsteen.net/songs/index.html). At this writing, it is complete through *Working on a Dream*. For the lyrics to officially unreleased songs, as well as an astonishing number of lyrical variants heard in concerts and recording sessions, the best resource is the Lyric section of the Italian Killing Floor site (http://www.brucespringsteen.it/Brucex.htm).

These latter two sources point to an important reason why I couldn't have written this book in the twentieth century: the digital age has thoroughly changed scholarship, and almost entirely for the better. The goals and even the methods of biography are the same as the ones I learned back in graduate school, but the resources at my disposal as a biographer on this project are ones that I could hardly have imagined way back then. Killing Floor is just one example of this, as is the digital extension of *Backstreets* magazine to www.backstreets.com. Under the impressive direction of Christopher Phillips, this latter site has served as a clearinghouse for all things Springsteen from all over the web and the world. Especially in writing about the most recent decade of Springsteen's life, I have found the site immeasurably valuable in pointing me toward artifacts and performances about which I might otherwise not have known.

For my purposes, however, the most valuable Springsteen site has been the UK-based Brucebase (http://brucebase.wikispaces.com/), run by Pete Russell, which contains a history of all Springsteen recording sessions; a thorough catalog of hundreds of bootlegs; a chart of the first and last performances of all his songs; setlist aggregation charts for his first half-dozen E Street tours; and a list of every live performance Springsteen has given going back to 1964. The vast majority of these listings contain complete setlists, and many of them include links to Johanna Pirttijärvi's Storyteller project, which attempts to transcribe virtually every word that Springsteen has said onstage. As I have done with other biographers, I have disagreed with the operators of Brucebase at a number of points on their interpretation of facts, but I am frankly in awe of their gathering of so many facts on one easily navigable website with very helpful hyperlinks.

ABBREVIATIONS

Alterman	Eric Alterman, *It Ain't No Sin to Be Glad You're Alive: The Promise of Bruce Springsteen*, 2nd ed. (Boston: Little, Brown, 2001)
Clemons and Reo	Clarence Clemons and Don Reo, *Big Man: Real Life and Tall Tales* (New York: Grand Central Publishing, 2009)
Cross	Charles R. Cross, ed., *Backstreets: Springsteen, the Man and His Music* (New York: Harmony Books, 1989)
Eliot	Marc Eliot, with Mike Appel, *Down Thunder Road: The Making of Bruce Springsteen* (New York: Simon & Schuster, 1992)
Goodman	Fred Goodman, *The Mansion on the Hill: Dylan, Young, Geffen, Springsteen, and the Head-On Collision of Rock and Commerce* (New York: Random House, 1997)
Guterman	Jimmy Guterman, *Runaway American Dream: Listening to Bruce Springsteen* (Cambridge, MA: Da Capo, 2005)
Kirkpatrick	Rob Kirkpatrick, *Magic in the Night: The Words and Music of Bruce Springsteen* (New York: St. Martin's, 2009)
Marsh, *Born*	David Marsh, *Born to Run: The Bruce Springsteen Story* (New York: Dell, 1981)
Marsh, *Glory*	David Marsh, *Glory Days: Bruce Springsteen in the 1980s* (New York: Pantheon, 1987)
Marsh, *On Tour*	David Marsh, *Bruce Springsteen on Tour, 1968–2005* (New York: Bloomsbury, 2006)
Marsh, *Two Hearts*	David Marsh, *Bruce Springsteen—Two Hearts: The Definitive Biography, 1972–2003* (New York: Routledge, 2004)
Sandford	Christopher Sandford, *Springsteen: Point Blank* (New York: Da Capo, 1999)
Santelli	Robert Santelli, *Greetings from E Street: The Story of Bruce Springsteen and the E Street Band* (San Francisco: Chronicle Press, 2006)
Songs	*Bruce Springsteen Songs*, 2nd ed. (New York: HarperEntertainment, 2003)
SSC	Springsteen Special Collection, Jersey Shore Center of Music Archives, Monmouth University, West Long Branch, NJ

Ties   *The Ties That Bind: Bruce Springsteen A to E to Z*, ed. Gary
         Graff (Canton, MI: Visible Ink Press, 2005)
TIYL   *This Is Your Life: Bruce Springsteen*
Williams Paul Williams, "Lost in the Flood," *Crawdaddy!*, Oct. 1974

WALK-IN MUSIC: SEVEN NIGHTS TO ROCK

xi   **"Johnny Bowker"** See Stan Hugill, comp., *Shanties from the Seven Seas: Ship-board Work-Songs and Songs Used as Work-Songs from the Great Days of Sail*, 2nd ed. (Mystic, CT: Mystic Seaport, 2003), 213. Scott Reynolds Nelson, *Steel Drivin' Man: John Henry—The Untold Story of an American Legend* (New York: Oxford University Press, 2006), 76, places the origin of the phrase "rock 'n' roll" in a slightly later period, to the songs sung by those forging railroad tunnels.

xii **Spirituality** Springsteen, speech for U2, Rock and Roll Hall of Fame Induction Ceremonies, New York, NY, 14 March 2005.

xiii **music provided you** Springsteen, during "Remember When the Music," Harry Chapin Tribute, New York, NY, 7 Dec. 1987.

xiv **unique life** Raymond Williams, *The English Novel from Dickens to Lawrence* (London: Chatto & Windus, 1970), 192.

xv   **structures of feeling** Ibid.

Chapter 1. I'M QUICK TO LEARN (1964–1968)

General Sources: Marsh, *Born*, ch 2; Eliot, ch. 1; Sandford, ch. 2; Alterman, ch. 1; Marsh, *On Tour*, ch. 1; Santelli, ch. 1; Kirkpatrick, ch. 1; http://brucebase.wikispaces .com/1949-1964; http://brucebase.wikispaces.com/1965; http://brucebase.wikispaces.com/ 1966; http://brucebase.wikispaces.com/1967; http://brucebase.wikispaces.com/1968. The best audio source for this period is *The Bruce Springsteen Story*, vols. 1 and 2 (E Street Records), which contain both sides of the 1966 Mr. Music single and both of the 1967 Left Foot sets.

3   **the first song** E.g., before "Twist and Shout," Cleveland, OH, 9 Aug. 1978.

3   **faltered** Glenn C. Altschuler, *All Shook Up: How Rock 'n' Roll Changed America* (New York: Oxford University Press, 2003), 161.

4   **Billboard singles charts** Ben Fong-Torres, *The Hits Just Keep On Coming: The History of Top 40 Radio* (San Francisco: Backbeat Books, 1998), is a solid history of Top 40 radio and very instructive in particular on the role played by the Gavin Report in the institutionalization of that format. In characterizing the transformation of American pop in the mid-1960s, I have also drawn on Jonathan Gould, *Can't Buy Me Love: The Beatles, Britain, and America* (New York: Three Rivers Press, 2007), Dave Marsh, *The Heart of Rock and Soul: The 1001 Best Singles Ever Recorded* (New York: Da Capo, 1999), Greil Marcus, *Like a Rolling Stone: Bob Dylan at the Crossroads* (New York: Public Affairs, 2005), and Geoffrey O'Brien, *Sonata for Jukebox: An Autobiography of My Ears* (New York: Counterpoint Books, 2004).

6   **searching for my father** Introduction to "Angel Eyes," Los Angeles, CA, 19 Nov. 1995.

7   **She was no stiff** Springsteen, speech for Bob Dylan, Rock and Roll Hall of Fame induction ceremonies, New York, NY, 20 Jan. 1988.

7   **Chantays' "Pipeline"** In the studio in the late 1970s, Springsteen used this song at least once as a warmup exercise for his band before a recording session.

12 **probable setlist** Since we have no recording of the Castiles at this gig, just their

setlist, we can only speculate whether a number of these performances (particularly "Never on Sunday" and "Summertime") were modeled on the guitar-based arrangements that the Ventures had featured on their albums *Mashed Potatoes and Gravy* and *The Ventures Play Telstar, The Lonely Bull*.

12 **one original song** "Sidewalk" was a song that Springsteen finished when two fans brought it to him after a teen-club gig near Fort Monmouth probably just a few weeks before. It remained popular enough to be requested at a Springsteen gig years later, long after the Castiles had broken up.

14 **as he still did** As Bruce would remember, the other band members *made fun of my voice*. See Q&A session, *DoubleTake* concert, Somerville, MA, 19 Feb. 2003. This was a solo acoustic benefit concert for *DoubleTake* magazine, and Springsteen's running commentary throughout it provides one of the best glimpses ever into his songwriting process. Recordings of this concert circulate among fans.

15 **new Hullabaloo Club** By the fall of 1966, both *Shindig* and *Hullabaloo!* were no longer on television, but the latter show at least left a fascinating residue in its wake: the Hullabaloo Clubs, which promised, in the newspaper ads advertising the Castiles' October appearance at the Middletown club, "TV's Hullabaloo Scene."

15 *fluorescent orange* Introduction to "It's Hard to Be a Saint in the City," Bryn Mawr, PA, 31 Oct. 1973.

16 *didn't even know* Introduction to "The River," Los Angeles, CA, 30 Sept. 1985.

16 **lowest club** David Henderson, *'Scuse Me While I Kiss the Sky: The Life of Jimi Hendrix* (New York: Bantam Books, 1983), 81.

17 **alternated gigs at the Café Wha?** For an extensive and extensively researched reasoning as to exactly when the Castiles played the Café Wha?, see http://bruce base.wikispaces.com/001166+New+York, in which the Brucebase team has really outdone itself. Checking its account, I find only one relatively minor factual discrepancy: the James Coburn film that was shot at the Café Wha? was *The President's Analyst*, rather than *In Like Flint*, as George Theiss remembered it.

19 **"Wake Me Shake Me"** As "Shake Me Wake Me," this song had originally been a Four Tops single, but the Castiles' version is clearly modeled on the Blues Project's.

20 *[I]f you ever played* Introduction to "It's Hard to Be a Saint in the City," Bryn Mawr, PA, 31 Oct. 1973.

21 *what did I* Introduction to "The River," Los Angeles, CA, 30 Sept. 1985.

22 **By 1962** Sheila Weller, *Girls Like Us: Carole King, Joni Mitchell, Carly Simon and the Journey of a Generation* (New York: Atria Books, 2008), 126.

Chapter 2. I PUSHED B-52 AND BOMBED 'EM WITH THE BLUES (1968–1971)

General Sources: Marsh, *Born*, ch. 3; Eliot, ch. 1; Sandford, ch. 2; Alterman, ch. 1; Marsh, *On Tour*, ch. 1; Santelli, ch. 1; Kirkpatrick, ch. 1; http://brucebase.wikispaces.com/1969; http://brucebase.wikispaces.com/1970; and http://brucebase.wikispaces.com/1971, and http://brucebase.wikispaces.com/Castiles percent2C+Steel+Mill percent2C+BS+Band+-+Studio+Sessions. I also owe an extraordinary debt in this chapter to Daniel Wolff's brilliant *4th of July, Asbury Park: A History of the Promised Land* (New York: Bloomsbury, 2005), not only his own chapter on 1970 but also his absorbing overall history of the town. For an absorbing glimpse into the full world of the Upstage, from its preorigins down to its dissolution in the wake of the 1970 riots, I highly recommend Carrie Potter Devening's inexplicably little-read *For Music's Sake: Asbury Park's Upstage Club and Green Mermaid Café—The Untold Stories* (Bloomington: Author House, 2011). The hundreds of pictures alone, culled from Tom Potter's own copious collection, are an invaluable window onto a now-vanished era.

For this period of Springsteen's career more than for any other, unofficially released recordings are essential to understanding the evolution of his sound, and I have sought out quite a few of them. In addition to the recordings cited below, I was also able to obtain privately circulating CDRs of the Sept. 1969 Richmond concert by Child in Richmond mentioned in the text, portions of an April 1970 Steel Mill concert at Monmouth College, a Nov. 1970 date at the Sunshine In, and a Nov. 1971 show at the Student Prince.

24 **a number of Cream songs** In some ways, this repertoire list makes Earth seem like an early Eric Clapton tribute band: over half the songs on it had been performed by the Yardbirds, Cream, or John Mayall's Bluesbreakers. Even the older songs the band performed ("Sittin' on Top of the World" and "Back Door Man") were probably drawn not from their original recordings but from recent covers by Cream and other blues-influenced rock musicians.

27 **The Upstage was** "Big Danny Gallagher" in Santelli, "Remembering the Upstage," in Cross, 36.

28 **decidedly male** There is no record of any woman other than den mother Margaret Potter ever participating in any of the jams. Moreover, three of the ten "Rules" posted on the wall of the Upstage seemed to assume that any woman present had to be an ornament rather than an artist. "2. Naked girls will not be tolerated for more than three or four hours at a time"; "4. Topless girls must stay at least three years away [*sic*] from the nearest male"; and "7. Girls wearing hot pants will sit by fire extinguishers." For more on this list, see below.

28 **In those days** Van Zandt quoted in *Ties*, 398.

28 **half-jokey rules** This list of rules may have been the most unusual, heretofore unmentioned artifact on display in the Rock and Roll Hall of Fame and Museum's 2009–11 exhibit *From Asbury Park to the Promised Land: The Life and Music of Bruce Springsteen.*

28 **shortly after midnight** Santelli, 10.

29 **came up very politely** Margaret Potter quoted in Joseph Dalton, "Bruce Springsteen: Made in the U.S.A.—My Hometown," *Rolling Stone*, 10 Oct. 1985.

30 **musically discriminating** See Miles Davis, with Quincy Troupe, *Miles: The Autobiography* (New York: Touchstone, 1989), 288.

30 **sort of chi-chi-chiffon** Iggy Pop, *I Need More* (Los Angeles: 2.13.61 Publications, n.d.), 80–81.

30 **a music that arose** LeRoi Jones, *Blues People: Negro Music in White America* (New York: William Morrow, 1963), 82.

31 **girls were not going** Federici quoted in *Ties*, 148.

31 **moment in American pop** The organ was an instrument that bridged myriad styles in early-1969's Top 40, from the "ride, Sally ride" chords of Sly and the Family Stone's "Everyday People," James Brown's "Give It Up, Turn It Loose," Creedence Clearwater Revival's "Proud Mary," and the Bob Seger System's "Ramblin' Gamblin' Man," to the more lugubrious riffs that underlay Tommy James's "Crimson and Clover," the Zombies' "Time of the Season," Joe Simon's "Games People Play," and Marvin Gaye's revisionist cover of Gladys Knight and the Pips' "I Heard It Through the Grapevine." All these songs were in the *Billboard* Top 40 for 15 Feb. 1969, the probable week of Springsteen's first meeting with Federici.

32 **Hey man** Santelli, "Remembering," 36.

32 **I didn't care** Ibid., 101, 100.

32 **Danny Federici's testimony** See Santelli, "[Interview with] Danny Federici," *Backstreets*, nos. 34–35 (Fall 1990/Winter 1991): 44.

32 **A weekend outing** Springsteen, speech for Creedence Clearwater Revival, Rock

and Roll Hall of Fame Induction Ceremony, Los Angeles, CA, 12 Jan. 1993. Interestingly enough, Springsteen incorrectly dates the Pandemonium stand during this speech as occurring in 1970, the year of the July riots in Asbury Park discussed below.

32 **run him off** Sandford, 38.

33 *played behind* Springsteen, Creedence speech, Los Angeles, CA, 12 Jan. 1993.

33 **a heavy metal band** Cross, "[Interview with] Little Steven Van Zandt," *Backstreets*, no. 6 (1983): 7.

34 **interest in** See Nancy Zaroulis and Gerald Sullivan, *Who Spoke Up? American Protest against the War in Vietnam, 1963–1975* (New York: Holt, Rinehart and Winston, 1984), 217.

34 **the great silent majority** Richard M. Nixon, "Address to the Nation on the War in Vietnam," 3 Nov. 1969, available at http://www.watergate.info/nixon/silent-majority-speech-1969.shtml.

36 **Fuck this whole thing** Gregg's memory of Duane was first shared in Cameron Crowe, "The Allman Brothers Story," *Rolling Stone*, 6 Dec. 1973, 54.

37 **Hammond B-3** Federici and Springsteen salvaged the B-3 from a Trenton basement just before their first Pandemonium date, and Federici rebuilt it, as he did nearly all the instruments that he owned throughout his career.

38 **We'd thought we'd go** Roslin quoted in Santelli, 11.

38 **Fillmore Recording Studios** *Live at the Matrix* (Great Dane Records) reproduces most of one of the band's 13 Jan. 1970 sets at that club; *The Unsurpassed Springsteen*, vol. 1 (Yellow Dog Records), includes all three of the tracks recorded in San Francisco in Feb. 1970.

38 **someone in his organization** It is in the very least suggestive that Graham doesn't even mention Springsteen in his autobiography until describing the 1988 Amnesty International tour. One would think that if he had had a hand in the 1970 offer, he would at least have made passing reference to it.

39 **psychic twin** It is not clear when Springsteen and Van Zandt met for the first time. Much like their slightly elder Manhattan contemporaries Martin Scorsese and Robert DeNiro, they seem to have kept popping up in the same places for four or five years in the late 1960s before they officially worked together. In 1966, the Shadows were on the same bill as the Castiles at the Surf 'n' See in August, and they headlined at the Hullabaloo in Van Zandt's hometown of Middletown in November the night after the Castiles played there. According to one story that Springsteen has told, that may even have been where they met, two years before the Upstage had opened. See Springsteen, introduction to "No Surrender," Sydney, Australia, 24 March 1985.

40 **almost one per day** James T. Patterson, *Grand Expectations: The United States, 1945–1974* (New York: Oxford University Press, 1996), 717–18.

40 **diffuse, decentralized, irrational** Daniel Patrick Moynihan, "Memorandum for H. R. Haldeman," 10 March 1970, collected in Steven R. Weisman, ed., *Daniel Patrick Moynihan: A Portrait in Letters of an American Visionary* (New York: Public Affairs, 2010), 219.

41 **These hippies** Rick Perlstein, *Nixonland: The Rise of a President and the Fracturing of America* (New York: Scribner, 2008), 495.

42 **"Run through the Jungle"** Fogerty explains his inspiration for this song at length in Craig Werner, *Up around the Bend: The Oral History of Creedence Clearwater Revival* (New York: Avon Books, 1999), 126–27.

42 **[n]ot surprised** Wolff, *4th of July*, 192.

42 **[n]ot the tight strut** This breathtakingly perfect description is from Wolff, *4th of July*, 176, and is implicitly based on Sancious's memories of dancing at the Upstage.

43   *[T]here's a weird thing* Introduction to "I Am the Doctor," Richmond, VA, 23 May 1970.

43   **few engagements booked** *Right the Fuck On!* (Palace Records) reproduces a Jan. 1971 Steel Mill concert at D'Scene, and indicates how Springsteen was already moving much closer to soul and R&B even before that band officially broke up.

45   **Hey, why don't we** Santelli, "Remembering," 36–37.

46   *Are you ready* Introduction to "It Takes a Lot to Laugh, It Takes a Train to Cry," Union, NJ, 15 May 1971. This concert is reproduced on *The Bruce Springsteen Story*, vol. 5 (E Street Records).

46   **We tried to get a guy** Santelli, "Remembering," 37.

46   **one cookin' band** Duane Allman quoted in the Brucebase listing for this 27 March 1971 concert.

47   **my band** Peter Knobler and Greg Mitchell, "Who Is Bruce Springsteen and Why Are We Saying All These Wonderful Things about Him?" *Crawdaddy!*, March 1973, 30.

48   **telling friends** See Charles Cross, "[Interview with] Southside Johnny," *Backstreets*, no. 19 (Winter 1987).

48   **It wasn't like we had** Sancious quoted in Wolff, *4th of July*, 199.

49   **the cops jumped in** Dunn quoted in Peter Guralnick, *Sweet Soul Music: Rhythm and Blues and the Southern Dream of Freedom* (New York: Harper & Row, 1986), 355.

49   **I think the Allman Brothers** Daniels quoted in Kemp, *Lullaby*, 103.

49   *It's all happening* Introduction to "Come On," Asbury Park, NJ, 17 July 1970.

49   **what it must have been like** Wolff, *4th of July*, 198.

50   **Damrosch Park** This July 1971 concert is actually one of the most widely available from this period and is reproduced on *The Bruce Springsteen Story*, vol. 6 (E Street Records).

50   **the farther away** *Exit through the Back Door* (Yellow Cat Records) contains a good sampling of several early-1972 sets at Richmond's Back Door that setlists would suggest are representative of the late period of the Bruce Springsteen Band.

51   **Upstage, when you think** Kenn quoted in Santelli, "Twenty Years Burning Down the Road: The Complete History of Jersey Shore Rock 'n' Roll," *Backstreets*, no. 21 (Summer 1987): 21.

51   **Renaissance would end** Van Zandt, foreword to Richard Neer, *FM: The Rise and Fall of Rock Radio* (New York: Villard, 2001), ix. Van Zandt used almost exactly the same periodization in his speech for the Hollies, Rock and Roll Hall of Fame Induction Ceremonies, New York, NY, 15 March 2010, during which he dated the golden age of rock 'n' roll as running from 1951 to 1971.

Chapter 3. DETHRONE THE DICTAPHONE, HIT IT IN ITS FUNNYBONE (1971–1972)

General Sources: Marsh, *Born*, ch. 4; Eliot, chs. 2–5; *Greetings* ch. of *Songs*; Sandford, chs. 2–3; Alterman, ch. 2; Guterman, ch. 2; Marsh, *On Tour*, ch. 1; Kirkpatrick, ch. 1; Clemons and Reo, 26–48; http://brucebase.wikispaces.com/1972; http://brucebase. wikispaces.com/Demo+-+Studio+Sessions; http://brucebase.wikispaces.com/Greetings+ From+Asbury+Park+-+Studio+Sessions.

52   **the night before** That was the night Duane Allman died in a motorcycle accident in Macon, GA. Bruce and the band were supposed to open for the Allmans again when the Georgians returned to Asbury Park in November, but for obvious reasons the date was canceled.

53 **Bo Diddley** Indeed, Springsteen covered "Bo Diddley's a Gunslinger" at least once in 1972.

55 **whose career path** Farrell had written the 'Shirelles' "Boys," which the Beatles covered on their first album, and later started the Wes Farrell Organization, a group that included a number of smaller music publishing firms under its umbrella, such as Pocketful of Tunes, the one for which Appel and Cretecos worked.

56 **looking for singer-songwriters** Lopez quoted in Eliot, 53.

56 **Springsteen's version** See *Songs*, 6–7.

57 **what song Springsteen performed first** Based on Appel's description, I suspect that it was the truly horrible "She's Leaving," which Bruce had performed with his band several times at the Student Prince that fall.

57 **derivative** The rise and fall of the melodic line on the song's title phrase echoes a similar technique in "It's Now or Never," Aaron Schroeder and Wally Gold's rewrite of "O Sole Mio" for Elvis Presley back when Springsteen was in junior high.

57 **very weird line** Appel quoted in Eliot, 55. For those curious about the lines in question, Appel quotes them.

59 **solo acoustic performer** Although he has never said so, it seems reasonable to assume that the songs he performed for Appel and Cretecos this second time were the ones that had worked best with those tough Bay Area audiences.

59 **twisted autobiographies** *Songs*, 7.

59 **argument with his mother** The greatest surprise here—especially for an early Springsteen song—is that the opening verse shows the boy's father sympathetically taking his son's side.

60 **venerable AABA form** Charles Hamm, *Yesterdays: Popular Song in America* (New York: W. W. Norton, 1979), 422.

61 **I just looked** Appel quoted in Eliot, 56.

61 **in the car** Springsteen speech for Bob Dylan, Rock and Roll Hall of Fame Induction Ceremonies, New York, NY, 20 Jan. 1988.

62 **oddly comforting** For a time, even Springsteen's memories of his own life during this period may have been subtly influenced by Scaduto's volume. In early 1972, the singer was no longer living in Challenger East but in Asbury Park itself, above Margaret Potter's abandoned beauty salon, just two doors down from the old site of the Upstage. In recent years, Springsteen has indeed remembered living above the salon when he had his breakthrough as a songwriter, but in recalling this period onstage during the 1970s, he was much more likely to speak of living over a *drugstore* rather than a beauty parlor (e.g., introductions to "For You," Uniondale, NY, 3 and 9 June 1978), so much so that these remarks influenced Dave Marsh's initial account of this period in *Born to Run* (e.g., p. 57).

Both descriptions are technically accurate—as the late Big Danny Gallagher testified to Allen C. Scheer in "Danny Gallagher, the Original Big Man," *Backstreets*, no. 29 (Summer 1989): 14, Bruce lived on the third floor of the building, the old salon was on the second floor, and the still-active Park Drug was on the first—but Bruce's relatively recent reminiscences of the salon (in 1998's *Songs* and in the 2005 *Storytellers* taping) are far more detailed and evocative than his more cursory 1970s references to the drugstore. This suggests that he didn't spend all that much time in the latter establishment.

So why mention the drugstore during the 1970s rather than the more familiar salon? Scaduto describes Dylan as living "above [a] drugstore" at one point during his post-college time in Minneapolis, a city that served much the same function in terms of Dylan's development that Asbury Park served in terms of Springsteen's. See

Anthony Scaduto, *Bob Dylan* (London: Helter Skelter Books, 1996), 34. That early in Springsteen's career, his own narrative of his rise to success understandably still bore echoes of the stories that had made him believe he could indeed succeed.

63   **Of all the guys** Scaduto, *Dylan*, 11.

63   **lyrics first** Ibid., 80.

63   **write the verses** *Songs*, 6–7.

63   **conscious journalistic approach** Scaduto, *Dylan*, 116.

63   **their seed** *Songs*, 7.

63   **on the way** Scaduto, *Dylan*, 127.

64   **worked to find** *Songs*, 7.

64   **unconscious songs** Scaduto, *Dylan*, 178.

64   **older songs** Dylan quoted in Greil Marcus, *Like a Rolling Stone: Bob Dylan at the Crossroads* (New York: Public Affairs, 2005), 33.

65   **cheap, broken** Ibid., 113.

65   *It was bye bye* Between "Growin' Up" and "It's Hard to Be a Saint in the City," Los Angeles, CA, 7 July 1978. These performances and the transition between them are featured on Springsteen's 1986 live set.

65   **exclusive recording agreement** The relevant contracts are fully reproduced in appendix A of Eliot.

66   **Barbra Streisand** In different accounts, he mentions other Columbia acts like Neil Diamond, Chicago, Paul Simon, and (of course) Bob Dylan, but amazingly the explicit parallel to Streisand is a constant in all versions of this story.

66   **Hammond's calendar** Dunstan Prial, *The Producer: John Hammond and the Soul of American Music* (New York: Farrar, Straus & Giroux, 2006), 270. To be fair, Hammond's calendar probably wasn't that full in the spring of 1972. Unlike Clive Davis's discoveries, many of the well-known acts with which Hammond was associated were by that point dead or living in seclusion.

67   **grinning easily** John Hammond, with Irving Townsend, *On Record: An Autobiography* (New York: Summit Books, 1977), 391.

67   **Who's your boy?** Ibid.

67   **extraordinary piece** Ibid. Appel (Eliot, 68) remembers Bruce leading off with "If I Was the Priest," but most other sources agree that this song was elicited later at Hammond's prodding.

67   **You were right** Prial, *Producer*, 271.

67   **really far out** Hammond, *On Record*, 391. As many others would do in the years to come, Hammond had falsely assumed from the singer's name that he was at least partially Jewish. Interestingly enough, Hammond apparently saw Bruce's Catholicism from the first as a potential marketing hook (see Eliot, 69).

68   **may have made** This is Appel's recollection, quoted in Eliot, 69.

68   **someone made a phone call** Both Hammond and Appel claim to have set up this impromptu gig (see Hammond, *On Record*, 393, and Eliot, 70). Although Hammond almost certainly had more local pull, the brevity of his version of events is a little less convincing than Appel's account of confusion and last-minute scrambling. According to Springsteen (Prial, *Producer*, 274), he and Appel actually went around to various clubs in Manhattan on foot, including the Bitter End, finally persuading the managers of the Gaslight to give the young singer a slot.

68   **neither hide nor hair** And here, of course, the hall of mirrors of multiple, conflicting reminiscences of the same events continues: Springsteen told Duncan Prial (*Producer*, 268) that Hammond walked up to him as soon as he walked off the stage and proclaimed, in stereotypically Hammondesque fashion, "That was mah-velous, Bruce. Just mah-velous."

Ultimately, what all these accounts may tell us is how those whirlwind two days felt to the three men involved: Hammond smoothly delighted at suddenly finding himself back in the game; Appel uncomfortable with being out of the loop, even when things appeared to be going extraordinarily well; and Springsteen gleefully bemused at the quasi-magical manner in which his success finally seemed to be unfolding.

68 **we loved him** Eliot, 70; Hammond, *On Record*, 393. Hammond apparently never said who "we" were, possibly meaning to imply other Columbia executives he was hoping to impress with his new discovery. In his autobiography, though, he claimed that he watched at least part of the show with "[a] noted guitar player." This detail could be another one of Hammond's self-dramatizations. But it is suggestive to note that one of the performers scheduled to play at the Gaslight au Go Go that night was blues legend Charlie Musselwhite. Musselwhite was scheduled to come on after ten, with newcomer Garland Jeffreys set to open for him around nine. It would have been unusual for a headliner to be at a club four hours before he hit the stage, but not unheard of, especially if he wanted to check out the room in advance on this, the first night of his gig at a recently remodeled club.

70 ***down to your boys*** Introduction to "The E Street Shuffle," New York, NY, 15 Aug. 1975.

70 **"For You"** Appel (quoted in Eliot, 56) remembers "For You" as being one of the songs Springsteen played in his office on Valentine's Day, but this seems unlikely since it was missing not only from the Hammond audition but also from all three sets of demos that Bruce cut during the spring. It begs credulity that a lyric this strong, had it existed, would have been omitted when a song like "Mary, Queen of Arkansas" showed up on every one of those occasions.

71 **either CBS or Sioux City** The Sioux City demos and unreleased Blauvelt recordings from the summer of 1972 are scattered across a number of sets, but most are available on *Before the Fame* (Pony Express Records, 1998, 2 discs) and *The Unsurpassed Springsteen*, vol. 4 (Yellow Dog Records, 1993).

73 **playing in a bar** Marcello Villela, "[Interview with] Clarence Clemons," *Backstreets*, no. 17 (summer 1986): 19.

75 **More than those of any other song** This paragraph not only quotes from but builds on the extended exegesis of this lyric that Springsteen gave during his 4 April 2005 taping at the Two River Theatre in Red Bank, NJ, for the VH1 series *Storytellers*. Bruce's postperformance breakdown of this song's lyrics are one of that show's undeniable highlights.

Chapter 4. ENDLESS JUKE JOINTS AND VALENTINO DRAG (1972–1975)

General Sources: Marsh, *Born*, chs. 5–11; Eliot, chs. 6–10; Goodman, chs. 10, 12; *Wild and Innocent* and *Born to Run* chs. of *Songs*; Sandford, ch. 3; Alterman, ch. 3; Guterman, chs. 2–3; Marsh, *On Tour*, ch. 2; Santelli, chs. 2–3; Kirkpatrick, chs. 2–3; Clemons and Reo, 29–65, 70–75, 265–66, 268 ("Jungleland" solo), 316; http://brucebase.wikispaces.com/1973; http://brucebase.wikispaces.com/1974; http://brucebase.wikispaces.com/1975; http://brucebase.wikispaces.com/The+Wildpercent2C+The+Innocent+percent26+The+E+Street+Shuffle+-+Studio+Sessions; http://brucebase.wikispaces.com/Born+To+Run+-+Studio+Sessions. The current pressings of *Wild and Innocent* reflect the original mixes and 1980s digital remasters of the albums, but the thirtieth-anniversary reissue of *Born to Run* (Sony, 2005) contains significantly improved digital remasterings of that album, as well as *Wings for Wheels: The Making of Born to Run*, a full-length documentary on DVD, on which I have drawn in this chapter. Louis Masur, *Runaway Dream: Born to Run and Bruce Springsteen's American Vision* (New York: Bloomsbury, 2009), which was published after I had already drafted the initial version of this chapter, also sheds interesting sidelights on the same material.

78   **a very fine young songwriter** Springsteen's album wasn't due out until November, but CBS did send a camera crew down to record their young artist at one point, giving us the first widely available video of Springsteen before a live audience. Although the complete video for at least one of these Max's sets may still exist in Columbia's archive, the most widely circulated version (*TIYL*, vol. 1, disc 1), contains only "Henry Boy" and "Growin' Up," the opening and closing of a single set.

78   **"Henry Boy"** Appel insists Bruce played this song in his office in February (Eliot, 56), but that is almost certainly wrong.

80   *a bishop and his wife* Introduction to "Bishop Danced," New York, NY, 31 Jan. 1973.

81   **Maxanne Sartori's afternoon show** This in-studio visit is reproduced on *WBCN Studios 1973* (Great Dane Records, 1992), and selections from a number of 1973 and 1974 appearances on other FM stations are available on *Radio Waves* (Great Dane Records, 1990).

81   *When this is over* Ossining, NY, 17 Dec. 1972.

82   **western themes** He could even have revived such old Bruce Springsteen Band favorites as "Don't You Want to Be an Outlaw?," "Cherokee Queen," and "If I Was the Priest," pairing them perhaps with "Balboa vs. the Earthslayer," which he had written in late summer. That last song is one of those for which we now have only a title, but Appel thought it was one of Springsteen's best: it was the song he had wanted him to sing if he had gotten the Super Bowl slot.

83   **January stand at Max's** The 31 Jan. 1973 performance, at which "Thundercrack" was probably premiered, was recorded for the syndicated radio program *The King Biscuit Flour Hour*. The most widely available current recording of this concert is *Max's Kansas City Night* (Crystal Cat Records, 2008).

83   **new set-closer** It may have been during that same week at Max's that Springsteen introduced another, even more famous marathon set-closer: "Rosalita," which set colorful words about a Latina girlfriend with overprotective parents to the tune of "Henry Boy," the song with which he had opened his solo set at the club back in August.

83   **the whopper about** This song has been called by many names over the years. In his "Songs" appendix to *Born* (272), Marsh actually lists it under three titles ("Contessa," "Hey Santa Ana," and "The Guns of Kid Cole"). On *Tracks*, Springsteen definitively named it "Santa Ana," but on bootlegs it circulates under a number of titles.

84   **Jackson Browne** Browne had been introduced to Springsteen by David Blue in Manhattan at the Bitter End, and he had invited him up onstage for an impromptu set. This happened on 4 Sept. 1972, probably when Bruce was playing an unadvertised gig at Max's for ready cash.

84   **I remember thinking** Henley quoted in Marsh, *On Tour*, 55.

86   **"The Fever"** This recording was probably for copyright purposes, and they may have recorded "You Mean So Much to Me" at this session for the same reason.

87   **musically cluttered** Dave Bourdon, "Rock Music Fans Get Perfect Show," *Binghamton Press and Sun-Bulletin*, 14 June 1973, SSC.

88   **may have been hoping** During the entire year that Sancious was in Richmond, Bruce doesn't seem to have performed "It's Hard to Be a Saint in the City" or "Growin' Up," two songs whose studio recordings are unimaginable without Sancious's piano accompaniment, live. From the Kenny's Castaways gigs through the Chicago dates, Bruce was usually the one at the piano during these performances. As the author of these songs, he obviously had a feeling for them, but he probably knew that his own piano playing on them couldn't possibly match Sancious's.

89   **Now in Blauvelt** Sancious had rejoined the rest of the band informally during some of their recent performances in Maryland, Virginia, and DC and officially

during the Fat City stand, and so before he came into the studio, he had already played live on several of the numbers that he was being asked to improve.

91   **as the verses go on** Even though both the second and the third verses of "New York City Serenade" were stripped from the abandoned "Vibes Man," it's interesting to note that in the later song the order of the two sketches that they trace are reversed. The new order allows the narrator to move more firmly into the scene with each of his three portraits: viewing Billy and Diamond Jackie in the first verse at a remove; then moving in the second verse from watching the Fish Lady to specifically asking her if he can take her hand; and finally giving advice unhesitatingly in the third verse to the seemingly profligate Vibes Man.

91   **returned to Max's** "New York City Serenade" seems to have been mostly finished by the time of the Max's stand. The biggest difference between the surviving studio tracks and the Max's performance is the atavistic survival of a few lines of the lyrics of "Vibes Man" in the Fish Lady verse. This suggests that the instrumental tracks may have been pretty much locked by this point, but Springsteen may not have finalized his vocal track, on which the final version of the lyric was added. The 18 July 1973 performance at Max's is reproduced on *The Unsurpassed Springsteen*, vol. 2 (Yellow Dog Records, 1993).

94   **dance with no exact steps** *Songs*, 25.

96   **When I listen to Bruce Springsteen** Lester Bangs, "Hot Rod Rumble in the Promised Land," *Creem*, Nov. 1975, 82.

96   *Last summer* Introduction to "New York Song," Bryn Mawr, PA, 24 April 1973.

97   **on the same path** Her first album, *Give It Up*, had made it to no. 138 on the albums chart—not as stellar a debut as *Jackson Browne*, but still a good starter position.

99   **Sam McKeith** McKeith, who was African American and who had frankly taken Springsteen on around the time of the CBS signing because he didn't want his client list to be restricted to black acts, had been initially unimpressed by the singer. Like many who encountered Springsteen's music during this early phase, McKeith was slowly won over during 1973 by his live performances, particularly with his band.

100   **slapping a bumper sticker** Clyde Hadlock, "Some Kind of Zoo in Hell," *Daily Kent Stater*, 20 Jan. 1974, SSC.

101   **monopop** As Christgau put it in one interview, this was the time in the midtwentieth century when "[e]verybody listened to the same music on the radio." Steve Horowitz, "'My Tastes Don't Evolve; They Broaden: An Interview with Robert Christgau," *Pop Matters*, 17 Oct. 2006.

101   *music provided you* Spoken interlude during "Remember When the Music," New York, NY, 7 Dec. 1987. This performance was at a tribute gala for the late Harry Chapin, and despite his acoustic guitar and harp rack, Springsteen's generic tilt at this concert was in strong contradistinction to almost every other performer on the bill, most of whom hailed from the folk community (most notably Pete Seeger and Peter, Paul, and Mary). "Remember When the Music," the song that Chapin's widow asked Springsteen to sing at the tribute, clearly refers to a glorified folk music past ("when the music was made with boxes strung of wood and wire"), but the comments that Springsteen wove into his performance of the song cleverly shifted it so that its meaning now seemed to refer to the pop music of his youth.

101   **feel out the arrangement** *Songs*, 44.

101   **Ronettes-inspired sound** Springsteen quoted in Goodman, 270.

103   **a new drummer** The dates get a little confused here. Some sources suggest that the fight with Lopez was in January, but surviving recordings indicate that Lopez was definitely onstage in Cleveland on 1 Feb. 1974 (Springsteen introduces him during "Thundercrack"). Similarly, there's some suggestion that Carter was

recruited during Springsteen's dates in Atlanta during early February, but if Springsteen had already recruited a new drummer by that point, why did he have to cancel concerts in February after Lopez's departure? The sequence of events I've presented here is the easiest way to reconcile most accounts: Clemons's arrest predated Lopez's fight; in between, the band met Carter in Atlanta but no attempt was made to recruit him until after Lopez had been fired.

105 **sort of observant** Landau quoted in Eliot, 115.

106 **The early show that night** The early show at Harvard Square Theatre on 9 May 1974 is available on *Rock 'n' Roll Punk* (E Street Records, 1999).

106 **projected song cycle** Among the songs new to Landau that Springsteen had ready at this point for his next album and might have performed that night were "A Love So Fine," "Angel Baby," "Jungleland," "She's the One," "She's So Fine" (aka "Angel Blues" or "Ride On Sweet William").

106 **street trash rockers** Landau, "Growing Young with Rock and Roll," *Real Paper*, 22 May 1974.

107 **a bit of Eventide** Arthur quoted in David Simons, *Studio Stories: How the Great New York Records Were Made: From Miles to Madonna, Sinatra to the Ramones* (San Francisco: Backbeat Books, 2004), 186.

109 **if you're doing your job** Weinberg quoted in Charles R. Cross, "Interview with Max Weinberg," *Backstreets*, no. 11 (Fall 1984): 20.

110 **three nights at Max's** This may have been in early Nov. 1973, although Hall and Oates were the opening act of record in the newspaper advertisements for that stand. It may have been that the owners of Max's were throwing unbilled work Aukema's way, as they had thrown similar work Springsteen's way a little over a year before.

110 **the New York shore** Bittan quoted in "Roy Bittan" (interview conducted 29 July 1992), in Ermanno Labianca, *Local Hero: Bruce Springsteen in the Words of His Band* (Milan: Great Dane Books, 1993), 23.

111 **putative headliner** This was the last time that Springsteen would ever open for anyone, except at charity events.

112 *couple of new boys* Introduction to "Cupid," New York, NY, 4 Oct. 1974.

112 **didn't even bother to mention** Michael Sangiacomo, "Jungle Land, Springsteen Style," *Philadelphia Inquirer*, 4 Nov. 1974; Lloyd Traven, "Springsteen Rocks Kirby," *Lafayette*, 22 Nov. 1974, SSC.

113 **presented his songs** Neer, *FM*, 197.

113 **"So Young and in Love"** Truth be told, this last number worked much better as an instrumental called "A Love So Fine." This is also the song that would be called "Paradise by the C" on the three-disc live set.

113 **full string sections** Conventional wisdom holds that "Backstreets" was unrecorded until the move to the Record Plant the following spring, but the strings on several takes are too close to the ones used on such confirmed earlier tracks as "Jungleland," "She's the One," and "Born to Run." All of these probably date from 914 in 1974 rather than the Record Plant in 1975, because (a) it's hard to believe that strings were being put back onto "Born to Run" once the bootleg single had caught fire on so many FM stations and (b) Suki Lahav can clearly be heard on one of the "Jungleland" takes, and she was definitely back in Israel by the time the band began recording in Manhattan.

For all discarded tracks from this period, the best source is *War and Roses: The Definitive "Born to Run" Outtakes, 1974–1975*. The two alternate takes of "Backstreets" here are also well supplemented by a third variation on *Deep Down in the Vaults*, vol. 2.

114 **Billy Joel concert** This was on 14 Dec. 1974. During the encores, Springsteen joined Joel onstage for, of course, "Twist and Shout."

115 **first recorded performance** This version of the song, the earliest one we have, is commonly called "Wings for Wheels." Since the Main Point benefit was later broadcast, there are several widely circulating recordings of it, including *You Can Trust Your Car to the Man with the Star* (Labour of Love, 1997).

115 **widening his perspective** Interestingly enough, Springsteen introduced the final version of the song at the Bottom Line, New York, NY, on 14 Aug. 1975, as being *a song about this guy from California and this girl from Indiana and how they met in the same place.*

116 **open and close** Another scheme would have called for all the album's songs to take place in a single day, possibly with the first side opening with an alarm clock going off.

117 **the piano part** Bruce originally wrote the song on piano and has performed it frequently on piano with no other accompaniment throughout his career, particularly on the *Born to Run* tour.

118 **considerable debate** Ontologically, some fans insist that it started with the massive 1971 live outfit that arose in the wake of Steel Mill's collapse, while others hold that it did not truly begin until the summer of 1975 when Steve Van Zandt finally joined the fold.

118 **This band has spent** Clemons and Reo, 56. One reason to doubt this story, however, is that Sancious wasn't even in the band at that point and wouldn't be for the next nine months. For Sancious's version of how the name came about (which would seem to place the naming in late March of 1974), see Santelli, 24.

119 **You hook on to Bruce** Clemons quoted in Jay Cocks, "Rock's New Sensation: The Backstreet Phantom of Rock," *Time*, 27 Oct. 1975.

120 **virtually unique** During this time, the only other pop performer who fronted a band anywhere near as well known was Prince, and the membership of his outfit was much more like a revolving door, changing from the Revolution to the New Power Generation, for example, as the artist's vision shifted from one phase to another.

120 **The band always** After "Thunder Road," Somerville, MA, 19 Feb. 2003. *The key to this song*, he added during this concert, *was the fadeout. Intimate Night* (Godfather Records) reproduced this concert and is an essential recording for anyone who is interested in Springsteen's own understanding of his song process.

121 **half a dozen bars** See especially "Thunder Road (Alternate Take no. 3)" on *War and Roses*.

121 **personal rather than communal** There was a sax break in the final version of the song, a wonderful sax break at the end, but it was there to convey the narrator's triumphant ride out of town, not to give the crowd at the Student Prince a few bars to dance to.

Chapter 5. TONIGHT'S GONNA BE EVERYTHING THAT I SAID (1975–1976)

General Sources: Marsh, *Born*, chs. 1, 12–13; Eliot, ch. 11; Sandford, ch. 4; Marsh, *On Tour*, ch. 3; Santelli, ch. 4; Clemons and Reo, 66–69; http://brucebase.wikispaces.com/1975. Eric Meola, *Born to Run: The Unseen Photos* (San Rafael, CA: Insight Editions, 2006), sheds interesting light on the publicity process surrounding the album's release.

122 **surprising surge of support** Once again, the chronology is very confusing here. Appel told Marc Eliot that the student interview was at "Brown" (Eliot, 121). Springsteen did play Brown and give an interview to a student reporter backstage, but that was on 26 April 1974, before he ever went into the studio to record "Born to Run." If Segelstein was indeed the person whose mind was changed, the most

reasonable guess would be that this happened during the late winter or early spring of 1975—i.e., between the time that Appel and Springsteen had leaked "Born to Run" and when the band started recording at the Record Plant. There are no concerts that fit the bill.

However, because Appel also refers in the same section to an upcoming "*Rolling Stone*" interview around the time of the meeting with Segelstein, my best guess is that Appel means to suggest that these events happened in *October* 1974. Even though this would have been before "Born to Run" was distributed to DJs, it had been recorded. Bruce did play Princeton that month (not Brown) and did have an interview coming up with *Crawdaddy!* (not *Rolling Stone*, whose reporters would not interview him in depth until late 1975, just before the release of *Born to Run*). This still doesn't explain why, if Segelstein's mind had changed, the label support didn't really arrive for another six months, but it seems the most likely reconciliation of the story with the verifiable facts.

123 **rock 'n' roll album** John Rockwell, "New Dylan from New Jersey? It Might As Well Be Springsteen," *Rolling Stone*, 9 Oct. 1975.

124 **Wolff has shrewdly pointed out** Daniel Wolff, *4th of July, Asbury Park: A History of the Promised Land* (New York: Bloomsbury, 2005), 209.

125 *something from our new album* Introduction to "Tenth Avenue Freeze-Out," Providence, RI, 20 July 1975.

126 **added in the spring** Van Zandt may have played with the band on 9 March, their last performance until the Palace date in Providence in July, but Van Zandt's addition to the band is usually placed in May.

126 **tastemaker** Maureen Orth, Janet Huck, and Peter S. Greenberg, "Making of a Rock Star," *Newsweek*, 27 Oct. 1975.

127 **simulcast on WNEW** There are several available recordings of the Bottom Line shows, but the best, *The Punk Meets the Godfather* (Godfather Records, 1991), is based on the WNEW simulcast of the early show on 15 Aug. 1975.

127 **When I think** Springsteen made this comment in a post on www.savethebottom line.com.

128 **punk poetry** John Rockwell, "Springsteen's Rock Poetry at Its Best," *New York Times*, 29 Aug. 1975.

128 **magnificent album** Greil Marcus, "Born to Run," *Rolling Stone*, 9 Oct. 1975.

129 **the complete monument** Winner quoted in Robert Christgau, "Yes, There Is a Rock-Critic Establishment (But Is That Bad for Rock?)," *Village Voice*, 26 Jan. 1976, available at http://www.robertchristgau.com/xg/rock/critics-76.php.

129 **With the successful mass-marketing** James Miller, *Flowers in the Dustbin: The Rise of Rock 'n' Roll, 1947–1977* (New York: Simon & Schuster, 1999), 325.

130 *Seasons come* Introduction to "Does This Bus Stop at 82nd Street?," Philadelphia, PA, 31 Dec. 1975.

130 **Hammersmith Odeon** The concert-length video *Hammersmith Odeon, London '75*, included in the thirtieth-anniversary *Born to Run* set, is a good document of the first heady phase of Brucemania. CBS has also made it available as an audio album. For a good summary of the British hype leading up to this concert, see Sandford, 98–99.

130 **Button incident** Reported in "Random Notes," *Rolling Stone*, 1 Jan. 1976.

131 **Marsh and Landau** Sinclair quoted in Goodman, 284.

132 **the first victory** Christgau, "Establishment."

133 **He's able to say** Orth, Huck, and Greenberg, "Making," 62.

133 **the Asbury Jukes** The Jukes begun as a loose assembly of players called the Blackberry Booze Band that played Thursdays and Sundays at the Stone Pony, a relatively new club that had opened in Asbury two years before. The band played

R&B and soul, styles of music Bruce still adored, even if his own work seemed to be moving away from them. When the group got its record deal, Springsteen gave them two songs he'd had kicking around for the last two or three years, "The Fever" and "You Mean So Much to Me," neither of which he thought would work on one of his own albums. He would even end up writing the liner notes for that first Jukes album, his most detailed offstage memoirs of the Asbury Park scene five years before. For his part, Steve Van Zandt had given the band "I Don't Want to Go Home," the ode to compulsive all-night jamming that he had been inspired to write five years earlier while he was out in Vegas with the Dovells.

133 **all these people** Jay Cocks, "Rock's New Sensation: The Backstreet Phantom of Rock," *Time*, 27 Oct. 1975.

134 **You know the Blauvelt Diner?** Arthur quoted in David Simons, *Studio Stories: How the Great New York Records Were Made: From Miles to Madonna, Sinatra to the Ramones* (San Francisco: Backbeat Books, 2004), 186.

Chapter 6. I'LL BE THERE ON TIME AND I'LL PAY THE COST (1976–1979)

General Sources: Marsh, *Born*, chs. 14–17; Eliot, chs. 12–14 and Appendix A (which reproduces almost 90 pages of documents relating to the Springsteen-Appel lawsuit and is invaluable); Goodman, chs. 13–14; *Darkness* chapter of *Songs*; Sandford, chs. 4–5; Alterman, ch. 4; Guterman, ch. 3; Marsh, *On Tour*, chs. 4–5; Santelli, ch. 4; Kirkpatrick, ch. 4; http://brucebase.wikispaces.com/1976; http://brucebase.wikispaces.com/1977; http://brucebase.wikispaces.com/1978; and http://brucebase.wikispaces.com/Darkness+On+The+Edge+Of+Town+-+Studio+Sessions. Frank Stefanko, *Days of Hope and Dreams: An Intimate Portrait of Bruce Springsteen* (New York: Billboard Books, 2003), and Lynn Goldsmith, *Springsteen: Access All Areas* (New York: Rizzoli, 2000), shed interesting light on how consciously Springsteen was crafting his image during this period. Although it became available after I had already drafted this chapter, I have also drawn on *The Promise: The Making of "Darkness on the Edge of Town,"* Thom Zimny's authorized documentary on the making of *Darkness* (which generously samples Barry Rebo's footage from Springsteen's late-1970s rehearsals, recording, and performances) in revising it.

138 **more frankly autobiographical** Before then, most of the stories Bruce told were either purposefully exaggerated attempts at humor or spur-of-the-moment personal revelations. One might count the long story about the first time that he met Clarence that served as a preface to the slow version of "E Street Shuffle" for a number of dates in August and September of 1975 (including the Bottom Line shows) as the beginning of this trend, but that was more in the realm of myth and legend. At most, that story represented a transition between the more "colorful" anecdotes of Bruce's life he told on his first two CBS tours and these new stories (like the one preceding "Pretty Flamingo"), in which he tried to connect the performance of a song to an affecting moment in his life.

138 **first recorded version** Introduction to "Pretty Flamingo," Ann Arbor, MI, 23 Sept. 1975.

138 *never found out* Introduction to "Pretty Flamingo," Memphis, TN, 29 April 1976. This concert, from which I will quote several times, is available on *Knock on Wood* (RR Records).

138 **hitting the big time** *Has anybody got the Wild and the Innocent album here?*, he asked the audience before performing "Incident on 57th Street" at the Ellis. *I only ask sometimes 'cause some people think that the last album out was the first one we put out.* (Introduction to "Incident on 57th Street," Memphis, TN, 29 April 1976.)

138 **the night before** Introduction to "Growin' Up," Nashville, TN, 28 April 1976, reported in *Nashville Banner*, 29 April 1976.

138 *You go to New York* Introduction to "Growin' Up," Memphis, TN, 29 April 1976.

139 *If we came in* Introduction to "It's My Life," Memphis, TN, 29 April 1976.

139 **surviving recordings** I've listened to a number of performances of this song on this tour, and the most striking one extant is from Springfield, MA, on 22 Aug. 1976. It is reproduced on *Down in Jungleland* (Winged Wheel Records).

141 *wrote the book* After "Knock on Wood," Memphis, TN, 29 April 1976.

141 **his elders** Quoted in Robert Christgau, "Yes, There Is a Rock-Critic Establishment (But Is That Bad for Rock?)," *Village Voice*, 26 Jan. 1976, available at http://www.robertchristgau.com/xg/rock/critics-76.php.

141 *just a prisoner* Probably after "Raise Your Hand," Louisville, KY, 2 April 1976.

141 **first walked onstage** Ronnie Tutt quoted in Peter Guralnick, *Careless Love: The Unmaking of Elvis Presley* (Boston: Little, Brown, 1999), 599–600.

142 **You wouldn't wear** Goldsmith, "Introduction," *Access*.

143 **making much money** According to the 31 March 1976 audit reproduced in Eliot (301), advances were charged against Springsteen's artist royalties rather than his writer royalties. Through the completion of *Born to Run*, that account showed a deficit of $5,727.64, indicating that Mike Appel really was playing things as close to the bone as he could.

144 **The last straw** When Landau joined the production team for *Born to Run*, it required a new agreement between Laurel Canyon Productions and CBS Records (dated 13 April 1975) that was specifically limited to Springsteen's third album and to which neither Springsteen nor Landau was a direct party.

145 **such changes, adaptations** Contract reproduced in Eliot, 275.

145 **not evil but** Springsteen and Tallent comments taken from Zimny, *Promise*.

145 **The full accounting** When Laurel Canyon's books were audited in the spring of 1976 at Springsteen's request, the corporation was found to owe Springsteen only $20,149, a drop in the bucket given the quantity of the moneys that had been moving through it. Just ask Billy Joel.

146 **I have been cheated** Remarks during deposition quoted in Eliot, 200. Incredible as it may seem, Springsteen did not seem to fully understand at first that a deposition is all on the record. His attorney explained this to him during a recess, and after this his testimony became much more circumspect.

147 *I've got like* Introduction to "Tenth Avenue Freeze-Out," Red Bank, NJ, 2 Aug. 1976.

147 **I have started** Quoted in David McGee, "Bruce Springsteen Claims the Future of Rock & Roll: Believers and Betrayers: 'A Textbook Example of a Naive Musician Learning the Meaning of Money,'" *Rolling Stone*, 11 Aug. 1977.

149 **six months earlier** The E Street Band played two shows at the Spectrum on 25 and 27 Oct. 1976, only their second and third headlining arena shows ever, after one date in Phoenix earlier in the month. The second of these shows is reproduced on *Spirit of '76* (Crystal Cat Records) and serves as a good example of the concerts on the latter half of the Lawsuit tour.

149 **entered the studio** *The Promise: The Darkness on the Edge of Town Story* (Columbia, 2010), a three-CD, three-DVD set chronicling the evolution of Springsteen's fourth album, was released as I was in the final stages of writing this volume. The set reproduces one of Springsteen's songwriting notebooks for this period, and as usual every page yields fresh insights into his compositional process. The audio discs contain a highly necessary remix of *Darkness on the Edge of Town* itself, as well as two discs' worth of discarded tracks, a few of which were previously unknown even to the most dedicated fans. Even more than on *Tracks*, however, a

number of the songs on *The Promise* have been augmented, with twenty-first-century performances added to the 1977 base recordings. For historical purposes, I have still based most of my conclusions on the unaugmented (if lower-quality) recordings on *Lost Masters II: One-Way Street* (Labour of Love Records), *Lost Masters III: Rattling the Chains* (Labour of Love Records), and *The Definitive Darkness Outtakes* (E Street Records). Most of this material is also contained on the six-CD compilation *The Unbroken Promise: Lighting Up the Darkness Sessions* (Godfather Records).

150   **There were also** Fairly complete takes of these three songs were recorded during some of the earliest sessions at Atlantic Records Studios in the summer of 1977. Given the slowness with which lyrics were coming to Springsteen on this project, this suggests that these three songs had been worked out before he and the band arrived in the studio. In particular, in *The Promise*, there is Rebo-shot footage of Springsteen singing a mostly complete "One-Way Street" during the sessions the band held at his home in Holmdel, NJ, which almost certainly predated the first Atlantic sessions in June 1977.

150   **clearly placeholders** Most comically, in the first surviving vocal that August for the already titled "Badlands," Springsteen seems to sing righteously and indignantly that *the pizza don't come*. What he probably meant was *the peace that don't come*. In the past, he would have polished that kind of easily misheard lyric before he ever got into the studio.

151   **shared an emotional temperature** The sheer inarticulate power of this emotion may explain why tracks like "Breakout," "Bring on the Night," and "Because the Night" couldn't quite come into focus that fall. The rage of their choruses was clear from the outset, but the specific verses that could lead articulately between such outbursts proved more elusive.

152   **the implicit setting** See introduction to "Racing in the Street," Portland, OR, 24 June 1978: *Back in Asbury Park they got this Circuit, it's formed from Kingsley Avenue and Ocean Avenue. It's a mini Indianapolis 500.* The earliest take of "Prove It All Night" had also set that song's action on the Circuit: the lyrics on this take are a blending of the lyrics of "Something in the Night" and the eventual lyrics of this song. Even on *Born to Run*, both "Night" and "Born to Run" were set on the Circuit. (The *Palace* Amusements Arcade was just off Kingsley, almost at the southern edge of the street where it ran off southwest onto Cookman.) After *Wild and Innocent*, Springsteen may have been through with the boardwalk, but he was obviously not yet through with Asbury Park, especially the Circuit.

154   **spitballing songs** Among several dozen others, there were two more Bo Diddley–style numbers ("Goin' Back" and "Preacher's Daughter"), two R&B ballads ("Hearts of Stone" and "Talk to Me"), yet another New York song ("Taxi Cab"), and, most deliriously of all, an intentional "frat rock" number ("Sherry Darling") that was written mostly because, as he recalled years later at the *DoubleTake* concerts, "All that summer I was stuck in the studio, and I just wanted to go to the *beeeeach*."

154   **something like a tone poem** This is in Zimny, *Promise*.

156   *That kind of character* After "Darkness on the Edge of Town," Somerville, MA, 19 Feb. 2003.

156   **my adult voice** *Songs*, 69.

156   **true rock legend** The footage of the end of the Pistols' Winterland show can be found at http://www.youtube.com/watch?v=cebSJMdbTzc&feature=related. For more complete accounts of this show, one of the most thoroughly dissected in the history of rock 'n' roll, see in particular Greil Marcus, *Lipstick Traces: A Secret History of the Twentieth Century* (Cambridge, MA: Harvard University Press,

1989), Version One; Jon Savage, *England's Dreaming: Anarchy, Sex Pistols, Punk Rock, and Beyond* (New York: St. Martin's, 1992), ch. 4; and Legs McNeil and Gillian McCain, *Please Kill Me: The Uncensored Oral History of Punk* (New York: Grove Press, 1996), ch. 34; all of which should be followed by a reading of John Lydon, with Keith and Kent Zimmerman, *Rotten: No Irish, No Blacks, No Dogs* (New York: Picador, 1994), in which the singer gives his own very grounded and not at all symbolic reading of the event, especially in "Segment 01: Never Mind the Situationists; This Was Situation Comedy."

157   **New York punk** While Springsteen was ensconced at the Record Plant in 1977 trying to complete *Darkness on the Edge of Town*, both Lou Reed and Patti Smith were there too, working on the albums that would become *Street Hustle* and *Easter*. Although he had made disparaging remarks about Springsteen two years earlier in an interview for the initial issue of *Punk* magazine, in 1977 Reed asked Springsteen to perform a spoken rap on the title track of *Street Hustle*, "because," as he later told a reporter, "he really is of the street." See Victor Bockris, *Transformer: The Lou Reed Story* (New York: Simon & Schuster, 1994), 291. As for Smith, by the summer of 1977, she and Springsteen had become friends and performed together several times. As he was homing in on the essence of his fourth album, Springsteen gave Smith the uncompleted "Because the Night," because he knew she could finish it, as he was unable to do. No matter how people may view them in retrospect, in the late 1970s Reed, Smith, and Springsteen were kindred spirits: fellow bridge and tunnel kids whose lives had been saved by both New York City and rock 'n' roll.

Springsteen also had considerable ties to the younger New York punks, Reed and Smith's spiritual godchildren, as it were. In March of 1978, while Springsteen was mostly occupied with the mixes of *Darkness*, he guested on the Dictators' "Faster and Louder." When the Ramones played the Fast Lane in Asbury about a year after that, Bruce and Joey (not Dee Dee, of course), hit it off, and the elder singer wrote a song for their band to record, the same way he had written a song for Elvis two years earlier. (The song, which Joey's band ultimately rejected, was "Hungry Heart.")

As far as the British punks were concerned, there is the significant case of Clash frontman Joe Strummer. Like Peter Gabriel, Strummer attended Springsteen's Nov. 1975 show at the Hammersmith Odeon and was utterly entranced, both by the length of the show—"That's the way to do it!" he thought—and by the idea that you could turn the streets of your hometown into the stuff of rock myth. Strummer quoted in Chris Salewicz, *Redemption Song: The Ballad of Joe Strummer* (New York: Faber and Faber, 2006), 137.

158   **Dave Marsh for one** As Marsh would explain in the Springsteen biography he was already working on at the time of the lawsuit, "Rock and roll is about promises—covenants between the audience and the star. . . . This is a central tenet of *Mystery Train*" (*Born*, 201). Marsh's implication was that Springsteen may have found himself echoing at this moment the whooping cry from Little Richard that Marcus highlights in the prologue to his volume: "HE GOT WHAT HE WANTED BUT HE LOST WHAT HE HAD!" See Greil Marcus, *Mystery Train: Images of America in Rock 'n' Roll Music* (New York: E. P. Dutton, 1976), 3.

158   **The best popular artists** Marcus, *Train*, 7.

159   **That last verse** After "Darkness on the Edge of Town," Somerville, MA, 19 Feb. 2003.

159   **You wanna ride** Springsteen quoted in *Ties*, 105.

160   **the bootleg albums** Despite the way he would later feel about such activities,

Bruce occasionally started his second sets on this tour with an explicit acknowledgment that the concert was almost certainly being bootlegged. Many of the
1978 shows are available in what E Street Radio later euphemistically called "fan-
based recordings," and I have consequently been lucky enough to listen to over a
dozen of them. Among the shows that most fans cite as classics are the 7 July show
at the Roxy in Los Angeles (*Roxy Night* [Crystal Cat Records]); the 9 Aug. show at
the Agora Ballroom in Cleveland (on *Summertime Blues* [E Street Records]), the
19 Sept. show at the Capitol Theatre in Passaic (*Pièce de Résistance* [Great Dane
Records]); and the 19 Dec. show at the Paramount Theatre in Portland (on *Paramount Night* [Crystal Cat Records]), as well as the two Winterland concerts,
which I will discuss in more detail below.

This is also the first tour for which there are considerable video records, most
obviously *Houston '78 Bootleg: House Cut* in the *Promise* set (which cleverly uses
video shot off the Jumbotron at that concert). In addition, vol. 1, disc 1, of *TIYL*,
contains pro-shot and amateur-shot performance videos from the tour, as well as
TV interviews and news reports that publicized it. Finally, *Classic 78* (Apocalypse
Sound) provides some interesting performance video from the 8 July concert in
Phoenix, as well as a very fun drop-in with Southside in Cleveland.

160 **"Because the Night"** Patti Smith's completed version of this song was released
in the spring and peaked at no. 13 on the *Billboard* Hot 100 in April. The version
Springsteen sang in concert later in the year was with a slightly different set of
lyrics that he had managed to complete at some point during early 1978. For the
specifics of Springsteen and Smith's serial collaboration on this song, see their
wonderful interviews on this topic in Zimny's *Promise*.

160 **Black Sabbath** They even played at many of the same venues that year as Bruce
did: the Milwaukee Arena in mid-August, a little over two months after the E
Street Band had been there; Madison Square Garden at the end of that month,
just four days after Bruce had finished a three-night stand there.

161 *the first song* Introduction to "The Promise," Philadelphia, PA, 26 May 1978.

162 **the two Winterland shows** Thanks to the KMET simulcast, the 15 Dec. show
has been widely available for decades. For my purposes, I have used *Winterland
Night* (Crystal Cat) as a reference point. The 16 Dec. concert is less widely available, but it still circulates as a CDR among collectors.

163 *I remember when* Introduction to "Prove It All Night," San Francisco, CA, 15
Dec. 1978. As Springsteen revealed to Steve Van Zandt on an April 2011 episode
of Van Zandt's *Underground Garage* program on Sirius XM Satellite Radio, this
song is musically based on the Animals' 1965 "Please Don't Let Me Be Misunder-
stood." So, in a way, several of the pieces of the three-year-old "It's My Life" set
piece were present in this concert, even if that cover itself was not specifically
performed.

163 *How many of you guys* Introduction to "Good Rockin' Tonight," San Francisco,
CA, 16 Dec. 1978.

163 *Is San Francisco* Introduction to "Prove It All Night," San Francisco, CA, 16
Dec. 1978.

164 *Back in 1974, 1975* Between "Racing in the Street" and "Thunder Road," San
Francisco, CA, 16 Dec. 1978. See, for example, the same transition in Los Angeles, CA, 7 July 1978. Springsteen made clear in other iterations of this story that
this road trip happened just before the beginning of the *Darkness* sessions. The
place itself, Thunder Mountain Park, off Route 80 near Imlay, Nevada, was built
by Chief Rolling Mountain Thunder (aka Frank Van Zant, no relation to Steve
Van Zandt), a member of the Creek nation, in 1968 after he returned from service in the Vietnam War. Whether the road sign was inspired by Springsteen's

song, or by the Robert Mitchum movie from which he had taken his title, or just by Van Zant's post-Vietnam rechristening, has never been satisfactorily explained.

166   *I wanna tell* Middle of "Raise Your Hand," San Francisco, CA, 15 Dec. 1978. For another version of this monologue, see the 7 July 1978 performance at the Roxy, which is reproduced on *Live/1975–85*.

Chapter 7. AIN'T NOBODY LIKE TO BE ALONE (1979–1982)

General Sources: Marsh, *Born*, ch. 18–19; Marsh, *Glory*, chs. 2–7; Eliot, ch. 15; *River* and *Nebraska* chs. of *Songs*; Sandford, ch. 5; Alterman, ch. 5; Guterman, chs. 3–4; Marsh, *On Tour*, ch. 6; Santelli, ch. 5; Kirkpatrick, chs. 5–7. http://brucebase.wikispaces.com/1979; http://brucebase.wikispaces.com/1980; http://brucebase.wikispaces.com/1982; http://brucebase.wikispaces.com/1979+solo+-+Studio +Sessions; http://brucebase.wikispaces.com/The+River+-+Studio+Sessions; http://bruce base.wikispaces.com/1981+solo+-+Studio+Sessions; "Phase 1" of http://brucebase.wiki spaces.com/Born+In+The+USA+-+Studio+Sessions. The definitive recorded source for Springsteen's rehearsals and studio work for this period is the *Lost Masters* series (Labour of Love Records), vols. 4–15, to be supplemented by *The Definitive River Outtakes Collection* (E Street Records, 2 discs).

167   **even come close** His last two albums had respectively gone to no. 3 and no. 5 on the *Billboard* albums chart, but as individual tracks "Born to Run" had gone only to no. 23 on the singles chart in 1975 and "Prove It All Night" only to no. 33 three years later. And those had been Springsteen's most successful 45s. "Tenth Avenue Freeze-Out" and "Badlands" hadn't even cracked the Top 40, "Spirit in the Night" hadn't cracked the Hot 100, and "Blinded by the Light" had, as indicated, been a hit only for someone else.

169   **early-1979 home recordings** Springsteen's early-1979 home demos are on *Lost Masters*, vol. 8, and supplemented by additional tracks on *Lost Masters*, vols. 4, 6, and 9, and *the Definitive River Outtakes* that are labeled as such.

169   **Harmony vocals** In performance, harmony vocals tended to show up during the live shows in the covers, particularly the early-'60s covers that he and the band had performed in 1974 and 1975. Rich harmony vocals à la the Beach Boys had been considered for several of the songs on *Born to Run*, particularly the title track, but had ultimately been omitted from the album's final mixes.

169   **his fifth album** To date, Springsteen's fifth album has not received the box set treatment accorded both *Born to Run* and *Darkness on the Edge of Town*. However, Springsteen has officially released fourteen of the discarded tracks from these sessions on other albums, most notably as the bulk of disc 3 of *Tracks*. *Lost Masters*, vols. 4, 11, and 14 date mostly from before the No Nukes concerts, but for other specific tracks see the "On the Tracks" listing for this album on Brucebase.

170   *the rabbi got up* The full monologue is very suggestive, particularly considering how Springsteen's life would change over the next ten years. Most interesting is his later statement that *if you don't make that connection, you just . . . you know, I used to, like, stay in my room . . . and write a song. . . .* This version is from introduction to "Stolen Car," Uniondale, NY, 29 Dec. 1980, but he made similar remarks before the song throughout his next tour.

172   **two charity concerts** At the time of this writing, *No Nukes*, the film that documented the MUSE concerts, has still not been released on DVD, although used VHS copies remain available from some dealers. Raw footage from the concert is available on *TIYL*, vol. 1, disc 2, and quite a bit of the film is available in pieces on YouTube.

172   **The exuberance** Marsh, *Born*, 247–48.

173 **the home demos** *Lost Masters*, vol. 7, contains over a dozen of these home recordings from early 1980.

173 **rehearsals in Holmdel** Audios from a number of the band rehearsals in Holmdel from late 1979 are available on the *Lost Masters* series (particularly vols. 7 and 12) and on the first disc of the *Definitive River Outtakes*. A video of these rehearsals is also in circulation among fans. It's rough, but it provides interesting insights into how Springsteen went about trying to craft a work he meant to be a "band album."

173 **second round of recording** *Lost Masters*, vols. 11, 13, and 15, and *Definitive River Outtakes*, disc 2, contain a plethora of alternative takes from this second phase of recording the album.

173 **seemed almost haphazard** All in all, over fifty complete songs had been recorded during these sessions. If Bruce had truly wanted the two-disc set to clearly communicate his range, he could have devoted individual discs or sides to particular impulses (as Neil Young had done the previous year on the instant classic *Rust Never Sleeps*). He could have put out a fun disc and a serious disc, an album of numbers meant to be performed live (as his labelmate Billy Joel had just done with *Glass Houses*) or a sober, more explicitly political album than even *Darkness* had provided (as no pop-centered artist currently seemed willing to do).

173 **certain happiness** Hilburn and Springsteen in Robert Hilburn, "Springsteen: Out on the Streets," *Los Angeles Times*, 19 Oct. 1980, SSC.

174 *All you guys* Introduction to "Darkness on the Edge of Town," Tempe, AZ, 5 Nov. 1980.

174 *I never did good* Introduction to "Independence Day," Tempe, AZ, 5 Nov. 1980.

175 *I don't know what* Introduction to "Badlands," Tempe, AZ, 5 Nov. 1980. This recording of "Badlands" is actually the one featured on *Live/1975–85*, although the spoken introduction is omitted. For a full audio clip, see http://www.youtube.com/watch?v=NGoBcNXa3mM, which unfortunately does not have synchronized video to accompany it.

176 **values** Rosalynn Carter quoted in Kevin Mattson, *"What the Heck Are You Up To, Mr. President?": Jimmy Carter, America's "Malaise," and the Speech That Should Have Changed the Country* (New York: Bloomsbury, 2009), 93. Mattson's book is, not incidentally, the best treatment ever of 1979's place in U.S. cultural history.

177 **a white heat** The Three Mile Island accident occurred on Wednesday, 28 March 1979, and he and the band recorded at least two takes of "Roulette" less than a week later, on Tuesday, 3 April.

178 **songs about cars** Even if we restrict ourselves to songs we know Springsteen rehearsed or recorded with the band, an excellent car-themed album could be made out of "I'm a Rocker," "Cadillac Ranch," "Ramrod," "Sherry Darling," "Living on the Edge of the World," and "Held Up without a Gun" on side 1; and "Stolen Car," "Drive All Night," "The River," "Chevrolet Deluxe," and "Wreck on the Highway" on side 2.

178 **love song to a car** This same sort of uniquely male emotion lies at the heart of *Christine*, the 1983 horror novel written by longtime Springsteen fan Stephen King, although it is unlikely that King heard a recording of "Chevrolet Deluxe" before he wrote his book.

178 **Billy** One can't help wondering if "Billy" here (and perhaps in "The Promise" as well) is a more scannable substitution for "Bart," as in Bart Haynes, the drummer from the Castiles who died in Vietnam.

179 **In a nation** Carter, "Crisis of Confidence" speech, originally delivered 15 July 1979, available at http://www.pbs.org/wgbh/americanexperience/features/primary-resources/carter-crisis/.

180 **made sense of** The phrase is psychologist Howard Gardner's, quoted in Lou

Cannon, *President Reagan: The Role of a Lifetime*, 2nd ed. (New York: Public Affairs, 2183), 111. Gardner's comments here are worth reading in full, since his analysis of Reagan's "multiple intelligences" in light of his training as a performer rather than a lawyer makes his cognitive development sound extremely similar to Springsteen's (e.g., "Actors find it easier to mimic than to understand. . . . They are kids who often have difficulty with the usual school stuff, but they can parrot things back and get reinforcement from others.") For other striking similarities between Reagan's and Springsteen's psyches when the two men entered public life, see Cannon's ch. 11 ("The Loner").

181   **the freest society** Ronald Reagan, "A Vision for America," 3 Nov. 1980, available at http://www.reagan.utexas.edu/archives/reference/11.3.80.html.

181   **almost certain bet** Marcus, "The Next President of the United States," *New West*, 22 Dec. 1980, reprinted in *In the Fascist Bathroom: Punk in Pop Music, 1977–1992* (Cambridge, MA: Harvard University Press, 1999), 163.

181   **one-off covers** Even though he had been listening to country music seriously for at least three years, the fall of 1979 was the first time he regularly covered country songs in concert, slipping "The Yellow Rose of Texas" in before "Cadillac Ranch" in Dallas shortly after the election, and then including "Waltz across Texas" as part of the no longer geographically bounded "Detroit Medley" during the encores in Austin. During late November, Springsteen added Hank Williams's "I Hear a Lonesome Train" and Elvis Presley's "Mystery Train" to these train-themed encores in Maryland and at Madison Square Garden.

182   *a fighting song* Introduction to "This Land Is Your Land," Uniondale, NY, 31 Dec. 1980. This New Year's Eve concert produced one of the most famous Springsteen bootlegs of all time and is widely available on *Nassau Night* (Crystal Cat).

184   **"Rockin' All Over"** Perhaps better known in Europe as a 1977 Status Quo single.

184   *I think everybody* Introduction to "Johnny Bye Bye," Manchester, England, 13 May 1981.

185   *I remember* Introduction to "Johnny Bye Bye," Los Angeles, CA, 20 Aug. 1981.

186   *I'm used to* Introduction to "Who'll Stop the Rain?," Los Angeles, CA, 20 Aug. 1981.

187   **wasn't getting married** According to Sandford, 190, Springsteen did propose around this time to his current girlfriend Joyce Hyser, but she declined, and shortly afterwards they broke up.

187   *some missing part* Introduction to "Spare Parts," Worcester, MA, 25 Feb. 1988.

188   **all my rock 'n' roll answers** Springsteen quoted in James Henke, "Bruce Springsteen: The *Rolling Stone* Interview," *Rolling Stone*, 6 Aug. 1992.

188   **writing new songs** The definitive source for Springsteen's home recordings of late 1981 and early 1982 is *How Nebraska Was Born* (Godfather Records).

189   **reign of terror** Warren Burger, "Annual Report to the American Bar Association," 8 Feb. 1981, available at http://heinonline.org/HOL/LandingPage?collection=journals&handle=hein.journals/wolj67&div=15&id=&page=.

189   **sure brought me** Robert Coles, *Bruce Springsteen's America: A People Listening, a Poet Singing* (New York: Random House, 2005), 113.

189   **start treating 17 yr. old** This quotation comes from Reagan's 22 Dec. 1976 radio commentary, the script of which is reproduced in *Reagan in His Own Hand* (New York: Simon & Schuster, 2001), 400–01, 403.

191   **found the atmosphere** *Songs*, 135.

191   **only about half** Songs like "They Killed Him in the Streets," "Ruled by the Gun," "James Lincoln Dear," and "Jesse James," all of which he was apparently still working on during this period, were all left off the tape he made for Landau.

192 **set in the Garden State** "Atlantic City" obviously fits this bill, and "State Trooper" and "Open All Night" are both explicitly set on the New Jersey Turnpike. Elsewhere, the narrator of "Mansion on the Hill" is located in *Linden town*, the auto plant named in the first line of "Johnny 99" is in *Mahwah*, and "Losin' Kind" takes place *south of the Camden line*. "Reason to Believe" takes place on *Highway 31*, but as Springsteen's cover note to Landau revealed, the real highway was Route 33 to Millstone, NJ, which was west of the Turnpike, nearer New Brunswick. (The number was probably altered to allow for a better rhyme.) Most fascinating of all was "Highway Patrolman," whose lyrics would seem to set its action in eastern Michigan, near both Ohio and the Canadian border. However, Springsteen stations Patrolman Joe Roberts at a barracks in *Perrineville*, the name of a community in New Jersey. It is west of Freehold on Route 33 (the same highway that inspired "Reason to Believe"), and *the Michigan line* mentioned in this song may very well be connected with Michigan Avenue in Brick, NJ, near Freehold Regional (which plays a central role in the events of "Used Cars"). The one stumper here is "Child Bride," which refers to Stovell, a community that doesn't seem to appear anywhere in the United States. The song also refers to Route 95, which is the numerical designation of the New Jersey Turnpike.

193 **Old-school country** He wasn't the only rocker exploring those genres during this period. Ersatz punk Elvis Costello's music took a similar turn, with the release that same fall of *Almost Blue*, which featured a cover of George Jones's "A Good Year for the Roses," among other country songs. Costello saved his truly alarming live recording of Leon Payne's "Psycho"—a bizarre number that offered up a homespun backwoods version of Norman Bates—for one of his B-sides.

194 **displaced Alabaman** Sandford, 14.

194 **the band reassembled** The first recordings they did that February were actually backing tracks for *On the Line*, Gary U.S. Bonds' follow-up to *Dedication*.

194 **up-tempo rocker** Reproduced in *Songs*, 140.

196 **that turbulence** Landau quoted in Marsh, *Glory*, 116.

196 **full-band arrangements** Even more interestingly, though, the songs on the 3 Jan. tape that did work with the band, songs like "Born in the U.S.A.," "Downbound Train," and "Pink Cadillac," seemed the least tied to the specifics of the New Jersey landscape: the former song generally casts its final action near *the gas fires of the refinery*, while the latter two have no real spatial or geographical referents.

197 **the bravest** Steve Pond, "*Nebraska* Album Review," *Rolling Stone*, 28 Oct. 1982.

197 **most personal record** Rockwell quoted in *Ties*, 255. Of course, Bruce had written songs since *The River* that did offer answers, or at least dreamed of them— songs like "Follow That Dream" and "This Hard Land"—but the recordings of those songs had never made it out of the studio.

197 **most single-minded work** Pond, "Review."

Chapter 8. THIS GUN'S FOR HIRE (1982–1986)

General Sources: Marsh, *Glory*, chs. 8–21; Eliot, ch. 16; Goodman, ch. 16; *Born in the U.S.A.* ch. of *Songs*; Sandford, chs. 6–7; Alterman, ch. 6; Guterman, ch. 5; Marsh, *On Tour*, ch. 7; Santelli, ch. 6; Kirkpatrick, chs. 7–8; http://brucebase.wikispaces.com/ Born+In+The+USA+-+Studio+Sessions, http://brucebase.wikispaces.com/1983; http:// brucebase.wikispaces.com/1984; http://brucebase.wikispaces.com/1985; http://brucebase .wikispaces.com/1986.

The five BITU videos are on the first disk of *Complete Video Anthology*; TIYL, vol. 1, disc 2, contains an interesting rehearsal performance of "Dancing in the Dark," as well as some clips from the final show in LA well over a year later.

198   **Springsteen's recent ones** *Born to Run* had moved six million units, and *Darkness* and *The River* about that many combined. Even *Greetings* and *Wild and Innocent,* initially greeted with relative indifference by American record buyers, had eventually sold two million each in the wake of *Born to Run's* release

199   **Springsteen music was everywhere** My favorite example of how widely known Springsteen was in the early 1980s is the opening chapter of *The Talk Show Murders,* a 1982 detective story by 1950s polymath Steve Allen, in which the first victim of the book's celebrity-focused serial killer is a working-class rock star named "Elmo Finkstetter." Surely, if the man who made Elvis sing "Hound Dog" in a tux to an actual canine cares enough to parody you like that, your fame must precede you nearly everywhere in the U.S.A.

199   **rock 'n' roll fable** Hill's comments are from his liner notes to the film's soundtrack album, which was released by MCA in 1984. Significantly, Hill got everyone's favorite faux Springsteen, Jim Steinman, to write songs for the film, songs on which Roy Bittan and Max Weinberg among others played, as they had for fellow Steinman mouthpiece Bonnie Tyler.

199   **dozen polished tracks** These included "Born in the U.S.A.," "Downbound Train," "Glory Days," "Darlington County," and "Working on the Highway" (the rewritten version of "Child Bride"), not to mention "Cover Me" (a song he had almost given to both Gary U.S. Bonds and Donna Summer), as well as such in-studio experiments as "I'm on Fire" and "I'm Going Down."

200   **muscles have swelled** "Random Notes," in *Rolling Stone,* 12 May 1983.

200   **more home recordings** Most of Springsteen's early-1983 home recordings are on *Lost Masters* (Labour of Love), vols. 16–19.

201   **these new sessions** What 1983 band recordings we have are mostly on disc 3 of *Tracks* and *Lost Masters* (Labour of Love), vol. 19. The beautiful "None but the Brave" from this same period was officially released on the third disc of *The Essential Bruce Springsteen.*

201   **vinyl copies** One of the few things for which the singer might have been grateful to Ronald Reagan was the fact that on 24 May 1982 the president signed into law a new bill that made "record piracy and counterfeiting" a much more serious federal crime. While CBS's initial efforts to enforce these laws with regard to Springsteen's work mostly focused on foreign-made live recordings, the new laws also had an immediate dampening effect on the so-called studio boots: anyone could record a concert off the radio and dupe it, but what was the percentage in the highly risky move of sneaking tapes out of the Power Station or the Hit Factory when the corresponding penalties had been increased so much? On Springsteen's shifting attitude toward bootlegging, see Clinton Heylin, *Bootleg: The Secret History of the Other Recording Industry* (New York: St. Martin's, 1996), 181.

205   **contains a group** *Songs,* 165, 167.

206   **so small at first** Interestingly enough, MTV had launched in New Jersey well before it was available in New York City.

207   **Bruce's old stuff** Baker quoted in *Ties,* 27.

207   **a financial gold mine** In 1983, when they were first introduced, CDs had been responsible for only about $17.2 million. In early 1984, sales in the new format were taking off briskly, on track to total $103.3 million by the end of the year.

207   **was like Moses** Steve Knopper, *Appetite for Self-Destruction: The Spectacular Crash of the Record Industry in the Digital Age* (New York: Free Press, 2009), 10, 13.

208   **But you don't** Teller quoted in Goodman, 342.

209   **the most over-qualified** Springsteen, acceptance speech, Rock and Roll Hall of Fame Induction Ceremonies, New York, NY, 15 March 1999.

210   **locked in the Sony vaults** Indeed, Scialfa's remarks in "The Patti Scialfa Story," *Backstreets*, no. 11 (Fall 1984): 7.

211   **Okay, fellas** Springsteen, acceptance speech, Rock and Roll Hall of Fame Induction Ceremonies, New York, NY, 15 March 1999. To be fair, the last time the band had traveled with a female vocalist, it had added offstage drama as well as onstage drama to the tour. During the 1974 tour, Springsteen and Suki Lahav had an affair, and it almost broke up the Lahavs' marriage. On the basis of that experience, the other members of the band did know how complicated it could get, and Springsteen's delay in announcing this last new addition to the band may have been an acknowledgment that no one wanted to see a repeat of that situation.

212   **more wholesome place** This may be the only time that Brian De Palma has ever increased the perceived wholesomeness of material under his control.

214   **the songs from** This also partially reflects the split between sides 1 and 2 of *Born in the U.S.A.* during its original vinyl and cassette releases.

215   **quasi-autobiographical song** The audience at Alpine Valley, for example, picked up on the Pavlovian trigger to cheer when Bruce mentioned *a kid with a guitar in his hand* during the song's final verse. *Alpine Valley Night* (Crystal Cat) documents this concert and is in my opinion one of the most essential recordings for understanding the early stages of the *Born in the U.S.A.* tour.

217   **the other part** Mario Cuomo, keynote address to the Democratic National Convention, San Francisco, CA, 16 July 1984, available at http://www.americanrhetoric.com/speeches/mariocuomo1984dnc.htm.

217   **our Nation** Jesse Jackson, address to the Democratic National Convention, San Francisco, CA, 18 July 1984, available at http://www.americanrhetoric.com/speeches/jessejackson1984dnc.htm.

217   **If we allow** Quoted in Gil Troy, *Morning in America: How Ronald Reagan Invented the 1980s* (Princeton: Princeton University Press, 2005), 148.

217   **statism** Ronald Reagan, "Remarks on Accepting the GOP Presidential Nomination," Dallas, TX, 23 Aug. 1984, reprinted in *Speaking My Mind: Selected Speeches* (New York: Simon & Schuster, 1989), 212–13.

218   **When I was a kid** Introduction to "Born to Run," Largo, MD, 25 Aug. 1984.

218   **wholesome cultural portent** George Will, "A Yankee Doodle Springsteen," *Washington Post*, 13 Sept. 1984, A19.

219   **the Great Reconciliation** Troy, *Morning*, 118.

219   **Backstage** Will, "Yankee Doodle."

219   **scheduled stump appearance** Through the intercession of the promoters who had booked the Civic Centre show, the president's campaign had even asked Springsteen to attend the rally. This suggests that they, like Will, were more disingenuous than self-consciously duplicitous in seeking to connect the two men's ideologies.

219   **America's future rests** Reagan, "Remarks at a Reagan-Bush Rally in Hammonton, New Jersey," 19 Sept. 1984, available at http://www.reagan.utexas.edu/archives/speeches/1984/91984c.htm. See "Remarks at a Rally in Fairfield, Connecticut," 26 Oct. 1984, in *Speaking*, 235–46, for other local variations added to the speech in New Jersey, including names of local officials, sports teams, produce, a fiftieth-wedding anniversary, and an acknowledgment of Mrs. Mamie De Marco in the audience, who had just celebrated her eighty-ninth birthday.

220   **extol unrestricted individualism** On Friday night, Springsteen even dropped the Elvis and *you have to fight for it* comments, and simply told the audience, *I've always considered myself pretty fortunate 'cause when I was a kid, I dreamed about something and I get to live out a little piece of my dream every night. Here's hoping you get to live out a little piece of yours*, a hopeful conceit that almost couldn't

sound closer to the spirit in which the president had tried to cite him. See introduction to "Born to Run," Philadelphia, PA, 15 Sept. 1984.

220 **Revolutionary War monument** This speech had been a part of the tour since mid-July. In it, Springsteen talked about the Revolutionary War monument in Freehold and how he had never really appreciated it (except as a possible backdrop for Castiles publicity photos), but how a trip down to the Mall in Washington back in the spring before the tour started made him appreciate such monuments more—especially after seeing Bart Haynes's name etched in granite on Maya Lin's two-year-old Vietnam Veterans Memorial. *Monuments are there*, he concluded, *so that you always remember and so that you'd never forget that this is your hometown.* See introduction to "My Hometown," Philadelphia, PA, 17 Sept. 1984.

220 ***Well, the President*** Introduction to "Johnny 99," Pittsburgh, PA, 21 Sept. 1984.

221 **haves and have-nots** In "Mansion on the Hill," the first song he had tried to write for *Nebraska*, Springsteen came surprisingly close to Governor Cuomo's metaphor of the two cities, but that song ended optimistically, hinting that the wealth its narrator had seen as a child he now possessed as an adult. Interestingly, Springsteen sang "Mansion on the Hill" in Pittsburgh on 21 Sept., for the first time in over two months, and introduced it with an honest confession: *sometimes I see myself outside that house, and sometimes I see myself inside it.* See introduction to "Mansion on the Hill," Pittsburgh, PA, 21 Sept. 1984.

221 ***It's a long walk*** Introduction to "My Hometown," Pittsburgh, PA, 21 Sept. 1984. The next night, on 22 Sept., his remarks before "The River" explicitly linked that song to the failure of the American dream (even if some Reaganites in the audience might remember that it had been written during the Carter administration), and he dedicated it to the members of United Steelworkers of America Local 1397.

221 **favorite Springsteen song** Reporters had asked the Reagan campaign what the president's favorite Springsteen song was. After a few days, the best that its staff could come up with was "Born to Run," setting loose several jokes from late-night comedians, not to mention an impossible-to-erase image of the first lady strapping her hands across sweet Ronnie's engines.

221 **a few generations** Reagan, *Speaking*, 238, 243.

222 ***but it's no good*** Introduction to "Born to Run," Buffalo, NY, 24 Sept. 1984.

222 ***Rolling Stone*** On the patriotic side, he also refuted the rumor that had been going around for the last four months that, on the cover of his new album, he was actually urinating on the American flag.

222 ***They can use*** Introduction to "My Hometown," Tempe, AZ, 8 Nov. 1984.

223 **"(They Call Me) Bruce"** Springfield's song had actually been recorded in 1978, the year of *Darkness*, but it was being packaged as a single now, in order to cash in on the much huger Springsteen mania set off by *Born in the U.S.A.*

224 **I knew** Springsteen quoted in Eliot, 240.

225 **I'm taking a dip** Phillips quoted in Sandford, 269.

225 ***Someday*, I'd like** Kurt Loder, "Bruce Springsteen: The *Rolling Stone* Interview," *Rolling Stone*, 6 Dec. 1984.

226 **Maxwell's** If you just saw the Sayles video, you couldn't tell, but the truth was that the bands at Maxwell's were usually much hipper than this. Maybe Bruce Springsteen circa 1972 could have played there, if it had booked music back then, but twelve years later the club hosted groups like the Feelies, Yo La Tengo, Sonic Youth, Tiny Lights, and Robyn Hitchcock and the Egyptians. These were the sorts of barely popular bands that were starting to be known as "college rock" or even "alternative music," bands that were being self-consciously marketed by their (usually independent) labels as *not* of the New Top 40 or MTV.

229   **the bubble is** Springsteen quoted in Sandford, 266.

233   **One of the things** Plotkin quoted in Michael Goldberg, "The Springsteen Christmas," *Rolling Stone*, 4 Dec. 1986.

233   **characterized these groupings** Marsh, *Glory*, 420.

235   **Apollo and Bugs Bunny** William Gibson, *Spook Country* (New York: G. P. Putnam, 2007), 128.

235   **car-stereo bombast** James Wolcott, "The Hagiography of Bruce Springsteen," *Vanity Fair*, Dec. 1985.

235   **Bruce assembled the band** The most striking account of this incident is in Eliot, 241–42, and distinctly places it in the fall of 1986, just before the live set was released, and not in a later year.

Chapter 9. WHAT I NEED IS SOME PROOF TONIGHT (1986–1992)

General Sources: Marsh, *Glory*, ch. 22; Eliot, ch. 17; *Tunnel, Human,* and *Lucky* chs. of *Songs*; Sandford, chs. 7–8; Alterman, chs. 7–8; Guterman, chs. 5–6; Marsh, *On Tour*, ch. 8; Santelli, ch. 7, Kirkpatrick, chs. 8–9; Clemons and Reo, 168–72; http://brucebase .wikispaces.com/1987; http://brucebase.wikispaces.com/1988; http://brucebase.wikispaces .com/1989; http://brucebase.wikispaces.com/1990; http://brucebase.wikispaces.com/1991; http://brucebase.wikispaces.com/Tunnel+Of+Love+-+Studio+Sessions; http://brucebase .wikispaces.com/Human+Touch+-+Studio+Sessions; http://brucebase.wikispaces.com/ Lucky+Town+-+Studio+Sessions.

239   **onstage at Le Zenith** *TIYL*, vol. 2, disc 1, has footage of the Geldof/Lewis performance.

240   **a sham** Sandford, 274.

242   **a long foreground** He apparently made some solo recordings in LA in early 1986, toward the end of the mixing of the live set, but none of these tracks has ever surfaced among collectors. Indeed, because of the paucity of studio bootlegs, not to mention live premieres of new material from this period, we cannot be sure of the exact order of composition for these new relationship-based songs.

243   **center** *Songs*, 191.

243   **the Italian bastardization** Ken Emerson, *Always Magic in the Air: The Bomp and Brilliance of the Brill Building Era* (New York: Penguin Books, 2005), 61.

243   **The song's original bridge** The finished lyric of "Brilliant Disguise" is *Songs*, 206; the draft to which I refer was on display in *From Asbury Park to the Promised Land*.

245   **may not have been inspired** On the other hand, it may have been even more inspired by Dylan's studies in painting with Norman Raeben, which in turn led to the dissolution of his marriage with Lownds. See Sean Wilentz, *Bob Dylan in America* (New York: Doubleday, 2010), 137–40.

246   **changed drastically** In Elvis Costello's 2003 cover of "Brilliant Disguise," the song wholly loses its *baion* basis when presented in a countrified arrangement.

247   **small venues** "Random Notes," in *Rolling Stone*, 14 Jan. 1988.

249   *when I walked back* Introduction to "Spare Parts," Worcester, MA, 25 Feb. 1988. *TIYL*, vol. 2, disc 1, has footage of five songs from opening night of the *Tunnel of Love* tour, but I am also basing some of my account on my own experience of the performance.

250   *I know one of* Introduction to "Born to Run," Worcester, MA, 25 Feb. 1988.

250   **"Fast Car"** Chapman's similarly acoustic song reached *Billboard*'s Top 10 a few months later, in the summer of 1988, although Springsteen could theoretically have heard a prerelease copy.

251   *my favorite song* Introduction to "Born to Run," Worcester, MA, 28 Feb. 1988.

251   **much wider variety** Such variety was in stark contrast to the covers one heard in the tour's actual encores, which were usually the same from night to night. Except for the occasional substitution of "Love Me Tender" for "Can't Help Fallin' in Love" (an even stiffer and more stately embalming of King Elvis), Springsteen and the band always played the same five numbers: the solo acoustic "Born to Run"; followed by the sing-along on "Hungry Heart"; "Glory Days"; one or the other of the Elvis ballads; "Rosie"; and then a Detroit medley that included the same interpolations of "I Hear a Train," "Sweet Soul Music," and "Shake."

253   **type of connection** Steve Pond, "Bruce Springsteen's *Tunnel* Vision," *Rolling Stone*, 5 May 1988.

254   **Whatever** Sandford, 274, 290.

256   **I play my songs** Quoted in Wensley Clarkson, *Sting: The Secret Life of Gordon Sumner* (New York: Thunder's Mouth Press, 1999), 197.

257   **If you believe** Human Rights Now! press conference, Barcelona, Spain, 10 Sept. 1988. *TIYL*, vol. 2, disc 2, has video of performances from the Toronto and Buenos Aires dates of the Human Rights Now! tour.

258   **"Chimes of Freedom"** Springsteen premiered this inspired cover on 3 July in Stockholm, just after he made the announcement that he would be touring for Amnesty. His version cut and restructured Dylan's long, rambling song (originally inspired by the assassination of John F. Kennedy), picking out stanzas that both preserved the lyric's narrative line and highlighted many of the types of individuals whose conditions Amnesty International sought to publicize and alleviate. The first part of the concert was broadcast live on Westwood One, and this premiere performance of "Chimes of Freedom" was subsequently made available on an EP, without the political speech that preceded it.

258   **Oh, I'm going out** Springsteen quoted in James Henke, "Bruce Springsteen: The *Rolling Stone* Interview," *Rolling Stone*, 6 Aug. 1992.

259   **get off the wheel** Sandford, 304.

259   *I'm here in Prescott* Introduction to "Sweet Little Sixteen," Prescott, AZ, 29 Sept. 1989.

260   **I questioned all** Henke, "Interview."

263   **peculiarly hot again** Two essential box sets (*Phil Spector: Back to Mono, 1958–1969* and *The Complete Stax-Volt Singles, 1959–1968*), which would be well received on their release, were being prepared at the exact same time that Springsteen was taking his own, separate retro turn.

266   *figured the situation* Introduction to "My Hometown," Los Angeles, CA, 16 Nov. 1990. Until recently, the second night of the Christic Institute shows was more widely available on *Christic Night* (Crystal Cat). More recently, both nights have become available in soundboard recordings on *The Christic Nights: Persic Recordings* (EV2).

267   **ego validators** Sandford, 315.

267   **I've played onstage** Henke, "Interview."

267   *looking at him* Introduction to "My Hometown," Los Angeles, CA, 17 Nov. 1990.

268   *it's been awhile* Introduction to "Brilliant Disguise," Los Angeles, CA, 16 Nov. 1990.

268   *I'd appreciate if* Introduction to "Darkness on the Edge of Town," Los Angeles, CA, 16 Nov. 1990.

268   *But you don't* Introduction to "Reason to Believe," Los Angeles, CA, 16 Nov. 1990.

269   **female genitalia** "Spirit in the Night" and "Spare Parts," to choose only two of

his most obvious earlier songs, had focused far more on male genitalia. Chronologically, the revision of Sonny Boy Williamson's "Cross My Heart" that he had recorded with Jackson, Bittan, and Porcaro earlier in the year was probably his first reference to female genitalia.

272 **almost perfectly captured** Not surprisingly, Marsh's selections coincided very neatly with Springsteen's covers in performance and sound check on his 1988 tour. In many ways, his book and that tour seem to have been in dialogue with each other.

272 **always been fluid** Patti Scialfa had been considered a Juke for a while before she joined the E Street Band, and once and future Cat Bobby Bandiera had been a fairly steady member of the lineup since 1985.

274 **a clear echo** Springsteen's first publicly released use of the word *piss* in his "Better Days" also echoes Van Zandt's use of the word in the "Better Days" he had written for Lyon.

275 **best of these** This is not to say that there were no clunkers among these tracks. "Leap of Faith" in particular showed that he hadn't wholly gotten over his slide into psychobabble of the previous year.

276 **how self-contained** Apparently, though, Springsteen didn't completely trust drum machines yet: Gary Mallaber played drums on all the tracks.

Chapter 10. I'LL KEEP MOVIN' THROUGH THE DARK (1992–1995)

General Sources: *Greatest Hits* ch. of *Songs*; Sandford, ch. 9; Alterman, ch. 8; Guterman, ch. 6; Marsh, *On Tour*, ch. 9; http://brucebase.wikispaces.com/1992; http://brucebase .wikispaces.com/1993; http://brucebase.wikispaces.com/1994; http://brucebase.wikispaces .com/1995; http://brucebase.wikispaces.com/1993+solo+-+Studio+Sessions; http://bruce base.wikispaces.com/Greatest+Hits+-+Studio+Sessions

279 **did neither** Both "Sad Eyes" and ""Goin' Cali" eventually appeared on the final disc of *Tracks*, and "Trouble River" would become one of the three bonus recordings included on *18 Tracks* the following year.

279 **seasoned "road guys"** "Random Notes," *Rolling Stone*, 28 May 1992.

280 **I never had** "Zachary Alford" (interview conducted 9 July 1992), in Ermanno Labianca, *Local Hero: Bruce Springsteen in the Words of His Band* (Milan: Great Dane Books, 1993), 70.

282 **chocolate cities** Douglas Massey and Nancy Denton, *American Apartheid: Segregation and the Making of the Underclass* (Cambridge, MA: Harvard University Press, 1993), 124.

283 **It really felt** Quoted in James Henke, "Bruce Springsteen: The *Rolling Stone* Interview," *Rolling Stone*, 6 Aug. 1992.

283 *the veil got* Introduction to "If I Should Fall Behind," Los Angeles, CA, 5 June 1992.

284 **a demand for** George H. W. Bush, "Remarks on Civil Disturbances in Los Angeles, California," Washington, DC, 30 April 1992, available at http://bushlib.tamu .edu/research/public_papers.php?id=4241&year=1992&month=all.

284 **looting that was done** Ice Cube quoted in Hillburn, *Corn Flakes with John Lennon and Other Tales from a Rock 'n' Roll Life* (New York: Rodale Books, 2009), 188.

287 **Bottom Line showcase** I have been unable to locate a recording of that performance, on 6 May 1992.

287 *Just be yourself* Introduction to "57 Channels," Los Angeles, CA, 17 Nov. 1990.

287 **troublemaking television set** This is a reference, of course, to the widespread

urban legend that Elvis Presley shot out his television set at least once, when Robert Goulet was appearing on *The Mike Douglas Show.*

287 **We've abandoned** Quoted in Henke, "Interview."

288 **the CNN effect** For an early example, see Livingston's conversation with Vice Admiral Jack Shanahan in "The 'CNN Effect': Television and Foreign Policy," *America's Defense Monitor* (Center for Defense Information), produced 7 May 1995. A transcript of this video is available at http://www.cdi.org/adm/834/tran script.html.

289 **changed political landscape** Around the same time, Tom Petty had home-produced a much slighter but undeniably new song called "Peace in LA" that for the most part hastily stated the obvious.

291 **contradictory a response** Addressing the Commonwealth Club in San Francisco a week and a half after Springsteen's television appearance, Vice President Dan Quayle emphasized not the economic causes of societal problems but rather what he called a "poverty of values." Even more explicitly than Springsteen, Quayle blamed television for the recent outbreak of what he redundantly called "lawless social anarchy." Among other things, he held sitcom character Murphy Brown's recent decision to raise a child out of wedlock on her own to account for the many single-parent households among the nation's poor. See Dan Quayle, "Speech to the Commonwealth Club," San Francisco, CA, 19 May 1992, available at http://www.commonwealthclub.org/archive/20thcentury/92–05quayle-speech.html.

As Quayle spoke these words, Steve Van Zandt was preparing three remixes of "57 Channels" that built on the rudimentary sound collage that Springsteen had used for his television appearance. Quayle's indictment of Murphy Brown made it into the mix, as did Joan Rivers crying for "Gossip! Gossip! Gossip!" and television sex therapist Dr. Ruth Westheimer suggesting that the audience "use a little imagination." In what seemed like a clear indication that neither Van Zandt nor Springsteen was happy with any of their political alternatives that election year, one sound bite of religious broadcaster and former presidential candidate Pat Robertson questioning whether Democratic presidential nominee Bill Clinton was "morally upright" enough to be commander in chief was immediately followed by a Nick at Nite announcement for an upcoming episode of *Green Acres*, seemingly implying that Governor Clinton might not be irredeemably immoral but that he was still very much from the backwoods. And running throughout all three mixes was a loop of the most common chant among protesters after the Simi Valley verdict: "No justice no peace!" Columbia issued all of Van Zandt's mixes on a "CD Maxi-Single," and it is well worth a listen if you can find it.

293 ***two years in*** Introduction to "Man's Job," Los Angeles, CA, 5 June 1992. Because of the radio simulcast, many recordings of this performance are available, the most widely circulating being *The Boss Is Back* (Kiss the Stone Records).

293 ***hiring the National Enquirer*** Introduction to "Human Touch," Los Angeles, CA, 5 June 1992.

294 ***I can see*** Middle of "Glory Days," Los Angeles, CA, 5 June 1992.

294 **much-publicized** Henke, "Interview."

295 **slightly but noticeably** When the Hot 100 switched for the week ending 30 Nov. 1991, newer artists like P. M. Dawn and Naughty by Nature suddenly moved up a few positions on the chart and a more old-fashioned artist like Roberta Flack suddenly shot down ten positions (although it would have been only two positions if this new system of measurement had been used throughout).

296 **bossa nova** Townshend quoted in Ty Burr, "Rock Opera Wizard: Pete Townshend Cranks It Up," *Entertainment Weekly*, 25 June 1993, available at http://www.ew.com/ew/article/0,,307041,00.html.

297   **When you have** Alex Coletti quoted in *Ties*, 195.

297   **performance Springsteen taped** Like Springsteen's subsequent *Storytellers* special for VH1, his *MTV Plugged* exists in a number of forms. At the taping, Springsteen performed twenty-four songs, but less than half made it on air. He did eventually issue a CD of the performance, *In Concert: MTV Plugged*, but on a much slower schedule than most *Unplugged* guests: a limited release in Europe in April 1993, with a permanent worldwide release waiting until Aug. 1997 (i.e., after the end of the *Tom Joad* tour). The CD contained just thirteen tracks, but two others ("Growin' Up" and "The Big Muddy") appeared on CBS's 1995 promo CD *Bruce Springsteen: Live and Rare*. A DVD of *Plugged* was finally issued in 2004 (five years after Springsteen had actually reunited with the E Street Band); it included nineteen of the songs from the original taping, but out of the original sequence in which Springsteen played them. CDs and DVDs of the complete taping circulate among fans, and even with their stops and starts for technical issues they feel a little more like a concert than the officially issued versions do.

298   **Joe Ely** Born in Amarillo and raised in Buddy Holly's hometown of Lubbock, Ely had a long and varied history in the music industry, one that superficially followed a constant downward path. His only charting country single ("All My Love") had come in 1977, his only charting pop album in 1981, and 1992 had seen him as part of the Buzzin' Cousins, the group that had backed John Mellencamp in *Falling from Grace*, his feature film debut. If it wasn't the Mellencamp film that piqued Springsteen's curiosity, it may have been the recommendation of sometime friend Joe Strummer, who had befriended Ely during one of the Clash's U.S. tours, excited to finally meet a real live Texan cowboy.

299   **two nights later** Incredibly, the night between these two concerts, Springsteen appeared as the last, previously unannounced guest on the final episode of *Late Night with David Letterman*.

301   **It didn't work** *Songs*, 261.

301   **exquisite** Sandford, 348.

301   **called in Tommy Sims** This may have been at the same session when Sims and Springsteen cut a cover of "Gypsy Woman" for a Curtis Mayfield tribute album.

302   **popular art** Academy Award acceptance speech, Los Angeles, CA, 21 March 1994.

303   **Joe Grushecky** The Southside Johnny or Bobby Bandiera of the Iron City, a man who sounded like Neil Diamond singing Mellencamp songs, Grushecky was a legendary local musician who (much like Joe Ely) simply couldn't get a break on the national scene. Two decades into a career that didn't seem to be going anywhere, Grushecky thought he had one last big album in him, even if he didn't have a recording contract anymore. He asked Springsteen to help out with the album, and Springsteen obliged, offering him not only time in Thrill Hill West but also the band with whom he himself was currently recording, including Zack Alford on drums. Although none of Springsteen's own recordings from that fall have ever surfaced, two of the tracks that he produced for Grushecky ("Chain Smokin'" and "Never Be Enough Time") would end up on Grushecky's next album. In February, a band including Shane Fontayne and Zack Alford (who were supposed to be working at Thrill Hill West on Springsteen's next album) recorded "Homestead," a song about a displaced steelworker that Springsteen had cowritten with Grushecky. When Springsteen and family headed back to Rumson that summer, Grushecky did too, recording five songs at Thrill Hill East that August, including "Dark and Bloody Ground," yet another Springsteen-Grushecky collaboration. As with "Homestead," the words to the song appear to have been Grushecky's, the music Springsteen's. That fall, Springsteen even sat in

with the Houserockers for a date at Marz American Style in Long Branch, around the time they cut the last three tracks for Grushecky's album at Thrill Hill East, where Springsteen was concurrently conducting far more disappointing sessions with Fontayne, Simms, and Alford. Springsteen didn't perform on these tracks, he only produced, but Scialfa did lend her unmistakable backing vocals to "Comin' Down Maria."

306   **ambivalence** *Songs*, 262.

308   **more like a** Parke Puterbaugh, "*Greatest Hits* Album Review," *Rolling Stone*, 6 April 1995.

Chapter 11. LOOK IN THEIR EYES, MOM, YOU'LL SEE ME (1995–1997)

General Sources: Joad ch. of *Songs*; Sandford, ch. 10; Alterman ch. 9; Guterman, ch. 6; Gene Santoro, *Highway 61 Revisited: The Tangled Roots of American Jazz, Blues, Rock & Country Music* (New York: Oxford University Press, 2004), ch. 22; Marsh, *On Tour*, ch. 10; Kirkpatrick, ch. 10; http://brucebase.wikispaces.com/The+Ghost+Of+Tom+Joad+-+Studio+Sessions; http://brucebase.wikispaces.com/1995; http://brucebase.wikispaces.com/1996; http://brucebase.wikispaces.com/1997.

310   *a song about* Introduction to "Dry Lightning," New Brunswick, NJ, 21 Nov. 1995. This first appearance of the 1995–97 tour is available on *This Ain't No Rock 'n' Roll Show* (Doberman).

310   *Do you want* Introduction to "It's the Little Things That Count" (following "The Wish"), Dublin, Ireland, 20 March 1996. This is one of the best recordings from the 1995–97 tour, available on *On the Floor in Dublin* (Doberman). *Brixton Night* (Crystal Cat), a more widely available recording of the Brixton Academy show from a little under a month later, is also quite good, especially for the "Pilgrim in the House of Love" speech.

310   *This is the* See, for example, introductions to "It's the Little Things That Count" Berkeley, CA, 29 Nov. 1995, and Washington, DC, 5 and 6 December 1995.

312   *is kind of* Introduction to "Highway 29," Dublin, Ireland, 20 March 1996.

312   **I think it's** Introduction to "Straight Time," Dublin, Ireland, 20 March 1996.

315   **if it had been implemented** Proposition 187 was approved by a significant majority of California voters but was subsequently declared unconstitutional by federal judges.

315   **evocative images** Arax quoted in Sandford, 369.

316   **alone with a guitar** Parke Puterbaugh, "*Greatest Hits* Album Review," *Rolling Stone*, 6 April 1995.

316   **to play drums** Max Weinberg wasn't available for regular West Coast sessions, since he now had a permanent job with Conan O'Brien on the East Coast.

321   **best days** William J. Clinton, "Remarks at the University of Chicago in Chicago, Illinois, 23 August 1996."

323   **irrational exuberance** Alan Greenspan, "The Challenge of Central Banking in a Democratic Society," Washington, DC, 5 Dec. 1996, available at http://www.federalreserve.gov/boarddocs/speeches/1996/19961205.htm.

324   **over twenty-two years** As Bruce memorably recalled in an interview for Taylor Hackford's documentary *Hail Hail Rock and Roll*, which Berry apparently liked so much that he reprinted it as the introduction to his essential autobiography.

325   **I don't know** Koppel interview quoted in *Ties*, 338.

325   *It was the deep* Introduction to "Angel Eyes," Los Angeles, CA, 19 Nov. 1995. In some ways, Springsteen's reenvisioning of Sinatra's contribution to American popular music here presages the one that Jay-Z would make in the twenty-first century, most resonantly in "Death of Autotune" on *The Blueprint* 3 and the

"Main Event" concert he gave at Madison Square Garden in Sept. 2009 as a specific echo of Sinatra's own Oct. 1974 "Main Event" concert at the same venue.

326   *I got a couple*   Introduction to "Adam Raised a Cain," New Brunswick, NJ, 21 Nov. 1995.

326   *What do I*   Introduction to "Darkness on the Edge of Town," New Brunswick, NJ, 21 Nov. 1995.

327   **his movie songs**   "Missing," of course, was almost impossible to perform live, being even more dependent than "Streets" on studio effects.

328   *My wife always*   Introduction to "Red Headed Woman" (following "Pilgrim in the Temple of Love"), London, England, 24 April 1996.

329   *a great song*   For example, introduction to "Red Headed Woman," Akron, OH, 25 Sept. 1996.

329   **For the most part**   Even on this very serious occasion, however, Springsteen was self-aware enough to include one song that attempted to burst any bubble of self-importance that might be growing around him. Far and away his most entertaining performance at the concert was of "Riding in My Car," a children's song Guthrie had written and one of the silliest and least political things he had ever done. *I was going through this Guthrie songbook*, he told the audience, *I said*, "*Hmmm, automobiles. . . . That's my business, Mr. Guthrie, no disrespect, but that's my business.*" See introduction to "Riding in My Car," Cleveland, OH, 29 Sept. 1996. Springsteen dove into this trifle with gusto, and you can hear from the audience's reaction how well it went over. *Shit, why didn't I think of that?*, Springsteen kidded after finishing it, *Directness, directness . . .* See introduction to "Plane Wreck at Los Gatos (Deportees)" (following "Riding in My Car"), Cleveland, OH, 29 Sept. 1996. Excellent recordings of both these performances appear on *'Til We Outnumber 'Em* (Righteous Babe); less pristine recordings of all Springsteen's performances at this concert appear on *USA Blues*, vol. 2 (Crystal Cat).

331   *There's a scene*   Introduction to "Across the Border," Akron, OH, 25 Sept. 1996.

333   **These concerts succeeded**   As far as I am concerned, these late New Jersey concerts yielded the most essential live recordings of the 1995–97 tour: *Freehold Night* (Crystal Cat), which documents the St. Rose of Lima appearance; and *Asbury Park Night* (Crystal Cat), which documents the third and last of the Asbury shows. Recordings of the first two Asbury shows are also circulating among fans, and the version of "I Wanna Marry You" that Springsteen did on the second night may have been his sweetest performance of the song ever.

333   **words**   Award ceremony speeches, Stockholm, Sweden, 5 May 1997.

334   *to continue to*   Banquet speeches, Stockholm, Sweden, 5 May 1997.

Chapter 12. BAPTIZED IN THESE WATERS, AND IN EACH OTHER'S BLOOD
         (1997–2005)

General Sources: *Live* and *Rising* chs. of *Songs*; Sandford, ch. 10; Alterman, epilogue and afterword; Guterman, chs. 1 and 7; Marsh, *Hearts*, introduction and ch. 23; Marsh, *On Tour*, chs. 11–13; Santelli, ch. 8; Kirkpatrick, chs. 11–12; Clemons and Reo, 87, 127–29; http://brucebase.wikispaces.com/The+Seeger+Sessions+-+Studio+Sessions (first two sessions); http://brucebase.wikispaces.com/1997; http://brucebase.wikispaces.com/1998; http://brucebase.wikispaces.com/1999; http://brucebase.wikispaces.com/2000; http://brucebase.wikispaces.com/2001; http://brucebase.wikispaces.com/2002; http://brucebase.wikispaces.com/2003; http://brucebase.wikispaces.com/2004; http://brucebase.wikispaces.com/Tracks+-+Studio+Sessions; http://brucebase.wikispaces.com/The+Rising+-+Studio+Sessions; http://brucebase.wikispaces.com/The+Essential+-+Studio+Sessions; http://brucebase.wikispaces.com/Devils+ percent26+Dust+-+Studio+Sessions.

340   **headed to the** Springsteen, liner notes to *We Shall Overcome: The Seeger Sessions* (CBS, 2006).

342   **the informality** Ibid.

344   **how little they overlapped** The only songs featured in both works were "Born in the U.S.A." and "This Hard Land," the former because Springsteen had included the *Nebraska* take of the song on *Tracks*, the latter because he was counting it as an officially released song on *Greatest Hits*.

345   **If he added** Interestingly enough, the only other song that we know he even considered on any of these occasions was "Sad Eyes," from the *Human Touch* sessions, which he rehearsed on 8 Dec. 1998 before appearing on *Late Night with Luuk* in Stockholm. Significantly, it's a discard from his 1990s solo work, which occupies at most one-fourth of *Tracks*. The DVD *Charlie Rose: November 20, 1998* (Charlie Rose Inc., 2006) reproduces what was probably the most detailed interview Springsteen gave at the time of the *Tracks* release.

346   **on Lincoln's birthday** He recorded it at the same session at which he recorded "Give My Love to Rose," his contribution to *Kindred Spirits: A Tribute to the Songs of Johnny Cash*.

347   *but not least* Acceptance speech, Rock and Roll Hall of Fame Induction Ceremony, New York, NY, 15 March 1999. *Rock and Roll Hall of Fame & Museum: Live* (Time Life DVD, 2009) includes the band's performances of "The Promised Land" and "Tenth Avenue Freeze-Out" from that night, but on different discs. It also includes abridged versions of Bono's induction speech and Springsteen's acceptance speech, both of which may be found in full in *Ties*, 521–26.

347   *my great band* These nine performers, it should be pointed out, had all shared a stage together fewer than a dozen times before, since Nils and Patti had joined the band for four brief years after Steve had left it.

348   *rebirth* Introduction to "Land of Hope and Dreams," Asbury Park, NJ, 18 March 1999; introduction to "Land of Hope and Dreams," Barcelona, Spain, 9 April 1999.

348   *reeducated and rededicated* Acceptance speech, Rock and Roll Hall of Fame Induction Ceremony, New York, NY, 15 March 1999.

348   **about the band** A little closer look at the contents of *Tracks* suggests that this shift may not have been quite so sudden. The sixty-six recordings of *Tracks* were meant to document the length and breadth of Springsteen's studio work, but thirty-two of those recordings, almost half the total, were drawn from a five-year period, from 1979 through 1984—the same period that accounted for 60 percent of the live set's contents. When one recognizes that only one of the *Tracks* recordings (the original acoustic version of "Born in the U.S.A.") comes from the *Nebraska* sessions, it grows clearer still that, even if *Songs* was a reasonable document of Bruce Springsteen's career, *Tracks* was, like the live set, much more clearly focused on the E Street Band.

348   *Brothers and sisters* Before "Take 'Em as They Come," Los Angeles, CA, 23 Oct. 1999. This concert is documented on *Los Angeles Night* (Crystal Cat), which is one of the best records of the earliest legs of the revival tour. *TIYL*, vol. 4, disc 1, contains video recordings of a number of performances from the revival tour.

349   *not life everlasting* Middle of "Light of Day," Barcelona, Spain, 9 April 1999.

349   *because you're alone* Middle of "Tenth Avenue Freeze-Out," Washington, DC, 31 Aug. 1999.

349   *river of life* Middle of "Tenth Avenue Freeze-Out," Los Angeles, CA, 23 Oct. 1999.

350   **devastatingly effective treatment** The fact that the song also spoke of the doubts that might prevent the singer from crossing a *river* clearly linked it to the "Tenth

Avenue Freeze-Out" monologue, as the individualized vocals linked it most nights to this tour's arrangement of "Out in the Street" (which usually appeared just before "Tenth Avenue," at the center of the show).

350 **break down** Craig Werner, *A Change Is Gonna Come: Music, Race & the Soul of America*, rev. ed. (Ann Arbor: Univ. of Michigan Press, 2006), 31.

351 **No one makes** Ibid., 31, 219–20, 352–53. Werner speaks of this as a show on the *Rising* tour, but the songs he lists fit the setlist from the 9 Sept. 1999 show at the Palace.

353 **vast right-wing conspiracy** The first person widely noted as using the phrase "right-wing conspiracy" was then first lady Hillary Rodham Clinton, in a *Today* show interview with Matt Lauer on 26 Jan. 1998, quoted in Ken Gormley, *The Death of American Virtue: Clinton vs. Starr* (New York: Crown, 2010), 418. Clinton, of course, was as steeped in the political templates of the Nixon era as any American liberal: her first job in Washington, DC, after law school was as a staff counsel to the House of Representatives' 1974 impeachment inquiry. In truth, the Nixon of the early 1970s was both more paranoid and more liberal than the most prominent Republican of the late 1990s, Newt Gingrich. Judged by the standards of Gingrich's Contract for America, Richard Nixon would have fallen somewhere to the left of current president Bill Clinton.

353 **sexual harassment** For one of the earliest conceptualizations of sexual harassment, see Mary P. Rowe, "Saturn's Rings," in *Graduate and Professional Education of Women* (Washington, DC: American Association of University Women, 1974), 1–9. For a narrative memoir that similarly places the phrase's origins in the mid-1970s, see Susan Brownmiller, *In Our Time: Memoir of a Revolution* (New York: Dial Press, 2000), 281.

353 **someone's "daughter"** The most prominent example of this was Vincent Bugliosi's portrait of Charles Manson as an evil genius who brainwashed dutiful American daughters into what Jean Murley has memorably called "killer Barbies." For Murley's feminist analysis of popular accounts of hippie-generated Nixon-era crimes like Manson's, see *The Rise of True Crime: 20th Century Murder and American Popular Culture* (New York: Praeger, 2008), 63–68.

355 **only now returning** The songs turned up in sound checks night after night for two or three months, much like the covers with which Bruce had been almost obsessed on the *Tunnel of Love* tour.

355 **"American Skin"** This song started showing up in sound checks only in late April 2000.

358 **antipolice rant** That Springsteen had done benefit concerts for the families of New Jersey police officers slain in the line of duty, most memorably one in Red Bank in early 1998 on a double bill with Jon Bon Jovi, didn't matter.

358 **limousine liberal** All these reactions are gathered by Alterman from previously published newspaper reports: Tierney on p. 283, Mulshine on p. 284, and Lucente on p. 279.

359 **This is what** *Songs*, 298. *Live in New York City* (Columbia DVD, 2001) contains performances from the last two revival tour concerts at Madison Square Garden, but it rearranges them in a less effective fashion. The first disc contains the condensed concert originally broadcast on HBO, and the second disc contains eleven "bonus" tracks. This means that, as far as this tour's tent poles go, "Tenth Avenue Freeze-Out" and "Land of Hope and Dreams" are on disc 1, while "Light of Day" and "If I Should Fall Behind" are on disc 2. More detrimentally, "American Skin" closes out the HBO concert/disc 1, where it seems very jarring immediately after "Land of Hope and Dreams."

365 **the city's interior** To read the city's geography into Springsteen's song, the *blood*

red circle depicted in the lyric's first verse can't be down on Cookman Avenue, because Cookman runs through a purely commercial district. Springsteen's song is about an area where people live, quite possibly Springwood Avenue, with its "block after abandoned block, the weeds waist-high." See Daniel Wolff, *4th of July, Asbury Park: A History of the Promised Land* (New York: Bloomsbury, 2005), 233.

365 **the soul gospel** *Songs*, 307.

365 **sense of loss** Springsteen seemed similarly preoccupied with the idea of racial reconciliation in another, much lighter song he wrote and recorded that fall, called "Let's Be Friends (Skin to Skin)." Indeed, if there was any theme that could unite a number of Springsteen's recent songs enough to build an album around them, it was this idea of racial reconciliation and repair, a desire to rebuild the country into some kind of postpluralist unity after the ever-increasing culture wars of the last three and a half decades.

366 **I went to** Quoted in Brian Hiatt, "Bruce Springsteen: Working-Class Superhero," *Rolling Stone*, 24 Dec 2009, 58.

367 **some kid rolled** Ibid.

367 **We've lost so** Gail Sheehy, *Middletown, America: One Town's Passage from Trauma to Hope* (New York: Random House, 2003), 89.

367 **Of the many** *Songs*, 304.

368 **Anything up-tempo** Eliza Truitt, "It's the End of the World as Clear Channel Knows It," *Slate*, 17 Sept. 2001, http://www.slate.com/id/1008314.

369 **"Fire and Rain"** For the true story of the song's genesis and referents, see Geoffrey O'Brien, *Sonata for Jukebox: An Autobiography of My Ears* (New York: Counterpoint Books, 2004), 266ff.

369 **Greil Marcus later** Marcus, *The Shape of Things to Come: Prophecy and the American Voice* (New York: Picador, 2007), 305.

371 **Psychologically everyone needed** McAuliffe quoted in the liner notes to *The Concert for New York City* (Sony, 2001).

373 **wider approach to publicity** *TIYL*, vol. 4, disc 2, contains the *Today Show* performances; *Nightline UpClose: Bruce Springsteen* (ABC News, 2009) contains both episodes of Springsteen's extended 2003 pre-*Rising* interview with Ted Koppel.

373 **From a marketing** Card quoted in Elisabeth Bumiller, "Bush Aides Set Strategy to Sell Policy on Iraq," *New York Times*, 7 Sept. 2002, available at http://www.nytimes.com/2002/09/07/us/traces-of-terror-the-strategy-bush-aides-set-strategy-to-sell-policy-on-iraq.html.

374 **Focus on war** Quoted in Frank Rich, *The Greatest Story Ever Sold: The Decline and Fall of Truth in Bush's America* (New York: Penguin Books, 2006), 55.

374 **intelligence and facts** Quoted ibid., 239.

376 *cry out from* Introduction to "You're Missing" (following "Empty Sky") Melbourne, Australia, 20 March 2003. *Live in Barcelona* (Columbia DVD, 2003) is a good document of the beginning of the *Rising* tour, when "Mary's Place" in particular was still fresh.

377 **major combat operations** Bush, "Speech aboard the USS Abraham Lincoln," 1 May 2003, available at http://www.washingtonpost.com/ac2/wp-dyn/A2627-2003May1.

377 *a particular time* Introduction to "Land of Hope and Dreams," Flushing, NY, 4 Oct. 2003.

380 *public service announcement* Introduction to "Land of Hope and Dreams," East Rutherford, NJ, 15 July 2003.

381 **his favorite song** At the same debate, in an unconscious echo of Ronald Reagan's dubiously stated preference for "Born to Run," Senator Dick Gephardt named "Born in the U.S.A." as his personal favorite.

381 **Bruce Springsteen had it right** Delia Rios, "Campaigns Strike Chords with the Music of America," *Arkansas Democrat-Gazette*, 5 Sept. 2004, available at http://epaper.ardemgaz.com/Repository/getFiles.asp?Style=OliveXLib:ArticleToMail&Type=text/html&Path=ArDemocrat/2004/09/05&ID=Ar00800.

382 **I don't think** Springsteen, "Chords for Change," *New York Times*, 5 Aug. 2004, available at http://www.nytimes.com/2004/08/05/opinion/05bruce.html.

383 *we need a* Introduction to "No Surrender," Miami, FL, 29 Oct. 2004.

383 **America does not** Evans and Kristofferson quoted in Chris Willman, *Rednecks and Bluenecks: The Politics of Country Music* (New York: New Press, 2005), 98, 13. Willman's underappreciated book is one of the best books available about modern country music and an essential source on the second culture wars that beset American popular music during this period.

Chapter 13. A MILLION DIFFERENT VOICES SPEAKING IN TONGUES (2005–2008)

General Sources: Marsh, *On Tour*, ch. 14; Kirkpatrick, ch. 12 and update; Clemons and Reo, 93, 187–203; http://brucebase.wikispaces.com/2005; http://brucebase.wikispaces .com/2006; http://brucebase.wikispaces.com/2007; http://brucebase.wikispaces.com/ The+Seeger+Sessions+-+Studio+Sessions (third session and miscellaneous studio and live recording); http://brucebase.wikispaces.com/Magic+-+Studio+Sessions.

386 **[W]hat tends to be** Brian Hiatt, "Bruce Kicks Up 'Dust,'" *Rolling Stone*, 6 April 2005, archived at http://www.greasylake.org/articles_record.php?articles1Page=11 &Id=270&release_title=Devils+ percent26+Dust&concert_date=.

387 *the* **Tom Joad**–*rules* Introduction to "Youngstown," Asbury Park, NJ, 21 April 2005.

388 **the** *Storytellers* **taping** Although at least two concerts in Boston on the *Devils and Dust* tour were pro-shot (presumably for eventual video release), the only officially released video from that tour is *VH1 Storytellers* (Columbia Video, 2005). As usual, Springsteen is less adventurous here at the beginning of a tour than he would be at the end.

388 *I haven't tried* Introduction to "Two Faces," Dallas, TX, 28 April 2005.

389 **move things around** In Seattle that August, however, he apparently did take his crew totally by surprise and ended up filling time the same way he had planned to do during Evan's delivery: by telling an Italian joke. See introduction to "This Hard Land," Seattle, WA, 11 Aug. 2005. The same thing happened toward the end of the tour in Uniondale, NY, but by then Bruce had apparently figured out what Patti could have told him fifteen years before: the Italian jokes never worked. See introduction to "Highway Patrolman," Uniondale, NY, 9 Oct. 2005.

389 *kind of got away* Introduction to "Real World," Dublin, Ireland, 24 May 2005.

389 *sons and mothers* Introduction to "Jesus Was an Only Son," Dublin, Ireland, 24 May 2005. Springsteen made similar statements introducing this song most nights of the tour.

390 **larger, emergent whole** For a good survey of the concept of "emergence" as it relates to the internet, see Steven Johnson, *Emergence: The Connected Lives of Ants, Brains, Cities, and Software* (New York: Scribner, 2001).

390 **Backstreets.com had taken** These posts are archived at http://www.backstreets .com/setlists2005.html.

390 *When I get* Introduction to "You're Missing," Buffalo, NY, 18 July 2005.

390 *No, I can't go* Introduction to "The Promised Land," Seattle, WA, 11 Aug. 2005.

390 *I've been in* Introduction to "Long Time Comin'," Buffalo, NY, 18 July 2005.

391   *a back-to-back* Brucebase has no Storytellers transcript for this concert, but the quotation may be found at http://www.backstreets.com/setlists2005.html.

391   *a night of debuts* Introduction to "Cynthia," Columbus, OH, 31 July 2005.

392   *The audiences've just* Introduction to "The Promised Land," Seattle, WA, 11 Aug. 2005.

392   *Got a few* Introductions to "The Ties That Bind," "I Wanna Marry You," and "Two Hearts," Asbury Park, NJ, 4 Oct. 2005.

392   *I don't think* Introduction to "Independence Day," Rochester, NY, 6 Oct. 2005. Usually I've cleaned up any ad-lib repetitions in Springsteen's stage chatter, but in this case it captures his mood so well that I left it exactly as uttered.

393   *You guys can do* Introduction to "I Wanna Marry You," Hartford, CT, 7 Oct. 2005.

393   *Richie from Germany* Introductions to "Growin' Up" and "Blinded by the Light," Madison, WI, 15 Oct. 2005.

393   *Scott Greenstein and* Introduction to "Two for the Road," East Rutherford, NJ, 17 Nov. 2005.

394   *an outtake from* Introduction to "Song for Orphans," Trenton, NJ, 21 Nov. 2005. Most sources place this as the tour premiere, but my own memory of the 16 Nov. concert at the Continental Airlines Arena in East Rutherford is that he premiered it there. I have not been able to locate a recording of that concert to confirm my memory, so I will assign it to the Trenton date. Both of the concerts in Trenton that closed the tour circulate on CDRs among fans and are well worth listening to.

394   **He's finally become** Marsh, *On Tour*, 300.

395   **a cult object** In 2400, Sub Pop Records had released an all-star tribute called *Badlands: A Tribute to Bruce Springsteen's "Nebraska,"* which featured rerecordings of the album's ten songs by Chrissie Hynde, Los Lobos, Deana Carter, Ani DiFranco, and others, with bonus performances of three of the other 1982 tracks that had been considered for either that album or the legendary E Street hybrid that fans always referred to as "Electric Nebraska."

395   *to get women* Springsteen and Platt quoted in the Backstreets account of this event, which is archived at http://www.backstreets.com/newsarchive11.html.

396   **Best Rock Vocal** This was Springsteen's third win in four years in that category— once the Grammy voters finally notice you, they never forget you.

397   *I don't know* Introduction to "The Promised Land," Asbury Park, NJ, 4 Oct. 2005.

398   **when it was released** The album was released with Seeger's blessings, but in most interviews that he gave about it the elder singer sounded vaguely suspicious of Springsteen's unabashed embrace of pop success.

398   **the town where** Bush quoted in Douglas Brinkley, *The Great Deluge: Hurricane Katrina, New Orleans, and the Mississippi Gulf Coast* (New York: William Morrow, 2006), 636.

398   **Springsteen's version** Although it wasn't widely known at the time, Springsteen had already recorded the performance of this song at a closed 13 April rehearsal, and it would soon be offered on his website as a free internet download.

400   **a   brothel   with** This   quotation   comes   from   http://www.myspace.com/chocolategeniusinc.

400   *Let's check the key* Introduction to "My Oklahoma Home" (following "Cadillac Ranch"), Asbury Park, NJ, 26 April 2006.

400   *our first gig* Introduction to "O Mary Don't You Weep," New Orleans, LA, 30 April 2006.

401   *a song that* Introduction to "My Oklahoma Home," New Orleans, LA, 30 April 2006.

401   *from Lake View* Introduction to "How Can a Poor Man Stand Such Times and Live?," New Orleans, LA, 30 April 2006.

401   **inevitable YouTube video** This video is at http://www.youtube.com/watch?v=211vkFbgvx0.

401   *there's about a* Introduction to "When the Saints Go Marching In," New Orleans, LA, 30 April 2006.

402   *left over from* Introduction to "My City of Ruins," New Orleans, LA, 30 April 2006.

402   **whose own band** Chocolate Genius had participated in the *Nebraska* concert back in January.

402   **a more dramatic** Randy Lewis, "Music Fits Moment at New Orleans Fest," *Los Angeles Times*, 2 May 2006, archived at http://articles.latimes.com/2006/may/02/entertainment/et-jazzfest2.

403   *a roll of* Introduction to "We Shall Overcome," Holmdel, NJ, 25 June 2006.

403   *what we're trying* Introduction to "When the Saints Go Marching In," Holmdel, NJ, 25 June 2006.

404   *not what we're trying* Video of this performance is available at http://www.youtube.com/watch?v=voXHqkN2k9Q.

405   **Isn't this the pits?** Scialfa quoted in "Springsteen-Scialfa Update," *RedBank-Green* 26 Aug. 2006, available at http://www.redbankgreen.com/2006/08/springsteenscia.html.

405   *Patti sends her love* Introduction to "Magic," Dallas, TX, 13 April 2008. For examples of this from the Sessions tour, see introduction to "Long Black Veil," (following "Cadillac Ranch"), Amsterdam, Netherlands, 16 May 2006; and introduction to "Long Time Comin'," Rotterdam, Netherlands, 13 Oct. 2006. As partial confirmation of these statements, when Scialfa rejoined the Sessions tour in Ireland in November 2006, all three of their children were with her.

406   *a kind of* Introduction to "Long Walk Home," London, England, 11 Nov. 2006.

406   **tour was over** *Live in Dublin* (Columbia Video, 2007) combines performances from the last three nights of the Seeger Sessions tour and shows the Sessions Band at the peak of its form.

406   **E Street Radio** That *lost number on a dial* would have been 10 on Sirius, 58 on XM, and 6010 on the Dish Network.

407   **most opaque lyrics** In "Your Own Worst Enemy," for example, it's hard to tell if the Bush-era culture of surveillance is the song's subject or only its underlying metaphor. Similarly, "You'll Be Coming Down" can only be construed as a song about contemporary politics if the privileged young beauty whom its narrator addresses can be seen as a metaphorical stand-in for the Bush administration at its moment of most unquestioned ascendance.

409   **If we didn't** This is from Springsteen's eventual eulogy for Federici, which is archived at http://www.brucespringsteen.net/news/index_archive.html.

412   *the things that we* Introduction to "Livin' in the Future," New York, NY, 28 Sept. 2007.

412   *our smash, smash* Introduction to "Magic," Los Angeles, CA, 29 Oct. 2007.

412   **almost no effort** A remix of "Girls in Their Summer Clothes" would briefly hit no. 95 on the chart in early February.

413   **the political songs** This was even more true in mid-October, when the band finally nailed an arrangement of "Your Own Worst Enemy."

414   *all Europeans should* Introduction to "Livin' in the Future," Copenhagen, Denmark, 8 Dec. 2007.

414   *I do feel* Introduction to "Livin' in the Future," Montreal, Canada, 2 March 2008.

415   **rock star** Lynn Hulsey and Laura A. Bischoff, "Obama Draws Crowd of 11,420 at Nutter Center Rally," *Dayton Daily News*, 25 Feb. 2008, available at http://www.daytondailynews.com/n/content/oh/story/news/local/2008/02/25/ddn022508obamaweb.html.

416   **The pundits** Barack Obama, keynote speech, Democratic National Convention, Boston, MA, 27 July 2004, available at http://www.pbs.org/newshour/vote2004/demconvention/speeches/obama.html.

416   **Making change** Clinton and Obama quoted in Patrick Healy and Jeff Zeleny, "At Debate, Two Rivals Go after Defiant Clinton," *New York Times*, 8 Jan. 2008, available at http://www.nytimes.com/2008/01/06/us/politics/06dems.html?page wanted=2&_r=1.

417   *We need a* Introduction to "The Promised Land," Milwaukee, WI, 17 March 2008.

417   **more insightful version** Like "American Skin," "A More Perfect Union" was praised in some quarters and condemned in others, but in this case there could be no doubt that the actual text of the work was known. By Wednesday morning, 1.2 million people had viewed the clip of the speech on YouTube. By the end of the week, 2.5 million people had viewed it, nearly as many people as had downloaded Flo Rida's "Low," the no. 3 single in the country that week, more hits than www.brucespringsteen.net would typically get in an entire month. If being a "rock star" candidate means getting people to listen to thoughtful speeches about our national character in the same numbers that they download dance tracks . . . well, then, American politics needs more "rock stars."

417   **a Springsteen fan** "White House DJ Battle," *Blender*, 13 Aug. 2008, available at http://www.blender.com/guide/61382/whitehousedjbattle.html.

418   **"nobody crowds you"** The Obama endorsement was posted on Springsteen's website on 18 April 2008 and is archived at http://www.brucespringsteen.net/news/index_archive.html.

418   **perfecting our imperfect union** Barack Obama, *The Audacity of Hope: Thoughts on Reclaiming the American Dream* (New York: Vintage Books, 2008), 427.

418   *I've spent most* Introduction to "The Rising," Philadelphia, PA, 4 Oct. 2008, archived at http://www.brucespringsteen.net/news/index_archive.html.

419   **so early in the year** Coming as it did on 16 April, the announcement was probably timed to coincide with the home stretch of campaigning before the Pennsylvania primary six days later. No matter what its presidential politics, Pennsylvania had been Springsteen country for almost three and a half decades. The singer's support just might help sway the older, less-educated, working-class white male Democratic voters whom Senator Obama seemed to have more problems attracting.

Chapter 14. COME TOMORROW, NONE OF THIS WILL BE HERE (2008–2009)

General Sources: Clemons and Reo, Prologue, 204–9, 219–22, 226–27, 258–64, 269–72, 287–93, 302–14 (Harley Davidson show), 315, 343–57; http://brucebase.wikispaces.com/2008; http://brucebase.wikispaces.com/2009; http://brucebase.wikispaces.com/Working+On+A+Dream+-+Studio+Sessions.

421   *a good building* Introduction to "Racing in the Street" (following "Waitin' on a Sunny Day"), Rochester, NY, 6 March 2008.

421   *knock this building down* After "American Land," Rochester, NY, 6 March 2008.

421   **the last time Danny** The performance is available on *Magic Tour Highlights*, a

digital EP Springsteen issued in July whose proceeds benefited the Danny Federici Melanoma Fund.

422 *Roy, you better* Introduction to "Sandy," Tampa, FL, 22 April 2008.

422 *the highest hill* Introduction to "Growin' Up" (following "Sandy"), Tampa, FL, 22 April 2008.

422 *when I lost you* Middle of "Darkness on the Edge of Town," Tampa, FL, 22 April 2008.

422 *Thank you so much* Introduction to "I'll Fly Away," Tampa, FL, 22 April 2008.

423 **change the vibe** There had even been a series of local radio contests to "pick a song for Bruce Springsteen's concert," but at stop after stop audiences didn't seem to be aware of these contests when Bruce mentioned them from the stage (which may say more about the decline of radio in the twenty-first century than even "Radio Nowhere" did).

423 *The quality of* Introduction to "For You," Portland, OR, 28 March 2008.

423 **an expected part** Interestingly enough, Bruce usually did it just after "Spirit in the Night," a song that the band was now doing many nights in implicit tribute to Danny.

424 **Wheel of Elvis** Costello would use it again on his 2011 tour.

426 **On stage** Springsteen, "Super Bowl Journal," posted Feb. 2009, archived at http://www.brucespringsteen.net/news/superbowljournal.html.

426 **concert on 31 July** This account is partially based on the description archived at http://www.backstreets.com/setlists2007.html, but mostly based on my own recollections of the concert.

428 **You are in** Scialfa quoted in David Fricke, "Bringing It All Back Home," *Rolling Stone*, 5 Feb. 2009, 78.

428 **while later I** This is from Rourke's message posted on www.brucespringsteen .net. Springsteen's and Rourke's versions of events differ slightly (phone call vs. letter; a request for a song vs. a spontaneous act of gratitude), but they seem to agree on the timing of the contact, as well as the fact that the actor reached out to the singer in some manner first.

428 **backstage after the show** Clemons and Reo, 205.

429 **I know a** Golden Globes acceptance speech, Los Angeles, CA, 11 Jan. 2009.

430 **18 January 2009** *The Official Inaugural Celebration* DVD (Presidential Inaugural Committee, 2010) includes all Springsteen's performances at the We Are One pre-inaugural concert.

431 **At my age** Quoted in Jon Pareles, "Springsteen Polishes His Dreams for America," *New York Times*, 29 Jan. 2009, available at http://www.nytimes.com/2009 /01/29/arts/29iht-bruce.1.19774940.html.

432 **the *Magic* tour** *London Calling: Live in Hyde Park* (Columbia Video, 2010), recorded 28 June 2009 at London's Hard Rock Calling Festival, is a good document of the middle of the *Working on a Dream* tour, although the sign requests are a little less adventurous than at most other concerts.

434 **"Wrecking Ball"** They had sound-checked the song in Chicago ten days before, but there they had played it more slowly. The greatest similarity between the two versions was Sooz's sweet violin line.

434 **almost anagogic** This is one case in which the bootleg recording is surprisingly preferable to the officially released one. In the single of "Wrecking Ball" that Springsteen released in early 2010, the piano is brought up in the mix and the drums down, thus ruining one of the arrangement's most effective aspects. Moreover, on the most widely available alternative recording of the song's first performance (as a bonus track on Godfather Records' *Rocking Down the Giants* bootleg of the second show of this stand), the harmony vocals give me shivers in a way that

they never do in their muted presentation on the official version. The *London Calling* DVD includes Springsteen's official video for "Wrecking Ball" and combines footage from several of the final Giants Stadium shows and also significantly remixes what the original audiences heard live.

435   **knee-slide across the stage** A move that was spontaneous during a rain-soaked onsite rehearsal a few days before the performance, but carefully planned for the day itself, right down to which pair of boots might give Bruce the greatest stopping power.

435   **You can't tell** Clemons and Reo, 271.

437   **22 November in Buffalo** A good recording of this essential concert is available on *Greetings from Buffalo Dream Night* (Crystal Cat).

HOUSE LIGHTS UP: MEET ME IN A DREAM OF THIS HARD LAND

General Sources: http://brucebase.wikispaces.com/2010; http://brucebase.wikispaces.com/2011.

439   **Myspace page** Evan James's music (without his last name) can be found at http://www.myspace.com/evanjamesmusictime/.

442   **That's what you** Springsteen, "Super Bowl Journal."

PERMISSIONS CREDITS

INDEX

Note: Page numbers in *italics* indicate a photograph or illustration.

Academy Awards ceremony (1994), 302
Achtung Baby (U2), 294
"Across the Border," 314–15, 327, 343
"Across the Borderline" (Cooder), 252–53, 264
"Action in the Streets," 148
"Adam Raised a Cain," 151, 152, 231
Aerosmith, 80
Ahmanson Theatre (L.A.), 85, 95
"Ain't Got You," 242, 246
"Ain't That Peculiar" (Gaye), 52
Alamo Bay (film), 317
Alfano, Bob, 18–19, 20, 24
Alford, Zach, 280–81, 285, 286, 303, 481
Allen, Steve, 474
"Allentown" (Joel), 322
"All I'm Thinkin' About," 343
Allman, Duane, 36–37, 46, 51, 456
Allman, Gregg, 36
Allman Brothers Band, the, 36–37, 44, 45, 49, 62, 70
"All Night Long" (Lyon), 274
"All or Nothin' at All," 263, 279
"All That Heaven Will Allow," 242–43
"All the Way Home," 273
Alpha Sounds, 103
Alpine Valley Music Theatre (East Troy), 214–15, 475
"America" (Simon and Garfunkel), 64
America: A Tribute to Heroes, 367–68, 369
American Babylon (Grushecky), 324
"American Idiot" (Green Day), 380, 416
"American Land," 398, 403, 421, 432
"American Skin," 355–61, 363, 365, 370, 380, 391, 434, 490
Amnesty International, 256–58
A&M Studios, 223–24, 246, 274–76
"Angel, The," 58, 67, 71, 76, 172, 278, 328, 437
"Angel Eyes" (Sinatra), 325–26

Animals, the, 8, 9, 17–18, 139, 251, 253, 469
Anthology of American Folk Music, 341
Antique Center (Red Bank), 404–5
antiwar movement, 34–35, 40–43, 177, 185–86, 286
Appel, Mike, 54–61, 65–70, 81, 85, 88, 97, 99, 102, 105, 108–9, 111, 112, 113–15, 119–20, 123, 124–25, 131, 437; lawsuit against, 143–49, 169
Appel, Steve, 102–3
"Arabian Night," 59, 67, 68, 71, 76, 82, 155
Arax, Mark, 315
Arcade Fire, 412, 440–42
arena rock, 348
Are You Experienced? (Hendrix), 19
Arizona State U. (Tempe), 174–76, 180–81, 197, 222–23
Armstrong, Billie Joe, 380
Aronofsky, Darren, 428–29
Arthur, Brooks, 107, 134
Asbury Jukes, the, 133–34, 148, 159, 210
Asbury Park, N.J., 17, 20, 22, 26–32, 45–47, 50–51, 61, 92, 247, 364–65; "Circuit," 152–53, 164, 467; riots, 41–42, 283. *See also specific venues*
Asbury Park Night, 483
"Atlantic City," 183, 188, 196, 206, 212, 213–14, 289, 315, 473
Atlantic City, N.J., 7, 183
Atlantic Highlands, N.J., 43, 59, 86
Atlantic Studios, 151, 467
Aukema, Niki, 110
Aykroyd, Dan, 168
Azito, Tony, 56, 57

"Baby Doll," 57, 74
"Baby I" (Castiles), 14–15, 18, 21, 35
Back in the USA (MC5), 105

"Back in Your Arms," 304, 307, 425
"Backstreets," 113, 123, 124, 161, 234, 314, 462
Backstreets.com, 391, 398–90
"Badlands," 151, 152, 161, 163, 202, 234, 252, 348, 354, 363, 432, 467, 470
Badlands: A Tribute to Bruce Springsteen's "Nebraska," 488
"Bad Moon Rising" (CCR), 256
Baez, Joan, 357
Bahler, Tom, 224
Baker, Arthur, 206–7, 210, 212, 217, 223, 227
Baker, Ginger, 195
"Balboa Park," 315–16
"Balboa *vs.* the Earthslayer," 460
"Ballad of the Self-Loading Pistol, The," 82
"Bamba, La" (Valens), 4, 7
Band, the, 36, 53, 62
Bandiera, Bobby, 198, 247, 259, 364, 395, 479
Bangs, Lester, 96, 128, 157
"Barefooting" (Parker), 239
Batlan, Mike, 190, 200
Beach Boys, the, 8, 84, 153
Beacon Theatre (N.Y.), 140–41
Beatles, the, 5, 6, 8–10, 13, 17–20, 55, 267, 439
Beaver, Ninette, 188
"Because the Night," 160, 264, 467, 469
"Beechwood 4-5789" (Marvelettes), 100
Bell, Barry, 224
Belmar, N.J., 118
Berkeley Community Center, 162
Berns, Bert, 4–5
Berry, Chuck, 47, 84, 184–85, 187, 281, 324
"Be True," 170, 172, 249, 255, 314
"Better Days," 274–75, 276, 287, 319; video, 279
Better Days (Lyon), 273, 274
Biff Rose, 83
Big Man's West (Red Bank), 198, 209
"Big Muddy, The," 275, 311, 481
"Big Payback, The," 196
Billboard charts, 4, 9, 127–28, 174, 198–99, 207, 214, 247, 270–71, 294–96, 307, 412–13
"Billy Rose" (Baez), 357
Biograph (Dylan), 232, 234
"Bishop Danced," 80–81, 82
Bittan, Roy: marriage, 258; musical range, 110–11, 117–18; other gigs, 305–6; recordings, 120, 150, 154, 194–95, 201, 265–66, 303, 410–11; recruitment, 73; songs cowritten with Springsteen, 261–63, 264; on *Streets of Fire* soundtrack, 474; synthesizer playing, 194–95; tours and live concerts, 112, 113, 164–65, 209–11, 279–80, 347, 422
Bitter End (N.Y.), 97, 458

Black Eyed Peas, the, 415
Black Oak Arkansas, 100
Black Rock Coalition, 281
Black Sabbath, 29–30, 33, 43, 160, 469
Blackstone, 109
Blackwell, Richard, 88
"Blinded by the Light," 75–76, 94, 127, 148, 155, 159, 202, 204, 470
"Blind Spot," 307
Blondes Have More Fun (Stewart), 168
Blondie, 80, 90, 168
Blood, Sweat and Tears, 84
"Blood Brothers," 306, 421–22
Blood on the Tracks (Dylan), 245
Blood Sex Sugar Magik (Red Hot Chili Peppers), 294
"Blowing Down the Road" (Ely), 329
"Blowin' in the Wind" (Dylan), 256
Blue, David, 460
Blue Cross Arena (Rochester), 433
Blues Magoos, the, 17, 19
Blues Project, the, 19, 24
blues revival, 29–31
"Bobby Jean," 201–2, 214
Body Count, 358
Bolton, Michael, 270, 272
Bonds, Gary U.S., 199, 377, 474
Bon Jovi, Jon, 246, 273, 302, 364, 485
Bono, 325, 384
Booker T and the MGs, 48
"Book of Dreams," 388
"Boom Boom" (Hooker), 253, 255
Boomtown Rats, 152
Boorstin, Daniel, 375
bootleg recordings, 165, 201, 343–44, 358, 491
Bootleg Series, Volumes 1–3 (Dylan), 273
Border, The (film), 252, 314
Bordonaro, Jon, 133
"Born in the U.S.A.," 195–96, 213, 214, 223, 286, 345, 357, 376, 379, 383, 430, 440–42, 467, 473, 474; Freedom Mix, 223
Born in the U.S.A.: album, 200–211, 286, 376, 436–37; thirtieth-anniversary box set, 393, 395; tour, 211–23, 226, 228–29, 233, 257
Born on the Fourth of July (Kovic), 162–63
"Born to Be Wild," 426, 427
"Born to Run," 106, 107–8, 113–15, 117, 121, 122, 123, 124, 126, 127, 146, 151, 161, 167, 207, 220, 221–22, 250–51, 257, 388, 462, 470, 478
Born to Run: album, 106–8, 113, 122–33, 157, 269, 436–37; tour, 125–27, 137–42
Born to Run (box set edition), 393, 395
Boston Garden (Boston), 87
Bottom Line (N.Y.), 126–27, 285, 287, 293
Bowie, David, 61, 83, 132

"Boys" (Shirelles), 457
Boyz II Men, 270
Bradley, Tom, 284
Bragg, Billy, 399
"Breakout," 467
Brickman, Marc, 112
"Bridge over Troubled Water" (Simon and Garfunkel), 369
"Brilliant Disguise," 243–44, 246, 248, 268, 311, 408, 477; video, 247
Bringing It All Back Home (Dylan), 72
"Bring on the Night," 170, 467
"Bring Them Home," 398, 402–3
Brinkman, Marc, 137–38, 170–71
British Invasion, 5, 8–10, 17, 24–25, 29
Bromberg, David, 81
"Brothers under the Bridge," 309–10, 318
"Brothers under the Bridges," 201–2, 314
Brown, Jason Robert, 369
Browne, Jackson, 64, 65, 97–98, 102, 227, 268, 460
"Brown Eyed Handsome Man" (Berry), 201
Brownsville Station, 81
Bruce Springsteen: Live and Rare, 481
Bruce Springsteen Band, the, 47–50, 52–54, 61, 69–77, 83, 169
Bruce Springsteen & the E Street Band Live/1975–85, 230–36, 240–41
Bruce Springsteen XXPlugged, 298, 481
Brunman, Glen, 141–42
Bruno, Frank, 340
"Buffalo Gals," 398, 399, 400
Buffalo Springfield, 62
Burdon, Eric, 49
Burger, Warren, 189
Burgess, Sonny, 317
Burke, Michael, 23, 24
Burnette, Billy, 280
Bush, George H. W., 271, 281, 284, 285, 291, 307, 319, 374
Bush, George W., 374–75, 377, 378–79, 381, 384, 396, 398–99, 401, 416
"Bye Bye Johnny," 192
"BYOB" (System of a Down), 379
Byrds, the, 8, 53, 62, 169, 170, 172, 178, 251

Cactus, 52
"Cadillac Ranch," 176, 178, 257, 400
Café Wha? (N.Y.), 16–17, 19, 21, 25, 453
Cafferty, John, 199, 219, 223
"Call on Me" (Bland), 100
"Candy's Boy," 154
"Candy's Room," 154, 408
Capital Centre (Largo), 218
Carboy, Gerald, 108
Card, Andrew, 373–74, 375

Carey, Mariah, 270, 297
Carr, Barbara, 300
Carr, Kristen Ann, 299, 300
Carter, Deana, 488
Carter, Ernest "Boom," 103, 108, 119, 142, 210, 281, 347, 461–62
Carter, Jimmy, 174, 177–78, 179–81, 417
"Car Wash," 201
Cash, Johnny, 251
Cassady, Neal, 128
Castiles, the, 11–23, 24, 26, 31, 169, 452–53
"Cathy's Clown" (Everly Brothers), 15
Cats on a Smooth Surface, 198, 210, 246, 247
"Cautious Man," 254, 388
CBGB (N.Y.), 28
"Chain Smokin'" (Grushecky), 481
Change Is Gonna Come, A (Werner), 351
Chapin, Harry, 247, 387, 461
Charlie's Place (Cambridge), 104–6, 131
Chatzy, Jeremy, 340
Checker, Chubby, 7
"Checkpoint Charlie" (Van Zandt), 226
Cheech and Chong, 80, 118
Cheers (Long Branch), 259
Cheney, Dick, 374
Cherlin, Harvey, 48
"Cherokee Queen," 460
"Chevrolet Deluxe," 178–79
Chicago (band), 87–88, 93
Chicago Transit Authority, 34
Chicanos, 314–16, 327
"Chicken Scratch" tour, 147, 437, 466
Child, 31–38, 42. *See also* Steel Mill
"Child Bride," 194–95, 473
Childe Harold (Washington, D.C.), 99
"Chimes of Freedom" (Dylan), 258, 478
Chinnock, Billy, 198
Chinnock, Danny, 420
Chlan, the, 17, 18
Christgau, Robert, 101, 132–33, 149, 271
Christic Institute, 268–69, 287
"Christmas in Washington" (Earle), 320
Ciambotti, Gia, 292
Cichon, Walter, 11, 51
Cinnamon, 108
"Circus Song," 80, 82, 86
City Auditorium Arena (Omaha), 141–42
Civic Arena (Pittsburgh), 220–21
Clancy, Liam, 80
Clapton, Eric, 29, 296, 297, 298, 454
Clash, the, 468
Clear Channel Entertainment, 368–69
Clearwater Music Festival (Asbury Park), 366
Clearwater Swim Club (Atlantic Highlands), 43, 59
Clements, Grace, 322

Clemons, Clarence: aging, 435; arrest, 102; death, 436; marriages, 187, 427; recordings, 86, 88, 91, 116, 119–20, 121, 195, 246; Red Bank club, 198; solo album, 199; solo career, 305–6; Springsteen and, 73–76; stories about, 138; Temple of Soul album, 366; tours and live concerts, 79–84, 95, 99, 112, 126, 209, 256, 347, 350, 368

Cleveland Stadium, 324

Cliff, Jimmy, 184, 298

Clifford, Mark, 340

Clinton, Bill, 319, 321–22, 333, 352–53, 355, 480

Clinton, Hillary, 416–17, 430, 485

CNN, 288–89

Cobain, Kurt, 157

Cochran, Eddie, 106

Cocks, Jay, 128, 140

coffeehouses, 22, 56, 58–59, 97

"Cold Hard Facts of Life, The" (Wagoner), 193

Cold Spring Harbor (Joel), 85

Coleman, Fred, 18

Coleman, Ornette, 301

Coliseum (L.A.), 228–29, 230

Colts Neck, N.J., 188, 190–92, 339–40, 405

Columbia Records: Appel lawsuit, 144–46, 147–49, 169; promotion of Springsteen, 85, 93, 97–98, 102, 122, 207–8, 241, 395; Springsteen's audition, 66–69; Springsteen's deal, 85; Springsteen's first profits with, 142–43; Springsteen's first recording, 69–77

compact disc format, 207

Concert for New York City, The, 369, 371

Confidential newsletter, 3–4

Conspiracy of Hope tour, 256

Convention Center Theatre (Dallas), 127

Convention Hall (Asbury Park), 364, 373, 378, 399

Cooder, Ry, 252–53, 314

Cook, Paul, 156

Cooke, Sam, 251, 351, 371

"Cop Killa" (Ice Cube), 358

Corgan, Billy, 321

Costello, Elvis, 341, 424, 473, 477

Count Basie Theatre (Red Bank), 436

"Countin' on a Miracle," 370, 388

country music, 36–37, 192, 193–94, 317, 472

"Courtesy of the Red, White, and Blue" (Keith), 379, 380, 416

"Cover Me," 208, 219, 223, 248, 474

"Cowboys of the Sea," 56, 58, 71, 82

Cox, Courteney, 212, 327

Crawdaddy, 98, 101, 105, 159, 464

Crazy Horse, 80

Crazysexycool (TLC), 294

Cream, 24, 37, 454

Creedence Clearwater Revival, 36, 42, 170, 181–82, 187, 379, 383

Creem, 104, 157

Crenshaw, Marshall, 303

Cretecos, Jim, 55–61, 65–69, 102, 145

crime and violence in America, 188–92

Crosby, David, 8

Crosby, Stills, and Nash, 64, 216–17

Crosby, Stills, Nash, and Young, 360

Cross, Charles, 390

Crossing Guard, The (film), 303

"Cross My Heart," 279, 479

"Crush on You," 178, 426, 438

Crystals, the, 111

Curtis, Kelly, 381

"Cynthia," 201, 391

Cyrus, Billy Ray, 294

Damrosch Park (N.Y.), 50

"Dance Dance Dance," 48

dance mixes, 206–7

"Dancing Fool" (Zappa), 168

"Dancing in the Dark," 203–5, 206–7, 210, 214, 215, 217, 219, 253, 318, 372, 429; video, 211–13, 216, 226

"Dancing in the Streets" (Vandellas), 49, 368–69

Dangerous (Jackson), 294

Dan Hicks and His Hot Licks, 84

Daniels, Charley, 49

"Daring Young Man on the Flying Trapeze, The," 404

"Dark and Bloody Ground" (Grushecky), 481

"Darkness on the Edge of Town," 155–56, 159, 162–63, 204, 229, 268, 293, 312–13, 318, 324, 422

Darkness on the Edge of Town: album, 149–56, 158–59, 161, 194, 269, 317, 436–37; tour, 160–66, 167, 233

"Darlington County," 474

Dave Clark Five, 8

Davis, Clive, 66, 72, 85, 94, 104, 111, 203

Davis, Miles, 30

"Dead Man Walking," 327, 328, 355

Dead Man Walking (film), 313

Deal Park Recreation Center, 44–45

Definitive Darkness Outtakes, The, 467

"Déjà Vu All Over Again" (Fogerty), 382–83, 407

Demme, Jonathan, 299–301, 305, 319

Dennis, Carolyn, 292

Denny, Reginald, 283

De Palma, Brian, 211–12, 475

Derek and the Dominoes, 297

"Desaparecidos, Los" (Van Zandt), 226

"Detroit Medley," 137, 141, 182, 423, 478

"Devils and Dust," 378–79, 380–81, 383, 396–97, 398, 406, 408, 429

Devils and Dust: album, 378–81, 385, 394, 407–8; tour, 385–95, 407, 423, 426, 428

"Devil's Arcade," 406–7

Diallo, Amadou, 355–57, 359, 361

Diamond, Neil, 55

Dictators, the, 468

Diddley, Bo, 9, 47, 53

"Didn't I?" (Gentry), 379

DiFranco, Ani, 329, 330, 488

Digable Planets, 351

DiLea, Eddie, 259–60

DiLea, Matty, 240, 259–60

DiLea, Tony, 259–60

Dinkins, Barbara, 48

Dion, 127

Diplomat Ballroom (N.Y.), 25

disco, 167–68

Dixie Chicks, the, 383

"Doctor My Eyes" (Browne), 97

Dodgers Stadium (L.A.), 377

"Does This Bus Stop at 82nd Street?," 63, 70, 71, 74, 130

Dole, Bob, 353

"Don't Look Back," 148, 149, 151

"Don't Worry Baby" (Beach Boys), 153

"Don't You Want to Be an Outlaw (Just like Jesse James)?," 54, 460

Doors, the, 29

"Doo Wah Diddy," 9

"Do Re Mi" (Guthrie), 330

DoubleTake concerts, 453, 467

Dovells, the, 70

"Downbound Train," 188–89, 194, 473, 474

Downtown Tangiers Rhythm and Blues Band, 44

Dr. Zoom and the Sonic Boom, 45–47, 49, 79, 88

"Dream Baby Dream" (Suicide), 388, 391

Dreams from My Father (Obama), 418

Drifters, the, 243

"Drive All Night," 150, 154, 173, 177

Dropkick Murphys, the, 440

"Dry Lightning," 309, 310, 318, 325, 327

Duckett, John, 6

Duke University (Durham), 139–40

Dunn, Duck, 49

Dyke and the Blazers, 40

Dylan, Bob, 36, 121, 132, 251, 287, 292, 324, 330; "Basement Tapes," 340–41; at Café Wha?, 16; Scaduto's book on, 61–63, 457–58; Shea Stadium performance, 377–78; as singer-songwriter, 55; songs, 8, 47, 114, 178, 245, 251, 258, 343; Springsteen compared to, 85, 98; Springsteen influenced by, 61–65, 72, 158, 232, 234, 273; Springsteen's first meeting with, 127; Springsteen's performances with, 302–3

Eagle, Larry, 340

Eagles, the, 84

Earle, Steve, 320

Earth, 24–32, 42, 47, 74

East Troy, Wisconsin, 214–15

Easy Rider (film), 53

Eddie, John, 303, 366

Eddie and the Cruisers (film), 199, 223

Ed Sullivan Show, The, 6, 7, 12, 109, 185, 267, 332, 439

Edwards, Henry, 128, 130–31

18 Tracks album, 346

EJ Thomas Hall (Akron), 331–32

Ellis Auditorium (Memphis), 137–42

Elwood, Philip, 38

Ely, Joe, 298–99, 317, 324, 329, 440, 481

Emerson, Kenneth, 104, 105–6, 243

Emiritas Stadium (London), 423–24

"Empty Sky," 372, 375, 376, 377, 390

"Entertainer, The" (Joel), 114

En Vogue, 281

Epsilons, the, 109

"Erie Canal," 385

Espinoza, Maria, 59, 75

Essential Bruce Springsteen album, 388, 395

E Street Band: All Area Access passes for, 182–83; appearance, 142; beginnings, 118–21; *Born in the U.S.A.* recording, 200–205; *Born in the U.S.A.* tour, 211–23, 226, 228–29; *Born to Run* tour, 137–42; "Chicken Scratch" tour, 147, 437, 466; *Darkness* recording, 149–56; greatest-hits package, 305–8; at Hall of Fame Springsteen induction, 346–47; *Magic* recording, 409–11; *Magic* tour, 411–14, 420–27; revival tour, 346, 348–64; *Rising* recording, 365, 369–73; *Rising* tour supporting, 373–78; *River* tour, 174–76, 181–87, 199; at Rock and Roll Hall of Fame opening, 324; on *Saturday Night Live*, 375; Ronnie Spector sessions, 148; Springsteen's disbanding of, 235–36, 246, 429; *Tunnel of Love* tour, 247–56, 278; on Vote for Change tour, 383

"E Street Shuffle, The," 94, 95, 116, 126, 159, 204

"Evacuation of the West," 86

Evans, Sara, 383

Evans, Terry, 263

Everly Brothers, the, 251

"Ev'ry Breath You Take" (Police), 257

Expo Theater (Fort Monmouth), 248

"Eyes on the Prize," 398

"Factory," 154, 163, 174, 361
"Fade Away," 177
Farrell, Wes, 55, 457
"Fast Car" (Chapman), 250
"Fast Song, The," 150, 154
Fast Times at Ridgemont High (film), 303
Fat City (Seaside Heights), 88, 461
Federici, Danny: accordion playing, 31, 80–81, 84, 92, 110; cancer, 409–10; in Child, 31–38; death, 420–22, 428; early life, 12; final performance, 413–14; marriages, 247; in Moment of Truth, 44; musical strengths, 117, 292; organ playing, 37, 86, 94, 110; other gigs, 305–6; recordings, 195, 343; song in memory of, 436; in Steel Mill, 38–43; tours and live concerts, 79–84, 209, 235, 298, 316, 333, 347; at Upstage, 31–32
Feigenbaum, Bobby, 48
Fenway Park (Boston), 377
"Fever, The," 83, 86, 113–14, 160, 346, 393, 465
"57 Channels and Nothin' On," 269, 286–91, 302, 304, 310, 316, 358, 480
Fillmore East (N.Y.), 25, 205
Fillmore Recording Studios, 38
"Fire," 150, 154, 160, 167, 241, 425
"Fire and Rain" (Taylor), 369
"Fist Full of Dollars." *See* "Atlantic City"
Flack, Roberta, 351
Flemington, N.J., 12
Flintstones, The, 199
"Float Away" (Marah), 440
Floyd, Eddie, 141, 165, 168, 234
Fluhr, Curt, 13, 17, 18–19
Fogerty, John, 42, 184, 186, 302, 382, 407
folksingers, 22, 24, 330–31, 340–42
"Follow That Dream" (Presley), 184, 188, 473
Fontayne, Shane, 280–81, 285, 290
Ford, John, 319, 331–32
"Fortunate Son" (CCR), 379, 382
"For You," 70, 153, 387, 459
"4th of July, Asbury Park (Sandy)," 92, 93, 94, 106, 141, 202, 231, 414, 421, 422
"Frankie," 147, 149
Franklin, Aretha, 351
Freedom No Compromise (Van Zandt), 241
"Freehold," 59
Freehold, N.J., 5–6, 10–14, 17, 20, 25, 26, 31, 32, 139, 187–88, 192–94, 232, 333, 361, 476
Freehold Night, 483
"Free Your Mind" (En Vogue), 281
"Froggie Went a Courtin'," 385
"From Small Things," 248
"Fuck tha Police" (NWA), 282
"Fugitive's Dream," 200
"Fun Fun Fun" (Beach Boys), 99

"Funk Broadway" (Dyke and the Blazers), 40
"Funk Song," 53, 83
Funky Divas (En Vogue), 281
Funky Dusty and the Soul Broom, 44–45
"Further on Up the Road," 370
"Fuse, The," 370

Gabriel, Peter, 227, 257–58
Gallagher, Big Danny, 32, 46, 420
"Galveston Bay," 317, 320, 327
Gandolfini, James, 373–74
Garden State Arts Center (Holmdel), 403–4
"Garden State Parkway Blues," 35, 40, 83
Gardner, Howard, 471–72
gas crisis, 177–78
Gaslight au Go Go (N.Y.), 68, 458
Gavin, Bill, 3–4
Geffen, David, 145
Geldof, Bob, 235, 239
Gentry, Montgomery, 379
"George Bush Don't Like Black People" (Legendary K. O.), 396
Gerry and the Pacemakers, 8
"Get Up Stand Up" (Marley), 258
"Ghost of Tom Joad, The," 307, 309, 318–19, 320, 326, 327, 331–32, 334, 343, 363, 432
Ghost of Tom Joad, The: album, 309–14, 316–25, 327–29, 394; tour, 326–27, 328, 329, 332–34, 340, 343, 392
Giants Stadium (Meadowlands), 227, 299, 393, 413, 427, 433
Gibson, William, 235
Gilbert, Liz, 66
"Gino Is a Coward" (Washington), 248–49
Giordano, Charlie, 340, 414, 420, 424
"Girls in Their Summer Clothes," 409, 489
"Girls Just Want to Have Fun" (Lauper), 203, 207
"Give the Girl a Kiss," 154
Glaub, Bob, 266
"Gloria" (Them), 303, 425
"Gloria's Eyes," 263, 279
"Glory Days," 195, 208, 240, 257, 259, 274, 294, 326, 423, 474, 478; video, 226
Glory Road, 45
Goffin, Gerry, 244
"Goin' Back," 467
"Goin' Back to Georgia," 37, 39–40, 47, 48
"Goin' Cali," 279
"Goin' Down Slow," 40
"Golddigger" (West), 396
Golden Age of Rock 'n' Roll, The (Sha Na Na), 100
Goldsmith, Lynn, 167, 394
Goodman, Fred, 131
"Good Man Is Hard to Find, A," 388
Good Morning America, 399

"Good Rockin' Tonight," 163, 165

Gordon, Robert, 154, 167

gospel impulse in music, 351–52, 354, 363, 365, 418

Gotham Playboys, the, 339–40, 342, 364, 397, 399, 400

Graham, Bill, 38, 156–57, 162–66

Graham, John, 23, 24

Grand Ole Opry (Nashville), 137

Grant, Amy, 280

Grapes of Wrath (film), 319, 331–32

Grapes of Wrath (novel), 318–19, 320, 331–32

Grateful Dead, the, 19, 36

Greatest Hits album, 305–8, 311, 316, 324

Green, Bobby, Jr., 283

Greenberg, Peter S., 128

Green Day, 380, 416

Greene, Bob, 129

Greene, Richard, 246

Green Mermaid (Asbury Park), 22, 27, 30, 44

Greenspan, Alan, 323

Greetings from Asbury Park, N.J.: album, 69–77, 81, 84–85, 98, 107, 278, 345, 394, 407–8, 437, 439; tour, 79–84

Grin, 205

"Growin' Up," 65, 67, 68, 70, 71, 74, 79, 138, 234, 393, 422, 460, 481

Grushecky, Joe, 303, 304, 322, 324, 343, 364, 377, 384, 392, 440, 481–82

"Guilty (Send That Boy to Jail)," 37, 39, 53

Gulf War, 288–89, 441

Guralnick, Peter, 49

Guthrie, Jack, 329, 395

Guthrie, Woody, 16, 63, 182, 329–30, 340, 398, 399

"Gypsy Biker," 407, 426, 481

Hadlock, Clyde, 100

Hammersmith Odeon, London '75 (video), 464

Hammond, John, 62, 66–69, 76–77, 78, 85, 93, 98, 105, 247, 459

Hanks, Tom, 300

"Happy," 276–77, 278, 295

Hard Day's Night, A (film), 8

"Hard Times" (Foster), 432

Harris, Emmylou, 376

Harry, Debbie, 90

Harry's Roadhouse (Asbury Park), 384

Hartford, John, 80

Harvard Square Theatre (Cambridge), 118–19

Hatfield, Bobby, 263

"Have Love Will Travel" (Berry), 253

Havens, Richie, 84

"Have You Forgotten?" (Worley), 379

Hayes, Isaac, 49

Haynes, Bart, 10, 13, 15–16, 20, 51, 179, 229, 476

HBO, 365

"Heart of Glass" (Blondie), 168

Heart of Rock and Soul, The (Marsh), 242, 272

"Hearts of Stone," 154, 467

heavy metal, 29–30, 33

Hedgerow Farm (Middletown), 364

"Heist, The." *See* "Meeting across the River"

"Held Up without a Gun," 177, 179, 424, 425

Helm, Levon, 341

"Help Me" (Ten Years After), 30

Hendrix, Jimi, 16, 19, 24, 45, 281

Henhoff, Nat, 64

"Henry Boy," 78–79, 460

Herman, Dave, 98, 126–27

Herman's Hermits, 8, 17

"Hey Hey My My" (Young), 157

"High Hopes" (McConnell), 307

"Highway 29," 309, 311–12, 314, 320, 327

"Highway Patrolman," 303, 314, 473

Hilburn, Robert, 173, 284

Hill, Walter, 199

Hit Factory (N.Y.), 201, 205, 246, 306, 318, 346, 365, 476

"Hitter, The," 343

"Hobo's Lullaby" (Guthrie), 329

"Hold On I'm Comin'" (Sam and Dave), 19

Hollywood Center Studios Soundstage, 291

"Hollywood Kids," 58

Hollywood Palace, 12

Holmdel, N.J., 169

Holmes, Delores, 48, 368

"Homestead" (Grushecky), 322, 481

"Honeymooners, The," 242

Hooker, John Lee, 16

House of Blues (Sunset Strip), 302

"House of the Rising Sun, The" (Animals), 9

Houserockers, the, 342

"How Can a Poor Man Stand Such Times and Live?" (Reed), 398, 400, 401

"How Can I Keep from Singing?," 398

HSBC Arena (Buffalo), 390–91, 437, 439

Huck, Janet, 128

Hullabaloo!, 12, 453

Hullabaloo Clubs (N.J.), 15, 17, 20, 25, 26, 33

Human Rights Now! concert tour, 256–58, 273

"Human Touch," 264–65, 279, 437; video, 279

Human Touch: album, 269, 278–79, 281; tour, 279–82, 291–94, 298–99

"Hungry Heart," 170, 172, 174, 202, 478

Hunter, Ian, 280

Hurricane Katrina and aftermath, 392, 396–99, 406

Hynde, Chrissie, 488

"I Am a Patriot" (Van Zandt), 226

"I Can't Help Falling in Love" (Presley), 184

Ice Cube, 284, 358

"Iceman," 388

"Idiot's Delight," 392

"I Don't Want to Go Home" (Van Zandt), 273, 465

"If I Had a Hammer," 398

"If I Should Fall Behind," 275, 300, 310, 350, 354, 363, 376, 485

"If I Was the Priest," 54, 56, 58, 67–68, 71, 460

"I Guess That's Why They Call It the Blues" (John), 203

"I Live for Cars and Girls" (Dictators), 115

"I'll Fly Away," 422

"I'll Work for Your Love," 408, 414, 426

"Imagine" (Lennon), 369

"I'm a Rocker," 178

"I'm Goin' Down," 368, 474

"I'm on Fire," 194, 368, 388, 417, 425, 474

"I'm Turning into Elvis (and There's Nothing I Can Do)," 307, 318

"Incident on 57th Street," 94, 96, 114, 301, 423

"Independence Day," 152, 163, 173, 174, 176, 361, 392, 406

Indianapolis, Indiana, 421

Indian Runner, The (film), 303

Ingraham, Laura, 383

"Innocent Man, An" (Joel), 203

Internet and social media, 386–87, 389–90, 393, 402–3, 423, 439–40

"In the Midnight Hour" (Pickett), 396–97

"In the Wee Small Hours of the Morning" (Sinatra), 325

"Into the Fire," 370, 372

Invisible Republic (Marcus), 341

Iovine, Jimmy, 280

Iraq War, 376–77, 380–81, 397, 398, 407

Iron Butterfly, 29–30, 33, 34, 37

Isley Brothers, the, 5, 8

"It Hit Me like a Hammer" (Lewis), 272

"It's Been a Long, Long Time" (Van Zandt), 273

"It's Hard to Be a Saint in the City," 59–61, 65, 67, 68, 70, 71, 95, 116, 138, 422, 460

"It's My Life" (Animals), 139–40, 148, 151, 181, 469

"It's the Little Things That Count," 309, 310, 318, 327

"It Takes a Lot to Laugh, It Takes a Train to Cry" (Dylan), 61

"I Wanna Be with You," 150, 170

"I Wanna Marry You," 177

"I Want You" (Dylan), 114

"I Will Follow Him" (March), 9

"I Wish I Were Blind," 263, 266

Izod Center (Meadowlands), 433

Jackson, Mahalia, 351

Jackson, Michael, 207–8, 294

Jackson, Randy, 262–63, 265–66, 276

"Jackson Cage," 174, 176

"Jacob's Ladder," 398

James Cotton Band, 34

"James Lincoln Dear," 188, 472

"Janey Needs a Shooter," 82

Jaywalkers, the, 44

Jay-Z, 440, 482–83

"Jazz Musician," 66, 71, 76

"Jeannie I Want to Thank You," 39

Jeffreys, Garland, 280

"Jenny Jenny" (Tutone), 406

Jersey Artists for Mankind, 233

"Jersey Girl" (Waits), 234

"Jesse James," 342, 399, 472

"Jesus Was an Only Son," 392, 393

Jive Five, the, 14

Joel, Billy, 35, 85, 114, 148, 203, 322

Joe's Place (Cambridge), 104

Johansen, David, 90

Johanson, Jai Johanny, 37, 49

John Cafferty and the Beaver Brown Band, 198, 199, 219

"John Henry," 385, 399

John Mayall's Bluesbreakers, 454

"Johnny 99," 188–89, 196, 220, 229, 388, 399, 400, 432, 473

"Johnny Bye Bye," 184–85, 188, 200

Jones, Jesus, 270–71

Jones, LeRoi, 30

Jones, Ricky Lee, 170

Jones, Steve, 156

Joplin, Janis, 29

Jordan, Steve, 379

Joshua Tree, The (U2), 280

Journey to Nowhere (Maharidge), 317

Joyce Garrett Singers, the, 430

Joyful Noize, the, 73–74

Jukes, the, 154, 272–73, 400, 464–65, 479

"Jump" (Van Halen), 203

"Jungleland," 106–7, 111, 113, 114, 119, 123, 124, 125, 165, 195, 423, 435–36, 462

"Keep the Car Running" (Arcade Fire), 412, 440

Keith, Toby, 379, 416

Kelly, Arthur and Ann, 408

Kenn, Sonny, 50–51, 198

Kennedy, Cleopatra, 292

Kenny's Castaways (N.Y.), 80, 84, 460

Kent State University shootings, 40–41

Kerry, John, 381–82, 383, 396, 407, 417

Kihn, Greg, 303

Killer inside Me, The (Thompson), 314

King, Bobby, 263, 292–93

King, Carole, 55, 141, 208, 244

King, Curtis, 432

King, Rodney, 282–86, 291, 356
"Kingdom of Days," 432
Kingsmen, the, 5, 15
Kings of Leon, the, 440
Kinks, the, 12, 17–20
"Kitty's Back," 93, 94, 95, 408, 414
Klein, Joe, 182
"Knock on Wood" (Floyd), 141, 168
Knopper, Steve, 207
Koppel, Ted, 373
Koppelman, Charles, 85, 94–95, 102, 129
Kovic, Ron, 162–63, 222, 382
Kragen, Ken, 224
Kravitz, Lenny, 270
Kriss Kross, 294
Kristofferson, Kris, 384
KSAN (radio station), 163

"Lady and the Doctor," 71
Lahav, Louis, 88, 111–12, 116
Lahav, Suki, 88, 111–12, 210, 248, 462
Landau, Jon: as critic, 132–33; first meeting
    with Springsteen, 105–6, 131–32;
    Springsteen quote, 111; as Springsteen's
    producer, 123, 126, 130–31, 143–44, 149,
    150, 190, 191, 195, 196, 200, 203, 208,
    228, 230–31, 232, 241, 279, 305–6, 331,
    381, 384
"Land of Hope and Dreams," 353–54, 363,
    372, 376, 377–78, 485
"Last Carnival, The," 436
"Last to Die," 407
Late Night with Conan O'Brien, 305
Late Show with David Letterman, The, 307,
    327, 373
Laurel Canyon Productions, 65–69, 102, 120,
    143–46, 149, 466
"Layla" (Clapton), 296, 297
"Leap of Faith," 479
"Learning to Fly," 272
"Leavin' Train," 263, 266
Ledin, Tomas, 333
Led Zeppelin, 29–30
Left Foot, The (N.J. club), 18
Legendary K. O., 396
Legends, the, 12
Leiber, Jerry, 243
Lennon, John, 184, 369
Leo, Kid, 104, 114
"Let It Be" (McCartney), 215
"Let's Be Friends," 370
"Let's Go Tonight," 154
"Let's Roll" (Young), 367
"Letter from an Occupant" (New
    Pornographers), 369
"Let the Four Winds Blow" (Domino), 100,
    109

"Let the Music Play" (Shannon), 203
Levine, Arnold, 206
Lewinsky, Monica, 352, 353
Lewis, Huey, 239, 270, 272
Lewis, Jerry Lee, 84, 324
Lewis, Randy, 402
"Light of Day," 249, 253, 349, 363, 485
"Like a Rolling Stone" (Dylan), 61, 65
Limbaugh, Rush, 383
"Line, The," 314, 320
"Lion's Den," 344, 354–55
Liszt, Greg, 399
Little Anthony and the Imperials, 14
"Little Girl like You," 200
"Little Latin Lupe Lu," 307
"Little Queenie" (Berry), 426
Little Royal and the Swing Masters, 103
Live in New York City album, 366, 485
"Living on the Edge of the World," 188
"Living Proof," 274–75, 286, 290–91, 311, 313,
    437
Livingston, Steven, 288
"Livin' in the Future," 407, 412, 413, 414
Lobos, Los, 488
"Local Hero," 275, 287, 429
"Loco-Motion, The" (King), 141
Loder, Kurt, 222, 225
Lofgren, Nils: aging, 435; first meeting with
    Springsteen, 205–6; guitar sound, 280;
    joins E Street Band, 209–11; recordings,
    246, 306; tours and live concerts, 212,
    214, 235, 258, 347, 350, 366, 424
Lomax, Alan, 402
Lone Justice, 280
"Lonesome Day," 370
Long Branch, N.J., 26–27, 92, 133–34
"Long Goodbye, The," 264, 279
"Long Time Comin'," 299, 343, 390–91
"Long Walk Home," 406–8, 418, 429, 431
"Look into My Window" (Castiles), 22
"Loose Ends," 171, 172, 424
Lopez, Vini: on Appel, 56; with Bruce
    Springsteen Band, 47–50, 52–54, 69–77;
    in Child, 30–38; with Dr. Zoom, 44–47;
    fight over finances, 102–3, 461–62; "Mad
    Dog" nickname, 26; in Moment of
    Truth, 44; Pandemonium meltdown, 33,
    125; recordings, 93, 95, 344; Springsteen
    scouted by, 26–27, 28; in Steel Mill,
    39–43; stories about, 138; tours and live
    concerts, 79–84, 333, 347
Los Angeles, Calif., 199–200; Rodney King
    beating and riots, 282–86, 287–88, 289,
    291, 293–94, 356
Los Angeles Times, 284, 315
"Losin' Kind, The," 188–89, 473
"Lost in the Flood," 70, 71, 76, 84, 387

Lost Masters II: One-Way Street, 467
Lost Masters III: Rattling the Chains, 467
"Louie Louie" (Kingsmen), 5, 15
"Love Me Tender" (Presley), 478
"Lovers in the Cold," 113, 115, 117
Lowell, Lisa, 210, 276, 385, 399
Lownds, Sara, 245, 477
Lucente, Bob, 358–59, 361, 380
"Lucky Man," 242
"Lucky Town," 275, 285, 389
Lucky Town: album, 273–79, 281; tour, 279–
    82, 291–94, 298–99
Lundvall, Bruce, 144–45
Luraschi, Johnny, 45
Lydon, Johnny (Johnny Rotten), 156–57, 158,
    159, 251
Lyon, Southside Johnny, 133–34, 147, 154,
    200, 258, 272–73, 302

Madison Square Garden (N.Y.), 87, 172, 181–
    82, 254, 256–57, 299, 348, 356, 359–61,
    369, 437, 485
"Magic," 407, 413
Magic: album, 384–85, 406–11; tour, 411–14,
    420–27
Magovern, Terry, 252, 315, 413
Maharidge, Dale, 317
Main Point (Bryn Mawr), 81, 87–88, 99, 103–
    4, 114–15, 116–18, 463
Mallaber, Gary, 285, 316, 479
"Man at the Top," 202–3, 214–16
Maness, Jay Dee, 246
Manfred Mann, 8, 9, 138, 148
Manhattan's Dictators, 115
Manion, Ed, 342
Manniello, Vinny "Skibots," 13, 18–19
"Mansion on the Hill," 192, 268, 276, 361,
    473, 476
"Man's Job," 262, 263, 279
"Many Rivers to Cross" (Cliff), 298
Marah, 440
March, Little Peggy, 9
Marcus, Greil, 65, 128, 158, 166, 181, 341, 369
Margaret and the Distractions, 27
Marley, Bob, 184, 258
"Marrakesh Express" (Crosby, Stills, and
    Nash), 64
Marsalis, Branford, 258
Marsh, Dave, 16, 61, 104, 105, 123, 125, 131,
    132–33, 143, 158, 172, 195, 211, 233, 240–
    41, 242, 272, 300, 394, 468
Martin, George, 5
"Mary, Queen of Arkansas," 67, 71, 76, 172,
    278, 354–55
"Mary Lou." *See* "Be True"
"Mary's Place," 371, 375

Marz American Style (Long Branch), 482
Marziotti, Frank, 11, 13
Maslin, Janet, 104, 105–6
Matawan, N.J., 13–14
Matchbox Twenty, 413
Matrix, 47
Matt's Saloon (Prescott), 259–60
Max's Kansas City (N.Y.), 78–79, 82–83, 84,
    87, 91–93, 99, 126, 461
Maxwell's (Hoboken), 226, 476
McAuliffe, John, 371
McCartney, Paul, 296
McConnell, Tim, 307
McGovern, George, 175
McGuinn, Roger, 169
McKee, Maria, 280
McKeith, Sam, 99
McLaren, Malcolm, 156
McLean, Don, 56
McLoone's Rum Runner (Sea Bright), 247
McVeigh, Timothy, 320
Medley, Phil, 4–5
"Meeting across the River," 124, 127, 188, 301
Melcher, Terry, 410
Mellencamp, John, 281, 292, 481
Mellon Collie and the Infinite Sadness
    (Smashing Pumpkins), 321
Men without Women (Van Zandt), 226
Mermaid Avenue (Billy Bragg & Wilco), 399
"Merry Christmas Baby," 241
Miami Horns, the, 147, 342
Miami Vice, 290
"Michael Row the Boat Ashore," 385
"Middle of the Road" (Pretenders), 203
Middletown, N.J., 12, 15, 17, 20, 25, 364
Midler, Bette, 132
Mile High Band, 259–60
Miller, James, 129
"Millworker" (Taylor), 322
"Missing," 303, 304, 370
Mitchell, Joni, 64, 65, 69, 71, 97, 330
Mitch Ryder and the Detroit Wheels, 137
"Mixed-Up Confusion" (Dylan), 63
Mizelle, Cindy, 400, 432
Moby Grape, 19
Moment of Truth, the, 26, 44
"Mona," 163
Mondale, Walter, 216–17
"Monkey Time, The" (Lance), 94, 371
"Monkey Wash Donkey Rinse (Zevon), 262
Monmouth Arts Center (Red Bank), 146–47
Montana Flintlock, 56
Moore, Sam, 50, 151, 263
"Morning Has Broken" (Stevens), 368
Morrison, Van, 235, 251, 281
"Mother's Little Helper" (Rolling Stones), 35

Mothers of Invention, the, 17, 35
Motifs, the, 11, 13, 18, 26, 31
"Motownphilly" (Boyz II Men), 270
"Motown Song, The" (Stewart), 270, 272
Mottola, Tommy, 270
"Mr. Jones" (Castiles), 21
Mr. Music (Bricktown), 14–15
"Mr. Tambourine Man" (Byrds), 8
"Mrs. McGrath," 385, 398
MTV, 206, 207, 211–13, 247, 271, 281
MTV Unplugged, 296–98, 481
MTV Video Music Awards, 373–74
Muller, Bobby, 196, 382
Mulshine, Paul, 358, 359
Muni, Scott, 104, 114
Municipal Auditorium (Austin), 127
"Murder Incorporated," 306, 308, 361; video, 307
Murphy, E., 303
Muscle Shoals sound, 37, 48
Musicians for Safe Energy (MUSE), 172, 175, 185
Musselwhite, Charlie, 459
"My Back Pages" (Byrds), 178, 318
"My Beautiful Reward," 274, 275, 277, 388
"My Best Was Never Good Enough," 314, 318, 320, 327, 387
"My City of Ruins," 364–65, 367–68, 369, 373, 377, 400, 410
"My Father's House," 196, 204, 389
My Father's Place (N.Y.), 99
"My Generation" (Who), 17
"My Hometown," 201, 208, 220, 221–22, 229, 230, 231, 232, 245, 256, 257, 293, 361–63, 376, 406, 476
"My Lover Man," 269
"My Oklahoma Home" (Cunninghams), 400, 401
Mystery Train (Marcus), 158, 400

Nassau Coliseum (Uniondale), 182, 234, 241
National, the, 440
National Sports Stadium (Harare), 257
"Native American" (Van Zandt), 241
"Natural Magic," 48
Ndegeocello, Me'shell, 281
"Nebraska," 188, 192, 196
Nebraska album, 190–99, 242, 246, 268–69, 317, 389–90, 394, 395
Neer, Richard, 98–99, 104, 113, 126, 132
Nelson, Paul, 132–33
Neon Boys, the, 90
"Never Be Enough Time" (Grushecky), 481
Never Say Die! (Black Sabbath), 160
Neville, Aaron, 270
Newark Star Ledger, 358

New Jersey: map of, viii; September 11 terrorist attacks and, 366–73; Shore region, 25–27. See also specific towns and venues
Newman, Randy, 132
New Orleans Fairgrounds, 337
New Orleans Jazz and Heritage Festival, 400–402
New Pornographers, the, 369
New Shrewsbury, N.J., 15
Newsweek, Springsteen on cover of, 128, 130
"New Timer, The," 317, 320
New West, 104, 181
New York, N.Y.: in 1970s, 90–91; clubs in, 16–17; Diallo shooting, 355–57, 359, 361; September 11 terrorist attacks, 366–73
"New York City Serenade," 89–91, 96, 111, 116, 117, 127, 461
New York Dolls, the, 80, 90
New York Guitar Festival (2006), 395
"New York Morning Love," 22
New York Post, 408
"New York Song," 88–89, 91, 96
New York Times, 128, 130, 197, 358, 468–69
Nichols, Terry, 320
Nicholson, Jack, 127
Nick of Time (Raitt), 270
Niedecken, Wolfgang, 324
"Night," 127, 137, 161
Night Ranger, 35
"99 Luftballons" (Nena), 203
914 Sound Studios, 70, 79, 82, 85–87, 88, 106–8, 113, 134
Nirvana, 157, 295
Nixon, Richard M., 34, 100
"No Fun" (Stooges), 156
"None but the Brave," 425
No Nukes concerts, 394, 470
"No Surrender," 201–2, 214, 377, 381–82, 383, 407
"Nothing Man," 304, 370
"Not the Only One" (Raitt), 296
NWA, 282
Nyro, Laura, 145

Obama, Barack, 415–19, 421, 429–30, 440–41
Obama, Michelle, 417
O'Brien, Brendan, 365, 370, 378, 379, 381, 406, 410–11
O'Brien, Geoffrey, 369
O'Brien, Mark, 368
Odin, 80
Off Broad Street Coffee House (Red Bank), 22, 24, 25
"Oh Angelyne." See "River, The"
"Ohio" (Crosby, Stills, Nash, and Young), 360

"Oh Mary Don't You Weep No More," 385
Oklahoma City bombing, 320
"Oklahoma Hills" (Guthrie), 329, 395
"Old Dan Tucker," 385
Oldham, Spooner, 37
Oliver's (Boston), 83, 86, 99
"One Shot of Happy, Two Shots of Sad"
    (Bono), 325
"One Step Up," 247, 265, 311
"One Way Street," 150
"Only the Good Die Young" (Joel), 35
"Only the Lonely" (Orbison), xiv
"On the Dark Side," 219
Ooze and Oz Productions, 25
"Open All Night," 188, 213–14, 399, 400, 473
Operation Desert Storm, 288, 290
Orbison, Roy, xiv, 43, 241, 247
Orchid Lounge (Ridgewood, N.J.), 45
organ in pop music, 37–38
Orth, Maureen, 128
"Out in the Street," 176, 180, 213, 363
"Out of Limits" (Marketts), 5
"Outside Lookin' In," 150
"Over the Rise," 269
"Owner of a Lonely Heart" (Yes), 203

Palace (Auburn Hills), 351
Palace Theatre (Providence), 125
Pandemonium (Wanamassa), 32, 33, 59, 125, 187
"Paradise," 371, 377, 388
"Paradise by the C," 161
Paramount Theatre (Asbury Park), 333, 386–
    87, 392, 398
Parliament, 351
Parrish, Lydia, 402
"Part Man, Part Monkey," 249, 263, 387
Partridge Family, the, 55, 57
Paul's Mall (Boston), 81, 92–93
"Pay Me My Money Down," 385, 402
"Peace in LA" (Petty), 480
"Peace Train" (Stevens), 368
Pearl Jam, 365, 381
Pechanec, Brenda "Bubbles," 259–60
Pelton, Shawn, 266
Pender, Mark, 342, 385
Penn, Sean, 303
"People Get Ready" (Mayfield), 354
"Peter Gunn Theme" (Mancini), 201
Petty, Tom, 169, 173, 270, 272, 480
"Phantoms," 86
Philadelphia (film), 299–301, 319
Philips Arena (Atlanta), 355
Phillips, Christopher, 390
Phillips, Julianne, 224–26, 229, 239–40, 241–
    42, 244, 245, 249, 254–55
Pickett, Wilson, 40, 396–97, 398
"Pilgrim in the House of Love," 328–29, 408

"Pink Cadillac," 201, 473
"Pink Houses" (Mellencamp), 203
"Pipeline" (Chantays), 7
"Planet Rock" (Bambaataa), 207
"Plane Wreck at Los Gatos (Deportee)"
    (Guthrie), 329–30
Platt, John, 395–96
Plotkin, Chuck, 194, 232–33, 280
Pocketful of Tunes, 56–61, 98
Pogues, the, 342
"Point Blank," 361
Pointer Sisters, the, 167
Point Pleasant, N.J., 69, 79–80
Polar Music Prize, 333–34, 347
politics, American, 100, 174–81, 184, 215–23,
    229, 255–57, 268, 286–91, 307, 314–16,
    319–23, 326–27, 334–35, 352–53, 361–63,
    366–73, 374–76, 379–83, 395–97, 406–8,
    411–12, 415–19, 432, 433–36, 479–80
Pond, Steve, 196–97, 252, 253, 264
"Pony Boy," 279
Pop, Iggy, 30
Popkin, Paul, 18–19
pop music: early 1960s, 8–9; early 1990s, 270–
    72, 294–96; mid-1990s, 330–31
Poppos, Patty, 393
Porcaro, Jeff, 262–63, 265–66, 279
Potter, Margaret, 27, 30, 50–51, 454
Potter, Tom, 27, 28, 50–51
Power Station (N.Y.), 199, 206, 476
power trios, 24–25
"Preacher's Daughter," 467
Presley, Elvis, 4, 7, 109, 133, 141–42, 149, 154,
    157, 163, 184–85, 187, 207–8, 217–18,
    244, 261, 329, 457
Preston, Billy, 84
"Pretty Flamingo" (Manfred Mann), 138, 148,
    428–29
Price, Alan, 12
"Price You Pay, The," 171, 172, 177
Prince, 200, 281, 463
Prine, John, 258
Projections (Blues Project), 19
"Promise, The," 146–47, 147, 148, 149, 152,
    154, 155–56, 158, 161, 346
Promise, The: The Darkness on the Edge of
    Town Story, 466–67
"Promised Land, The," 154, 182, 252, 256,
    262, 351, 360, 377, 403, 432, 484
"Protection," 248, 249
"Prove It All Night," 151, 163, 213, 467, 469,
    470
psychedelic rock, 17–20
Public Enemy, 286
Public Image Ltd., 158
punk, 90, 156–57, 203
Puterbaugh, Parke, 308, 316

Quayle, Dan, 480

"Racing in the Street," 152–53, 155–56, 164
"Radio Nowhere," 406, 426, 429
Raeben, Norman, 477
Rage against the Machine, 365
"Raise Your Hand" (Floyd), 141, 147, 165, 234, 258
Raitt, Bonnie, 97–98, 105, 268, 270, 272, 296
Ramm, Curt, 434
Ramones, the, 90, 160, 468
"Ramrod," 172, 176, 178, 363, 423
"Randolph Street," 193
rap, 271, 295
Reagan, Ronald, 174, 176, 180–81, 186, 189, 197, 214, 215–23, 229, 319, 334, 361, 374, 375, 377, 383, 402, 417, 429, 474
"Real Love, The" (Seger), 272
"Real Man," 279
Real Paper, 105, 129
"Real World" (B.S. and Bittan), 261–62, 263, 264, 387, 389
"Reason to Believe," 262, 387, 413, 473
Record Plant (N.Y.), 119, 122–26, 143, 151, 160, 171, 177, 462
Record Report (Gavin letter), 3–4
Red Bank, N.J., 22, 24, 25, 26, 108, 175, 198, 209. See also specific venues
"Red Headed Woman," 269, 328–29, 408
Rednecks and Bluenecks (Willman), 487
Red One, the, 214
Redwood Curtain (Wilson), 314
Reed, Blind Alfred, 398
Reed, Lou, 84, 90, 93, 96, 128, 132, 329, 468
Reid, Vernon, 281
"Rendezvous," 148, 149, 163, 344
"Reno," 343, 408
"Restless Nights," 438
"Resurrection," 35–36, 39, 53, 228
rhythm and blues, 40, 49–50, 82, 263
Richards, Keith, 235
Richmond, Va., 34, 38–39, 43, 50, 52, 460
"Riding in My Car" (Guthrie), 483
Rifkin, Marty, 316–17, 343, 399–400
Righteous Babe label, 329
"Right Here, Right Now," 271
"Ring of Fire" (Cash), 100
"Rising, The," 372, 373, 376, 430
Rising, The: album, 365, 369–73; tour, 373–78, 380
"River, The," 171, 172, 177, 178, 182, 193, 229, 234, 241–42, 245, 256, 258, 361, 476
River, The: album, 168–74, 176–79, 194, 214, 242, 317, 376, 394, 423, 437; tour, 174–76, 181–87, 199, 206, 233
Robbins, Tim, 313, 316
Roberts, Rick, 80

Rock and Roll Hall of Fame and Museum (Cleveland), 324, 345, 346–47, 384, 484
Rock and Roll Hall of Fame & Museum: Live, 484
"Rockaway the Days," 202
rock improvisation, 29–31
"Rockin' All Over the World" (Fogerty), 184
Rocking Down the Giants, 491–92
Rockwell, John, 128, 132–33, 197
Rogers, Angel, 292
Rogues, the, 14, 15, 18
Rolling Stone, 85, 104, 105, 123, 128, 131, 149, 196–97, 222, 252, 253, 264, 294, 305, 343, 386
Rolling Stones, the, 8, 12, 13, 29, 35, 168, 173, 218
"Roll of the Dice" (B.S. and Bittan), 261, 263, 279
Ronson, Mick, 280
"Rosalita," 93, 96, 99, 100, 124, 140, 151, 212, 213, 242, 380, 460
Rose Center and Planetarium (N.Y.), 373–74
Roseland (N.Y.), 303
Rosenberg, Richie "La Bamba," 342
"Rosie," 478
Roslin, Vinnie, 11, 31–38, 38, 39
Rossi, Carlo, 103
"Roulette," 171, 177, 179, 183, 245, 249, 289, 315, 357
Rourke, Mickey, 258, 428–29
"Route 66," 303
Rove, Karl, 374
Roxy (L.A.), 127
Royal Albert Hall (London), 328
Royko, Mike, 129
Rubber Club (L.A.), 258
"Ruled by the Gun," 188, 472
Rum, Sodomy, and the Lash (Pogues), 342
Rumble Doll (Scialfa), 299
Rum Runner (Sea Bright), 259
Rumson, N.J., 204, 231, 241, 273, 364
"Run through the Jungle" (CCR), 42, 184

"Sad Eyes," 265, 266, 279, 391, 484
"Saga of the Architect Angel, The," 82
Sam and Dave, 19, 50
Sancious, David: with Bruce Springsteen Band, 47–50, 52–54, 69–77; leaves band, 108, 110, 119, 142, 281; musical strengths, 116, 117, 209–10; other gigs, 79, 210, 257; recordings, 88–89, 91, 93–94, 95, 263, 460–61; tours and live concerts, 103; at Upstage, 28, 44–47
Sandford, Christopher, 194, 254
Sandy Hook, N.J., 247
San Francisco music scene, 18, 19, 37–38, 58–59

Sangiacomo, Michael, 112
"Santa Ana," 86, 393
"Santa Claus Is Coming to Town," 100, 163, 230, 231
Santelli, Robert, 38, 344, 345
Sartori, Maxanne, 81, 104, 114
Satellite Lounge (Cookstown), 50, 103
Saturday Night Live, 285–86, 287, 290–91, 374–75
"Say Goodbye to Hollywood" (Joel), 148
Sayles, John, 162, 226, 240, 476
Scaduto, Tony, 61–63, 457–58
Scaggs, Boz, 111, 170
Schaefer Music Festival (Central Park), 111
Schechter, Bill, 227
Sciaky, Ed, 104, 113–14, 114, 132
Scialfa, Patti: birth of children, 266–67, 302; in Jukes band, 479; marriage, 269–70, 404–5, 408, 427; on-stage tribute to, 427; pregnancies of, 263, 266, 270, 276, 299; recordings, 246, 342, 343, 399; recruitment, 73; Sinatra, 325; solo albums, 258, 299, 378; Springsteen and, 254–55, 258–59, 260, 261, 264–65, 293–94, 304, 313, 324; tours and live concerts, 210–11, 214, 248, 252, 254–55, 333, 347, 350, 364, 368, 413
Scott, Little Jimmy, 301
Scott, Toby, 196, 232, 343–44
Searchers, the, 8
"Secret Garden," 304, 307
"Seeds," 229, 357, 432
Seeger, Pete, 329, 340–42, 385, 397–99, 404, 441
Seeger sessions, 397–99, 413, 427
Segelstein, Irwin, 113, 122, 463–64
Seger, Bob, 270, 272, 379
Seldin, Norman, 13–14, 73–74
September 11 terrorist attacks, 366–73
"Series of Dreams" (Dylan), 273
Sessions Band, 337, 402–4, 414, 422, 432, 434
"Seven Angels," 263, 266
Sex Pistols, the, 156–57, 165
Shadows, the, 26, 39, 455
"Shake Rattle and Roll," 324
Sha Na Na, 84, 100
Shangri-las, the, 14
Shankar, Ravi, 258
Shea Stadium (N.Y.), 377
Sheehan, Cindy, 398
"Shenandoah," 385
"Sherry Darling," 173, 176, 467
"She's Leaving," 457
"She's So Fine," 106, 115
"She's the One," 113, 125, 126, 462
Shindig, 12, 453

Shipbottom Lounge (Point Pleasant), 74
Shock'n Y'all (Keith), 379
Shoreline Amphitheatre (Mountain View), 235
"Shotgun" (Walker), 100
Shrine Auditorium (L.A.), 325
Shurtleff, Jeffrey, 180
"Shut Out the Light," 222
"Sidewalk" (Castiles), 12, 453
Siebert, Thomas L., 333
Sierras, the, 10
Simon, Paul, 369
Simon and Garfunkel, 64, 330
Sims, Tommy, 280–81, 285, 301, 481
"Sinaloa Cowboys," 315–16, 330
Sinatra, Frank, 325–26
Sinclair, John, 131
singer-songwriter movement, 55–56, 63–65, 78–79
singles, releasing, 107–8
Sioux City Music, 68–69, 71, 78–79, 343–44
"Sister Christian" (Night Ranger), 35
"Sister Theresa," 35
Sly and the Family Stone, 49
Smashing Pumpkins, the, 321
"Smells like Teen Spirit" (Nirvana), 295
Smith, Fred "Sonic," 305
Smith, Harry, 341
Smith, Patti, 80, 90, 93, 132, 305, 468, 469
Smith, Tommy, 41
"Solidarity" (Van Zandt), 226
Some Girls (Rolling Stones), 168
"Something about You" (Four Tops), 248
"Something in the Night," 147, 149, 151, 152, 154, 467
"Something to Talk About," 272
"Song of the Orphans," 80, 82, 394
Songs (book), 191, 344–45, 346, 347–48
Sonny and the Starfires, 26, 32
Sony showcase concert, 291, 307
SOS Racisme! concert, 256
"Soul Driver," 262, 263, 269
"Souls of the Departed," 275–76, 290, 357, 371
Soundworks West (L.A.), 262–63
"So Young and in Love," 113, 161
"Spanish Johnny," 315
"Spare Parts," 245, 246
Spector, Phil, 100, 107, 119, 127, 410–11
Spector, Ronnie, 148
Spectrum (Philadelphia), 87–88, 149, 161, 433, 436–37, 466
"Spirit in the Night," 74–75, 82, 115, 140, 161, 231, 424, 470
Sports Arena (L.A.), 185–86, 252–53, 433
Springfield, Rick, 223
Springsteen, Adele Zirilli (mother), 7, 21, 59, 422

Springsteen, Bruce, 135, 237, 337; accusations against, 356–57; aging, 409–10, 435–36; ambivalence about success, 146–47, 235, 236, 304; appearance, 142, 200; Appel lawsuit, 144–46, 147–49, 169; autobiographical themes, 54, 59, 64, 75–76, 138–40, 152–53, 165, 192–94, 203–5, 215, 234–35, 242, 264–65, 279, 310–12; awards, 333–34, 346–47, 396–97; band's financial problems, 102–3; birthdays, 259, 339–40; in California, 261–70; charity or benefit concerts, 172, 175, 185–86, 195, 235, 247, 256–57, 261, 268–69, 329–30, 333, 364, 367–68, 369, 384, 385, 392, 395, 436; community organizing viewed by, 429–30; "cowboy" persona, 53–54; criticism of, 128–31, 383; desire for children, 240, 245, 260; disinterest in school, 13, 17, 20, 22, 34; divorce, 255, 258; draft deferment, 20; drugs viewed by, 185; early life, 6–23, 192–94, 457–58; fatherhood, 266–68, 269–70, 273, 295, 298, 302, 311; guitars, 7, 10, 13, 29, 69; harmonica playing, 121; homes, 199–200, 204–6, 231, 265–66, 339–40, 405; home studios, 190–92, 200, 231, 237, 241, 265–66, 276, 299–300, 303, 317, 339–40, 405; house-hunting, 187–88; ideology, 176–81, 197, 221–22, 319–23, 352–53, 379–80, 381–82; influence, xiv; integration of covers into sets, 99–100, 181–82, 251, 472; lack of Top 10 singles, 167; marriage to Phillips, 224–26, 229, 239–40, 241–42, 244, 245, 249, 254–55, 427; marriage to Scialfa, 269–70, 404–5, 408, 427; motorcycle trip, 259–60; multiracial bands, 48–50, 73–76, 91, 101–4, 281; musicians recruited, 108–12; on-stage monologues and stories, 139–40, 148, 163–65, 175, 182, 183, 217–18, 221–22, 229, 234, 249–50, 268, 287, 310, 326, 331–32, 349–50, 411–12, 437–38, 465, 476; personal insights in songs, 64, 96–97, 146–47, 151–52, 155–56, 170–72, 197, 241–42, 269, 275–76, 311–16, 333–34; piano playing, 387, 460, 463; political comments and views, 174–76, 180–81, 185–86, 215–23, 228–29, 234, 255–57, 307, 326–27, 334–35, 352–53, 361–63, 373–76, 381–82, 391, 395–97, 406–8, 411–12, 415–19; requests taken on tours, 423–26; revisiting of early songs, 312–13, 388–95, 407–8, 423–26; Rock and Roll Hall of Fame induction, 73, 345, 346–47; on Rodney King riots, 283, 293–94; Scialfa and, 210, 254–55, 258–59, 260, 261, 264–65, 293–94, 304, 313, 324; second auditions, 11, 58–60; songwriting skills development, 61–65, 82–83, 86–87, 89–90, 150–51, 312–14, 410, 453; Southern and country influences, 36–37; stage personas, 81, 161–62, 212–13, 286–87, 293–94, 326–27, 350–52; therapy, 188, 249, 260–61, 266–67; topical songs, 176–79, 183, 188–90, 197, 252, 275–76, 286–91, 299–301, 317–18, 326–27, 355–61, 364–65, 370–71, 383, 432; ukulele playing, 392; writer's block, 258, 261–63, 303–4, 343, 428. *See also specific albums, groups, songs, performance locations*
Springsteen, Doug (father), 6, 17, 21–22, 32, 139–40, 154, 163, 195, 344–45, 420, 422
Springsteen, Evan James (son), 266–67, 273, 298, 339, 439–40
Springsteen, Ginny (sister), 6, 7, 11, 13, 21, 171
Springsteen, Jessica Rae (daughter), 276–77, 295, 298, 339, 405
Springsteen, Pam (sister), 6, 21, 164, 200, 303
Springsteen, Sam Ryan (son), 302, 339, 405
St. Paul, Minnesota, 211–13
St. Pete Times Forum (Tampa), 421–22
Stadio Comunale (Turin), 254
"Stand on It," 201
Starkweather, Charles, 188
Starr, Edwin, 228–28, 376
Starr, Kenneth, 352, 353
State Theater (New Brunswick), 326
"State Trooper," 389, 473
Stax Records, 48–49
Steel Mill, 38–43, 48, 53, 83, 151, 205, 210, 463
Steel Pier (Atlantic City), 7
Steely Dan, 71
Stein, Chris, 90
Stein, Jeff, 211
Steinbeck, John, 319, 320, 331, 334
Steinman, Jim, 474
Steppenwolf, 29–30
Stevens, Cat, 368
Stevens, Gary, 14
Steve van Zandt and the Big Bad Bobby Williams Band, 44–45
Stewart, Amii, 168
Stewart, Rod, 168, 227, 270, 272
Sting, 256–58, 266
"Stolen Car," 171, 172, 173, 177, 178, 241–42, 309, 311, 389
Stoller, Mike, 243
Stone Pony (Asbury Park), 27, 142, 152, 198, 210, 232, 246, 247, 258, 302, 364, 366, 378, 384, 385

Stooges, the, 30, 156
Storytellers (VH1 show), 385, 388, 408, 481
"Straight Time," 309, 311, 312, 320, 327
"Street Fightin' Man" (Rolling Stones), 218, 228–29
"Streets of Fire," 151, 163, 199
Streets of Fire (film), 199
"Streets of Philadelphia," 300–302, 304, 305, 307, 316, 318, 327, 329, 370; video, 301
Streisand, Barbra, 66, 458
strip clubs, 408–9
Strummer, Joe, 468
Student Prince (Asbury Park), 33, 50, 52, 68, 73, 82, 152, 420
Sub Pop Records, 488
Suicide, 388
Summer, Donna, 168, 199, 208, 248, 474
"Summertime Blues," 424–25
"Sun City" (Van Zandt), 227–28, 252, 256
Sunshine In (Asbury Park), 33, 43, 44, 45–47, 70, 152
Super Bowl appearance, 435
"Surfin' Bird" (Trashmen), 5
Surf 'n' See Club (Sea Bright), 14, 15, 17, 18
"Surprise Surprise," 438
"Suspicious Minds" (Presley), 244, 303
Suydam, Arthur, 339
Sweet Lies (film), 239
"Sweet Little Sixteen" (Berry), 260
synthesizer rock, 203
System of a Down, 379

Taliefero, Crystal, 291–92
"Talking in Your Sleep" (Romantics), 203
"Talk to Me," 154, 467
Tallent, Garry: at Alpha Sounds, 103; Appel viewed by, 145; with Bruce Springsteen Band, 47–50, 52–54, 69–77; with Dr. Zoom, 44–46; Jersey Artists for Mankind, 233; in Moment of Truth, 44; other gigs, 305–6; recordings, 93, 95, 195, 246, 273, 316–17, 410–11; tours and live concerts, 79–84, 113, 209, 212, 298, 347, 362; tuba playing, 44
Tapestry (King), 55, 208
"Taxi Cab," 467
Taylor, James, 65, 69, 322, 369
"Tears in Heaven" (Clapton), 296
Teendezvous, Le (New Shrewsbury), 15, 20, 22, 23, 25, 26, 33
Television, 90
Teller, Al, 208
Tellone, Albee "Albany Al," 88
Temple of Soul, 366
"Tender Years," 223
"Tenth Avenue Freeze-Out," 124, 126, 132,

147, 159, 204, 268, 349, 363, 375–76, 382, 470, 484–85
Ten Years After, 30
Terkel, Studs, 322
"Terry's Song," 413
Testa, Philip, 183
Tharpe, Sister Rosetta, 354
"That's What You Get" (Castiles), 14–15, 18, 21
Theiss, George, 10–12, 14–15, 18–19
Them, 8, 424–25
"Then She Kissed Me" (Spector), 426
"There Goes My Baby" (Drifters), 243
"(They Call Me) Bruce" (Rick Springfield), 223
"They Killed Him on the Street," 188, 472
"30 Days Out," 263
"This Hard Land," 298, 305, 306, 308, 316, 318, 327, 345–46, 473, 484
"This Land Is Your Land" (Guthrie), 182, 184, 234, 330
"This Train," 354
Thompson, Jim, 314
Thompson, Marc Anthony, 400
Three Mile Island nuclear plant, 171, 177
Thriller (Jackson), 207–8
Thrill Hill East studio, 276, 342, 343–44, 364–65, 378, 429, 481
Thrill Hill West studio, 237, 276, 317, 323, 378, 481
"Thundercrack," 82–83, 86–87, 344, 393, 408, 425, 433, 460
"Thunder Road," xiv, 116–18, 120–21, 123, 124, 126, 140, 148, 151, 152, 153, 156, 164–65, 182, 191, 202, 213, 231, 233, 268, 314, 318, 334, 348, 360, 423
Tierney, John, 358, 359
"Ties that Bind, The," 163, 169–70, 392
"Tiger Rose," 317
Tillotson, Johnny, 14
Timberlake, Justin, 413
Time magazine, 128, 140
"Times They Are A-Changin'" (Dylan), 343
Today Show, 373, 399, 412
"Tom Joad" (Guthrie), 329–30
Toms River, N.J., 25
Tone, 108, 142, 210
Tonight Show with Jay Leno, The, 327
"Tougher than the Rest," 247, 388
"Town Called Heartbreak, A" (Scialfa), 413
Townshend, Pete, 235, 239
T-Pain, 413
Tracks: album, 242, 343–48, 394, 423; tour, 346, 348–64
Tradewinds (Sea Bright), 324
"Train Song, The," 37